D1230555

Lafayette in the Age of the American Revolution

Bust of Lafayette by Jean-Antoine Houdon, now on display in the rotunda of the capitol at Richmond, Virginia, where it faces Houdon's statue of Washington.

Lafayette in the Age of the American Revolution

SELECTED LETTERS AND PAPERS, 1776–1790

Volume V • January 4, 1782–December 29, 1785

STANLEY J. IDZERDA *and*
ROBERT RHODES CROUT, *Editors*

Carol Godschall *and* Leslie Wharton,
Assistant Editors

CORNELL UNIVERSITY PRESS

ITHACA AND LONDON

This book has been published with the aid of a grant from the National
Historical Publications and Records Commission.

First published 1983 by Cornell University Press.
Published in the United Kingdom by Cornell University Press Ltd.,
Ely House, 37 Dover Street, London W1X 4HQ.

International Standard Book Number 0-8014-1576-4
Library of Congress Catalog Card Number 76-50268
Printed in the United States of America
*Librarians: Library of Congress cataloging information
appears on the last page of the book.*

*The paper in this book is acid-free, and meets the guidelines for permanence and
durability of the Committee on Production Guidelines for Book Longevity of the Council on Library Resources.*

THE PAPERS OF THE MARQUIS DE LAFAYETTE

Sponsored by the Cornell University Libraries,
the National Historical Publications
and Records Commission, and the
National Endowment for the Humanities

ACKNOWLEDGMENTS

The appearance of almost any work of documentary history is the result of cooperative consultation. So has it been with this volume. We deeply appreciate the assistance we have received from libraries, institutions, archives, museums, specialists, foundations, and dedicated collectors. Their support and encouragement have made this volume possible.

Dependable and continued financial support for this project has come from the National Historical Publications and Records Commission and Cornell University Libraries. In addition, this volume has received important contributions from the National Endowment for the Humanities, the Gebhard-Gourgaud Foundation, the Port Ulao Foundation, the Surdna Foundation, the Athwin Foundation, the O'Shaughnessy Foundation, the Bigelow Foundation, and the St. Paul Foundation. Generous support also came from Walter Annenberg on behalf of the Annenberg Foundation in honor of the Honorable and Mrs. William P. Rogers. Other generous individuals, who wish to remain anonymous, have provided needed financial support, and we gratefully recognize them.

We extend special thanks to the archivists and staff of the National Historical Publications and Records Commission. Richard Sheldon, Sara Dunlap Jackson, and Mary Giunta deserve particular thanks for their prompt and dependable responses to our many requests. They may be deservedly proud of thir significant contribution to many documentary projects. We also appreciate the steadfast cooperation and encouragement of the director and staff of the Cornell University Libraries, notably the Department of Rare Books and Manuscripts and Interlibrary Services. The staff of St. Benedict College also contributed much of their time and energies to the preparation of this volume.

We have received much help from the staffs of the National Archives, the Manuscript Division of the Library of Congress, and the Skillman Library of Lafayette College in the preparation of this volume. We also got generous assistance from the staffs of the New-York Historical Society, the Clements Library of the University of Michigan, the Henry L. Huntington Library and Art Gallery, the Houghton Library and the Fogg Art Museum of Harvard University, the Pierpont Morgan Library, the Yale University Library, the American Philosophical Society Library, the Massachusetts Historical Society, the Boston Athenaeum, the Connecticut State Library, the Connecticut Historical Society, the Eleutherian Mills Historical Library, the Chicago Historical Society, the Joseph Regenstein Library of the University of Chicago, the Lilly Library of Indiana University, the American Antiquarian Society, the Glassboro State College Library, the New York Public Library, the Columbia University Libraries, the Haverford College Library, the Pennsylvania Academy of the Fine Arts, Independence National Historical Park, the Historical Society of Pennsylvania, the University of Pennsylvania Library, the Charleston Library Society, the South Carolina Historical Society, the Mount Vernon Ladies Association, the Virginia State Library, the Virginia State Historical Society, the Alderman Library of the University of Virginia, the Anderson Museum of the Society of the Cincinnati, the United States Senate Commission on Art and Antiquities, the National Portrait Gallery of the Smithsonian Institution, the Museo del Prado in Madrid, the Royal Archives of Windsor Castle and the Public Record Office in London, the Österreichische Nationalbibliothek in Vienna, and the Landesbibliothek in Weimar.

We also thank the officials of the Archives Nationales and the Archives du Ministère des Affaires Etrangères in Paris, the Service Historique des Armées in Vincennes, and the Bibliothèque Municipale de Nantes. As with earlier volumes, we continue to owe an immense debt of gratitude to Mme Chantal de Tourtier-Bonazzi, Conservateur aux Archives Privées in the Archives Nationales. She has continually provided us with sage advice and interceded on our behalf when we encountered problems related to our work.

Private collectors make a special contribution to documentary history when they are generous enough to share their collections with projects such as this. We are fortunate to have received the cooperation of Mme André Balleyguier, who allowed us to publish and quote from her Lafayette material. M. and Mme René de Chambrun have provided us with copies of Lafayette material from the Château de La Grange—Bléneau, for which we are most grateful. We also extend hearty thanks to others who have preferred to remain anonymous.

A unique contribution to French-American history occurred in the 1960s when Arthur H. Dean brought to Cornell University the Chavaniac and Blancheteau collections of Lafayette material, now known as the Arthur H. and Mary Marden Dean Collection. Mr. Dean's unwaivering and generous support for this project has been gratifying. We offer him our profound thanks for his friendship.

Many libraries, archives, and individuals have given us permission to reproduce the materials in this volume. We thank them and credit them in the provenance notes to the documents and in the list of illustrations.

We also acknowledge our debt to the editors and staffs of the papers projects of other eighteenth-century figures. They have not only assisted us in locating obscure documents, but have on occasion shared with us their insights and perceptions gained over many years of study. Particularly helpful to this volume were the Papers of George Washington, the Papers of Thomas Jefferson, the Adams Papers, the Papers of Nathanael Greene, the Papers of General Friedrich Wilhelm von Steuben, the Papers of Benjamin Franklin, the Papers of Robert Morris, the Papers of John Jay, and the Papers of Henry Laurens.

Finally, a cheerful and diligent staff is a boon to any enterprise. We especially thank the assistant editors of earlier volumes, Linda J. Pike and Mary Ann Quinn, for their perceptive advice and support. Our editorial burdens have also been lightened by the talents of editorial assistants Margaret John and Judith Slein and the help of others who assisted us: Rita Guerlac, Gerry Idzerda, S. Kristin Malloy, Rita Smidt, S. Rosalinda Wagner, and Victoria Williams. On many occasions our editor at Cornell University Press, Barbara Salazar, has come to our rescue with her unique talents, and we especially thank her for her diligence.

While the list of acknowledgments is long, it does not dilute our sense of obligation to each contributor to this enterprise, and we share with every one, as Lafayette did with his colleagues, that sense of companionship in this noble struggle.

STANLEY J. IDZERDA
ROBERT RHODES CROUT

Ithaca, New York

CONTENTS

Introduction   xxi
Editorial Method   xxvii
    Selection, xxvii; Transcription, xxvii; Translations, xxviii;
    Annotation and Index, xxix
Guide to Editorial Apparatus   xxxi
    Textual Devices, xxxi; Descriptive Symbols, xxxi;
    Location Symbols, xxxii; Short Titles, xxxiii
Chronological Outline   xxxvii

PART I. FRANCE AND THE PEACE
JANUARY 4, 1782–MARCH 2, 1783
    From George Washington, January 4, 1782   2
    To George Washington, January 18, 1782   4
    From the Comte de Vergennes, January 23, 1782   6
    To the President of Congress, January 29, 1782   6
    To John Jay, January 30, 1782   7
    To George Washington, January 30, 1782   8
    To Benjamin Franklin, February 12, 1782   10
    To Benjamin Franklin, [February 16–March 15, 1782]   13
    From John Adams, February 20, 1782   14
    To Benjamin Franklin, February 25, 1782   15
    To the Comte de Vergennes, March 20, 1782   15
    To the Comte de Vergennes, March 20, 1782   17
    To John Adams, March 27, 1782   18
    To John Jay, March 28, 1782   19
    To Robert R. Livingston, [March 30, 1782]   20
    To George Washington, March 30, 1782   21
    To George Washington, March 31, 1782   25
    From John Adams, April 6, 1782   25
    To George Washington, April 12, 1782   26
    To Henry Laurens, April 14, 1782   28
    Proposals for the French Campaign in North America, April 18,
    1782   30

To John Jay, April 28, 1782   33
Franklin's Account of the Peace Negotiations with Great Britain,
  [May 1782]   34
To John Adams, May 7, 1782   36
From John Adams, May 21, 1782   37
To Benjamin Franklin, June 12, 1782   39
To Benjamin Franklin, [June 20, 1782]   40
Minutes of the Assembly of June 24, 1782, of the Worthy Lodge
  of Saint John of Scotland of the Social Contract   41
To Benjamin Franklin, [June 25, 1782]   42
To Robert R. Livingston, June 25, 1782   43
To George Washington, June 25, 1782   48
To George Washington, June 29, [1782]   49
From the Comte de Ségur, July 7, 1782   51
To Henry Laurens, August 20, 1782   53
To the Comte de Vergennes, September 10, 1782   54
To Benjamin Franklin, September 12, 1782   55
To Benjamin Franklin, September 17, 1782   56
From Benjamin Franklin, September 17, 1782   57
To Benjamin Franklin, [September 21, 1782]   59
From John Adams, September 29, 1782   59
To John Adams, October 6, 1782   60
From George Washington, October 20, 1782   62
To George Washington, October 24, 1782   64
From Robert R. Livingston, November 2, 1782   66
To the American Peace Commissioners, November 21, 1782   68
To the Comte de Vergennes, November 22, 1782   69
To George Washington, December 4, 1782   72
To Benjamin Franklin, December 6, 1782   74
To John Jay, December [26], 1782   75
To [the Comtesse de Tessé], January 1, 1783   77
From Robert R. Livingston, January 10, 1783   78
From John Jay, January 19, [1783]   79
To William Carmichael, January 20, 1783   81
To William Carmichael, January 29, 1783   83
To William Carmichael, February 2, 1783   83
To the President of Congress, February 5, 1783   84
To the President of Congress, February 5, 1783   85
To Robert R. Livingston, February 5, 1783   86
To Robert R. Livingston, February 5, 1783   88
To George Washington, February 5, 1783   90
To the Comte de Vergennes, February 5, 1783   93
To John Jay, February 15, 1783   94
To the Comte d'Estaing, February 18, 1783   97
To the Comte de Vergennes, February 18, 1783   98
To the Conde de Floridablanca, February 19, 1783   99
From the Conde de Floridablanca, February 22, 1783   101

Note on Correspondence with the Conde de Floridablanca,
February 22, 1783   102
To Robert R. Livingston, March 2, 1783   102

PART II. CONSOLIDATING THE PEACE, WITNESSING THE TRIUMPH
MARCH 19, 1783–DECEMBER 23, 1784
To Jean-François Joly de Fleury, March 19, 1783   110
To the Comte de Vergennes, March 19, 1783   112
From George Washington, March 23, 1783   113
To Adrienne de Noailles de Lafayette, March 27, 1783   117
From George Washington, April 5, 1783   119
John Adams to James Warren, April 16, 1783   121
To George Washington, April 19, 1783   124
To William Carmichael, April 27, 1783   126
To Sir Henry Clinton, April 30, 1783   127
From Robert R. Livingston, May 1, 1783   128
Recommendation of Lafayette for the Cross of Saint Louis, May
5, 1783   131
To the American Peace Commissioners, May 12, 1783   131
To George Washington, June 10, 1783   132
From Nathanael Greene, June 10, 1783   133
To the Comte de Vergennes, June 12, 1783   134
From George Washington, June 15, 1783   135
To John Adams, June 16, 1783   136
From Henry Knox, June 16, 1783   137
To the Comte de Vergennes, June 17, 1783   139
From the Comte de Vergennes, June 29, 1783   140
To Henry Laurens, July 6, 1783   141
To the President of Congress, July 20, 1783   142
To the Comte de Vergennes, July 21, 1783   144
To George Washington, July 22, 1783   145
Address of Nobles of Langeac to Lafayette, [August 4, 1783]   147
To the President of Congress, September 7, 1783   148
To George Washington, September 8, 1783   151
To Jeremiah Wadsworth, September 28, 1783   154
From George Washington, October 12, 1783   155
To Benjamin Franklin, [October 20, 1783]   157
From George Washington, October 20, 1783   158
To [Mme de Simiane?], October 21, 1783   158
From George Washington, October 30, 1783   159
To George Washington, November 11, 1783   162
To William Temple Franklin, November 19, 1783   165
To William Carmichael, November 20, 1783   166
To Benjamin Franklin, [December 13, 1783]   167
Observations on Commerce between France and the United
States, [December 13, 1783]   168

To the Comte de Vergennes, December 16, 1783   176
From Charles-Alexandre de Calonne, December 18, 1783   178
To George Washington, December 25, 1783   179
From Charles-Alexandre de Calonne, December 25, 1783   182
To Robert Morris, December 26, 1783   182
To James McHenry, December 26, 1783   184
To Henry Knox, January 8, 1784   186
From Charles-Alexandre de Calonne, January 9, 1784   189
To Robert Morris, January 10, 1784   190
To George Washington, January 10, 1784   191
To Charles-Alexandre de Calonne, January 31, 1784   193
From George Washington, February 1, 1784   194
From Thomas Mullens, February 5, 1784   196
To Charles-Alexandre de Calonne, February 10, 1784   198
To Charles-Alexandre de Calonne, February 26, 1784   198
To Charles-Alexandre de Calonne, March 5, 1784   199
To Jeremiah Wadsworth, March 7, 1784   200
To John Adams, March 8, 1784   201
From Charles-Alexandre de Calonne, March 8, 1784   203
To Robert Morris, March 9, 1784   204
To George Washington, March 9, 1784   205
To George Washington, March 9, 1784   208
From Henry Laurens, March 15, 1784   210
From John Adams, March 28, 1784   211
From Henry Laurens, March 31, 1784   212
To John Adams, April 9, 1784   213
To [Simon-Nicolas-Henri Linguet], April 20, 1784   214
To the Comte de Vergennes, [May 10, 1784]   215
To George Washington, May 14, 1784   216
From Robert Morris, May 19, 1784   218
To Benjamin Franklin, [May 20, 1784]   220
To John Adams, June 2, 1784   222
From John Adams, June 11, 1784   223
From Charles-Alexandre de Calonne, June 11, 1784   224
From Charles-Alexandre de Calonne, June 16, 1784   225
From the Maréchal de Castries, June 17, 1784   226
To Adrienne de Noailles de Lafayette, [June 20, 1784]   226
To John Adams, June 25, 1784   227
To Adrienne de Noailles de Lafayette, June 25, 1784   229
To Adrienne de Noailles de Lafayette, June 28, 1784   231
To the Comte de Vergennes, June 28, 1784   232
To Samuel Adams, August 7, 1784   233
Address of the Committee of Officers of the Late Pennsylvania
   Line, with Lafayette's Reply, [August 9–10], 1784   233
To Adrienne de Noailles de Lafayette, August 13, 1784   235
To Adrienne de Noailles de Lafayette, August 20, 1784   237

Address of the Citizens of Baltimore to Lafayette and His Reply,
    September 1, 1784   240
James Madison to Thomas Jefferson, September 7, 1784   241
To the Comte de Vergennes, September 15, 1784   243
Barbé de Marbois's Journal of His Visit to the Territory of the
    Six Nations, September 23–October 8, 1784   245
To the Commissioners of Congress, September 30, 1784   253
Robert Morris to the President of Congress, September 30, 1784   254
Account of Lafayette's Meeting with the Six Nations, October
    3–4, 1784   255
To Adrienne de Noailles de Lafayette, October 4 and 10, 1784   260
To John Jay, October 7, 1784   263
To Alexander Hamilton, October 8, 1784   263
To George Washington, October 8, 1784   264
To Thomas Jefferson, October 11, 1784   266
To the Prince de Poix, October 12, 1784   267
To the Comte de Vergennes, October 12, 1784   269
James Madison to Thomas Jefferson, October 17, 1784   271
To Alexander Hamilton, October 22, 1784   275
To David Humphreys, October 31, 1784   276
Recommendation for James, November 21, 1784   277
From George Washington, December 8, 1784   279
Address to the Continental Congress, [December 11, 1784]   280
Congress to Louis XVI, December 11, 1784   282
To [John Jay, December 12, 1784]   282
To the President of Congress, December 12, 1784   284
To James Madison, December 15–17, 1784   285
To George Washington, December 17, 1784   287
To Samuel Adams, December 19, 1784   288
From George Washington, December 23, 1784   289

PART III. STRENGTHENING THE BONDS
JANUARY 23–DECEMBER 29, 1785
To Adrienne de Noailles de Lafayette, January 23, 1785   292
To John Jay, February 8, 1785   293
From George Washington, February 15, 1785   295
From [the Marquis de Condorcet], February 24, 1785   299
To William Carmichael, March 10, 1785   300
To Nathanael Greene, March 16, 1785   302
To Patrick Henry, March 16, 1785   305
To Richard Henry Lee, March 16, 1785   306
To James Madison, March 16, 1785   309
From James Madison, March 20, 1785   310
To the American Commissioners, April 8, 1785   315
To Alexander Hamilton, April 13, 1785   317
To Jeremiah Wadsworth, April 16, 1785   318

To [John Adams], May 8, 1785   320
To Henry Knox, May 11, 1785   321
To George Washington, May 11, 1785   322
To George Washington, May 13, 1785   324
To Pierre-Samuel Du Pont de Nemours, May 30, 1785   327
To Patrick Henry, June 7, 1785   328
To Henry Knox, June 12, 1785   329
Verses Sung to Lafayette at Lyons, [June 23, 1785]   330
To Jeremiah Wadsworth, July 9, 1785   331
To John Adams, July 13, 1785   333
To John Jay, July 14, 1785   335
From George Washington, July 25, 1785   336
To [Mme de Tessé], August 7, 1785   340
From George Washington, September 1, 1785   342
To Thomas Jefferson, September 4, 1785   345
To [Thomas Boylston], October 4 [November 4?], 1785   349
To the Comte de Vergennes, November 16, 1785   350
To Rabaut de Saint-Etienne, November 20, 1785   351
To [Thomas Boylston], November 20, 1785   352
To Jeremiah Wadsworth, December 3, 1785   353
To James McHenry, December 3, 1785   354
From John Adams, December 13, 1785   355
From John Adams, December 20, 1785   357
To [the Marquis de Castries], December 29, 1785   358

Appendix I: French Texts   361
Appendix II: Calendar of Omitted Letters   427
Index   445

ILLUSTRATIONS

Lafayette   *frontispiece*
    Marble bust by Jean-Antoine Houdon, 1787. Courtesy of the Vir-
    ginia House of Delegates, Richmond, Virginia.

Benjamin Franklin   12
    Oil by Charles Willson Peale, 1785. Courtesy of the Pennsylvania
    Academy of the Fine Arts, Joseph and Sarah Harrison Collection.

Henry Laurens   52
    Oil by John Singleton Copley, 1781. Courtesy of the Library of
    Congress, Washington, D.C., from the collection of the Architect
    of the Capitol.

Engraved dinner invitation from Lafayette to Franklin, April 5,
1785   58
    Courtesy of the American Philosophical Society Library,
    Philadelphia.

Signature page of the Preliminary Articles of Peace between
the United States and Great Britain, November 30, 1782   73
    Courtesy of the Public Record Office, London.

John Jay   95
    Detail of oil, head by Gilbert Stuart, c. 1782, balance of figure by
    John Trumbull, c. 1785. Courtesy of the National Portrait Gallery,
    Smithsonian Institution, Washington, D.C.

Charles III of Spain   100
    Oil by Goya. Copyright © Museo del Prado, Madrid. All rights
    reserved.

Robert R. Livingston   129
    Oil by Charles Willson Peale, c. 1782. Courtesy of Independence
    National Historical Park Collection.

Henry Knox   138
  Oil by Charles Willson Peale, 1783. Courtesy of Independence
  National Historical Park Collection.

Elias Boudinot   152
  Oil by Charles Willson Peale. Courtesy of the Art Museum,
  Princeton University. Gift of Mr. and Mrs. Landon K. Thorne
  for the Boudinot Collection.

George Washington   163
  Terra cotta bust by Jean-Antoine Houdon, 1785. Courtesy of
  the Mount Vernon Ladies' Association of the Union, Mount
  Vernon, Virginia.

Eagle Badge of the Society of the Cincinnati   177
  Originally owned by Tench Tilghman. Courtesy of the Anderson
  House Headquarters and Museum, Society of the Cincinnati,
  Washington, D.C.

Charles-Alexandre de Calonne   181
  Oil by Elizabeth Vigée-Lebrun, 1784. Reproduced by kind permission of the Lord Chamberlain, St. James's Palace.

Blank diploma of the Society of the Cincinnati.   206
  Courtesy of the Beinecke Rare Books and Manuscript Library,
  Yale University.

Benjamin Franklin   221
  Plaster bust by Jean-Antoine Houdon, 1786–91? Courtesy of the
  Boston Athenaeum.

John Adams   228
  Oil by John Singleton Copley, 1783. Courtesy of the Harvard
  University Portrait Collection, bequest of Ward Nicholas Boyl-
  ston, 1828.

Letter of Anastasie de Lafayette to George Washington, June
18, 1784   239
  Courtesy of the Department of Rare Books, Cornell University
  Libraries, Arthur H. and Mary Marden Dean Collection.

François Barbé de Marbois   246
  Engraving, unsigned, undated. Courtesy of the Library of Congress, Washington, D.C.

Marquis de Lafayette with James Armistead Lafayette   278
  Engraved by Noel Le Mire from a painting by Jean-Baptiste Le
  Paon. Courtesy of the Virginia Historical Society, Richmond.

Letter of Louis XVI to Congress, May 10, 1785   283
  Courtesy of the National Archives, Washington, D.C.

Richard Henry Lee   307
    Oil by Charles Willson Peale, 1784. Courtesy of Independence
    National Historical Park Collection.

George Washington   326
    Oil by Charles Willson Peale, 1784. Courtesy of Fogg Art Muse-
    um, Harvard University. Grenville L. Winthrop Bequest.

Joseph II   334
    Engraving by J. P. Pichler after the painting by Heinrich Füger.
    Courtesy of the Bildarchiv und Porträtsammlung, Österreichische
    Nationalbibliothek, Vienna.

Prince Henry of Prussia   341
    Plaster bust by Jean-Antoine Houdon, c. 1784. Courtesy of the
    Nationale Forschungs- und Gedenkstätten der Klassischen
    Deutschen Literatur in Weimar, Goethe-Nationalmuseum,
    Weimar.

Lafayette   346
    Oil by F. G. Bevelet, 1788. Reproduced by permission of Fogg
    Art Museum, Harvard University, courtesy of an anonymous
    owner.

Autograph inscription to Lafayette in presentation copy of
Jefferson's *Notes on the State of Virginia*   348
    Courtesy of the Tracy W. McGregor Library, University of Vir-
    ginia, Charlottesville.

The Marquis de Castries   359
    Oil by Joseph Boze. Courtesy of the Musée National du Château
    de Versailles.

MAPS

Western Europe   103
The United States after the peace of 1783   217
Europe in the 1780s   303

INTRODUCTION

The victory at Yorktown was a stunning military success for the forces of France and the United States. Yet in its wake persistent questions remained: Could an acceptable peace treaty be negotiated? If so, could the weak confederation of American states survive as a political entity? The letters and documents in this volume follow Lafayette's efforts to transform the military victory of 1781 into a diplomatic, political, and commercial success that would ensure the fruits of peace. This volume focuses on Lafayette's continuing struggle to help the young nation to survive the early postwar years.

It begins with Lafayette's return to France at the beginning of 1782, when he had become "the hero of two worlds." Louis XVI, for example, responded to a congressional commendation of Lafayette: "The justice that you render the Marquis de Lafayette confirms more and more the opinion that we ourselves have of his zeal and talents and can only add to the desire we have that he experience new marks of our satisfaction." Among these marks were the rank of *maréchal de camp* with seniority rights from the capture of Yorktown and, later, membership in the Order of St. Louis, remarkable accomplishments for such a young man.

Throughout France, Lafayette's exploits in America were the subject of popular poems, pictures, pamphlets, and songs. His every public appearance became an opportunity for general celebration. Lafayette had become in his own country the personification of the American Revolution; his dispatch to Congress reported that his reception by the French people demonstrated that "nothing weighs so much with the nation and her sovereign as an ardent zeal for the cause of America."

Lafayette had intended to remain in France for only a short time, just long enough to give an account of the situation in the United States and to assist in the plans for the next military campaign. Under instructions from Congress, he was to assume two roles in France: consultant and assistant to Franklin in obtaining supplies, and adviser to all American ministers. Lafayette termed his role "aide-de-camp" to the ministers. His first project was to promote another loan for the Americans. This was no easy task, for skeptical French officials believed that the Americans themselves had not made enough sacrifices. Lafayette also pressed for a combined military and naval operation against New York City and Charleston, important cities still occupied by British troops. After a month of lobbying, Lafayette succeeded in securing the loan and eliciting assurances that an expeditionary force would be sent.

During the months that followed, British agents made a number of peace overtures to the American commissioners, all short of the one critical concession: recognition of the United States' independence. Lafayette stayed on in the hope that he might be useful in the negotiations, and in fact he served Franklin well at Versailles. But he slowly grew disenchanted with the pace and demeanor of the diplomacy, in which, he concluded, "cheating is considered as a Very clever improvement." Finally, in late October, having decided that negotiations were proceeding too slowly, Lafayette accepted the rank of second in command of the combined Spanish-French expedition that was to relieve the United States. This honor involved a force of twenty thousand men and fifty ships of the line, gathering at Cadiz.

For the next two months Lafayette fulfilled the responsibilities of quartermaster general for the expedition, assembling supplies, mobilizing armaments. On January 20, however, a preliminary peace treaty was signed at Paris, and the expedition was canceled. Though Lafayette found himself denied the opportunity of another campaign in America, he did have the honor of dispatching a vessel to the United States with the first news of the preliminary treaty.

Lafayette now set out for the Spanish court, where, dressed in his American uniform, he paid his respects to Charles III and talked with Floridablanca, his foreign minister. He obtained the formal acceptance of the credentials of the American chargé d'affaires and an invitation for him to attend an ambassadorial reception. Lafayette devoted the remainder of his time in Spain to working on the thorny issue of the United States' boundaries. He returned to France when he had had some success.

With the war at an end, Lafayette decided to devote his major energies to strengthening the bonds of peaceful intercourse between France and the United States before returning to America. This volume reflects his intense interest in the commercial relationship between the two countries and his attempts to improve its regulation and encourage its growth. The commercial treaty of 1778 had authorized the opening of one or more free ports. Lafayette successfully urged the addition of Lorient, a port much favored by American merchants. His concern about the future of French–American trade was echoed in a series of letters to a succession of French comptrollers general.

Finally, in December 1783, he set down in writing his extensive observations. Lafayette spoke of the minute details of trade that he had observed in America: the preference for square nailheads; the manner of folding linen. He also raised major issues: the role of French colonial trade in French–American relations, the bad effects of France's internal duty system, its state monopolies, and the short-term credit of its financiers. He advised the shapers of France's economic policy, "It is clear that direct trade is the best policy for buying tobacco and selling our own goods."

In the months that followed, Lafayette continued to urge reform of France's commercial mechanisms. He urged modification of the port fee system, especially the admiralty, anchorage, and pilotage fees; and he won some concessions. Calonne ordered the Farmers General to give American tobacco preferential treatment; he abolished the export duty on French *eaux-de-vie* shipped to America.

Lafayette also assumed responsibilities in the Society of the Cincinnati, founded in the spring of 1783 to preserve the friendships that the war had fostered among the officer corps. He agreed to preside over the French officers who had served in the American army, and who constituted a distinct branch of American membership in the Society. The emergence of the Society drew criticism from those who feared that the hereditary nature of its membership might lay the groundwork for an American nobility, and Lafayette was sensitive to those concerns. Yet there was a great flurry among Frenchmen to be included in its membership, and Lafayette soon found himself barraged by their requests. For France the Society was a welcome innovation, and Louis XVI granted it special honors by permitting its badge the distinction of being the only foreign decoration (beside that of the Order of the Golden Fleece) that French subjects could wear publicly. He also ordered it displayed from the same buttonhole as the Cross of St. Louis.

Throughout the period included in this volume, the relationship between the Lafayettes and the Washingtons continued to grow. They exchanged gifts and warm letters, and the Lafayette family portrait appeared in the most prominent place in Mount Vernon. Lafayette's filial devotion for Washington continued, as did the influence of Washington's ideas. Lafayette was particularly awed by Washington's desire to resume his private life once the victory of the Revolution was assured. Washington's June 1783 Circular Letter to the States, his original valedictory address to the nation, provided not only Washington's comment on the critical problems facing the young nation but also his vision of America's future. Lafayette responded to it: "My Heart Has Been a Partaker in the Glory of My dear General from whom Every thing that is Great and Good So Naturally flows that it gives a good grace to His Heroic Actions."

When Lafayette finally returned to the United States in August 1784, he found Americans filled with a deep appreciation of his love for his adopted country. They besieged him with honors and banquets. Lafayette's frustrated desire throughout the war was finally realized— he saw the American flag flying over New York City. Saint-Jean de Crèvecoeur recalled seeing Lafayette there, seated at the head of a table so large that a hundred tablecloths were required to cover it, while "the flag of America, unfurled on the roof of the house, . . . waved in the breeze, [reflecting] the joy of our hearts as well as the solemnity of the occasion that was being celebrated."[1] This scene of celebration was repeated across ten states of the American confederation. Yet the tour was more than a personal triumphal procession. Lafayette took every opportunity to promote what he considered to be the most critical issue facing the United States, the need for a stronger American union. To this end he spoke before the state legislatures of Pennsylvania, Massachusetts, Rhode Island, Maryland, Virginia, and New Jersey. Lafayette also offered his services as blood brother of the Iroquois nation and his association with the French crown to promote a peaceful settlement of the hostilities between the United States and the Iroquois at the peace negotiations at Fort Schuyler. Noting Lafayette's significant role there, James Madison concluded, "The commissioners were eclipsed."

In addition to his work on political issues, Lafayette renewed his association with the American scientific community. Harvard College gave him an honorary doctor of laws degree; and at a session of the American Philosophical Society, he presented a paper on "animal magnetism," which reflected his continuing interest in the experiments of Mesmer.

In an address before the American Congress, Lafayette returned to the major theme of his tour by publicly acknowledging the efforts of all those who sought "to strengthen the Confederation, preserve public faith, regulate trade, and in a proper guard over continental magazines and frontier posts, in a general system of militia, in foreseeing attention to the navy, to insure every kind of safety." He concluded with his hope that the United States would continue to be an "immense temple of freedom" that would "ever stand a lesson to oppressors, an example to the oppressed, a sanctuary for the rights of mankind!" Lafayette's vision of America had not gone unnoticed, for Washington himself wrote

---

[1]*Lettres d'un cultivateur . . .* (Paris, 1787), 3:317–18.

with some embarrassment to Henry Knox: "Would to God our own countrymen . . . could view things by that large and extensive scale."[2]

Upon his return to France in January 1785, Lafayette resumed his role as promoter of American causes with renewed vigor. His Monday soirées became famous in Paris as the "American dinners," evenings devoted to discussing American ideas and reveling in the company of American friends and acquaintances. Lafayette was now a benefactor to Americans throughout Europe. He offered to oversee the education of his friends' sons in France. In Paris, he urged the French navy to purchase American timber and hemp, the city of Paris to use American whale oil for illumination. He toured the south of France, promoting American trade at Nîmes and Lyons. At the courts of Frederick the Great and Joseph II he provided enticing accounts of the opportunities waiting in American markets and in the commodities that Americans had to sell.

Because tobacco continued to be the major American staple that affected the French market, Lafayette shared Jefferson's desire to end the Farmers General's monopoly over its sale in France. Upon his return from central Europe, he began a major effort to see that monopoly ended. But reform of commercial regulations was not the only change Lafayette sought. When he took action for the cause of Protestant rights in France, it may have been his American experience that inspired him. Lafayette knew the time for reform was at hand.

Though he was not a republican in the modern sense of the word, Lafayette strongly favored constitutional government founded on popular support. At this time he expressed his reservations about the despotism of Frederick the Great of Prussia and his clear support for the cause of the Patriot forces in the United Provinces. He also began to give active support to the abolition of slavery.

This volume continues to reveal a Lafayette that scholars have failed to notice, a Lafayette who by 1782 was mature beyond his years. As his old antagonist, Horatio Gates, put it, Lafayette was an "old head upon young shoulders."[3] Not merely a boy in transition, he was a man who clearly saw and understood that the revolutionary ideology of the American conflict was "in earnest" rather than a "rehearsal" for future events. He continued past the silencing of the guns to participate in leadership decisions in both France and America. The mythical Lafayette is not found in these volumes. The mortal Lafayette who appears here emerges as a fully formed character intent on making a difference in the future of his country.[4]

[2]Fitzpatrick, *Writings of Washington*, 28:5.
[3]Gates to Franklin, August 16, 1784, PPAmP: Franklin Papers.
[4]For another interpretation, see Louis Gottschalk, *Lafayette between the American and the French Revolutions, 1783–1789* (Chicago, 1950), p. vii.

EDITORIAL METHOD

SELECTION

Nearly three thousand first- and second-party Lafayette documents are available to us for the period 1776–1790. We shall publish about three-fifths of them in these volumes. The choice of documents depends on the exigencies of space and the desire to avoid needless repetition. We intend to provide material sufficient to illuminate the events in which Lafayette participated, his motives and character, and those of the people with whom he lived and worked. The selections include first-party material: letters and documents written by Lafayette himself; second-party material: letters and documents addressed to Lafayette; and some third-party material: contemporary letters, journals, and documents that contain information about Lafayette. Some of the third-party material is extracted from longer documents; we have reproduced only the portions relevant to Lafayette. In such cases, the letter *E* is placed as a superscript after the title of the document. First- and second-party documents that we do not print are listed in Appendix II.

TRANSCRIPTION

In our transcription of the manuscripts we retain the original spelling. If it is unusual enough to cause confusion, the correct spelling follows in brackets. The thorn (as in "ye") is transcribed as "th." Punctuation is retained as found, except for dashes at the ends of sentences, which are replaced by periods. A minimum of additional punctuation is supplied when necessary for clarity. Apostrophes are supplied for possessive forms. When the writer's punctuation is unclear, we follow modern usage. Original capitalization is also retained, except that each sentence is made to begin with a capital letter and names of persons and places and personal titles are silently capitalized. Lafayette's use of capitals increased during the period of this volume, and in some instances he wrote over lower-case letters to capitalize them. We have tried to reproduce his capitalization, but in cases where it is unclear we follow modern usage. Abbreviations are not spelled out unless they are not readily recognizable; contractions are retained. Superscript letters are brought down to the line.

When the manuscript has been damaged or contains an illegible passage, if no more than four letters are missing, we supply them silently. If more than four letters or entire words are missing, we supply them in brackets, with a question mark within the brackets if the conjecture is doubtful. Gaps that cannot be filled are explained in brackets in the text; for example, [*illegible*], [*torn*]. The writer's interlineations or marginal notes are incorporated into the text without comment. Slips of the pen are silently corrected. Words underlined once by the writer are printed in italics. Passages written in cipher and deciphered interlinearly are printed in large and small capitals. Signatures are printed in large and small capitals. Addresses, endorsements, and docketing are not transcribed but are included in the provenance note if they are contextually significant. The dateline is placed at the head of each document regardless of its position in the manuscript.

The greatest problems arise in the materials that were altered in preparation for the publication of *Mémoires, correspondance et manuscrits du Général Lafayette, publiés par sa famille:* Lafayette's Memoir of 1779 and his letters to his family and to George Washington. Many changes have been made in these manuscripts in pencil and nineteenth-century ink. Words, sentences, and even paragraphs have been scribbled over or marked for deletion with slashes or brackets, and words and phrases have been added in the margins and between the lines in Lafayette's nineteenth-century hand. It is likely that he made or approved all the changes, because copies of the letters and memoir which Lafayette sent to Jared Sparks in 1829 conform to the text of the amended manuscripts. Most of the changes Lafayette indicated were incorporated in the texts printed in the *Mémoires*. A comparison of the printed texts with the amended manuscripts reveals further changes, but these alterations follow the pattern Lafayette established. The majority of the changes are purely stylistic, and we disregard them. We have attempted to print the text as Lafayette first wrote it. When a significant passage has been deleted on the manuscript or omitted from the *Mémoires*, we print it in angle brackets. All other significant changes are explained in the notes.

TRANSLATIONS

The French materials in this volume are translated into English because these documents would otherwise be either unintelligible or poorly understood by too many readers. Our experience and knowledge of eighteenth-century French has enabled us to offer what we believe to be accurate translations, particularly of idioms and technical terms; more important, our effort has been to catch the nuance and tone of the French language of that time, when epistolary style often depended on the status of the correspondents as well as the subject discussed. Translators' rationales are rarely convincing to those who have an intimate grasp both of the era and of the language being used. For those readers, the French texts of all translated documents are printed in Appendix I.

The letter *T* is placed as a superscript after the title of every translated document. The same superscript follows passages translated in the notes, but we do not print the French texts of those passages. In the translations, spelling, capitalization, and punctuation are modernized.

ANNOTATION AND INDEX

Notes to the text follow each document. The first note gives the provenance and other necessary information about the document and is unnumbered. The numbered notes provide clarification, information, and explanation of materials in the text. In our annotation we have tried to take into account the pattern of Lafayette's life and thought and the fact that the best commentary on his letters usually is to be found in the other documents. When we cite documents that are printed in our volume, we identify them by title and date only. The source citation is given for all other items mentioned in our notes.

All proper names are identified in the Index; people and places are given space in the annotation only when the information is immediately required for an understanding of the text.

GUIDE TO EDITORIAL APPARATUS

TEXTUAL DEVICES

[roman]   Conjectural reading for missing or illegible matter (a question mark follows when the reading is doubtful); interpolated explanation of gallicisms; matter taken from another copy or added to the manuscript. See notes for each document.

[*italic*]   Editorial comment inserted in the text.

⟨roman⟩   Matter deleted in the manuscript, or in Lafayette, *Mémoires,* but here restored. See provenance note for each document.

⟨*italic*⟩   Docketing or marginal reply to issues raised in the document.

SMALL CAPITALS   Matter written in cipher and deciphered interlinearly.

DESCRIPTIVE SYMBOLS

AD	Autograph document
ADS	Autograph document signed
AL	Autograph letter
ALS	Autograph letter signed
AM	Autograph manuscript
AMS	Autograph manuscript signed
D	Document
DS	Document signed
E	Extract
ET	Extract, translation
L	Letter
LbC	Letter-book copy
LS	Letter signed
M	Manuscript
T	Translation

LOCATION SYMBOLS

American repositories (with abbreviations as in the National Union Catalogue of the Library of Congress):

CSmH	Henry E. Huntington Library and Art Gallery, San Marino, California
CSt	Stanford University Library, Stanford, California
CU-BANC	Bancroft Library, University of California, Berkeley, California
Ct	Connecticut State Library, Hartford
CtHi	Connecticut Historical Society, Hartford
CtNhHi	New Haven Colony Historical Society, New Haven, Connecticut
CtY	Yale University Library, New Haven, Connecticut
DeGE	Eleutherian Mills Historical Library, Greenville, Delaware
DLC	Manuscript Division, Library of Congress, Washington, D.C.
DNA	National Archives and Records Service, Washington, D.C.
DSI	Smithsonian Institution, Washington, D.C.
ICHi	Chicago Historical Society, Chicago, Illinois
ICN	Newberry Library, Chicago, Illinois
ICU	Department of Special Collections, Joseph Regenstein Library, University of Chicago, Chicago, Illinois
InU	Lilly Library, Indiana University, Bloomington
MH	Houghton Library, Harvard University, Cambridge, Massachusetts
MSaE	Essex Institute, Salem, Massachusetts
MWA	American Antiquarian Society, Worcester, Massachusetts
MeHi	Maine Historical Society, Portland
MiU-C	William L. Clements Library, University of Michigan, Ann Arbor
N	New York State Library, Albany
NHi	New-York Historical Society, New York
NIC	Department of Rare Books, Cornell University Libraries, Ithaca, New York
NN	New York Public Library, New York
NNC	Rare Book and Manuscript Library, Columbia University, New York
NNPM	Pierpont Morgan Library, New York
NjGbS	Glassboro State College Library, Glassboro, New Jersey
NjHi	New Jersey Historical Society, Newark
NjMoHP	Morristown National Historical Park, Morristown, New Jersey
OClWHi	Western Reserve Historical Society, Cleveland, Ohio
PEL	David Bishop Skillman Library, Lafayette College, Easton, Pennsylvania
PHC	Haverford College Library, Haverford, Pennsylvania
PHi	Historical Society of Pennsylvania, Philadelphia
PPAmP	American Philosophical Society Library, Philadelphia
PPT	Temple University Library, Philadelphia
PPU	University of Pennsylvania Library, Philadelphia

RNHi   Newport Historical Society, Newport, Rhode Island
RPJCB   John Carter Brown Library, Providence, Rhode Island
ScC   Charleston Library Society, Charleston, South Carolina
ScHi   South Carolina Historical Society, Charleston
Vi   Virginia State Library, Richmond
ViHi   Virginia Historical Society, Richmond

Foreign repositories:

AAE   Archives du Ministère des Affaires Etrangères, Paris
ALG   Archives, Château de La Grange, Courplay
AN   Archives Nationales, Paris
BMN   Bibliothèque Municipale, Nantes
PRO   Public Record Office, London
SHA   Service Historique de l'Armée, Château de Vincennes

SHORT TITLES

Arneth and Flammermont, *Correspondance secrète du comte de Mercy-Argenteau:* Alfred d'Arneth and Jules Gustave Flammermont, eds., *Correspondance secrète du comte de Mercy-Argenteau: avec l'empereur Joseph II et le prince de Kaunitz,* 2 vols. (Paris: Imprimerie Nationale, 1889–91).

Bachaumont, *Mémoires secrets:* Louis Petit de Bachaumont, *Mémoires secrets pour servir à l'histoire de la république des lettres en France, depuis MDCCLXII jusqu'à nos jours,* 36 vols. (London: John Adamson, 1781–89).

Bigelow, *Works of Franklin:* John Bigelow, ed., *The Complete Works of Benjamin Franklin,* 10 vols. (New York: G. P. Putnam's Sons, 1888).

Boyd, *Jefferson Papers:* Julian Parks Boyd, ed., *Papers of Thomas Jefferson,* 19 vols. to date (Princeton: Princeton University Press, 1950–).

Burnett, *Letters of Congress:* Edmund C. Burnett, ed., *Letters of the Members of the Continental Congress,* 8 vols. (Washington, D.C.: Carnegie Institution, 1921–36).

DAB: Allen Johnson, ed., *Dictionary of American Biography,* 12 vols. (New York: Scribner, 1957–73).

Diary and Autobiography of John Adams: L. H. Butterfield, ed., *Diary and Autobiography of John Adams,* 4 vols. (Cambridge: Belknap Press of Harvard University Press, 1961).

Diplomatic Correspondence, 1783–1789: The Diplomatic Correspondence of the United States of America, from the Signing of the Definitive Treaty of Peace, 10th September 1783, to the Adoption of the Constitution, March 4, 1789, 7 vols. (Washington, D.C., 1833–34).

Doniol, *Histoire:* Jean-Henri Doniol, *Histoire de la participation de la France à l'établissement des Etats-Unis d'Amérique,* 5 vols. (Paris, 1884–92).

Ferguson, *Papers of Robert Morris:* E. James Ferguson, ed., *The Papers of Robert Morris, 1781–1784,* 4 vols. (Pittsburgh: University of Pittsburgh Press, 1973–78).

Fitzpatrick, *Writings of Washington:* John C. Fitzpatrick, ed., *The Writings of*

George Washington, 39 vols. (Washington, D.C.: U.S. Government Printing Office, 1931–44).

Gottschalk, *Between:* Louis Gottschalk, *Lafayette Between the American and the French Revolutions, 1783–1789* (Chicago: University of Chicago Press, 1950).

Gottschalk, *Letters of Lafayette:* Louis Gottschalk, ed., *The Letters of Lafayette to Washington, 1777–1779*, rev. ed. (Philadelphia: American Philosophical Society, 1976).

Hansard, *Parliamentary History: The Parliamentary History of England from the Earliest Period to the Year 1803 . . .*, 36 vols. (London: T. C. Hansard, 1806–20).

Hening, *Statutes:* William Walter Hening, *The Statutes at Large: Being a Collection of All the Laws of Virginia, from the First Session of the Legislature in the Year 1619*, 13 vols. (Richmond, 1819–23).

Henkels, *Confidential Correspondence of Robert Morris:* Stan V. Henkels, ed., *Catalogue No. 1183: The Confidential Correspondence of Robert Morris* (Philadelphia, [1917]).

JCC: Worthington C. Ford, ed., *Journals of the Continental Congress, 1774–1789*, 34 vols. (Washington, D.C.: U.S. Government Printing Office, 1904–37).

JHD: Journal of the House of Delegates of the Commonwealth of Virginia: begun and held in the town of Richmond . . . 1781, 3 vols. (Richmond: T. W. White, 1827–28)

LAAR: Stanley J. Idzerda et al., eds., *Lafayette in the Age of the American Revolution: Selected Letters and Papers, 1776–1790*, 5 vols. to date (Ithaca: Cornell University Press, 1977–)

Lafayette, *Mémoires: Mémoires, correspondance et manuscrits du Général Lafayette, publiés par sa famille*, 6 vols. (Paris, 1837–38). Letters written in English are translated into French.

Madison Papers: William T. Hutchinson and William Rachal, eds., *Papers of James Madison*, 12 vols. to date (Chicago: University of Chicago Press, 1962–).

Metra, *Correspondance secrète:* François Metra, *Correspondance secrète, politique et littéraire, ou Mémoires pour servir à l'histoire des cours, des sociétés et de la littérature en France, depuis la mort de Louis XV*, 3 vols., reprint of 1787–90 ed. (Geneva: Slatkine, 1967).

Morris, *John Jay:* Richard Brandon Morris, *John Jay, the Nation and the Court* (Boston: Boston University Press, 1967).

Recueil des anciennes lois françaises: Recueil général des anciennes lois françaises, depuis l'an 420 jusqu'à la révolution de 1789 . . . avec notes de concordance, table chronologique et table générale analytique et alphabétique des matières, par M. Jourdan, 29 vols. (Paris: Belin-Le-Prieur, 1821–33).

Rice and Brown, *Rochambeau's Army:* Howard C. Rice, Jr., and Anne S. K. Brown, trans. and eds., *The American Campaigns of Rochambeau's Army, 1780, 1781, 1782, 1783*, 2 vols. (Princeton: Princeton University Press; and Providence: Brown University Press, 1972).

Richard Henry Lee Correspondence: Richard H. Lee, *Memoir of the Life of Richard Henry Lee, and His Correspondence with the most distinguished men in America and*

Europe, illustrative of their characters, and of the events of the American Revolution. By his grandson . . . , 2 vols. (Philadelphia: H. C. Carey and I. Lea, 1825).

Ridley, "Diary": Herbert E. Klingelhofer, "Matthew Ridley's Diary during the Peace Negotiations of 1782," *William and Mary Quarterly*, 2d ser., 20 (January 1963):95–133.

Rutland, *Papers of James Madison:* Robert Allen Rutland et al., eds., *Papers of James Madison*, 10 vols. (Chicago: University of Chicago Press, 1962–77).

Smyth, *Writings of Franklin:* Albert Henry Smyth, ed., *The Writings of Benjamin Franklin*, 10 vols. (New York and London, 1905–7).

Stevens, *Facsimiles:* Benjamin F. Stevens, *Facsimiles of Manuscripts in European Archives Relating to America, 1773–1783*, 25 vols. (London, 1889–98).

Syrett, *Hamilton Papers:* Harold C. Syrett et al., eds., *Papers of Alexander Hamilton*, 2 vols. (New York: Columbia University Press, 1961).

Virginia Council Journals: H. R. McIlwaine et al., eds., *Journals of the Council of the State of Virginia*, 4 vols. (Richmond: Virginia State Library, 1931–32).

Virginia State Papers: Calendar of Virginia State Papers and Other Manuscripts . . . preserved in the Capitol at Richmond, 11 vols. (Richmond, 1875–93).

Warren–Adams Letters: Massachusetts Historical Society, *Warren–Adams Letters, Being Chiefly a Correspondence among John Adams, Samuel Adams, and James Warren, 1734–1814*, 2 vols. (Boston, 1917–25).

Washington Diaries: Donald Jackson, ed., *The Diaries of George Washington*, 6 vols. to date (Charlottesville: University Press of Virginia, 1976–).

Wharton, *Diplomatic Correspondence:* Francis Wharton, ed., *The Revolutionary Diplomatic Correspondence of the United States*, 6 vols. (Washington, D.C., 1889).

CHRONOLOGICAL OUTLINE

(Italics indicate major historical events in which Lafayette did not participate.)

1757
  September 6. Lafayette born at Chavaniac, in Auvergne.
1759
  August 1. Father killed at the Battle of Minden.
1760
  April 5. Birth of sister, Marie-Louise-Jacqueline, who died three months later.
1763
  February 10. Treaty of Paris. France, defeated in Seven Years' War, gives up all claims in North America.
1770
  April 3. Mother dies.
  May. Inherits a large fortune from his grandfather.
1771
  April 9. Becomes a *sous-lieutenant* in the King's Musketeers.
1773
  April 7. Becomes a lieutenant in the Noailles Dragoons.
1774
  April 11. Marries Adrienne de Noailles.
  May 19. Becomes a captain in the Noailles Dragoons.
1775
  Summer. Stationed at Metz; at a dinner given by his commander, the Comte de Broglie, hears the Duke of Gloucester speak of the American revolt.
  December 15. Birth of daughter, Henriette.
1776
  June 11. Placed on reserve status.
  December 7. Signs agreement to serve as a major general in the American army.

1777

February. Buys *La Victoire,* in which he plans to carry a party of French officers to America.

February 21–ca. March 9. Visits London.

April 20. Sails from Pasajes, Spain, for America on *La Victoire.*

June 13. Arrives at North Island, South Carolina.

July 1. Birth of daughter Anastasie in Paris.

July 27. Arrives at Philadelphia; reports to Congress.

July 31. Appointed major general, but without command; invited to join Washington's military "family."

September 11. Wounded in the leg at the Battle of Brandywine.

October 3. Death of daughter Henriette in Paris.

October 17. Burgoyne surrenders to Gates at Saratoga.

November 25. Lafayette commands at a skirmish at Gloucester, New Jersey.

December 1. Receives command of a division.

1778

January 23. Selected by Congress to lead an "irruption" into Canada.

February 6. French-American treaties of alliance and commerce signed in Paris.

February 19. At Albany. Decides the Canadian expedition is not feasible. Assumes command at Albany.

March 31. Leaves Albany to resume command of his division at Valley Forge.

May 4. Congress ratifies the French-American treaties.

May 18. Lafayette given command of an independent detachment to obtain intelligence of British movements and interrupt British communications.

May 20. Leads retreat from Barren Hill.

June 28. Battle of Monmouth.

July 11. D'Estaing arrives off New York.

July 22. Lafayette appointed to the command of a detachment ordered to Rhode Island to serve under Sullivan.

August 8–9. British evacuate works on northern end of Rhode Island; American forces under Sullivan occupy them.

August 11–14. Hurricane batters French and British fleets off Rhode Island; Howe withdraws to New York.

August 21. D'Estaing sails for Boston.

August 30–31. Lafayette assists in evacuation of American troops from Rhode Island.

September 14. Franklin elected minister plenipotentiary to France.

October 5. At Fishkill. Challenges Carlisle to a duel.

October 13. Requests leave from Congress to return to France.

1779

January 11. Lafayette sails from Boston for France on the *Alliance.*

February 6. The *Alliance* reaches Brest.

February 12. Lafayette arrives at Versailles; confers with Maurepas.

February 12–19. Under house arrest in Paris.

March 3. Named lieutenant-commander of the King's Dragoons with the rank of *mestre de camp.*

March 14–31. Discusses plans with the French ministers for a raid on Irish and English coasts. An expedition under Lafayette and Jones decided upon.

April 12. Aranjuez Convention confirms the alliance of France and Spain.

May 22. Lafayette-Jones expedition abandoned; ordered to take command of the King's Regiment of Dragoons.

June 13. Ordered to Versailles to meet with Vaux, who will command the troops in Normandy for a joint French-Spanish expedition against England; made *aide-maréchal-général-des logis* under Vaux.

June 16. Spain's official declaration of grievances presented to the British ministry; Spain institutes siege of Gibraltar.

October 9. American and French defeat at Savannah.

November. Expedition against England abandoned.

December 24. Birth of Lafayette's son, George Washington.

December 26. British fleet and troops under Clinton sail from New York for Charleston, South Carolina.

1780

January 8–16. Rodney captures Spanish convoy and Spanish blockading squadron.

January–February. Lafayette discusses with French ministry plans for an expeditionary force to be sent to America.

February 29. Catherine II issues Declaration of Armed Neutrality.

March 20. Lafayette sails from Rochefort for America on *L'Hermione.*

April 26. Arrives off Boston Harbor.

May 10. Arrives at Washington's camp, Morristown, New Jersey.

May 12. Americans surrender at Charleston.

July 10. French expeditionary force under Rochambeau and Ternay arrives off Newport.

July 24–ca. August 5. Lafayette confers with Rochambeau and Ternay at Newport.

August 15. Assumes command of light division.

August 16. Gates's defeat at Camden.

September 21–22. Lafayette attends Hartford Conference with Washington, Rochambeau, and Ternay.

September 25. Benedict Arnold's treason discovered.

September 29–30. Lafayette sits on court-martial of Major André.

October 7. Battle of Kings Mountain, South Carolina.

October 14. Washington appoints Greene commander of the southern army.

November 26. Washington orders Lafayette's light corps disbanded.

December 15. Ternay dies.

December 20. Britain issues manifesto authorizing reprisals against United Provinces (unofficial declaration of war).

December 30. Detachment under Benedict Arnold arrives at Portsmouth, Virginia.

1781

January 4. Lafayette attempts to negotiate with the mutineers of the Pennsylvania Line.

January 5–7. Arnold occupies Richmond.

January 20–27. Mutiny of New Jersey Line.

February 20. Lafayette appointed to command expedition against Arnold in Virginia ("Portsmouth expedition").

March 1. Articles of Confederation formally ratified.

March 8. Destouches's squadron leaves Newport for the Chesapeake.

March 16. Battle of Cape Henry ("First Battle of the Capes"). Destouches returns to Rhode Island.

March 30–31. Lafayette visits Washington's mother in Fredericksburg and goes to Mount Vernon.

April 6. Washington orders Lafayette's detachment to South Carolina to join Greene.

April 21. Lafayette takes command of American troops in Virginia.

April 24. British under Phillips and Arnold land at City Point, Virginia. Cornwallis' army marches from Wilmington, North Carolina, to join Phillips.

April 25. Lafayette arrives at Fredericksburg. *Phillips's army enters Petersburg, burns warehouses; Greene's troops repulsed at Hobkirks Hill, near Camden.*

April 29. Lafayette's detachment arrives at Richmond.

April 30. Finding Richmond defended, Phillips withdraws his troops and sails down the James River.

May 1. Greene orders Lafayette to remain in Virginia and officially gives him command of the troops in that state.

May 6. The Comte de Barras arrives at Boston from France to command the French squadron in America.

May 9. Spanish capture Pensacola.

May 10. British evacuate Camden.

May 11. British garrison surrenders fort at Orangeburg, South Carolina.

May 12. British surrender Fort Motte, South Carolina.

May 13. British reinforcement of 1,800 men sails from Staten Island to join Phillips.

May 15. British surrender Fort Granby, South Carolina.

May 20. Cornwallis's army joins Arnold's at Petersburg; Cornwallis takes command.

May 20–25. In camp at Richmond.

May 22. Washington and Rochambeau confer at Wethersfield, Connecticut, and agree on a joint expedition against New York City.

May 24. Cornwallis's army leaves Petersburg for expedition into Virginia.

June 1–21. French army leaves Newport to join Washington's army on the Hudson.

June 2. French forces under De Grasse capture the garrison on Tobago.

June 10. Wayne, with 1,000 Pennsylvania troops, joins Lafayette.

June 11–14. Lafayette's army maneuvers between British army and Continental stores by means of an abandoned road.

June 15–16. Cornwallis occupies Richmond.

June 19. Steuben, with Virginia Continentals and militia, joins Lafayette.

June 21. Cornwallis evacuates Richmond, begins march to Williamsburg; Lafayette's army follows.

June 25. Cornwallis occupies Williamsburg.

June 27–July 4. In camp near Williamsburg.

July 4. Cornwallis evacuates Williamsburg, begins march to Portsmouth.

July 6. Battle of Green Spring against Cornwallis.

July 9–24. Tarleton's Legion makes an unsuccessful expedition to destroy military stores in Virginia. ·

July 21–24. Combined American and French armies reconnoiter area around New York City.

August 2. Cornwallis occupies Yorktown and Gloucester and begins to fortify them.

August 14. Washington and Rochambeau learn that De Grasse is sailing for the Chesapeake.

August 18. British evacuate Portsmouth and its supporting posts.

August 19. American and French armies begin march from Philipsburg to Virginia.

September 2. De Grasse's fleet arrives at Yorktown; French marines placed under Lafayette's command.

September 5. De Grasse's fleet engages British fleet under Graves off the Virginia Capes ("Second Battle of the Capes").

September 10. Comte de Barras's squadron arrives in the Chesapeake with siege cannon and supplies.

September 14. Washington and Rochambeau arrive in Williamsburg.

September 26. Lafayette visits De Grasse's flagship. The last of the French and American troops arrive in Williamsburg.

October 3. Lauzun's Legion and Mercer's infantry skirmish with Tarleton's Legion near Gloucester.

October 14. Redoubt No. 10 captured by troops under Lafayette's command.

October 16. Cornwallis' forces attempt a retreat across York River but are forced back by a severe storm.

October 19. Cornwallis surrenders.

November 4. De Grasse leaves the Chesapeake for the West Indies.

November 8–10. Presides over court-martial of spies Lawrence Marr and John Moody in Philadelphia.

November 23. Congress instructs its ministers abroad to confer with Lafayette.

December 5. Notified of promotion to *maréchal de camp* pending end of American war.

December 23. Sails for France on board the *Alliance.*

1782

January 17. Lafayette arrives in Lorient from America.

January 21–22. Arrives in Paris during celebration for birth of dauphin; honored by queen; pays respects to Louis XVI.

February 12. British surrender St. Kitts to the French.

February 25. Vergennes endorses loan of 6 million livres to the United States.

March 20. Lord North resigns as prime minister of Great Britain.

March 27. Rockingham-Shelburne coalition replaces North ministry.

April. British emissary arrives in Paris for peace negotiations.

April 12. Rodney captures de Grasse at the Battle of the Saints.

April 16. Last of the United Provinces recognizes American independence.

April 18. Lafayette presents proposals for further French campaigns in North America.

June 17. Parliament passes the Enabling Act.

June 24. Lafayette received into Masonic lodge of Saint-Jean d'Écosse du Contrat Social.

July. Rockingham becomes British prime minister; peace negotiations begin in Paris.

September. Britain successfully defends Gibraltar against Spanish siege.

September 7. French emissary leaves for England for secret talks with Shelburne.

September 17. Birth of Lafayette's daughter Marie-Antoinette-Virginie.

September 24. Britain's agent in Paris receives revised commission to treat with the "thirteen United States."

October. Proposed Franco-Spanish expedition against the British West Indies under d'Estaing.

October 8. Commercial treaty between the United States and the United Provinces.

October 24. Lafayette accepts position of quartermaster general of Franco-Spanish expeditionary force.

November 30. Britain and the United States sign preliminaries to peace.

December. British forces evacuate Charleston.

December 2. Lafayette joins Franco-Spanish expedition at Brest.

December 23. Lands at Cadiz.

December 24. Major French force in the United States, under command of Vioménil, departs.

1783

January 6. Petition from unpaid American soldiers read to Congress.

January 20. Great Britain, France, and Spain sign preliminaries to peace.

February 1. Franco-Spanish expedition called off.

February 5. Lafayette writes Washington requesting appointment as American representative at treaty ratification in London.

February 14. Sends *Le Triomphe* to United States with news of preliminary peace.

February 15. Arrives at Madrid to work toward Spanish recognition of American minister.

February 22. House of Commons accepts peace but condemns concessions.

February 24. Shelburne resigns.

March. American tobacco merchants complain to Lafayette of difficulties with the Farmers General.

Mid-March. Lafayette returns to Paris and accepts rank of *maréchal de camp*.

March 19. Approaches French ministers about trade concessions for United States.

March 23. Lafayette's news about provisional peace arrives in Philadelphia via *Le Triomphe*.

March 29. Lefèvre d'Ormesson replaces Joly de Fleury as controller of finances.

April 3. Fox-North coalition takes power in Great Britain.

April 8. Catherine, empress of Russia, issues manifesto announcing annexation of the Crimea.

April 10. Congress passes resolution of approval and thanks for Lafayette's services to the United States while in Europe.

May 5. Lafayette recommended for the Cross of St. Louis.

May 13. Society of the Cincinnati established near Fishkill, New York.

June. Robert Livingston resigns as secretary of foreign affairs.

June 28. *Arrêt du conseil* establishes regular packet service between France and United States.

July 2. British order in council prohibits all trade between British West Indies and United States.

August 22. Spain officially receives American chargé.

September. Peace of Versailles.

October 29. Congress resolves to appoint Adams, Franklin, and Jefferson commissioners to negotiate treaties with maritime powers of Europe.

October 31. Congress receives minister from United Provinces.

November 3. Continental army is mustered out.

November 4. Calonne replaces d'Ormesson as controller of finances.

November 25. British forces evacuate New York.

December 13. Lafayette sends Calonne observations on American commerce in France.

December 17. Fall of Fox-North coalition.

December 23. George Washington resigns as commander in chief.

1784

January 9. Lafayette informed of four free ports for American merchants in France.

January 13. Elected to membership in Charleston Library Society.

February 10. Addresses Calonne about trade restrictions on American commerce.

March 24. American Intercourse Bill extended by Parliament.

May 4. First general meeting in Philadelphia of the Society of the Cincinnati.

May 14. Official *arrêt du conseil* proclaims Lorient a free port.

May 19. Robert Morris requests Lafayette's help with further trade concessions for America.

June 28. Lafayette sets sail for America.

July 19. Alliance between France and Sweden.

August 4. Lafayette arrives in New York City; received by State Assembly in Trenton.

August 9. Honored in Philadelphia by former officers of Pennsylvania Line.

August 12. Addresses American Philosophical Society on mesmerism.

August 17–28. Visits Mount Vernon.

August 19. Congress adjourns.

August 30. *Arrêt du conseil* further lessens trade restrictions on American merchants.

September 14. Lafayette receives freedom of New York City.

September 23. Arrives Albany; decides to travel to Fort Schuyler to negotiate with Indians.

September 29. Arrives with French chargé at Fort Schuyler.

September 30. Feted by Indians at Oneida Castle.

October. Connecticut confers citizenship on Lafayette and his son.

October 2. American commissioners arrive at Fort Schuyler.

October 3. Lafayette addresses Indians.

October 4. Indians respond to Lafayette; he departs.

October 5. Treaty negotiations begin between Indian nations and American commissioners.

October 7. Lafayette visits battlefield at Saratoga.

October 15. Arrives Boston; *Nymphe* placed at his disposal.

October 19. Lafayette honored by Massachusetts State Assembly and Boston merchants on third anniversary of Yorktown.

October 20. Receives honorary degree from Harvard University.

October 22. Treaty negotiated with Indians.

October 24. Lafayette honored at dinner of Rhode Island chapter of the Cincinnati.

November 10. Commercial alliance between France and the United Provinces.

November 15. Lafayette arrives at Yorktown; on to Williamsburg.

November 17. Louis XVI offers to mediate between Austria and the United Provinces.

November 18–28. Lafayette meets with Washington in Richmond; returns to Mount Vernon.

December 1. Lafayette and George Washington part.

December 3. Austria proposes creation of kingdom of Burgundy.

December 6–11. Lafayette visits Congress at Trenton; receives standard surrendered by Cornwallis.

December 11. Congress praises Lafayette in letter to Louis XVI. Lafayette takes leave of Congress, appealing for national unity.

December 18. Maryland House of Delegates approves citizenship for Lafayette and his male heirs in perpetuity.

December 20. Governor Clinton and other officials bid Lafayette farewell in New York.

December 21. Jay takes oath of office as secretary for foreign affairs.

December 23. Lafayette sails for France.

1785

January 20. Lafayette arrives in France from American tour.

January 24. Speaks to provincial estates at Brittany. *States General accept French mediation in dispute between Austria and United Provinces.*

January 25. First meeting of New York Society for Promoting the Manumission of Slaves.

February 14. Congress authorizes $80,000 to treat with Barbary States.

February 24. Adams chosen minister plenipotentiary to Great Britain.

March 7. Congress accepts Franklin's resignation as minister to France.

March 10. Jefferson chosen to replace Franklin.

March 30. Lafayette requested to secure munitions for Virginia.

May. Takes up cause of Protestants in France.

May 7. Proposal made to buy American whale oil to light Paris in response to Lafayette's efforts.

June. Spanish chargé arrives in United States.

June 1. George III officially receives Adams as American minister.

June 7. Lafayette authorizes purchase of estate in French Guinea for experiment in emancipating slaves.

August. Urges suppression of French tobacco monopoly to aid American merchants.

August–October. Tours German states.

August 4. Arrives at Prince Henry's country estate in Rheinsberg.

September 2–3. Arrives in Vienna; presented to Emperor Joseph II.

November 8. Treaty of Fontainebleau.

November–December. Lafayette persuades Castries to purchase naval stores from United States.

November 10. Treaty of alliance between France and United Provinces.

November 17. Calonne informs Lafayette of diminished duties on American fish oils.

1786

Works for French trade concessions for the United States as a member of the "American Committee."

August. Buys plantation in Cayenne for experiment in slave emancipation.

1787

February 22–May 25. Attends Assembly of Notables.

May 24. Calls for toleration of the Protestants and reform of the criminal law.

1788

November 6–December 12. Attends Second Assembly of Notables; supports doubling of the Third Estate.

1789

March 26. Elected deputy to the Estates General from Auvergne.

June 27. Joins with the Third Estate, which had constituted itself as the National Assembly.

July 11. Presents draft for the Declaration of the Rights of Man and the Citizen.

July 13. Chosen vice-president of the National Assembly.

July 14. Fall of the Bastille.

July 15. Lafayette proclaimed commandant of the Paris National Guard.

October 5–6. Leads Paris National Guard to Versailles; brings the king to Paris.

1790

June 19. Supports decree abolishing titles of nobility.

July 14. Presides at Federation ceremony of the National Guard.

1791

June 21. Flight of the king to Varennes.

July 17. Demonstration at the Champ de Mars dispersed by the National Guard.

October 8. Lafayette resigns as commandant of the Paris National Guard.

1792

ca. January 1. Takes command of the Army of the Center at Metz.

May–August. Commands the Army of the Left.

August 10. Arrest of the king.

August 19. Lafayette impeached by the Convention. Emigrates and is captured by the Austrians.

September 18, 1792–September 19, 1797. Imprisoned at Wesel, Magdeburg, Neisse, and Olmütz.

1795

October 24. Joined by wife and daughters in prison at Olmütz.

1797

September 19. Released from prison under the terms of the Treaty of Campo-Formio.

November. Moves to Lemkühlen, Holstein.

1799

ca. January. Moves to Vianen, Holland.

November 9–10 (18 Brumaire). Establishment of the Consulate.

1800

January. Lafayette establishes residence at La Grange.

1807

December 24. Death of his wife, Adrienne.

1815

Begins first of several terms in the Chamber of Deputies.

June 18. Waterloo.

June 22. Lafayette insists on Bonaparte's abdication.

1824

August 16. Arrives in New York for American tour.

1825

September 9. Sails for France.

1830

July 28–30. Plays leading role in Revolution of 1830.

August 16–December 26. Commandant of National Guard of the Realm.

1834

May 20. Death in Paris.

Lafayette in the Age of
the American Revolution

PART I

FRANCE AND
THE PEACE

January 4, 1782–March 2, 1783

At all Events, When My Advice is Asked for, No Court, No Country
No Consideration Can Induce Me to Advise a thing that is not
Consistent With the dignity of the United States.

To John Jay, February 15, 1783

When Lafayette returned to France in January 1782 from the victory
at Yorktown, he was bedecked with honors and attention. Now he was
realizing all the dreams he had dreamed during the often frustrating
and dangerous years of American campaigning. He returned to the
promise of a promotion in the French army, one usually reserved for
men many years his senior. His connections in French society and
government suggested that a person of his accomplishments and station might soon expect to consolidate his place among the ranks of
French leadership.

Yet Lafayette's chief desire was either to serve the American peace
commissioners as "political aide de camp" or to return to America and
participate in the final campaign to force the remaining British troops
out of America. Not only did Lafayette don his cherished American
uniform on as many occasions as possible; he seemed eager to assure
everyone that until final peace and American independence were at-
tained, he would continue to concentrate his energies on America's
interests and needs.

Such aspirations meant that Lafayette would have to continue to
serve as intermediary and diplomat, as well as military strategist. Perhaps Ségur was correct in his assessment that in this role Lafayette
would "add the olive branch to the laurel." Certainly Lafayette's advice
to the French foreign minister, Vergennes, proved invaluable in securing a final loan to the continually destitute Americans. As for the peace
negotiations, Lafayette's ambitions to play a larger role were almost
certainly doomed to disappointment. With his usual brashness, he of-

fered to go to England and assist in the negotiations, a proposal that would certainly have offended the British. And as the negotiations in France wore on, his truly dual loyalty to France and America began to hinder his effectiveness. Neither side could trust him completely in the arcane maneuvers that led to the preliminary articles of peace. Certainly Adams and Jay became cooler toward him as their distrust for Vergennes increased.

Eventually it seemed best for Lafayette to leave the negotiations and take up his sword again. He went to Cadiz to take part in the mighty expeditionary force as second in command, under his friend Admiral d'Estaing. The campaign was to begin in the West Indies and then move northward to clear the British from Charleston and New York City. To be second in command of more than seven thousand Bourbon troops was a clear honor for Lafayette as long as he could reconcile the position with his orders from Congress and Washington. Yet this last military victory was not to be. Nevertheless, with the signing of the preliminary treaties Lafayette still had the unique pleasure of being the first to dispatch the news to America, on one of d'Estaing's fastest frigates, aptly named *Triomphe*.

From George Washington

Philadelpa. 4th. Jany 1782

My dear Marqs.

I cannot suffer Colo. Gemat to leave this City—for France—without a remembrance from me, to you.

I have remained at this place ever since you left it, and am happy in having discovered the best disposition imaginable in Congress to prepare vigorously for another Campaign. They have resolved to keep up the same number of Corps, as constituted the Army of last year and have urged the States warmly to compleat them. Requisitions of money are also made, but how far the abilities, and inclinations of the states individually to tax heavily will coincide with the views of Congress is more than I am able, at this early period, to inform you.[1] A further pecuniary aid from your generous nation, and a decisive Naval force upon this Coast in the latter end of May or beginning of June—unlimited in its stay and operations—would, unless the Resources of Great Britain are inexhaustible, or She can form powerful alliances, bid fair to finish the War in the course of next campaign with the Ruin of that People.

The first, that is an aid of money, would enable our Financier to support the expences of the War with ease and credit without anticipating, or deranging those funds which Congress are endeavouring to establish, and which will be productive though they may be slow in the establishment. The second, a Naval superiority, would compel the enemy to draw their whole force to a point, which would not only disgrace their Arms by the relinquishment of Posts, and the States which they affect to have conquer'd—but might, eventually, be fatal to their Army—or by attempting to hold these Posts be cut off in detail. So that in either case, the most important good consequences would result from the measure.

General Lincoln has accepted his appointment of Secretary at War. Proper plans of oeconomy are adopting in every department—and I do not despair of seeing, ere long our affairs under much better management than they have been; which will open a new field—productive it is to be hoped, of a fruitful harvest.

As you will have received—in a more direct channel than from hence—the news of the surprize & recapture of St. Eustatia by the Arms of France—I shall only congratulate you on the Event; and add, that it marks, in a striking point of view, the genius of the Marqs. De Boullié for Enterprize—and for intripidity & resources in difficult circumstances. His conduct upon this occasion does him infinite honor.[2]

I shall be impatient to hear of your safe arrival in France—and to receive such communications as *you know* will be interesting to the cause we espouse, and in which we are Actors.

Though unknown to Madam La Fayette I beg you to present me to her as one of her greatest admirers. Be so good also, as to make a tender of my best wishes to Duke de Lauzen and other Gentlemen of the Army of Count de Rochambeau who may be in the circle of your friends, & with whom I have the honor of an acquaintance. With sentiments of purest affection—& most perfect regard, I am My dear Marqs. Yr. assurd friend & obt. Hble. Servt.

G. WASHINGTON

P.S.   Jany. 5th.
Since writing the foregoing, I have had the letter and Resolves herewith sent, put into my hands by the Delegates of Virginia in Congress.[3] I have a peculiar pleasure in becoming the channel through which the just and grateful plaudits of my native State, are communicated to the Man I love.

G.W.

By advices just received from So. Carolina the Enemy have evacuated all their Posts in that State & have centered their whole Force in Charlestown. Wilmington is also evacuated, & North Carolina freed of its Enemys. The disaffected part of the State are suing for mercy and executing, it is said, some of their own leaders for having mis-guided them.

ALS (DLC: George Washington Papers, Series 4), draft.
1. On October 3 and November 2, 1781, Congress resolved to call upon the states to raise $8 million for the war effort; it also set quotas for each state (*JCC*, 21:1087–92). The first quarterly payment came due on April 1, 1782, but not a single state made payment.
2. Bouillé captured the island of St. Eustatius from its British occupiers on November 25, 1781.
3. The Virginia House of Delegates voted a resolution of thanks to Lafayette on December 17, 1781. Noting particularly his "generous endeavours to preserve the civil rights of the citizens . . . ," the House also voted to have Lafayette's bust made in Paris and presented to him (*JHD*, December 17, 1871, p. 43).

To George Washington

L'Orient January 18he 1782

My Dear General

I thank My Stars there is a Good Opportunity to let You know that After an Happy Voyage of 23 days I am Safely Arrived in L'orient, and that My family and friends are In a Very Good Health, Which Circumstances, My Dear General, I am Sure Will afford You Some Satisfaction. We Are Arrived Last Night, and are Setting out this Morning in Great Speed for Versailles and Paris, So that I Have But the time to Scrible a Line, and Beg leave to Request Your Excellency Will please to let My friends know of My Safe Arrival. However Happy I am to Be in France, and to Enjoy the Sight of My friends, I Anticipate the pleasure to find Myself again in a few Months on the American Shore, and to feel that Unspeakable Satisfaction I Ever Experienced when after an Absence I Could once More Arrive at Head Quarters.

As I am just Arrived I Cannot Be Very Particular in My Intelligences. From what I pick up on the Shore I find that Lord Cornwallis's down fall Had a glorious Effect, and was properly felt in France, England, and Indeed throughout Europe. The Birth of a Delphin Has Given a General Satisfaction to the french Nation, and from Attachement to the Queen I Have Been Made Particularly Happy By this Event.[1] The taking of Statia is a Clever affair, and I Never Read of a Prettier *Coup de Main*.[2] The Dutch Will no doubt Be Greatly pleased with the Conduct of the french. Old Count de Maurepas is dead.[3]

Charlus is Adjutant General of the Gendarmerie of France which is father Commands.[4] It Appears that the Convoy from Brest to the East and West indias Has Met with an Accident. 23 vessels it is Said are taken. I am not Much Acquainted with Particulars. But from a Bad Event we May derive Some Good if it is an Inducement to do what we Have Been talking about.

Be So kind, My Dear General to present My Best Respects to Mrs. Washington and My Compliments to the family and George and to My friends of the Army. On My Arrival I found a letter from Madame de Lafayette for America wherein She desires Her Most affectionate Compliments to You.

Adieu, My Dear General, we are Ready to Go and Yet when I think You are So Many thousand Miles off I Cannot Leave writing to You. Viscount de Noaïlles, Gal. Portaïl, Gouvion and all the detachement of Your Army Now at L'orient Join in Presenting their Respects to You, and I, My Dear General, I Need only Adding that I am forever Your Grateful and Respectfull friend

LAFAYETTE

Count de Charlus Being Major General of the Gendarmerie I am told the prince de Broglio a Son to the General will take His place in Your Army.

By an American Gentleman I am told that Mr. Deane after Endeavouring to Apolozige for Arnold's Conduct and Speaking as well as Arnold Acted is gone to the Austrian Flanders, So that there is no doubt of His Being a traitor.[5]

ALS (PEL: Hubbard Collection).

1. "Delphin": The dauphin, Louis-Joseph, was born on October 22, 1781.

2. Statia: The capture of St. Eustatius by Bouillé on November 25, 1781.

3. The Comte de Maurepas had died in November 1781.

4. The Comte de Charlus, son of the Marquis de Castries, had come to know Washington while serving with the French forces in America during 1780–81. Charlus returned to France after the seige of Yorktown.

5. As the American agent in Paris in 1776, Silas Deane had signed the agreement for Lafayette's commission in the American army on December 7, 1776. (*LAAR*, 1:17). Congress recalled Deane in 1778 to answer charges of irregularities in the conduct of his official duties. He returned to Europe in 1780; in 1781 he wrote some letters to friends in America, proposing an early reconciliation with England. The letters came into the hands of the North ministry, which had them printed in the New York *Royal Gazette* from October through December 1781, when Lafayette was still in America.

From the Comte de Vergennes[T]

Versailles, January 23, 1782

If I had had a moment to myself, Monsieur le Marquis, I would have been able to embrace you and give you all my felicitations. I should have sent them to you in America. You will find them expressed in the enclosed letter, which bears the date of December 1 but was not sent owing to lack of opportunities. It may give you material for some reflection, and I have a great need to discuss some with you, Monsieur le Marquis. I am not wonderfully pleased with the country you left; I find it rather inactive and very demanding.

Please give me the earliest opportunity to talk with you; I need your insights to clarify my thoughts.

I flatter myself that your time overseas has not altered the sentiments that you promised me would continue. Mine for you can have no limit but that of my existence. On that foundation remains the tender and sincere attachment with which I have the honor to be, Monsieur le Marquis, your very humble and very obedient servant,

DE VERGENNES

All the packets from America were delivered to me.

ALS (NNPM: Lafayette Collection, vol. 2), translation. For the enclosed letter congratulating Lafayette on his participation in the victory at Yorktown, see *LAAR*, 4:444–47.

To the President of Congress

Paris January 29h 1782

Sir

On My Arrival at L'orient, I Had the Honor to Write a Letter, Which, I Hope, Your Excellency Has Received.[1] My Stay in France Has Been So Short, that I Cannot Be Very Particular, But Have Given Mr. Franklin Notice of this Opportunity.[2] He Was Pleased to Accept of My Services as a Political Aid de Camp. The Difficulties Governement is Under to Assist us With Monney, Have No Doubt Been Related By Mr. Franklin. But as I know their zeal And Good Intentions towards us, I Have Had Pointed Conversations on the Subject.[3] Whatever they will think In their Power to do, Will of Course Be Communicated By Cher. de la Luzerne. Every Part of the time I Am Absent from America, Shall Equally Be Employed in Endeavours to promote the Wiews of Congress.

The Reception I Have Met with Is the More flattering to Me, as it Evinces Nothing Weighs So Much With the Nation and Her Sovereign, as an Ardent zeal for the Cause of America, and Honorable testimonies of Her Confidence.[4]

Requesting Your Excellency Will lay Before Congress a New Homage of My Respect and Gratitude I Have the Honor to Be With Great Personal Regard Sir Your Excellency's Most obedient Humble Servant

LAFAYETTE

ALS (DNA: RG 360, PCC 156, pp. 264–66). John Hanson was serving as President of Congress at the time.

1. Lafayette wrote Hanson from Lorient on January 18, 1782 (DNA: RG 360, PCC 156, pp. 260–61).

2. "Opportunity": to send dispatches on a reliable conveyance across the Atlantic. Franklin did send some dispatches dated January 28, presumably on the same ship that carried this letter (see Wharton, *Diplomatic Correspondence*, 5:136–37).

3. Franklin heard from Lafayette within a few days after his arrival at Lorient (Lafayette to Franklin, January 22, 1782 [PPAmP: Franklin Papers, vol. 24, pt. 1, letter 39]). On January 28 Franklin wrote to Robert Morris, ". . . our good Friend the Marquis whom I have just now seen, has been at my Request with all the Ministers, spent an hour with each of them, pressing with all the Arguments possible a farther Supply of Money for the ensuing Campaign; and being better acquainted with Facts he was able to speak with greater Weight than I could possibly do" (Ferguson, *Papers of Robert Morris*, 4:133).

4. Franklin wrote to Robert Livingston on March 4, 1782:

The Marquis de la Fayette was at his return hither received by all ranks with all possible distinction. He daily gains in the general esteem and affection and promises to be a great man here. He is warmly attached to our cause; we are on the most friendly and confidential footing with each other, and he is really very serviceable to me in my applications for additional assistance [Wharton, *Diplomatic Correspondence*, 5:214].

To John Jay

Versailles January 30h 1782

Dear Sir

On My Departure from America, I Have Been Intrusted With Dispatches for You, Which it Has Been Recommended to me to forward By a Safe Opportunity. I dare not Send them By Post, and Still less Will I put them in the Hands of Spanish Expresses. But as there is No Private Person Going towards Madrid, I will Make use of the first french Courier that Will Be Dispatched to Mr. de Montmorin.

As Every Piece of Intelligence is of Course Contained in the Inclosed letters, I Will only Add that a Small Expedition of the Ennemy from Canada Had Been Checked By the Gallantry of Lt. Clel. Willet, and that after the Evacuation of Wilmington, and a little Success of Gal. Greene Against a fort in Carolina, the Ennemy are Now Confined to Penobscot, Newyork, Charlestown, and Savahna.[1] That they May Be driven from all, or at least from One of the two Important Posts, and that Some further Assistance May Be obtained from Hence, is the Ardent Wish of My Heart, and is not Quite Stranger to My Voyage this Side of the Atlantic. Whenever a Communication Betwen You and me May Be Productive of Advantages to America, or of Some Personal Agrement to You, I shall ever Consider Myself Happy and Honoured By a Correspondance With Mr. Jay for whom I Entertain the Highest Respect, and whom I Beg to Be Convinced that My Attachement is not less Sincere than the Regard I Have the Honor to Be With Der. Sir Your Most obedient Humble Servant

LAFAYETTE

I Beg My Best Compliments May Be Presented to My friend Carmichael[2] and my Respects to Mrs. Jay.

ALS (London: Royal Archives, Windsor Castle: The Correspondence of Chief Justice Jay. With the gracious permission of Her Majesty Queen Elizabeth II).

1. Marinus Willett defeated the Tories in their last major raid in the Mohawk Valley of New York in late October 1781. After Nathanael Greene's December 1 attack on the fort at Dorchester, South Carolina, the British in that state retreated to Charleston.

2. William Carmichael was John Jay's secretary in the American legation.

To George Washington

Versaïlles January 30h 1782

My Dear General

Having landed Some Days Ago at l'orient, I Had the Pleasure to inform You of My Safe Arrival, and Hope the letter will Have a Prosperous Passage. You Easely Imagine, My Dear General, that no time Was lost in posting off to Paris, where I found My family and friends in Perfect Health. My Daughter and Your George are Grown up So Much that I find Myself Great deal older than I Aprehended.[1] The Short Stay I Have Hitherto Made Cannot Have fully Apprised me of all Circumstances. There is Nothing Very Important lately Happened. For I trust, Before this Reaches You, You will Have Heard of the Unlucky turn of the Weather that forced the out ward Bound Convoys

to put up Again in the Harbour of Brest. Measures Had Been taken to
Be Before Hand with the Ennemy in Every Quarter of the World. It is
trüe Rodney, it is Said, Has also Been obliged to Return.[2] Lord Cornwallis Has Been taken in a Merchant Vessel, and Ransomed By a
french Privateer. We Heard Nothing of Arnold.[3] Should He Be
Brought into Some Harbour, I Shall Make it My Business to obtain His
Being delivered as an American deserter. It is Said Lord George Germaine is Going to Quit His Post.[4]

As I told you My opinion of the Ministers, And Also the degree of
friendship that Subsists Betwen Me and Each of them, I will only Add
that, I am Hitherto Much Satisfied with their zeal and Good Intentions
for America. But find it Very difficult, Next to Impossibility to Get
Monney. On My Arrival Mr. Franklin told me Nothing Could Be Expected.[5] However I Had Some Conversations on the Subject. I Hope,
Betwen us, Some thing May Be obtained, But Would not Have Mr.
Moriss to Be Sanguine. What May Be done, Cher. de la Luzerne will of
Course Announce. But Congress will Be Mistaken if they Build upon
Expectations of Monney from this Quarter. However, I will Exert My-
self for the Best, to Promote that, and Every other Wiew which May Be
Interesting to America. As to Grand operations or More Minute Cir-
cumstances of Supplies, tho' I Have Had Conversations on the Subject
with the king and His Ministers, I Cannot as Yet write You Any thing
Particular, and Will Endeavour to do it By the first Good Opportunity.

It is Generally thought in this Quarter, that the Exertions of America
are not Equal to Her Abilities.[6] Nothing Can Operate So Much for
further Assistance As Pointed Assurances of A Numerous, well
Cloathed and well fed Army for the war. Congress ought to Be Very
Careful of that Matter. For You May depend upon it, England are
Determined to play a desperate Game and to try at least an other
Campaign. Will it Be a defensive one in America, and offensive Elsewhere, or the Reverse of that, I Cannot as Yet Ascertain. But I think
the Evacuation of Newyork and Charlestown, is as far from their ideas
for Next Campaign, as the Very Evacuation of London. And to Get out
of it, they Must Be driven.

The Reception I Have Met with from the Nation at large, from the
king and from My friends will I am Sure Be pleasing to You and Has
Surpassed My Utmost Ambition. The King Spoke of You to me in
terms of So High A Confidence, Regard, Admiration, and Affection
that I Cannot forbear Mentionning it. I Have Been the other day
Invited at the Marechal's de Richelieu, with all the Marechals of France
where Your Health was drank with Great Veneration, and I was Requested to present you with the Homages of that Body. All the Young
Men of this Court are Solliciting a permission to Go to America. I must
tell you that the News about Cardinal de Bernis, was only a Rumour

propagated in the Provinces, and it Appears the king Means to Be His own first Minister.[7] Madame de Lafayette Requests I will present Her Respectfull and Affectionate Compliments to You and to Mrs. Washington. Viscount de Noaïlles Begs leave to offer His Best Respects. Be So kind to Present Mine to Mrs. Washington, and My Compliments to the family, to George, to My friends in the Army. Adieu, My Dear General, However Happy in My Situation Here, I Could not Have a Moment's Rest, Had I not a Certainty that Nothing is doing in America, that My Services Could not for the Present Be of Any Use to You, and that the light Compagnies Have joined their Respective Regiments.[8] It is Alwaïs Pleasing for My Heart to Repeat the Homage of the Respect and Attachement that Make me for Ever Your Most Affectionate friend

LAFAYETTE

The Next time I write to Your excellency it will Be in Cyphers and More Particular.

ALS (PEL: Hubbard Collection).

1. "Your George": George-Washington Lafayette.

2. The convoys from Brest were bound for India and the West Indies with supplies, troops, and additional ships of the line. Despite the foul weather, Admiral Rodney had succeeded in leaving England in mid-January; he arrived in the West Indies a full month before the French squadron.

3. Cornwallis and Benedict Arnold left New York City in the same convoy in mid-December and arrived safely in England in mid-January.

4. Even after Yorktown, George Germain, secretary of state for the colonies, had remained adamant in his opposition to American independence. He resigned in early February.

5. During this same month Franklin was writing to his American colleagues John Adams, John Jay, and Robert Morris about the limits of French aid and the need for the Americans to help themselves (Smyth, *Writings of Franklin*, 8:357–58, 364–66, 373–74).

6. See Vergennes to Lafayette, January 23, 1782.

7. Rumors had it that the Cardinal de Bernis would replace Maurepas (Bachaumont, *Mémoires secrets*, November 25, 1781, 18:163).

8. The light infantry corps commanded by Lafayette in America had been made up of select troops on temporary assignment from regiments in the regular army.

To Benjamin Franklin

Paris. February 12th 1782.

Dear. Sir.

I had the night before last, the pleasure to see Mr. Franklin, and gave him some account of the situation our affair was in, at that time. I ca[n] for the present be more paticular and will relate what has past respecting the letter of M. De Vergennes and the several articles a list of which has been put into my hands.[1]

I have represented to the Marquis De. Castries, that his assistance was absolutely necessary on the occasion. Had he not been rather short of means he would have aided us more completely; but advised you should request M. De. Veymerange to find a large vessel of 1200 tons or two of 600 each but not less, and know from him what is the price demanded to carry our stores.[2] It will be better not to mention the Marquis de Castries, and by those means we may lay before him every proposition that will be made. So that if they are exaggerated, or if no vessel can be found, we will avail ourselves of his assistance and authority.

The same Minister has also requested I would as soon as possible give him an exact memorandum of the stores on account of the United States, that are to be sent by the convoy of March; the number of tons is to be exactly specified. I will solicit for a protection to the very mouth of an American harbor. Should the vessels and officers be French they will probably better understand, and keep close with the commander of the escort. The Minister has also very judiciously observed, that we must not accept of any vessel under the size of 600 tons. He says the stores must immediately be collected at Brest, and the account of them be given to him as soon as possible. The moment the propositions from M. Vermerange are come to hand, I offer my services to carry them to Versailles and render the bargain as advantageous as possible to the United States.

Your excellency having requested my opinion respecting the importance of the several articles in a French list amounting to 1050 tons I will only say that clothing, camp-equippage, and powder are the most essential. Small arms come next with their flints &c. The howitzers and carriages I would reserve for the last. But if two vessels of 600 tons each may be easily procured at a cheap rate I should think it important to send under that convoy every-thing that is already bought and is destined to North America.

I had the other day the honor to explain to Mr. Franklin the reasons why I imagined the *Alliance* was entitled to the indulgence of a cruise, which has been positively promised by Congress.[3] Should it be your Excellency's opinion, that she ought to cruise for some weeks, and then return to your commands towards the end of March, M. De Castries has promised that Barry will be permitted to get all American sailors in any French harbor for whom he will make an application.

I have had several conversations respecting the situation of American affairs. I am in a few days to be called into a committee of the three Ministers,[4] which I have requested, because I think it better to debate with them all, than to divide my opinion into separate conferences. In every answer to their questions I will endeavor to fulfil the views of your Excellency, and in case you are satisfied with your aid-de-Camp, I am perfectly happy.

Benjamin Franklin, whose intermittent suffering from gout and a painful bladder stone induced him to rely heavily on Lafayette as his intermediary with the French court.

This is a very long epistle. I will now put an end to it, but not before I have presented your Excellency with the homage of the affection and respect, I have the honor to be with, Dear Sir, Your Excellency's, most obedient, humble servant

LAFAYETTE

P.S.)

I hope M. De Guichen will have gone with these last north east winds.[5] Rodney has been some time on his way. There is a convoy going from Cork towards the end of this month, notice of which might be sent to Barry. All the ships of the line, with some troops have left New-York.[6]

L (MH: Sparks Mss 16, fols. 320–23; by permission of Houghton Library, Harvard University), copy.

1. Vergennes's February 6 letter to Franklin dealt with the state of French-guaranteed Dutch loans to the Americans. Appended to it was a summary of the poor state of American accounts (AAE: Correspondance politique, Etats-Unis, vol. 20, fols. 272–73).

2. Veimerange, intendant general for the French army, was responsible for logistic arrangements for Rochambeau's expeditionary force in America. Franklin replied later that day that he would try to see Veimerange (DLC: Benjamin Franklin Papers). Veimerange attempted to intercede with Castries to obtain transport for American supplies but to no avail (Veimerange to Franklin, March 11 [PPAmP: Franklin Papers, vol. 24, p. 135]).

3. When Congress decided to use the Continental frigate *Alliance* to take Lafayette to France, it instructed Captain Barry to make the quickest voyage possible and to risk no engagements until after Lafayette's safe arrival (Ferguson, *Papers of Robert Morris*, 3:260–63).

4. Vergennes, Ségur, and Castries.

5. Guichen's convoys for India and the West Indies did not get out of Brest until the middle of February.

6. These were British ships of the line from Admiral Digby's squadron, sailing to join Hood and Rodney in the West Indies.

To Benjamin Franklin

[February 16–March 15, 1782]

Mis. de Lafayette's Best Respects Waït Upon Mr. Franklin and Would Be Much obliged to His Excellency for a Copy of His Memorial to the french Court As He Intends Pressing Upon this Subject in a letter to Count de Vergennes.[1]

The Mis. de Lafayette Begs Also to know at What time Captain Barreay Has Sett out for l'Orient, and When His Courier is Expected Back. Count de Vergennes Appears Unwilling to Decide Any thing Before Cher. de la Luzerne's dispatches Have Been Received.[2]

What is the Day and Hour Which Mr. Franklin Has Appointed for a Meeting of the three Ministers Agreable to What He was pleased to Say on tuesday last.[3]

AL (DLC: Benjamin Franklin Papers).

1. On February 15 Franklin wrote Vergennes that he had found the foreign minister's February 6 account of the French-guaranteed Dutch loans to be in error. The following day, he sent Vergennes a revised *aperçu* (*AAE:* Correspondance politique, Etats-Unis, vol. 20, fols. 272–73). Lafayette wrote a note to Vergennes advising him that the aid would be best used "not paying old debts but prosecuting the war with vigor, and by that they become immediately useful to the success of the next campaign"[T] (Stevens, *Facsimiles,* no. 1641).

2. Barry wrote Franklin on February 27 that he had returned to Lorient from cruising for prizes. On February 29 he received Franklin's February 10 letter instructing him to take on board supplies for America (DNA: RG 360, PCC 137, vol. 1, p. 510). Barry refused and left for America on March 15.

3. See Lafayette to Franklin, February 12.

From John Adams

Amsterdam Feb. 20. 1782.

My dear General

Yesterday Major Porter, brought me, your kind favour of the first of this month, together with Some Letters from America, in one of which is a Resolution of Congress of the 23d of November "That the Secretary of foreign affairs acquaint the Ministers Plenipotentiary of the United States, that it is the desire of Congress that they confer with the Marquis de la Fayette, and avail themselves of his Informations relative to the Situation of publick affairs, in the United States."[1] This Instruction, is So agreable to my Inclinations, that I would undertake a Journey to Paris, for the Sake of a personal Interview with my dear General, if the State of my Health, and the Situation of affairs, in which I am here engaged did not render it improper.

Permit me, however, to congratulate you, on your Arrival with fresh and unfading Laurels, and to wish you all the Happiness, which the Sight of your Family the applause of the Public and approbation of your Sovereign can afford you. I Should be extreamly happy in your Correspondence, Sir, and if there is any Thing in this Country which you would wish to know, I Should be glad to inform you as far as is in my Power. This Republick is ballancing between an alliance with France and America, on one hand, and a Mediation of Russia for a Separate Peace on the other. The Byass is Strong for Peace but they dont See a Prospect of obtaining it, by the Mediation. They are determined however to try the Experiment, but are So divided about it that all is Languor and Confusion. I fancy they will oscillate for Some time, and at last finding the Negotiations for a Separate Peace, an Illusion, they will join themselves to the Ennemies of their Ennemy.

Upon your Return to America, I Should be obliged to you, if you would Say to Some of the Members of Congress, that if they Should think fit to recall me, it is absolutely necessary in my humble opinion that they Should have Some other Person here invested with the Same Powers. With the Sincerest Affection and Esteem, I have the honor to be, my dear General, your most obedient and humble Sert.

LbC (MHi: Adams Papers).
1. *JCC*, 21:1135.

To Benjamin Franklin

Paris february 25h 1782

Mis. de Lafayette's Most Respectfull Compliments Waït on Mr. Franklin and Has the Honor to Inform His Excellency that in Compliance With His directions He Had Last Evening a Conference with Count de Vergennes. The Minister Said He Wished to Make Himself the Communication to Mr. Franklin, when Asked for it By Him, So that the Sum Will Be immediately Communicated, and I Heartly Wish it Was not less difficult to obtain its Augmentation.[1]

The Petition will Be presented this Evening to Mis. de Castries, and the Answer Sent to Passy as Soon as Possible.[2]

Mr. Franklin Cannot Render His friend More Happy than in Employing of Him for the Service of America, and He feels a particular pleasure in Avoiding for the doctor the trouble of Journeys to Versaïlles where His Peculiar Situation Calls Him two or three times a Week.

AL (PPAmP: Franklin Papers, vol. 24, no. 100).
1. The "Sum": a 6-million livre loan from France. For Franklin's account, see his March 4 letter to Robert Morris in Ferguson, *Papers of Robert Morris*, 4:340–46.
2. See Lafayette to Franklin, February 12, note 2.

To the Comte de Vergennes[T]

Paris, March 20, 1782

You asked me the other day, Monsieur le Comte, to send you a written account of my letters about Spain. Owing to the good will of

Congress, which asked all its ministers to correspond with me, I am instructed about the American offers and the Spanish reluctance to treat with them. It may be diplomatic to hide this feeling, but it would be quite unjust to attribute the obstacles to those who are trying to solve them.

On July 2, 1781, the ministers heard from Mr. Jay that Congress, informed of the objection to the treaty, had decided to yield the issue in question, which concerned navigation on the Mississippi, and Mr. Jay requested that someone be appointed to work out the articles with him.[1]

On July 21, the minister announced that he would present the letter to His Majesty.[2]

On September 19, the minister announced that he *would propose* to the king the nomination of a person charged with conferring with Mr. Jay; that he would present to the king a letter from Mr. Morris concerning that assistance for which he gave him some hope.[3] Finally, the minister requested the propositions that would become the basis of the treaty.

On September 22, the propositions were sent.

On September 27, a letter from the minister announced that a person would be named to confer and added that the instructions would be given before the court left for the Escorial.

On October 5, as the court was on the verge of leaving, Mr. Jay wrote to the minister and informed him that he would await his orders at the Escorial. The minister answered that he would write him as soon as he had something definite on the matter.

On December 10, the minister announced the nomination of don Bernardo del Campo, whose instructions would be ready in eight or ten days.

On December 27, M. del Campo gave as an excuse for his not taking up the matter, that his instructions were not completed; they were not yet begun and he did not know when they would be. This M. del Campo is first secretary to the minister.

On February 1, 1782. M. del Campo repeated the excuse of December twenty-seventh. On February 16, same excuse.

When Mr. Jay addresses himself to the minister, the minister is sometimes busy, sometimes sick, and he referred Mr. Jay to don Bernardo del Campo. And don Bernardo del Campo, not having received instructions, could only promise to talk to the minister about it.

This lack of health, of time, or of instructions has caused them, up to now, to neglect all the memorials that the American minister has presented.

I do not permit myself, Monsieur le Comte, to judge here the policies of a court that I have so many reasons to respect. But the Americans, with good reason, wish that the details of their conduct not be unknown to the king and that he whose treaties have been based on generosity and openness not doubt that, in their negotiation with Spain, his American allies are lacking neither good faith nor good will.

According to the hopes of September 19, we had imagined that Spain's aid would go beyond the modest amount America had received; but the remaining bills of exchange, amounting to 25,000£, would have been protested if Mr. Franklin had not used the money at his disposal, and I see, Monsieur le Comte, that France's right to the glory of this revolution and to the gratefulness of the Americans could not honestly be shared by any other European power.

M. de Vauguyon's dispatches will surely inform you of the state of American affairs in Holland. According to the information I received from Mr. Adams, it seems that they are taking a turn for the better.[4] I beg you to accept, Monsieur le Comte, the homage of the respectful attachment with which I have the honor to be your very humble and obedient servant,

LAFAYETTE

ALS (AAE: Correspondance politique, Etats-Unis, vol. 20, fols. 438–39), translation.

1. In order to "remove every obstacle" to a commercial treaty and an alliance with Spain, Congress resolved on February 15, 1781, that Jay should be permitted to yield the free navigation of the Mississippi by the Americans (*JCC*, 19:151–54). The alliance would involve Spanish recognition of American independence and ensure financial aid, the chief objects of Jay's mission to Spain.

2. The "minister" referred to is the Conde de Floridablanca, first minister to Charles III.

3. Robert Morris, the American superintendent of finance.

4. John Adams had advised Lafayette on March 10 that the provinces of Friesland, Holland, Gelderland, Zeeland, and Overijssel had acknowledged the sovereignty of the United States (MHi: Adams Papers).

To the Comte de Vergennes[T]

March 20, 1782

You were busy, Monsieur le Comte, and I did not want to talk to you about business, but Mr. Franklin spoke to me about an idea that he asked me to communicate to you.

He says that the English ministers exaggerate the obstacles that France would bring to the peace; Mr. Forsh, a tool of Lord North, will not give them an account of his mission.[1] A private letter from Mr.

Franklin to a friend, who is also a friend of the *new* ministers, could without inconvenience let them know your response.[2]

L.F.

ALS (AAE: Correspondance politique, Etats-Unis, vol. 20, fol. 440), translation.

1. Nathaniel Parker Forth ("Mr. Forsh"), an agent of Lord North, had met secretly with Vergennes to discuss separate peace negotiations between France and England. Vergennes refused the offer and so informed Franklin and the Spanish ambassador to France (Richard B. Morris, *The Peacemakers* [New York, 1965], pp. 252–56).

2. Since there was much speculation that Lord North would soon be out of office (he resigned that same day), Lafayette probably meant that negotiation with Forth would be futile. Lafayette was probably suggesting contact with David Hartley, a friend of the Rockingham Whigs and Franklin's correspondent.

To John Adams

Paris March 27h 1782

My Dear Sir

I Beg You Will Accept My Best thanks for the two letters You Have Been Pleased to write Giving the Particulars of Your Situation in Holland, and favouring me With Your Opinion Upon the Operations of the Next Campaign.[1]

I am Happy to find You Are likely to Get the Better of British Cabals, and Hope our Independance Will Be Soon Aknowledged throughout the United Provinces. Such a Measure from a Republican and Commercial Nation Will prove Particularly Agreable to America. You Will Vastly oblige me, My Dear friend, to Let me Hear of the Progress of Your Negotiations, and I Do Assure You that Independant of Public Considerations, the High Regard and Warm Attachement I feel for You, Will Greatly Contribute to My Satisfaction.

On My Departure from America I Have Been Desired By Dr. Moriss to Represent the Necessity of a Pecuniary Assistance. It Has Been Granted, But four or Six Millions are Wanting to Make up the Sum. Could it Be Possible to find them in Holland Upon American Credit?

The defensive plans of Gal. Connway are So Very absurd, that I think With You a General Evacuation Will probably take place.[2] However we ought not to Be too Sanguine. *In all Cases,* I am Entirely of Your Opinion about What *we ought to do.*[3] I Cannot write So Confidentially By post as I would wish, and Will Be More Particular when an Opportunity offers. I Had a letter from Mr. Jay. Things there as Usual. General Washington writes me that Every thing in the Several Departements is taking a Good turn, and Great Improvements are Made. He Appears Much Satisfied with the Present Situation of Affairs.[4]

You are to Receive a Visit, not from a friend—that I Had from the Ministers Here.[5] You Will Vastly oblige me With the Particulars. But let me know, what I am to Say, and Not to Say. The Next Safe opportunity I will write You a Confidential letter, and wish it was in Your Power to let me Have a Cypher to Correspond with you. I will Remain Some weeks more in France, and am Sure Congress will Approuve of the Delay. With the Highest Regard and Most Sincere Affection I Have the Honor to be Dear Sir Yours

LAFAYETTE

ALS (MHi: Adams Papers).

1. Letters of February 20 and March 10.

2. On February 22 General Henry S. Conway had moved in the House of Commons that George III be advised that the American war no longer "be pursued." The motion lost by one vote. On February 27 he reintroduced the motion, explaining that he meant not a withdrawal from the places held by British troops (a "defensive war"), but a renunciation of "offensive war," "a war in which attempts were made by an army, to possess themselves of what they had not before." The motion carried without a division (Hansard, *Parliamentary History*, 22:1030, 1068, 1085).

3. Adams's March 10 letter had urged Lafayette to secure a fleet and funds to capture the British troops as they evacuated (MHi: Adams Papers).

4. Jay's letter of March 1 has not been found. Washington had written Lafayette on January 4 of his pleasure to discover "the best disposition imaginable in Congress to prepare vigorously for another Campaign." He also forwarded news of the British removal to Charleston from the Carolina back country (DLC: George Washington Papers, Series 4).

5. Maryland native Thomas Digges was being sent by the North ministry to sound out Adams on separate peace negotiations.

To John Jay

Paris March 28h 1782

My Dear Sir

I take the Opportunity of a Spanish Courier's Going to Madrid to let You know that St. Kitts Has Been taken By the french.[1] The Intelligence Has Been Received Yesterday, and it is the More pleasing as British Accounts Had Rendered us Very Uneasy Upon the fate of the Expedition.

Your letter of the 1st Having Come to Hand I Made What Communications I thought to Be Serviceable.[2] But Will Be More Particular upon this Point. You know the Bills Have Been Immediately Accepted By Mr. Franklin.

It Was Said the British Ministers Would Resign and A New Set Be Introduced. But the Matter is at least Very doubtfull. You Will Certainly Hear of the dutch Being about Aknowledging our Indepen-

dance. As a french man and of Course a zealous lover of the House of
Bourbon I Earnestly Hope the king of Spain Will not leave to Halland
the Credit of first Entering Into this Measure. Generosity and frankness are the Pillars of the Spanish Character, We Shall Certainly Experience Both in the Negotiation that is Going on Betwen that Court and
the United States.[3]

I Beg, My dear Sir You will present My Respects to Mrs. Jay and
Remember me to My friend Carmichaell.[4] I will write to You Both By
the Next Safe Opportunity. With the Highest Regard I Have the
Honor to Be Your Affectionate Humble Servant

LAFAYETTE

ALS (NNC: John Jay Papers).
1. The British West Indian island of St. Kitts surrendered to the French on February
12.
2. The letter has not been found. Jay had discovered that the Spanish government
would not cover the bills of exchange presented to him in Spain.
3. These flattering comments indicate that Lafayette assumed the text of his letter
would be transmitted to the Spanish ministers.
4. William Carmichael had assisted Lafayette in his 1777 departure from France while
serving as Silas Deane's secretary. See *LAAR,* 1:43–44.

To Robert R. Livingston[T]

[March 30, 1782]

As for Spain, I have a letter from Mr. Jay whose negotiations are not
advancing, and it is the Spaniards' fault. After having conferred with
Dr. Franklin about it, I sent the ministers of France an account in which
I represented the conduct of the Court of Madrid from the point of
view that seemed best to demonstrate how badly they have behaved, I
ended by telling them how unjust it would be to accuse the Americans
of delays that should be attributed only to Spanish slowness.[1] This
government seems convinced of our difficulties in dealing with the
Madrid Court, Dr. Franklin has taken charge of some letters of exchange drawn on Spain. You will learn through M. le Chevalier de La
Luzerne, that a Mr. Forth came from England to Paris, spoke to M. le
Comte de Vergennes, impressed upon him that advantages could be
given to France, etc. M. le Comte de Vergennes's reply was as he has
declared, that France will never negotiate without her allies. Mr. Forth
returned to London.[2] This proves that independence is the only obstacle to peace for them; they will probably try to make some deceptive
propositions to America, and I desire it in order that the Congress will

have a new occasion to speak to them with firmness and generosity. I was very satisfied with M. le Comte de Vergennes's reply. Keep all this secret until M. le Chevalier de La Luzerne talks to you about it. Please tell Mr. Morris that so far it has not been possible for me to get an addition to the millions of livres for this year, but I am watching for an occasion to obtain an increase, and I will not let it escape. I wrote Mr. Morris that I did not think the desired sum could be entirely fulfilled.[3] Every means of bringing operations to the Continent, and of getting a little more money, the occasions to serve our cause in case the English really want to negotiate, will be seized by me with the patriotic zeal that attaches me to the United States. In the situation things are in, I think I should remain here yet a while, and I think the Congress will approve my conduct.

The dispositions of the king of France, the minister of France and the French nation, are just as we could want. I speak of them without bias; France is the only true friend on which America should count in Europe. The situation is so uncertain, that we must make greater efforts than ever before. A good army in America will do more to bring peace than one can imagine. The minority is no more our friend than the majority. The king of England is more irritated than humiliated, it is thus necessary to convince him firmly of the impossibility of conquering us. If this campaign is vigorous, it will certainly be the last.

LAFAYETTE

LS (PHC: Charles Roberts Autograph Letters Collection), translation. The entire letter (except for Lafayette's signature and the name of the addressee) is in code. An unsigned copy is in DNA: RG 360, Miscellaneous PCC, Letters Relating to Spain and the Barbary States.

1. See Lafayette's first letter to Vergennes, March 20.
2. See Lafayette's second letter to Vergennes, March 20, note 1.
3. Lafayette to Robert Morris, March 20 (Henkels, *Confidential Correspondence of Robert Morris*, item 271).

To George Washington

Antony March the 30h 1782

My Dear General

The Sailing of the Alliance Has Been So Unexpected That Mr. Franklin and Myself Have not Been Able to Send the Dispatches We Intended to forward By that Opportunity. There is Now a french Cutter that is Pretty Suddenly Sent of To America. I expected to write By a frigat which is to Sail in a Short time. But Cannot Let this Opportunity Slip a way, Before I Have the pleasure to Remember me to You, and Let You Hear of My Wellfare.

The taking of Mahon Has taken place Sooner than Was Generally Expected. Gal. Murray and Gal. Draper are about Quarrelling, As Generally Happens after a Misfortune Betwen British Commanders.[1] The Siege of Gibraltar is Going on. The Capture of St. Kitts Has Been the Better felt in England As upon a letter from Sir Samüel Hood the Sanguine Part of the Nation Had Conceived Hopes to Preserve this island. Many provinces in Holland are about Aknowledging American Independance. There is a Great Confusion Among the Parliamentary Part of the British Nation. Some are of opinion This is a *finesse* of Lord North, Who Wishes to throw Upon Parliament the Blame of Having Given up their Colonies. It Has Been long Said He would Retire. But He Has Hitherto kept His place, and the Opposition Members do Not Well Agree together. However we Have just got intelligence that a change of Ministers was going to take place.[2]

I Have wrote to Mr. Lewingston about NEGOCIATIONS of PEACE, about FRENCH MONEY, and About SPAIN and Have Requested He Would Communicate My Letter to Your Excellency.[3] We Must not Hope for SPANISH MONEY, nor Notwistanding their Compliments for DUTCH MONEY.

As to the ideas You Gave me in writing, I Have Represented them in the Strongest light Imaginable.[4] I Had With KING OF FRANCE a long Conversation About it. I Had Many With FRENCH MINISTERS. They Have plans about WEST INDIES. They also are Stopped By SPAIN and Without SPANISH SHIPS, I am affraïd BRITISH FLEET there Will Somewhat Exceed FRENCH SHIPS or at least Be upon a Parr. DUTCH SHIPS are Not to Be Rekoned. To Get SPANISH SHIPS in AMERICA is the Great Affair. Without it MARITIME SUPERIORITY is Very difficult, the More So, as they are Not Stranger to Some Ideas About GREAT BRITAIN which However Appears to me far from Being Settled. Tho' Nothing is fixed upon the Afore Mentionned points, I am Inclined to Believe in CHARLESTON more than in NEW YORK. For My Part I Much Prefer the former. But am affraïd SPAIN will offer Obstacles. They alwaïs are for WEST INDIES. Had I only to Manage FRENCH MINISTERS it would Be a much Easier Work. I think we May Hope for operating in SEPTEMBER.

Many People are of opinion the Ennemy Mean to Evacuate Newyork and Charlestown. For My Part I am not so Sanguine, and think it Would Be a Great Mistake for us to Calculate upon this Supposition Either in France or in America.

Under the Present Circumstances, My dear General, those of foreseen NEGOCIATIONS, or at least Possible, and the Unfixed Situation of those I Have Just Now Mentioned I think it Consistent with Your

Instructions, and perhaps Useful to America that I Should Remain Some time in Europe, that I May Avail Myself of Circumstances and Opportunities. I Hope, My dear General, You Will Approuve of My Conduct. May I flatter Myself that an Expectation of Being Useful, Having Somewhat detained My Departure, I will Neverthless Be Considered as a Candidate for the Command of the light Infantry—a Command Which is the Utmost of My Ambition, which Will not displease that Corps—and as on the Moment I Cease to Be Useful, the Moment a Determination is taken, I Hope Sailing for America, I flatter Myself the Infantry will not Be drawn [out] Before I Can present Myself Among the Candidates.

There Will Be a decision Before MAY and one FRENCH SHIP May Carry it immediately for WEST INDIES and an other do the Same for AMERICA. I will Have No time lost.

In the Present Situation of Affairs, We Must, I think, Prepare Vigourously, and I Hope to fulfill your Wishes, at least So far as Respects CHARLESTON.

I So perfectly know the Sentiments of Congress, and those of the Nation that I am Sure not only their Desicions upon Political Points, But also the Expression of them Will Add a New Lustre to the Idea they Have Given of their liberality and Noble Spirit. I am Sure, My dear General, that Every thing Considered, You will find I am Much in the Right to Waït a few weeks, and See what turn Affairs are taking. To Serve our Noble Cause is the Utmost of My Ambition, and I Will embrace Every Measure that May Be Productive of that End.

I will also add, My dear General, that Every thing I write in this letter Being the Result of the Confidence that Has Been placed in Me, I Must write for you alone, and this is As Confidential as the Most Secret Parts of our Correspondance.

Since I left America, I Had one letter from You By the Hermione.[5] I am Very Happy to Hear that a Spirit of Oeconomy and Arrangement is diffused throughout Every Departement, and for Many Reasons I Hope we May Have a Numerous Army for the Operations of the Campaign.

I Have Been for a few days at this Country Seat with Marquis de Castries who during the Holydays Comes to take Some Respite of Ministerial Cares. We are United By an Intimate friendship, and am Happy to find that Since He is at the Head of the Navy we Have Had a Serge of Successes. Had it not Been for the Storm that Mr. de Guichen Met with on His leaving Brest, we Should not, Independant of the Spaniards, Have lost an Instant of Maritime Superiority in the West Indias.

Now, My dear General, I will Speack to You of My Private Concerns.

Independant of My Situation at Court, and Among My Societies, the
Marks of affection I Every day Receive from the People at large, Render me as Happy as I Can Possibly Be. Such Influence as I May Have
Will Be truly precious to me whenever it Can do Some little Good to
our Adorable Cause. I Am Perfectly Satisfied with the Dispositions of
this Governement. Both Nations will for Ever Be attached to Each
other. And I See Both are So Much the object of British Envy and
treachery that It Will Ciment Among them an Eternal Amity and Alliance. Mde. de Lafayette Requests I will present to you Her Most
Affectionate and Respectfull Compliments and Also to Mrs. Washington whom She Most fervently prays to Make after the war a Voyage
to France, and Spend Some time in our family, where We Would Be So
very Happy to Receive You. Be pleased, My dear General, to Remember
Me Most Affectionately to the family, and to present My Best Respects
to Mrs. Washington. My Compliments waït upon George. I Had a letter
from Him and wish I Had Received one from My friend Tilmangh.[6]
Be So kind My dear General to Pay My Most affectionate Compliments
to Gal. Greene, Gal. Knox, and all my friends in the Army. I am So
Hurried this time, that I Cannot write to them. When Tilmangh writes
to McHenry and Hamilton I Beg He will Remember me to them.[7]
Adieu, My dear General, Most Respectfully and affectionately I Have
the Honor to Be Your tender and for Ever your Best friend

                                                         LAFAYETTE

Vicount de Noaïlles, Count de Charlus, Duke de Lauzun,[8] and all the
officers of Your Army Request their Best Respects to Be presented to
Your Excellency. The officers are about Returning to join their Respective Corps.

ALS (PEL: Hubbard Collection). Words written in cipher and deciphered between the
lines are shown here in small capitals.
   1. "Mahon": Port Mahon, chief city of Minorca. General Murray and General Draper
were the governor and lieutenant governor of Minorca. After the British garrison succumbed in February 1782 to a long French-Spanish siege, General Draper immediately
pressed a long series of misconduct charges against his superior.
   2. North resigned as prime minister on March 20; an unstable Rockingham-Shelburne
coalition took office on March 27.
   3. See Lafayette to Robert R. Livingston, March 30.
   4. Washington had written Lafayette on November 15, 1781, "No land force can act
decisively unless it is accompanied by a Maritime superiority" (LAAR, 4:436).
   5. Washington to Lafayette, January 4 (see Lafayette's March 27 letter to John Adams,
note 4).
   6. "George": George Augustine Washington. Tench Tilghman was Washington's
aide-de-camp. The letter from George A. Washington has not been found.
   7. McHenry and Hamilton had both been on Washington's staff with Lafayette.
   8. These officers had served under Rochambeau in the French expeditionary force in
America.

To George Washington

Antony March the 31st [1782]
We Have Certain Intelligence, My Dear General, that Lord North is out of place. He Has Himself Announced that Event in Parliament, and Said a New Minister Should Be Named in the Course of two or three days. It is Generally Believed Marquis de Rockingam Will Replace Him. Charles Fox is likely to Get Into Administration, and there Will not Be Better principles to Be found in the New Ministry than in the former. Can those people think that By Covering the trap With New leaves they May Better take in the People of America? Having felt the Pulse of France, they Will do the Same With America. I am glad of if, Because it Will Give Congress an Opportunity to Appear to Advantage.

Adieu, My dear General, let me once More tell you that With the Highest Respect, with all the tenderness and Warmth of a Heart devoted to you I Have the Honor to Be Your Most obedient Servant and forever affectionate friend

LAFAYETTE

ALS (PEL: Hubbard Collection).

From John Adams

Amsterdam April 6st. 1782.
My dear General,
I am just honored now with your's of 27st. March. All things were working rapidly together here for our good, untill on the 3d instant, the Russian Ministers at the Hague presented the Memorial which You have seen in the Gazettes.[1] This will set twenty little Engines to work, to embroil and delay: but I believe that in the Course of four or five Weeks We shall triumph over this which I take to be the last hope of the Anglomanes. The Voice of this Nation was never upon any occasion declared with more Unanimity, & the numerous Petitions have already done an honor and a Service to the American Cause, that no artifice can retract or diminish.

As to the Visit, Mr. Franklin is informed of the whole.[2] It is nothing.

The new British Ministry are in a curious Situation. There is but one sensible Course for them to take, and that is to make the best Peace they can with all their Enemies. We shall see whether they have Resolution & Influence enough to do it.

As to Credit here, I am flattered with hopes of it, provided a Treaty is made, not otherwise. Whether that will be done and when I know not. I can never foresee any thing in this Country, no not for one day, and I dare not give the smallest hopes.

Your confidential Letter had better be sent by the Comte de Vergennes's Express to the Duke de la Vauguyon.[3] I hope We shall have a good Account soon of Jamaica.

I am extreamly sorry, that Mr. Jay meets with so much delay in Spain. The Policy of it is totally incomprehensible.

Am happy to find that your Sentiments correspond with mine, concerning what We ought to do, and have no doubt that all will be well done in time. What is there to resist the French and Spanish Force in the West Indies? or in the Channel? or in N. America? or in the E. Indies? If my Dutchmen fairly concert Operations with France and Spain, and the Seas are kept with any Perseverance, all the Commerce of G. Britain is at stake. Yet your Caution not to be too sanguine is very good. Spain does not yet seem to be sufficiently awake and the English Admirals under the new Ministry will do all they can.

I fancy they will try the last Efforts of Despair this Summer, but their Cause is desperate indeed. Never was an Empire ruined in so short a time, & so masterly a manner. Their Affairs are in such a state, that even Victories would only make their final Ruin the more compleat. With great Affection & Esteem, I have the honor to be &ca.

LbC (MHi: Adams Papers).
1. The Russian intermediaries Markov and Prince Gallitzin presented a memoir to the States General which included a letter from Fox to the Russian ambassador at London, offering a separate peace treaty to the United Provinces. For the text, see the *Mercure de France*, April 13, 1782.
2. See Lafayette to Adams, March 27, note 5.
3. Vauguyon was the French minister at the Hague.

To George Washington

Paris April the 12h 1782

My Dear General

However Sensible I am that our Cause May Be Better Served By My Presence Here, than it Could Possibly Be at this Period By My Returning to America, I Cannot Refrain from A Painfull Sentiment at the Sight of Many french officers Who Are Going to Join their Colours in America. I Shall, thank God, follow them Before Any thing Passes that May Have Any Danger or Any Importance. But I am So far from the Army, So far from Head Quarters, So far from American Intelligences, that However Happy I am Rendered Here, I Cannot Help ten times A day Wishing Myself on the other Side of the Atlantic.

This letter, My Dear General, Is Intrusted to Count de Segur, the Eldest Son of the Marquis de Segur Minister of State and of the War Departement Which in France Has a Great Importance. Count de Segur Was Soon Going to Have a Regiment, But He Prefers Serving in America, and Under Your orders. He is one of the Most Amiable, Sensible, and Good Natured Men I Ever Saw. He is My Very Intimate friend. I Recommend Him to You, My dear General, and through You to Every Body in America Particularly in the Army.[1]

A few Recruits are Going out With this Convoy, and Will Be Protected By a frigat. They are Destined to fill up the Regiments, and prove Nothing either for or Against Any Operation in the Campaign. Mr. Franklin Has not Been able to Procure Vessels to take in Some Stores He Has Got at Brest. I Have Requested Marquis de Castries to let us Have what He Could Spare. It Will for this time Amount to Nothing or Very little. But He promised me We Should Have thousand tons in the Next Convoy—and Upon the whole I like it Better, as the Convoy will Sail under a Better protection and two Months Before JULY.

Inclosed I Send you, My dear General, the Copy of a letter lately written By a french Cutter.[2] I Have little to Add on one Article, But that My Expectations are Encreasing about CHARLESTON. But SPAIN will Insist upon WEST INDIES. We Expect Intelligences About what they Mean at last to do in Every Quarter With SPANISH SHIPS. Upon which I will Conclude With KING OF FRANCE and FRENCH MINISTERS. I do not forget FRENCH MONEY. The Moment I know Better one of FRENCH SHIPS will let you Have a full Account.

The New Ministry Have not as Yet Done Any thing of Importance. As Holland Was about Aknowledging Independance, England Has Endeavoured to take a Way their Attention from it and Has proposed peace to them Under the Mediation of Russia. Nothing as Yet is finally Settled. I Hope we May then get the Better of British Cabals; I Have Requested Mr. Lewingston to Communicate a few Words I Have writen in Cyphers upon Political Subjects.[3] Admiral Barrington With twelve Ships of the Line is to go out and His Destination Has Been kept Very Secret. Some People Imagine He is Going to take a Way the troops from Newyork and Charlestown Which it is Not much in their

Power to Reinforce.[4] It is Said Lord North Was Rather Glad of an opportunity to leave the Helm at So Critical a period, and would not Have His Name Affixed to a Disadvantageous peace.

Mr. Laurens is in England upon His Parole.[5] I intend writing this day to Him By a private Opportunity, and Will Advise Him, if Possible, to Get a permission to Go out of Great Britain. I wish He Was in France where, if exchanged, He Might Confer with the other Commissioners upon the Affair of Peace.

I Beg, My Dear General, You Will present My Best Respects to Mrs. Washington. Mde. de Lafayette, Your Son George,[6] and My daughter join in the Most affectionate Compliments to you and to Her. Remember me, My dear general, Most tenderly to the family, and the Gentlmen of the Army. Most Respectfully I Have the Honor to Be Your Excellency's Most obedient Servant and affectionate friend

LAFAYETTE

ALS (PEL: Hubbard Collection). Coded passages deciphered between the lines appear here in small capitals.

1. On this same date Lafayette wrote separate letters of introduction for the Chevalier de Lameth, the Prince of Broglie, and the Comte de Ségur, addressing them to Washington, Alexander Hamilton, Robert Morris, Henry Knox, and Benjamin Lincoln.

2. Lafayette's letter of March 30 to Washington.

3. See Lafayette to Livingston, March 30.

4. The New British Ministry was planning to remove all troops from America and use them to strengthen the West Indies and Halifax. Barrington's mission in April was to cruise near Brest on the lookout for French convoys.

5. Henry Laurens had been captured at sea in September 1780, while on his way to take up his post as U.S. commissioner to the United Provinces. He was a prisoner in the Tower of London from October 1780 until his parole in December 1781. In June 1781 Congress had named him one of five peace commissioners; the others were Adams, Franklin, Jay, and Jefferson.

6. "Your Son George": George-Washington Lafayette.

To Henry Laurens

Paris April 14h 1782

My Dear Sir

Our Separation Has Been So Long, our Correspondance So Interrupted that I Bless the Happy Opportunity Which is Now Offered. How often Have I Wished for the times When it Was So Very Convenient for us to Communicate With Each other.[1] Those times, I know, are Present to Your Memory, And You Are Happy to think this friendship of ours Has in Some Instances Been Productive of Public Good.

Whilst I Lamented I Had not Seen You, An Account of Your Misfor-

tune Reached Head Quarters. What I felt on the Occasion, I Hope it is
Needless for me to Mention. The treatement You Met With is So Very
Strange that one is at a loss What to Admire the More, its folly or Its
Insolence.[2] The Law of Nations Being Unrespected, Retaliation Was
the only Pledge We Had of their Not Blundering You Into the Most
Dreadfull Misfortunes. But I Could not Help feeling Proud at the
Noble, Steady Conduct of My Respectable friend, Whom Every In-
stance Has proved to Be a trüe Representative of America.

Every Public Intelligence is Sufficiently known and Private Communications are not Alltogether Safe. Let me Only tell You, that on My
Departure a Spirit of Arrangement and Oeconomy Was Diffused
throughout Every Departement. Every thing there is Improving Very
fast, and Upon a Rememberance of our former Difficulties, our York
town and Valley forge times, You Must feel With me on the Success of
the Noble Cause in Which We Are Engaged. General Washington,
Your Son, and Your friends When I last Heard from them Were in
Perfect Health, and Clel. Laurens Had Joined Greene's Colours in the
Defence of His Native State.[3]

The Late Change of Ministry is So far Pleasing As Wiggish Appearances, tho' in an Ennemy, Cannot fail to Be Agreable. As a french
Man, as An American I Very little Care Who Governs Great Britain.
Never Shall I forgive (tho' it is pretty Well Paid for) British Haughti-
ness and Cruelty to us Poor Rebels. But, on Account of Humanity at
large, I Heartly Wish tho' I am far from Believing, the Sacred flame of
liberty May Some what Be kindled in that Quarter. The British Minis-
try Are Going to fall into a Mistake. Too late it is By far to think of
Partial Negotiations. In the Mean while they are Loosing time and
Ground, and By and By they Will See their Error When I Hope a
General peace Will take place.[4] Mr. Franklin's letters, and My Verbal
Communications to Mr. Young Will Make you Acquainted with our
Opinion.[5] On Every Account, I Must, My Dear friend, Insist on the
Part that Respects Your Parole and Exchange.

Some public Business I am Charged With By Congress Have to this
Moment Differed My Return. I Hope Sailing in the first Days of May,
and (In Case I Cannot See You) I will Be Happy to Receive Your
Commands. With the Warmest Attachement and the Highest Regard I
Have the Honor to Be Your Most Obedient Servant and Affectionate
friend

LAFAYETTE

P.S. At the time of Your Misfortune Mde. de Lafayette Made Vain
Efforts to Contrive Her letters to You.[6] I just now Hear You Have not
Received Some Monney You Expected, and I know You Hate Accept-

ing any offer from the people about you. Give me leave to Inclose a
Small letter of Credit which will Be Enlarged if Convenient. Mr. Young
is in Hurry and I must of Course Be in Haste. Adieu.

ALS (ScHi: Henry Laurens Papers).

1. Lafayette had developed a friendly relationship with Laurens after the Battle of
Brandywine in September 1777; they corresponded regularly during the time Laurens
served as president of the Continental Congress, between November 1777 and December 1778 (see *LAAR*, 1 and 2, *passim*).

2. "The treatement": Laurens's incarceration in the Tower of London.

3. "Your son": Henry Laurens, Jr.; "Clel. Laurens": John Laurens, another son.

4. This section was written with the expectation that it would be forwarded to the new
ministry.

5. "Young": Moses Young, Laurens's secretary.

6. See the letter of Adrienne Lafayette to the Comte de Vergennes on behalf of
Laurens in October 1780, shortly after Laurens had been captured (*LAAR*, 3:202–3).

Proposals for the French Campaign in North America[T]

Paris, April 18, 1782

So little is known of the enemy's plans, and ours depend so much on
our allies, that for the moment it is impossible to decide on a campaign
plan.[1] Our present operations, especially in the Antilles, are subject to
still uncertain circumstances. But there are some political questions on
which a decision can be reached and some military dispositions which
will surely be made, and which, following those of the enemy, may be
easily changed according to circumstances.

Sent by America to give an account of its situation, and by General
Washington to fix upon a plan of cooperation, I add to these titles that
of a Frenchman who relates everything to the interests of his country
and that of a man honored by your confidence who freely presents his
private opinions.

The Americans are tired of the war, and the people long for an end
to their sufferings. But the most tempting propositions, made by ministers once cherished and still revered, will obtain nothing contrary to the
terms of the treaty nor even to the requirements of gratitude. In these
circumstances, however, I advise that none of the requested aid be
reduced; it should be the last, and it will crown all the rest. At the least,
we should furnish the supplies on the list Mr. Morris sends, which
amounts to an inconsiderable sum.[2]

The evacuation of New York and Charleston are still problematical.
In both cases we must either take the ports that give the British a
foothold or take the troops that they think should be posted elsewhere.

But above all it is necessary for the allied fleet to be in the Chesapeake during the winter season. Any operation in the Antilles will have succeeded or failed; facilities for the refreshment and recovery of the crews and provisions for the allied fleet will be found only on the coast of the United States.[3] If the enemy do not withdraw their troops, it is militarily and politically useful to take offensive action. If they do withdraw their troops, we must try to intercept them or escort those of M. de Rochambeau. Since this movement of the fleet is necessary even for the continuation of the war in the West Indies, there can be no objection to my assuring General Washington that during the winter the allied fleet is positively to proceed to North America.

Given this base of operations, the choice must be left to the general. New York and Charleston alone could fully occupy such an armament. The other posts are unimportant, or rather, because they are distant, they would distract the fleet from the major objects of its attention.

In the course of exploring the modes of operation, the necessity of augmenting the French division was recognized. This is a point agreed upon in the committee, on which it is useless to repeat myself. The change in ministers and measures has produced new speculations. Here is one that, because of the consequence, seemed to me should be interesting.

The closer peace approaches, the more we should gain control of the principal points. Newfoundland, with its banks, is an important one. Taking the key to it away from the enemy, or taking possession of it before the negotiations, assures us of a great advantage.

Occupied by other objectives, watched over and followed by the enemy, neither a part nor the whole of the allied fleet can make this expedition, which would take away its superiority or waste its time. It is from Brest, a point of departure somewhat closer, that one can hope to surprise Newfoundland.

If nothing is attempted in the English Channel during May, the obstacles will only keep increasing, and these kinds of operations will be given up; the very next operation will then be the sending of both ships and troops to American waters for the autumn.

Three thousand men and a few warships that would carry some of them would leave Brest around the end of May and would be off Newfoundland sometime in July. This expedition and the one to Penobscot would not last beyond the end of August. If it left earlier, had favorable winds, and did not go to Penobscot, this force would lose much less time. It would then join M. de Grasse, as M. de Barras did, but with this difference: the enemy would not be expecting it. Then, if there are no operations on the continent, all the French forces will proceed to the Antilles.

The evacuation of the British posts may be premature; in that case, the allied fleet will be occupied only with the enemy fleet and army. It is no longer on the continent but in the West Indies themselves that the Newfoundland forces will effect their junction.

Is it better to destroy or preserve the Newfoundland forts? Is it appropriate to have the Americans cooperate? Cannot Penobscot be taken by an American force under the protection and direction of the Newfoundland generals? Once the expedition is decided upon, it would be easy to settle these details.

If these expeditions do not take place, General Washington will proceed against Canada. The weakness of the enemy, the disposition of the people, and the efforts of New England and the state of New York give us high hope of success.

By concerning ourselves with Newfoundland and Penobscot and with preparations against New York or Charleston, we could then, in case of evacuation, turn the plans for Canada against Detroit, Niagara, and other outposts, which greatly lengthen the campaign. The secondary point of discussion, that of boundaries, would be demolished by facts, and as this news would come at about the same time as news from India and the Antilles, everything would be ready at the end of the winter for a general peace.[4]

LAFAYETTE

P.S. As part of our dispositions are general and preliminary, it is of utmost importance that they be communicated immediately to General Washington. This is the only means of ensuring, in any event, that the necessary preparations are made.

AMS (AAE: Mémoires et documents, Etats-Unis, vol. 2, fols. 95–96), translation. The proposal was sent with a cover letter to Vergennes on April 24.

1. The "allies" referred to here include the United Provinces and Spain, as well as the United States.

2. This list was probably that enclosed in Morris to Franklin, November 27, 1781, under the title "Invoice of Articles necessary to be imported from France for the Next Campaign in addition to those remaining on hand in the United States and on a supposition that the Cargo lost in the Ship Marquis de la Fayette is replaced. . ." (PPAmP: Bache Collection of Franklin Papers). Lafayette had carried the letters to Franklin, and Morris had instructed Franklin to share their contents with him (Ferguson, *Papers of Robert Morris*, 3:264).

3. The West Indies depended on North America for their food supplies during much of the war.

4. "The secondary point of discussion": the first point of discussion with Britain was its recognition of the independence of the United States.

To John Jay

Paris April 28h 1782

Dear Sir

The Opportunity I Now Embrace is offered By The Prince of Masserano Who Sets of this Minute for Spain, and Intends to Act a Part in the Darling Siege of Gibraltar. I Will Communicate a few intelligences Which it May Be Agreable for You to know and Which I Hope I May Safely Intrust to this Conveyance.

Holland is Now Quite Determined, and Has Agreed to Aknowledge our Independence. They are About Making A Treaty of Commerce and Have Received Mr. Adams in His Public Character.[1]

I Will Also Give You an Account of what Has lately Past Respecting Negotiations.

A few days Before the fall of the late Ministry France Had Some Advances Made to Her Under Hand Wherein it Appeared the Great point was to Make Her Abandon American Independence. The Answer Was Very proper, Very finely Expressed, and Such as Would please Every American Mind.[2]

Some time After that Mr. Adams Was Applied to at the Hague. He also Said Independance Was the first Step, and Nothing Could Be done But in Concert With France.[3]

The New Ministry Have Sent Emissaries to the french Administration, to Mr. Adams, and to Mr. Franklin.[4] The french Ministers Have Repeated that treating Was out of the Question Untill American Plenipotentiaries Were Admitted Into the Negotiations. Mr. Adams, and Mr. Franklin Have once More Said that America Was Not less Averse to a Separate peace, and that Any Attempt Was Nothing But a loss of time.

Under those Circumstances, I think we must Very Soon know What the Intentions of the Ennemy Are, either to try the Event of this Campaign or to Propose a General Negotiation.

Mr. Mitton Who Commanded an Important Convoy Has Safely Arrived into Martinique Harbour. He Has Under His Care a Vast Quantity of Military Stores Much Wanting for the french fleets, and His Safe Arrival Affords us Great Satisfaction.[5]

Some Vessels Going Under Convoy to the East Indias Have Met An English Squadron and have obliged to Put Back. It is feared Some transports May Be taken, But Nothing Material.

I am in Hopes a Northern Power, not of the first Rate, Will Before long Enter Into a treaty of Commerce. But I Request from You the Utmost Secrecy. The telling of it to You Alone Cannot Be a Breach of Confidence.[6]

I Beg the Whole of this letter May Be Considered as Confidential, and I do Not know What Communications Have Been Made to Your friends. God Grant them a Good Success at Gibraltar. I wish the devilish Rock Was out of the Way. Most affectionately and Respectfully Yours

LAFAYETTE

My Best Respects Waït Upon Mrs. Jay, and My Compliments upon My friend Your fellow Sufferer.[7]

ALS (NNC: John Jay Papers).

1. On April 16 the last of the United Provinces, Gelderland, agreed to recognize the independence of the United States. Six days later the States General resolved to recognize John Adams as envoy.

2. Vergennes told the emissary that France could not negotiate with England unless the English court were willing to confer with its allies on equal terms, which meant recognition of American independence at minimum.

3. A reference to the Digges mission; see Lafayette to Adams, March 27, note 5.

4. The Earl of Shelburne's agent Richard Oswald met with Franklin on April 12 and with Vergennes on April 17. The parolee Henry Laurens met with Adams to discuss peace terms.

5. French naval captain Mithon de Genouilly had arrived in Martinique on February 14, escorting a convoy of twenty-two vessels (*Mercure de France*, April 27, 1782).

6. On April 24 Franklin advised Swedish ambassador Creutz of his authority to negotiate a commercial treaty with him (DLC: Benjamin Franklin Papers).

7. "Your fellow sufferer": Carmichael.

Franklin's Account of the Peace Negotiations with Great Britain[E]

[May 1782]

The coming and going of these Gentlemen was observ'd, and made much Talk at Paris: And the Marquis de la Fayette, having learnt Something of their Business from the Ministers, discoursed with me about it.[1] Agreable to the Resolutions of Congress, directing me to confer with him and take his Assistance in our Affairs, I communicated with him what had past. He told me that during the Treaty at Paris for the last Peace, the Duke de Nivernois had been sent to reside in London, that this Court might thro' him, state what was from Time to Time transacted, in the Light they thought best, to prevent Misrepresentations and Misunderstandings.[2] That such an Employ would be extremely agreable to him on many Accounts; that as he was now an

American Citizen, spoke both Languages and was well acquainted with our Interests, He believ'd he might be useful in it; and that as Peace was likely from Appearances to take Place, his Return to America was perhaps not so immediately necessary. I lik'd the Idea and encourag'd his proposing it to the Ministry. He then wish'd I would make him acquainted with Messrs. Oswald & Grenville, and for that End propos'd meeting them at Breakfast with me, which I promis'd to contrive if I could, and endeavour to engage them for Saturday.

Friday Morning, the 10th. of May I went to Paris, and visited Mr. Oswald. I found him in the same friendly Dispositions, and very desirous of doing Good, and seeing an End put to this ruinous War. But I got no farther Light as to the Sentiments of Lord S[helburne] respecting the Terms. I told him the Marquis de la Fayette, would breakfast with me tomorrow, and as he Mr. Oswald, might have some Curiosity to see a Person who had in this War render'd himself so remarkable, I propos'd his doing me the same Honour. He agreed to it chearfully. I came home intending to write to Mr. Grenville, whom I supposed might stay and dine at Versailles, and therefore did not call on him. But he was return'd, and I found the following Note from him.

Paris May 10th.

Mr. Grenville presents his Compliments to Mr. Franklin, he proposes sending a Courier to England at 10 o Clock to night, and will give him in Charge any Letters Mr. Franklin may wish to send by him.

I sat down immediately and wrote the two Short Letters following, to the two Secretaries of State. . . .[3]

And I sent them to Mr. Grenville with the following Note;

Mr. Franklin presents his Compliments to Mr. Grenville, with thanks for the Information of his Courier's Departure, and his kind Offer of forwarding Mr. F[ranklin's] Letter who accepts the Favour and encloses two.

The Marquis de la Fayette and Mr. Oswald, will do Mr. Franklin the honour of Breakfasting with him to morrow between 9 and 10 o Clock. Mr. Franklin will be happy to have the Company also of Mr. Grenville if agreable to him. He should have waited on Mr. Grenville to Day at Paris, but he imagined Mr. G[renville] was at Versailles.

Passy, Friday May 10th.

To which Mr. G[renville] sent me this Answer.

Mr. Grenville presents his Compliments to Mr. Franklin and will with great Pleasure, do himself the Honour of breakfasting with Mr. Franklin to Morrow between 9 and 10 o Clock. Mr. Grenville was at Versailles to day, and should have been sorry that Mr. Franklin should have given himself the Trouble of calling at Paris this Morning. The Courier shall certainly take particular care of Mr. Franklin's Letters.

Paris Friday

The Gentlemen all met accordingly, had a good deal of Conversation at and after Breakfast, staid till after One o Clock, and parted much pleas'd with each other.

M (DLC: Benjamin Franklin Papers), extract.

1. "These Gentlemen": Richard Oswald and Thomas Grenville, the emissaries of Shelburne and Fox.

2. "The last Peace": the Peace of Paris of 1763, which closed the Seven Years' War. It took some months for Lafayette to realize that his peculiar dual loyalty would mean that he would not be trusted with significant diplomatic secrets by either the French or the American officials. Further, as he wrote Adams on October 6, "I have no Public Capacity to be led into Political Secrets . . ." (MHi: Adams Papers).

3. The editors omit the text of Franklin's letters to Charles J. Fox and Lord Shelburne.

To John Adams

Paris May the 7h 1782

I Heartly Give You Joy, My Dear Sir, Upon the Happy Conclusion of Your Dutch Negotiations.[1] Every Body Here Congratulates me not only As a Zealous American, But Also as Your Long Professed friend and Admirer. And tho' the Court Air Has not So Much Altered My Republican Principles as to Make Me Believe the Opinion of a king is Every thing, I Was the other Day pleased to Hear the king of France Speack of You to me in terms of the Highest Regard. This Dutch Declaration, in the Present Crisis, I take to Be Particularly Important. To the Victory You Have Gained, I Wish You May Join a Successfull Scarmish, and Bring About an Useful Loan of Monney. I Had a letter from Mr. Lewingston Dated february the 19he.[2] Nothing Important in it, But that He Urges the Necessity of a Pecuniary Assistance And the Advantages We are to Derive from Operations In North America.

As this Opportunity is Safe, I May tell you the french Succour for this Year Does Not Exceed Six Millions of Livres. So far as Respects Operations I Have My Hopes.

Mr. Franklin Has the other Day Communicated a letter from You, and I Entirely Coincide With Every Sentiment You Have therein Expressed.[3] It Suffices to Say the letter Respected Propositions of Peace. I Am Entirely of Your Opinion, that Should England Amuse us With Emissaries, Not Vested With Proper Powers, it is Not Consistent With the Dignity of America to Continue the Correspondance.

But I do not Believe it Will Be the Case. Mr. Oswald Has Returned to Mr. Franklin. A Gentleman is Expected to Count de Vergennes. It Appears they Wish for a General Peace. Our Independance to Be the Ground of it. It Remains to know How they Understand it. The treaty to Be Negotiated at Paris.[4]

I Heartly Wish for Peace. This Campaign, in Europe at least, is Going to Be a Spanish One. I think it the Interest of America to Have a peace, at Such Conditions, However, Without Which I Had Rather fight for ten Years longer. I May, I Hope, Before long Converse With You at Paris. For in the Present Situation of Affairs, You Will no doubt think it the Sentiment of Congress and the People at large, that My Presence at the french Court is likely to Serve our Cause Better than My Immediate Return to America.

Mr. Franklin is Very Desirous You Would Come Here, and I am the More Anxious for it, As Either Before My Departure Which I Continue to Annonce as Immediate, or in Case Propositions are Seriously Made I Have a Great Desire to Converse freely With You.

This Will Be Delivered By Mr. Ridley.[5] So that I Have Been More Confidential than I Should Have Hazarded to Be By Post. Mr. Jay will Have little objection to Come, and As Mr. Franklin Says, the Spaniards Had four Years, We May Give them forty.[6] With the Highest Regard and Most Sincere affection I Have the Honor to Be Dear Sir Your obedient Hbe. Servant

LAFAYETTE

ALS (MHi: Adams Papers).
1. Formal recognition of Adams as American envoy to the United Provinces.
2. Letter not found.
3. Adams had written Franklin on April 16 an account of his meeting with Henry Laurens in which he had told Laurens that he could not discuss the peace terms with him (as a prisoner) on any other basis than as "one private citizen conversing with another" (MHi: Adams Papers).
4. Lord Shelburne had sent Richard Oswald to Paris early in April to discuss peace preliminaries with Franklin. He returned to Paris on May 4 with the understanding that a peace was to be negotiated there and that the ministry's secretary of state, Lord Fox, would dispatch Thomas Grenville to begin discussions with Vergennes.
5. Matthew Ridley, a merchant and agent for the state of Maryland in Europe.
6. In a letter of April 22, urging Jay to leave Madrid to assume his duties as peace commissioner at Paris, Franklin commented, "Spain has taken four years to consider whether she should treat with us or not. Give her forty, and let us in the meantime mind our own business" (Bigelow, *Works of Franklin*, 9:198).

From John Adams

Hotel des Etats Unis de
L'Amerique, a la Haye
May 21. 1782

My dear General

Yours of the Seventh of this month, was Yesterday brought me, by Mr. Ridley, and I thank you for your kind Congratulations, on the

Progress of our Cause in the Low Countries. Have a Care, however, how you profess Friendship for me: there may be more danger in it, than you are aware of.

I have the Honour, and the Consolation to be a Republican on Principle.—that is to Say, I esteem that Form of Government, the best, of which human Nature is capable. Almost every Thing that is estimable in civil Life, has originated in under Such Governments. Two Republican Towns, Athens and Rome, have done more honour to our Species, than all the rest of it.—a new Country, can be planted only by Such a Government.—America would at this moment have been an howling Wilderness in habited only by Bears and Savages, without Such forms of Government, and it would again become a Wilderness under any other. I am not however an enthusiast, who wishes to overturn Empires and Monarchies, for the Sake of introducing Republican Forms of Government.—and therefore I am no King Killer, King Hater or King Despiser.—There are Three Monarcks in Europe for whom I have as much Veneration as it is lawfull for one Man to have for another. The King of France, the Emperor of Germany and the King of Prussia, are constant objects of my Admiration, for Reasons of Humanity Wisdom and Beneficence which need not be enlarged on. You may well think then, that the Information you give me, that "the King of France was pleased the other day to Speak to you, of me in terms of the highest Regard", gave me great Pleasure.[1]

I Shall do all in my Power to obtain here a Loan of Mony but with very faint hopes of Success.—In short, there is no Mony here but what is already promised to France, Spain, England Russia Sweeden Denmark, the Government here, and what will be fatal to me is the East India Comany have just opened a Loan for Nine Millions of florins under the Warrantee of the States of Holland and with an augmented Interest.

My Hopes of a Speedy Peace, are not Sanguine.—I have Suspicions of the Sincerity of Lord Shelburne, Dunning and others of his Connections which I wish may prove groundless: but untill they are removed, I Shall not expect a Peace.—Shelbourne affects to be thought, the Chatham of the Day, without any of his great Qualities.[2]—I much fear that all their Maneuvres about Peace will turn out, but Artifices, to raise the Stocks. The British Cabinet is So divided, that my Expectations are not very high. Let Us be upon our Guard and prepared for a Continuance of the War. The Spaniards will demand Cessions and the Dutch Restitutions, which the English will not yet agree to, if they Should get over all the Claims of France and America.[3]

I Should be very happy to have a personal Conversation with you, but this will hardly take Place, untill full Powers arrive in Paris from

London[4] and I know very well that whether in America or Versailles or Paris, you will be constantly usefull, to America, and Congress will easily approve of your Stay where you are, untill you shall think it more for the publick Good to go elsewhere. With great affection and Esteem I have the Honor to be &c.

LbC (MHi: Adams Papers).

1. See Lafayette to Adams, May 7.

2. "Chatham": William Pitt the Elder, deceased proponent of conciliation with America.

3. Spain wanted the cession of Gilbraltar, and the Dutch wanted restitution for their ports seized in India and Ceylon.

4. As one of the official American peace commissioners, Adams was reluctant to leave his post in the Netherlands until English envoys with "full powers" to negotiate a peace settlement had arrived in Paris.

To Benjamin Franklin

Paris June 12h, 1782

My Dear Sir

Major Ross Having Called Upon me this Morning, and Having Said that in the Mean while You Give His lordship's Conditional Disharge it Was Your Opinion I Should Give that of the Aids de Camp at the Bottom of which You will Express Your Approbation of the Measure, I Request You Will please to Have the Piece Drawn up in the Way that Appears to You the Most properly Expressed.[1]

When General Lincoln Has Been Released His family Were Exchanged With Him, and it May Serve as a precedent, Particularly Now that Negotiations are Said to Be likely to take place.[2]

Congress are So Very Strict, and General Washington So Very Cautious Upon the exclusive Rights of Governement *alone* in Settling all exchanges that I Cannot take Great deal Upon Myself. I am without Instructions whatsoever, and Have no Powers of Any kind. But Congress know My Intentions are Good, and I Cannot Be accused of a Propensity towards the British Nation. I think therefore that if I Am Authorised By Your advice I May Concur With You in Releasing the family of the General you Have Discharged, Provided it is in the Same Conditional Way. That is in Case the exchange is Immediately Made By Congress, or Has Been Agreed to Even Before We write this piece. Be pleased therefore, My dear Sir, to Have it Drawn up in the Way that appears Most Convenient to Every Party, Provided it does not Commit Either You or Me (for you know that in our American Governement one Must Be Cautious) and after it is writen fair, Leave a place for My Name to Be put in and Be pleased to write You think the Conditional exchange of these Gentlemen (So far as you know it) Consistent With the Sense of Congress, and that you Advise me to Agree to the Measure, or any thing that Appears to You Will Answer the Purpose.[3] Most Respectfully and Affectionately Yours

LAFAYETTE

I think with You, My dear Sir, We must in this Moment Do every thing we Can to Show our Good dispositions, So as to let the Ennemy Have the Blame in Every Miscarriage of Negotiations—and Personally I wish to Act politely By Lord Cornwallis.

ALS (DLC: Benjamin Franklin Papers).

1. Lord Cornwallis had asked to be released from his parole so that he could return to military and diplomatic duties; Franklin had provided a release conditional upon the approval of Congress after Lafayette had expressed his views on the subject (see Smyth, *Writings of Franklin*, 8:530–40). Major Alexander Ross was now requesting a similar release for himself and Cornwallis's other aides-de-camp.

2. General Benjamin Lincoln had been captured with the British took Charleston in 1780. On the release of his "family"—his aides—see Washington to Lafayette, December 14, 1780, note 6 (*LAAR*, 3:260).

3. In his journal for June 12, Franklin reported that Lafayette had sent him "the Drafts of a limited Discharge, which he should sign, but requested my Approbation of it, which I made no Difficulty, tho' I observ'd he had put into it that it was by my Advice. He appears very prudently cautious of doing any thing that may seem assuming a Power that he is not vested with" (Smyth, *Writings of Franklin*, 8:540).

To Benjamin Franklin

Versailles thursday Morning [June 20, 1782]

My Dear Sir

Agreable to Your Desire I Have Waïted Upon Count de Vergennes and Said to Him what I Had in Command from Your Excellency.[1] He Intends taking the king's orders this Morning, and Expects He Will Be Able to Propose Mr. Grenville a Meeting for to Morrow where He will Have Him to Explain Himself Respecting France and Her Allies, that He May Make an official Communication Both to the king and the Allied Ministers. What Count de Vergennes Can Make out of this Conversation Will Be Communicated By Him to Yr. Excellency in Case You are able to Come in the other Case I Will Waït Upon You to Morrow Evening with Every Information I Can Collect.[2] I Have the

Honor to Be very Respectfully My dear Sir Your obedient Servant and affectionate friend

LAFAYETTE

ALS (PPAmP: Franklin Papers, vol. 25, no. 101).

1. Thomas Grenville's original instructions had authorized him to negotiate with France only, a point the French government opposed. Grenville met with Franklin on June 15 to advise him that the instruction had been changed, enabling him to negotiate with France or "the Ministers of any other Prince or *State*". The phrase concerned Franklin because it appeared to exclude Grenville from negotiating directly with the Americans. On the evening of June 17, Lafayette went to Franklin's residence to inform him that Vergennes was satisfied with the phrase. Because of Franklin's illness, Lafayette returned to Versailles to explain Franklin's apprehensions about the phrase (Smyth, *Writings of Benjamin Franklin*, 8:511–13, 516–20, 522–23, 541–47).

2. On June 24 Franklin and Jay went to Versailles, where Vergennes informed them of his generally positive reply to Grenville. Grenville's instructions, however, required further modification because d'Aranda felt that the failure to make specific mention of his monarch's name would be an affront to dignity (Doniol, *Histoire*, 5:117–18).

*Minutes of the Assembly of June 24, 1782, of the Worthy Lodge of Saint John of Scotland of the Social Contract*ET

June 24[, 1782]
in the Orient of Paris

The year of True Light 5782, on the twenty-fourth day of the fourth month, the worthy lodge of Saint John of Scotland of the Social Contract, mother lodge of the Scottish Rite in France, was duly convened and regularly assembled under the geometric points[1] known by the children of light only, Brother de Rouillé, worshipful, illuminating, and brothers de Chevey and Guibert, in the absence of the two overseers, inspecting the columns of the south and of the north. The proceedings were opened in the customary manner, reading given of the last tracing board.[2] The worthy lodge gave it the Masonic honors. . . .

A brother master of ceremonies having announced that Brother de Lafayette was at the outer door and asking entry into the temple, the worshipful having sent several Scottish knights preceded by two masters of ceremonies to receive this confrere. The worthy lodge, while receiving Brother de Lafayette with the honors usually rendered only to Masons of the highest degree, wished to give him a discernible token of the value that it set on his military talents, of which the example sets the pattern for heroes.

Brother de Lafayette having been seated in the east,[3] though not of high masonic rank, the worshipful commended him by the usual grand honors, and after he had responded in the usual manner to the honors just received, he was taken to the foot of the throne, where he swore the obligation of affiliation to follow in the future the regulations that the worthy lodge does observe and will observe.

Brother Gauthier, charged by the worthy mother lodge with drawing up a list carrying all the deeds that it had done since the dispatch of its last tablet to every regular lodge, gave an account to the worthy mother lodge of the work he had done, which was approved and given honors in the usual manner. The worthy mother lodge ordered that it be printed as well as the list of officers and members it had received and affiliated since the last dispatch, and that all be sent duly signed, stamped, and sealed to every regular lodge, charging its secretary general to sign it by order of the worthy mother lodge and to hold executing it for the present deliberation.

Brother de Lafayette, obliged to cover the duties of his civic pursuits, having asked permission of the worshipful to withdraw, the worshipful had him escorted with the same honors as on his introduction to the temple. . . .

D (André Lebey, *La Fayette ou le militant franc-maçon*, 2 vols. [Paris, 1937], 1:48–49), extract, translation. The current location of the manuscript is unknown. The Lodge of the Social Contract was the principal lodge of the Scottish Rite of Masons in France.
  1. The "geometric points": the Masonic expression for the four parallelogram sides of the temple.
  2. "Tracing board": a missive sent to a temple or any Masonic writing.
  3. The east was the place of honor, occupied by the worshipful and other dignitaries.

To Benjamin Franklin

St. Germain tuesday [June 25, 1782]

My Dear Sir

You Have Been Acquainted that Mr. de Castries's Courier Was to Go to Morrow Evening, and I intend taking the Same Opportunity to write to Congress and General Washington. But as I want to Justify My Delay, Upon the trüe Motives of it, those of Public Utility, and American Wellfare, I Hope Your Excellency Will please to Mention fully the Matter to Congress, and By Making them Sensible of Your opinion Respecting this Measure, to let them know that My Services Here, for Some Weeks to Come, May Be of Some Use to the interest of America.[1]

I Have Just Happened to Hear of Mr. Jay's Arrival and Will waït Upon

Him to Morrow Evening when I Will Also Call at Passy to Pay You My Respects.[2] You Will oblige me to talk with Mr. Jay Respecting our opinion on the Subject I Have Mentionned. With Every Sentiment of Affection and Regard I Have the Honor to Be My Dear Sir Your Most affectionate friend

LAFAYETTE

ALS (DLC: Benjamin Franklin Papers).

1. In his June 25 report to Robert Livingston, Franklin wrote, "The Marquis de Lafayette is of great use in our affairs here, and as the campaign is not likely to be very active in North America, I wish I may be able to prevail with him to stay a few weeks longer" (Smyth, *Writings of Benjamin Franklin*, 8:550).

2. Jay arrived in Paris from Madrid on June 23. Two days later Lafayette wrote him a letter of welcome requesting that Jay tell Congress why Lafayette's presence was needed in France. On June 28, Jay wrote to Livingston:

> I have had the satisfaction of conferring with the Marquis de La Fayette on several interesting subjects. He is as active in serving us in the cabinet as he has been in the field, and (there being great reason to believe that his talents could be more advantageously employed here than an inactive campaign in America would admit of there) Dr. Franklin and myself think it advisable that he should postpone his return for the present. [Wharton, *Diplomatic Correspondence*, 5:527]

To Robert R. Livingston

St. Germain June the 25h. 1782

Dear Sir

The Reasons for Which Instead of Coming I Have Now the Honor to write Will Be Explained in a Letter I take the Liberty to Adress to Congress.[1] I Will therefore Immediately Enter Into the Matters I Wish to Relate. Mr. Franklin Will No Doubt Be Very Particular in His Informations. It is Needless for me to Enter Into Such Details as Will of Course Be Communicated to Congress By their Ministers. But as they Have Been pleased to Order I should Give My Opinion, I Will Have the Honor to tell You What I think Upon the Several transactions that Have lately taken place.

Before the Change of Ministry, the old Administration Had Sent people to feel the pulse of the french Court and of the American Ministers. They Had Reasons to Be Convinced Neither of the two Could Be Deceived Into Separate Arrangements that Would Break the Union, and Make Both their Ennemies Weaker. In the Mean while a Cabal Was Going on Against the old Ministry. New Appointements took place, and it is not known How far Lord North Would Have Gone towards a General Negotiation.

It Had Ever Been the plan of Opposition to Become Masters of the Cabinet. But, While Everyone of them United Against Ministry, they

Committed this Strange Blunder Never to Think What Would Become of them After their Views Had Been fulfilled. They Were Made Ministers, and Upon the first day they did not know How to Divide the prey, Upon the Second they perceived they Had different Interests and different Principles to Support, Upon the third they were Intriguing Against Each other, and Now the British Ministry Are So Much Divided, that Nothing But their disputes, Can Account for their Indecision in Public Affairs.

The Marquis of Rockingham Has Nothing of a Minister But the Parade of Levees, and Buzy Appearance. He is led By Mr. Burke. He is also Upon the Best terms With Charles Fox. The Principles of the Later Every Body knows. That party it Appears is on one Side of Administration.

The Duke of Grafton, and Lord Camden think it their Interest to Support Lord Shelburne, whom However they Inwardly Dislike. The Earl of Shelburne Seems to Have By far the Greater Share in the king's Confidence. He is Intriguing, Unprincipled, and Upon a Pretence to follow Lord Chatam's opinions, He Makes Himself Agreable to the king By Opposing American Independance. He is, they Say, a faithless Man, Wishing for a Continuation of the War By which He Hopes to Raise His own Importance, and, Should the Rockingham party fall, Should Lord Shelburne Be forced to Divide power with an other party, He is Not far, it is Said, from Uniting With Lord North and Many others in the old Administration.

The king Stands Alone, Hating Every one of His Ministers, Grieving at Every Measure that Combats His Revengefull Dispositions, and Wishing for the Moment when the Present Ministry Having lost their Popularity, Will Give Way to those He Has Been obliged to Abandon for a time.

Such is the Position in Which they Stand, and I am Going to Relate the Measures they Have taken towards a Negotiation.

It Appears Lord Shelburne on one Hand, and Charles Fox on the other Went on Upon the plan Lord North Had Adopted to Make Some Private Advances, But they Neither Communicated Their Measures to Each other, Nor Said at first Any thing of it in the Cabinet.[2] Count de Vergennes Said that France Could Never think to Enter into a treaty But in Concert With Her Allies, and Upon Being told that America Herself did not So much Insist upon Asking for Independance, He Answered People Need Not to Ask for What they Have Got. Mr. Adams in Holland, Mr. Franklin in Paris Made Such Answers as Were Consistent With the Dignity of the United States, But as Well as Count de Vergennes they Expressed a Sincere desire for peace Upon liberal and Generous terms.

From the Very Begining, Mr. Adams Has Been Persuaded that the British Ministry Were not Sincere, that the Greater Part of them Were Equally Against America as Any In the old Administration, and that All those Negotiations Were not Much to Be depended upon. His Judgment of this Affair, Has Been Confirmed By the Events, tho' at present the Negotiation Has put on a Better out Ward Appearance.

Mr. Franklin's pen is Better able than Mine Can Be, to Give You all the Particulars through Which Mr. Grenville a Young Man of Some Rank is Now Remaining In Paris With Powers to Treat With His Most Christian Majesty and all other Princes or States Now at War with Great Britain.

I shall only Remark that in Late Conversations with Count de Vergennes Mr. Grenville Has Considered the Aknowledgement of Independance as a Matter Not to Be Made a Question of, But to Be At once and Previously declared. But Upon Count de Vergennes's writing down Mr. Grenville's Words to Have them Signed By Him, the Gentleman Instead of this Expression the king of England Has *Resolved* At once to Aknowledge &ca., insisted to Have the Word is *Disposed* Made use of in what He Intended to Be Considered as His official Communication. He Has Also Evinced a Backwardness in Giving Mr. Franklin a Copy of His Powers, and their Ministry are So Backward Also in Bringing Before Parliament a Bill Respecting American Independance, that it does not show a Great Disposition towards a Peace, the Preliminaries of which Must Be An aknowledgement of America as a Separate and Independant Nation.[3]

It is Probable that Within these two Days Mr. Franklin Had Some Communication with Mr. Grenville Which May throw Some Light Upon the late Points I Have Just Now Mentioned.

Mr. Jay is Arrived from Madrid. Mr. Laurens, it Seems, Intends to Return Home. Mr. Adams's Presence in Holland is for the Moment Necessary.[4] A few days Will Make us Better Acquainted With the Views of Great Britain, and Since the Ministers from Congress Have thought I Must for the Service of America tarry Here Some time longer, I Shall Under their Directions Devote Myself to Promote the Interests of the United States. The footing I am Upon at this Court Enables Me Some times to Go Greater lengths than Could Be done By a foreigner. But Unless an Immediate Earnest Negotiation which I am far from Hoping Renders My Services Very Useful, I Will Beg Leave to Return to My Colours, and Be employed in a Shorter Way to Ensure the End of this Business than Can Be found in Political Dissertations.

I Have Communicated the Opinion of Mr. Adams, Such as I found it in His letters. Mr. Franklin's Ideas Will Be Presented By Himself, and also those of Mr. Jay Both of which must Be Preferable to Mine, tho' I do not Believe they Much differ. But from What I Have Collected By Communications with Your Ministers, With those of the french, and By Private Intelligences I Conclude

1st. that the British Ministry are at Variance Betwen themselves, Embarassed upon the Conduct they ought to Have, and not Very firm in their Principles and their Plans 2dly that Negotiations Will go on Slowly, Will Serve to Establish principles, and facilitate a treaty, But that the king of England and Some of the Ministers Have not lost the Idea of Breaking the Union Betwen France and the United States, 3dly that the Situation of England, Want of Men and Monney, the efforts France Intends to Make Will Reduce the former to a Necessity to Make Peace Before the End of Next Spring. America Will no doubt Exert Herself, and Send Back Every Emissary to Her Plenipotentiaries Here—for the Ministry in England are Now Deceiving the People with the Hope that Gal. Carleton is Going to Operate a Reconciliation, and with Many Histories of the Same Nature.[5]

In the Course of this Affair We Have Been perfectly Satisfied With the french Ministry. They Have Proved Candid and Moderate. Mr. Jay Will write About Spain. Very little is to Be Said of them, and By them Very little is to Be done. It Appears Holland is Going on well, and I Believe Mr. Adams is Satisfied Except upon the affair of Monney which is the difficult Point, and goes on Very Slowly.[6]

BY ALL I CAN SEE, I JUDGE THAT IF AMERICA INSISTS ON A SHARE IN THE FISHERIES, SHE WILL OBTAIN IT BY THE GENERAL TREATY; THIS POINT IS TOO NEAR MY HEART NOT TO MENTION IT.[7]

The News of Count de Grasse's Defeat Has Been Very Much felt in France, and the Whole Nation Was Made truly Unhappy By this Disagreable Event.[8] The General Cry of the people Was Such that I do not Believe Any french Admiral Will in Any Case take Upon Himself to Surrender His own Ship. The people at large Have perhaps Been too Severe, and Governement Have not Pronounced as there is to Be a Court Martial—But I Was Happy to See a patriotic Spirit diffused through Every Individual. The States of Several provinces, the Great Cities, and a Number of different assossiations of Men Have offered ships of the line to a Greater Number than Have Been lost.[9] In the Mean while Governement are Using the Greatest Activity, and this Has Given a Spur to the National Exertions. But Independant of the Stroke in itself, I Have Been Sighing Upon the Ruin of the plans I Had proposed towards an Useful Cooperation Upon the Coasts of our America.[10] My Schemes Have Been Made Allmost Impracticable, and My Voyage (the Case of Negotiations excepted) Has not Been By far So Serviceable to the public as I Had Good Reasons to Expect.

The Spaniards are Going at last to Besiege Gibraltar. Count D'Artois the king of France's Brother, and Duke de Bourbon A Prince of the Blood are Just Setting out to Serve there as Volunteers. They Intend to Begin in the first days of September—So that We May Expect one Way or other to Get Rid of that Incumberance, and let the Siege Succeed or Miscarry We May Expect Hereafter to Make use of the Combined forces of the House of Bourbon.

We are Waïting for Intelligences from the East Indias where it Appears We Have Got a Superiority and are Entitled to Expect Good News from that Quarter. The Ennemy Had Some dispatches By land, But either our operations are of a later date, or they only Have published a Part of their Intelligences.

Paris June the 29h, 1782

Mr. Franklin and Mr. Jay Will Acquaint You With Count de Vergennes's Answer to Mr. Grenville, and Also with what Mr. Grenville Has Said Respecting the Enabling Act.[11] This Act, and Also The Answer to Count de Vergennes Are Every Day Expected in Paris, and The Way in Which Both Will Be Expressed May Give us a pretty just idea Upon the present intentions of the British Ministry. The only thing that Remains for me to inform You of is that Under the pretence of Curiosity, Admiration, or private Affairs, England Will probably Send Emissaries to America, Who Cannot Hope to Insinuate themselves Under Any other But a friendly Appearance. With the Greatest Regard and a Warm Affection I Have the Honor to Be, My Dear Sir Your obedient Humble Servant

LAFAYETTE

ALS (DNA: RG 360, PCC 156, pp. 282–92.) A passage written in code and deciphered interlinearly appears here in small capital letters.

1. On June 29, Lafayette wrote to the Congress: ". . . upon Mr. Franklin's and Mr. Jay's Request, I Have Determined Not to Depart Untill an Answer from the British Court Has More fully Explained Their Trüe Intentions." Elsewhere in the letter he explained that Franklin and Jay had based their request on the unlikelihood of an immediate military campaign in America and the probability that Versailles would be the site of peace negotiations (DNA: RG 360, PCC 156, pp. 294–95).

2. Shelburne's private emissary to France was Oswald and Fox's was Grenville; neither discussed his mission with the other because each minister assumed he had responsibility to treat with France and its allies.

3. This "bill Respecting American Independence" was the "Enabling act" Lafayette mentions later in this letter. Passed on June 17, 1782, and signed by the king on June 19, it "enabled" the king to negotiate with the Americans.

4. These were the three other peace commissioners appointed with Franklin.

5. Shelburne had authorized General Carleton and Admiral Digby to make a final effort in America for peace and reconciliation; both Washington and the Congress refused to treat with them during May 1782, and the effort failed (*JCC*, 22:263).

6. John Adams wrote to Livingston on July 5 that although he had engaged the Dutch for a loan of 5 million guilders, it would be optimistic to expect receipt of more than 1.5 million by the end of the year (Wharton, *Diplomatic Correspondence*, 5:594).

7. The cod and haddock fishing grounds off Nova Scotia and Newfoundland remained a prize sought by England, France, and the United States to the end of the treaty
negotiations.

8. The Battle of the Saints in the Caribbean on April 12 pitted Admiral de Grasse
against Admiral Rodney. In the defeat, de Grasse lost eight ships and was himself captured with his flagship. See Lafayette to Washington, June 25, note 1.

9. Louis XVI's younger brothers, the Duc d'Orléans and the Comte d'Artois, had
offered to provide a 110-gun ship; the Prince de Condé made a similar offer on behalf of
the Estates of Burgundy; the municipality of Paris had done likewise; and there was
much talk of opening a popular subscription for more vessels (*Mercure de France*, June 8,
1782).

10. See Lafayette's April 18 memorandum to Vergennes.

11. See Franklin to Livingston, June 29 (Wharton, *Diplomatic Correspondence*,
5:533–35).

To George Washington

St. Germain June the 25h 1782

My Dear General

How it is Possible for me to Be Here at this Period You Will Hardly
Be able to Conceive, and I Confess I am Myself more and More Sur-
prised at these Strange Delays. Both duty and Inclination Lead me to
America, and tho' it is Not probable You are Active in the field, Yet the
Possibility of it is to me A torment. But from the Moment I Engaged in
our Noble Cause, I Made it My Sole point to Sacrifice Every thing to its
Better Success. The Hope to fix a plan of Campaign Has long kept me
Here, when Count de Grasse's defeat Has Ruined the Schemes of
Ministry and My own Expectations.[1] I Would then Have Immediately
Sailed, when Negotiations Have kept me Here, and the American Min-
isters Have Declared they Wanted My presence in this part of the
World. I am Myself Sensible of it, and know, in Case of a treaty, I May
Better Serve our Cause, By the Situation I am in, with Governement,
and My knowledge of America, than I Could do in any other Capacity
during an inactive Campaign. I therefore Have thought, Considering
Your Principles and Your Sentiments, that You Will Approuve My
Submitting to Remain a fortnight longer in this place, and Unless
things Become More forward than they Now Promise to Be, I Hope By
the 20he of Next Month to Set Sails for America, and to Proceed
towards Head Quarters.

The Political Situation of Affairs, and the Intelligences We get Have
Been By me Communicated to Mr. Lewingston whom I Have Re-
quested to Impart My long letter to Your Excellency, and therefore
Will not trouble You With Repetitions.[2]

A few Days Ago, Upon Motives which He Will Account for to Congress, Mr. Franklin thought Proper to grant Lord Cornwallis a Conditional Exchange. With this I Had Nothing to do, and Much Less yet With the Exchange of the Sailors that Had Been detained in England. The only Business I Have Middled with is that of Lord Cornwallis's Aides de Camp. They Represented that Gal. Lincoln's aids Had Been Exchanged Along With Him, that Orders Had Been Sent By Lord Shelburne, In Consequence of Which the British Commander in chief Must By this time Have Proposed their Exchange to You for officers of the Same Rank at Your Choice, that there Was Hardly Any Doubt But What the Business Was Now Effect. Under Those Circumstances, at a time of Negotiations for peace, and With the Advice of Doctor Franklin I Consented to Give the Inclosed *Conditional* Disharge—But did not think it Consistent with My duty to Go further.[3] I am obliged to Mylord Cornwallis, and Wish to treat Him Well and His Aids. But as I know the ideas of Congress and Your Delicacy Upon the Subject, tho' I thought Something ought to Be done in the Present Circumstances, I Made it a point to Act With Caution, and I Hope Your Excellency Will not think I went farther than I ought to Have Done.

COUNT DE GRASSE Has So foolishly taken a Way MARITIME SUPERIORITY that I am at a loss. I Hoped CHARLESTON Would follow JAMAICA and perhaps NEW YORK HARBOUR and NEW YORK Would Have Been Also tempted. They will Send 28 [FRENCH SHIPS] to 26 [WEST INDIES]. The difficulty is to Bring SPANISH SHIPS to AMERICA, and for that We Must Have Had Some Advantage in WEST INDIES, and a french Commander in Chief. As I do not think NEGOCIATIONS will Be So forward as Some people expect I will Be Very Careful to improve Every opportunity to Bring on What I think to Be Useful on the Subjects I Have just Mentioned.

ALS (PEL: Hubbard Collection). Passages in code deciphered between the lines appear in small capitals. Undeciphered code appears in brackets.
1. The "expectations" were that De Grasse would take Jamaica and then use his fleet to relieve the coastal cities of America held by the British.
2. Lafayette to Livingston, June 25.
3. Enclosure not found. For the conditional discharges of Cornwallis's aides, see Lafayette to Franklin, June 12.

To George Washington

Paris June the 29h [1782]
Mr. Grenville Says, My Dear General, that the Enabling Bill Has Past Both Houses.[1] How it Will Be Worded, I do not know. We also Expect

Some Answer to a few lines Count de Vergennes Has Given to Mr. Grenville. But I am affraïd those people are not Sincere.

I Had no letter from You this Age, My dear General, and As I Hope You Have wrote Some times I Guess Many of My letters Have Shared the Same fate. I envy the pleasure the Gentlemen of the french Army Will Have on their landing Upon the American Shore, and feel the More tired of these Political Concerns, as I am truly Vexed Not to join the Army, and to Remain in A city, three thousand Miles from You, in the Midst of a Campaign. I do not Believe it Will Be an Active one, and Yet Being at Such a Distance, I feel an insupportable degree of Uneasiness.

I Request, My Dear General, You Will Present My Best Compliments to My friends in the Army. I am truly Ashamed to let them Be in the field, and to keep at Such a distance from them. They will think I am much altered from what they Have known me to Be, Unless You are pleased, My dear General, to let them know that Your political people[2] Have kept me Here for Motives of public utility, and that Never Could I Make a Greater Sacrifice to My zeal for America than When I delay so much My Return to the Army where I Heartly Wish I Could Be Immediately transported.

Made. de Lafayette is well, and I Hope in the Course of Some Months Your God Son will Have a Brother. She Requests Her Best And Most Affectionate Compliments to Be presented to You, and My little family does the Same, as they are taught Before all to Revere and to love General Washington.

Be pleased, My dear General, to present My Most affectionate Respects to Mrs. Washington. My Best Compliments waït upon the family, and I do Assure You I Had much Rather Be one of them than to Be Here Speaking of the peace of 48, the Peace of 63,[3] the Bazis and Conditions of a treaty, and Be Busy to distinguish Betwen truth and falsehood in a line where Cheating is Considered as a Very clever improvement.

Adieu, My Dear General, I Hope You Will approuve My Conduct and in Every thing I do I first Consider what Your opinion Would Be Had I an opportunity to Consult it. I Anticipate the Happiness to Be Again With You, My dear General, and I Hope I Need not Assuring You that Nothing Can Exceed the Sentiments of Respect and tenderness I Have the Honor to Be With Your Most Hble Servat and for ever Your Most devoted Affectionate friend

LAFAYETTE

ALS (PEL: Hubbard Collection).
1. On the Enabling Act, see Lafayette to Livingston, June 25, note 3.
2. "Your political people": the peace commissioners and agents of Congress.

3. A reference to the treaties concluding the War of the Austrian Succession and the Seven Years' War. The phrase "British Fleet" has been inserted here on a misunderstanding by the decoder that Lafayette's underlining indicated use of a code word.

From the Comte de Ségur[T]

Rochefort, July 7, 1782

I received, my dear Lafayette, your friendly letter, and I was extremely touched.[1] I love you madly and I cannot console myself that I am not traveling with you. You are going to play a very honorable role, and one that is very difficult to play. You will have to reconcile the French and American characters, deal tactfully with opposing interests, and fill the measure of your glory to overflowing by adding the olive branch to the laurel leaves.[2] And you will even have to act against your own inclination by helping to put a definite end to the horrible scourge to which you owe your fame. I am very sorry not to be able to talk with you freely at the moment I most desire it. But letters are not safe enough, and I haven't anything to tell you but things I would not want to be read. I foresee that you are going to be more revolted than ever at English arrogance, stupid Spanish vanity, French inconsistency, and despotic ignorance. You will see that the cabinet tries one's patience as much as a battlefield, and that as many stupid things are done in a negotiation as in a campaign. You will see especially how essentials are sacrificed to form, and you will say more than once, "If chance had not made me one of the principal actors, I should certainly not stay in the theater." But the more obstacles you encounter, the more merit you will gain. How could you not succeed in all you desire, for you have genius and good fortune. To have that is to have half again as much as it takes to be a great man. Farewell, my friend. I expect to leave the day after tomorrow, consoling myself rather philosophically for going two thousand leagues for nothing, but not consoling myself for not finding you in a place that I find full of your name and your deeds.[3] I shall carry out all your commissions, and I shall point out the patriotic sacrifice you are making in temporarily exchanging your sword for a pen. I request that you love my wife, hug my children, take my place with my father, and join us as soon as you can to sound the charge or beat the farewell retreat.

L (courtesy of Mme André Balleyguier, Paris), translation.
1. Letter not found.
2. The olive branch for the peacemaker as well as the laurel wreath for the war hero.
3. Ségur sailed on July 15 to serve under Rochambeau in America.

Designated one of the official American peace commissioners after his release from the Tower of London, Henry Laurens signed the preliminaries of the treaty with Great Britain.

To Henry Laurens

Paris August the 20h 1782

My Dear Sir

With an Heartfelt Satisfaction I Have Received Your Wellcome favor of the 6h Inst., and Have Been Made truly Happy In the Recovery of My Correspondance With My Good and Respectable friend.[1] The Honor of Getting Acquainted With Your Son, and My Dear Clel. Laurens's Brother Has Been to Me an Additional pleasure.[2] I Hope in a fortnight I Will Be Able to Pay My Respects to the Remainder of the family, and Had it Not Been on Account of Your Health Should Be Very Angry With You for Your Passing So Near Paris Without Paying us a friendly visit.[3]

I am Sorry to Hear, My Dear Sir, Your Health is So Much Impaired and Strongly Advise You to Pay a Great Attention to Its Recovery. I Expect the pleasure to know from You How You Do, and Your letters Will Ever Afford me a Sincere Satisfaction.

The Conduct of the Ennemy towards You Has Been So Very Unjust, Absurd, and Barbarous, that I am Glad You Intend to Represent it Properly to Congress. Thank God, You are out of their Hands, and I think, Hereafter, The Climate of England Will Ever Disagree With You, and the Behaviour of the Ennemy Will Still Encrease The proper Idea You Have from the Begining Entertained of that Haughty, Barbarous Nation.

I Have Been Enquiring for the Gentleman to Whom the Bill Was directed. He Will Not Be in town Before Sunday, at Which time My Secretary Has orders to Waït Upon Him With a letter from me,[4] and I Will Endeavour to Manage that Affair in the Best Way I Can.

You Ask me How the Work of Peace is Going on. Well, My Dear friend, it Does not Go on Very fast. Mr. Fitzherbert, lately an Envoy to Bruxelles, is Now in Paris and Has Powers to treat With three of the Belligerent Nations. Mr. Oswald Will Have Powers to treat With America. But Negotiations Must all go the Same Step, and from the Character You Gave me of Lord Shelburne,[5] from other Informations it Appears the Intentions of that Minister are not Easy to Be known; nor His Protestations Safe to Be Depended Upon. It is for the Present difficult to form an Opinion, But in the Mean While I See With Pleasure that The American Plenipotentiaries and the Ministers of France do Perfectly Understand, and Are Perfectly Satisfied With Each other.

Mde. de Lafayette is Very Much obliged to Your Attention. She Has

Heartly felt for You in Every Circumstance of Your Captivity, and She Would think Herself Very Happy in the Honor of Your Acquaintance.[6]

I Wish You a Better Health, My dear friend, and With the Highest Regard, the Most Perfect Attachement I Have the Honor to Be Your Affectionate and Most obedient Humble Servant

LAFAYETTE

I am Sorry You do not Accept of the Appointement of Congress. I Would Be Very Happy to Go over With You to America, and Intend Setting out Before Long. But Will Be able in a few days to Be more Particular on that Point.

ALS (ScHi: Henry Laurens Papers).

1. A fragmentary copy of Laurens's letter of August 6 is in NN: Bancroft Transcripts.

2. "Your Son": Henry Laurens, Jr.; Lafayette had served in several campaigns in America with Colonel John Laurens.

3. Laurens's health had been broken by more than a year as a prisoner in the Tower of London. He refused to serve as a peace commissioner, and went instead to southern France to recuperate.

4. Letter not found.

5. In his August 6 letter to Lafayette, Laurens had characterized Shelburne's strengths as "duplicity and dissimulation."

6. See Lafayette to Laurens, April 14.

To the Comte de Vergennes[T]

Paris, September 10, 1782

I hoped to have the honor of seeing you today, Monsieur le Comte, and together with Mr. Jay, I was to talk to you about the scruples that are holding up our negotiations.[1] We shall bring you the instructions and resolutions of Congress, and your opinion will govern the response of the plenipotentiaries; but our extracts are not ready, and on the basis of what you told me, I do not see any disadvantage in delaying this consultation for a day. It is, I think, tomorrow, Monsieur le Comte, that Mr. Jay will be able to go to Versailles, and in any case I shall have the honor of dining with you and of bringing you the homage of the tender and respectful attachment with which I have the honor to be your very humble and obedient servant,

LAFAYETTE

Please do not take the trouble to reply.

ALS (AAE: Correspondance Politique, Etats-Unis, vol. 22, fol. 214), translation.

1. Concerns centered around the issue of allied unity and the attempts of Britain to deal separately with the United States. The British commissioner had powers to negotiate only with France, the United Provinces, and Spain. In addition, the American commissioners wished Britain to acknowledge the independence of the United States before treaty negotiations, while the British ministry seemed to be equivocating on the issue.

Coincidentally Lafayette transmitted to Franklin a proposal from Vergennes that the British peace commissioner be empowered to negotiate with the plenipotentiaries of the United States for a treaty whose first article would expressly renounce any British claims over the United States (DLC: Benjamin Franklin Papers). Richard Oswald received a revised commission on September 24, permitting him to treat with "the thirteen United States of America" (Wharton, *Diplomatic Correspondence*, 5:748–49). This, together with recognition of U.S. independence as the first article of the preliminary peace terms, satisfied the American commissioners.

To Benjamin Franklin

Paris September the 12h 1782

Dear Sir

Inclosed I Have the Honor to Send You a Letter that Relates to our Continental Stores, and When I am able to Get the Account of them You Have Seemed to Desire, I Will Immediately Communicate it to Your Excellency.[1] I fear the Army is in Want, and of Course Am Particularly Interested in Their Safe and Speedy Departure. If You Approuve of it, I Will Waït Upon M. de Castries, and from Him know Every Particulars About the Convoy.[2]

By a Very Good Information, tho' Not Ministerial, I Have found That Mr. Reyneval Has Been truly Intended to Go, or Perhaps is Gone, in Which I Confess I Have Been Mistaken.[3] Having at once Put two Questions to Count de Vergennes, it Appears He Answered But one of them, But Had I Sooner Received Your Letter, I Would Have Been More Pointed in My Enquiries With that Minister.[4]

Upon Recollection, I Cannot Help thinking Mr. Jay Had Some Notion of My knowing Mr. Rayneval's Departure, and Having With You Some Reserve about it Which it Was But Proper to Return. When I thought of it, it Made me Smile, and As it Was the 11he September I Might Have Spoke to Him pretty Much the Same Way As Scipio did to the Romans Upon a Mistaken Notion of Theirs.[5]

Be pleased, My Good friend, To Let Me know How You do, and Accept the Tender Assurances of the High Respect and Warm Attachement I Have the Honor to Be With Your obedient Hbe. Sert. and Devoted friend

LAFAYETTE

ALS (PHi: Benjamin Franklin Papers).

1. This may have been the September 10 complaint from the firm of Lamarque, Fabre et Cie. about Alexander Gillon's departure without repaying money it had advanced to him (PPU: Benjamin Franklin Papers). On Gillon's activities, see *DAB*.

2. On September 5 a convoy of eighty vessels arrived at Brest. Under protection of a French squadron, it set sail on September 10 (*Mercure de France*, September 21 and October 19, 1782).

3. Gérard de Rayneval, *premier commis* of the French foreign ministry, had left for England on September 7 for secret talks with Lord Shelburne. The American merchant and agent for Maryland, Matthew Ridley, had already informed John Jay of the trip on September 9 (Ridley, "Diary," p. 104).

4. Franklin's letter has not been found, but it was an inquiry of the purpose of Rayneval's trip (ibid., p. 112). Matthew Ridley gives Lafayette's account of his meeting with Vergennes:

> On mentioning Reneval's being gone to England—he avowed but said he had not informed Mr. Jay of it.—Hearing then the nature of the business etc.—that he had received a Confidential Letter from Lord Shelburne—that it required secrecy and he had thought to keep it secret the only way was to send Reneval to England. The Marquis said he asked him what Shelburne said about America. Vergennes replied assez Convenable. He said he was surprised how Mr. Jay could get knowledge of it that it had been known to only two or three Persons. [Ridley, "Diary," p. 112]

For the text of the proposed treaty preliminaries, which de Grasse carried to Vergennes from Shelburne, see Doniol, *Histoire*, 5:104.

5. Jay assumed that Rayneval's departure meant France and England would negotiate for peace separately. On September 21 Jay and Lafayette had a sharp exchange over the significance of Rayneval's mission (see Wharton, *Diplomatic Correspondence*, 6:21, 29; Ridley, "Diary," pp. 107, 112; F. Monaghan, ed., *The Diary of John Jay during the Peace Negotiations of 1782* [New Haven, 1934], p. 14). Jay's confidant, Ridley, assumed the worst of Lafayette's interest:

> I find the Marquis to be meddling in the Affairs of Peace he is continually inquisitive as to what is passing wishes to be present at all Mr. Jay's Interviews with those appointed to treat on the part of England wants to know everything passing and as regularly conveys all to Comte de Vergennes and without doubt to the Marquis de Castries as he is his Relation. In short he is a politician who seeks to profit of time and Circumstances in order to advance himself in France. full of Ambition and not without Intrigue. Feels his consequence and Influence and profits of it to force himself into the knowledge of what relates to us under the character of an American. [Ridley, "Diary," p. 107]

Lafayette felt he was being charged with deceit or disloyalty to the American cause. Since the accusation came on the anniversary of his wounding at the Battle of Brandywine (September 11, 1778), it reminded him of Scipio the Elder, who, when he was accused of crimes against Rome, replied, "This is the anniversary of the day I conquered Hannibal. I am going off to sacrifice; let those who wish stay here and accuse me."

To Benjamin Franklin

Paris September 17h 1782

My Dear Sir

Every Child of Mine that Comes to Light is a Small Addition to the Number of American Citizens. I Have the pleasure to Inform You that, tho' She Was But Seven Months Advanced, Mde. de Lafayette Has this

Morning Become Mother of a Daughter Who However Delicate in Its Begining Enjoys a Perfect Health, and I Hope Will Soon Grow Equal to the Heartiest Children.

This Reminds me of our Noble Revolution, into Which We Were forced Sooner than it ought to Have Been Begun. But our Strength Came on Very fast, and Upon the whole I think We did *at least* as Well as Any other people. They Asked me What Name My Daughter is to Have. I Want to Present Her as an offering to My Western Country. And As there is a Good *Sainte* By the Name of Virginie, I Was thinking if it Was not Presuming too Much to Let Her Bear a Name Similar to that of one of the United States. With the Highest Regard and Most lifely Affection I Have the Honor to be My dear Sir Your obedient Humble Servant

LAFAYETTE

Forgive the Hand writing, But I am in Hurry.

ALS (PPU).

From Benjamin Franklin

Passy, Sept. 17. 1782

Dear Sir

I continue to suffer from this cruel Gout: But in the midst of my Pain the News of Madm. de la Fayette's safe Delivery, and your Acquisition of a Daughter gives me Pleasure.

In naming our Children I think you do well to begin with the most antient State. And as we cannot have too many of so good a Race, I hope you & Mde. de la Fayette will go thro' the Thirteen. But as that may be in the common way too severe a Task for her delicate Frame, and Children of Seven Months, may become as Strong as those of Nine, I consent to the Abridgement of Two Months for each; and I wish her to spend the Twenty-six Months so gained, in perfect Ease, Health & Pleasure.

While you are proceeding, I hope our States will some of them new-name themselves. Miss Virginia, Miss Carolina, & Miss Georgiana will sound prettily enough for the Girls; but Massachusetts & Connecticut, are too harsh even for the Boys, unless they were to be Savages. That God may bless you in the Event of this Day as in every other, prays Your affectionate Friend & Servant

B. FRANKLIN

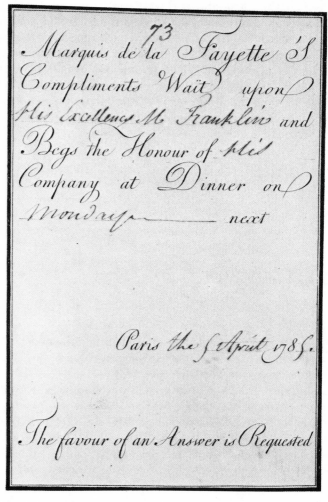

73

Marquis de la Fayette 'S
Compliments Wait upon
His Excellency M. Franklin and
Begs the Honour of His
Company at Dinner on
Monday ———— next

Paris the 5 April 1785.

The favour of an Answer is Requested

An invitation to Franklin to attend one of the Lafayettes' Monday-night "American dinners," at which they entertained principally Americans who were visiting Paris.

To Benjamin Franklin

Paris Saturday Evening [September 21, 1782]

I am Very Sorry, My Dear Sir, I Have not the Pleasure to Waït Upon You this Evening. But Mr. Jay Called at Half Past Eight and told me He Had Considered of the Affair Now in Question; And Before Any thing Was Determined He Wants to Have a long Conversation With You.[1] He Will Be at Passy to Morrow Morning. For My Part I See You Will not of Course Give me Any Commands to Count de Vergennes, and Will therefore Confine Myself to a Conversation Upon General terms. Late as it is I will Not trouble You, and Wish You a Better Night. To Morrow Evening I Will do Myself the Honor to Pay My Respects to You.

AL (PPAmP: Franklin Papers, vol. 42, no. 135).

1. "The Affair Now in Question": whether the Americans should proceed to negotiate with the British before they recognized American independence. Jay and Adams opposed the idea. Franklin's views, as summarized by Ridley, were that it was "a pity to keep 3 or 4 millions of People in War for the sake of Form" (Ridley, "Diary," p. 112). Oswald's revised commission, authorizing him to negotiate with "the United States of America," reached Paris on September 24. For its text, see Morris, *John Jay*, 2:360–62.

From John Adams

The Hague Sep. 29. 1782

My dear General

I Should have written you, Since the 29 of May, when I wrote you a Letter that I hope you read, if it had not been reported Sometimes that you was gone and at other times that you was upon the Point of going to America.

This People must be indulged, in their ordinary March which you know is with the Slow Step. We have however at length the Consent of all the Cities and Provinces, and have adjusted and agreed upon every Article, Word, Syllable, Letter and Point, and Clerks are employed in making out five fair Copies for the Signature which will be done this Week.[1]

Amidst the innumerable Crowd of Loans which are open in this Country, many of which have little Success, I was much afraid that ours would have failed. I have however the Pleasure to inform you, that I am at least one Million and an half, in Cash, about Three Millions of Livres which will be a considerable Aid to the operations of our Financier at Philadelphia, and I hope your Court, with their usual Goodness will make up the rest that may be wanting.

I am now as well Situated as I ever can be in Europe. I have the Honour to live, upon agreable Terms of Civility with the Ambassadors of France and Spain; and the Ministers of all the other Powers of Europe, whom I meet at the Houses of the French and Spanish Ministers as well as at Court, are complaisant and Sociable. Those from Russia and Denmark are the most reserved. Those from Sardinia & Portugal are very civil.

The Ministers of all the neutral Powers consider our Independance as decided. One of those even from Russia Said So not long ago and that from Portugal Said it to me within a few Days. You and I have known this Point to have been decided a long time: But it is but lately, that the Ministers of neutral Powers, however they might think, have frankly expressed their opinions. And it is now an Indications that it begins to be the Sentiment of their Court, for they dont often advance faster than their Masters in expressing their Sentiments upon political Points of this Magnitude.

Pray what are the Sentiments of the Corps Diplomatick at Versailles.? What Progress is made in the Negotiation for Peace? *Can any Thing be done before, the British Parliament, or at least the Court of St. James's, acknowledge the Sovereignty of the United States absolute and unlimited?*[2]

It would give me great Pleasure to recive, a Line from you, as often as your Leisure will admit. With great Esteem I have the Honour to be, Sir your most obt.

LbC (MHi: Adams Papers).
1. The treaty of commerce with the United Provinces was signed on October 8. For Adams's account of its significance, see his October 8 letter to Robert Livingston, in Wharton, *Diplomatic Correspondence*, 5:803–5.
2. On this issue, see Lafayette to Franklin, September 21, note 1.

To John Adams

Paris October the 6h 1782

My Dear Sir
Your favor of the 29h last Has Safely Come to Hand, for Which I am the More Obliged to You, as I Set the Greatest Value By The Honor of Your Correspondance. I Have Been Long Waïting for a Safe Oppor-

tunity To Write, and Will Endeavour This May Stir Clear of the Post Offices, As the Itching fingers of Clarks Do not Permit Any Secret to Pass Unnoticed.

I Am Happy to Hear You Have Walked on With our dutch friends to the Wished for Conclusion of The treaty of Commerce. Admit the Wonders You Have Performed in that Country, I Greatly Rejoice at Your Having Succeeded in Monney Matters. The More So, as I Aprehend Our financier[1] Needs Much An European Assistance, and The Great Expenses they Have Made in this Country Give Me But little Hope to Obtain a further Supply than The Six Millions, and the Ballance of Accounts Which Have Been Determined Upon Since the time I Arrived from America.

M. Jay Advances But Slowly With the Spaniards. In fact, He Does not Advance at All, and tho' Count d'Aranda Has Got Powers, Tho' He Has With a Pencil Drawn an Extravagant Line This Side of the Mississipy, Yet Untill Powers Are Exchanged Upon an Equal footing, and Untill the Spanish Pencil is transported three Hundred Miles West Ward, There is No doing Any thing towards Settling a treaty With that Nation.[2]

As to the Grand Affair of Peace, there are Reasons to Believe it Will take Place. Many Attempts Have Been Made to treat Upon an Unequal footing, Which By the Bye Was a Very Impertinent Proposal. But We Stood firm, deaf, and dumb, and As France Refused to Enter Into Business Untill We Were Made to Hear and to Speack, at Last, With Much Reluctance, And Great Pains, His Britannic Majesty and Council Were Safely Delivered of A Commission to treat With Plenipotentiaries from the United States of America.

In Case We are to judge from Appearances, One Would think Great Britain is in Earnest. But When We Consider the Temper of The king and His Minister, the foolish, Ridiculous issue of the Attempt Against Gibraltar, The Collection of forces at Newyork the Greatest Part of Which are Destined to the West Indias, and The Combination of the American, french, Spanish, Dutch Interests on the One Hand, and those of a Haughty Nation on the other, it Appears Probable that five or Six Months Will Pass Before The Work of Peace is Happily Concluded. But that it Will Be Concluded Before Next Summer Appears to me the Most Probable Idea that Can Be formed Upon this Matter.

We Have Letters from America as Late as the 6h September. M. de Vaudreuïl and His Squadron Had Arrived at Boston. It Was Said Charlestown Would Be Evacuated and the troops Sent to Newyork. There is a Rumour of *Madras* Having Been taken. At Least We May Look for Good News from The East Indias.[3]

As I Have No Public Capacity to Be led into Political Secrets, I Beg

You Will Consider these Communications as Confidential, and Have
the Honor to Be With the Highest Regard My dear Sir Your obedient
Hble. Servant

LAFAYETTE

ALS (MHi: Adams Papers).

1. "Our financier": Robert Morris, U.S. Superintendent of Finances.

2. Jay was to negotiate as peace commissioner with the Conde de Aranda, the Spanish
minister to France, but Aranda refused to let Jay see his commission. Jay then refused to
negotiate without an exchange of documents. In a confrontation witnessed by Lafayette
on September 26 in Vergennes's antechamber, Aranda told Jay that they could not
exchange powers because Spain had not yet acknowledged U.S. independence. Lafayette
then broke in to say "that it would not be consistent with the dignity of France for her ally
to treat otherwise than as independent," a remark that appeared to Jay "to pique the
Count d'Aranda not a little." Vergennes interceded in the row, urging Jay to negotiate
with Aranda. Jay replied, "Both the terms of my commission and the dignity of America
forbid my treating on any other than an *equal footing*" (Jay to Livingston, November 17,
1782, in Wharton, *Diplomatic Correspondence*, 6:45).

On the issue of boundaries, Aranda had sent Jay a map in early August with his
proposals: "from a lake near the confines of Georgia, but east to the Flint River, to the
confluence of the Kanawha with the Ohio, thence round the western shores of Lakes Erie
and Huron, and thence round Lake Michigan to Lake Superior" (ibid., 6:23). The
Americans wanted the Mississippi River as the western boundary.

3. The rumored capture of Madras did not occur.

From George Washington

Verplanks point 20th. Oct 82

My dear Marqs.

Whilst I thought there was a probability of my letters finding you in
France I continued to write to you at Paris. After that, I ceased to do so,
expecting the more agreeable pleasure of embracing you in America.
Your favor of the 29th. of June, placing the time of your departure
from thence on a contingency, and our latest advices from Europe,
reporting that the Negociations for Peace were nearly in the same state
as at the commencement of it, I shall renew my corrispondence.

I approve, very highly, the motives which induced you to remain at
your Court, and I am convinced Congress will do the same. The Campaign, as you supposed has been very inactive. We formed the junction
with the French Corps (whch. is now Encamped on our left ten miles
distant) the Middle of September; and have remained in perfect unison
with them ever since their arrival. It may I believe with much truth be
said, that a greater harmony between two armies never subsisted than
that which has prevailed between the French & american since the first

junction of them last year. I had prepared a beautiful Corps for you to command, that would not, I am convinced either in their appearance or action, have discredited any officer, or Army whatever. It consisted of all the light Infantry of the Northern Army to which Sheldon's Legion would have been added. But we have done nothing more than to keep a watch upon the enemy this Campaign except restraining them from detaching; which I believe has been the consequence of our junction, & lying here. A few German Troops, & Refugees have been sent to Hallifax; from thence it was supposed they were to proceed to Canada. This took place before I came into the Field, which was on the last day of August. The Cold weather puts us in mind of warm fire sides; & the two armies will seperate for this or some other purpose, in the course of a few Days. The French Army will go Easterly—we Northerly, & shall fix our Cantonments in the Vicinity of West point.

The Enemy in New York make no scruple of declaring their intention of evacuating Charles town. Many Transports went from the former about a Month ago; with design, it was said, to take of [f] the Garrison; but whether it is to be brought to the last mentioned place or carried to the West Indies is mere matter of conjecture—very probably the British Troops may go to the latter & the foreigners to the former. Time only will shew this, as indeed it may another thing—viz—that the late changes in the British Councils may prevent the evacuation of it at all. With respect to New York, various opinions have prevailed—some thought the speedy evacuation of it inevitable—others, that it would be delayed till the spring, while a third set, less sanguine than either of the other two, believed that nothing short of Military force would ever free the City of them. Their whole design being, to amuse the Belligerent Powers, & deceive America till they could put their Marine & other matters in a more prosperous train for prosecuting the War. The first, it is certain were in an error, because the Troops are still at New York, but wch. of the other two may be right your knowledge from what is transacting on the European theatre enables you to judge better of than I. Certain it is, the loyalist & Refugees in New York are very much alarmed & know not what to expect. As certain it is Sir Guy Carleton holds himself in readiness to evacuate, or perform any other movement with his Army, while he endeavors assiduously in the mean while to propogate the favourable disposition of Great Britain to grant every thing America can require. Their Transports have wooded & watered, & lay ready for any Service. So have the Ships of War under Admiral Pigot; but I believe they are designed for the West Indies, with *part* of the Troops at New York more than for any other purpose.

You will have heard before this Letter can reach you, of the loss of the L'Eagle. It will be unpleasant therefore to repeat it. Every body laments the misfortune, & pities poor L'Touche.[1] Duke Lauzen has been very sick but is now recovering fast—tho' very thin, & pale.

Poor Laurens is no more. He fell in a trifling skirmish in South Carolina, attempting to prevent the Enemy from plundering the Country of Rice. Genl. Lee is also dead—he breathed his last at Philadelphia about a fortnight ago. Your Aid G.W. has had an intermittant fever ever since April & by the last Accts. of him from Mount Vernon where he is, he was very low & weak.[2] As I despair of seeing my home this Winter I have just sent for Mrs. Washington who will think herself honoured by yours & Madm. La Fayettes notice.[3] Make a tender of my best respects to her, & offer a blessing in my name to your Son, & my Godson. Present me also to Count Charlux & others with whom I have the honor of an acquaintance. The Count de Noailles will have the trouble of reading, a letter from me.[4] Adieu My dear Marqs. Believe me to be, what I really am your sincere friend & most affectionate Humble Servt.

G. Washington

ALS (DLC: George Washington Papers, Series 4).

1. Latouche had commanded the frigate *Hérmione,* which brought Lafayette to America in 1780. While returning to America in September 1782, in command of the frigate *Aigle* (carrying the Baron de Vioménil, the Duc de Lauzun, the Marquis de Laval, the Prince de Broglie, the Comte de Ségur, and others), Latouche found his vessel being pursued by British frigates. The vessel ran aground as it attempted to escape up Delaware Bay. Though his passengers escaped, Latouche was captured (see Rice and Brown, *Rochambeau's Army,* 1:79–80).

2. John Laurens died at the Battle of Combahee Ferry, South Carolina, on August 27. The disgraced former general Charles Lee died in Philadelphia on October 2. On Washington's continuing concern for the ailment of his nephew George Augustine Washington, see his letter to him in Fitzpatrick, *Writings of Washington,* 25:342–43.

3. Letter to Martha Washington not found.

4. Washington's October 18 letter to the Vicomte de Noailles congratulated him on his appointment to the King's Cavalry (ibid., 25:273–74).

To George Washington

Paris October 24 1782

My Dear General

My Last Letter Has Informed You that in Case Peace is Not Made, and our Plans do not Immediately take place at this Court, I Would think it Consistent With My zeal for our Cause, and My Obedience to Your Intentions, to take a Round About Way to Serve our Military Purposes.[1] Under those Circumstances, I Have Accepted to Go this

Winter With Count d'Estaing, But tho' I am to Reenter Into the french line as a Marechal de Camp from the Date of Lord Cornwallis's Surrender, I Will However keep My American Uniform, and the out Side as Well as the Inside of an American Soldier. I Will Conduct Matters, and take Commands as an officer Borrowed from the United States, as it Were Occasionally, and Will Watch for the Happy Moment When I May join Our Beloved Colours.[2]

My Seeing WEST INDIES, Will I Hope Bring about and Insure the thing We Want, or Any other You May Wish. In Seeing WEST INDIES I Will Have With me MARITIME SUPERIORITY. A Vessel Will go to America in a fort Night. What I write to You Has Been Given to me Under the Greatest Secrecy, and Untill I am at Liberty to Mention it, I Beg it May Be for You *Alone*. When Matters are Better Settled, I will Be More Particular, in the Mean While You May prepare Your Orders to me. As there Will Be private Communications, and they Might Be Sent By two Ways, I Was thinking officers Could Be dispatched. George Wanted to Make a Voyage. McHenry Had the Same Desire.[3] You know that with me George Will Be Well taken Care of. I Give those Hints Before Hand. Your Excellency Will fully Hear from me By the Next Vessel. I Hope NEW YORK May take place about JUNE.[4] What I am doing Was the only Way.

In a Month time We Must know if England is Willing to Make peace, and if it not Made shortly after the Meeting of parliament, it is Certain that an other Campaign Becomes Necessary. I do not intend to Set out Before that time.

Clel. Gouvion is not, I Suppose, Immediately Wanting, and I Have Presumed to think Your Excellency Will not Be displeased at My keeping Him With me.

My Best and most Affectionate Respects Waït Upon Mrs. Washington, And My tenderest Compliments Upon the family and My other friends. Mde. de Lafayette joins with me in presenting You and Mrs. Washington with Assurances of Her love and Respect. You know My Heart, My dear General, and I Need not telling You How Respectfully How Affectionately I Have the Honor to Be Your Most Obedt. Hbe. Servant and Devoted friend

LAFAYETTE

ALS (PEL: Hubbard Collection). Coded passages deciphered between the lines appear here in small capitals.

1. Lafayette wrote to Washington on October 14: "I Have Requested Clel. Gouvion to Tell You, What It is Better not to write, About My Plans in Case of PEACE, and in Case it Gives Way to ideas in WEST INDIES. The last I consider as the only Way to Help Your Views, and As We Must if the Short Road Will not do, take the longer to Arrive To the Same End" (PEL: Hubbard Collection).

2. D'Estaing was to command a French-Spanish expeditionary force against Jamaica.

Lafayette hoped that when the winter campaign ended, the French contingents would then mount an attack on the North American continent.

3. George Augustine Washington and James McHenry, former aides of Lafayette.

4. The projected attack on New York by the Americans and D'Estaing's French forces.

From Robert R. Livingston

Philadelphia 2d Novr 1782

Dear Sir

The confusion occasioned by the misfortune of the Eagle & the delay that the Gent. who saved their baggage experienced in geting here prevented my receiving your favor of the 25th. & 29th. July till the last of Sepr. tho' I had acknowledged the rect. of other letters by the same conveyance much earlier.[1]

Your Letter contained so much important matter that it was laid before congress for knowing it would be advantagious to you & place your assiduity & attention to their interests in the strongest point of light I chose to consider most of yours as [a] public letter. This last was particularly acceptable as neither Mr. Franklin or Mr. Jay had been so explicit as we had reason to expect. Our system of politics has been so much the same for a long time tending only to one point a determination to support the war till we can make peace in conjunction with our allies that the whole history of our cabinet amounts to nothing more than a reiteration of the same sentiments in different language & so plain is our political path so steadily do we walk in it that I can add nothing to what I have already written you on that subject.

The events of the campaign are as uninteresting. The inactivity & caution of the enemy have given us leisure to form the finest army this country ever saw while they conspire to render that army useless for the present. The troops are gone into winter quarters our[s] at Fishkill Westpoint & its vicinity. The French as far east as Hartfort TO AVAIL THEMSELVES OF CIRCUMSTANCES & BE READY TO EMBARK IN CASE THE BRITISH SHOULD EVACUATE NEW YORK tho of this there seems at present very Little probability. This day we are informed from New York that 14 sail of the line one of forty guns & 7 frigates sailed from thence the 26th. We cannot learn that they had troops on board or under their convoy. MR. DE VAUDRUIL STILL CONTINUES AT BOSTON WHERE HE HAS MANY REPAIRS TO MAKE & MUCH TO DO BEFORE HIS SHIPS CAN SAIL.[2] The Manifique is lost I believe without hope of recovery. She will however be well replaced by the America which all accounts concur in calling a fine ship.[3] But unless your fleet is very considerably strengthened in these seas another campaign may slip away as uselessly as the last for I see no reason to suppose while Lord Shelburne is at the head of administration that the negotiations for peace will wear a serious aspect. I believe with you that his royal master is set upon risking every thing rather than acknowledge our indepen- dance & as he possesses the art of seduction in a very eminent degree it will require more firmness to resist his solicitations than is generally found among courtiers. I am very much pleased to hear that the seige of Gibralter is at last undertaken with some prospect of success. This I sincerely wish [*blank space*] England has found in that single fortress a more powerful ally than any other she could make in Europe. It has for the most part employed the navy of Spain & cost them five ships of the line. You need feel no anxiety on the score of an appology for yr. absense. Every body here attributes it to its true cause & considers it as a new proof of your attatchment to the interests of America. The papers I send with this will serve to confirm this assertion.[4] I thank you for the acquaintance of the Prince de Broglio & Count De Segur. They handed me your letters the day I unfortunaly was about to leave town.[5] They have however promised to be here this winter & to give me an opportunity of consoling myself for your absense by the atten- tions they will enable to shew to those you love. Your brother in law is gone I find to the seige of Gibralter.[6] I beg you to write particularly to remind him of his American friends. He shall hear from me by the first opportunity. In the mean while tell him that he will not do justice to our expectations if he neglects to promote the great objects which we discussed together a little before he left this foreseeing then that he would eer long be called to Spain. I ought not to conclude this without informing you that the chair of State is transfered to Mr. Boudinot Mr. Hansons term having expired.[7] I am my Dear Sir with the warmest affection & the sincerest regard & esteem Your Most Ob. Hum: Servt.

AL (NHi: Robert R. Livingston Papers), draft. Coded passages deciphered between the lines appear in small capitals.

1. Livingston almost certainly means July here rather than June. On the misfortune of the *Aigle*, see Washington to Lafayette, October 20, note 1.

2. Vaudreuil's squadron was a remnant of the French fleet that had been defeated in the Battle of the Saints in April.

3. The *Magnifique*, from Vaudreuil's squadron, was lost at the entrance to Boston Harbor on August 9; Congress voted to offer the French the *America* as a substitute on September 3 (*JCC*, 23:543).

4. This was probably a copy of the congressional resolution of October 4, declaring the United States' determination to adhere to its agreement not to conclude any peace or truce with England without the consent of France.

5. Lafayette's April 12 letters of introduction for the Comte de Ségur and the Prince de Broglie are in NHi: Robert R. Livingston Papers.

6. The Vicomte de Noailles.

7. The "chair of State": presidency of the Continental Congress.

To the American Peace Commissioners

Paris November the 21st 1782

Gentlemen

Since the Early Period When I Had the Happiness To Be Adopted
Among The Sons of America, I Ever Made it My Point To Do That
Which I Thought Would Prove Useful To Her Cause or Agreable to
Her Citizens. After We Had Long Stood By ourselves, France Did join
in our Quarrell, and So Soon as Count D'Estaing's Departure Made My
Presence Unnecessary, I Had a Permission to Return to France Where,
Among other things, I Endeavoured to Impress this Court With The
Propriety To Send a Naval force, and An Auxiliary Army To Serve
Under the orders of General Washington. The Plan of a Descent in
England Lengthned My Negotiation, The Succour Was at Last Sent,
and Arrived at a Critical Period. It Prevented Evils, But Did not Pro-
duce Any Great Immediate Good Untill That Naval Superiority Which
Had Been Promised Was Sent to Cooperate With us, and Helped us in
the Capture of Lord Cornwallis.

This Event Ended the Campaign in Virginia, and The Army I Had
Commanded Was of Course Separated. Congress Gave me Leave to Go
to France, and to Return at Such Time as I Should think Proper. I Had
it in Command To Make Some Representations at this Court, and The
General's Particular Instructions Were By all Means to Bring a Naval
and Land Assistance to Operate in our America.[1]

Count de Grasse's Defeat Having Ruined our Plans, I Now Was
Despairing to fulfill the Intentions of Congress and The orders of My
General, When it Was Proposed to me to Serve in The Army Under
The Direction of Count D'Estaing.[2] This Has Appeared to me The
only Way I Had To Serve My Views, I Had the Honor to Consult you
about it, and Upon Your Approbation of The Measure, I Consented to
Accompagny Count d'Estaing in His Expeditions, Provided it Was in
My Capacity, and Even Under the Uniform of an American officer,
Who Being for a time Borrowed from the United States, Will obey the
first order or take the first Opportunity to Rejoin His Colours.

Had I not Been Detained By You, Gentlemen, Upon Political Accounts Which You Have Been pleased to Communicate to Congress, I
Would Have Long Ago Returned To America.[3] But I Was With You of
Opinion, That My Presence Here Might Be Useful, and Since it Appears Matters are not Ripe for a treaty, My first Wish is Now To Return
to America With Such force as May Expell the Ennemy from The

United States, Serve the Views of Congress, and Assist Your Political Measures. When, or How this May Be Effected I Am Not Yet Able to Determine, or I would not Be at liberty to Mention, But, However Certain I Have Been of Your Opinion, I Think it A Mark of Respect to Congress not to Depart Untill I Have Your Official Approbation of the Measure. With the Highest Respect I Have the Honor to Be, Gentlemen Your obedient Humble Servant

LAFAYETTE

ALS (ICN: Herbert R. Strauss Collection).

1. See the November 23, 1781, resolution of Congress and Washington's letter of November 15, 1781 (*LAAR* 4:440–41, 435–37).

2. On the projected expeditionary force to the West Indies, see Lafayette to Washington, October 24, above.

3. While both Jay and Franklin had indicated to Congress that Lafayette was useful to them, they did not initiate proposals that Lafayette defer his return to America. On November 23 Lafayette presented this letter to the three commissioners "for our Approbation of his going out, with the C. D'Estaing. He recites in it that he remained here by our Advice, as necessary to the Negotiations. This nettled both F. and J. I knew nothing of it, not having been here, and they both denied it" (*Diary and Autobiography of John Adams*, vol. 3, p. 71).

To the Comte de Vergennes[T]

Paris, November 22, 1782

When I left America, Monsieur le Comte, I was charged with presenting its position here, and in the critical circumstances in which it finds itself, Congress requests me particularly to set forth to you its financial needs. It is in accordance with their leave of absence and their instructions that I have come here, and when, without their approval or a stated rank in the French army, I am about to undertake operations that they are unaware are beginning,[1] I must at least carry out their commissions and above all ease my conscience with the opinion that in this delicate moment I take the liberty of submitting to you.

The dispatches of Congress have arrived; those of the Chevalier de La Luzerne have not yet.[2] Something may have gone wrong in his offices or on board the American ship, and if these letters are delayed it would be a pity to fall into postponements and uncertainty. You know America too well, Monsieur le Comte, to need to be enlightened by this last dispatch. Besides, I have talked too much with the king's minister on the subject in question not to know that he will recommend giving the help America believes it urgent to request.

The papers Mr. Franklin showed you in confidence contain at least some news.[3] They were addressed to him, and if you fear the news is exaggerated, I must add that private information, my intimate knowledge of the country, and the judgment it is easy for me to form of the present situation finally all unite, Monsieur le Comte, in persuading me of the necessity for this pecuniary assistance.

When I consider America, Monsieur le Comte, it is natural for me to adopt a Frenchman's point of view. It is in this capacity alone that I am examining the dangers of British influence. The people are war-weary, but right now they love France and hate England. Bestowing help at this moment is an act all the more useful in that it puts the seal on all the previous ones. It restores courage and silences the British emissaries who constantly accuse France of wanting to stir up the fire without extinguishing it. I do not dwell on these calumnies, Monsieur le Comte; their absurdity should, I hope, guarantee their impact. But it is no less useless to dwell upon the weak pecuniary efforts of the American people. From this point of view, I confess, they are very much to be blamed. One can say that there is little money in the country, and I can attest that the British left less of it than is believed; this money is still either within their lines or in the buried strongboxes of the Royalists. One might add that in this period of confusion, the states have not been able to take suitable steps to impose and collect taxes; and that, moreover, the extent of the country and the widely scattered population make tax collection difficult. One might also observe the difference between present taxes and those that were one of the grounds for discontent. Finally, Monsieur le Comte, the Americans would say that their commerce has suffered cruelly this year. But while I think that these excuses, although quite valid, are not sufficient, I can easily see that Congress, Mr. Morris, and all the leaders of the Revolution are concerned lest lack of money make them fail. It is clear that they must try to get funds, and to succeed they must take all measures that will not endanger the Revolution itself.

Since they have not been able to obtain any, Monsieur le Comte, I believe it becomes necessary, for the success and the glory of the common cause, to make one last and generous effort in favor of the Americans. If we compare the sums they are asking with the advances made to our allies in the last war, and especially if we recognize the degree of interest we had in supporting them, the help the Americans judge indispensable will no longer seem exorbitant.

M. de Rochambeau's army is leaving America, and if New York is not evacuated, this premature action seems to call for compensation. These troops cost thirteen million. They are taking the place of other troops in the West Indies and, moreover, do not cost as much. Instead of dispatching two regiments, six million was given. In the present situation, could we not give at least what the minister of finance had surely set aside for the annual maintenance of this army? I should think also that, if the war continues, especially if it is prolonged by interests that concern neither the Americans nor their allies, we would consider it necessary at least to help them a little during the campaign.[4] Would not this projected assistance, combined with the unforeseen economy of M. de Rochambeau's army, come close to the hopes America seems to have formed?

Perhaps we will remember that this continent is the only place where we have had great success. The reason is simple enough, since everything there works to our advantage and runs counter to our enemy. In the happy event that we bring our forces there, we must find an army able to cooperate. There has never been a better army than the American; but if the army's patience is finally exhausted, if Congress is torn between the difficulty of keeping it and the difficulty of disbanding it, if we must finally anticipate an upheaval instead of conducting an offensive operation, not only will it be impossible to attack enemy positions, but it will also be easy for them to withdraw from these posts, as well as from Canada, and these surplus troops, no longer retained in North America, will be directed against our islands.

From a political point of view, it would seem still more urgent to help the Americans. I do not fear a peace between them and England, and if we carry the war there I am convinced we should have a great success. But to strengthen the bonds of friendship still more, to assure them of the means to operate against the enemy, I would not like us to refuse this urgent and final request. America's intentions are excellent; we have nothing to fear but the impossibility of their continuing, and yet America would never consent to set aside the duties of the alliance or those of gratitude. But in closing, Monsieur le Comte, it is impossible for me not to give you my opinion. I give it from the depths of my heart and, without flattering myself that it will replace that of the Chevalier de La Luzerne, I should reproach myself for not having told you how urgent and necessary I believe assistance is. Accept, I pray you, Monsieur le Comte, the tribute of affectionate and respectful attachment with which I have the honor to be your very humble and obedient servant,

LAFAYETTE

ALS (AAE: Correspondance politique, Etats-Unis, vol. 22, fols. 477–79), translation.

1. "Operations": D'Estaing's expedition to the West Indies.

2. Lafayette did not expect Vergennes to approve further financial aid without La Luzerne's assessment of American military prospects.

3. In his November 8 letter to Vergennes, Franklin had sent the following: excerpts of Livingston to Franklin, September 5, 13, and 18; Morris to Franklin, September 27, September 28, and October 7; Morris to Adams, September 27; and the September 14

and October 3 resolutions of Congress (AAE: Correspondance politique, Etats-Unis, vol. 22, fols. 196, 233, 243, 275–79, 295–96, 363, 280, 234–35, 328–29).

4. The interests "that concern neither the Americans nor their allies": Spain's obsession with the recovery of Gibraltar.

To George Washington

Brest December the 4h 1782

My Dear General
Most Secret Intelligences

My former Letters Have Acquainted You That, However Talkative Were Politicians About Peace, an Expedition Was Going to take place the Command of which is Given to Count d'Estaing. I Have Also Added that Upon Being Requested to Go, I Have Willingly Accepted of it, as I thought it the Means, the only Means in the World to Bring About What You Have Directed me to obtain. Clel. Gouvion Must Be With You, and I Refer You, My Dear General, to the letter I wrote By Him, as Well as to Some Notes I write to Him as I Have a full Cypher With that Gentleman.[1] WEST INDIES is the first object. SPAIN in the Way. We Have Got Here 9 Ships of the Line to Set out With the first fair Wind. Your Excellency knows that Count d'Estaing is Gone to Spain. We Shall Have MARITIME SUPERIORITY. Please to Prepare Propositions, and Notions about NEW YORK, CHARLESTON PENOBSCOT, NEWFOUND-LAND One FRENCH SHIP is to Be Sent to AMERICA, and then By Your orders to WEST INDIES. I shall write the Next Opportunity.

Inclosed, My dear General, I Have the Honor to Send you the Copy of a Letter to Congress.[2] I Hope You Will be able to tell them You are Satisfied with My Conduct. Indeed, My dear General, it is Necessary to My Happiness You Will think So. When You are absent, I Endeavour to do the thing Which You Seem Likely to Have Advised Had you Been present. I love you too much to Be one Minute Easy Unless I think You Approve of My Conduct.

Peace is Much talked of. I think, *Betwen us*, Much of the difficulty Must lay with the Spaniards—and Yet I do not think the Ennemy are Very Sincere. They Have Been Heaping Chicanes and finesses upon the affair of Limits for America, and So on.[3] It is My opinion that, in the Bottom of their Hearts, they are determined, if they Can, to try What turn Next Campaign Will Give to their Affairs and God Grant We May Make it a Vigorous one, Particularly about NEW YORK.

I Have Arrived Here But Yesterday Morning. I Have Much of Public Business upon My Hands. So that in Requesting My Best Respects to

Article 9th

In case it should so happen that any Place or Territory belonging to Great Britain, or to the United States, should be conquered by the Arms of either, from the other, before the Arrival of these Articles in America, It is agreed that the same shall be restored, without Difficulty, and without requiring any Compensation.

Done at Paris, the thirtieth day of November, in the year One thousand seven hundred Eighty Two

Richard Oswald

John Adams

Franklin

John Jay

Henry Laurens

Signature page of the preliminary peace articles between Great Britain and the United States, whose signing on November 30, 1782, frustrated Lafayette's hopes for the French-Spanish expedition against the British West Indies.

Be presented to Mrs. Washington, and My Compliments to the family, George and My friends in the Army I Will only add the Expression of the Most tender and Gratefull Respect I Have the Honor to Be With, My dear General Your obt. Sert. and affect. friend

LAFAYETTE

ALS (PEL: Hubbard Collection). Coded passages deciphered between the lines appear in small capitals.

1. Lafayette had written to Washington on October 14, "I have requested Clel. Gouvion to tell you, what it is better not to write, about my plans in case of PEACE, and in case it gives way to ideas in W. INDIES" (Gottschalk, *Letters of Lafayette,* pp. 254–56). In two letters of December 3 to Gouvion, Lafayette informed his aide that he was sending the vessel *Serpent* to America to carry Washington's orders and Gouvion to Saint-Dominque, and would meet him there (NIC: Dean Collection).

2. For fear that Americans might misinterpret his voyage to Spain and the West IUdies, Lafayette wrote to Congress on December 3:

I Could not Suffer to think that Any Member of Congress Might from public Report, Imagine, that I Enlarge So far their Permission as to follow pursuits that Would not Particularly Promote the Views of America—and as they do not Choose Being Intruded Upon with Minute Details of Military plans, Let it Sufice to Say that I Beg Leave to Refer them to the Opinion of General Washington. [DNA: RG 360, PCC 156, pp. 300–302]

3. The Spanish were also proposing that the western boundaries of the United States be five hundred miles east of the Mississippi, and were therefore unwilling to grant free navigation on that river. See Lafayette to Adams, October 6, note 2.

To Benjamin Franklin

On Board the *Censeur* Brest Road December
the 6h 1782

Dear Sir

After Having Been two days out of the Road, a S. W. Wind obliges us to Come Back Again, and I fear it Will Give time for Lord Howe to Embarass our Passage.[1] No Letter from You Has yet Come to Hand, Which I am Very Sorry for, as I Impatiently Waït for information Upon our Monney Affairs. I Have not Yet Received Your Answer to My Consulting Letter.[2] But I know the Opinion of the three Gentlemen in the Commission, and You Have Also thought that I ought not to detain the fleet on My Account. And as I am Still more Anxious to do the Best, than to Appear to Have done So, My Conscience is Easy, and I Would Willingly loose the Credit of Past Exertions, Rather than to Neglect an Opportunity of Making New Ones. Mr. de Rayneval's Speedy Return Makes me Hope That Peace is not far at a distance. I Would Be Much Obliged to You for Your Opinion. In Case Men of Some Rank Are Sent By France, I do not know who Will Be the person.

If it is Not the One We Spoke About together, it Will Be The Usual Ambassador, My uncle the Mquis. de Noaïlles.[3] This if You please (Entre Nous) Unless You think Useful to Communicate it, Under Secrecy, to Your Colleagues.

As to My Part, if Matters Were So Ripe as to Admit of My Return, Nothing Would More Highly please me than the Happiness, Any How, to Serve America, and More Particularly in the Capacity of a Man Honoured With Her Confidence.

An Express is Sent to Versaïlles, By Whose Return I Hope to Hear from You, and I do not think the Weather Will Permit us to Set out Before that time. Requesting My Compliments to Be Presented to Your Grandson I Have the Honor to Be With Every Sentiment of affection and Respect Your Excellency's Most obedient Humble Servant

LAFAYETTE

ALS (PPAmP: Franklin Papers, vol. 26, no. 89).

1. Lafayette feared interception by a British squadron under Admiral Howe. With nine ships and 6,000 soldiers on board, the convoy was a fair prize.

2. The letter to the American Peace Commissioners of November 21.

3. Lafayette still thought he might be selected as intermediary at the British court. He wrote to Franklin on December 8 that he was sailing with the fleet "and Untill Peace is Ascertained, Will Continüe in Promoting the Wiews Which You Have decided to Be the Most Advantageous to America." He remarked, "In this Affair, it is Useless to observe that My Personal Interest Has Been by me Entirely Given Up" (DLC: Benjamin Franklin Papers).

To John Jay

Cadix December the [26] 1782

Dear Sir

My Letters to Doctor Franklin Have Hitherto Acquainted You With Every thing that Related to Me.[1] I Have Been With the Convoy As far as Cape Ste Mary, and then I Came in a frigat to this Port. On My Way I Have Dispatched a Vessel to General Washington, and Have Communicated Particulars of our Situation, as Well as Proposals for Military Operations.

The Convoy I Came With is Coming In, a Good Number of french and Spanish Ships Are getting Ready, the french Division at Gibraltar is Going to Embark, So that We Intend to Sail With a powerfull Reinforcement.

On My Arrival at this Place, I Have Been told that our American preliminaries are Agreed Upon for Which I Heartly Rejoice With You.[2] But Am Sorry to Hear That Mylord Shelburne Has Not Been

Candid With the french.[3] Should He think That America May forget
Treaties, He Will Be Much Disappointed. This May Be for The United
States A New Opportunity to Shine in their Political Character. In Case
it Becomes Necessary to Go on With Military Operations, I Very Much
Hope they Will Be Successfull.

In the first Moments I Saw Count d'Estaing He Asked for My Opinion Upon the Present Political Situation of our Affairs. It Appears that
the Spanish Court, and Count de Montmorin Himself Wanted Him to
take those Informations. My Answer Was That America Had Made
treaties, and Would Stand By them—that Her Steadiness Was Equal to
Her Spirit—But that Unless they Give Monney, No Efforts Can Be
Expected. Upon this Monney Affair, I Was Very Urging. Count d'Es-
taing Has wrote to Count de Montmorin a Private letter Which is to Be
Laid Before the Spanish Court.[4] I Have wrote one to Carmichael By
Post Which is to Be Oppened By Count de Florida Blanca.[5] I Have So
Far Conquered My Hatred to Count O'Reïlly as to Speack freely With
Him Upon this Matter. I do not Much Expect from the Attempt. But
As No American Plenipotentiary Was Committed, As limits and Every
Political idea Was out of the Way, I Have thought there Was not Amiss
in Seizing the present Opportunity—to tempt them into an offer to
Lend us Monney from the Havanna. I do not Believe it Will Succeed,
But there is No Harm in the trial.[6]

You Will Greatly oblige me, My dear Sir, to keep me Acquainted
With Every thing that is Interesting to America. My Heart is in it, You
know, and Your Communications Will Be Very Well Come. I Live With
Mr. Harrison and Am Very Happy in His Acquaintance. But Your
letters Had Better Be Sent to Mde. de Lafayette With a Particular
Recommendation.

Be pleased to Remember me Most Affectionately to Mr. Franklin,
Mr. Adams, and Mr. Laurens, and to let them know Any thing in this
letter that Appears Worth Communicating. My Best Compliments
Waït Upon Doctor Bancroft.

I Request, My dear Sir, You Will Be So kind as to Present My Best
Respects to Mrs. Jay and to Receive the Hearty Assurance of the High
and Affectionate Regard I Have the Honor to Be With Dear Sir Your
obedient Humble Servant

LAFAYETTE

ALS (NNC: John Jay Papers).

1. Lafayette had written to Franklin on December 4, 6, and 8 from Brest.

2. The preliminaries to the U.S.-British peace treaty had been agreed to on November
30. For the text, see Morris, *John Jay*, 2:432–36.

3. On November 20 Shelburne had proposed that France concede one of its islands,
Guadeloupe or Martinique, along with Dominica or St. Lucia to England as compensation for British withdrawal from Gibraltar. In exchange, Spain would cede the eastern

half of Hispaniola to France. Before the proposal could be acted upon, however, the British cabinet added further terms that made it unacceptable to the French.

4. On November 29 D'Estaing had written a proposed plan of campaign for the joint expedition (AAE: Correspondance politique, Espagne, vol. 609, fols. 304–29).

5. Letter not found.

6. Conde Alexander O'Reilly, the governor of Cadiz, had extended his hospitality to the Jays in 1780 (Morris, *John Jay,* 1:699, 705). This gesture may have encouraged Lafayette to approach him with the idea of a Spanish loan.

To [the Comtesse de Tessé]ᵀ

Cadiz, January 1, 1783

The convoy of which I took leave fifty miles away has since experienced a thousand vexations. It finally came into port with the Toulon convoy. All those troops are joining the French and the more than five thousand Spanish troops at Gibraltar. Whatever Vaudreuil may say, M. d'Estaing is in command of both land and sea forces. I am the quartermaster general for the French and Spanish troops, and although M. de Falkenhayn had wanted to stay on, I have to clear things only with M. d'Estaing, who told the troops to follow the orders I give and shows me his usual friendship and trust. . . . I shall say nothing to you about Cadiz. Its greatest merit is that it is less Spanish than the other cities. Besides, I do not want to infringe upon the rights of those returning from Gibraltar to describe it, and my journals will all be from the other world. I shall not write in them that I see M. le Comte O'Reilly every day; my principles have little in common with those of the governor of Louisiana. I had planned not to see him, but without him one can procure nothing here, and the public good requires that I sacrifice my aversion. If I judge by the manner in which I am regarded by the troops, M. de Ségur's fears were ill founded, but I am very well off where I am. I hope our campaign will go better than the last one, and above all I hope that a good peace will arive to make all my preparations unnecessary.

While we are considering what has been done and trying to make it better, while we are bored with many necessary details, the navy is also making all its preparations. We have M. de La Motte-Picquet. There was another general officer, M. de Bausset, but he had an uncivil tongue and I hope to persuade M. d'Estaing simply to send him away. I shall go on board *Le Terrible* and M. d'Estaing *Le Majestueux;* these two ships will be closest together.

Shall we have peace, my dear cousin, and must we still fight in order to understand one another? My own grand adventure seems to be settled, and America is sure of her independence. Humanity has won its case, and freedom will never again be without a refuge. Let our success now give rise to a general peace, let France regain her stature and her advantages, and I shall be perfectly happy, for I am not philosophical enough not to have a personal stake in public affairs.

L (NIC: Dean Collection), fragmented copy, translation.

From Robert R. Livingston

Philadelphia 10th. January 1783

Dear sir

I was honoured by yours of the 14th of October last. It contains much useful information, and upon the whole exhibits a pleasing picture of our Affairs in Europe.[1] Here the scene is more checkered with good and evil. The last I think predominates. The want of money has excited very serious discontents in the Army. They have formed Committees. A very respectable one with General McDougal at their head is now here.[2] Their demands tho' strictly just are such as Congress have not the means of satisfying. The States upon whom they call complain of inability. Peace is wished for with more anxiety than it should be. Wearied out with the length of the war the People will reluctantly submit to the burdens they bore at the beginning of it. In short peace becomes necessary. If the war continues we shall lean more upon France than we have done. If peace is made she must add one obligation more to those she has already imposed. She must enable us to pay off our Army [or] we may find the reward of her exertions and ours suspended longer than we could wish.

Charles town is at length evacuated. The Enemy made a convention with General Greene and were suffered to depart in peace. In one of the papers I send you, you will see their general Orders at going off.[3] The embarkation of your Army before the war in this Country had closed gave me some pain.[4] Their stay might have answered useful political purposes, and they been at hand to operate against New York, which they will not otherwise quit.

Congress saw this in its true light, but were too delicate to mention it. I enclose their resolutions on being apprized of it.[5] You speak of operations in America. I agree with you that they devoutly to be wished both by France and by us, but if they are to depend upon operations in the West Indies it is ten to one but they fail. The machine is too complex. If it is to be worked in any part by Spanish Springs the chance against it is still greater, for whatever the latter may be in Europe in the West Indies they loose their elasticity.

The great cause between Connecticut and Pensylvania has been discided in favor of the latter.[6] It is a singular event. There are few instances of independent States submitting their Cause to a Court of Justice. The day will come tho' when all disputes in the great republic of Europe will be tried in the same way, and America be quoted to exemplify the wisdom of the measure. Adieu my dear Sir, continue to love this Country, for tho' she owes you much she will repay you all with interest when in Ages to come she records you with her Patriots and Heroes. I have the honor to be Dear sir with the sincerest Esteem and Regard your most obedt. humble servant

(signed) ROBT. R. LIVINGSTON

Enclosed the Resolutions of Congress on the French Army leaving America.

LbC (DNA: RG 360, PCC 118, p. 378).

1. Lafayette had written to Livingston that the British envoy in Paris had sufficient authority to begin negotiations. He also advised him of the lack of success in Gibraltar and of D'Estaing's project (NHi: Robert R. Livingston Papers).

2. A petition from disgruntled soldiers and officers led by General Alexander McDougall was read to Congress on January 6. It warned that if the army were not paid, "the most serious consequences were to be apprehended." Its text is in DNA: RG 360, PCC 42, vol. 6, fol. 61.

3. The evacuation occurred in mid-December. An article headed "Evacuation of Charlestown," reprinted from the January 4 issue of *Rivington's New-York Gazette*, appeared in several Philadelphia newspapers. For example, see *The Pennsylvania Packet*, January 9, 1783.

4. The reference is to the departure of the major French force, under the command of Vioménil, on December 24.

5. The text of the resolutions of January 1 noted the understanding that the French troops would "return whenever an object should offer, in which they might effectually co-operate with the troops of the United States." It also assumed that the "departure was dictated by a conviction that they could elsewhere be more usefully employed against the common enemy" (*JCC*, 24:1–2).

6. In 1753 Connecticut had chartered the Susquehannah Company to settle the Wyoming Valley of Pennsylvania, territory within the boundaries of Connecticut's original charter. In accordance with Article 9 of the Articles of Confederation, a special court was convened in November 1782 to decide jurisdiction over the area, and it decided on December 30 in Pennsylvania's favor (ibid., 24:31–32).

From John Jay

Rouen 19 Jany 1782 [1783]

Dear Sir

Accept my thanks for your obliging Letter of the 26 Decr. last, which the Marchioness was so kind as to send me Yesterday. I congratulate you on your safe arrival at Cadiz, and you have my best wishes that the same good Fortune you have hitherto experienced, may continue to attend you.

The State of my Health making a Change of Air, and exercise adviseable I left Paris ten Days ago on an Excursion into Normandy. Hence I suppose it has happened that I have neither heard of nor seen your Letters to Dr. Franklin.

If I am not mistaken a Copy of the american preliminaries has been sent to Spain; and I flatter myself that Count de Montmorin will think them perfectly consistent with our Engagements to our allies—It appears to me singular that any Doubts should be entertaind. of american good Faith; for as it has been tried & remains inviolate they cannot easily be explained on Principles honorable to those who entertain them. America has so often repeated & reiterated her Professions and assurances of Regard to the Treaty alluded to, that I hope she will not impair her Dignity by makeg. any more of them; but leave the continued Uprightness of her Conduct to inspire that Confidence which it seems she does not yet possess, altho she has always merited.

Our warmest acknowledgments are due to you for the Zeal you manifest to serve America at all Times and in all places—but Sir I have little Expectation that your Plan of a spanish Loan will succeed. I confess that I am far from being anxious abt. it. In my opinion America can with no Propriety accept Favors from Spain and for my own part I would rather borrow money to repay what we have recd. from her, than submit to pick up any Crums that may fall from her Table.

My absence from Paris has deprived me of the means of Information, & therefore I cannot at present gratify either your wishes or my own on that Head. God knows whether or no we shall have peace.[1] A variety of contradictory Reports daily reach me, but they deserve little Credit. It is again said that Charlstown is Evacuated. That may be—It is also said the Enemy have left New York; but I adhere to my former opinion, and do not believe a word of it—Mrs. Jay writes me that Mr. Oswald is gone to London, but for what Purpose I am ignorant. Thus my dear Sir are we held in a State of Suspence which nothing but Time can remove. I propose to return next week to Paris and shall then write to you again. Adieu I am with perfect Respect & Esteem Dr. Sir your most obt. Servt.

AL (London, Royal Archives, Windsor Castle: The Correspondence of Chief Justice Jay. With the gracious permission of Her Majesty Queen Elizabeth II).

1. The following day Jay received word from Paris that the preliminary articles of peace had been agreed to on January 18 and that they were to be signed January 20 (Morris, *John Jay*, 2:487–88).

To William Carmichael

Cadix January the 20th. 1783

Dear Sir,

Your Letter of the 14th. has this day come to hand.[1] The occasion of it I lament, but it becomes my duty to answer.

From an early period I had the happiness to rank among the Foremost in the American Revolution—in the affection & confidence of the People, I am proud to say, I have a great Share—Congress honors me so far as to direct I am to be consulted by their European Ministers which circumstances I do not mention out of Vanity, but only to shew that in giving my Opinion I am called upon by dictates of Honor & Duty which it becomes me to obey.

The measure being right, it is beneath me to wait for a private Opportunity; Public concerns have a great weight with me, but nothing upon Earth can intimidate me into Selfish considerations: To my Opinion you are entitled, & I offer it with the Freedom of a heart that ever shall be independent.

To France you owe a great deal; To Others you owe nothing: as a Frenchman whose heart is glowing with Patriotism, I enjoy the part France has acted & the connection she has made; as an American I acknowledge the obligation & in that I think true Dignity consists: but Dignity forbade our sending abroad Political forlorn hopes & I ever objected to the Condescention; the more so, as a French treaty had secured their Allies to you & because America is more likely to receive advances than to need throwing herself at other People's head.[2]

The particulars of the Negociation with Spain I do not dwell upon—in my Opinion they were wrong, but I may be mistaken. Certain it is that an exchange of Ministers ought to have been, & now an exchange of powers must be upon an equal footing. What England has done is nothing either to the Right, or to the Mode—the Right consisted in the People's will; the Mode depends upon a consciousness of American Dignity—But if Spain has hitherto declined to acknowledge what the Elder Branch of Bourbon thought honorable to declare, yet will it be too strange that England ranks before her in the date & the Benefits of the acknowledgment.

There are more Powers than you know of who are making advances to America—some of them I have personally received, but you easily guess that no treaty would be so pleasing as the one with Spain—the three natural Enemies of Britain should be strongly United—the French Alliance is everlasting; but such a treaty between the Friends of France is a new Tie of confidence & affection—the Spaniards are slow in their motions but strong in their attachments—from a regard to them, but still more out of regard to France, we must have more patience with them than with any other Nation in Europe.

I has hitherto been kind not to help Spain in exposing the weak side of her policy; so that when England is encouraged by a want Union in her Enemies no part of the faults be laid upon the United States.

But peace is likely to be made, and how then can the Man who advised against your going at all, propose your remaining at a Court where you are not decently treated? Congress, I hope, & thro' them, the whole Nation, do not intend their Dignity to be trifled with & for my part, I have no inclination to betray the confidence of the American People—I expect we are going to have peace, & I expect Spain is going to act by you with propriety; but, should they hesitate to treat you as a public Servant of the United States, then, however disagre[e]able is the task, Mr. Carmichael had better go to Paris where France may stand a Mediator & thro' that generous & common Friend, we may come to the wished for connection with the Court of Spain. With an high regard & sincere affection, I have the honor to be, Dear Sir, your Obednt. Humbe. Servnt.

LAFAYETTE

LS (DNA: RG 360, PCC 156, pp. 308–11). Though the letter bears the word "copy," it carries Lafayette's signature.

Lafayette sent this letter in the expectation that Spanish officials would intercept it in the public mails (see Lafayette to Carmichael, January 29). When John Jay went to Paris in June for the peace negotiations, William Carmichael stayed behind as acting chargé d'affaires.

1. The letter has not been found. It probably dealt with Carmichael's lack of recognition by the Spanish court and the possibility that he might be recalled. Carmichael wrote to Livingston on January 18: "I availed myself of the Letters which the Marquis de la Fayette had done me the honor to address me from Cadiz; I know that these hints have been conveyed to the Ministry & am assured underhand that I shall have soon reason to be satisfied" (DNA: RG 360, PCC 88, p. 340).

2. "Political forlorn hope": in military usage, a "forlorn hope" was a small body of troops assigned to make the first breach in a rampart or fortification. Few were expected to survive.

To William Carmichael

Cadix january the 29th 1783

My dear Sir

As there is a Safe Express Going to Madrid, I Have the Honour to Inclose the Copy of a Letter which the Spanish Ministry May Have thought proper to detain.[1] My Opinion is the Same, and Weither in Public, or Private Communications, I shall Ever declare Against Any thing that Would Commit the Dignity of the United States. My last letter Has Been Calculated for Inspection, and Yet, When a Private Opportunity offers, I Have Nothing to Alter in the Opinion You Are pleased to Ask. That letter, I think, if not Already Communicated, Had Better Be Shown to the french Ambassador. So far as Respects me, I Wish My Sentiments to Be known, and Shall Ever glory in the Name of the Warm and faithfull friend to America.

Should peace take place, and Now I Hardly Question it, I think I Will pay a Visit to My friends on the other Side of the Atlantic. Adieu, My dear friend Yours for Ever

LAFAYETTE

ALS (CtY: Benjamin Franklin Collection).
1. Enclosure not found; it is almost certainly the letter of January 20 to Carmichael.

To William Carmichael

Cadix february the 2d 1783

My dear Sir

Your favor By Count de Montmorin's Courier Has Been timely Received, and I just Snatch the Opportunity To Congratulate You Upon the News of a General peace.[1] Remember the times, My Good friend, When We Have Made our first Acquaintance.[2] Now our Cause is Gained, and the Rememberance of Past labours Adds to the Enjoyement. I Have determined to Go to Madrid, and Cannot think of leaving this Country Before I Pay My Respects to the king. I am also very desirous to Know Count de Florida Blanca. So that about the 12he I will Be With You. In the Mean while I am Yours

LAFAYETTE

ALS (DNA: RG 233, HR 27A-G7.4 Papers of William Carmichael, Tray 742, item 103).
  1. Letter not found.
  2. Carmichael had assisted Lafayette in his 1777 trip to America (*LAAR* 1:43–44, 50).

To the President of Congress

                                                       Cadix february the 5h 1783
Sir

What Ever Dispatch I Made in Sending a Vessel, I don't flatter My-self to Apprise Congress with the News of a General Peace. Yet Such are My feelings on the Occasion, that I Cannot Differ Presenting them With My Congratulations. Upon their knowledge of My Heart I More depend, than Upon Expressions that Are So far Inadequate to My Sentiments. Our Early times I Recollect With a Most Pleasing Sense of Pride. Our Present ones Make me Easy and Happy. To futurity I Look forward in The Most Delightfull Prospects.

Former letters Have Acquainted Congress that Upon My intending to Leave France, I Had Been detained By their Commissioners. To My Letter of the 3d December, I Beg Leave to Refer them for a further Account of My Conduct.[1] Now the Noble Contest is Ended, and I Heartly Rejoice at the Blessings of a Peace. But 49 Ships and twenty thousand Men are Now Here Whom Count D'Estaing was to join With the Combined forces in the West Indias—and During the Summer they Were to Cooperate With our American Army. Nay it Had Lately Been Granted, Whilst Count D'Estaing Acted Elsewhere, that I Should Enter St. Laurens River at the Head of a french Corps. So far as Respects me, I Have no Regret, But Independant of Personal Gratifications, it is known that I Ever Was Bent Upon the Addition of Canada to the United States.[2]

On the Happy Prospect of a Peace I Had Prepared to Go to America. Never did an Idea Please me So Much As the Hope to Rejoice With those to Whom I Have Been a Companion in our Labours. But Howev-er Painfull the Delay, I Now Must differ My Departure. In the Dis-charge of my Duty to America, No Sacrifice Will Ever Be Wanting, and When it Has Pleased Congress to Direct their Ministers Should Consult With me, it Became My first Concern to *Deserve* their Confidence. From My Letter to Mr. Lewingston, An opinion May Be formed of our Situation in Spain.[3] My Advice Has Been Called Upon and I Have Given it. My Presence is Entreated, and Instead of Sailing to America, I

Am Going on a journey to Madrid. Being So far on My Way, and Mr. Jay Being at Paris, it is, I think, Better for Me to Go there. But Unless Congress Honour Me With Any Commands, I Shall Embark in the Course of June, and am Panting for the Moment When I May Again Enjoy the Sight of the American Shores.

Now, Sir, our Noble Cause Has Prevailed, our Independance is firmly Settled, and American Virtue Enjoys its Reward. No Exertions, I Hope, Will Now Be Wanting to Strengthten the foederal Union. May the States Be So Bound to Each other, as Will for Ever Defy European Politics. Upon that Union, their Consequence, their Happiness Will Depend. It Now Becomes the first Wish of a Heart, So truly American, that No Words Can Express its Gratefull, Unbounded, and Eternal Affection. With the Highest Respect I Have the Honour to Be Sir Your Excellency's Most obedient Humble Servant

LAFAYETTE

ALS (DNA: RG 360, PCC 156, pp. 312–14).
1. On the December 3 letter to Congress, see Lafayette to Washington, December 4, 1782, note 2.
2. Lafayette's first independent command in American in 1778 was an assignment to invade Canada (*LAAR*, 1:243–384).
3. See following letter.

To the President of Congress

Cadix february the 5h 1783

Sir

Having Been at Some Pains to Engage a Vessel to Go to Philadelphia, I Now find Myself Happily Relieved By the kindness of Count d'Estaing. He is Just Now Pleased to tell me that He Will Dispatch a french Ship, and By Way of Compliment Upon the Occasion, He Has Made Choice of the Triumph. So that I am not Without My Hopes to Give Congress the first tidings of a General Peace, and I am Happy in the Smallest Opportunity to Do Any thing that May Prove Agreable to America.[1] With the Highest Respect I Have the Honor to Be Your Excellency's Most obedient Hbe. Servant

LAFAYETTE

ALS (DNA: RG 360, PCC 156, p. 336).
1. Lafayette's news of the general peace, sent on the *Triumph*, was the first to reach America (*JCC* 25:940).

To Robert R. Livingston

Cadix february the 5h 1783

Dear Sir

On the 7h December I Had the Honour to write to You from Brest,[1] and My Letters down to that Date Have Contained Accounts of our Political Affairs. Since Which time I Have Been taken up in Preparations of a Plan, that Would Have turned out to the Advantage of America. Indeed it Exceeded My first Expectations, And to My Great Surprise, the king of Spain Had Not only Consented His forces should Cooperate With us, But On the Consideration to obtain a Necessary Diversion, He Had Been Induced By Count d'Estaing to Approuve My Being detached into Canada With a french force. Nay, Had the War Continued, I think that, if not for love, at least on political Motives, they Would Have Consented to offer a Pecuniary Assistance.

The Conditions of the Peace I do not dwell upon. I Hope they are Such as Will Be Agreable in America. They Have no doubt Been Sent from France, and the Part of it that Respects the United States Will Have Been Immediately forwarded for their Ratification. I do not Hope to Send You the first tidings of a General Peace. Yet I Have Prevailed Upon a Small Vessel to Alter Her Course, and My own Servant is Going With the Dispatches to Prevent Either Neglects, or other Accidental Delays.[2]

On the Moment of My Arrival at Cadix, I Begun With Mr. Carmichael a close Correspondance. It at first Respected Monney Matters, But Soon, took a Still More Important turn. Having Been officially Asked My Advice Upon His future Conduct, I Gave it in a letter of which the Inclosed is a Copy.[3] Whatever light My opinion May Appear in at Madrid or Else where, I think it is Consistent With the Dignity of the United States. Now, Sir, As I Was Enjoying the Hope to Be in a few Weeks on the American Shore, I Had from Carmichael a letter, and an other was writen to Mr. Harrison, wherein He Requests My Assistance at Madrid.[4] How far it May Serve Him I do not know. But Since I am thought Useful, I differ Every other Prospect, and to My zeal for the Service of America, I Readily Give up Personal Gratifications. On My Arrival at Madrid, I Will Have the Honor to Give You My Opinion of our Situation there. Among the Spaniards We Have But few Well Wishers, And as they at the Bottom Hate Cordially the french, our Alliance tho' a political, is not A Sentimental Consideration. But I Wish a Settlement of Boundaries May Remove the More Immediate Pros-

pects of dispute. It is, I Believe, Very Important to America. The More
So as She Became A Natural Ally to France, A Natural Ennemy to
Britain. But for Ever the Spaniards Will Be Extravagant in their ter-
ritorial Notions, and Very jealous of the Encrease of American Wealth
and Power. But it is Good Policy for us, to Be Upon friendly terms
With them, and I Wish on My Return to Paris, I May Carry for Mr. Jay
Some Hope, Better to Succeed in His Spanish Negotiation.

I Have just Heard that Both Floridas Were Given to Spain. It Ac-
counts for Lord Shelburne's Condescentions in fixing our Southern
Limits. The People of Florida Will, I Hope, Remove Into Georgia. But
the Spaniards Will Insist Upon a Pretended Right to An Extent of
Country All along the Left Shore of Mississipy. Not that they Mean to
Occupy it, But Because they are Affraïd of Neighbours that Have a
Spirit of liberty. I am Sorry those People Have the Floridas. But as We
Cannot Help it We Must Endeavour to frustrate Lord Shelburne's
Wiews, Which I Presume are Bent Upon a dispute Betwen Spain and
the United States. A day Will Come, I Hope, When Europeans Will
Have little to do on the Northen Continent, and God Grant it May Ever
Be for the Happiness of Mankind and the Propagation of liberty.

On the Perusal of My Letter to Carmichael, I Beg You Will Remember it is Calculated to Undergo the Inspection of Both Cabinets at
Versaïlles and Madrid, and to Be a Proof Against the Unfriendly Con-
structions of a Spanish Ministry. Be pleased to tell Mr. Moriss I Re-
member His Want of Monney Extends farther than Occasions of War.
At the time of My Leaving France, I Had Been Made to Hope. But do
not know for the Present What Has taken place. On My Arrival at
Madrid I Will Be Very Attentive to that Point, But Shall take Care to
Preserve the dignity of the United States of which I Have a Proper, and
Most Exalted Sense.

In My determination to Go to Madrid I Have Consulted With Mr.
Harrison a Gentleman Whose Residence at this place Enables Him to
know a Great deal about the Spaniards. He Has to this Moment Acted
as a Consul in this place. So far at least as to Serve His Country Men,
and Spend His own Monney. For He Has No Public Character, and
What He Has done, He Undertook at Mr. Jay's Request. There ought,
I think to Be a Consul at this place, and if the Appointement is differed, Several Inconveniences Will Be laid Upon the American trade.
There is no Gentleman, Exclusive of What His Volontary Services Deserve, Who Could Better fill the Place than Mr. Harrison, and Was I to
take the freedom to Advise, I Would Warmly Recommend Him for the
Appointement.[5]

So far as We know of the Spanish Preliminaries, they Give up their
Claim Upon Having Gibraltar But keep Mahon, and Have the two

Floridas. The Islands of Providence are Returned to England. We Hourly Expect a french Courier. Tabago Excepted, they Give up their Conquests in the West Indias, and Have St. Lucia Again. Before the Vessel is Gone, I Hope to Be More Particular. As to American Preliminaries they Have long Ago Been Sent to Philadelphia.

While I Was writing a french Courier is Arrived. Enclosed You Will find an Extract of the Preliminaries Such as they are Sent to me.[6] May I Beg You Will please to Communicate My letter to Gal. Washington. Tho' it is a public one, I May Ask the favor from You, as I Would otherwise Have Sent Him a Copy of it.[7] With the Highest Regard I Have the Hr. to Be Your obedient Humble Servant

LAFAYETTE

I Have just Received a Note from the french Ambassador at Madrid Where By I find that My Letter Had A pretty Good Effect.[8]

ALS (DNA: RG 360, PCC 156, pp. 316–20).

1. Lafayette's December 7 letter to Livingston included some information about the French force gathering at Brest. It also contained a commendation of the activities of William Temple Franklin (MHi: Robert R. Livingston Papers).

2. See Lafayette to Congress, February 5, "Having Been . . . ," note 1.

3. Lafayette to Carmichael, January 20, 1783.

4. Letters not found. Richard Harrison wrote to Livingston on February 7 that Lafayette had intended to sail for Philadelphia, "but on communicating to him a Letter from Mr. Carmichael intimating that his presence might be of use at Court, he sacrificing his private wishes to the public service immediately changed his plan & yesterday set out for Madrid" (DNA: RG 360, PCC 92, pp. 421–22).

5. While Richard Harrison continued to act as an unoffical agent of the United States at Cadiz, Congress took no action toward appointing consuls for Spain until 1785 (JCC, 29:722–24, 831).

6. Enclosure not found.

7. Livingston forwarded a copy on March 29 (DLC: George Washington Papers, Series 4).

8. Note not found. This was probably a reference to Lafayette's January 20 letter to Carmichael.

To Robert R. Livingston

Cadix february the 5h 1783

Most Private

Your friendship to me, My dear Sir, and the Affection I Have for you, Command My Most *Confidential* Communications. As public Affairs Have the first place With me, let me tell you that our Articles of Confederation ought to Be Revised, and Measures Immediately taken to Envigorate the Continental Union. Depend upon it there lies the danger for America. This last Stroke is Wanting, and Unless the States Be Strongly Bound to Each other, We Have to fear from British, and Indeed from European Politics. There ought to Be delegates from Each State, and perhaps Some officers Among them, one of whom I Would Be Happy to Be, Who, towards Next fall Would Meet together, and Under the Presidence of Gal. Washington, May Devise Upon Amendements to Be Proposed in the Articles of Confederation, limits of States &c. &c. &c.[1] As to the Army, I Hope their Country Will Be Gratefull, I Hope the Half Pay Affair May Be terminated to their Satisfaction.[2]

Now, My dear Sir, I am Going to Intrust you With My Private Concerns. First of all, I Wish the people of America to know that When I Have lengthned My furlough, it Was for their Service—and at the Request of their Commissioners—that Upon My Embarking in a french Expedition, it Was With a View to Join you in the Summer With forces Adequate to Every plan Gal. Washington Had directed me to Promote—that Moreover A Canadian Expedition Was to take place—that Now Instead of Sending a Vessel, I Was Going Myself to America—But that Entreaties from Your Resident at Madrid Have forced me to go there, and probably from there to Paris—But that in the Month of june I am to Embark for America. I Confess, My dear Sir, I Have a Great Value for My American popularity, and I Want the people at large to know My Affection to them, and My zeal for their Service. The Best Way to Manage it is to Have a Resolve of Congress Published, By Way of Answer to My letters, wherein their Approbation of My Conduct Will Comprehend the Above Mentionned Matters.[3]

Here is an other thing Which Would Highly flatter me and Lies Within Your departement. A Ratification of the treaty Will Be Sent By Congress to the Court of England. It is But an Honorary Commission that Requires only a few Weeks, and Even a few days Attendance. The Sedentary Minister You May Send or With me, or after me, or What I Would like Better at the time When Great Britain Has Sent Her's to you. So Many Greater Proofs of Confidence Have Been Bestowed upon me By Congress, that I May freely tell you My Wishes upon this Very pleasing Mark of their Esteem. Upon My leaving England, I Have Been Considered there as an Enthusiastic Rebel, and Indeed a Young Madman.[4] I Would Well Enough like to Present Myself there in the Capacity of an Extraordinary Envoy from the United States—and tho' Upon My Committing So far the french Ambassador I Have Been With Him on pretty Bad terms—Now our friendship Has Revived and I am in a Situation to Lead Him into My Measures, and to know His Secrets Without telling Him Mine.

As to the choice of a Minister (this Commission Being only A Compliment) I think it is a Very Difficult task. I Advise to take a Gentleman who Had No Connection With the Great Men in England. Our friend Hamilton Would Be a Very proper choice. You ought to Bring it About. Are You Acquainted With Clel. Harrison who Was in the General's family. There are few men So Honest and Sensible. But I Hope You May Send Hamilton, and He knows Better than all the British Councils.

In Case Congress Were pleased to do for me What I Have So Much at Heart, I Would Beg You to Send Mr. McHenry to me, a Member in the Maryland Senate.This My dear Sir, is Entirely Confidential—for You, and *for you alone*. Should the General Be in Philadelphia You May Show it to Him; Adieu, My Best Respects Waït Upon Your lady and family. Most affectionately I am Yours

LAFAYETTE

Should you think it of Any Use to Have printed the last Paragraph of My letter to Congress, I will Be glad of it, as the opinion of one who knows Europe, May Have Some Weight With the people.

ALS (DLC: Alexander Hamilton Papers).

1. On December 6, 1782, Lafayette wrote to his friend Mme Simiane, ". . . if peace were concluded I owe a visit to the Americans and I still count on taking a hand in their constitution . . ."ᵀ (NIC: Dean Collection).

2. On discontent among the officers over the lack of pay, see Livingston to Lafayette, January 10, note 2.

3. Congress passed a resolution of approval and thanks for Lafayette's services in Europe on April 10, 1783, about two weeks after this letter arrived. The resolution stated "that Congress are satisfied with the reasons which have prevailed with Major-General the Marquis de la Fayette, for his stay in Europe, and his consequent absence from his command in the army of the United Stated, and have a high sense of the new proofs he has exhibited of his zeal in the cause of the said states, and of his constant attachment to their interests and welfare" (*JCC*, 24:234).

4. Just before his first voyage to America in 1777, Lafayette had visited England as the guest of the French ambassador, his wife's uncle (*LAAR*, 1:8–9).

To George Washington

Cadix february the 5h 1783

My Dear General

Were You But Such a Man as Julius Caesar or the king of Prussia, I Should Almost Be Sorry for You at the End of the Great tragedy Where You are Acting Such a Part. But With My dear General I Rejoice at the Blessings of a Peace where our Noble Ends Have Been Secured. Remember our Valley forge times, and from a Recollection of

Past dangers and labours, We Still Will Be More pleased at our Present Comfortable Situation. What a Sense of Pride and Satisfaction I feel When I think of the times that Have Determined My Engaging in the American Cause! As for You, My dear General, Who truly Can Say You Have Done all this, What Must Your Virtuous and Good Heart feel on the Happy Instant Where the Revolution You Have Made is Now firmly Established. I Cannot But Envy the Happiness of My Grand Children When they Will Be about Celebrating and Worshipping Your Name—to Have Had One of their Ancestors Among Your Soldiers, to know He Had the Good fortune to Be the friend of Your Heart, Will Be the Eternal Honour in Which they Shall Glory—and to the Eldest of them, as long as My Posterity Will Last, I Shall Delegate the favour You Have Been pleased to Confer Upon My Son George.

At the Prospect of a Peace, I Had Prepared to Go to America. You know me too Well, My dear General, Not to Be Sensible of the Pleasure I Anticipated in the Hope to Embrace You, and to Be Reunited With My fellow Soldiers. Never did Any thing Please me So much as the delightfull Prospect I Had Before me. But on a Sudden I Have Been obliged to differ My Darling Plan, and as I Have at Last Been Blessed With a Letter of Yours, I know You Approuve of My Lengthtening My furlough Upon Political Accounts.[1] The Inclosed Copy of a letter to Congress, and My official letter to Mr. Lewingston Which I Request Him to Communicate to You, Will fully Inform You of the Reasons that Urge me to Post off to Madrid. From there, it Will Be Better for me to Go to Paris, and in the month of june, I Will Embark for America. Happy, ten times Happy Will I Be in Embracing My dear General, My father, My Best friend Whom I love With an Affection and a Respect Which I too Well feel, Not to know it is Impossible for me to Express it.

In My letters to Congress, You Will Also See that, Independant of the Plans I Had Been Permitted to propose to You, In the Execution of Which We Were to Have An Immense Naval and Land force, it Had Been at last obtained I Should Enter Canada. I Had My Hopes to Embrace You at Mont Real, or at least to Be Met there By a detachment from the Army. The Necessity of a diversion Was the Ground Upon Which We Had obtained the king of Spain's Consent. But Now those Schemes are Over, and We Must Rejoice at the Happiness of those You Have Rescued from the Hands of British tyranny.

Now, My dear General, that You are Going to Enjoy Some Ease and Quiet, Permit me to Propose a plan to You Which Might Become Greatly Beneficial to the Black Part of Mankind. Let us Unite in Purchasing a Small Estate Where We May try the Experiment to free the Negroes, and Use them only as tenants. Such an Exemple as Yours

Might Render it a General Practice, and if We Succeed in America, I Will Chearfully Devote a part of My time to Render the Method fascionable in the West Indias. If it Be a Wild Scheme, I Had Rather Be Mad that Way, than to Be thought Wise on the other tack.

I am So Anxious, to Hear from You, My dear General, and to let You Hear from me that I Have Sent My own Servant With a Vessel upon Whom I Have prevailed to Set Him a Shore on the Maryland Coast. Before I leave France, I Hope I Receive Your Answers, and I will Be directed Where to find you on My Arrival. Upon that Intelligence I depend to Regulate My Course, and if You are at Home I Shall Steer for the Bay of Chesepeake.

Independant of My Public Letter to Mr. Lewingston, there is a Private one Which He Will Also Communicate. Amongst the Many favors I Have Received, I Would take it as a Most flattering Circumstance in My life to Be Sent to England With the Ratification of the American treaty.[2] You know it is But an Honorary Commission, that Would Require the Attendance of a few Weeks, and if Any Sedentary Minister is Sent, I Would Have the pleasure of introducing Him. This, My dear General, is Entirely Confidential.

Your Influence, My Dear General, Cannot Be Better Employed than in inducing the people of America to Strengthen their foederal Union. It is a Work in Which it Behoves You to Be Concerned. I look Upon it as a Necessary Measure. Depend Upon it, My dear General that European Politics Will Be Apt to Create divisions Among the States. Now is the time When the Powers of Congress Must Be fixed, the Boundaries Determined—and Articles of Confederation Revised. It is a Work in Which Every Well Wisher to America Must Desire to Be Concerned. It is the finishing Stroke that is Wanting to the Perfection of the temple of Liberty.

As to the Army, My dear General, What Will Be its fate? I Hope their Country Will Be Gratefull. Should the Reverse Be the Case, I Would Indeed feel Very Unhappy. Will part of the Army Be kept together? If Not, I Hope We Won't forfeit our Noble titles of officers and Soldiers in the American Army. So that in Case of Danger We May Be Called upon from Every Quarter, and Reunite in the defense of a Country Which the Army Has So Effectually, So Heroïcally Served. I long to know What Measures Will Be taken. Indeed, My dear general, I depend upon Your Goodness for a Very Minuted letter—not only on public Accounts, But also Because I Want to Be Acquainted With Every one of Your Personal Concerns.

Adieu, Adieu, My dear General, Had the Spaniards Got Common Sense I Could Have Dispensed With that Cursed trip to Madrid. But I am Called Upon By a Sense of My duty to America. I Must Go, and the differ the Happy Voyage. My Best, Most Affectionate Respects Waït Upon Mrs. Washington. Now We are Going to Quarell, for I Must Urge Your Returning With me to France. Her Accompagning You there, is the Best Way I know off to Compromise the Matter, and So she Will Make Mde. de Lafayette and Me Perfectly Happy.

I Request Your Excellency Will please to Present My Compliments to Tilmangh, George, and all the family.[3] Remember me to all My friends in the Army. I am So Hurried in Sending the Vessel a Way that I Will Write to them By other Opportunities. They know My love to them, and I Have a Grateful Sense of their friendship. Be So kind My dear General, to Remember me to Your Much Respected Mother. Her Happiness I Heartly Partake. Adieu, once More, My dear General. With Every Sentiment of Love and Respect I am for Ever Your Most devoted and Affectionate friend

LAFAYETTE

ALS (PEL: Hubbard Collection).
  1. See Washington to Lafayette, October 20, 1782.
  2. Washington wrote to Livingston on March 29, 1783, about Lafayette's wish to be "the bearer of the Ratification. How far it is consistent with our National honor, how far motives of policy make for or agt. sending a foreigner with it . . . I pretend not to determine, but if there is no impropriety, or injustice in it, I should hope that Congress would feel a pleasure in gratifying the wishes of a Man who has been such a Zealous labourer in the cause of this Country" (Fitzpatrick, *Writings of Washington*, 26:267). Livingston replied on April 9 that nothing would give him greater pleasure, but he recommended against it because of Congressional distrust towards France. He also added: "The honor of the nation seems to require that it should be represented by a native— that it should not appear to act under the foreign influence—too close a connection with France might undo her foes jealous of us—the court of St. James might consider this an insulting step" (DLC: George Washington Papers, Series 4). Washington withdrew his endorsement of the idea on April 16, explaining, "There is no Man upon Earth I have a greater inclination to serve than the Marquis La Fayette; but I have no wish to do it in matters that interfere with, or are repugnant to, our National policy, dignity, or interest" (Fitzpatrick, *Writings of Washington*, 26:327).
  3. Tench Tilghman and George Augustine Washington, aides to Washington.

To the Comte de Vergennes[T]

Cadiz, February 5, 1783

I congratulate you, Monsieur le Comte, and rejoice with you on the successful conclusion of your labors. My first idea was to go to America, but a sentence in your letter made me think that you advise me to return to France.[1] M. d'Estaing is my witness that this made up my mind, and since you did not think of my making that voyage, it is

because you think my return is more advisable. In the course of the
summer I shall ask the king's permission to go to Philadelphia.

As a result of Mr. Carmichael's solicitations, M. d'Estaing's opinion,
and what I hear from M. de Montmorin, I shall hold myself ready to
give the Spanish minister the opinion of a man who knows America
and who, being French, will arouse his ill humor less. I shall write you
from Madrid, Monsieur le Comte, but I did not want to delay giving
you a succinct account of my conduct and adding my congratulation to
the assurance of my respect and attachment.

LAFAYETTE

ALS (AAE: Correspondance politique, Espagne, vol. 610, fol. 200), translation.
1. Letter not found.

To John Jay

Madrid february the 15h 1783

Dear Sir

I am Happy in this private Opportunity to write to You, and Have
long Wanted Safe Means to do it Confidentially. The Same Reason, I
Suppose, Has Prevented My Hearing from You to this Moment. But as
I am just Arrived at Madrid, and the Gentleman Who Carries this is
just Setting out I Shall only Write a few lines.

My feelings on the Occasion of a General peace are Better known to
You than I Could Express them. They are Consistent With My zeal for
our Cause, and My love to America, and More I Cannot Say.

On My leaving Paris I Had Great Hopes of our plans. On My Arriv-
ing at Cadix, I found they Had Succeeded Beihond My Expectations,
Nay, Besides the Most Advantageous Cooperation With America, Par-
ticulars of which I Will Relate, I Had Some Hopes Monney Might Be
Got for that Purpose. Upon this I wrote to Mr. Carmichael. I Had the
Honor to Give You an Account of My Conduct and Ideas on the
Occasion, But Your Answer Has Not Come to Hand.[1]

Upon the Prospect of a Peace, I Had a Letter from Mr. Carmichael
Wherein He Entreats My Advice upon His future Conduct. He Had
No letters from Paris. My Advice Being Asked for, I Gave it in a letter a
Copy of Which I Enclose, and Sent it By post for the Perusal of the
Court of Spain and probably of the Court of Versaïlles With Spanish
Constructions Upon it.[2]

I am told El Campo on His journey to Paris is Instructed to Settle
Matters With You, and I Wish it at last May Be Upon a Proper footing.[3]

John Jay, whose frustrations in dealing with an intransigent Spanish court led him to question the reliability of the French-American alliance as well.

I Had determined Upon Going to America But Had A Letter from Mr. Carmichael Wherein He Entreats My Coming to Madrid, and Says I May Be Useful in Reasoning With this Ministry. I Gave up My favorite Plan, and Contenting Myself With Sending a letter to Congress, I Have posted of to Madrid Where Now I am and Had only a Short Conference With the french Ambassador, and an other With Mr. Carmichael Whose ideas, I am Happy to find, Coincide With Mine on the line We ought to follow.

In the few days I Remain Here I Would Wish 1st to Induce this Ministry to Give El Campo liberal Instructions 2dly to See that the American Chargé d'Affaires Be Officially Received 3dly to Advize their Proposing to You a loan of Monney. My Expectations are Very Small. But I Have Been Invited Here. The little I Can do I must Exert to the Utmost. Whatever Disposition I find them in, I Will Hasten to Paris, and Give You Every Intelligence I Can Collect. I look Upon Myself as Your Political Aid de Camp. If I May Any How Serve America, I am Happy and Satisfied.

At all Events, When My Advice is Asked for, No Court, No Country, No Consideration Can Induce Me to Advise a thing that is not Consistent With the dignity of the United States.

By the Month of june I Intend taking up Again My Plan of a Voyage to America. Untill that time I Have Nothing to do, and towards the tenth of March, I Will offer Myself to You With Spanish Intelligences, and a Great zeal to do Any thing that May Serve the Public.

I Beg My Best Respects to Be Presented to Your Colleagues. I do not Write to them, and in this letter they May See What You think Worth Communicating. My Most Respectfull Compliments Waït Upon Mrs. Jay. I Have Hardly time Enough left to write a line to Mde. de Lafayette,[4] and in Great Haste Subscribe Myself Most Respectfully and Affectionately Yours

LAFAYETTE

P.S.

Mr. Littlepage Having Been pleased to Come into My family for the Expedition, I Have Advized Him to go With me on My journey to Paris. His Voyage to America is But little differed, and it May prove Agreable to Him to know the Best part of France.

ALS (NNC: John Jay Papers).
1. See Lafayette to Jay, December 26, 1782, and Jay's reply, January 19, 1783.
2. See Lafayette to Carmichael, January 20.
3. Bernardo del Campo, Floridablanca's undersecretary, was to go through Paris on his way to London to negotiate with the British. Jay wrote to Livingston on April 7 that the Spanish ambassador on March 29 had advised him to return to Madrid "and there complete the treaty, for that in their opinion, it ought to be concluded either at *Madrid* or

Philadelphia" (Henry Johnston, ed., *The Correspondence and Public Papers of John Jay*, [New York, 1890–93], 3:38).
   4. Letter not found.

To the Comte d'Estaing[T]

Madrid, February 18, 1783

I have received your letter, Monsieur le Comte, and thank you warmly for the trouble you are taking for *Le Triomphe*.[1] Thanks to your precautions, I have hopes that nothing untoward will happen to it, and I am sure it will be well received in Philadelphia. The British are going to send the son of the Duke of Norfolk to Philadelphia, and that proves that they do not do things halfway. M. d'Adhémar has been made ambassador to London, and the Marquis of Carmarthen is to come to Paris. I have been staying with M. de Montmorin here, Monsieur le Comte. He shows a friendship for me that I find very touching. I find him much to my liking, besides, because he knows and likes you. Yesterday we went to court, and neither my dress nor my principles prevented the king from receiving me graciously.[2] Later I had a conversation with M. de F.B. and this minister is to come here tomorrow to continue it.[3] I have found many prejudices, no knowledge of the whole situation, and a facial expression too stiff to be warm. Without consoling him on the misfortune of independence, I am devoting the week to preaching to him to turn it to advantage, and then I shall quickly leave for France, to which I am recalled by terrible anxiety about the fate of one of my aunts.[4]

I am distressed, Monsieur le Comte, to see your arrival at Paris delayed. I was hoping to greet you here and shall always be happy when I can offer you in person the tribute of my respect and affection.

AL (AN: Fonds de la Marine, C[7] 157, dossier Lafayette), translation.
   1. D'Estaing had written to Lafayette on February 11 that the *Triomphe's* departure was delayed by adverse winds (AN: Fonds de la Marine, B[3] 801, dossier 3).
   2. Lafayette wore his American major general's uniform to his February 17 audience with King Charles III (Lafayette, *Mémoires*, 2:60). For his comments about Charles's views on the Americans, see Lafayette to Livingston, March 2, 1783.
   3. "F.B.": Floridablanca.
   4. Lafayette's aunt Marguerite-Madeleine de Lafayette, known as Mlle du Motier.

To the Comte de Vergennes[T]

Madrid, February 18, 1783

Upon my departure from Cadiz, Monsieur le Comte, I had the honor to write you a few lines and report to you the reasons that postponed my American journey.[1] M. le Comte de Montmorin also thought that I could be useful at Madrid, and I asked him to advise me on the line of conduct I should maintain there. Thanks to M. d'Estaing, I have been able to write to Congress, and in speaking to them of the peace, I have not let them be unaware of how advantageous the campaign plan was. After presenting me to the king, M. le Comte de Montmorin took me to see M. de Floridablanca. Whatever is done here for the United States will never be done enthusiastically, but setting aside American interest, I think it is even more important for France to mitigate these Spanish prejudices and repugnances. When I talked with M. de Floridablanca, it seemed to me he liked America little and did not know it at all, that he was astonished at each act of condescension by England, and that the misfortune of independence makes more impression here than the need to gain some advantage from it. If they abide by the British boundaries,[2] it is for fear of a dispute that would fulfill Lord Shelburne's object. If they receive Mr. Carmichael it is because they are afraid of seeing Mr. Jay arrive, whom they do not like as much. Natural dilatoriness combines with an uncommon repugnance, and although M. de Floridablanca seems well enough disposed, I predict that the Spanish treaty will give us a fair amount of trouble. That minister should be here tomorrow, and the following day we shall pay him another visit. I would think myself fortunate, Monsieur le Comte, if through my knowledge of the country I could make the minister a bit confident about it, and if by pressing for the reception of Mr. Carmichael or the establishment of a few basic principles, we could bring Spain a little closer to the United States. Since M. le Comte de Montmorin is writing you, and since Mr. Carmichael, as well as I, informs him of all these steps, I shall only add that I shall spend the whole week here and shall do my utmost to enlighten the prejudices of the Spanish ministry. Free America is an unknown to them, and the advantage of having been there stands me in the stead of other knowledge that I lack. If I can be of service to the views of M. de Montmorin and Congress, I would be even happier to contribute to them, for present feelings in Spain make me foresee some very unpleasant difficulties.

On the subject of England, Monsieur le Comte, you must be very well satisfied, and I congratulate you with all my heart. From the letters I receive, I learn of the arrangement for commissions and embassies. It is yet another task for you, after that of the peace. Farewell, Monsieur le Comte. Accept, I beg of you, the tribute of the warm and respectful attachment with which I have the honor to be your very humble and obedient servant,

LAFAYETTE

ALS (AAE: Correspondance politique, Espagne, vol. 610, fols. 246–47), translation.
1. Lafayette to Vergennes, February 5.
2. "The British boundaries": the boundaries of the United States that the British had agreed to in the peace preliminaries, especially the Mississippi River as the western boundary and the St. Mary's River as the southern boundary. For the boundaries Spain had proposed, see Lafayette to Adams, October 6, 1782, note 2. Also see Lafayette to Livingston, February 5, "On the 7th Dec."

To the Conde de Floridablanca[T]

Madrid, February 19, 1783

Monsieur le Comte,

Having had the honor to confer with your excellency on matters related to the United States and having soon to report to the American Congress, I would like to impress upon my mind the result of our conversations. In place of the indifference and even the discords that another nation would like to predict, I am pleased to take to the United States a description of your good intentions. I owe this happy result to you, Monsieur le Comte, and to ensure that this description is complete—to assure myself that I am forgetting nothing—let me first submit to Your Excellency my report to Congress.

His Catholic Majesty wishes that lasting trust and accord be established between him and the United States. He is determined, for his part, to do everything he can to maintain it. The American chargé d'affaires is henceforth welcome, and Your Excellency will deal with the interests of both nations. Before presenting Mr. Carmichael to the king, Your Excellency, who wishes to show every possible regard for Mr. Jay, is waiting only until the Comte d'Aranda notifies him of your intentions.[1]

With respect to the establishment of boundaries, His Catholic Majesty is adopting those of the preliminaries of November 30 between the United States and the Court of London.[2] His fear of raising a subject of dispute is the only objection he would have to the free navigation of the

Lafayette's accounts of the American Revolution awakened the fears of Charles III that the successful rebellion of the British colonies would inspire the Spanish colonies to revolt.

Mississippi. Virginia tobacco and matters related to shipping will be the subject of reciprocal agreements in the treaty, and in accordance with America's production, arrangements useful to her finances will be made in the treaty. When I had the honor of speaking to you in favor of a decrease in the duties on cod, you replied to me that you would have to give France the same advantage, and that by virtue of long-standing treaties the British would claim that they, too, should have it. But you will, in any case, do everything in your power to satisfy America.

It would give me extreme pleasure, Monsieur le Comte, to go into all the details of the ties I foresee between Spain and the United States, but I am not the one for this pleasing task. The ministers of Congress and the minister you will send there must attend to it, and I confine myself to recalling the general ideas you have given me. A word from you will assure me that I have not forgotten anything. The intentions of His Catholic Majesty and Your Excellency's candor leave no room for false representations. The alliance of the House of Bourbon with the United States is based on common interests. It will be all the stronger for the affection and trust that Your Excellency wishes to establish.

This is the result of our conferences, Monsieur le Comte, as I have formulated it, and the account that I plan to give, though I have no formal mission to do so. I know the sentiments of Congress, and I know all the value they will place on your intentions. In allowing me to submit to them what I have learned, you incur my personal gratitude, and I add my acknowledgment of it to the testimony of the respect with which I have the honor, etc.,

LAFAYETTE

L (DNA: RG 360, PCC 59, vol. 4, pp. 319–21), copy, translation, marked "true copy" in Lafayette's hand, and enclosed with his March 2, 1783, letter to Robert Livingston.
1. Jay was so advised on March 29; see Lafayette to Jay, February 15, note 3.
2. "Boundaries": especially the western boundary of the United States, at the Mississippi River.

From the Conde de Floridablanca[T]

[Prado,] February 22, 1783

I cannot better carry out your wishes than by asking your permission to give you my reply herewith. You have understood perfectly everything I have had the honor to convey to you about our intentions with regard to the United States. I shall add only that although His Majesty's inclination is at present to follow the boundaries established by the treaty between the British and the Americans of November 30, 1782, he expects to obtain information that will inform him whether there are difficulties or disadvantages in this plan, and to settle this question amicably with the United States. I have the honor to be, Monsieur le Marquis, your very humble and obedient servant,

FLORIDABLANCA

L (DNA: RG 360, PCC 59, vol. 4, pp. 321–22), copy, translation.

Note on Correspondence with the Conde de Floridablanca[T]

Madrid, February 22, 1783

When I received the Conde de Floridablanca's reply, I asked him for an explanation of the added clause regarding boundaries. He replied that the boundaries set between the British and the Americans had been accepted in principle, that his remark applied entirely to utterly unimportant details that he would like to obtain from the Spanish commanders, which would be settled in a friendly fashion and would do no harm to the general principle. I asked him in the presence of the French ambassador if he would give me his word of honor on this.[1] He replied that he would, and that I could hold him to it before Congress.

Signed,

LAFAYETTE

DS (DNA: RG 360, PCC 156, p. 322), translation. This note appears at the bottom of the copy of Floridablanca's letter.
    1. Montmorin wrote to Jay the same day that Lafayette was leaving for Paris. He added, "He is your friend, your adopted compatriot, and will be counted by posterity among the numbers who contributed most to the great revolution in which you were one of the principal actors" (Morris, *John Jay*, 2:497).

To Robert R. Livingston

Bordeaux March the Second 1783

Dear Sir

Upon the News of a General Peace, I Had the Honor to write to You, and took the Liberty to Adress Congress in a Letter of Which the Inclosed is a duplicate.[1] Those dispatches Have Been Sent By the *tri-*

Western Europe

umph a french Vessel, and By Her You Will also Have Received a Note of the General Preliminaries.

The Reasons of My Going from Cadix to Madrid Being known to You I Shall only Inform You that upon My Arrival there I Waïted upon the king and Paid a Visit to Count de Florida Blanca. Independant of My Letter to Mr. Carmichael of Which You Have a Copy, I Had Very Oppenly Said that I Expected to Return With Him to Paris. So that After the first Compliments, it Was Easy for me to turn the Conversation Upon American Affairs. I did it With the More Advantage as I Had Before Hand fully Conversed With Mr. Carmichael, who Gave me His Opinion Upon Every Point, and I was Happy to find it Coincided With Mine.

In the Course of our Conversation, I Could See that American Independance Gives Some Ombrage to the Spanish Ministry. They fear the Loss of their Colonies and the Success of our Revolution Appears to Be An Encouragement. Upon this their king Has pretty Odd Notions, as He Has Indeed Upon Every thing. The Reception of Mr. Carmichael they wanted to Procrastinate, and Yet they knew it Must Be done.[2] In offering My opinion to Count de Florida Blanca I did it in a Pressing and a Very free Manner. I Rejected Every Idea of delay and Was the Happier in My Moral and Phisic Description of America, and of Each of the States, as Count de Florida Blanca Appeared to me to know Very little Upon these Matters. While I Abated their fears from our Quarter, I Endeavoured to Awaken them Upon other Accounts. It is Useless to Mention the Particulars of this Conversation which lasted Very long and Which He promised to lay Before the king. Two days after He Said He Would Pay me a Visit at Madrid.

Agreable to the Appointement I Waïted for Count de Florida Blanca, and there in presence of the french Ambassador He told me that the king Had determined Immediately to Receive the Envoy from the United States. Our Conversation Was Also Very long, and I owe Count de Montmorin the Credit to Say that not only at that Moment, But in Every Instance Where He Could take Advantage of Count de Florida Blanca in our favor He threw in all the Veight of the french Influence.

It Was on a Wenesday that I Had Count de Florida Blanca's Visit. Agreable to the Spanish Stile He Endeavoured to delay our Affairs. I took the liberty to Say that on Saturday I Must Set out and it Was at last fixed that on friday Mr. Carmichael Should deliver His Credentials and on Saturday Would Be Invited to the dinner of the foreign Ministers.

As to More Important Matters, I Conversed upon the Affair of limits, Upon the Navigation of the Mississipy, to the last of which Points I found Him Very Repugnant. I Spoke Upon the Cod fish duties. I

Wanted to Have a Preference Engaged for in writing Upon all Bargains Respecting tobacco and Naval Stores. In a Word I did My Best,
and Would Have Been More Particular in Point of Monney, Had not
the Minister's Answer Put it out of My Power to do It in Any other Way
But Such as Was Inconsistent With the dignity of the United States.

As Count de Florida Blanca Was taking leave I told Him that My
Memory Must Be Some What Aided. I Proposed writing to Him, and
Getting from Him an Answer. To this He first Objected and Afterwards Consented telling However that His Word Was as Good as His
writing—and as I Had Been Some times Haughty With Him in Behalf
of America, He Added that Spain Was Sincere in Her Desire to form
an Everlasting friendship, But did not Act out of fear. I Had Before
observed that it Was on the Account of Spain, that I Wished for a Good
Understanding Betwen Her and America.

The Reading of My Letter, a Copy of Which I Inclose, Will Better
inform You of the Points that Have Been either Wholly or Partially
Granted. I Endeavoured to Make the Best of our Conversation and to
Engage Him as far as I Could. On the other Hand I kept our Side Clear
of Any Engagement, Which it Was Easy for me to do in My Private
Capacity. I did not Even Go So far as General Professions. But Since I
Had Been Called there Wanted only to Induce Him into Concessions
that Might Serve the Purposes of Mr. Jay. My Letter Was Delivered on
thursday. The Next day I Accompagnied Mr. Carmichael Who is Much
and universally Beloved and Respected in that Country. On Saturday
Before dinner I Received the Answer Which for fear of Ambiguities I
Had Requested to Be Given at the End of the letter. A Sentence of the
Answer I Made Him Explain Before the french Ambassador. Herein
are joined those Copies, and I keep the Original for Mr. Jay Whose
Political Aide de Camp I Have Been. I Have of Course Referred to
Him Every thing and this Negotiation, Wherein He Has Exercised the
Virtue of Patience Will now Require His Care and His Abilities.

The Ministers of Some Powers, Prussia Among them, Having Asked
me if Congress Would Be Willing to Make Advances towards them, I
Have Answered that the United States ought in My Opinion not to
Make But to Receive Advances.

In the Mean time I was Emploïed in Conversation With Count de
Florida Blanca I Have not Neglected Speaking Upon the Same Subject
With the other Ministers. Mr. de Galvez in Whose departements the
Indias Are, Appears Much Averse to the English Limits. He Has for
the Present Sent orders to the Spanish Governors to Abide By those
limits, and an Offical Copy of those orders Has Been Promised to me.
But Mr. de Galvez Was of Opinion that those limits Would not do. I
Have therefore thought it Proper Officially, By writing, and Before

Witnesses So Effectually to Bind them, that the Affair of limits Cannot Now But Be Settled on their Side. Independant of their Hand writing, France, through Her Ambassador is a Witness to the Engagement— and yet Being in a Private Capacity, I took Care Not to Engage America to Any thing.

Never Was a Man further from a Partiality to Spain than I am. But I think I Now Have Left them in a Sincere and a Steady Intention to Cultivate the friendship of America. The french Party at that Court Will Be for it and Both Ideas Will Be joined together. They labour Under fits of territorial Madness. They Have an ill Understood, and an ill Conducted Pride. It is disagreable to treat With them, and their own Interest does not Persuade them out of their Prejudices. But tho' they Had Rather there Was not Such a thing As North America, they are truly and Earnestly desirous to Maintain a Good Harmony, and live in friendship and Good Neighboourly Union With the United States. Mississipy is the Great Affair, and the Mention of it in My letter is the Most favorable Construction I Could Snatch in our Conversations. It is, I think, the Interest of America to Be Well With Spain—at least for Many Years—and Particularly on Account of the french Alliance—So that I Very Much Wish Success to Mr. Jay's Negotiations. I Have Advised Mr. Carmichael to Continue His Conferences, and I think they Will Be of Service.

On My Arrival at this Place, I Hear that Lord Shelburne is out of place, and Has Been Succeeded By My lord North.[3] But I Cannot Give it as Certain. The American flag Has Already Made its Appearance Before the City of London.[4]

The Ruin of Carthage Was the Last Sencence in Every Speech of a Roman Patriot. Upon the Same principles of an Unbounded zeal for America, Can I Be permitted to Repeat that Every American Patriot Must Wish that the foederal Union Betwen the States May Soon Receive an Additional Strength. Upon that Intimate Eternal Union, their Happiness, their Consequence depend.

Hoping that My Volonteering Excursion to Madrid May Have Somewhat Prepared the Way to fulfill the Intentions of Congress, and Hastening to join Mr. Jay Whose Abilities Will Improve the Account I am Going to lay Before Him, I Have the Honor to Be With the Most Affectionate Regard Dear Sir Your obedient Humble Servant

LAFAYETTE

ALS (DNA: RG 360, PCC 156, pp. 344–50). Enclosed with this letter were Lafayette's correspondence with Floridablanca, February 19–22, and his notes on their correspondence.

1. These were the letters of February 5.
2. While Floridablanca invited Carmichael to a dinner for the diplomatic corps before

Lafayette left, the Spanish did not receive him officially as charé until August 22 (Carmichael to Jay, August 23, in Morris, *John Jay*, 2:574).

3. On February 22 the House of Commons passed a series of resolutions that accepted the peace but condemned its concessions. Shelburne resigned the following day under pressure from the unlikely coalition of Lord North and Charles James Fox. After a month of wrangling, the coalition succeeded to the ministry, and Lord North became secretary of state.

4. On February 5 the Nantucket vessel *Bedford* made entry at the London customhouse.

PART II

CONSOLIDATING THE PEACE, WITNESSING THE TRIUMPH

March 19, 1783–December 23, 1784

As to My Going to America, I first Went for the Revolution, and not for the war, and Warfaring was truly A Secondary Incident, which in Support of the Rights of Mankind Had Become Necessary. Now I am Going for the people, and My Motives are, that I love them, and they love me—that My Arrival will please them, and that I will Be pleased With the Sight of those whom I Have Early joined in our Noble and Successfull Cause.

To John Adams, April 9, 1784

As Lafayette turned his attention from warmaking, he genuinely reveled in the peace and immediately began efforts to expand and solidify friendly relations between his native country and his adopted one. Concerned with perpetuating the alliance between France and the United States, he seemed to be guided by the hope that mutual commercial interests would bind the two nations to each other in friendship. For a person whose entire life had pointed toward military achievement, Lafayette proved to be remarkably attentive to commercial and business matters, as his "Observations on the Commerce between France and America" of 1783 reveals. Yet he also displayed ignorance—typical of people of his position in society—about the morass of commercial regulations that constrained French-American trade by a nearly inextricable network of privileges and fees.

Lafayette continued his efforts to gain free ports for American produce arriving France, to reduce restrictions on American commerce, and to expand trade between the United States and the French West Indies. His learning also continued apace. Occasionally he could report small victories in his efforts to unshackle commerce. As he became more deeply involved in trade, Lafayette advised and assisted American trade officials and individual merchants from all quarters. Some he had known in America; others came with recommendations from old friends. An American community gathered around his dinner table in

Paris, composed of traveling Americans, those sympathetic to America's aspirations, and French men and women interested in discussing new ideas.

When the Society of the Cincinnati was established in the summer of 1783, Washington asked Lafayette to represent the European officers who had served under American command and to determine the qualifications of candidates. Lafayette also worked on behalf of many French veterans who sought membership in the order, whose emblem was one of only two non-French military decoration French officers could wear. Along with this delicate task, Lafayette felt obliged to defend the society from American and European detractors who charged that the hereditary principle of its membership was detrimental to republican virtue.

After countless delays that added up to a year and a half, Lafayette finally returned in triumph to the scenes of his glory for the last five months of 1784. The American people responded to their Marquis with parades, banquets, accolades, and interminable speeches. Lafayette always responded by turning the compliments back to America. Surely the high points of his tour were the visits to his beloved fatherly mentor, Washington. Elsewhere he took an active part in promoting the efforts of the Indian commissioners in New York and urging Boston merchants to send their goods to France. Nearly everywhere in the ten states he visited he urged his American friends to rebuild and strengthen the American confederation's central authority.

Lafayette received certificates and honorary citizenships, but the focal point of his trip may well have been his appearance before the Congress to bid it farewell. There he summarized his views on the importance of French-American amity, and he reiterated the meaning of America's revolutionary labors to the world. "May this immense temple of freedon ever stand a lesson to oppressors, an example to the oppressed, a sanctuary for the rights of mankind!" The Americans had offered Lafayette all the republican honors his heart could desire. He was now filled with optimism for the results that this revolutionary struggle could augur for the rest of mankind.

To Jean-François Joly de Fleury[T]

Paris, March 19, 1783

I went to see you, Monsieur, and was especially sorry to miss paying you my respects since a trip to Auvergne will deprive me of that pleasure for some time. But there is one subject about which I cannot delay speaking to you, and I am compelled by my love for the public good, by the confidence with which I am honored, and by my knowledge of American affairs to take the liberty of doing so.

It is by trading with the United States that we shall derive great advantage from the war, from our expenditures, and from the revolution. But because we have lost time attaining that object, and at a time when the English are making up for their errors, I think it particularly important to decrease the number of impediments our commercial system presents to the Americans. It is unnecessary to say, Monsieur, that I do not propose to go into the details of administration here, but after much reflection on the common interest and on the particular disposition of our allies, I am convinced of two truths that my duty as a citizen requires me to suggest to you. The first is that it is up to us to obtain almost all the American trade. The second is that, because of the restrictions we place on trade, we are in imminent danger of losing most of it.

It is not my place to indicate the remedies; it would take too long to cite all the instances. But I cannot refrain from mentioning the two tobacco ships that were recently chased out of Lorient, and that immediately set course for England because of their difficulties with the Farm.[1] Having gained the right to reflect on the interests of France and America, I am unhappy to think that in repulsing American trade instead of attracting it, we serve the English much better than they can serve themselves.

Some ports have already been given to the Americans, and surely it will be deemed necessary to add others. I have had the honor of discussing this with M. le Comte de Vergennes and shall limit myself in what I write him today on the subject.[2] But we are now dealing with a matter in which the Americans are very interested, and since the officials at Bayonne are creating great difficulties for them, it must be hoped that we shall avoid increasing them by obstructing their trade with Spain.[3] Because of the location of this port, only the hope of this easy communication can attract the Americans to it. Without going into the details submitted to you by the deputies of Bayonne, and though a soldier has the right to judge that the coast offers an excellent position in this kind of war, I limit myself to the duty of warning you that a greater constraint on the markets would have a bad effect on American merchants.

The reflections I am submitting to you, Monsieur, are more than excused by the patriotism that motivates them. Accustomed to this kind of confidence, I am pleased to deserve it through my frankness and zeal, and I confess that at this moment I am very alarmed about our commercial interests with the Americans. It is with great pleasure,

Monsieur, that I shall bring you upon my return the homage of the respectful attachment with which I have the honor to be, Monsieur, your very humble &c.

LAFAYETTE

L (AAE: Correspondance politique, Etats-Unis, vol. 23, fols. 247–49), copy enclosed in Lafayette to Vergennes, same date; translation.
   1. During March 1783 there were a number of complaints about the difficulties American tobacco merchants were having with the Farmers General in Nantes, Lorient, and other ports. The Farmers General had a monopoly over tobacco sales, and the low prices they offered, together with their complex regulations, caused many American tobacco merchants to prefer the markets of London and Amsterdam.
   2. See following letter.
   3. Bayonne had long been a center for smuggling tobacco overland into Spain.

To the Comte de Vergennes[T]

Paris, March 19, 1783

I am leaving for Auvergne, Monsieur le Comte, and unless I receive orders from you, I shall be away for about three weeks. But if I can be useful to you at all, be good enough to write me at the Château de Chavaniac, near Brioude, and I shall be happy to come and bring you both my public zeal and my private attachment.

The deputies from Bayonne came to see me. They are very grateful for your interest and very worried about the campaign of the Farms and *Régies*.[1] Your views are too close to our own to permit me to give mine here. But though I am not specifically entitled to do so, I thought my duty as a citizen would suffice to justify a letter to M. de Fleury. You will find here a copy of my letter, and I very much hope you approve of it. One cannot repeat too often that after a great war and a fine peace, it would be ridiculous to lose the fruit of so much blood and so many expenditures, and to do it to please a class of people who please no one. After having taught England a lesson, let us accept the one she is now giving us and try to ensure that when the Americans find they get along with their friends as well as they do with their enemies, they are not forced to give their preference to the latter.

While diminishing the natural disadvantages of Bayonne, and also opening the port of Marseilles and making Dunkirk as advantageous as possible, I hope, Monsieur le Comte, that you will decide in favor of Lorient instead of Port-Louis.[2] Port-Louis is very small and offers none of the conveniences of Lorient, and Lorient is very agreeable to the Americans. As to the general advantages of trade, it would be very important were a prompt decision to prevent the renewing of trade relations between the United States and England.

Please be good enough, Monsieur le Comte, to present my respects to Mme la Comtesse de Vergennes. I went several times to see her but was not fortunate enough to be able to pay my respects to her. Please accept the assurance of my tender and respectful attachment.

LAFAYETTE

ALS (AAE: Correspondance politique, Etats-Unis, vol. 23, fols. 345–46), translation; enclosing Lafayette to Joly de Fleury, March 19, 1783.

1. The deputies of the Bayonne chamber of commerce were seeking the return of Bayonne to its traditional status as a free port outside of the administrative domain of the tax-collecting Farmers General and *régisseurs* (AAE: Mémoires et documents, France, vol. 2011, fols. 143–56).

2. Port-Louis is at the entrance to the bay on which Lorient is situated.

From George Washington

Hd. Qrs. Newburgh 23d. Mar. 1783

My dear Marqs.

I have to acknowledge the honor of your favors of the 14th. & 24th. of October and 4th. of Decr; to thank you for the warm and affectionate expression of them; and to congratulate you & Madame La Fayette on the birth of a daughter. Virginia I am perswaded, will be pleased with the Compliment of the name; and I pray as a member of it she may live to be a blessing to her Parents.

It would seem that none of my Letters (except one by Colonel Gemat) had reached you when you last wrote. I do not know how to acct. for this. My last letter to you went by the Chevr. Chartellux which could not have arrived. The others were committed to the care either of the Chevr. de La Luzerne or our Secretary of Foreign affairs at Philadelphia, to be forwarded by such conveyances as might offer.[1]

I am fully perswaded My dear Marqs. of your Zeal in the American Cause. I am sure you adopted the plan you are now in the execution of as the most likely, tho' a little circuitous, to serve it—and I shall express to Congress who I know have an exalted opinion of your zeal, abilities & faithful Services, my entire approbation of your conduct; & the purity of the motives which gave rise to it. Your pursuit after honor and glory will be accompanied by my warmest wishes, & you have my sincerest congratulations on your promotion, & Command in the French Army.

As it is your wish, I have given Colo. Gouvion my consent to meet you at the rendezvous appointed him—& he sets out with all the alacrity of a friend to attend it.[2] You must receive him as a precious loan because I esteem and value him and because it is to you only I would part with him. I should be happy if I could speak decidedly upon any plan of operation on the American Theatre in which the Naval & Land forces of His most Christian Majesty could be combined—but such is the state of our finances—such the backwardness of the States to Establish funds—& such the distress of the Army for want of them that I dare give no pointed assurances of effectual cooperation lest I should, unintentially, be guilty of deception—especially as my estimates & sentiments respectg. the ensuing Campaign are now pending before Congress for decision.[3]

Last year, while I had the prospect of a vigorous campaign before me (founded on the hope of succours from your Court) I took a comprehensive view of the Enemies situation & our own—arranged the whole under different heads—and digested plans of attack applicable to each. This I have put into the hands of Colo. Gouvion to Copy for you—and with the alterations occasioned by the change of circumstances—& such other information as you will receive from this Letter & from him will enable you to Judge as fully as I can do (in my present state of incertitude) what can be attempted with such a force as you can bring at either of the places mentioned therein.[4]

No Requisitions by Congress, have yet been made of the States for Men—whether this proceeds from the present state of the public funds & little prospect of bettering them, or the hope of Peace—or partly from both, does not lye with me to decide—but so the fact is—so far indeed were they from requiring men to recruit the Battalions of last year that several of them have been reduced, and the Non-Commissioned & privates incorparated in their respective State Lines. This however has no otherwise reduced our efficient force than by the diminution of Commissioned Officers—but all Corps that are not fed with Recruits must dwindle, from the deaths, desertions, & discharges incident to them—the last of which you well know, operates more powerfully in our army than most others. Our present force, tho small in numbers is excellent in composition—and may be depended upon as far as the first are competent. About June the *total* of *this Army* exclusive of *Commissiond* Officers may be computed at 9000 & by October it will have decreased near 1000 men by the discharge of so many men whose term of Service will have expired.

I am impressed with a belief that *no* Militia could be drawn out *previous* to the arrival of a French fleet, and Land force on the Coast. I am not *sanguine* that *many* could be had afterwards—but certain it is, there would be great difficulty in subsisting & providing for them, if it should be found necessary to call for their aid; hence it appears, that little or no dependence is to be placed on any other Troops than the Continentals of this Army. These would require very little previous notice for an operation against New York, which is the only Post of importance the enemy have within the United States; and indeed the only one against which they could move for want of transportation, or the means to obtain it.

Penobscot is a secondary object; unassailable but by means of a Naval superiority—with wch. the place might soon be carried with out the aid of American Troops; to call for which would spread the alarm and waste time for an unnecessary purpose.

Motives, My dear Marqs., of friendship and candor have given birth to the freedom of this communication, on my part—good sense & prudence will point it to proper objects, on yours—and on your honor & discretion I can firmly rely. It only remains for me to add, for your farther information, that since May last (when my thoughts on the plan of Campaign for 1782 were digested as they are now sent to you) Charles Town & Savanna having been evacuated—& Troops (Recruits principally) having arrived from Europe; the Enemies Posts have been strengthned—New York agreeably to the Estimates of General Greene and Major Burnett, which I enclose, by 3000 men;[5] Hallifax & Canada from European and other Accts., by the like number—and Penobscot by 3 or 400 more—these being the only changes which have happened since my statement of the Enemys force in May last, you will be able to bring the whole into one view & determine accordingly. It is reported that a number (some say seven) British Regiments are about to Embark for the West Indies; by other accts. the whole are said to be going thither but there is not, I believe, any orders for either yet come to hand—in this momt. everything with them is suspend[ed].

Your polite & friendly offer to my Nephew, claims my grateful acknowledgements; I wish he was in a condition to avail himself of it. He has been in a declining state of health near 12 Months—but was something better the last time I heard from him. McHenry has left the Military & embraced a Civil walk of life; by which act he has disqualified himself from answering your purposes.[6] The Vessel you gave us room to expect is not arrived; but Gouvion will go to Philadelphia & seek a passage from thence.[7] He can tell you more forcibly than I can express it how much we all love & wish to embrace you—when, how, or where this will happen you best can tell. For myself particularly, I hope it is unnecessary to repeat to you, that whether during the continuance of the War—or after the olive branch shall have extended itself over this Land (for which I most devoutly pray) I shall be happy to see you on Columbias shore. The Inhabitants of my humble Cottage will salute you with the Richest marks of grateful friendship wch. to a mind susceptible as yours is will be a greater feast than the luxuries of the East; the Elegancies of Europe—or the ceremonies of a Court can afford. Adieu—believe me always My dear Marquis Yr. Most Obedt. & affecte.

G.W.

P.S. Under cover of this Letter, you will receive a duplicate of the one written to you by the Chevr. Chattellux, and a Copy of my letter to Congress approving your conduct.[8]

ALS (DLC: George Washington Papers, Series 4), draft.

1. Since Lafayette left America, Washington had written him on January 4 (by Colonel Gimat) and October 20, 1782 (both above), and on December 15, 1782 (in Fitzpatrick, *Writings of Washington*, 25:433–35).

2. In November 1782 Lafayette had sent Gouvion to America to see Washington and inform him of Lafayette's plans in the event of a continuation of the war (see Lafayette to Washington, December 4, 1782). Washington did not send Gouvion back to France until June 1783 (see Washington to Lafayette, June 15, 1783).

3. On January 30, 1783, Washington wrote Congress, presenting his estimates of the army's needs for the coming campaign and hinting that he would like to undertake a full-scale siege of New York (Fitzpatrick, *Writings of Washington*, 26:82–86). Congress resolved that "such are the present situation and prospects of these states that it would be inexpedient at this time to determine upon the plan, or to enter upon the expensive preparations which it would require" (*JCC*, 24:142). On February 26 Robert R. Livingston wrote Washington, enclosing the resolutions of Congress, but Washington insisted that in spite of the current negotiations, the Americans would have to fight one more campaign. See Washington to Congress, March 19, 1783, in Fitzpatrick, *Writings of Washington*, 26:237–38.

4. Washington's memorandum of May 1, 1782, containing his plans, is in ibid., 24:194–215.

5. On December 19, 1782, Greene forwarded to Washington his and Major Burnet's estimates of the troops the British sent to New York from Charleston (DLC: George Washington Papers, Series 4).

6. In his letter to Washington of October 24, 1782 (above), Lafayette suggested that Washington could dispatch an officer to carry his confidential communications to Lafayette, and suggested either George Augustine Washington or James McHenry. McHenry had since been elected a member of Congress from Maryland.

7. Lafayette had written Washington on October 24 that a ship would sail for America in a fortnight with plans for the coming campaign. This letter was written the same day the *Triumph* arrived in Philadelphia, bearing news of the provisional treaty.

8. Washington's letter to Lafayette of December 15 (Fitzpatrick, *Writings of Washington*, 25:433–35), was probably the one carried by Chastellux. Lafayette had requested Washington, in his letter of December 4, to communicate to Congress his approval of Lafayette's furlough in France. Washington accordingly wrote Congress on March 23: "Congress have had too many unequivocal proofs of the Zeal, the attachment to, and important exertions of this young nobleman in the American Cause, to entertain a doubt of the propriety of his present absence. Sure I am that his return will be as soon as he can make it subservient to the Interest of this Country. These being my Sentiments I communicate them without reserve" (ibid., 26:250–51).

To Adrienne de Noailles de Lafayette[T]

Chavaniac, March 27, 1783

I received your lovely letter yesterday,[1] my dear heart, and this is the first occasion on which I could write you. You received a note written at Brioude that informed you of the day of my arrival. It was shortly before nightfall that I found myself again in the château where I had left two very dear people who are there no longer.[2] The first moment was terrible for my aunt, her cries and her grief were enough to frighten one. But she gradually recovered, and despite the abundance of her tears, an immense change has taken place since my arrival. I found her horribly changed and aged; but now she has more strength, spends the day out of her room, comes to the table and eats something. Since my arrival, the house has been full of people, and she is busy doing the honors. For myself, I have given up all formalities and think only of my aunt. She talks to me about my affairs and about her own, and I tell her about you, our children, and America. We broached the affair of the Chevalier de Chavaniac; she wants to pursue it, and if she does she really must try to win.[3] But I would prefer that she give up all her property, which would enable us to arrange things as we please. She still wants to go to Langeac, at least for the moment. But I hope that this summer we shall persuade her to come to Paris. I rejoice in the change my presence has brought about in her, and in truth it is miraculous.

As for me, my dear heart, it would be very sweet for me to be here if I could find again what I left behind. But each pleasant impression is saddened by this perception: remembering things brings back memories of people. There is not a corner in this house, not a tree around it, where I do not feel as if I am about to see my aunt and Mme d'Abos again, and I must pay painful attention in order to comprehend that of the three of us I am the only one still living.

Let us talk of our own affairs a bit, my dear heart, and I shall tell you first that I consult your little memorandum at every step. The subdelegate was here yesterday and will return Saturday. He is awaiting the order for a grant of 80 septiers and a loan of 150. I shall have each village name its representatives, and I would like the government to allow me to construct public granaries, to which I would add some of my grain, which would provide a bank of grain for seed. Thirty thousand francs are expected for your establishment, and that will do a great deal of good. You have rendered an immense service to the country.[4] On Monday I shall see a committee of parish priests, and we shall see what better things can be done. I plan to leave again on Thursday because it is indispensable to my aunt that I stay until then. She doesn't know the extent of the sacrifice I am making for her. But I know your heart, and I know you would insist on my staying here. It will be ten or eleven days. I shall dine in Brioude, sleep in Issoire; Friday I shall dine in Clermont, and Monday I hope to dine in St. Germain.

It is a great joy for me, my dear heart, to think that you share all my sentiments, and this thought gives me double the pleasure in communicating them to you. I have not spoken of your health, but I thank you very much for having told me about it. What you tell me about it is very necessary to me; you know well what I would say to you about it. Please give my compliments to the doctor. Do not neglect to have the work on our house hastened.[5] My aunt loves you tenderly, is very touched by your concern, and is writing you, I think, today. I have carried out your commissions, which are much appreciated. I gave her poor Anastasie's portrait. Have one made of George and Virginie and also have a copy made of the little picture you have of me. If all that is ready, I can send it to her when I arrive. A thousand affectionate greetings to mama and my sisters. I embrace our children. Farewell, my dear heart, take care of yourself, look after your health, love me always, and with that be certain of my happiness.

ALS (ALG, courtesy of the Comte de Chambrun), translation.

1. Letter not found.

2. Lafayette was visiting his father's sisters, Charlotte de Chavaniac, who was mourning the recent death of her sister, Madeleine de Lafayette (Mlle du Motier), Mme d'Abos, Mme de Chavaniac's daughter, had died in childbirth in 1778, while Lafayette was in America (*LAAR*, 2:230n–31n).

3. The Chevalier de Chavaniac was Mme de Chavaniac's brother-in-law. By the terms of their marriage contract, the parents of the chevalier and his brother, Mme de Chavaniac's husband, had agreed to leave one-third of their estate to a chosen child of the marriage. After the death of Mme de Chavaniac's husband, the chevalier sued to obtain that third part of the estate. Though a court had declared in favor of the chevalier in 1782, Mme de Chavaniac was still contesting the decision (NIC: Dean Collection, Chavaniac Documents, ca. 1700–1789).

4. To provide relief for the peasants around Chavaniac, Lafayette wanted to establish a public granary. He and Adrienne de Lafayette had also undertaken a project to establish a spinning mill and school for spinning in Auvergne to provide employment for those who would otherwise be forced to migrate after the harvests. The subdelegate was an aide to the intendant of the province. In 1784 the plan for the school was approved and the French government granted 6,000 livres for its establishment.

5. Lafayette had purchased a home on the Rue de Bourbon in Paris, and it was being readied for occupation.

From George Washington

Head Qrs. Newburgh 5th. Apl 1783

My dear Marqs,

It is easier for you to conceive than for me to express the sensibility of my Heart at the communications in your letter of the 5th. of Feby. from Cadiz. It is to these communications we are indebted for the only acct. yet recd. of a general Pacification. My Mind upon the receipt of this news was instantly assailed by a thousand ideas—all of them contending for pre-eminence, but believe me my dear friend none could supplant, or ever will eradicate that gratitude, which has arisen from a lively sense of the conduct of your Nation; from my obligations to many illustrious characters of it, among whom (I do not mean to flatter, when) I place you at the head of them; And from my admiration of the Virtues of your August Sovereign; who at the same time that he stands confessed the Father of his own people, & defender of American Rights has given the most exalted example of moderation in treating with his Enemies.

We now stand an Independent People, and have yet to learn political Tactics. We are placed among the Nations of the Earth, and have a character to establish; but how we shall acquit ourselves time must discover—the probability, at least I fear it, is, that local, or state Politics will interfere too much with that more liberal & extensive plan of Government which wisdom & foresight freed from the mist of prejudice would dictate; and that we shall be guilty of many blunders in treading this boundless theatre before we shall have arrived at any perfection in this Art—in a word that the experience which is purchased at the price of difficulties and distress, will alone convince us that the honor, power, & true Interest of this Country must be measured by a Continental Scale; & that every departure there from weakens the Union, & may ultimately break the band, which holds us together. To avert these evils—to form a Constitution that will give consistency, stability & dignity to the Union; & sufficient powers to the great Council of the Nation for general purposes is a duty which is incumbent upon every Man who wishes well to his Country—and will meet with my aid as far as it can be rendered in the private walks of life; for hence forward my Mind shall be unbent; & I will endeavor to glide gently down the stream of life till I come to that abyss, from whence no traveller is permitted to return.

The Armament wch. was preparing at Cadiz, and in which you were to have acted a distinguished part would have carried such conviction with it, but it is not to be wondered at, that Great Britain should have been impressed with the force of such reasoning. To this cause I am perswaded, the Peace is to be ascribed. Your going to Madrid from thence instead of coming immediately to this Country, is another instance My dear Marquis of your zeal for the American Cause; & lays a fresh claim to the gratitude of her Sons, who will, at all times, receive you with open Arms; but as no Official dispatches are yet received, either at Phila. or New York of the completion of the treaty—nor any measures taken for the Reduction of the Army, my detention therewith is quite uncertain; to say then (at this time) where I may be at the epoch for your intended visit to this Continent is too vague even for conjecture—but nothing can be more true than that the pleasure with which I shall receive you will be equal to your wishes. I shall be better able to determine *then* than now on the practicability of accompanying you to France—A Country to which I shall ever feel a warm affection; & if I do not pay it that tribute of respect which is to be derived from a visit it may be ascribed with more justice to any other cause, than a want of inclination; or the pleasure of going there under the auspices of your friendship.

I have already observed, that the determinations of Congress, if they have come to any, respecting the Army, is yet unknown to me; but as you wish to be informed of *every thing* that concerns it, I do, for your satisfaction, transmit authentic documents of some very interesting occurrences which have happened within the last Six months—but I ought first to have premised, that from accumulated sufferings, & little or no prospect of relief, the discontents of the Officers last Fall put on the threatned appearance of a total resignation, till the business was diverted into the channel which produced the Address and Petition to Congress which stands first on the file herewith enclosed.[1] I shall make no comment on these proceedings—to one as well acquainted with the sufferings of the American Army as you are, it is unnecessary—it will be sufficient to observe that the more the Virtue & forbearence of it is tried, the more resplendent it appears. My hope is, that the Military [exit] of this valuable class of the community will exhibit such a proof of the amor patriae as will do them honor in the page of history.

These papers, with my last letter (which was intended to go by Colo. Gouvion—containing extensive details of Military Plans) will convey to you every information I can give—in the present uncertainty, worthy of attention.[2] If you should get sleepy, & tired of reading them, recollect, for my exculpation, that it is in compliance with your request, I have run into such prolixity.

I made a proper use of the confidential part of your Letter of the 5th. of Feby.[3]

The scheme, my dear Marqs. which you propose as a precedent, to encourage the emancipation of the black people of this Country from that state of Bondage in wch. they are held, is a striking evidence of the benevolence of your Heart. I shall be happy to join you in so laudable a work; but will defer going into a detail of the business, till I have the pleasure of seeing you.

Lord Stirling is no more—he died at Albany in Jany. last, very much regretted—Colo. Barber was snatched from us about the same time, in a way equally unexpected, sudden and distressing; leaving many friends to bemoan his fate.[4] Tilghman is on the point of Matrimony with a namesake & Couzin; Sister to Mrs. Carroll of Baltimore. It only remains for me now, My dear Marqs., to make a tender of my respectful Compliments in which Mrs. Washington unites, to Madame La Fayette; & to wish you, her, & your little offspring, all the happiness this life can afford. I will extend my Compliments to the Gentlemen, with whom I have the honor of an Acquaintance, in your circle. I need not add how happy I shall be to see you in America—& more particularly at Mount Vernon—or with what truth and warmth of Affection I am Yr. Most Obedt. & faithful friend

G. WASHINGTON

ALS (DLC: George Washington Papers, Series 4), draft.

1. The enclosures concerned the "Newburgh Affair" of March 1783. Anonymous letters were circulated among the Continental officers encamped at Newburgh, New York, fanning the flame of discontent as Congress continued to delay action on the petition for back pay and pensions the officers and soldiers had addressed to Congress in January. One of the anonymous letters proposed a meeting of generals to decide on a vigorous course of action to force Congress to act on the petition. Washington immediately called a meeting of generals to discuss the issue. On March 15 he addressed the assembled officers, pledging his strongest support for their demands. The officers received his address warmly and passed resolves affirming their support of Washington while condemning the inflammatory anonymous letters. See also Washington to Lafayette, June 15, 1783.

2. See Washington to Lafayette, March 23, 1783.

3. In his letter of February 5, 1783, Lafayette had told Washington that he would be flattered to be the official delegate to carry the ratified peace treaty to England. Washington mentioned Lafayette's request to Livingston. See Lafayette to Washington, February 5, note 2.

4. Colonel Francis Barber was crushed by a falling tree on February 11, 1783.

John Adams to James Warren

Paris April 16th. 1783

Dear Sir,

It is my Duty to unbosom myself to some Friend in Congress, upon whose discretion I can rely—and there is none to whom I can do it with more propriety than to you, of whose Patriotism & Friendship I have had so long Experience.

We are at Peace, but not out of danger. That there have been dangerous designs against our real Independence if not against our Union and Confederation, is past a doubt in my Mind—And We have cause to fear that such designs may be revived in various Shapes. Europe is generally sensible, that the United States in half a Century will, if they keep together, give the Tone to the World. This is not a flattering Idea to them, and We may depend upon it, there will be a Succession of vain Politicians, who will manoeuvre to break Us.

Let me beg of You to look up some old Papers in Mr. Thomson's office.[1] I mean the Contracts entered into with Monsieur de Coudrai and other French officers, the M. de la Fayette among others, by Mr. Deane, and Mr. Deane's Letters. If De Coudrai had been made Major General, older than Green, with the Command of the whole Artillery & all military Manufactures, subject only to the Command of Congress & the Commander in Chief, and if the Marechall M. had been that Commander in Chief, as was proposed, what would have been the Situation of our Army & Country?[2] In whose Power should We have been? Pursue the History of our foreign Affairs from that time to this, & see if all has been right. See if We have not Motives enough to think of standing on our own Legs, and judging for ourselves.

The Marquis de la Fayette is an amiable Nobleman, & has great Merit. I enjoy his Friendship, & wish a Continuance of it. But I will conceal nothing from You. I see in that Youth the Seeds of Mischief to our Country, if We do not take care. He was taken early into our Service & placed in an high Command, in which he has behaved well; but he has gained more applause than human Nature at 25 can bear. It has enkindled in him an unbounded Ambition, which it concerns Us much to watch.

The Instruction of Congress to their foreign Ministers to consult with him was very ill Judged.[3] It was lowering themselves & their Servants. There is no American Minister, who would not have been always ready & willing to consult with him; but to enjoin it & make it a Duty was an Humiliation, that would astonish all the World, if it was known. Your Ministers will never be respected, never have any Influence, while You depress them in this manner. Every Frenchman of Course, who knows, & enough do know it, will consider your Servants as mere Instruments in their Hands. If Dr. Franklin, Mr. Jay, Mr. Laurens, Mr. Dana have occasion for the Advice of the Marquis, it would be wonderful. It may be said that he is a convenient Go-between. I say for this very reason, it should have been avoided. There ought to be no Go-between. Your Ministers should confer directly with the Ministers of other Powers; and if they chuse at any time to make Use of a third Person, they ought to chuse him.

The Marquis may live these 50 Years. Ten years may bring him by the order of Succession to the Command of your Army. You have given him a great deal too much of Popularity in our own Country. He is connected with a Family of vast Influence in France. He rises fast in the French Army. He may be soon in the Ministry. This Mongrel Character of French Patriot & American Patriot cannot exist long— And if hereafter it should be seriously the Politicks of the French Court to break our Union, Imagination cannot concieve a more proper Instrument for the Purpose, than the Marquis. He is now very active— everlastingly busy—ardent to distinguish himself every way, especially to increase his Merit towards America, aiming as I believe at some Employment from Congress. Pains are taken to give him the Credit of every thing. Believe me, it is of infinite Importance, that you yourselves & your Servants should have the Reputation of their own Measures, and of doing your Service.

I know the Confederation of our States to be a brittle Vessel. I know it will be an Object of Jealousy to France. Severe Strokes will be aimed at it, & if We are not upon our Guard to ward them off, it will be broken—and what a Scene of Misery to our Country does this Idea open.

Amidst all the Joys, of Peace and the glorious Prospects before Us, I see in Europe so many Causes of Inquietude, that I cannot be longer easy without laying my thoughts open to a Friend. I have freely hinted at the Characters which have given me unutterable Distress, because they have endangered & dishonoured our Country—and I now give You my Apprehensions of another.

Our Country is a singular one. It is a Temple of Liberty, set open to all the World. If there is any thing on Earth worthy of being contended for, it is this glorious Object. I never had thro' my whole Life any other Ambition, than to cherish, promote & protect it, and never will have any other for myself, nor my Children. For this Object however, I have as much as any Conqueror ever had. For this I have run as great Risques & made as great Sacrifices, as any of the pretended Heroes, whose Object was Domination & Power, Wealth & Pleasure. For this I have opened to You Characters with Freedom, which it is to me personally dangerous to touch. But it is necessary, &, come what will, I will not flinch. These People know me. They know I stand in their Way, & therefore You will hear of Insinuations enough, darkly circulated to lessen me at Home.[4] I care not. Let me come home & tell my own Story. Your Friend

LbC (MHi: Warren-Adams Collection).
1. Charles Thomson was secretary of Congress.

2. Silas Deane, while American commissioner to France, had pledged commissions in the American army to a number of French officers, including Tronson Du Coudray and Lafayette. Although Congress was willing to confirm Du Coudray's commission, they found it impossible to satisfy his demands for seniority and command (see *LAAR*, 1:11–12, 15n).

"The Marechall M." is probably the Maréchal de Maillebois, whose comments on the conduct of the American war the American commissioners enclosed in their letter to the Committee of Secret Correspondence, February 6, 1777 (Wharton, *Diplomatic Correspondence*, 2:262).

3. On the Congressional resolutions of November 23, 1781, See *LAAR*, 4:440–41.

4. Adams seemed convinced that Franklin, Vergennes, and others were constantly plotting to harm American interests in favor of France. In addition, he believed his own reputation was being sacrificed to the lies and intrigues of this cabal, among others.

To George Washington

Olainville Near Paris April the 19h. 1783

My Dear General

Having Been told By Mquis. de Castries at Whose Country Seat I am, that He Now is Sending a Vessel to America, I Cannot Resist an Opportunity to write You a few lines. My Letter's journey By land Will Be Almost as long As its Voyage Across the Ocean, and the New England Porstmouth is Very far Distant to the Banks of the Potowmack—for I Suppose, My dear General, that You Intend Spending this Summer at Home, and Unless I am Prevented By the Answers of Congress, I Hope Before long to Partake of Your Country Pleasures.

Great Britain Having at Last Got a Ministry, Wherein the king Has five Votes, and the Rockingam Interest Has But four, Nothing Now Can Put a Stop to the Definitive treaty.[1] Mr. Laurens is Arrived, and Mr. David Hartley is Hourly Expected.[2] The Duke of Manchester is Also Coming As an Ambassador to France. A Bill Had Been Proposed in England, Which Greatly favours the American trade, But it Now Meets With Difficulties.[3] I Hope France Will Make Alterations in Her Commercial Scheme, Which in Some Respects is Very foolishly Regulated. It is a Business to Which I the More Earnestly Apply, as it Also Immediately Concerns the American Interest. Upon these Points I Consult With Mr. Barklay the Consul, and I Hope we May obtain Many Useful Amendments. To My Great Satisfaction Mr. de Fleury Has Been obliged to Resign. His Principles and His Views Were Quite opposed to Mine, And I Hope Mr. d'Ormesson His Successor Will Have a More liberal Way of thinking.[4]

There Has Been a Quarrel Betwen Russia and Turkey Which, Had our War lasted, Would Have Made me tremble for its Consequences.

But Now it May Be Amicably Ended, and at all Events, Nothing Now, thank God, Can Effect the Great Cause of America, and Mankind. The General Opinion is that the Dispute I allude to Will Be friendly Compromised.[5]

Doctor Franklin Has Applied for His Recall. Who is to Replace Him I do not know, But in Case, as I am told, Gal. Schuyller takes that Carrier [career], He is of all Men the Properest I know of for an Embassy to France. Hamilton Should Come out as His Secretary, and the More I think of it, the More I .Wish Schuyller May Be Induced to Accept of the Employement. I do not like to Middle With the foreign Choices of Congress, But I think You Will Serve the Public By Improving the Hint I take the liberty to Give Confidentially to You.[6]

Since the Letter of Which Cher. de Chattelux Was Bearer, Not a line from My dear General Has Come to My Hands.[7] But Now I Hope to Be More fortunate, and the Dangers of War Being over, I know there is No danger of Your forgetting to let Your Best friend Hear of Your Wellfare.

George's State of Health Makes me Uneasy. I Hope the Sea May Be Beneficial.[8] My three Children are Well, and their Mother Requests Her Respectfull Compliments to Be Paid to You and to Mrs. Washington. My Most Affectionate Respects Waït Upon Her and Upon You, My dear General, Whom I So tenderly love, And to Whom, So long as I Can Breath, I Shall Ever Be the Most Gratefull, Devoted, and Affectionate friend

LAFAYETTE

Our friend Cher. de Chattelux is Just Coming in and Requests His Affectionate Respects to Be Presented to You and Mrs. Washington.

ALS (United States Senate Commission on Art and Antiquities, Washington, D.C.).

1. On April 3, Charles James Fox and Frederick Lord North came into office in a coalition government, replacing the Shelburne ministry. As Fox was in favor of granting the Americans independence immediately and North was less ambivalent about establishing peace than Shelburne had proved to be, the Americans now expected a prompt end to the negotiations.

2. Henry Laurens had been in London, successfully lobbying against the enactment of trade bills on the United States (Wharton, *Diplomatic Correspondence*, 6:366). David Hartley, named by Fox to replace Richard Oswald in the negotiations, arrived in Paris on April 24, 1783.

3. The series of bills presented in the House of Commons in March and April provided for the provisional establishment and regulation of trade between England and the United States. Laurens objected to the opening of trade by act of Parliament and also to beginning trade while British troops remained in the United States.

4. To meet the enormous expenditure and debts of the state, Joly de Fleury increased taxes and tried to cut the expenses of the court. He was replaced on March 29 by Lefèvre d'Ormesson, a cousin of Adrienne de Lafayette.

5. There had been a number of disturbances in 1782 in the "neutral" border area between Russia and the Ottoman Empire, and Russia appeared to have ambitions to

annex the Crimea, which, by treaty with the Ottoman Empire, was nominally independent. Though Russia had sent troops into the area late in the year, there had been no military action, and the tensions seemed to have eased by the time Lafayette wrote this letter.

6. Franklin remained American minister in France until the summer of 1785, when Thomas Jefferson took the post.

7. Chastellux probably brought Washington's letter of December 15, 1782 (in Fitzpatrick, *Writings of Washington*, 25:433–35).

8. George Augustine Washington was in the West Indies trying to restore his health. See Washington to Lafayette, October 20, 1782.

To William Carmichael

St. Germain April 27h 1783

My Dear Sir

In Consequence of Your letters, I Have Applied to the Commissionners in Paris, and Particularly to Mr. Jay who told me Your Accounts are Waïted for, and where Settled, the Monney Shall Be Sent. You know Mr. Barklay is the Person Whom Congress Have Appointed for that Purpose.[1]

As to Still More Important Matters, Mr. Jay tells me He Has Been Assured from the Spanish Court that they were desirous to treat *With Him*, and that it Has Been Agreed Betwen Him on the One Part, and I think Count d'Arenda, and Mr. Gardochy on the other, that as Soon As a definitive treaty is Signed, He Will Repair to Madrid and there Resume the Negotiations.[2]

Be it as it Will, I Hope a Good, liberal, and Everlasting treaty will take place, that May Strengthten the Alliance Betwen the House of Bourbon and the United States of America.

Nothing New in this Quarter, But that Count d'Estaing Has Been Promised the first Vacant Governement of 30,000£.[3] Mr. Laurens is Here, and Mr. Hartlay is Either Arrived or Hourly Expected. Duke of Manchester is Also on His Way, and Mr. d'Adhemar will Set out in a few days. Littlepage Has Been Sick But Now does Very Well. Adieu, My dear Sir, Most Affectionately Yours

LAFAYETTE

My Most Affectionate Compliments Waït Upon Count de Montmorin. Remember me to Mr. Burgoing Mr. de Seran and all friends in Madrid.

ALS (CSmH: HK 222).

1. Letters from Carmichael to Lafayette not found. Jay had left Carmichael in Spain to prepare statements of Jay's and America's accounts in Spain. For their settlement, see

Morris, *John Jay*, 2:682–711. On November 18, 1782, Congress had appointed Thomas Barclay to examine and settle the accounts of all American representatives in Europe (*JCC*, 23:728–30).

2. The Spanish court had refused to recognize the American minister formally. Jay did not return to Spain, but he sailed for America in the fall of 1783.

3. There were two classes of provincial governorships in France. The first, available to princes of the blood and *maréchaux de France,* paid 60,000 livres per year; the second paid 30,000 livres and could be held by lieutenant generals of the army, such as D'Estaing. He was appointed governor of Touraine in 1785.

To Sir Henry Clinton

Sir   Paris April the 30th, 1783

Upon a Perusal of Your Printed Correspondance, I Must Beg Leave to trouble You With an Observation—Not that I Have Claims to Set forth, or Relations to Criticise. Whatever Be the Means, our Contest is Ended, and a Sentence in Your Letters June the 11th and August the 2d. is the only one I intend to Mention.

Having Said to Lord Cornwallis that He May Be Opposed By About 2000 Continentals, and, As Lafayette Observes, a Body of ill Armed Militia, You Are Pleased to Add, *full as Spiritless as the Militia of the Southern Provinces And Without Any Service,* Which Reads as if it Were a Part of My Intercepted Letters.[1]

How Far Your Description is Undeserved, Experience, I think, Has Proved, and that it Came from Me, No American Will Believe. But Your Correspondance is So Public, that, With a full Relyance on Your Candor and Politness, I Have taken the Liberty to transcribe the Passage, and to Return it to You, Sir, as its trüe Author.[2] At the Same, Sir, Permit Me to Assure You of the High Regard I Have the Honor to Be With Your Most obedient Humble Servant

LAFAYETTE

ALS (MiU-C: Clinton Papers).

1. As a result of the controversy over whether he or Lord Cornwallis was responsible for the British defeat at Yorktown, Clinton published a narrative of his conduct in 1783. A passage in Clinton's letter to Cornwallis of June 11, 1781, also quoted in an August 2 letter, read: "And your Lordship may possibly have opposed to you, from fifteen hundred to two thousand Continentals, and (as Lafayette observes), a small body of ill armed peasantry, full as spiritless as the militia of the southern provinces, and without any service" (*Narrative of L-G Sir Henry Clinton, K.B., relative to his Conduct during Part of his Command of the King's Troops in North America: Particularly to that which respects the unfortunate Issue of the Campaign in 1781* [London, 1783], pp. 114–15, 241).

2. Clinton replied to Lafayette on May 12, 1783:

In consequence of the letter you did me the honor to write me, I reread the publication in question, and I agree that that remark, which is assuredly mine from the way it is inserted, seems to be a part of your intercepted letter. You are assuredly entitled to receive this admission, but allow me at the same time to add my assurances of the esteem with which I have the honor to be, sir, your very humble, very obedient servant.[T] [MiU-C: Clinton Papers]

From Robert R. Livingston

1st May 1783 Philadelphia

Dear Sir

I am now to acknowledge your favor of the ——[1] by the Triumph & that of the 2d. March from Bordeaux. You were the happy messenger of glad tidings on both occasions. We had recd. no account of the signature of the general preliminaries or of the cessation of hostilities before her arrival. You can easily conceive the joyful reception it met with here where we began to be heartily tired of war—nor was it less welcome information to the army than to the other citizens of America. The second letter which promesses a happy settlement of all differences with Spain was flattering to those among us who knew the importance of her friendship both in a commercial & political view. Congress feel themselves under great obligations to you for the ardor you discovered in accelerating this happy event & the address with which you placed it in such a train as to make it difficult for the Spanish minister to go back from his engagements.

By this conveyance I send our ministers the ratification of the provisional articles.[2] Carleton & Digby have sent out their prisoners and we are making arrangments to send in ours—Congress having determined on there part to do not only all that good faith may require but by this mark of confidence to convince them that they have no doubt of the sincerity of their professions. Our ministers will shew you the letters that have passed between Carleton & me. Some among us from finding nothing yet done that leads to the evacuation of New York have been apprehensive that the British will affect delays on that subject till the Tories are satisfied which I can venture to tell you in confidence they never will be unless the british shall on there part repair all the cruel losses they have unnecessarily occasioned.[3] I this moment recd. a letter from the Genl. informing me that he had proposed a personal interview with Carleton in hope of learning something of his intentions with respect to the evacuation but I fear he will be deceived in this hope if I may judge from the debates of the 3d of March which prove that no orders had then been transmitted.[4]

You oblige me extreamly by the confidence you repose in me in your Letter of the ——.[5] You know how sincerely I wish to render you every

Robert R. Livingston, as secretary of foreign affairs, acquainted Congress with Lafayette's detailed accounts of American affairs in Europe.

service in my power & knowing this you will pardon or rather be pleased with the freedom that I shall speake of the business you mention. Both Hamilton & myself consider it as extreamly difficult to effect. Real obstacles present themselves which will render it delicate to make the attempt and objections which have no real weight will be thrown in by prejudice and partial interests which may I fear defeat my earnest wish to procure for you this concluding testimony of the friendship which this country owes you. But as the treaty is not yet come over I can say nothing certain and I hope to have an opportunity of writing to you more at large by the Triumph in which your domestic will return.[6] For general information I refer you to him & have the honor to be my Dear Sir with the sincerest attatchmt. Your Most Obt. Hume. Servt.

I can not leave writing without expressing how sincerely I agree with you in your wishes that unanimity may prevail & the band of Union among us be strengthened. No thinking man here but at the same time feels the necessity & laments the difficulty of effecting a measure on which our happiness so greatly depends. Congress have made some general arrangements in their finances which if adopted by the several states will render our national debt a national tie which time & experience may strengthen.[7] Our ministers will shew you those resolutions. I will not therefore unecessarily burden Coll. Ogden with them.

AL (NHi: Robert R. Livingston Papers), draft.

1. Left blank in draft; Lafayette's letter of February 5, 1783.

2. Congress ratified the provisional treaty on April 15, 1783 (*JCC*, 24:241–52).

3. Between March 24 and April 13, Livingston corresponded with Admiral Digby and General Carleton at New York on meeting the terms of the provisional treaty. As soon as they received instructions from England, the British commanders were willing to comply with Article 7, the cessation of hostilities and the release of prisoners. But they seemed reluctant about the last provision of that article, British evacuation of posts in America, until Congress met Article 5, the restitution of all confiscated Loyalist property. Livingston enclosed copies of this correspondence in his letter to the peace commissioners, April 21, 1783 (Wharton, *Diplomatic Correspondence*, 6:336, 337, 346, 348, 362, 363, 367–68, 369, 377, 386–87).

4. See Washington to Livingston, April 23, 1783 (Fitzpatrick, *Writings of Washington*, 26:348–49). On March 3 David Hartley had proposed in Commons an address to the king recommending the withdrawal of troops from New York, but he received no support. One member objected that no time could be set for the evacuation because of the large number of transport ships that would be required. Another supposed that New York was not to be evacuated until America had fulfilled the conditions of the treaty relating to the Loyalists (*The Parliamentary Register, or History of the Proceedings and Debates of the House of Commons*, 9 [London, 1783]: 390–91).

5. Left blank in draft; Lafayette's February 5 letter containing his request to be sent to England to deliver the ratified treaty.

6. On Lafayette's dispatch of his servant on *Le Triomphe* with news of the negotiation of the peace preliminaries, see Lafayette to Livingston, February 5, "On the 7th Dec."

7. On April 18, 1783, Congress passed a resolution intended to provide for payment of the war debt, calling for the states to give Congress the power for twenty-five years to levy import duties on specified items and a general 5 percent ad valorum duty on all

imported goods, the revenues from which would pay off $1.5 million of the debt annually. They also recommended that the states cede their territorial claims to Congress so that Congress could use those lands for debt payment. A congressional committee drafted a circular letter to the states explaining the resolution, and Congress approved it on April 26 (*JCC*, 24:257–62, 277–83). The request for power required unanimity from the states, which it never received.

Recommendation of Lafayette for the Cross of Saint Louis[T]

May 5, 1783

Monsieur le Marquis de Lafayette, who was born September 26, 1757, served from April 9, 1771, was made captain May 19, 1774, and *mestre de camp* March 3, 1779, went over to North America at the beginning of the war between America and England. The conduct that he showed there has been so distinguished that he gained the complete confidence of Congress as well as that of the king, and His Majesty, to reward him, decided to grant him the title of *maréchal de camp* dated from the nineteenth of October 1781.

As there is no article in the regulations determining the length of service required before a general officer is eligible to receive the Cross of Saint Louis, it is proposed that His Majesty award it to the Marquis de Lafayette.

He is twenty-six years old. He has had twelve years of service, of which nearly six were in America, where he was involved in everything and was very usefully employed for negotiating purposes, and he has finally obtained the rank of *maréchal de camp* through a very singular distinction and because of the zeal and talents that he has proved himself to possess.

D (SHA: Dossier Lafayette, LG 1261, 1st Series), translation. The recommendation was written by Minister of War Ségur and was approved by the king with the word "Bon" at the bottom of the page.

Created in 1693, the Cross of Saint Louis was awarded to distinguished French military men for their virtue and merit, and the services they had rendered.

To the American Peace Commissioners

Paris May 12th. 1783

Gentlemen,

Having yesterday conferred with Count de Vergennes upon some public Concerns, He requested I would tell you what, instead of troubling you with the Demand of a Meeting, I think better to mention in this Note.

The several Powers, said he, are going to make up their Treaties and when ready to sign, they will, of course meet to do it all together. The Mediation of the Emperor and that of Russia have been required, and under that Mediation the French Treaty will be sign'd. It now rests with America to know if she will conclude her Treaty under the Mediation or chooses to let it alone. There is no necessity for it But in case you prefer to have it, Count de Vergennes thinks it is time to join with England in making a combined Application to the Court of Vienna and that of Petersbourg.[1]

So far, Gentlemen, I have been requested to speak to you. I will add that from my last Conferences on the Subject I hope we may get the Harbour of L'Orient, as we have wished for the American Trade. Be pleased to accept the Assurances of my great & affectionate Respect

LA FAYETTE

LbC (DLC: Benjamin Franklin Papers).
1. Laurens acknowledged Lafayette's letter on May 13 and said he would bring up the matter as soon as Adams summoned the commissioners to meet (ScHi: Henry Laurens Papers). The Americans did not accept mediation, but worked with David Hartley, the British peace minister, through the spring and summer of 1783 on the details of a final treaty.

To George Washington

Paris June the 10the 1783.

My dear general.

Having received no answer to my letter by the Triumph, I may I think, flatter myself before long to hear from you, and I confess I am waiting with great impatience.[1] It is an age my dear general, since I had a line from you, and I have been So happily used to our intimate communications that it is very hard to me, not to know any thing of your ideas, your concerns, and your Sentiments on every occasion. God grant I may Soon have that long wished for letter. Upon its contents, my motions will be determined, and unless my presence here is ordered by Congress, I hope I may Soon be reunited to my dear general. Having fully explained myself in my letter by the Triumph, I have thought it useless to repeat my ideas in the Subsequent ones, and these lines are only intended to present doctor Bancroft Who is going by way of England to Philadelphia. I have long known him, first of all in England and afterwards in France where he ever appeared to me a

Sensible and a warm friend to our Cause. Agreable to that party Spirit, which to my great concern has ever divided our ministers or envoys in Europe, Doctor Bancroft has been praised by some and criticised by others. But I owe him the Justice to Say that his public opinions, and his Conduct have always appeared to me Such as becomes a Citizen of the United States.[2]

Your God Son, my dear General, is now under innoculation.[3] That piece of intelligence, tho' it is not very important is the only one I will give, for this letter will be long on its way and I intend taking Speedier opportunities. We are going to have a change in the Ministry and I fancy Mquis. de Castries will Soon resign. The destruction of the Ottoman Empire Seems to have been determined upon by Russia and the Emperor.[4] L'*Orient* has been made a free port for the American trade and I think is very advantageous.[5] When I am writing to you my dear general, I don't know Well how to Stop. But When I reflect this letter will be So long on the road, I must content myself with presenting my most affectionate respects to Mrs. Washington, my tender compliments to my friends, and to repeat you my dear general, that every Sentiment of filial love, respect and gratitude make me for ever. your devoted friend.

LAFAYETTE.

Mme de Lafayette and our little family present their respects to you and Mrs Washington.

L (MH: Sparks Mss 88; by permission of Houghton Library, Harvard University), copy.

1. See Lafayette to Washington, February 5, 1783.
2. Although Dr. Edward Bancroft had been a double agent working for the British, his duplicity was discovered only in the late nineteenth century (see *LAAR*, 1:14n, 36; 2:268–69).
3. George-Washington Lafayette was being inoculated against smallpox.
4. In June 1783 Russia began military action to annex the Crimea, which by treaty with the Ottoman Empire was to have maintained its independence.
5. For Lafayette's efforts on behalf of Lorient, see Lafayette to Vergennes, March 19, 1783. The formal *arrêt du conseil* proclaiming Lorient a free port did not come until May 14, 1784.

From Nathanael Greene

Head quarters Charles Town June 10th 1783

Dear Marquis

I wrote you a few days ago by Mr. Hunter of Virginia.[1] This letter goes inclosed to a Cousin of mine Mr. Griffin Greene with whom my brothers and my self are concerned in trade. He is bound to Bordaeux to look after an interest we have laying there in the Ship Flora which by some mismanagement has been idle there for many months past.

It is possible my Cousin may want a letter of credit to the amount of one thousand or twelve hundred pounds sterling. I shall be much oblige to you to give him this credit if he should have occasion for it in the management of his business; and for which I will be responsible. Your polite letter from Nantz authorises this liberty; and I hope you may not find it inconvenient.[2]

I will say nothing upon politicks by this uncertain conveyance. I am my dear Marquis Your Most obedt. humble Servt.

N. GREENE

ALS (NjGbS).

1. The letter has not been found. James Hunter was a Virginia munitions manufacturer.

2. No letter from Lafayette at Nantes has been found. Lafayette also wrote Greene on February 5, 1783, from Cadiz, offering to introduce Greene's business associates at the best commercial houses in France. In requesting that Greene send him his commands, Lafayette wrote: "You know me too well, I trust, to Stand Upon Ceremonies with me and from Such a friend as you, I Have a Right to Expect None" (DLC: Nathanael Greene Papers)

In his letter to Griffin Greene of June 10 (Ct), Nathanael Greene wrote: I have also inclosed you a letter to the Marquis de la Fayette desiring him to advance for you one thousand pounds sterling or to give you that credit if you should have occasion for it. He made me an offer of this sort, some little time past, but I am afraid he will leave Europe for America before you will see him and if he should not He may think I have taken his offer in too strong a light. Courtiers are flowing in language but timid & cautious in conduct. I dont wish to do injustice to the Marquis' generous intentions; but I wish not to raise your expectations too high, lest it should prove a disadvantage to you.

Lafayette did offer to advance Griffin Greene the money requested, but he did not need it at the time (Nathanael Greene to Lafayette, March 24, 1784, CSmH: GR 2467).

To the Comte de Vergennes[T]

Paris, June 12, 1783

I saw Sir James Jay, Monsieur le Comte, and learned with pleasure that you were to have a talk with him tomorrow about American trade. The subject is so important and time is so precious that I am happy every time the government turns its attention to it. Sir James Jay communicated his ideas to me, and I was satisfied with them. In principle, helping some firms here and in America seems to me advantageous; among the latter it would be fair, I think, to include Sir James's.[1] The twofold interest that motivates me will serve as an excuse for the liberty

I am taking, and I add to it the homage of my tender and respectful attachment.

LAFAYETTE

ALS (AAE: Correspondance politique, Etats-Unis, vol. 24, fol. 332), translation.

1. Sir James Jay, elder brother of John Jay, spent most of the war years in England. His memorandum on French–American trade suggested that the major impediment was the lack of available long-term credit—something that the British had supplied in abundance to their former colonies. Jay's plan was for France to lend financial support to some American mercantile houses in order to promote American participation in the French markets and sales of French manufactures in America (AAE: Correspondance politique, Etats-Unis, vol. 24, fols. 224–25).

From George Washington

Newburgh 15th. June 1783.

My dear Marqs.

You are too well acquainted with the merits of Colo. Gouvion to need my testimony either of his Services, abilities or worth; and yet, my wish to see them rewarded, induces me to repeat & even to impress them upon you. I do not take the liberty of bringing this officer directly before Monsr. the Count de Segur—but of the communication of my ideas of his deserts and my desire to serve him would contribute to procure him the Smiles of that Minister I should have no objection to their being offered in any manner your prudence shall dictate.

We remain here in a listless State, awaiting the arrival of the definitive Treaty; the uncertaintly of wch., added to the great Expence of subsisting the Army have induced Congress to Furlough (which, in the present case is but another term for discharging) all the Soldiers who stood engaged for the War.[1] This measure, tho' extremely distressing to the officers on acct. of their want of pay has been effected without any disorder & with less discontent than could possibly be expected. The three years men have been formed into Corps & will remain at West Point & in the Vicinity of it till the Treaty arrives & Congress shall have determined on a Peace establishment for this Country. The former, will put a period to my Military Services & carry me back to the walks of private life, & to that relaxation & repose which can not but be grateful to a mind which has been on the stretch for more than Eight Years a great part of wch. it has been embarrassed by a variety of the most perplexing circumstances.

Colo. Gouvion will give you a Pamphlet, containing a compilation of Original Papers which I have suffered the publication of to shew the

Origin the oeconomy, the Justice, & even the necessity of the Half pay, or Commutation of the Half pay, to the officers of this army which some of the States have been opposed to. The greatest part of these Papers accomd. one of my late letrs. to you but they will now appear in a more connected form.[2]

As I have little expectation that Gouvion will find you in France but much of seeing you hear soon, I shall add no more to this letter than my best respects to Madame De la Fayette & blessing to your little progeny. With the greatest attachment, & the most unalterable affecn. I am My Dr. Marqs. Yr. Most Obt. Servt.

G.W.

ALS (DLC: George Washington Papers, Series 4), draft.
1. On the resolutions of May 26, see *JCC*, 24:364–65.
2. Published at Fishkill, the pamphlet was *A Collection of Papers relative to Half-Pay and Commutation of Half-Pay granted by Congress . . . Compiled by permission of His Excellency General Washington from the Original Papers in his Possession.* For the letters related to the Newburgh Affair, see Washington to Lafayette, April 5, note 1.

To John Adams

Paris June the 16th 1783

The Mquis. de Lafayette Has the Honour to Present His Respects to Mr. Adams, and Acquaints Him He Had letters from America as late as the first of May, in one of Which Mr. Lewingston Refers Him to those He was writing to the Commissioners.[1] The Mquis. de Lafayette will to Morrow Before twelve do Himself the Honour to Call Upon Mr. Adams, and Communicate to Him what He Has Received.[2]

Count de Vergennes was Yesterday Expressing a desire to know if the last Dispatches to Mr. Hartlay were So Satisfactory as Duke of Manchester Assures them to Be.

AL (MHi: Adams Papers).
1. See Livingston to Lafayette, May 1, 1783.
2. On the same day Lafayette wrote a similar letter to Franklin and Jay (NNC: Jay Papers). Jay's reply completely ignored Lafayette's inquiry about David Hartley, who had replaced Oswald (ibid.). Hartley had written the commissioners on June 14, urging them not to be uncompromising on the issue of reciprocity and suggesting a temporary trade agreement (Wharton, *Diplomatic Correspondence*, 6:483–87). The Duke of Manchester, England's ambassador to France, had replaced Fitzherbert as negotiator of the treaties with Spain and France.

From Henry Knox

Westpoint June 16 1783

I am indebted to you my dear Marquis for several letters which I have had the pleasure to receive.[1] My Brother is indebted to you for much kindness, which he has pressed me to acknowledge with the greatest sense of gratitude.[2] And America is infinitely indebted to you for your assistance, in the moment of her deepest distress, and from thence up to the present auspicious period. She recognizes the favors she has received with an unbounded attachment to you. For myself I shall ever recur to the pleasures of Your friendship with the ardor of a lover, and my Harry Your Godson, shall be taught the same sensations.

From the information of the General It is supposed you may be on your passage to America. Therefore I shall not trouble you with details upon any subjects. Our system of policy will mend I believe? and it is the growing sentiment that there will be no dignity or safety but in a general Government unfettered by local or State policy. We shall have general funds and we shall be a united people. Our affection for France will be perpetual.

Colonel Gouvion will inform You of the society we have formed in which we have taken the liberty to involve a great number of the officers of the Army which [illegible word] under the orders of the Count Rochambeau.[3] We Consider you as an American and therefore one of us without any particular specification.

Permit me to press you to write me as frequently as your occasions may admit and be assured I shall be a punctual correspondent. Suffer Mrs. Knox & myself to present our respectful compli[ments] to the marchioness your Lady. I am my dear Marquis with great affection Your sincere friend & humble servt.

H. KNOX

ALS (MHi: Henry Knox Papers), draft.
1. Letters from Lafayette not identified.
2. William Knox went to Europe in 1781 on business.
3. Knox was one of the founders of the Society of the Cincinnati, which was established at a meeting of officers at Verplanck's House, near Fishkill, on May 13, 1783. The Society was to be an order to preserve the friendships established among the officers during the war and was intended also to raise funds for the widows and orphans of veterans. It took its name from Lucius Quintus Cincinnatus, who in 485 B.C. left his plow to lead Rome to victory against the Aequians and then, shunning further military and political power, returned to his farm. The French officers serving under French direction were to have an organization separate from the Americans.

Henry Knox, one of the founders of the Society of the Cincinnati.

To the Comte de Vergennes[T]

Paris, June 17, 1783

The American ministers have been to see you, Monsieur le Comte, and consequently I have nothing to say about their affairs. The mail brought me some letters from America, and I also suppose that you will have received some. In his letter of May 1, Mr. Livingston informs me of the public rejoicing at the news of a general peace; Congress was very pleased about what took place between the Spanish ministers and me. Prisoners have been exchanged, but the slowness in evacuating New York was beginning to cause displeasure, and General Washington was going to have an interview with General Carleton. The preliminary articles were ratified by Congress, and I am promised longer letters at the first opportunity.

Those from General Washington enclose fifty-four pages in which he sends me details about the army.[1] We have the same opinion about the necessity and the means of preserving union among the states. The army's affairs are taking a turn that does new honor to its virtue and patriotism. As soon as those affairs are put in order, the general will resume his private life. That, Monsieur le Comte, is the essence of my dispatches; I should also mention testimonies of attachment, respect, and gratitude to the king that General Washington expresses to me, and you would do me a great favor to be kind enough to tell the king of them.

The Americans seemed to be very tired of the war, and the news of peace was all the more pleasing. But if by misfortune it had been postponed, the general was preparing for a cooperative effort. The dissolution of the army will see the establishment of some commercial firms, and several officers are addressing themselves to me for advice. I am even expecting some of them to come here, and I very much want to have them establish connections with France.[2]

There is one point, Monsieur le Comte, on which I am often consulted, and I beg you to be kind enough to give me a ministerial answer. Under the denomination of free port, do you mean only a depot for American products with permission to reload them without duties? This would be far less than the notion the Americans have of it. Or is it, as they think, a port where all products of the realm, whether manufactured goods or raw materials, would come in without duties with a custom-house bond, like exports to the colonies, and once they have come in with the exemption, would be regarded as having come into a foreign country? Will the foreign raw materials or manufactured goods be admitted freely and without distinction into the free port, with permission to remain there if that is wished, to be sold and resold and change owners as often as desired, to be sent afterward to some completely different port without customs formalities? Meanwhile, of course, no article would go beyond the limits of the port except under the usual restrictions applicable in other parts of the realm. I ask you for this explanation, Monsieur le Comte, because I propose to communicate it to my friends so they can regulate their conduct by it.[3]

I ask your pardon for this long letter, Monsieur le Comte, and I beg you to give me news of your health. Accept the homage of my tender and respectful attachment.

LAFAYETTE

ALS (AAE: Correspondance politique, Etats-Unis, vol. 24, fols. 354–55), translation.
1. See Washington to Lafayette, April 5, 1783.
2. On July 17, 1783, Lafayette wrote letters to Vergennes and his cousin Lefèvre d'Ormesson, the minister of finance (AAE: Correspondance politique, Etats-Unis, vol. 25, fols. 46–47) introducing Matthias Ogden, who had been in Lafayette's Light Division (see *LAAR*, 3:173). Ogden, in partnership with other officers, hoped to establish trade connections with France, and Lafayette secured an invitation for him to a reception for Louis XVI (New Jersey Historical Society, *Collections*, 13 [1964]:151).
3. See Vergennes's definition in his letter to Lafayette, June 29, 1783.

From the Comte de Vergennes[T]

Versailles, June 29, 1783

I received, Monsieur, the letter you did me the honor of writing me on the seventeenth of this month. You want to know what is meant by free port.

We mean by this designation, Monsieur, a place where all merchandise, domestic as well as foreign, can be imported and from which it can be exported freely. You will understand from this definition, Monsieur, that all the merchandise from the north, without exception, can be imported into Lorient and exported without difficulty by the Americans. In short, as far as trade is concerned, Lorient will be considered foreign territory with respect to France. The prohibitions and duties established for foreign merchandise will not apply except in the case in which one wants to send foreign merchandise, subject to such duties or prohibitions, into the interior of the realm.

L (AAE: Correspondance politique, Etats-Unis, vol. 24, fol. 411), draft, translation.

To Henry Laurens

Paris July the 6th 1783

Dear Sir

I Have Been Honoured With Your kind letter for Which I offer You My Best thanks.[1] I Hope You May,find Some Benefit In Drinking Bath Waters, and the Pleasure of Your Correspondance Will Be Extremely Agreable. By your Colleagues You Will no doubt Be Acquainted With the Arrival of the Washington Packet. She Had a fine Passage and Carried over the Ratification of the Preliminaries. Our Intelligences Are Not, However, Quite Compleat, And the french Ship, Triumph, Must Now Be on Her Way to France. It Appears Mr. Lewingston Had a Mind to Resign, But Robert Moriss Had Determined to Remain in office, at Least Untill Many Arrangements Are Settled.[2] The Army Have Been Sent Home Upon furlough, and Will, they Say, Be Provided for at the time when the treaty Arrives. No Great Hurry, it Appears, in the Evacuation of Newyork. In Spite of the Preliminary Articles, they are Sending of[f] Negroes, Which infringement is Accounted for Upon this Principle, that When they Came within the British lines, it Was Promised them they Should Be Set free.[3] There is ten to one However those Men are Sent to West India Markets. General Washington Was Hearty and Happy, and I Have Been Warned that fuller intelligences Would Be Sent to me By the Triumph—So that I am waïting for Her. Nothing as Yet determined in the Diplomatic Line—So far I Can tell, But Have little trust on a letter that Must Be Delivered through So Many itching fingers in the Post offices.

Curious it is, My dear Sir, that Nothing Can Be Settled in the British Ministry. Since it Comes Round, the Pitt party Will Again Have their turn.[4] Who Ever Be there, it is Now So clear to them they Had Better Court the friendship of America, that Every Sensible Man, after a *Peace* is Effected, Will do His Best to obtain a *Reconciliation*—two very different things By the Way.

I Have Some days ago wrote to Mr. Knox and Doctor Bancroft, But as I do not Hear from them, I must give you a trouble which in Your present State of Health I wished to Avoid.[5] You know what Has past Betwen Sir Henry Clinton and Myself. Inclosed You will find My letter and His Answer, Both of which if it Has not Been Already done, I Beg You Will Have Printed in the Newspapers Under this Simple Head— *letter from the Mquis de Lafayette to Sir Henry Clinton*—and *Answer from Sir Henry Clinton to the Marquis*[6] But if Gal. Clinton is Near at Hand, I Beg

You Will pay Him a Compliment on the Occasion. He Cannot, I Should think Have Any objection to the Printing of those letters.

I Have a letter from Clel. Ogden who is just landed in France; and Notifies He Has dispatches to me.[7] In Case there is Any thing important I will do myself the Honor to Communicate My Intelligences. My little family are Well, and join With Mde. de Lafayette and Myself in presenting You, Miss Laurens, and Your Son With our Best Compliments. Adieu, My dear Sir, I Hope it is Needless for me to Assure You of the High Regard I Have the Honor to Be With very affectionately Dear Sir Your obedient Humble Servant

LAFAYETTE

ALS (ScHi: Henry Laurens Papers).
1. Laurens had written Lafayette from London on June 20, mentioning a recent crisis in the British government and informing Lafayette that he was leaving the next day for Bath (ScHi: Henry Laurens Papers).
2. Livingston resigned as secretary of foreign affairs in June 1783. Morris had told Congress in January that he would resign as superintendant of finance unless Congress took effective measures to establish substantial revenues by May (Morris to Congress, May 1 and 3, in Wharton, *Diplomatic Correspondence*, 6:399–403).
3. At Laurens's urging, the preliminary treaty between Britain and the United States called for the British to return all captured slaves to the Americans (David D. Wallace, *The Life of Henry Laurens*, [New York, 1915], p. 405). Sir Guy Carleton argued that the Negroes within British lines did not come under the provisions of the treaty because they had been freed by proclamations issued by the British officers under the authority of the king (substance of a conference between General Washington and Sir Guy Carleton, May 6, 1783, in Fitzpatrick, *Writings of Washington*, 26:402–5).
4. William Pitt the Younger and Lord Shelburne, the former prime minister, were in the opposition in Parliament.
5. Letters to William Knox and Edward Bancroft not found.
6. See Lafayette to Clinton, April 30, 1783, and note 2.
7. Letter not found.

To the President of Congress

Chavaniac in the Province of Auvergne
july the 20th 1783

Sir

Having Gone for Some days in the Country where I Was Waïting for the Arrival of the Triumph, I am Honoured With Your Excellency's favor of the 12th April which I Hasten to Aknowledge. It is for me a Great Happiness to think that Congress Have Been Pleased to Approuve My Conduct, and that an Early Intelligence Has Proved Useful to our American trade. To My Great Satisfaction I also Hear that My Endeavours in Spain Have Been Agreable to Congress.[1] Upon My

Arrival in Paris, I Made Mr. Jay Acquainted With My Proceedings and the Concessions I Had obtained from the Spanish Court (without Any on our Part) Where also Put into His Hands. Since Which I Could Have No More to Act in the Negotiation[s] wherein I Had taken the Part of a temporary Volonteer.

However Repeated May Have Been the Marks of Confidence Congress Have Conferred Upon me, they Ever fill up My Heart With a New Satisfaction. What You Have Mentionned Respecting Payement of Debts Will of Course Become My first, and Most Interesting Affair. I Have Warmly Applied to the french Ministry, and Will on that Point Sollicit the Confidence of the Gentlemen in the American Commission.[2] But upon Hearing of an opportunity, Could not an Instant differ to Aknowledge Your Excellency's letter. Agreable to the last dispatches, I am Waïting for the orders I Hope to Receive By the Triumph. Any Commands Congress May Have for me, Shall Be chearfully Executed By one of their Earliest Soldiers, Whose Happiness it is to think that at a less Smiling Moment He Had the Honour to Be Adopted By America, and Whose Blood Exertions, and Affection, Will in Her Good times, as they Have Been in Her Worse ones, Be Entirely at Her Service.

It Appears Russia is Determined Upon a turkish War, and Should they Give it Up Now, the Matter Would only Be Postponed. What Part the Emperor is to take, We Cannot at Present So Well determine. When Ever the Way is Oppened to me, I Endeavour to do that, Which May Prove Agreable to Congress, and Intend to keep them Acquainted With the Political Occurrences that May Happen. It is a pleasing Idea for me Now to think that Nothing Can derange our Glorious State of Liberty and Independance. Nothing, I Say, for I Hope Measures Will Be taken to Consolidate the foederal Union, and By those Means to defeat European Arts, and Insure Internal tranquillity. With the Highest Respect I Have the Honour to Be, Sir, Your Excellency's Most obedient Humble Servant

LAFAYETTE

P.S. Congress Have no doubt Received Accurate Accounts Respecting the affair of free ports. On My Arrival from Spain, I found that Baïonne and Dunkirk Had Been pitched upon and immediately Applied for L'Orient and Marseïlles.[3] L'Orient is By far the Most Agreable in the ocean, and We now Have got it. That Being done I again am applying for Bayonne that Has Some advantages, and Wish Congress would Send orders to Mr. Barklay. In the Mean while the More free ports we Have, the Better it is. That affair of free ports, the one Congress Have Recommended and the dispatches I am directed to Expect

By the Triumph Will determine the time, when, Having no More American Business Here, I may indulge my ardent desire to Return to the Beloved Shores of America.

LAFAYETTE

Congress know of the arrangement for Packet Vessels that Has Been proposed, where By they may Hear often from France. It is to take place in the Month of September.[4]

ALS (DNA: RG 360, PCC 156, pp. 352–55).

1. President of Congress Elias Boudinot, in his April 12 letter to Lafayette, thanked him for sending news of the signing of the provisional treaty. He also enclosed a copy of the April 10 congressional resolution approving Lafayette's continued stay in Europe (*JCC*, 24:234). Boudinot told Lafayette that the peace terms gave "universal satisfaction," except the lack of a time provision for American repayment of English commercial debts, which he hoped would be in the final treaty. He asked Lafayette to attend to this subject, which he feared might throw merchants back into the hands of their English creditors (Burnett, *Letters of Congress*, 7:135–36).

2. Lafayette wrote to the American Peace Commissioners on July 22, 1783, informing them that he had received instructions from Congress to attempt a postponement of British collection of American debts (MHi: Adams Papers). See also following letter.

3. On the free ports, see Lafayette to Vergennes, March 19, 1783.

4. The *arrêt du conseil* of June 28, 1783, established a regular packet service between France and America.

To the Comte de Vergennes[T]

Chavaniac, July 21, 1783

Upon returning here, Monsieur le Comte, I received letters from Congress dated April 12, and the president sends me a resolution approving my stay in Europe. But there is an important point with which Congress expressly charges me and upon which they direct me to apply to you. I do so with all the more confidence since through the inevitable consequences our trade is particularly involved in it.[1]

In drafting the preliminary articles, the American ministers did not fix any term for the payment of their debts to England. After a war such as this, in which some have been ruined, others have put everything into government bonds, and everyone has suffered from the depreciation of the paper currency, it is impossible for American merchants to pay their British debts immediately. They will need three or four years to do that, and their ministers will surely receive orders to this effect. But I should be very pleased, Monsieur le Comte, if they should be obliged to you also in this respect; the effect would be excellent in America. If they owe the reparation of this oversight to you, you will also render a great service to French trade. The impossibility of paying their debts will put American merchants in the hands of the British. One does not abandon a workman whose bill one cannot pay off, and if a clause on this subject is not added, the trade relationship that we want will suffer considerably.[2] Accept, I beg you, Monsieur le Comte, the tribute of my very warm and respectful regards.

LAFAYETTE

ALS (AAE: Correspondance politique, Etats-Unis, vol. 25, fol. 75), translation.
1. See preceding letter, note 1.
2. Vergennes replied on August 5 that it would be impossible to add a clause concerning repayment of the American merchants' debts. He explained that the British peace negotiator was authorized to make compromises in the interest of his king or his nation but had no power to interfere with individual rights governed by law (AAE: Correspondance politique, Etats-Unis, vol. 25, fol. 130).

To George Washington

Chavaniac in the Province of Auvergne

july the 22d. 1783

My dear General
    Your letter of the 10th of May is the Last one that Came Into My Hands for Which I Beg leave to offer You my Best thanks—and in Case former Answers do not Arrive, I Must Again tell you How Happy You made Your friend By Your letters Inclosing the Proceedings of the Army.[1] In Every instance, My dear General, I Have the Satisfaction to Love and to Admire You. The Conduct You Had on that Occasion Was Highly praised throughout all Europe, and Your Returning to a Private Station is Called the finishing Stroke to an Unparalleled Character. Never did a Man Exist Who So Honourably Stood in the Opinions of Mankind, and Your Name, if Possible, Will Become Still Greater in Posterity. Every thing that is Great, and Every thing that is Good Were not Hitherto United in one Man. Never did one Man live whom the Soldier, States man, Patriot, and Philosopher Could Equally Admire, and Never Was a Revolution Brought about, that in Its Motives, its Conduct, and its Consequences Could So Well Immortalize its Glorious Chief. I am proud of You, My dear General, Your Glory Makes me feel as if it Was My own—and While the World is Gaping at You, I am pleased to think, and to tell, the Qualities of Your Heart do Render You Still more Valuable than Any thing You Have done.
    Since My last, My dear General, I Have Received letters from Con-

gress, wherein I am directed to attend to a Particular Business Respecting the Payement of debts to Great Britain. I Have Immediately Applied to Count de Vergennes, and Will Endeavour, if not too late, to Succeed in that Important Affair. I Have Also writen to our American Ministers, and Upon that point Have Sollicited their Confidence.[2] Had they Spoken to me at the time of the Separate Preliminaries, the Matter Would Have Been Arranged to Mutual Satisfaction. It often Happens people do not Understand Each other, and Should they Be Brought to Right Again, they Hardly Could Be able to find out a Cause of Complaint. It Some times is the Case every where, and Some in the Commission Have Strong prejudices.[3] But it Would Be Improper for me to Give more than Private Hints. My Heart is So oppen to You, My dear General, that from You it is Impossible for me to Conceal Any thought.

Nothing New in Europe, But What Relates to the Russians and turks. The first Have Invaded the Krimée, preparations are Making Upon the Black Sea, and Russian Ships are Coming Round to the Meditarrean. The Expulsion of the turks from Europe Has Ever Been With Russia a favorite Scheme. It Appears Very Improbable to me, that We May Compromise Matters, in Which Case, an Attempt to that Revolution Would only Be differed. What Part the Emperor[4] Will take, is as Yet Very Uncertain, nor is it known what Prussia Will do about it. England is to Be Sure, determined to Stay Neutral, and Has not Much to do with Levant trade. As to France, She does not Wish to Quarrel With Any Body. Her desire is to prevent a Russian War, and it Appears She Will not do more, But What is Absolutely Necessary. Such, My dear General, is My private opinion of political Affairs in Europe.

It Had Been Said Mal. de Castries Would Resign—But Now for Certain He Remains in the Ministry. There Have Been New Disturbances in the British Cabinet. The definitive treaty is not Yet at an end. Its termination, the affair Recommended to me, the Arrival of the Triumph, and our Political Situation Will determine the Happy time When I Set Sails for America. In the Course of a fortnight, My dear General, I Hope to Be able to write You Very fully—But Hearing of an opportunity Could not let it Pass unnoticed. God grant, I May, Instead of writing Be Enabled to Come Myself. Adieu, My dear General, Mde. de Lafayette joins with me in Presenting our Best Respects to Mrs. Washington. She loves You With all Her Heart. My affectionate Compliments Waït Upon the family, George, and all our friends. Adieu, adieu, My dear General, Do often Remember Your Adopted Son, who With Every Sentiment of the Highest Respect and Warmest affection Has the Honour to Be Your obt. Hble. Servant and Most affectionate friend

LAFAYETTE

ALS (PEL: Hubbard Collection).

1. Washington's letter of May 10, 1783, is in Fitzpatrick, *Writings of Washington*, 26:420–22. Washington sent enclosures concerning the army in his letter to Lafayette of April 5, 1783 (above).

2. See Lafayette to Vergennes, July 21, 1783. Lafayette wrote the commissioners on July 22: "Knowing the Uneasiness of our American Merchants on that affair, I Cannot Help Partaking of it, and Would Consider it as a Great favor to Be acquainted With the Present Situation of things, and With the farther Measures You Might think Proper for me to Undertake" (MHi: Adams Papers). No reply from the commissioners has been found.

3. John Adams opposed any foreign interference with American negotiations, including Lafayette's. See Adams to James Warren, April 16, 1783.

4. Joseph II, Holy Roman emperor.

Address of Nobles of Langeac to Lafayette[T]

Sir,   [August 4, 1783]

The name of Lafayette, great in its origins, dear to the State, and spread through the annals of history, has just resounded gloriously in both hemispheres. It is you, Monsieur le Marquis, who, seconding the generous and beneficent views of the prince, fought against that arrogant and redoubtable insular people, the British, our enemies; you gave liberty to an oppressed people and attracted the attention of all Europe.

Gilbert de Motier de Lafayette, one of your ancestors, distinguished himself in the battle of Baugé, in Anjou. He contributed much to driving the British out of the realm and was made a *maréchal* of France.

Young and at an age when abilities barely declare themselves, heir of the hero's hatred against the enemies of the State, you applied yourself to following in his footsteps; your first campaigns were marked by the most valiant exploits, as witness Cornwallis, and already your glory has surpassed his. What dignity is not promised you by a valor so precocious and glittering?

You excited the admiration and gratitude of the French. The Auvergnats are indebted to you for the honor you do them, and especially those of us who have the honor of being your neighbor.

Also, all were eager to show you how pleased they are to see you and to render you the most respectful and deserved homage.

We did not have the honor of being the first, but our sentiments for and attachment to you are no less keen or respectful.

Please deign, Monsieur le Marquis, to accept the wine this town has the honor of offering you, in consideration of your birth and your merit; deign further to be persuaded that, if circumstances permit, it will be infinitely flattered to belong to you through its possessions, as it is yours in its heart.[1]

From Henry Mosnier, *Le Château de Chavaniac* (Le Puy, 1883), pp. 24–25, translated.
1. The feudal rights of the marquisate of Langeac, one of the most important seigneuries of Auvergne, were for sale at the time. Lafayette bought the marquisate in 1786. Traditionally, the *vin d'honneur* is offered by a municipality to a person of rank or newly elected official as a mark of its esteem.

To the President of Congress

Nancy September the 7th 1783

Sir

In Consequence of the Late Arrangements, the french September Packet is Going to Sail, and I Beg Your Excellency's Leave to Improve that Regular, Speedy, and Safe Opportunity. At the Same time, Congress Will Receive a definitive treaty Which So far as I may judge, is Very Similar With the Provisional Articles.[1] But Upon this Point, Since I Left Madrid, My Services Have not Been Wanting. From our Commissioners Congress Will of Course Receive Better Informations. This one object I must However Mention Which Respects American Debts. So Soon as I knew the Wishes of Congress, I did, as Ever I Shall in Such a Case, Earnestly Apply to the french Ministry And the American Commissioners—But Was Answered it Could not Be done and did not Even Consist With the Powers of the British Ministry—After Which, and at that time of the Negotiation, I Had no Means to Improve the Hint I Had Received from Your Excellency.[2]

As to Mercantile Affairs in France, Mr. Barklay Will Acquaint Congress With their Present Situation. Bayonne and Dunkirk Having Been Pointed out as American free Ports, and the opinion of Congress Not Being known, I took Upon Myself to Represent the Harbour of L'Orient Was preferable to either of those Above Mentioned. It Has Lately Been Made a free Port, and I Now Wish the Affair of Bayonne May Be Again taken Up. Those three Ports, With Marseïlles, Would Make a Very Proper Chain, and in the Mean while I Hope L'Orient Will Prove Agreable to the American Merchants.

There Now Exist in this kingdom Many obstacles to trade Which, I Hope, By little and little Will Be Eradicated, and from the Great Natural Advantages of this Country Over England, it Will of Course Result that a french trade, Generally Speaking, Must prove More Beneficial to

America. Upon Many Articles of American Produce, I Wish Preferences May Be obtained from this Governement, and Besides Commercial Benefits in Europe, Your Excellency feels that West India Arrangements Cannot Easely Be Adjusted With European Notions and Present
Costoms. Upon those objects, Mr. Barklay Had, and Again Will Have
Conferences With the Ministers. Circumstanced as We Now are, He is,
and the Commissioners also are, of opinion, that My Presence in France May Be Serviceable. As He Was pleased to Apply to me on the
Subject, Saying He Would Mention the Matter to Congress, and as
their orders I Was to Expect Have not Yet Reached me, I think it My
Present Duty, and it Ever Shall Be My Rule, to Do that In Which I
Hope to Serve the United States.[3]

Warlike Preparations are Still Going on in the Eastward. Immediately after She Had Signed a Commercial treaty with the turks, it Has
Pleased the Empress of Russia to Seize Upon the Krimée Under a
frivolous Pretence.[4] Her Armies are Ready to take the field, Stores and
troops Have Been Collected Upon the Borders of the Black Sea, and
the turks are Making Immense, But I think, Not Very formidable
Preparations. By our Last Accounts the Austrians Were Gathering
Upon those Limits of theirs Which Lead towards an Invasion of turkish
Provinces, and it is thought By Many, that for fear of the Plague, the
two Imperial Powers Will prefer Winter Operations. How far Matters
May Be Carried, or Compromised Cannot Yet Be Well determined.
What Part France, Prussia, and England Will take is Not Yet known.
The Levant trade Cannot But Be Interested in the Affair.

In Every American Concern, Sir, My Motives are So Pure, My Sentiments So Candid, My Attachement So Warm, So Long Experienced,
that from Such a Heart as Mine, Nothing, I Hope, Will Appear Intrud-
ing or Improper. Upon Many Points lately Debated, My opinions, if
Worth a Remark, are Well and Generally known, But I Must frankly
Add that the Effect Some Late transactions Have Upon European
Minds Cannot But Make me Uneasy.[5] In the Difficulties Which a Patriotic, and Deserving Army Have Met With, Europeans Have Been
Misled to See a Want of Public Gratitude. In the Opinions that Have
from Every Quarter Been Started, Europeans Have, I also Hope, Mistaken Partial Notions for a Want of Disposition to the foederal Union—
and Without that Union, Sir, the United States Cannot Preserve that
Dignity, that Vigour, that Power, Which Insures the Glory, the Happiness of a Great, liberal, and Independant Nation.[6] Nay, it would Become our ill fate, of us Who Have Worked, fought, and Bled in this
Cause, to See the United States a prey to the Snares of European
Politics. But I am only Mentioning the opinions of Many on this Side of
the Water, and In My Heart I Hope Every think Will Be Adjusted to

the Satisfaction of that part of the Citizens Who Have Served in the Army, and that other Part in the Civil line who During the War Have Simpathised With their troops. I, above all, Earnestly Hope, and Most fervently Pray, the Ennemies of liberty, or Such as are jealous of America, May not Have the Pleasure to See us deviate from the Principles of the foederal Union—and Upon a Recollection of My Introductory Apology, I Hope the observations I Humbly offer, will Be as kindly Received, as they are Respectfully and Affectionately Presented.

When it is thought My presence Here Can Be Dispensed With, or in Case the Situation of Affairs did persuade me it is More Useful in America, I Will not Wait for Any thing else to join a Wished for and Beloved Shore. Any orders, either to Come or to Stay, to do Such, or Such thing, in a Word Any Communi[cation] Whatever Congress are pleased to Give me, I shall Most chearfully Gratify Both duty and Inclination in obeying them, and As Every Moment in My Life is Devoted to love and Respect, So Will the Happiest Among them Be Employed to Serve the United States. With Every Sentiment of an Affectionate Regard I Have the Honour to Be Sir Your Excellency's Most obedient Humble Servant

LAFAYETTE

ALS (DNA: RG 360, PCC 156, pp. 356–63). The president of Congress was Elias Boudinot.

1. Unable to agree on additional commercial articles, David Hartley and the American commissioners signed the preliminary articles as the definitive treaty on September 3, 1783.

2. For Vergennes's letter, see Lafayette to Vergennes, July 21, 1783, note 2.

3. Thomas Barclay wrote to Robert Livingston on September 14:
. . . the Marquis de La Fayette, who is now in Lorain, thought proper some time ago to consult me on the propriety of his immediately Embarking for America. He seem'd much at a loss upon the Subject as on the one hand he suppos'd that he might be very usefull here as the Court of France seems determin'd on adopting some Commercial regulations respecting the Trade to be carried on between the United States and their West India Colonies. Upon considering the matter I did not hesitate to give the Marquis my opinion that it woud be best for him to remain in France, either untill he received the Command of Congress to return or untill the necessity of his going to America wou'd be more apparent. [DNA: RG 360, PCC 137, Appendix, pp. 309–11]

4. In a proclamation dated April 8 O.S. (April 19) and made public on July 21, Russian empress Catherine II officially annexed the Tauride Peninsula, citing the need for peace and security on the border. Russia and Turkey had just concluded a commercial treaty at Constantinople on June 21, ensuring Russia free navigation of the Black Sea.

5. This was a reference to the Newburgh Affair.

6. French concern for the stability of the American union had recently been exacerbated by the appearance of the text of Thomas Paine's *Crisis* no. 13 in the August 16 *Mercure de France*. There Paine had urged his readers to recognize that "that which must more forcibly strike a thoughtful, penetrating mind, and which includes and renders easy all inferior concerns, is the UNION OF THE STATES. On this our national character depends" (Philip S. Foner, ed., *The Life and Major Writings of Thomas Paine* [New York, 1945], p. 233).

To George Washington

Nancy September the 8th 1783

My Dear General

Your Wished for and Most Heartly Wellcome favours Have not this long While Reached me, and I Most Warmly Request You, My dear General, not to forget writing to a friend who Loves you With a filial and Unbounded affection. This letter is Going By the September Packet, and Here after there Will Be one Sailing Every Month, By Which, While in Europe, I Shall Most Exactly Adress My dear and Respected General. Along With My Dispatches, You Will Receive the definitive treaty. Since I Have Returned from Spain (which Affair By the Bye Has Been too Much Neglected) I Was not Much Consulted Upon Politics By the Commissionners. What I know of the Subject is, that After Many Earnest, and long delade [delayed] Hopes to get Much from England in definitive and Commercial Arrangements, the last Answer Has Been that the preliminary Articles Were Sufficient to Make up a definitive treaty.

Inclosed, My dear General, You Will find a Copy of My letter to Congress Where By You May judge Both of the Political Situation of Affairs, and of the Mercantile American Concerns, that for the present Detain me In Europe.[1] As to the first My Private Opinion is that a War Betwen the Russians and turks is Unavoidable—that the Emperor Will take a Part in it, and that Much depends Upon the king's of Prussia Determination to Become Either an Opponent or Partaker to the Division of the Ottoman European Provinces. As to France, the Revolution Cannot But Greatly Hurt Her trade, But if She Can Help it She Will Not Middle With those Wars. England is Much Embarassed in Her finances, But tho' She May loose a little, Will Rejoice at Every Event Which affects France With a greater loss. Such at least is My Private opinion in this Affair.

As to the American trade, it Has Been Represented that My presence Here Might Serve the United States, and to me, that Consideration Shall Ever Be a determining one. I Hope My Dear General Will Approuve My Conduct, Which Approbation, I Confess, in Every Instance Will Ever Prove Necessary to My Happiness and Self Satisfaction. But I Greave to Be so long from You, Such a distance, Such an Interval of time Cannot Agree With the tender feelings of a Heart Who Had taken the Happy Habit to live in Your family, Among My American friends, who, in Any Part of the World, never felt Himself So much at Home, as

Elias Boudinot IV, painted by Charles Willson Peale, can be seen holding the preliminaries to peace with Great Britain, which he signed during his tenure as president of Congress.

When He Was at Head Quarters. Untill I Return to America, My dear General, Untill I See You, and our fellow Supporters of our Noble Cause, My Mind Cannot Be properly Easy, and Every Mention, Every Rememberance of America Makes me Sigh for the Moment When I May Enjoy the Sight of our free and Independant Shores.

Many Months Ago, My dear General, I did Myself the Honour to write You on the Subject of the Bust the Assembly of Virginia Have Voted.[2] Not knowing if My thanks Ever Reached them, But knowing You Have Mentionned them My Uncertainty, I don't think I Can do Any thing further on the Subject, as it Would not Become me to Send to the Assembly House, (and to keep for me a Copy of) the Bust Which they Have Been pleased to Adorn With Honourable Inscriptions—So that I imagine Some Minister Here Will Be charged With the direction of that Monument of their Satisfaction, Which, I Confess, fills my Heart With a pleasing Sense of pride and Gratitude.

From My letters to Congress, You Will See I am Asking for their orders. While in Europe, I think I May Serve them in the Way of Information and Advice—the More So, if they Confine themselves to the Sending of Consuls. I may also on other Accounts prove Useful, but I must Anew Receive direct orders from them to that purpose. Never Shall I more glory, and Better Enjoy Myself than in the title of an Essential Servant to the United States.

By the Next packet, My dear General, I Will tell you what Commercial Arrangements Have taken place, and also What are My own Motions. But Should I Receive the least Hint, or See Myself that, By the Situation of affairs, Every Good Man's influence is Wanting upon the Spot, then, My dear General, No Public Affair (for My own are out of the Question) No Season of the Year, no Impediment in the World Can prevent My flying to a Beloved Country whose Happiness, Glory, and liberty, are dearer to me than my own life.

Your Circular letter, My dear General, as well as Your Modest Retirement, Have Had the Universal Applause of Europe—and My Heart Has Been a Partaker in the Glory of My dear General from whom Every thing that is Great and Good So Naturally flows that it gives a good grace to His Heroïc Actions.[3]

Should you think of Coming to Europe, of Seeing a Country where Your Name is Adored, I Need not tell you What Unexpressible Happiness I Would feel in Receiving You Under My Roof, in Making My House Yours, as Yours Has Been and for Ever I Hope Will Be Mine, and I flatter Myself I would know it timely Enough Not to Embark Myself in any journey, or Voyage to America, that Might Prevent the Happiness I Would derive from Your friendly, and thousand times Wellcome Visit.

Mde. de Lafayette and My three Children are Well and all the family join in their Respectfull and Affectionate Compliments to You and Mrs. Washington Whom I Beg You Will Present With My Most tender Respects. Tell Her She ought to Pay us a Visit Along with You, and to Come in Compagny With Her Grand Children. My affectionate Compliments waït Upon George, all the family, and all our friends. Please to Remember me to Mr. and Mrs. Lund Washington and to the Young lady.4

It is Said in England Your Retirement is Owing to Ambitious Wiews, and that You Intend Soon to Appear Again Upon the Stage. Adieu, My Dear General, My Heart is So well known to You that I Need not telling You How tenderly How Respectfully I shall Ever Be Untill My last Breath, My dear General Your Most obedient Humble Servant and Most Obliged Affectionate friend

LAFAYETTE

Our ideas Respecting the foederal Union and the Army So Much Coincide With Each other, that Nothing Needs Being Said Betwen us Upon those Important Matters.

ALS (PEL: Hubbard Collection), enclosing a copy of Lafayette to Congress, September 7, 1783.
   1. See preceding letter.
   2. Letter not found; see Washington to Lafayette, January 4, 1782, note 3.
   3. Lafayette was profoundly affected by Washington's circular letter to the states of June 1783, which read in part:
      The great object for which I had the honour to hold an appointment in the Service of my Country, being accomplished, I am now preparing to resign it into the hands of Congress, and to return to that domestic retirement, which it is well known, I left with the greatest reluctance. . . .
         . . . according to the system of Policy the States shall adopt at this moment, they will stand or fall, and by their confirmation or lapse, it is yet to be decided, whether the Revolution must ultimately be considered as a blessing or a curse: a blessing or a curse, not to the present age alone, for with our fate will the destiny of unborn Millions be involved. [Fitzpatrick, *Writings of Washington,* 26:483–96]
   The text of the letter appeared in French in the August 30 and September 6 issues of the *Mercure de France,* and in German in the Viennese *Historisches Portefeuille zur Kenntnis* . . . (2:385–404).
   4. Probably Eleanor ("Nellie") Parke Custis.

To Jeremiah Wadsworth

Nancy September the 28h. 1783

My dear friend

   With Infinite Satisfaction I Hear of Your Safe Arrival in Paris, and Now I long for the Moment When I Can Most Cordially Embrace, and Wellcome You in My House. My friendship to You, My dear Sir, I

Hope I Need not telling You Any thing about—therefore Shall Content Myself to Say I am Very Sorry I Cannot Immediately Set out to Paris—But am Nailed to this place By the Illness of an Intimate friend, Who Has Been at the point of death, and to whom, at the Present Period, My absence Would do infinite Harm[1]—But in a few days, I Hope to Be at liberty, and then Instead of Pursuing a journey I Had Intended to Flanders, I Shall Set out to Paris, Where I Hope to Be at the End of the Week, and where the pleasure to See you, and Mr. and Mrs. Carter will Be felt By me With Unexpressible Satisfaction.

In the Mean while, My dear Sir, Be pleased to Consider my House as Being Your own. Mde. de Lafayette will Be Happy to See You, and I Hope You will not think to Stand Upon Ceremonies with the family of Your Intimate friend. By a letter from Schuyller, I Hear of the Errand You are Upon, and to Begin the Business I Send You letters to the Several Ministers.[2] With Every Sentiment of Affection and Regard I Have the Honour to Be, My dear Sir Yours Most Sincerely

LAFAYETTE

ALS (Ct: Governor Joseph Trumbull Collection).

1. This was Roger de Damas, brother of Mme de Simiane (Lafayette to Adrienne, September 8, 1783, ALG, courtesy of the Comte de Chambrun).

2. The letter from Philip Schuyler has not been found, but it may have referred to Wadsworth and Carter's scheme to buy the monopoly rights to supply the Farmers General with American tobacco. Lafayette's letters to the French ministers not found.

From George Washington

Princeton 12th. Octor. 1783

My Dear Marqs.

While I thought there was a probability of my letters finding you in France, I wrote frequently to you there; and very long epistles too. My last was dated the 15h. of June. Between that, & the letter which must have been handed to you by the Chevr. Chartellux, I addressed three others, under the following dates—March 23d—April 5h.—& May 10h.[1] Subsequent to these I have been honored with your favor of the 19h. of April dated at the seat of the Marqs. de Castries; & of three more in June, recommendatory of Doct: Bancroft, Monsr. de Baune, and the Count Wengiezski.[2]

I should not have remained silent so long, had I not been in daily expectation of seeing you in this Country. The event My Dr. Marqs. which seems (by your last letters) to have been in some degree a let to this pleasure, will not I apprehend, ever take place. The late Secretary of foreign affairs (for at present there is none) with whom I have conversed confidentially on the subject of your wishes, as they are expressed in your favor of the 4h. of February, thinks, high as you really stand in the good opinion of Congress, & however great their inclination is to comply with your wishes, in almost every thing; yet, in *such a case as that,* it would be impracticable to obtain it, & for that reason impolitic to attempt it. Lest *he* should not have communicated these sentiments to you, motives of friendship have prompted me to do it without reserve.[3] To add after giving this information, how much it is my wish to see you in a Country which owes so much to your important services in the Cabinet, and in the Field; & how happy you would make your friends at Mount Vernon by considering that place as your home, would only be to repeat, what I persuade myself, you have long ago been convinced of: nevertheless, I cannot forbear urging it.

With anxious expectation we have been upon the lookout, day after day these four months for the arrival of the Definitive Treaty of peace. In equal expectation have we been the last two of the evacuation of New York by the British forces. On the happening of either of these events, I have placed my retirement to the walks of private life, & look forward to the epoch with heart-felt satisfaction: Till I get home & have time to look into the situation of my private concerns, which I already know are in a deranged state, & very much impaired, I can form no plan for my future life. I have it in contemplation, however to make a tour thro' all the Eastern States—thence into Canada—thence up the St. Lawrence, & thro' the Lakes to Detroit—thence to lake Michigan by land or water—thence thro' the western Country, by the river Illinois, to the river Mississippi, & down the same to New Orleans—thence into Georgia by the way of Pensacola; & thence thro' the two Carolina's home. A great tour this, you will say—probably it may take place no where but in imagination, tho' it is my *wish* to begin it in the latter end of April of next year; if it should be realized, there would be nothing wanting to make it perfectly agreeable, but your Company.

Congress have fixed upon the falls of Delaware for the residence of the sovereign power of these United States, & 'till a proper establishment can be made at it, & accomodations provided, they will hold their Sessions at ———.[4] By their desire I shall remain with them, 'till one of the events already mentioned takes place, & then shall bid a final adieu to public life.

I hope the Russians & Turks will accommodate their differences. I wish it from motives of universal benevolence, which I should be glad to see as extensive as the great Globe itself. And I wish it also, because the flames of War once kindled may draw in one power after another, 'till the regions most remote may feel the effects of it.

The Dutch Minister, after a passage of near 16 weeks, is just arrived at Philadelphia.[5] Many foreigners are already come over to that &

other places; some in the mercantile line—some to make the tour of the Continent—and some (employed) no doubt to spy out the Land, & to make observations upon the temper and disposition of its Inhabitants—their Laws, policy &ca.

No Peace establishment is yet agreed on by Congress—but the opposition which was given by the Eastern States to the half pay, or commutation of it for the officers, is begining to subside; it is to be hoped that every thing will soon go right, & that the people will get into a proper tone of thinking again.

Mrs. Washington left me a few days ago for Virginia (before the weather & roads shou'd get bad). Otherwise I am sure she would unite most cordially with me in respectful compliments to Madame La Fayette, & congratulations on the passage of my namesake, thro' the small-pox.[6] With every wish for your & her happiness—& with the most sincere friendship I am, My Dr. Marquis Your affecte. Servant

G. WASHINGTON

LbC (DLC: George Washington Papers, Series 2).

1. Washington's letters of March 23, April 5, and June 15, 1783, appear above. The letter carried by Chastellux (December 15, 1782) and that of May 10, 1783, are in Fitzpatrick, *Writings of Washington*, 25:433–35, 26:420–22.

2. Letter of April 19, above. Lafayette's letters of May 18, June 10, and June 12, introducing Wengiezski, Bancroft, and Beaune, are in Gottschalk, *Letters of Lafayette*, pp. 263, 265.

3. See Lafayette's letter to Washington, February 5, 1783.

4. At the bottom of the page, Washington noted for this point in the letter: "No place yet agreed on."

5. Congress formally received Pieter Johan van Berckel, the minister to the United States from the United Provinces of the Netherlands, on October 31, 1783.

6. On George-Washington Lafayette's innoculation, see Lafayette to Washington, June 10.

To Benjamin Franklin

Paris Monday Morning [October 20, 1783]

My Dear Sir

The famous William Pitt is just Arrived in Paris, and is Just Returning to London.[1] He Has Expressed a warm desire to Get Acquainted With You, and As I Hoped You Would Come to day to the American dinner, I Have Invited Him together With Lord Camden's, Duke of Grafton's Sons, and two other of His friends.[2] It is Possible You will Be Glad to know a Young Man Whose Abilities and Circumstances are So Uncommon—So that, Unless the Going Very Gently in a Carriage Hurts you, You will do me an Extreme pleasure to Dine With us, as You are the Center Upon Which Moves the Whole Party. But I Would not Have You do Yourself Any Harm on that Account. Most Respectfully and Affectionately Yours

LAFAYETTE

ALS (PPAmP: Franklin Papers, vol. 42, no. 140).
1. William Pitt, traveling in France with his friends James Edward Eliot and William Wilberforce, was called back to London unexpectedly to attend to state matters.
2. George Henry Fitzroy, Earl of Euston and son of the Duke of Grafton, was a member of Parliament for Thetford and friend of Pitt; John Jeffries Pratt was also one of Pitt's particular friends.

From George Washington

20. Octr. 83 Rocky Hill

Sir

I do myself the honor to transmit you herewith a Copy of the Institution of the Cincinnati a society formed by the American Officers before they seperated and Retired to private life.

The principles of the society the purposes for which it was formed and the qualifications necessary to become Members will fully appear by the Institution.[1] Should any of the Foreign Officers who are qualified by serving three Years in our Army wish to become Members, I must take the liberty to Request you to let them sign the Institution and pay the necessary sum into your hands.

Major L'Enfant who will have the honor to deliver you this, has undertaken to get the Order[2] of the society executed in France. He has directions to deliver you one of the first that are compleated, and you will please also to call on him for as many more as you may want. Maj. L'Enfant will inform you the price of them. The Diplomas shall be forwarded as soon as they can be made out. I am &c.

L (Anderson House Museum, The Society of the Cincinnati, Washington, D.C.), draft; enclosing a copy of the Institutions of the Society of the Cincinnati.
1. The Society of the Cincinnati was formed to perpetuate the memory of the war and the friendships formed among the officers. Hereditary memberships that would pass to the eldest son were open to all officers of the American army who had served three years or until the end of the war. The institution also allowed for honorary memberships and for the membership of officers who served in the French forces in America.
2. I.e., the badge.

To [Mme de Simiane?][T]

Paris, Tuesday morning October 21, 1783

... My dinner yesterday was a great success, Mr. Pitt had the support of five Englishmen, and there were a dozen rebels including the ladies.[1] After talking a bit about public affairs, Mr. Pitt left for London and left me very satisfied with his intellect, his modesty, his nobility, and a character as interesting as the role for which his position destines him. The attack in Parliament prevents him from coming to Paris, and he claims that as long as England remains a monarchy, one can scarcely expect to see me in London. Despite this joking, I would really like to go there someday. I shall pay little court to the king. I shall be saved by the Opposition. Since we won the match, I admit I take extreme pleasure in seeing the British. The humiliation of the war before last and their insolence during peacetime gave me a feeling of aversion toward them that only grew with the horrors with which they defiled America, and the association of their name with the word "tyranny" became unpleasantly habitual to my ears. But now I see them with pleasure, and whether as a Frenchman or as an American soldier or even as a private individual I find myself without embarrassment in the midst of this proud nation. My conversion, however, is not so complete that on all occasions I do not do them what harm I can. Though I am not so fatuous as to treat them as personal enemies, it is enough for me that they are enemies of the glory and prosperity of France, for in the matter of patriotism I can *shock* the public, as it is said I have done in the matter of sensibility.

L (NIC: Dean Collection), extract in the hand of Emilie de Tracy de Lafayette, translation. This letter was published under the date of [Oct. 1786] in Lafayette, *Mémoires*, 2:160–61, but was certainly written after the dinner with Pitt on October 20, 1783.

1. For four of the Englishmen with Pitt, see Lafayette to Franklin, October 20, 1783; one Englishman is unidentified. Wilberforce wrote of the dinner in his diary: "Dine Marquis de la Fayette's pleasing enthusiastical man: his wife a sweet woman. Dr. Franklin, Mr. Page [Littlepage?], Crillon's aid du Camp, young Franklin, Noailles, Madame Boufflers there. Free the Spanish Colonies" (R. I. and S. Wilberforce, *The Life of William Wilberforce* [London, 1838], 1:44).

The freeing of the Spanish colonies was probably the topic of conversation that dominated the evening. Neither Adams nor Jay was present; both were en route to England.

From George Washington

Princeton 30h. Octor. 1783

My Dr. Marqs.

As I persuade myself it would rather give you pain than pleasure, were I to apologize for any liberty I might take with you, which does not exceed the rules of propriety & friendship—I shall proceed without further hesitation or ceremony to beg the favor of you to send me of the plated wares (or what formerly used to be called French plate) the articles contained in the enclosed memorandm. to which, as I am not much of a connoisseur in, & trouble my head very little about these matters, you may add any thing else of the like kind which may be thought useful & ornamental, except Dishes, plates & Spoons—of the two first I am not inclined to possess any, & of the latter I have a sufficiency of every kind.

I shall esteem it a very particular favor if you would let me have these things as soon as possible, by the first Vessel which may sail after they are ready either to Alexandria, Baltimore, Philadelphia or New York. The last, on account of the Packets which are to sail twice in every month, might be the readiest conveyance to this Country, tho' it would not be so convenient for me afterwards. Nevertheless, (as I am desirous of getting the Plate, as soon as may be) I would rather have them sent to that place than wait for a conveyance to either of the others.

If you shou'd send these things to New York, be so good as to address them to Jacob Morris Esqr. (who now lives there) with a request that they may be forwarded to me by the stage, or any other ready & quick conveyance to Alexandria—or if this cannot be, then to hand them on to Colo. Biddle at Phila. who will, I am persuaded convey them from thence to me; as he would also do, if they should be sent to that place in the first instance directed to his care, by a Vessel bound to that Port. If they should be sent to Baltimore be pleased to direct them to the care of Colo. Tilghman, if there, or Saml. Purviance Esqr., if he is not.

I have not My Dr. Marqs. sent by this conveyance, money for the purchase of these articles: the reason is, I am altogether unacquainted with the prices of them—but a bill shall be remitted to you the moment I am informed of the cost; in the mean while I am sure you will have no hesitation in becoming responsible to the workman for the payment.

Altho' I promised not to apologise for giving you trouble in these matters, yet I cannot forbear assigning my reasons for doing it in this particular instance.

1st. then, because I do not incline to send to England (from whence formerly I had all my Goods) for any thing I can get upon tolerable terms elsewhere.

3d. [2d.] Because I have no correspondence with any Merchants or artisans in France.

3d. If I had, I might not be able to explain so well to them, as to you, my wants, who know our customs, taste & manner of living in America—and 4th. Because I should rely much more upon your judgment & endeavours to prevent impositions upon me, both in the price & workmanship, than on those of a stranger.

I have only to wish, in the last place, that they may be packed in a proper (permanent) case, that will bear tra[n]sportation in the first instance, & will be a proper repository afterwards when not in use, if it shou'd be found more co[n]venient to keep them there. With best respects to Madame La Fayette I am, &ca. &c.[1]

G.W_____N

A List of plated Ware to be sent to General Washington, by the Marqs. de la Fayette Vizt.

Every thing proper for a tea-table—& these it is supposed may consist of the following Articles—A Large Tea salver, square or round as shall be most fashionable; to stand on the Tea-table for the purpose of holding the Urn, teapot, Coffeepot Cream pot, china cups & saucers &ca.

A large Tea-Urn, or receptacle for the water which is to supply the tea pot, *at the table.*

2 large Tea pots—& stands for Ditto.

1 Coffee-Pot—& stand.

1 Cream Pot.

1 Boat or Tray, for the Teaspoons.

1 Tea-Chest—such as usually appertains to tea or breakfast tables—the inner part of which, to have three departments—two for tea's of different kinds—the other for Sugar.

If any thing else should be judged necessary it may be added, altho' it is not enumerated.

Also,

Two large Salvers, sufficient to hold twelve common wine glasses, each.

Two smaller-size Do. for 6 wine glasses, each.

Two bread-baskets—middle size.

A Sett of Casters—for holding, oil, Vinegar, Mustard &c.

A Cross or Stand for the centre of the Dining table.

12 Salts, with glasses in them.

Eight Bottle sliders.

Six large Goblets, for Porter.

Twelve Candlesticks.

Three pair of snuffers, & Stands for them.

And any thing else which may be deemed necessary, in this way. If this kind of plated Ware will bear engraving, I should be glad to have my arms thereon; the size of which will, it is to be presumed be large or small in proportion to the piece on which it is engraved.

G. W_____N

LbC (DLC: George Washington Papers, Series 2).

1. On December 4, 1783, Washington canceled his order for plated ware; he had been able to obtain some in New York City after the British evacuation. Washington's countermand was too late; Lafayette had already sent the items Washington requested. In a

letter of April 4, 1784, Washington acknowledged receipt of the plated ware and promised to reimburse him for the expense (Fitzpatrick, *Writings of Washington*, 27:258–59, 384).

To George Washington

Paris November the 11th 1783

My Dear General

However Scarce are American letters, yet as the Eyes of the World Are fixed upon you, I Now and then Hear what Becomes of My dear General. Your Visit to Congress,[1] Your Stay With the Army Untill the treaty Arrives, Your Having Been Voted a Statue,[2] are Events which Are known to Every one, and felt By me, So that what to Europe is an Information, to me proves to Be a Cause for the Most tender Emotions. But Now, My dear General, that You Are Enjoying the Sweets of Retirement, I Hope Your Absent friend Will Be Some what Benefited By it, and Your Letters Cannot But Be More Numerous than it Was possible to Have them in Your Busy times. The convenience of those packets is peculiarly precious to Me, and I Earnestly Beg You Will Every time Enable me to Bless the opportunity.

The Gazette I Have to Present, My dear General, is not Very interesting. Ottoman disputes Appear for a while to Be at an End. Russia Will keep what She Has Got. The Emperor Stands Ready, But Will not Move for the present. As to the turks, lucky they are Not to Be Attacked, for their Armies Cut a Bad figure.[3] The king of Prussia is quarrelling With Dantzick that He May Have an Opportunity to take Hold of that City.[4] Spain Has made a Ridiculous Bombardement of Alger, for which Every Body, and the Algerians too Have Laughed at Her.[5] France is Exerting Herself to Preserve Good Harmony in the East Ward, and for the Present Count de Vergennes Seems to Have Well Succeeded. As to England, She is much Engaged in Disputes With Ireland, and Very jealous of the Irish Volonteer Assossiation.[6]

M. d'Ormesson the french financeer is out of place, and in lieu of Him a M. de Calonne Has Been Named.[7] The queen Was lately pregnant, But Has Had a Miscarriage. Such are the present News at the Court of France.

My last letter from America is dated August the 20th.[8] The place of Residence for Congress Had not Been yet fixed Upon. I Hope, My dear General, your letter to the States Will Have a Good effect.[9] The More I think of it, the More I Examine European Notions, the Better

Terra cotta bust of Washington, which the sculptor Houdon left behind at Mount Vernon when he returned to Paris to execute a life-size statue of the general.

Am I Convinced that American Glory, Consequence, Wealth, and liberty depend Upon a tight Well framed foederal Union. At the Same time, it is to Be Hoped our Virtous Army Will not Meet with Ungratefull Proceedings. Every Honest Breast, Unless greatly Misled, must Be Shocked at the Idea. I am Very Impatient to Hear what Has Been done. In the Mean while, I am Collecting the Opinions of Every American Merchant Within My Reach—And My Exertions are Bent Upon Representing What May Be Most Advantageous in Mercantile Regulations. For tho' One Cannot Hope for a Compleat Success, Yet it pleases one to think that Some Good Measures May Be Influenced By a proper Representation. This Governement are Well Disposed to America, and it is far from Being the Case With the Ministers of Great Britain.

Mr. Jay, Mr. Adams, and Mr. Laurens are in England. Many English Gentlemen Have Been flocking to Paris, Some of them Eminent Characters—and By Some I Have Been told that it was Reported in England I Would Be Sent With the definitive Ratification—a Rumour for which I Cannot Account.

I am Waïting for letters from You, for orders from Congress. It is Also the Case with the Commissionners. Untill Dispatches Arrive, We Cannot know our fate. But Nothing in the World Can Prevent My Going in a little time. As you know what Has Been writen to Me, You Can Better judge what I will do. But it is At least Certain I shall in a few Months Embrace My dear General, Spend with Him the Spring and Summer, and Most Earnestly Entreat Him to let me Accompagny Him to France where His Presence Will Excite the Most Enthusiastic and Affectionate transports. Don't Be Angry with me, Madam, for You Must Come too, take along the Young girls, and then all Will Be Perfectly Right.

Oh that I Were at Mount Vernon, By the Side of My dear General, Reminding Him of His Past labours, and their Glorious Happy Conclusion! It Melts My Heart, only to think of it. I feel Uneasy—and What I Want I know to Be a Voyage to the free, the Beloved Shores of our America. Mde. de Lafayette, My three Children are presented to You with the Most tender Homage to Yourself and Mrs. Washington. Your George is in perfect Health.[10]

My Best Respects, My Most tender Compliments Waït Upon Mrs. Washington. Be So kind, my dear general, to Remember me to the inhabitants of Mount Vernon—to George[11]—to the family of Hdqrs—to all my friends—adieu, adieu, my dear general, it is not without Emotion that I present you with the affectionate Respects off Yr. obt. Hbe. Sert.

LAFAYETTE

ALS (PEL: Hubbard Collection).

1. Washington addressed the Congress at Princeton on August 26 (*JCC*, 24:521–23).
2. On August 7, 1783, Congress voted to erect an equestrian statue of Washington, but the resolves were not carried out.
3. Russia had already annexed the Crimea as part of its "Greek project" to force the Turks out of Europe, but the onset of winter prevented the Turkish and Russian armies from going to war.
4. Having divided Poland, Prussia hoped now to annex Danzig, a Polish port city.
5. The Spanish fleet had bombarded Algiers in August.
6. The Irish Volunteers, first established as a militia organization to protect Ireland from possible invasion by France during the American Revolution, soon aligned themselves with the Patriots in the Irish Parliament, who pressed for increased political independence from England and for parliamentary reform.
7. D'Ormesson resigned as controller of finances, and Charles-Alexandre de Calonne accepted the post on November 4.
8. Letter not identified.
9. Lafayette was referring to Washington's June 18, 1783, "Circular Letter . . . to the Governors of the Several States," which also included a plea for the states to grant stronger authority to Congress. See Lafayette to Washington, September 8, 1783, note 3.
10. George-Washington Lafayette.
11. George Augustine Washington.

To William Temple Franklin

Paris November the 19th 1783

My dear Sir

The object of My Wanting a Declaration of independence is to Have it Engraved in Golden letters at the Most Conspicuous part of My Cabinet, and When I Wish to Put myself in Spirits, I Will look at it, and Most Voluptously Read it over—So that you will oblige me to Procure it for me, printed if You Can, in order that a french workman May Be less apt to Make Blunders. Most affectionately Yours

LAFAYETTE

Do you know of Any American Gentleman that is Immediately Going to England? I want to give Him a letter to that Country.

ALS (PPAmP: Franklin Papers, vol. 105, no. 152).
Lafayette eventually placed his engraved copy of the Declaration of Independence on one side of a double frame, leaving the other side empty. He claimed he was waiting for a parallel declaration of French rights to hang beside it (Lafayette, *Mémoires*, 3:197; Gottschalk, *Between*, 53–54).

To William Carmichael

Paris November the 20th 1783

My Dear Sir

Your favor By Count de Montmorin Having Been long on its Way, and Montmorin's Papers Being Entangled Among His Baggage, it is But lately that I Could Get my friend Carmichael's letter.[1] I Heartly thank you for it, My dear Sir, and With the Same Sentiments I Give You joy for the termination of the Ceremonial part in Your Embassy.[2] Count de Florida Blanca is as Candid and Generous a Man as Ever Existed. I feel Happy in His Acquaintance. I am pleased to think it is With Him You Have Business to transact. Depend upon it, My dear Sir, Florida Blanca is too Sensible a Man not to Value the friendship of our America. To His Sound judgement You Will Be Indebted for favourable Promises. To His Honesty You May Apply for their faithfull liberal Execution. You like that Man and His Nation. I am Glad of it Because it Makes you More Comfortable at Madrid, and Because it Disposes you to Be an Agreable Negotiator. Great Britain is Ready to Become Munificent in Her Commercial treaties. It is the Interest of the House of Bourbon, it is Your own interest to Get the Start of them. Let liberal propositions Be Immediately Sent from Spain. No time is to Be lost. The One Who grants first Will gain 100 per Cent. Should a free trade Be Established Betwen Spain's islands and the United States, their Colonies Will flourish, and it will then Be so much Against the Interest of Americans to Interrupt such a Commerce, that they will join in Every war Against England, and to preserve the profits of a trade with the Spanish Islands, they will oppose any British tentative Against their Southern Continent.[3]

M. Jay is now in England and Will Spend Some time at Bath for the Recovery of His Health. Adams and Laurens are Also on that Side of the Water. Littlepage Has Gone to London. Wether He Embarks from thence, or Returns this Way Depends Upon Contingencies. He Expects letters from You and Nassau. The Affairs of Ireland Will I think Be Settled to the Satisfaction of the Volonteers. It is a Noble Assossiation, and I am pleased Both With their Measures and their probable Good Success.[4] No News from America. Nothing Settled Respecting their foreign Departement. Every thing, I fancy, Will Come at Once With the Ratification of the Definitive treaty. We Now Have Got Monthly Packets that are Very Convenient. So late down as the End of September, Congress Had not fixed Upon a place for their Residence and their five per Cent Impost was not yet Entirely Adopted.⁵ But All will Come on Right, and the idea of divisions Among the states is all together Groundless. You Have long Ago Heard that M. Jay does not intend Returning to Madrid.

Adieu, My dear Sir, I Beg You will present my Best Compliments to our friend Harrison, to Cher. de Burgoing, to all my Acquaintances at Madrid. With Every Sentiment of Affection and Regard I Have the Honor to Be Dear Sir Your obedient Humble Servant

LAFAYETTE

ALS (DNA: RG 233, HR 27A-G7.4, Papers of William Carmichael, tray 742, item 102).
1. Letter not found.
2. Ten days before the signing of the peace treaty, the Spanish king officially received Carmichael as chargé d'affaires for the United States.
3. Lafayette assumed that his letters to Carmichael would be opened before delivery and his remarks on American commerce and relations with Spain read by the Spanish government. For Lafayette's less guarded views on Spain and for his earlier attempt to influence Spanish policy with doctored letters, see Lafayette's letters to Livingston, February 5, 1783, and Carmichael, January 20, 1783.
4. See Lafayette to Washington, November 11, 1783, note 6. On November 10 the Irish Volunteer Association held a convention to propose parliamentary reform.
5. On the 5 percent tax, see Livingston to Lafayette, May 1, 1783, note 7.

To Benjamin Franklin

Paris Saturday Evening [December 13, 1783]

My Dear Sir

The Inclosed is a Paper I intend to Present to the Several Ministers, with the Hope it May Give them Some favourable ideas Upon the American trade. But Before I do it, I Wish of Course to Have Your Approbation. Be So kind, My dear Sir, as to Read it Over, and if You think it May Answer a Good Purpose, I Will in my private Capacity Give it to Marechal de Castries, M. de Vergennes,¹ and M. de Calonne. To Morrow about ten in the Morning I Hope Having the Honour to Call upon You in My Way to Versailles. With the Highest Respects I Have the Honour to Be Your obedient Servant and affectionate friend

LAFAYETTE

For this time Excuse the Scribbling.

ALS (PPAmP: Franklin Papers, vol. 42, no. 144), enclosing a copy of Lafayette's Observations on Commerce.
1. Gottschalk notes, "Vergennes should properly have been approached only after his two colleagues had come to some sort of agreement" (Gottschalk, *Between* pp. 44–45), but

Vergennes was correctly involved as *chef du conseil royal des finances* and a member of the Comité des Finances.

Observations on Commerce between France and the United States[T]

[December 13, 1783]

France must have anticipated great advantages to have sacrificed both its treasure and the blood of its citizens in the recent war. There are some advantages that no error can take from it, and while France has recovered its respect, France's rival is losing part of its commerce, an immense territory, and a large number of subjects, which Europe was hastening to increase. France has accomplished still more: it has protected itself from certain and immediate ruin. In the eyes of all who know the New World, it is clear that on the eve of the Declaration of Independence, England was assured of all our American possessions. But though we should bless that revolution for the benefits gained and the evils avoided, and though commonplace criticism is reduced to questioning whether that inevitable power of the United States, now isolated and at peace, would be better situated in a reunion with our rivals, there are still other advantages that seemed assured to us and that I see, with regret, are escaping us.

It would have been easier to develop commercial connections while the animosity of the war lasted, but even if we have waited until we have rivals, we have advantages over them. It is not that trade seems to me a matter of sentiment; the Americans love France, they are grateful and generous, and while we may criticize them for their excessive hatred (in regard to reprisals or refugees, for example), it would be too absurd to accuse them of love for England. Still, every merchant seeks a profit, and though the government of the United States favors us, its mercantile interests maintain a policy of impartiality. It must be admitted that the influence of commercial interests will go further still. It will little by little control the councils, where merchants play a major role. Since we are rivals of the British in both our manufactured goods and our sea trade, it is by these very means that our political rivalry will be decided someday.

When I speak of our advantages, I therefore confine myself to saying that in our first attempts to establish trade connections we shall find our advantages at the disposition of the Americans. Nature has given us some exclusive advantages; a little care will give us more. Instead of rejecting this trade, it would require less trouble to attract the greater part of it. Each delay, each mistake becomes a sure gain for England. In short, if America does not exist for us, it will exist for others, and if this truth is not worth some sacrifices, it is at least worth prompt and very serious consideration.

As I was involved early in this revolution, I must lament the slightest benefits my country neglects to gain from it. I must cherish everything that strengthens the natural alliance that common interest seems to me to require. If I had the experience of a merchant, I would write about trade with the United States. But I cannot make that claim, and if my reflections or the information I have gathered have given me some ideas, they are too imperfect to put forth in a memorial. I have told the king's ministers what I have learned or thought, and it is in obedience to them that I present a few notes on this important matter here.

Though the trade of the realm and the colonies is divided into departments, in relation to the United States it is indivisible. Looking at France and America, we see on the one side raw materials and on the other manufactured goods, which means a very profitable exchange for France. If this truth required an example, I would cite the large trade in linseed, which the former American colonies sold to Ireland. From the time the seeds were planted until America received the bleached linen, Ireland gained everything by supporting that crop. If we avoid ruining the trade, our broadcloth, our silks of every kind, our linens and fashionable clothing, etc. will find a considerable American market that with care can be further enlarged. And while the less refined manufactures will be closer to American taste (for I have seen that in Boston it is solely the rounded heads of our nails that keep them from being marketable, and that the Irish manner of folding linen influences its sale), we could cut the costs of our more refined manufactures by simplifying our methods. Some industries would not lose by adopting the British principle that employs one person for each task, and for each task only the necessary amount of energy. It is remarkable, for instance, that while the raw material produced in our colonies is better and less expensive than that of the British colonies, the cotton products of Rouen are more expensive since the peace than those of Manchester. The cost of our labor, the good taste and intelligence that distinguish us, all promise that we can imitate and surpass any kind of foreign product.

In establishing commercial relations, in creating a taste for our manufactures, we ought also to facilitate the export of our products. I hear the Americans expressing the wish that our trade with them would be on the same footing as our trade with our own colonies. They are alarmed by the unnatural imposition of internal duties. From the moment the product leaves the factory, with the cases unopened for fear of formalities that would be worse than the uncertainty about the contents, until they see it loaded aboard ship, they complain of those countless difficulties that afflict French merchants as well. These vexations lead to smuggling and cheating, and for a foreigner ignorant of our customs and language, they are even more intolerable. The British factories give credit on longer terms than we do, a reflection less unfortunate than the others but worth being noted. As for our wines and spirits, they give us an exclusive advantage over England. The taste for French wines increases daily; they are in demand in the North and are essential in the hot part of the country. One would have to eliminate that trade for Portugal, the Azores, or even Madeira to stand the comparison to France.

Here, then, is a new source of wealth to revive our productions and our manufactures. It would be stupid to dry up this channel of commerce, since it is much easier to promote it. But as this part of the New World produces good foodstuffs and not precious metals with which to pay our workers, we must follow the example of Ireland and encourage their farmers. While we return their furs to them manufactured into hats, muffs, etc., use their excellent iron, and import their lumber (as the British did before) for the construction of ships, to which we add our own sails, rigging, and so forth, we should also see that there is a profitable market in France for their indigo, rice, and tobacco. Their indigo, less refined than ours, has its own special use. American rice ought to be given preference over that of the Levant, even though that trade is well established. The most important commercial item is tobacco, but that trade is ruined by Messieurs the Farmers General. And if there is any nation favored for its cod, we must not forget that cod is virtually the money of New England. In short, if we want the Americans to buy French products, their means of selling to us cannot be increased too much.

Far from fulfilling this desired end, our present system has driven American trade away. The intricacies of our regulations are even more annoying than their cost. The Farm agents can do nothing but impede trade and can never settle anything. Time, so precious to a merchant, is as wasted over a slight obstacle as it would be over the most important matter. And then the long-awaited judgments of the company vary arbitrarily on each occasion.

On arriving in a French port, an American merchant wavers for fear of declaring too little and having his cargo confiscated or declaring too much and having to pay duties on what he does not have. In the case of cargoes of tobacco, an error in declaration is even more troublesome, for if one makes an error to one's disadvantage, one is accused of contraband, and that absurd accusation can be suspended only by a special order that establishes no precedents for future shipments. When reexporting their merchandise, the Americans wish to recover their entry duties, a privilege that they consider essential to trade.[1] For the moment, France has lost the tobacco trade. Since this peace, I believe, only two tobacco ships have arrived, and even this was the result of an earlier commitment; all others went to England and Holland, where manufactured goods were received in payment. One particular tobacco ship waited in France for nine months, during which time Messieurs the Farmers General would neither buy the cargo nor permit it to go on to Marseilles, where the Italians wanted it; it finally sailed for Amsterdam. Good tobacco currently sells in Philadelphia for 50 to 60 shillings a hundredweight. When it arrives in France, the various duties bring the cost to 54 livres in our money, and while in our ports it brings only 9 sous a pound, they say it sells for 16 sous in London and Amsterdam. Without going into details in which I may be mistaken, it is clear that direct trade is the best policy for buying tobacco and selling our own goods. Our competitors will go to any lengths to eliminate this trade, even if they take a temporary loss, and unless we enlighten the Farm's sense of patriotism, the lure of immediate gain and commitment to the old customs may jeopardize our mercantile and political interests.

These abuses have long restricted our trade, afflicted our citizens, and, it is generally agreed, offset the natural advantages we have over other nations. I do not claim to offer any new ideas but only to indicate what strikes the Americans as particularly important. It is even less my place to determine the remedies, though the example of other countries proves that some exist, and I shall only speak here of the issue of free ports, which has too long been neglected. The treaty promised two, and Marseilles and Dunkirk have always been free ports. When peace was settled, I suggested that Lorient would be very convenient for the Americans. The government was willing to name it a free port, and I was asked to see it done and to announce to the Americans a formal letter confirming it, which has not yet appeared.[2] The conclusion of that matter and the addition of Bayonne[3] would form a chain of four free ports adequate for American commerce. Perhaps it would be better for us if all the ports of France were free, but without digressing to this novel notion, without even mentioning here the merits of both Lorient and Bayonne, I shall only add that these arrangements ought to be made with the ministers of Congress and their consul in France.

Whatever the American imports may be, however, France fortunately has a very favorable balance of trade. So the problem is to find a way for the Americans to pay for the excess they buy from us, and only trade between the United States and the French colonies can provide one. Even if I had vast knowledge I would be afraid to risk an opinion on this important question. The French merchants and French colonists seem to disagree on this issue. It is said that both sides have good arguments, but this is roughly what has struck me about American trade during my talks with people less ignorant than I.

When the interests of American commerce are harmful to our trade, they must be ignored by our government, but I do not say the same for the interests of our farmers, our workers in France, and our fellow citizens in the colonies. The sale of their products and the resulting prosperity must be balanced against mercantile profits and must work for the greatest public good. It is less than eighteen years since the chambers of commerce unanimously opposed any trade between the colonies and foreign countries.[4] Since that time they have become more tolerant of trade in some articles. They even acknowledge now that it is better to get salted meat from America than from Ireland. But only after much debate did necessity force us to establish free ports at Saint Lucia and at Môle Saint Nicolas.[5] Among the merchants there is a diversity of opinion, and all this discussion makes me hope that we can establish a conciliatory system in which national and private interests will be in harmony.

When we got salted meat from Ireland, we were taking England's refuse, and there is no comparison between that meat and America's in point of price and quality. If American fish are allowed into our colonies, European markets will take more of our fish. Competition can be reestablished by imposing moderate duties, but as long as feeding the slaves depends on laws prohibiting the importation of foreign produce into the colonies, the slaves will be few and poorly nourished, will work little and die sooner. And finally, since we have slaves, should we not listen to the double voice of self-interest and humanity? The king's customs duties, the consumption of manufactured goods, and colonial agriculture will increase in proportion to the degree of commercial freedom. Are not the colonists themselves the best judges of the feeding of their slaves? And is it feared that they will give their slaves more than is necessary? If we take American cod and salted meat, we shall surely also get livestock, stave wood, and other products that the American continent has always produced. I must mention here that the existing free ports require an inconvenient and expensive coastal trade. If we are expecting to benefit from trade with the Spanish islands, let me remind you that their trade is limited to goats and the hides of cattle that run wild in the woods (the scarcity of pasturage does not permit them to raise cattle any other way). Only the island of Marguerite has some pasturage, but this minor trade can hardly be considered, since that island will gradually adopt our agricultural system. If we repulse their trade, the Americans would turn to the Spanish, and the Spanish are always paid in British manufactured goods. The negligence of the coastal patrols makes smuggling easy. Among those lazy Spaniards, whatever they promise, one can count on nothing that requires personal effort. But wood suitable for houses, for building and repairing ships, for casks, masts, and beams, and finally salted provisions (which we shall get from America whatever the regulations) are items in which Spain cannot hope to compete with America.

It is impossible to think that fish, salted provisions, in fact all the above-mentioned articles will not be admitted into our colonies. Flour, however, presents a greater difficulty that I do not know how to resolve. The colonists say that since the question of grain exports is still in doubt, we ought not to be so determined about requiring exports of French grain to our colonies.[6] Slaves use little flour, and if the grain merchant loses, the consumer and consequently the French laborer will gain from it. Our fields will be converted into vineyards; internal trade will offer an outlet for wheat. Since American flour is brought into European ports all the time (even France has taken some), it is cruel to stifle the colonies' growth by conferring monopolies from which only a few individuals will usually profit. French rum, molasses, and manufactured goods will go to the United States from the French islands, but the Americans will insist strongly on maintaining trade in sugar, at least for their own consumption. If they cannot get sugar from us or the British, they will encourage trade from Brazil or the Spanish colonies, to our detriment. If they are free to open a sugar trade with the British islands, they will reestablish commercial liaisons there that we ought to fear. The development of our colonies should concern us. Saint Lucia, for example, is thought of as a tomb, though it could become a flourishing island. If we stifled the growth of an enemy possession, wouldn't we believe we had done the enemy great harm? And since French trade does not suffice for the development of our colonies, why not allow them to sell their surpluses to allied consumers?

If we confined trade to certain islands or ports, limited the amount of sugar in each cargo, or even required security deposits from an agency controlling this commodity to the French consuls in the United States, would it not be possible to ensure that this commerce does not exceed the continent's needs, and that the Americans will find no profit in shipping our sugar to Europe? It is feared that difficulties will arise in enforcing these regulations, but cannot the same be said for all restrictions? If these restrictions do not regulate trade sufficiently to allow us to grant complete freedom, why are other restrictions so alarming that we adopt a complete prohibition of trade? It is reasonable, moreover, to attempt some experiments, and we should not start with those that would bring us useless regrets by making us lose a little-known trade. When we have examined this trade from every point of view, there is still one point worth considering. Since the United States is overflowing with produce, and our colonies and the United States have mutual needs that bring them closer together, it is to be feared that a refusal to grant legal commercial liberties will lead to general abuse. If trade is universally prohibited, the Americans and the colonists will violate all regulations without distinction. But the assurance of a lawful profit will do away with smuggling, and it is smuggling that creates vexations and animosities, loses the king's customs duties, destroys all plans to improve our trade, and undoes political ties.

If it is equitable to give only the surplus of our trade, even to our closest allies, if those allies are to be used only for the prosperity of our commerce, or rather for that of our farmers and workers, and if the trade of our colonies is to be used only for the advantage of the mother country, then we would undoubtedly be wrong to sacrifice our major shipping interests to our allies. It is said that our colonial shipping destroys more sailors than it trains, and the Americans generally do not expect a very rapid growth in their shipping. It is true that the Americans at present are eagerly moving to the frontiers, attracted by the valuable lands awaiting cultivation. American shipping, moreover, may be more costly than we think. While the Americans' wood is cheaper, their labor is not, and the cordage they use is largely imported from Europe. Their sailors are better paid and better fed, while their ships do not last nearly as long as ours. The Americans argue that if their ships were built cheaper, the French would buy some of them and make them French property. Finally, they claim that many other nations ship less expensively, so that they are not the ones to be feared in this respect.

If I have hazarded some ideas on American trade, I was encouraged to do so by the king's ministers and still more by the love of my country and my attachment to the United States. These motives, which I have the right to make known, would excuse some pretensions concerning matters I scarcely understand, but I cannot even reproach myself with that offense. I admit that the least significant merchant knows more than I, and if any of my ideas seem reasonable, they should be credited all the more since they are explained by one who is ignorant, and so are not shown off to advantage. I am not offering a proposal; I have gathered here, as requested, some notes on well-known truths or on American opinions that my private connections enabled me to hear. While for the prosperity of our trade, our agriculture, and our manufacturing we facilitate our exports, and to ensure payment favor

American imports, we must also, in looking after our shipping (and in anticipating both what is desirable and what cannot be prevented), see that the interests of our merchants join those of our manufacturing and our colonies to produce the greatest possible good for the realm. The king's ministers will know better than I how to fulfill these objectives, but there are two reflections that do not require any expert knowledge. The first is that if we waste time, we shall do ourselves irreparable harm. The second is that since the United States minister, the consul, and other American envoys are here in France, it is all the more important to consult them, as their talents and knowledge make their advice valuable, and their opinion will have great influence on the disposition of the United States.

LAFAYETTE

MS (AN: Marine B^7 460) in a secretary's hand, translation.

Lafayette sent copies of these observations to Morris, Franklin, and the French ministers Calonne, Castries, and Vergennes (for Vergennes's copy, see AN: Archives des Affaires Etrangères, B^{III}, vol. 442, fols. 21–37). On the copy he enclosed to Morris with his letter of December 26, 1783, he added:

> While I am Sending over this Memorial, I Beg leave to Observe it Was Intended to Point out the Inconveniences in the French trade. It Was therefore My object, on the One Hand to present them in their worst point of View, and on the other to Overlook the Advantages which that Commerce Has over other Nations. It would Have Been wrong in me Not to [observe] that this Memorial is not intended to Give a stated Account of the affair, But to obtain favourable Alterations Upon Particular points. [DNA: RG 360, PCC 156, pp. 374–91]

1. Britain and the United States practiced a system of drawbacks on import duties if the goods were immediately reexported without changing hands. This practice allowed captains to stop in many ports but pay duties only on the goods actually sold in each port.

2. Lafayette was instrumental in getting Lorient chosen over the smaller Port-Louis. See his letters to Vergennes, March 19; to the American commissioners, May 12; and to Congress, July 20, 1783.

3. On July 4, 1784, letters patent declared Bayonne to be outside the French customs area and outside the tobacco monopoly.

4. For most of the eighteenth century the merchants of designated French ports had exclusive rights to the trade with the French American colonies. In 1765, government policy shifted toward a modified system of exclusivity. The change produced heated debates. The chambers of commerce of the port cities strenuously opposed the measures, arguing for strict adherence to the principles of exclusivity, while colonial interests favored the changes. The free-port system in the West Indies continued to be limited.

5. In 1767 the government formulated a series of arrêts du consent to deal with colonial problems. The measures reaffirmed the principle of exclusivity while creating a free port in Saint Lucia and one in Saint-Domingue, with limited trade between the colonists and foreign nations. Wood, livestock, hides, resin, and tar would be imported for a modest duty; foreign ships could export syrups, rum, and manufactured goods.

6. Commerce in grain was severely limited within France until 1763, when many of the restrictions were removed. The following year a governmental edict allowed grain to be exported, and in 1774 internal trade was completely liberalized, though exports to foreign countries were prohibited. The 1774 edict drew heated criticism—Jacques Necker was one of its most vocal opponents—and controversy over the issue continued until 1788.

To the Comte de Vergennes[T]

Paris, December 16, 1783

Monsieur le Comte,

After witnessing the triumph of the noble cause that gathered them together, the American officers have laid down their arms to resume their peacetime occupations. But at the moment of parting, they wanted to exchange a pledge of their warm brotherhood and wished also to perpetuate their gratitude to France with the memory of their obligations.

It is with these intentions, Monsieur le Comte, that the Society of the Cincinnati has been founded. You know its bylaws, and I limit myself to carrying out the orders of General Washington, president of this association.[1]

In a letter brought me by Major L'Enfant, who has been charged with designing the insignia and having them made up, the general instructs me to receive the subscriptions and signatures and to distribute the distinctive emblems to all the officers in Europe who have fulfilled the necessary conditions in the army of the United States of America. I beg you then, Monsieur le Comte, to be so kind as to obtain the king's permission for those of us Frenchmen who appear to be eligible under the bylaws.[2]

The society flatters itself, Monsieur le Comte, that the insignia of its order will be accepted by the generals, admirals, and colonels of the French troops who served alongside the Americans, and the whole American army joins in requesting this permission from the king. Should he have the kindness to grant it, the next departure of the *Washington* will quickly bring them the news.

The society is very concerned, Monsieur le Comte, that its purpose be clearly understood in Europe and in America. Its bylaws will be published in foreign newspapers, but you will really oblige the association by having the enclosed article inserted in the *Gazette de France* under the heading of Paris.[3] I have the honor to be, with a warm and respectful attachment, Monsieur le Comte, your very humble and obedient servant,

LAFAYETTE

ALS (AAE: Correspondance politique, Etats-Unis, vol. 26, fol. 204), translation.

1. See Washington to Lafayette, October 20, 1783, note 1.

2. At that time the Golden Fleece was the only foreign order to which French officers were allowed to belong.

One of the original eagle badges of the Society of the Cincinnati, presented by Washington to his aide Tench Tilghman.

3. On December 23, 1783, the following appeared in the *Gazette:*

The American packetboat *Washington* arrived the eighth instant at Havre. On board this vessel came Major l'Enfant with the orders of the Society of Cincinnatus.

This association, whose rules will be published, was founded by the American officers as a monument to the fraternal love that brought them together in the same cause.

The characteristic mark of the society is the Bald Eagle, a species of eagle peculiar to America, which bears emblems related to the glory and honest disinterestedness of Cincinnatus, whose situation was analogous to that of the American officers. It will be suspended on a blue ribbon, dotted with white, betokening the alliance of the United States with France, and of their gratitude to her.

General Washington, president of the society, writes in that capacity to the Marquis de Lafayette to receive the acceptances of the officers of the American army at present in Europe who have complied with the prescribed terms, so that he may give them the honors of the order of Cincinnatus.

Major l'Enfant carried a letter to Comte de Rochambeau in which the Society presented the honors of the order to the generals and colonels of the French army who served in America, and also to the admirals who commanded our naval forces in that country.[T]

From Charles-Alexandre de Calonne[T]

Paris, December 18, 1783

I am, Monsieur, truly sorry not to have had the honor of seeing you when you were kind enough to take the trouble of coming to see me. I read with the greatest interest the observations on the commerce between France and the United States that you sent me.[1] I shall be delighted to discuss these issues with you, but as I am going to Versailles tomorrow, and from now until I leave have business to attend to and appointments to keep which would not allow me to give you as much time as I would like, I propose that we meet one day next week, whatever day is convenient for you, and ask that you inform me of the time you have chosen. You have, Monsieur, so many claims to universal esteem that you cannot doubt my feelings and the haste with which I shall contribute to the views that interest you. I have the honor to be, etc.,

DE CALONNE

L (DNA: RG 360, PCC 137, vol. 3, p. 529), copy, translation; inscribed "true copy" in Lafayette's hand. At the end of the letter, Lafayette wrote, "I Have Sent the Original over"; the original was probably enclosed with Lafayette to Morris, December 26, 1783.

1. See Lafayette's Observations, [December 13, 1783].

To George Washington

Paris December the 25te. 1783

Sir

On the Receipt of Your Excellency's letter, I took Measures to fulfill the Intentions of the Society in Which I Have the Honour to Be a member.[1]

As our Institution was differently interpreted, I wrote a letter to Count de Vergennes of which the inclosed is a Copy, and the Account I gave was printed in a Court Gazette which I Have also the Honour to send.[2] At a king's Council, this day was a week, it Has Been decided Count de Rochambeau, His Generals and Colonels, and also the Admirals should Be permitted to wear the Order, and a Very proper letter Upon the Subject Has Been writen By Marechal de Segur to M. de Rochambeau.[3]

As to our American officers, I Shall Examine into the claims of Every one—when the point is clear, deliver or Refuse the order, and in doubtfull Cases take the Advice of a Board of American officers Members in the Society.

No foreign Badge But the golden fleece is permitted to french men in this Service. From the distinction Shown to our Society, And the testimony it Bears of Having Acted a Part in this War, our Badge is Highly Wished and Warmly Contended for By all those who Hope they Have Some Claim to it. The Nation Have Been Very much pleased with the Attention our Society Has paid to the alliance, and Have found there is Some thing Very interesting in that Brotherly Assossiation.

Major L'Enfant is Employed in the Execution of Your orders. A Good Number of Eagles will Be Made in twelve days, when I intend to Call for the few American officers Now Here, and together to waït Upon the Generals and Admirals of the french Army With the Marks of the order.

Count d'Estaing Has Represented that Mr. de Bougainville Count Dillon, and, I think, two other Colonels were with Him auxiliary to our troops, and that Savahna, tho' the Attempt Was Unsuccessfull, Has Been Attended with Great fatigues and dangers.[4] The claim I think to Be Very proper, and as the Candidates are few, we Might act according to the known Sense of the Society. But claims are Raising for Captains of Ships, which Seem to me Quite an other affair, the Consideration of which, Cannot, in My Opinion, But Be differed Untill the Grand Society Meeting.[5]

Major L'Enfant Having it from You that M. de Vaudreuïl Had Been left out through Mere Mistake, and should Be Considered as the other Admirals, I Have Advised the Major to pay Him a Visit, and Will not Advise Him Against delivering to Him One of the Marks, which M. de Vaudreuïl Will not Wear Untill the official letter is Arrived. My Reasons for it are that Such a Mistake Could not But Hurt His feelings, and that, Circumstanced as He is, we ought not to give such an officer a ground of Complaints.[6]

In all these Matters, I Had nothing to do But to Hazard an opinion. Major L'Enfant knows Your orders and the Society's intentions. So far as Respects the Business entrusted to me, I shall execute it in the Best Manner I Can, and I am Glad to See our Society Meets with Approbation. Objections are Made, as is the Case in Every Novelty—the Hereditary part of the institution Has its Comments—[7]But the General Voice is in favour of our Brotherly Society, and General Washington's Name as President Adds a Weight to the Assossiation. With the Highest and Most affectionate Respect I Have the Honour to Be My dear General Your obedient Humble Servant

LAFAYETTE

ALS (Anderson House Museum, Society of the Cincinnati, Washington, D.C.).

1. See Washington to Lafayette, October 20, 1783.

2. See note 3 and text of Lafayette to Vergennes, December 16, 1783. The *Gazette de France* announced establishment of the Society and published its bylaws on December 23.

3. The Marquis de Ségur wrote to Rochambeau on December 18, 1783, informing him that the king was pleased to allow the French officers to accept the badge of the Society of the Cincinnati (Baron Ludovic de Contenson, *La Société des Cincinnati de France et la Guerre d'Amérique, 1778–1783* [Paris, 1934], pp. 24–25).

4. D'Estaing led French forces in a combined American and French expedition against British-held Savannah in September and early October 1779 (*LAAR*, 2:319n).

5. Under the Society's existing rules, naval captains were ineligible for membership, though army captains were. At the first general meeting, in May 1784, the society amended the provisions to admit naval captains (see Lafayette to Washington, March 9, 1784, and notes).

6. The Society's bylaws (enclosed with Washington to Lafayette, October 20, 1783) included a list of the French admirals and commanders who were to receive the Society's badge. The name of the Marquis de Vaudreuil, an admiral in d'Estaing's forces, was inadvertently omitted.

7. A number of Americans and Europeans protested the hereditary principle that allowed membership to descend through the eldest son. They were concerned that the Society might lay the groundwork for a hereditary aristocracy, which would be contrary to the principles of the American Revolution.

Charles-Alexandre de Calonne, French controller general of finance, worked with Lafayette to establish free ports for American trade.

From Charles-Alexandre de Calonne[T]

Versailles, December 25, 1783

I have read, Monsieur, with the greatest attention, the very interesting memorandum that you did me the honor to direct to me concerning the facilities we might provide the United States of America for their commerce with France.[1] The views this proposal sets forth, particularly on free ports that seem to be most suitable for American shipping, are very well thought out and seem to me likely to conform to the political interests of the state as well as to the king's finances, with the help of a few precautions that I shall take care of right away; and after I have conferred with M. le Comte de Vergennes on the measures necessary to prevent any difficulty, I shall hasten to make a report on it to His Majesty. His predispositions in favor of the United States of America are so well known that there is reason to expect that he will now gladly approve the means to ensure, facilitate, and extend the hoped-for commercial relations for the mutual benefit of the two nations. I shall be delighted to discuss this with your forthwith, and you can rest assured that I shall do everything in my power to conclude this matter as soon as possible. I have the honor to be, etc., etc.

DE CALONNE

L (DNA: RG 360, PCC 137, vol. 3, pp. 532–33), copy, translation; inscribed "true copy" in Lafayette's hand. At the end of the letter, Lafayette wrote, "The original letter Has Been Sent over"; the original was probably enclosed with Lafayette to Morris, December 26, 1783.

Lafayette wrote Vergennes on December 25, apparently before he received Calonne's letter:

I have seen M. de Calonne, Monsieur le Comte, and was very pleased by the hopes he has given me. He invited me to go to Versailles one day to confer with you there on matters related to American commerce. He authorized me to tell Congress, as if on my own account, that the government was going to attend to these matters; and to fend off as much as possible any ties with England, I shall send Mr. Morris, if you think it appropriate, both my memorandum and the government's assurance that it will attend to this commerce.[T] [AAE: Correspondance politique, Etats-Unis, vol. 26, fol. 251]

1. See Lafayette's Observations, [December 13, 1783].

To Robert Morris

Paris December the 26th 1783

Dear Sir

Altho' I Have not By this Opportunity Been Honoured with Any Commands from Congress, I Beg their Permission to Acquaint them through You with the Measures Respecting Commerce which it Has Been Both My duty and My inclination to pursüe.

On My Return from Spain I Heard that Bayonne and Dunkirk were the two ports pointed out for American trade. L'Orient was out of the Question, and Altho' it Was Wished for By the Ministers and Consul of the United States, their Having no positive order from Congress Seemed to them to forbear a timely Application. As I was a private Man, I thought I Might Make it Myself, and Every Difficulty I met with the Better Convinced me of the Importance there was in getting that Harbour. It Was at last fixed upon *in lieu* of Bayonne, and I was permitted to let it Be known to Mr. Barklay—But Mr. d'Ormesson Being Overburthened With the Details of His place, An Enormous time Was lost in Giving the Affair an official and Complete Conclusion.

Monsieur de Calonne Having Got into place, I Have Applied to Him as I do to Every Minister that Has Some thing to do with American Affairs. Inclosed You will find Answers from Him, and I Hope our Next Conference will finish the affair of L'Orient.[1] It Has Much pleased me to Hear from Colonel Gouvion that Your Opinion Respecting its Conveniency Coincided with Mine. But Since it Has Been decided we should obtain L'Orient, I Have Made an Application for an Addition of free ports—Because the more are Got, the Better it Will Be. Dunkirk, L'Orient, Bayonne, and Marseïlles will Be a Very proper chain. Bayonne With the Country Round it Oppens a Good Contraband trade With the Spaniards.

Upon the Receipt of Your letter September the 30th, Mr. Franklin Sent it to me Requesting I would Make what [use] of it I thought proper. I Had Extracts of it translated which I intend taking With me to Versaïlles.[2] Your Opinion will Have a Great weight in the Affair, Because of the Confidence Europeans Have in Your Abilities, and the Respect which is paid Here to Your character.

The Ideas Upon Commerce that Are Met with in this Country are far from Being allwaïs Right. To persuade people into their own Interest is Some times as difficult a Matter as it would Be to obtain a Sacrifice—But the Ministry and the people are Wishing for intimate Connections with America Upon a liberal footing. One of the Impediments is that the trade in France is Subject to Many [Inconveniences] which By little and little will Be Removed, and the other that the Merchants Here, and the farming interest about Bordeaux oppose Any foreign trade With the West Indias.

Those Oppositions I Have Been Every day Combatting in the Best Manner I Could—and at last Have determined to present Several Heads By Way of Memorial[3] which I will Comment in Conversation. It is Entirely in the Capacity of a frenchman that I write, and with as little

Appearance of Partiality as I Could. The Reason is obvious, and I Have sent a Copy of My Memorial to Every one of the Ministers. With it I enclose Mr. de Calonne's Answers and a Copy of an old letter from Mr. de Vergennes which You must Have got long Ago.[4] Should you think the Memorial Worth Reading to Congress or Any Committee, I Must Beg it May not go elsewhere as I do not wish it Being propagated.

In Every thing I do, I Need not Saying that I will Ask for directions from the Ministers of Congress, and I Very Much Wish to See them treating the Matter directly with this Governement. I the More Desire it, as I know the Intentions of Congress only from Hear Say, and Cannot Move a step in Cases where their Name is to Be Made use off with the Ministry. With the Highest Regard I Have the Honour to Be Dear Sir Your obedient Humble Servant

LAFAYETTE

ALS (DNA: RG 360, PCC 156, pp. 369–71), marked "Duplicate."

1. Calonne's letter of December 18, acknowledging receipt of Lafayette's Observations on Commerce, [December 13, 1783], and Calonne's December 25 letter to Lafayette, above.

2. Lafayette's Observations.

3. Extracts from Morris's letter were probably those added to a Foreign Ministry copy of Lafayette's Observations (AAE: Mémoires et Documents, Etats-Unis, vol. 2, fols. 100–103). They included, among other comments on American trade: "The people of Europe should consider that the means of this country to pay for the merchandise that they ply upon us is proportional to our wealth."[T]

4. Probably the letter Vergennes wrote to him on June 29, 1783, defining a free port.

To James McHenry

Paris December the 26th 1783

My Dear McHenry

Had You not Been Employed in Quartering the Continental Congress, I would find it Very ill in You not to Have writen By Colonel Gouvion. I wanted to Hear from You, about You, and then I wanted to know Your Opinion Upon Several Matters. My letter to Congress Will let You know what Intelligences We Have in this Quarter.[1] My letter to Mr. Moriss Will Acquaint them with some late Measures I Have taken Respecting American Commerce.[2] It Contains one letter from Mr. de Vergennes, two from M. de Calonne, and a piece from me to Gouvernement which I also inclose to You, and Which, for Reasons obvious, I Request May not Be Spread out of Congress. It is on that Account, and also for a Good translation that I send it to You, and thirdly Because that Entrusting temper which You know me to be possessed of, Now and then is Altered By the Selfishness of others. When I Hear, By Way of Exemple, that Your plenipotentiaries's letters, Rather Gave a Ground to think I Have not Been so Active as they in obtaining the last six Millions, I Cannot Help Remembering that Jay and Adams Never Went to Versaïlles But twice, I think, when I pushed them to it, that M. Franklin did Repose Himself upon me who went so far as to say that I Had Rather delay the departure of 8000 men and Nine ships waïting for me at Brest than to Go without an assurance of the six millions—in Consequence of which I went in My travelling dress to Count de Vergennes's and Upon His table wrote a Billet to Doctor Franklin intimating He should Have the Monney.[3] But Never Mind that, and Be so kind only as to take Care My Commercial efforts Be known in America, and also that Congress send instructions Respecting trade, least the Matter should Be Dropped as Has Been My very well Begun Spanish Negotiation.

The Institution of the Cincinnati Has pretty well succeeded in France. The officers who Have Been in America set a Great Value By the Mark of the Society. A few objections Have Been Made By the public to some parts of the institution which May be either mended or improved—But it Has Been found Very interesting, and even some what affecting, and people in General Have Been pleased with that Brotherly Assossiation.

[*Manuscript torn; top third of this page of text missing*] . . . of commerce. [*Part of line missing on tear*] . . . published that whereas I Have well Served America in the field and Cabinet, they expect my assistance in Settling their Commercial affairs with some European Nations. My Station in life, knowledge of Courts, and facility of Accompagnying those Sovereigns Both in their Camps of peace, and in their private parties, would Enable me to introduce to Advantage an American Consul. It ought to Be immediately settled, and orders sent By the Washington.

The Second point is that I do not choose to quit the American Service. It is the only Way I Have to Make a kind of official Representations in favour of America. Independant of that affectionate love for Her which Makes me proud of Being Among Her Citizens and [*manuscript torn; top third of this page of text missing*].

My Last letters Have Acquainted You of the Measures [I Have] taken with Respect to Madame Le Vacher. There is Very little to be Got—But I am in pursuit of the affair With the same Eagerness as if it concerned my own sister.[4] As to Mr. Chace a memorial Has Been Required from Him By the Naval Minister.[5]

As an ardent lover of America I am glad to Hear of the influence You are said to Have in Congress. As Your most affectionate friend I shall Be glad whenever You Have an opportunity to display Your abilities. If Congress do not send me Any Commands, I shall Most Certainly embark in the spring. If they Have Commands for me, I would Be thrice Happy to Receive You along with them, and to Make with you french and European travels. You ought to Make them charge you with some political commission to Courts in Europe, and I would like going as a volonteer with you. [*Manuscript torn; part a line missing*] Your family and our friends. Most affectionately I am for [*manuscript torn; several words missing*].

LAFAYETTE

The Washington Will probably arrive at the end of january. Your answers May Be Here at the end of March—for, if I am to go, I would like embarking for America in April. You may as soon as you Receive this write me By several opportunities in such a way as I will easely understand, altho' post offices will not comprehend it. By the way when I think of it, You ought to advise Congress writing for the general's statue which Has not yet Been ordered. Should not Greene be entitled to some Honour of the kind? Adieu, my dear friend.

ALS (CSmH: MH 157). The second leaf of the four-page manuscript is torn in half, so that the top portion of two pages of text is missing, as is half of the closing line, which was written along the left margin.

1. Lafayette's letter to Congress, December 26, 1783, contained news of the fall of the Fox-North government in England and brief mention of other European news. He concluded the letter by saying that unless Congress had commands for him in Europe, he would embark for America in the spring (DNA: RG 360, PCC 156, pp. 365–66).

2. See preceding letter.

3. Lafayette's letter to Franklin not found.

4. Jean Le Vaché Le Brun had married Ann Howard in Annapolis in September 1781; in August 1782 he left "for Europe," never to be heard from again. A deposition on the matter from the mayor of Annapolis is in PPAmP: Franklin Papers, vol. 55, no. 56.

5. Samuel Chase had written to Lafayette (letter not found) requesting help over the loss of his ship *Matilda*, which had been captured by a British frigate. Franklin wrote to Chase on January 6, 1784, that Castries had advised Lafayette that if Chase wished to pursue the matter, he should write an official report (Smyth, *Writings of Franklin*, 9:152–54).

To Henry Knox

Paris january the 8th 1784

I Have Been last time Very Unfortunate, My dear friend, and the Washington's departure Has Been So Sudden, that I Could not Send By Her Any thing More But official Copies, of Which the inclosed is a duplicate.[1] It Has Been to me a Great Happiness to Hear from You, and while we are Separated I Beg You will let me Enjoy it as often as Possible. You know my tender Affection to You, My dear Knox, it is Engraved in My Heart, and I shall keep it as long as I live. From the Begining of our Great Revolution which Has Been the Begining of our Acquaintance, we Have Been Actuated By the Same Principles, Impressed With the Same ideas, Attached to the Same friends, and We Have Warmly loved and Confidentially Entrusted Each other. The Rememberance of all that is dear to My Heart, and from Every Motive of tenderness and Regard I Set the Greatest Valüe By the Happiness of Your Possession as a Bosom friend. Let me therefore Beg You, My dear Knox, not to Be lazy in letting me often Hear from You. Your Brother is in London, and Enjoys a Good Health.[2] We Correspond Sometimes, and I am Very much Attached to Him. Before He Returns Home, I wish He may Again make a Visit to France, for which Purpose I intend writing to Morrow to Him.

By our last Accounts from America, We Hear that New York is Evacuated, and our peace Establishement finally Settled. I Hope also to Hear it is Under the Command of General Knox, Because our Stores, our Artillery, and What little Remains of our Worthy Army, in a Word Every thing Continental ought to Be kept in the Most perfect order.[3] The disbanding of our Army, I must Confess, Affects me with Some Painfull feelings—and Altho' it is a Proper Measure not to keep a Standing Army, Yet I Could not Help Sighing at the first News that the Continental Army was no More. We Have So intimately So Brotherly lived together, we Have Had So much to fear, so Much to Hope, we Have United ourselves through So many changes of fortune, that the parting Moment Cannot But Be Painfull. Would to god, our Brave Companions were Rewarded Agreable to their deserts![4] I Can't express the Anxiety I Have felt, and I do Still feel on the Occasion. In Every thing Relating to that I Beg You will Be Very Particular.

Our Assossiation Meets with Great Success. On thursday Next A Sufficient Number of Eagles will Be made to Answer Immediate Purposes.[5] I intend inviting all the American officers to My House, and Conduct them in a Body, with our Regimentals, to the General of the French Army to whom we will present the Marks of the Assossiation.[6] You will Receive Many Applications Relative to an Addition to the Brotherhod. But as Nothing Will Be decided Before the Assembly in May, I Have time to Send You My observations.[7]

I Have Been Much Employed in Rendering America What Services I Could in the Affairs of Her Commerce. What I Can do must Be Entirely done Before the Spring, when I intend Embarking for my Beloved shores of liberty. I Hope to Arrive in Good time for the Grand

Assembly. My delays in Europe are owing to motives of American public Service. My attachement Needs no Comment, from which my Good wishes are obvious, and as to my exertions they Have Been and shall ever Be as Affectionate as my Heart, as Constant as my love to the public, and the individuals in the United States.

M. Moriss Has Received the Copy of Representations I Have laid Before the Court of France—and this time, I let Him know that Dunkirk, l'Orient, Bayonne, and Marseïlles Have Been declared free ports for the trade of America.[8] I don't write You Any thing about English News. They are distracted in that island. What they Have done to day, will Be Undone to Morrow, and While Pilots are Boxing the National Ship goes a drift, Sometime one Way, and Some time an other.[9] But You will get english intelligences from Jay, Adams, Laurens, and Barklay who are on that Side of the Water. The Appearances of a Russian war are more Remote. At all Events, let America Be Strongly attached to Her Continental Union. Let a Continental policy Rule the policy of the States, and the land of freedom will Have little to do with European Quarrells.

My Best Respects Waït Upon Mrs. Knox, and Miss Lucy. I most affectionately and fatherly kiss my Son Harry.[10] Mde. de Lafayette is Very much obliged to Your kind Rememberance and Presents You and Mrs. Knox with Her Most affectionate Compliments. Remember me most tenderly to [Huntington?] and all our Brother officers whenever You Have the good fortune to meet one of them. Adieu, my dear Knox, I am Your affectionate friend

LAFAYETTE

ALS (MHi: Henry Knox Papers). This letter is dated January 8 in Lafayette's hand. In the margin, in another hand, is the inscription "from the Marquis de Lafayette 12 January 1784."

1. Lafayette's Observations on the Commerce between France and the United States, [December 13, 1783].

2. William Knox.

3. Washington resigned as commander in chief on December 23, 1783; Knox, the senior major general, was in command of the army.

4. The army had been mustered out November 3, 1783, before Congress settled on a plan for the payment of the soldiers (*JCC*, 25:703). A peacetime establishment of four regiments of infantry and one of artillery was ordered by Congress (*JCC*, 25:725).

5. The "eagle": the badge of the Society of the Cincinnati.

6. The French officers who served in the American army and those who served under the French command of Rochambeau were organized separately in the Society of the Cincinnati.

7. The first general meeting of the Society of the Cincinnati was to be held in Philadelphia on May 4, 1784.

8. See Lafayette to Morris, December 26, 1783.

9. The analogy of political confusion to sailors fighting for control of the helm appears in Plato's *Republic*, bk. 6, paragraph 488.

10. Lafayette was godfather to Knox's son Harry.

From Charles-Alexandre de Calonne[T]

Versailles, January 9, 1784

Sir,

I reported to the king the observations contained in the report you sent me concerning American trade and those you made to me in our last conference.[1] I am authorized to notify you that it is His Majesty's intention to grant the United States the ports of Lorient and Bayonne as open and free ports in addition to those of Dunkirk and Marseilles. The first of these ports is completely free, and the freedom of the second is restricted only with regard to tobacco, which is subject to a duty there. From now on, the Americans may dispatch their ships to these four ports and will experience no difficulty there. If need be, you can explain what is meant by *free ports* from the definition given by M. de Vergennes in his letter of last June 29.[2] The Americans will find, especially at Dunkirk, all the facilities they may want for the sale of their leaf tobacco, their rice, their stavewood, and other merchandise, as well as for the purchase of those goods that may suit them, such as linens, spirits, woolens, and so forth. It is even proposed that depots and warehouses be set up there, which will be provided for them on conditions very advantageous to their trade. I have given orders to the Farmers General to offer preferential treatment and reasonable prices in purchasing tobacco from North America, and in addition the United States will be as favored in their trade in France as is any other nation.[3] The complaints the Americans may address to you, or that Mr. Franklin and other American ministers (whom I shall be very pleased to see) may have to transmit to me on their behalf, will be carefully examined, and the government will not tolerate any kind of vexation to be caused them. All possible measures will also be taken to prevent shipments of defective merchandise; if any have been sent up to now, they must be attributed to the greed of only a few merchants of the lowest order. I shall take care of everything in regard to customs and duties that hinder commerce; it is an important subject and one that requires considerable work. Finally, Monsieur, you may depend on it that I, as well as M. le Maréchal de Castries and M. le Comte de Vergennes, shall always be ready to receive and listen attentively to subsequent requests and statements you think it necessary to make in favor of American trade. I have the honor to be, etc.,

DE CALONNE

P.S. The ports of Bayonne and Lorient will be made, like Dunkirk, entirely free.

L (DNA: RG 360, PCC 137, vol. 3, p. 535), copy, translation.
1. Lafayette's Observations, [December 13,] 1783; see also Calonne to Lafayette, December 25, 1783.
2. See Vergennes to Lafayette, June 29, 1783.
3. The requirement that American trade be received on a most-favored-nation status was based on Article 2 of the Treaty of Amity and Commerce (1778):
The most Christian King and the United States engage mutually not to grant any particular Favour to other Nations in respect of Commerce and Navigation, which shall not immediately become common to the other Party, who shall enjoy the same Favour, freely, if the Concession was freely made, or on allowing the same Compensation, if the Concession was Conditional. [Gilbert Chinard, ed., *The Treaties of 1778 and Allied Documents* (Baltimore, 1928), p. 25]

To Robert Morris

Paris January the 10th 1784.

Dear Sir,

On the twenty sixth of last Month I had the Honor to address you a Letter enclosing some Observations from me to the French Minister, and Answers from them to me, and also giving you an Account of some Measures which in my private Capacity I thought it my Duty to undertake.[1] I have been much encouraged by your verbal Opinion to Colo. Gouvion respecting L'Orient, which I had taken upon myself to recommend for a free Port. A Duplicate of my Dispatch of December the 26th. is going in this Packet, whereby you may See, that in the private applications I make, Congress cannot by any Means be in the least committed.

Since my last Letter I have had some Conferences with the Ministry respecting enforcing what I had presented in the Memorial. Enclosed you will find an original official Letter from Mr. de Calonne the Minister of Finances, wherein the Affair of the free Ports is finally settled, and some other Parts of my observations are answered. I beg Leave to submit to Congress the Propriety of it's being published in the News Papers, and for the Facility of a Translation, I enclose a fair Copy made out by a more legible Hand.[2]

LAFAYETTE

L (DNA: RG 360, PCC 156, pp. 392–3), copy.
1. See Lafayette to Morris, December 26, 1783.
2. See preceding letter. Morris transmitted extracts of Lafayette's letter and a copy of Calonne's to Congress on April 16, with the comment that Calonne's letter, showing "the labors of that young nobleman to have been crowned with the wished for success, will, I

doubt not, be pleasing to Congress, as it is certainly very interesting to the commerce of the United States" [Wharton, *Diplomatic Correspondence*, 6:794].

To George Washington

Paris january the 10th 1784

My dear General

The departure of the Washington Has Been So Sudden that I Could not get in time on Board the Particular letter which you ought to Have Received. So that My Correspondance [Has Been] Confined to an official Cincinnati letter, and a Bill of plated wares, which was not By Any means my intention.[1] Inclosed I Send you a duplicate of the letter Respecting our Assossiation.[2] Major l'Enfant tells me a tolerable Number of Eagles will Be made on thursday, when After Having Called together the American officers Now Here, and Examined their Claims to the Marks of the Institution, we shall in a Body, and with [our] American Regimentals waït Upon Count de Rochambeau, and the Admirals of the french troops, and present them with the Badges they are to wear. You will Receive many Applications On that Subject, and I Need Not telling you old Rochambeau wants to Be as Conspicuous as He Can in that, as you know He does in Every other Affair. But as Nothing Can Be decided Before the Month of May I will timely write, and I Hope I will myself tell you my opinions in the Several instances that will Be Submitted to You. In Case the Badge is Multiplied, it will loose its price in Europe—and yet, there are Some instances who are Entitled to Regard.

By our last Accounts from America, my dear General, we Hear that Newyork is Evacuated, and that our Army, our Virtous and Brave Army [Now] are disbanded. Its dissolution, However Expected and proper it is, Has not Been Heard of By me without a Sigh. How Happy I Have Been at the Head quarters of that Army! How affectionately Received in Every tent I Had a Mind to Visit! My Most fortunate days Have Been Spent With that Army—and Now that it is [No] more, my Heart shall Ever Reverence and Cherish its Memory. God Grant our Brother officers may Be treated as they deserve! Will not the Country Remember what Evils that Army Have guarded Her Against, what Blessings they Have insured to them? I am told there is a peace Establishement of 800 men—and My dear general Now is at Mount Vernon where He Enjoys those titles Every Heart Gives Him, As the Saviour of His Country, the Benefactor of Mankind, the Protecting Angel of liber-

ty, the pride of America, and the Admiration of the two Hemi-
spheres—and Among all those Enjoyements I know He will Most tend-
erly feel the pleasure of Embracing His Best His Bosom friend, His
Adopted Son, who Early in the Spring will Be Blessed with a direct
Course to the Beloved landing that leads to the House at Mount
Vernon.

There are no great News in France, But it is Not the Case in England
whose people Seem as it were distracted. Pitt's party Have for the
Moment Got in place, But the Majority in the Commons are So much
Against them that it is Impossible for them to Remain in the Ministry.
It is probable we will In a few days See Mr. Fox and Lord North
Restored to their former power, when they will Undo Every thing the
others Have Done.[3] Mrs. Jay, Adams, and Laurens are Either at Lon-
don or Bath, Mr. Barklay is in England, and our old friend Doctor
Franklin is Confined to His House By the Gravel.[4] Under those Cir-
cumstances I thought it My duty not to Neglect the Affairs of America.
But as I Have no Instructions, Nor Any public Authority, I Can only
Advise and influence Such Preparatory Measures, as I thing May Be
Agreable to the United States. Some time Ago I presented a Memorial,
Which together with Some letters from the Ministers I Have on the
26th of last Month Enclosed to Mr. Moriss. In Consequence of those,
and of Several Conferences I Had with the Ministers, they Have determined to put a final Hand to the Affair of L'Orient, which I Had long
Ago taken Upon Myself to Begin, and which Wanted a definitive Conclusion. By a letter of this day to Mr. Moriss I Send Him Some further
Parts of a Correspondance with the Ministry, Wherein it is officially
Announced that Dunkirk, L'Orient, Bayonne, and Marseïlles are the
four free ports Given to the trade of America. This Evening I Return
to Versaïlles, where there is to Be a Conference Betwen the foreign
affairs, Naval, and finances Ministers and Myself. As I Am little Acquainted with those Matters, I Consult upon them with Wadsworth. In
all this America Neither promises Nor Asks for Any thing, So that she
Cannot Be Committed—and Her Ministers Being either Sick or
Abroad, do not, *Betwen Us*, So much as to mention an [earnest] word of
the Mercantile interest of America in France. European Affairs are
about the Same as when I wrote you last. There is No probability of an
impending war—at least for Next Year. The Emperor is in Italy as a
traveller. Unless I Am Honoured with Some Particular Commands
from Congress, I intend embarking for America Early in the Spring,
and I Hope to Arrive in time for the Grand Cincinnati Meeting. Mde.
de Lafayette, Your Son George, and my daughters join in the Most
Respectfull Compliments to You, and Mrs. Washington. I Give Her joy
upon Your Peacefull Retirement into Private life. I Beg, my dear general, You will Remember me to George, Mead, Mr. and Mrs. Lund

Washington, to all your friends and Relations. Adieu, My dear general, Your most Respectfull and affec friend

LAFAYETTE

ALS (PEL: Hubbard Collection).

1. See Lafayette to Washington, December 25, 1783. The letter requesting Lafayette to buy plated ware is that of October 30, 1783.

2. Enclosure not found.

3. On December 17, 1783, George III dismissed the Fox-North coalition. He appointed William Pitt the Younger, an inveterate opponent of North and his American policy, as First Lord of the Treasury and Chancellor of the Exchequer.

4. Kidney stones.

To Charles-Alexandre de Calonne[T]

Paris, January 31, 1784

In our last conversation, Monsieur, I submitted to you some questions from American merchants. You asked me for a note on them, and your good intentions toward this trade and the prompt decisions that stem from them have revived my hopes. While the British parties argue, we can make up for the delays of whose disadvantages you have been so well aware.

The four free ports were granted; you are designating some public buildings there to be used as American warehouses. It is greatly to be desired that none of the four ports be without this advantage; the fee for the use of these warehouses should be at the lowest possible price. What should be definitely settled is the schedule of fees for anchorage, the Farmers General, and the admiralty courts—in short, all those fees that are levied in an indefinite and always inconvenient way. They are less useful to the king than they are inconvenient to private parties, and while it is urgent to set them at the lowest rate possible, I think it would be very important to sacrifice them entirely.

Seeing the difficulties of trade with France, Mr. Wadsworth and Mr. Carter, two very rich Americans, have abandoned all ideas of pursuing this kind of trade. I showed them your letter, and they decided to try some ventures. They bought some silks and other articles and sent them off to a ship that was to sail from Lorient. But as the route went through Monsieur's domain, they either had to pay the duties, which would absorb the profit, or, as they did, lose the opportunity to ship the goods and increase the expense by taking a detour.[1]

These gentlemen want to send forty thousand bottles of Champagne wine to America. It would be convenient for them to load it in Brest, and one of their ships is passing there on returning from England.

They ask whether they will experience any difficulties and what fees must be paid for the ship to enter and leave the harbor.

Mr. Nesbitt, a merchant in Lorient, sends word that M. Pignon told him that Virginia tobacco was being purchased for 45 livres tournois and Maryland tobacco for 40.[2] He is forced to take a loss on what he has already received, but his friends and he gave orders for their tobacco to go directly from America to foreign ports. This tobacco monopoly is a great misfortune for trade with America, but since Messieurs the Farmers General must buy it, I am trying to find out what their purpose can be in giving the Americans a distaste for bringing it here when the same quality sells for much more in other European ports.[3]

Mr. Wadsworth and Mr. Carter, about whom M. de Rochambeau's whole army can tell you,[4] made a very just observation to me. It is that England is decreasing the duties on articles exported to America, and if France were to do as much, for example, on mirrors and that whole branch of glassware, it would have an advantage over British manufactures.

When I receive your answer to these notes, sir, I shall report to the American merchants on what may concern them. They are encouraged by your activity and your determination, and it is very fortunate that you have come to divert the current that was carrying all the American trade to England. I have, etc.

L (DNA: RG 360, PCC 137, vol. 3, pp. 429–32), copy, translation; enclosed with Lafayette to Robert Morris, August 14, 1784 (DNA: RG 360, PCC 121, p. 107).

1. Many feudal domains and civil jurisdictions charged fees or tariffs for goods transported across their territory. In this case lands owned by the Comte de Provence, the king's brother, were between Lorient and the source of the manufactured silk.

2. Jonathan Nesbitt was a Philadelphia merchant who was in Lorient during the war. Michel Pignon was a member of the tobacco committee of the Farmers General.

3. The Farmers General had a monopoly on the purchase of all tobacco imported into France. In September 1783 they contracted with Jonathan Williams and William Alexander to provide them with 15,000 hogsheads of tobacco annually at 30 livres tournois. As tobacco was selling in Virginia and Maryland for 40 and 45 livres tournois, this portended great difficulties for American tobacco farmers willing to sell to France (Jacob M. Price, *France and the Chesapeake* [Ann Arbor, 1973], 2:741). See also Lafayette to Calonne, February 10, 1784.

4. Wadsworth and Carter had been efficient suppliers for Rochambeau's army in America.

From George Washington

Mount Vernon 1st. Feby. 1784

At length my Dear Marquis I am become a private citizen on the banks of the Potomac, & under the shadow of my own Vine & my own

Fig-tree, free from the bustle of a camp & the busy scenes of public life, I am solacing myself with those tranquil enjoyments, of which the Soldier who is ever in pursuit of fame—the Statesman whose watchful days & sleepless nights are spent in devising schemes to promote the welfare of his own—perhaps the ruin of other countries, as if this Globe was insufficient for us all—& the Courtier who is always watching the countenance of his Prince, in hopes of catching a gracious smile, can have very little conception. I am not only retired from all public employments, but I am retireing within myself; & shall be able to view the solitary walk, & tread the paths of private life with heartfelt satisfaction. Envious of none, I am determined to be pleased with all, & this my dear friend, being the order for my march, I will move gently down the stream of life, until I sleep with my Fathers.

Except an introductory letter or two, & one countermanding my request respecting Plate, I have not written to you since the middle of Octobr. by Genl. Duportail.[1] To inform you at this late hour, that the City of New York was evacuated by the British forces on the 25h. of Novembr.—that the American Troops took possession of it the same day, & delivered it over to the civil authority of the State—that good order, contrary to the expectation & predictions of Gl. Carleton, his officers & all the loyalists, was immediately established—and that the harbour of New York was finally cleared of the British flag about the 5h. or 6h. of Decemr., would be an insult to your intelligence. And to tell you that I remained eight days in New York after we took possession of the City—that I was very much hurried during that time, which was the reason I did not write to you from thence—that taking Phila. in my way, I was obliged to remain there a week—that at Annapolis, where Congress were then, and are now sitting, I did, on the 23d. of December present them my Commission, & made them my last bow—& on the Eve of Christmas entered these doors, an older man by near nine years, than when I left them, is very uninteresting to any but myself. Since that period we have been fast locked up in frost & snow, & excluded in a manner from all kinds of intercourse, the winter having been, & still continues to be, extremely severe.

I have now to acknowledge, and thank you for your favors of the 22d. of July & 8h. of September, both of which, altho' the first is of old date, have come to hand since my letter to you of October. The accounts contained therein of the political & commercial state of affairs as they respect America, are interesting, & I wish I could add that they were altogether satisfactory; & the agency you have had in both, particularly with regard to the Free ports in France, is a fresh evidence of your unwearied endeavours to serve this country; but there is no part of your Letters to Congress My Dear Marquis, which bespeaks the excellence of your heart more plainly than that, which contains those noble & generous sentiments on the justice which is due to the faithful friends & Servants of the public,[2] but I must do Congress the justice to declare, that as a body, I believe there is every disposition in them, not only to acknowledge the merits, but to reward the services of the army: there is a contractedness, I am sorry to add, in some of the States, from whence all our difficulties on this head, proceed; but it is to be hoped, the good sense & perseverance of the rest, will ultimately prevail, as the spirit of meanness is beginning to subside.[3]

From a letter which I have just received from the Governor of this State I expect him here in a few days, when I shall not be unmindful of what you have written about the bust; & will endeavour to have matters respecting it, placed on their proper basis.[4] I thank you most sincerely My Dear Marqs. for your kind invitation to your house, if I should come to Paris. At present I see but little prospect of such a voyage; the deranged situation of my private concerns, occasioned by an absence of almost nine years, and an entire disregard of all private business during that period, will not only suspend, but may put it forever out of my power to gratify this wish. This not being the case with you, come with Madame la Fayette & view me in my domestic walks. I have often told you; & I repeat it again, that no man could receive you in them with more friendship & affection than I should do; in which I am sure Mrs. Washington would cordially join me. We unite in respectful compliments to your Laday, & best wishes for your little flock. With every sentiment of esteem, Admiration & Love, I am, My Dr. Marqs. Your Most affecte. friend

G: WASHINGTON

LbC (DLC: George Washington Papers, Series 2).

1. Probably Washington to Lafayette, October 12, 1783.

2. See Lafayette to the President of Congress, July 20 and September 7, 1783.

3. Since payment of the officers depended on appropriations from the states, a final settlement to the officers' satisfaction was still in doubt.

4. The Virginia Assembly had commissioned a bust of Lafayette to be presented to him, but little had been done to ensure the fulfillment of the commission.

From Thomas Mullens

Liege the 5th. of february 1784.

Sir/

I Received your favour of the 20th. of Last Month with the Papers I Left with you inclosed, I am very much oblidged to you for the interest you have, and will be pleased to take for what regards me. I have no other proof of my Service in the american army But my Commission and the resolwe of Congress which you have Seen. All I Can Say is that I took on in the american Service in november 1776 with General Conway in Paris and that I Continued in the Service from that month till the end of november 1778. and Drew pay During the whole time. I parted with no other forlough or passport but my Commission and the resolve you have Seen.[1] I do give you my word of honor I never resigned and that my intention was to go back the following Summer if I had not been (as you Know) imployed with you, in Monsieur DeVaux army,[2] and after that, if I had not been Sent as Captain of guides with General Rochambeau to America I would have gone back to Serve there again, but you Know it was not in my power, as been employed for my own King and master. If any other person was charged With the Distribution of the order, and that they required prooffs of my Service in that Country, I would not Know to who I Should adress me Self to for a Certificat but to you, as being Very often Eye wittness to my way of Serving, and Beheavour. Not Knowing personaly the Gentlemen of the Committee I will ask it as a particular favour, of the marquis, to return them my hearty thanks for their good intentions in my behalf. I Suppose they are Some of the gentlemen whom I had the honor of Serving with in that Country. If So, they have Seen how I have Served there, and may judge if I have merited, the honor of wearing the Badge, with them or not.

General Lafayette has Shewed me a great deal of friendship where ever I met him, and even honored me with a promise of his protection, now I reclaim it, and beg he will write In my favour to the Committee or to his excellency, Genl. Washington who, I am Sure will not refuse me the honor of wearing the Badge.[3] I belive my Service in America with the french army, with the time I Served the american army, may Count a Letter in my favour. In short I Leave all to your Judgement and gooness of heart. And remains with the humblest respect, Sir, Your most humble and Devoted Servant—

MULLENS.

Capitaine D'infenterie

Basse Sauvenniere a Liege.

ALS (Anderson House Museum, Society of the Cincinnati, Washington, D.C.).

1. On June 11, 1778, Congress granted Mullens a brevet commission of lieutenant colonel (*JCC*, 21:586).

2. The Comte de Vaux commanded the troops for the projected invasion of England in 1779 (See *LAAR*, 2:275–337 *passim*).

3. On March 8, 1784, a board of French Continental officers presided over by Lafayette considered Mullens' petition and agreed to present his request for membership in the Society of the Cincinnati at the meeting of the Society's general assembly in May; Mullens was admitted.

To Charles-Alexandre de Calonne[T]

Paris, February 10, 1784

As I am on the point of writing to America, Monsieur, I would like to continue sending on favorable news in my letters. Having established the free ports, you must complete your work by ascertaining and perhaps even abolishing in those ports the fees of the admiralty courts, those for anchorage and piloting, and other hindrances to trade of which I had the honor to write you.[1] It would be worthwhile to reassure the Americans about the sale of their tobacco. I sent you some recent complaints, and I predict bad results from the instructions given by the Farm for Virginia tobacco.[2] It is now being obtained from the Ukraine, and generally instead of buying America's, the Farm is taking cheap tobacco of very poor quality. You have been so generous on the free ports that it would be inconsiderate to present a new idea of this kind, but several Americans have told me that if Le Havre had similar privileges, they would ensure increased purchases of the manufactured goods of Normandy and would facilitate the sale of articles made in Paris. A ship loaded in England would also come and pick up some French goods because of the tempting proximity and convenience. What I have the honor to tell you about it, Monsieur, should be attributed to the desire not to neglect any of the Americans' statements. Please accept the homage of my gratitude and of the respect, etc.

L (DNA: RG 360, PCC 137, vol. 3, pp. 433–34), copy, translation; enclosed with Lafayette to Robert Morris, August 14, 1784 (DNA: RG 360, PCC 121, p. 107).

1. Admiralty (charges for court duties), anchorage (one of the many harbor fees), and pilotage (a fee for having the ship brought safely into harbor) were only a few of the many separate charges.

2. See Lafayette to Calonne, January 31, 1784.

To Charles-Alexandre de Calonne[T]

Paris, February 26, 1784

Monsieur le Controleur Général will find here the reports he kindly entrusted to me, and in order to carry out his intentions I submit to him the views of the American merchants I have consulted.[1] The fees to be paid in the free ports are less annoying because of their cost than because of their multiplicity. Abolishing them entirely would perhaps be difficult, but they could be decreased first and then combined as a single fee, so much for a three-masted ship, so much for a two-masted one, and so on, so that they would not be delayed to determine how much water they draw. This method would deprive no one because the profits would be divided among those who have a claim to them. It would prevent the extortions and dishonesty to which foreigners may be subjected. It would remove all the encumbrances of that kind about which the Americans complain, and it would far surpass the British method. After this arrangement is made, two statements would have to be sent, one of the old fees and the other of the new form adopted, and this new regulation would be printed in all the American papers.

A ship is about to leave for America, and if Monsieur le Controleur Général will be good enough to make a decision on this subject and some other points in my letters, I shall hasten to carry out his views by communicating the dispositions he has made. If it is convenient for him to receive me either Saturday in Paris or Sunday at Versailles before or after the council meeting, I shall comply with the orders he will be kind enough to give me. I beg him to accept, etc.

L (DNA: RG 360, PCC 137, vol. 3, pp. 437–38), copy, translation; enclosed with Lafayette to Robert Morris, August 14, 1784 (DNA: RG 360, PCC 121, p. 107).
    1. Reports not identified.

To Charles-Alexandre de Calonne[T]

Paris, March 5, 1784

In order to comply with the intentions of Monsieur le Controleur Général, I went to M. Chardon's,[1] and although he had been bled twice, he was kind enough to attend to our business. He did not think this work could be done until we have new and more precise statements, but in accordance with the report he was to give today, I hope to receive two letters that will reassure the Americans about the disposition of the two departments.

Besides that letter that Monsieur le Controleur Général promised me, I take the liberty of telling him that the announcement of the four free ports was received in New York a month ago. Consequently, ships should be expected any day, and since only a mere formality remains to be taken care of, it would be desirable for it to be dispensed with as soon as possible. I even delayed the American officer in the hope that my Sunday trip to Versailles would enable me to send the printed statement.

In talking with the Americans about the importation of their flour to our colonies, one of them told me we could take steps to have them paid in part with wines and manufactured goods. This obligation to have contracts made with the Americans could be combined with the excellent idea of a modest duty, subject to drawback, which Monsieur le Controleur Général was kind enough to share with me—an idea that M. le Comte d'Estaing had also given me. I have the honor, etc.

                                                                        L.

L (DNA: RG 360, PCC 137, vol. 3, p. 441), copy, translation; enclosed with Lafayette to Morris, August 14, 1784 (DNA: RG 360, PCC 121, p. 107).
    1. Daniel-Marc-Antoine Chardon was commissioner for the inspection of shipping, fisheries, and maritime dues.

To Jeremiah Wadsworth

                                                    Paris March the 7th 1784

My dear Sir,
    Where this letter may Reach You, I Cannot tell, But Whatever Part of the World You are in, I Want to let You know that I very much Regret the pleasure of Your Compagny. I Had a Note from our Amiable friend Dated Calais March the 2d, Wherein She tells me You are all well, and Ready to push for the English Shore.[1] Had our Revolution Miscarried, I Could not Have Met a Briton But What I Would Have Quarrelled with Him. But in the Way it Went, I think We May Be at our Ease with them, Since it Becomes American Soldiers to Be kind to the Conquered.

    Colonel Gouvion's Compliments Waït Upon You. Altho' He is just from America, We May Suppose His Being Advised Not to Return there. But in all Cases, if He is to Be employed as a Principal and Confidential Man, I think it Worth our friend's While to Make the Voyage. The More So as it Will do Him Honour, and Enable Him to take place in [the] Military Establishement, if Such a one is Made that deserves His attention.[2] But What I wish Most is, His [Being] Soon Advised By His friends to Accompagny me in My Voyage.

    That Voyage, My dear Sir, is a pleasant idea to me. I Hope to Set off By the last days of April. The pleasure of Hearing from You Before that time Will Be Very Agreeable. I Beg also You Will let me know what Becomes of irish Politics. Should they depend Upon Such and

Such Ministries, Untill Ministers are Neither Scotch, Nor English, and Have No Need of British titles and British popularity, they will Be Soon Deceived in their Expectations. My Best Compliments Waït Upon Mr. And Mrs. Church. Most Affectionately Yours

L.F.

ALS (CtHi: Jeremiah Wadsworth Papers).
   1. Letter not found. This was probably Angelica Schuyler Church, "Carter's" wife. John B. Church (alias Carter) had been in France with his partner Jeremiah Wadsworth trying to obtain payment on bills due them from the Ministry of the Marine. Wadsworth, Church, and Church's wife were at Calais ready to embark for England.
   2. Lafayette was interested in furthering Gouvion's military career in either America or France. Since the peacetime army in America was negligible, Lafayette wrote the Marechal de Ségur on May 15, 1784, trying to secure Gouvion a staff position in the French army (NIC: Dean Collection).

To John Adams

Paris March the 8th 1784

My dear Sir

Before I Had a Pointed Reason to write, My friendship for You, and our Common zeal for the Public Had dictated it. But I must Begin With the Article that in My Mind Creates Some Uneasiness.

It is writen from Amsterdam that Mr. John Adams is Very Violent Against the Society of the Cincinnati and Calls it a *french Blessing*—and that He Says, altho' I Have long Announced an Intention to Go to America, I Never fulfill it, which Seems to Him a Want of zeal to Comply with the desire of My American friends.[1]

Was I to take the Matter Up, as a french Man, I Might tell You, that the french Court Had Not, that I know of, dreamt of the Society Before Count de Rochambeau Was writen to By General Washington[2]—and I Might Add that Orders, titles, and Such other foolish tokens of Vanity, Are Not More Valued in France, Not Even So Much, As they are in Germany, Russia, Spain, and Great Britain.

But As it is as An American that I Engaged, Bled, Negotiated, fought, and Succeeded in our Noble Cause, I only Want to Mark out My Conduct to You, Whom I Esteem, and Whose Esteem, in Point of Republicanism particularly, I Hold in the Greatest Value.

The Institution in itself I do not Examine. It is Worth paying Attention to it. Should it Be dangerous, it Must not Subsist. Should Some parts Be Exceptionable, Amendments Must Be Made. In Case it is quite Harmless, the American officers Might Be Indulged in that, as the

Country is not a little Indebted to them. Opinions Must Be Collected Because Opinions, of Honest Men May differ. *Lee* Was the Hero of Some,[3] General *Washington* Was Mine, and So on. I don't Enter into the Merits or demerits of the Society. I only want to Acquaint You with the Part I Have taken.

The Society's letters Respecting the french Army were directed to their Generals and Admirals. The Permitting of it, Has Been Considered at Versaïlles, as a Compliment Paid to a large and Meritorious Body of Americans, as a Badge of Union Betwen the two Countries, and I Had no Part to Act in the Business. The part I Acted, Was, 1stly to Accept for Myself, and deliver the Marks of the Society to American officers pointed out by Gal. Washington—2dly after it was Accepted By the french officers to deliver it to them in a polite and Brotherly Manner—and When I acted So, I was led By two motives—the One, Because, independant of the affectionate and dutiful Regard that Binds me to Our Gallant, patriotic Army, Independant of what Can Be Said in favour of that free Maçonnery of liberty, it Has Ever Been My duty and inclination to Set up in the Best light Every thing that is done By a Body of Americans—and When wrong Measures, Such as are Some times taken in County or town Meetings Have Been By me disputed for in foreign Compagnies, I will Be Still More desirous to See a Proper Respect Paid to the Measures of Such a Respectable Body as the American officers. My Second Motive is, that Independant of Any Propriety of the Institution in itself, Had I Amendments to Propose, it Should Be in America and Not in Europe, and that, on the Moment the Society is Unpopular, a two Words Resolve from an Assembly May Entirely destroy it, when, if danger is feared, I Heartily Would Consent to the destruction.

I Have not Entered into the Merits of the Assossiation. Your Opinion, and Mine, on the Subject, are not to Have Effect in Europe. Let us Reserve it for America, where it May Be of Use. I only Wanted My Conduct Not to Be Misrepresented to You—and As to My democratic principles, let it Be Remembered that at a time When Your Situation Was to the Worst, and My disobeing This Court Might Be Ruinous, I Went over a Volonteer in the Cause from which others Could not Recede Unless they Were Deserters.

As to My Going to America, You know I Came With an Instruction to Settle a plan of Cooperation. Count de Grasse's Misfortune Postponed it. Negotiations Came on, and You thought I Should Stay. Count d'Estaing Was Employed, and You thought I should Go with Him. I did not Set off Before the Affair of the Six Millions Was Settled, as You well know. When Peace Was Made, I Returned through Spain. The Minister and Consul wanted free ports, wished to Have l'Orient, and Had no Instructions to Ask officially. Instead of two that were Promised, four Have Been Given—Dunkirk, L'Orient, Bayonne, and Marseïlles. That Affair will Be Soon Concluded and Before the end of May I Shall Set out for America. Many Reasons of delay Might Be pleaded. But they did not So Much Weigh, with me as to Retard the Intended Visit.

This *Confidential* letter I Consider as a Personal Mark of Esteem for You, and Respect for Your Opinion. Altho' We Have differed in a few points, our fundamental principles are the Same. It is not to the Great Man I write, Because My popularity, thank god, is Established in the kind, liberal Hearts of the American Nation at large. It is to the Honest Man, Because, Altho' Your opinion Some times Has Seemed to me Wrong Your Principles Have Ever Been Right and I Greatly Valüe Your Esteem. Adieu, My dear Sir, let me Hear Some times from You and Believe me afectionately Yours

LAFAYETTE

ALS (MHi: Adams Papers). Lafayette took great care with the wording of this letter, to soften the impact of his remarks.

1. The source of Lafayette's paraphrasing of Adams' opinion remains unidentified. Adams believed that the society was a hereditary chivalric order and violated the Articles of Confederation. In a January 25 letter to Matthew Ridley, he had written, "I have been informed that this whole Scheme, was first concerted, in France and transmitted from thence, by the Marquis" (MHi: Adams Papers).

2. Washington's October 29, 1783, letter to the Comte de Rochambeau informed him of the establishment of and his election to membership in the society "to perpetuate those friendships which have been form'd during a time of common danger and sitress" (DLC: George Washington Papers, Series 4).

3. General Charles Lee.

From Charles-Alexandre de Calonne[T]

Versailles, March 8, 1784

I have studied very attentively, Monsieur, the representations you did me the honor to send me on the fees American ships are obliged to pay in the four free ports His Majesty assigned to them.[1] You complain, Monsieur, of the high cost of these fees, their multiplicity, and the ease with which people of bad faith use them to deceive foreigners ignorant of the French language and local customs. You request the abolition of the majority of these fees and that all those that are allowed to remain be combined into a single fee imposed according to the size of each ship (with three or two masts, and so on), to avoid the detailed manner of imposing the duty on the basis of the ship's tonnage capacity and the amount of water it draws. I must first observe to you, Monsieur, that on the one hand, the fees levied on American ships in French ports are the same as for other foreign ships, and that on the other, they do not exceed the fees levied by the British. But you state that the Americans are not informed of the nature and quality of the fees imposed in France, on their ships as on all others. I cannot, on that account, propose any decision to His Majesty before ascertaining, through definite information, what these fees consist of, for whose profit they are levied, and by what right they were established. To gain an understanding of these matters I have requested His Majesty to have orders sent to the admiralty courts in the four free ports so that these tribunals will send without delay a precise statement, certified by them, of all the fees of any kind that an American ship is obliged to pay when it enters or leaves port. When these statements reach me, I shall hasten to bring the results to His Majesty's attention, and then I can propose that he take official measures to decrease these fees as much as possible, to consolidate those that are kept, and to have them paid on the basis of ship size. This will be a new occasion for me to prove to the United States the favorable disposition of our court toward all that concerns them. You should be convinced that I allow no such opportunity to escape, and the decision His Majesty has just made on my report on the abolition of all duties on the export of our spirits is another proof of the attention he gives to all aspects of our trade with the United States. I flatter myself that you do justice to the desire I have to give you proof of all the sentiments I have pledged to you. I have the honor to be your very humble, etc.,

De Calonne

L (DNA: RG 360, PCC 137, vol. 31, p. 647), copy, translation. A marginal note in Lafayette's hand reads: "The Original Has Been Sent By the March packet from Lorient."
1. See Lafayette to Calonne, March 5, 1784.

To Robert Morris[E]

Paris March 9th. 1784.

Dear Sir

On the 10th of January I had the Honour to send you Mr. de Calonne's Letter wherein the Affair of the free Ports *Dunkirk, L'Orient Bayonne* and *Marseilles* is finally settled. Upon its Conclusion I thought my next Step was to enquire what Duties were paid there by American

Vessels, and I found them various in their Kind, multiplied in their Number, inconvenient in their Perception,[1] and so uncertain in their Rates, that American Merchants have to fear a confusion at least, and probably a series of Impositions. I therefore in my private Capacity and of course without committing the United States thought proper to address this Government—1st. to have those Duties entirely or at least in a Part abolished. 2ly. what remains of them to have reduced into one description, dependant upon the Vessels size and not the arbitrary Mode of Tonnage, and so clearly explained that every American Captain may know them before he leaves his Country. In Consequence of said Application I had a Letter addressed to me which I have the Honor to enclose. I have flattered myself that the Abolition of Duties upon exported Brandies would also be agreeable to America. The Propriety of publishing M. de Calonne's Letter I Beg leave to submit to Congress.

L (DNA: RG 360, PCC 137, vol. 3, p. 643), copy, extract. On May 27, 1784, a committee of Congress considered extracts of this letter and the enclosed letter from Calonne to Lafayette dated March 8, 1784. It resolved that they be sent along with other letters and records to Adams, Franklin, and Jefferson to assist them in their commercial negotiations in Europe (JCC, 27:471).

1. "Perception:" collection (of taxes or dues).

To George Washington

Paris March the 9th 1784

Sir

Your Excellency Has Been Acquainted With my first Measures Respecting our Society.[1] To My Letter Xber. the 25th I Beg Leave Particularly to Refer and Entrust this With Major l'Enfant Who is Returning to America.

Having in a Body Waïted Upon Count de Rochambeau, we delivered Him and His officers the Marks of the Assossiation. A Resolve of theirs for a Volontary Subscription Will Arrive in time to Be debated in the Grand Assembly.[2]

Many Claims Have Been Raised By french officers, Which it is not My Business to Present. But I Beg Leave to observe that Some of them, Like in Chevalier de Lameth's Case, are Entitled to Consideration. Count de Rochambeau, I am told, is writing on the Subject.[3]

Former dispatches Have Apologised for the Part We Have taken Respecting Count d'Estaing's officers.[4] The Neglect, We knew, Was not Intended—and, as also in Mr. de Vaudreuïl's Case, it Would Have

Blank diploma of the Society of the Cincinnati, bearing its insignia, an American bald eagle, and signed by its first president, George Washington.

Produced a Bad Effect.[5] The Captains in the Navy, Ranking as Colonels, Have Set up a Claim to the Assossiation. Some of them, La *Peyrouse*, La *Touche*, *Tilly*, Acted as Commodores.[6] It May Be Observed that American trade Will Have to do With Naval Officers.

At a Board of Officers Met at My House, the Claims of Several Gentlemen Were Introduced. Our Opinions are Submitted to the Assembly, and With them I enclose a list of Members who Have Signed and Paid, or to Whom, on Account of their Dispersion, the Institution are Yet to Be Sent. Clel. du Plessis Convinced us He Had not Resigned.

Our Brotherly Assossiation Has Met With General Applause. Not a dissenting Voice to Be Heard But on the Point of Heredity that Creates a debate Wherein Most of the Americans take the other Part. Who Can Question But What We do not on Any Account Wish to Injure those Sacred Republican Principles for which We Have Fought, Bled, and Conquered? and What Sacrifice Has not Been Made By us, in Support of those Principles? which, I am Sure, we are Ready to Repeat Upon Every Occasion?

There is an Unanimous Opinion of the officers Here which they Beg Leave to Present, wiz—that all American Officers in Europe Ought to Resort to a Committee of Which this City is a Natural Center, and that the Committee Be Instructed to Correspond With the Grand Assembly.

It Had Been My Fond Hope that I Could Have Arrived in time for the Begining of May—But American Concerns, an Account of Which I Give to Congress,[7] detain me for a few Weeks—and Now When I think this Letter Will Be Read Among Representatives from all the lines of the Army, My Heart is Glowing With all the Most Unbounded Sentiments of Affection and Gratitude. How Pleasing it is for me, to Recollect our Common toils, dangers, turns of fortune, our So Glorious Successes and that Lively Attachment Which United us With Each other Under our Beloved General. Never Can My Heart forget the Return of Affection I Have Particularly Obtained, the Numberless Obligations I am Under to My dear Brother Officers, and the Happy Hours, the Happiest in My Life, Which I Have Past in their Compagny. Before the Month of June is Over, I shall, thank God, Be Again With them, and Am Panting for the Instant When I May Be Blessed with a Sight of the American Shore. With the Highest Respect and Unbounded affection I Have the Honour to Be Sir Your Excellency's Most obedient Humble Servant

LAFAYETTE

ALS (Anderson House Museum, Society of the Cincinnati, Washington, D.C.), enclosing a list of members of the Society of the Cincinnati in France, March 8, 1784 (Anderson House Museum, Society of the Cincinnati, Washington, D.C.) and the Proceedings of a

Committee of French Continental Officers, March 8, 1784. This letter was read in the general meeting of the Society of the Cincinnati on May 7, 1784.

1. See Lafayette to Washington, December 25, 1783.

2. Since the French officers were granted honorary membership in the Society of the Cincinnati, they were not expected to pay membership dues. Since the bylaws allowed for voluntary contributions, however, the French officers decided to donate money to the general fund.

3. The Chevalier de Lameth had been wounded at Yorktown. Rochambeau's letter to Washington of March 1, 1784, recommending Lameth for membership, is in DLC: George Washington Papers, Series 4. Lameth was admitted to the Society.

4. The membership provisions of the society were unclear on whether those who served under D'Estaing at Rhode Island in 1778 and at Savannah in 1779 would be in the American branch or the French. At the May 1784 General Assembly of the American branch, the captains and superior officers under D'Estaing were admitted.

5. See Lafayette to Washington, December 25, 1783.

6. Lafayette wrote an extensive letter to Washington that same day supporting the claims to membership of naval captains, those who had served with D'Estaing, and other officers. Among them was General Thomas Conway, whom Lafayette recommended for membership to eliminate the chance that he might "become a pretence to a Sect who Have not Hitherto found Any Against me." Lafayette also supported the concept of an American committee in Europe, "as it is Calculated only for American purposes, and ought to Consist But of American officers for the time Being in Europe" (Gottschalk, *Letters of Lafayette*, pp. 278–81).

7. Lafayette's efforts were to secure commercial concessions (see his letter to Robert Morris, March 9, 1784).

To George Washington

Paris March the 9th 1784

My Dear General

Had I Not So Perfect a Confidence in Your friendship, I Would Very Much fear to tire You With My Scribbling of this day. But Cannot Leave My penn Before I Have Again Mentionned My tender Respectfull Affection to My dear General. I Want to tell you that Mde. de Lafayette and My three children are Well, and that all of us in the family Heartly join to Present their dutiful Affectionate Compliments to Mrs. Washington and Yourself. Tell Her that I Hope Soon to thank Her for a Dish of tea at Mount Vernon. Yes, My dear General, Before the Month of june is Over You will see a Vessel Coming Up Pottowmack, and out of that Vessel Will Your friend jump With a Panting Heart and all the feelings of Perfect Happiness. I intended to Have Gone Sooner, But a few Commercial Matters Still keep me Here. For Since No Body Middles with them, I Have Undertaken in My Private Capacity to do what is possible for one who Has Neither title, or Instruction. It is at least a Confort that in My private Capacity I Cannot Commit Congress, and that I never Speak But of what I know. Four ports Having Been declared free, I Send Mr. Moriss a Letter Respecting the duties to Be paid there.[1] And I Hope Congress will also publish that all duties Have Been Removed from the Exportation of Brandies.

Most of the Americans Here are indecently Violent Against our Assossiation.[2] Wadsworth Must Be excepted, and Doctor Franklin Said little. But Jay, Adams, and all the others warmly Blame the Army. You Easely guess I am not Remiss in opposing them—and However if it is found that the Heredity Endangers the true principles of democraty, I am as Ready as Any Man to Renounce it. You Will Be My Compass, My dear General, Because at this distance I Cannot judge. In Case Upon Better Consideration, You find that Heredity will injure our democratic Constitutions, I join with You By proxy in Voting Against it. But I So much Rely on Your judgement that if You think Heredity is a proper scheme I will Be Convinced that Your Patriotism Has Considered the Matter in the Best point of View. *To You alone,* I would Say So much, and I abide By your opinion in the Matter. Let the foregoing Be Confidential, But I am Sure Your disinterested virtue will weigh all possible, future Consequences, of Hereditary distinctions.

There are No News in this Moment that are worth Relating. What Respects Balons, Mr. l'Enfant Will tell.[3] The present English disputes are Some what Ridiculous. They must end in a dissolution of Parliament or an Union Betwen Pitt and Fox. Adieu, My dear General, Accept with Your Usual Goodness the Affectionate tribute of a Heart So Entirely devoted to You that No Words Can Ever Express the Respect, the Love, and all the Sentiments With Which You know it is glowing for You, and that Make me Untill my last Breath Your obedient Humble Sert. and affectionate friend

LAFAYETTE

My Compliments waït Upon George and all the family at Mount Vernon. Be so kind My dear general as to Remember me to all our friends. I am very Sorry the Hurry I was in to Serve You occasioned my Sending So Soon the plated wares.[4] Adieu, my dear general.

ALS (PEL: Hubbard Collection).
1. Lafayette to Morris, March 9, 1784.
2. "Assossiation": the Society of the Cincinnati.
3. Numerous balloon experiments took place in France over the fall and winter of 1783–84; the first ascent of a man in a free balloon was in November 1783.
4. See Washington to Lafayette, October 30, 1783.

From Henry Laurens

London 15 March 1784.

Sir.

Immediately after my return from Paris, I found it necessary to go to Bath, where I thought I had pretty well recovered my health, & was coming to London in order to make Preparations for my Voyage to America, hoping to have embarked in this Month, but I was again seized by the Gout in my Head, & in all parts of my Body, in the Month of January, & have never since been one Day well. At this Moment, I am wholly incapable of writing, & am going to submit to another dragging down to Bath, but not before I acknowledge with many thanks your polite & obliging Letter accompanied by a larger Paper,[1] delivered by Mr. Wadsworth, this Paper I shall leave under seal & your Direction in the Case of Mr. Bridgen, to be forwarded by the hand of a Friend; the Writer of that Piece, though he is pleased modestly to plead an unacquaintedness with the Subject, has in my Opinion acquitted himself abundantly well, one thing perhaps might have been added, that in case of a War between two great Powers, the distant People may be made infinitely serviceable to the Commerce of their best Friend, a Subject which requires the earliest attention.

The People here are talking about it, & about it goaded by Applications from the West India Planters, & some of the Merchants, they have deliberated & sometimes half promised, but hitherto, have done nothing; in the mean time the distant People, provoked by the Proclamation of the 2nd of July 1783, & the trifling Conduct which appeared at the Negotiations through that Summer, are shewing Signs of great resentment, the particulars of which undoubtedly you have learned;[2] I say now, as I said upon the grand occasion so far back as 1777. "*Be steady, &* all things will come right."

We are told that a Priest first discovered the Art of making Gun Powder, Military Men write Treatises upon Commerce, Colonel Lord Sheffield has just emitted a new Edition of his elaborate Treatise, with additions, particularly as I am informed of bitterness & invective, the first Publications of this Book certainly influenced the Conduct of last Summer.[3] No doubt the present will also have its Effect. I shall request Mr. Bridgen to send you a Copy on which you will form your own Judgement. Shakespear says, "There is a tide in the Affairs of Men which taken at the Flood leads on" &c, I forget the rest, & have not the Book by me, but you know it; I could wish our Friends would wisely embrace the Tide.

I have had no opportunity under so much sickness of hearing any thing from a neighboring Island,[4] but through the Channell of News Papers, otheways I should long since have contrived a Communication.

Our good Friend General Washington is as much admired, & spoken of in as high Strains, in this Country as in any other.

The new Ministry here seem at present to be fixed, but there are Watchmen ready to embrace the first Moment to unhorse them. I have it from as good Authority as the Case will admit of, that certain necessary business is to be accomplished, the Parliament dissolved, & a fair appeal made to the People, but had this been told me by the K— himself, I should nevertheless say, his Majesty may see cause to reconsider.

My Daughter who is so good as to act in this occasion as my assistant Secretary, desires to unite with me, in most respectful Compliments to Mons. le Marquis, & Madame de la Fayette; with every good Wish to their dearest Pledges—I have—the honor to be, with the highest Regard, My dear & much-esteemed Marquis Your obliged & most obedt. Servt.

L (MHi: Henry Laurens Papers, Kendall Collection), copy.
1. The letter has not been found; the paper was Lafayette's Observations, [December 13, 1783].
2. The British order in council of July 2, 1783, prohibited all trade between the United States and the British West Indies.
3. Sheffield's *Observations on the Commerce of the American States* (London, 1784), opposed any relaxation of the British Navigation Acts in favor of the United States.
4. Ireland.

From John Adams

The Hague March 28. 1784

Sir

I did not receive your Letter of the 8th. untill the day before yesterday. That I have not Seen with Pleasure, Approbation or Indifference, the Introduction into America, of So great an Innovation, as an order of Chivalry, or any Thing like one, or that has a Tendency to one, is very true. That I have been violent against it, is not So. I am not a violent Man. I have disapproved of this measure, with as much Tranquility and Self Recollection, and Phlegm, if you will, as if I had been a native fullblooded Dutchman. It is not more than two or three times, that I have had occasion to Say any Thing about it, and then it was not I who introduced the Subject and then I Said very little.

It is not my Intention to discuss the question. It is too ample a Field. But it is not done by the Sovereigns of our Country. What would be

Said, in any Nation of Europe, if a new order, was instituted by private Gentlemen, without consulting the Sovereign? It is against our Confederation and against the Constitutions of Several States as it appears to me.[1] It is against the Spirit of our Governments and the Genius of our People. Well may our Government be weak, if the Sovereign, the Confederation and Constitutions are thus neglected. It has and will unavoidably introduce Contests and Dissentions, than which nothing is more injurious to Republican States, especially new ones. I Sincerely hope our officers, whose Merits, no Man is more willing to acknowledge and reward than I am, in any way consistent with our Principles, will voluntarily, after a little reflection lay it aside. I have written nothing to America upon the Subject.

I See no motive of Reason or Prudence, for making a Mystery of our Sentiments upon this Subject in Europe or America, or for reserving them for America. It is a publick Thing about which every Man has a right to think for himself and express his Thoughts.

As to your going to America, Surely I have no Objection against it. Being asked whether you was going to America I answered that you talked of it, but I questioned whether you would go, as the War was over, and I knew of no particular Motive you might have to go. If you go I wish you a pleasant voyage, and an happy Sight of your Friends. With much respect

LbC (MHi: Adams Papers).
1. Both the Articles of Confederation and some state constitutions explicitly forbade inherited titles.

From Henry Laurens

Bath 31st March 1784

My dear General,

The day after I had the honor of writing to you the 15th. Instant I left London, I have been about a fortnight at this place constantly confined to the House. My Son who is charged not to pass thro' Paris without paying his respects at Hotel la Fayette and presenting Pamphlets and News Papers if he can find any thing in London worth your acceptance, will relate the condition in which he leaves me, very unfit for encountering a Sea Voyage, yet I determine very soon after his return to make an Effort for embarking.

You must have observed that what is called the American Intercourse Bill was extended by a new Bill previous to the late dissolution of Parliament to the 20th June.[1] I have not yet discovered what the new Ministers mean to graft upon it. Possibly next Saturday's London Gazette may disclose, in the meantime it appears the Merchants and Planters in the British West India Islands are resolved at all hazards to enjoy an open Trade with the United States. A very wealthy sensible Man whose Estate lies in Jaimaica was with me Yesterday, he assured me that continued Restrictions would produce an open and violent Opposition on the part of the Islands, that according to his last advice a sort of compromize had taken place in Jaimaica. The American Vessels were winked at while they lay at the mouth of a Port or River in Jaimaica, sold and discharged their Cargoes received their returns and went off with dispatch. The Ministry cannot be unacquainted with such irregular Proceeding, but it does not become me to dictate to their Wisdom. A little further irritation from this side will produce very formidable Resolutions on the other and the grand Question, which Country will suffer most detriment by partial or total Prohibitions, will be brought to the Test. With the highest Esteem and Respect, I have the honor to be, Dear Marquis, your obliged & most obedt. humble Servant.

L (MHi: Henry Laurens Papers, Kendall Collection), copy.

1. On March 24 the House of Lords approved a limited extension of the king's authority to regulate trade between the British Empire and the United States (*Journals of the House of Lords*, [London, 1509–], 37:70–71). The following day, George III prorogued Parliament.

To John Adams

Paris April the 9th 1784

Dear Sir

A friendly letter I wrote You, and the One I Receive is not so affectionate as usual. The Value I Set By Your Esteem, the Consequent fear least my Conduct Be Misrepresented to You, Such were the Motives that Actuated me. As to the Institutions Alluded to, I only Need Saying that My principles are Known.[1] If You Have writen Nothing, I did more, for whatever I thought Ought to Be Amended, I Submitted to the President of the Society—and I think, Every Man's influence, So far as it Goes, must Be Exerted for the Good of the public.[2] But it Has Been My principle, in foreign Countries, Not to Blame American Measures. I don't Say You are in the least wrong, particularly as You tell me You Never Spoke Unasked. I Have only told you, what in Similar Cases I Used to do—and I don't See the least Harm in doing other wise. As to

My Going to America, I first Went for the Revolution, and not for the war, and Warfaring was truly A Secondary Incident, which in Support of the Rights of Mankind Had Become Necessary. Now I am Going for the people, and My Motives are, that I love them, and they love me— that My Arrival will please them, and that I will Be pleased with the Sight of those whom I Have Early joined in our Noble and Successfull Cause. I may add, that Opinions of Honest men, when they Have Some Influence, do more or less prove Serviceable—and How Could I Refrain from Visiting a Nation whose I am an Adoptive Son, and where, particularly Among Your fellow Citizens, I Have experienced So Many Marks of Affection and Confidence. With Much Respect, and also with a Sincere Attachement I Have the Honour to Be Dear Sir Your obedient Humble Servant

LAFAYETTE

ALS (MHi: Adams Papers).
1. This is a response to Adams' March 28 letter to Lafayette.
2. See Lafayette to Washington, March 9, 1784 ("Your Excellency has been . . .").

To [Simon-Nicolas-Henri Linguet][T]

Paris, April 20, 1784

It is really true, Monsieur, that I have not forgotten M. Baumier, but thus far my recommendation is quite unavailing. I cannot imagine how all his hopes vanish one after the other, but this unfortunate man is truly persecuted by his star. If between now and my departure he is not in a better situation, I shall consent to take him with me to America. The trip I shall make, Monsieur, will be very short. My friends there have been waiting for me a long time, and although the revolution is over, the thirteen states still have to work on their federal constitution. Several persons are asking me to be a witness to their work in this connection; and when I yield to their friendship by going to see them, I would like to contribute some share of those talents that may serve America and consolidate still further, if possible, the temple of liberty. But at least I shall be a very approving spectator, and during the coming winter I shall come to renew the assurance of my tender attachment to you. It is equaled only by my gratitude for your interest and the value I place on your opinion. It is with these sentiments that I have the honor to be for all my life, Monsieur, your very humble and very obedient servant,

LAFAYETTE

ALS (InU: Lafayette Mss. I), translation.

Baumier has not been identified. No person of that name went to America with Lafayette in June 1784. Linguet had been involved in various libertarian causes in England and France.

To the Comte de Vergennes[T]

Paris, Monday [May 10, 1784]

Tomorrow, Monsieur le Comte, you will have a visit from Mr. Jay, who is returning to America. After taking leave of you, he wishes, if it is the custom, to take leave of the king, too. Although I am not very skilled in diplomatic etiquette, I told him that this seemed proper to me.[1]

Mr. Barclay received orders from Mr. Morris about which he wishes to confer with you. He also bears a letter from Dr. Franklin,[2] and it is all in connection with the affair of the seizures made in Brittany of which I have often had the honor of speaking to you.[3] I told him you would be busy tomorrow morning, but if you have the kindness to receive him around six o'clock, please give me your orders for that time or for any other that would suit you. Please accept, Monsieur le Comte, my tender and respectful homage.

LAFAYETTE

ALS (AAE: Correspondance politique, Etats-Unis, vol. 29, fol. 485), translation.

1. Jay and Lafayette apparently breakfasted together on the morning of May 10 to discuss matters before Jay's departure (Lafayette to Jay, May 9, 1784 [CtY: Benjamin Franklin Collection]).

2. Robert Morris had written to John Barclay on February 7 on the necessity to settle American accounts abroad promptly (PPAmP: Franklin Papers, vol. 48, no. 22d). Franklin prepared a memorandum on May 10 on the state of Le Ray de Chaumont's disputed accounts, over which the two were seeking Ferdinand Grand's arbitration (PPAmP: Franklin Papers, vol. 54, no. 125(10)).

3. In 1779 the *Alliance*, under American flag and commission but sailing at French expense, had captured the Irish vessel *Three Friends*, freighted to the account of the Bordeaux firm Forster Frères. The Forsters appealed to the French government, which indemnified them in an *arrêt du conseil* of May 30, 1780. When the *Alliance* arrived at Lorient in February 1783, the Forsters had its prizes seized for payment. At Franklin's urging, Castries ordered the seizure vacated in March. On the grounds that the *Alliance* was an American vessel, the French government referred the entire matter to the Congress. On May 11, 1784, Congress determined that it was strictly a French matter and returned the question of indemnification to the French government (*JCC*, 27:369).

To George Washington

Paris May the 14th 1784

My dear General

To My Great Satisfaction, My Departure is fixed Upon the tenth of Next Month, When I intend leaving Paris, and Immediately Embarking for America. My Course will Be Straight to Pottowmack, and I do Most feelingly Anticipate the pleasure of our Meeting at Mount Vernon. There is Nothing New in France, But that the Affair of the free Ports is Quite Settled, and that Nothing yet Has Been done Respecting the Intended Regulations for Commerce Betwen America and the West Indias. Governement are Very friendly to the Interest of the United States, But labour Under Many difficulties, the Strongest of all is the Complaints of flour Merchants, Manufacturers, and Raisers in the Country Round Bordeaux.[1] There Has Been a Pretention Set up a Vienna By the Empress of Russia, for a Preeminence of Her Ambassador over ours, Which is foolish and Groundless, and from Which She Must Certainly desist.[2] Some Portuguese Disputes Respecting a Settlement in Africa Have Been decided to the Satisfaction of France.[3] Mr. Pitt's party will Be the Stronger in the New Parliament. But Charles Fox Comes in as a Member for Wesminster, and Will Head an Opposition. The Situation of Ireland is Critical, the lord lieutenant's Conduct Has Been foolish, and Some Resolutions of the people are very Spirited.[4] A German doctor Called *Mesmer* Having Made the Greatest discovery Upon *Magnetism Animal*, He Has Instructed scholars, Among Whom Your Humble Servant is Called One of the Most Enthusiastic.[5] I know as Much as Any Conjurer Ever did, which Remind's me of our old friend's at Fiskills Enterwiew with the devil that Made us laugh So Much at His House, and Before I Go, I will Get leave to let You into the Secret of Mesmer, which You May depend Upon, is a Grand philosophical discovery.

Mr. Jay is Gone this Morning to Dover where He intends embarking for America. He Has taken Care, of A family picture, Including Mde. de Lafayette, our Children, and Myself which I Beg leave to Present to My dear General, as the likenessess of those Who are Most Affectionately devoted to Him.[6]

The Whole family join with me in the Most Respectfull Compliments to You, and Mrs. Washington. Be So kind, My dear General, to Remember me to the other Inhabitants of Mount Vernon, and to all friends that You May Happen to See. Adieu, My dear General, Be

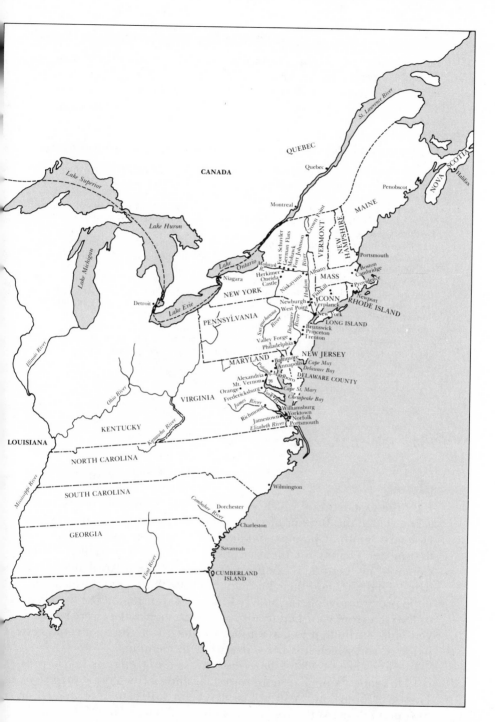

The United States after the peace of 1783.

pleased with Your Usual kindness, to Receive the tender wishes of one
who More than Any Man Existing May Boast of Being, Your excellency's Most Affectionate, Respectfull friend and Humble Servant

LAFAYETTE

ALS (PEL: Hubbard Collection).

1. Bordeaux grain producers and manufacturers wanted France to retain a monopoly
of the flour trade to the West Indies.

2. The dispute was between the Russian and French ambassadors regarding prece-
dence at court functions (M. de Flassan, *Histoire général et raisonnée de la diplomatie fran-
caise, ou de la politique de la France. . .* , [Paris, 1811], 7: 376).

3. In July 1783 the Portuguese established a fort at Cabinda with the aim of excluding
other Europeans from the slave trade of the region. France sent an expedition to eject
the Portuguese in 1784.

4. Lord Rutland's intransigence on the issue of parliamentary reform led many members of the Irish Parliament to oppose sending the customary address of thanks to the
lord lieutenant that spring.

5. Lafayette was one of the inner circle of Mesmer's disciples. Mesmer postulated a
principle of "animal magnetism," which he claimed operated in a manner similar to
magnetism in metals. With this principle he attempted to cure a variety of disorders,
from convulsions and hysteria to seasickness.

6. The portrait did not go on the ship with Jay. Lafayette seems to have entrusted its
transportation to John B. Church (Lafayette to Adrienne de Lafayette, June 25, 1784).
The portrait reached Washington in the summer of 1785 (Fitzpatrick, *Writings of Washington*, 28: 205–10).

From Robert Morris

Office of Finance 19. May 1784

Dear Sir,

By the Opportunity which your friend Mr. Constable offers I now
acknowledge the Receipt of your several favors of the twenty sixth of
December tenth of January and ninth of March last. Accept I pray you
my sincere Thanks for them all. I also enclose for your Perusal the
Copies of my Letters to Congress of the sixteenth of April and of this
date.[1] To these I add their Resolutions of the third Instant which will I
hope prove agreeable to you.[2] If I have not transmitted the Copies of
or Extracts from your Letters to Congress so soon as they were received
you must attribute it to Circumstances which I on the Spot could best
judge of and which it is not worth while to mention.

In pursuance of what I have just now said to Congress I shall pro-
ceed to request your Exertions for establishing a free Port at the Isle of
France or Bourbon.[3] You will easily obtain sufficient Information in
Europe to direct your Applications on this Subject And M. Constable
will I think be able to give you some useful Information as to the
Consequences of it upon this Country. I confess that it appears to me to

be the probable Means of Establishing, at that Port, the most extensive and useful Commerce with India that has ever yet existed. To France and to America it will be most particularly useful because *we* shall trade freely and without Risque to such Port—and *you* will undoubtedly furnish us with all those Articles of India Goods which we should otherwise go in Search of to India or procure from other Nations. This will form an Object of near twenty Millions of Livres annually or calculating both the Export and Import Cargoes it will amount to about thirty Millions and consequently cannot be less than five Millions clear Adavntage to France. And if it be considered that this is so much taken from her commercial Rival we may estimate it as being an Object of ten Millions annually. Such being the Importance of it with Respect to America alone what may we not calculate on for the other Countries who may incline to Trade thither? But besides this great Commercial Consideration there are others of a political Nature. Such as the encrease of your Seamen. The Advantage of a Place of Arms Marine Arsenal &ca. in that critical Position. These I shall not dwell upon because I do not wish to go out of my Depth.

Returning then to a commercial View of the Subject I consider it as almost certain that America would find it more advantageous to trade with that Port than to go on to India. And hence I draw one very strong Inference that we should not only be by that Means brought into a closer political Connection with France but that France would hold a much larger Share of all our other Commerce than she would without such an Establishment. I will not trouble you with my Reasons because I think they will not escape you. But before I close my Letter I must observe that altho this Commerce may and undoubtedly will yield you a Revenue yet there is Danger in Beginning with Revenue too soon. Let the Port be first made free to all the World and let good and intelligent Commissioners or Intendants be appointed to transmit Information of the Commerce carried on. If there be no Duties there will be no false Entries and thus in two or three Years the Court will be able to Act with their Eyes open and in the mean Time the enriching of your own Subjects is always of sufficient Consequence even if Revenue be put entirely out of the Question. If on the other hand you only free the Port by Halves [&] leave it subject to Duties and Restrictions The Commerce may never take it's Course that Way And always Remember that the Commission received by your Merchants from such a Commerce is alone of vast Importance. With sincere Esteem and Respect I am Sir Your most obedient & hum. Servant

R.M.

LbC (DLC: Robert Morris Papers).
1. Morris's letters to Congress contained recommendations on French trade. With

them he sent letters from Lafayette reporting on the French commercial concessions (DNA: RG 360, PCC 137, pp. 523, 639).

2. Congress had resolved on May 3 that a letter be written to Lafayette "expressing the high sense which Congress entertain of his important services, relative to the commerce of France and these United States, and particularly to free ports. . ." and suggesting that an opening of trade with the French West Indies would be greatly appreciated (*JCC,* 26:332–33).

3. The Isle de France (now Mauritius) and Bourbon (now Réunion) were French colonies in the Indian Ocean east of Madagascar. American trade with the Isle de France was begun by 1785.

To Benjamin Franklin

Versaïlles thursday Morning [20 May 1784]
My dear Sir

I intended Having this day the pleasure to See You, But am obliged to Stay Here for the Queen's Concert, and Will do Myself the Honour to Call Upon You to Morrow Morning. There I Will lay Before You a letter I Have Received from Mr. de Calonne.[1] I am glad to Hear the Washington is Soon Expected, and Hope we May Get Intelligences Before My departure which is fixed on the 12th of june.

There is an other point Upon which I Beg leave to offer my Opinion, and Since, on the Opposite Side, Under Governement Banners, I perceive a Respected Veteran, to whom I Have Had the Honour to Be a fellow Soldier, I Beat A parley, and am Sure He Will like My proposition. That Mesmer is the true preacher of Magnetism Animal, to Which By the Way He Has Been Much Helped By Your electric discoveries, is a truth which No Body Will deny. That Deslon Has treacherously Broken His faith, trampled Upon the Most Sacred Engagements is a More disputable. That While Mesmer Intended Acquiring a great glory and a great fortune, He Has not Been Such a fool as to Impart His Whole System to One Man who Might Claim a share in the Honour and Profit is also pretty Clear. That Baron de Breteuïl, out of a private picque to Mesmer, Has Sent to Deslon, in order *to know Mesmer's doctrine which does not Exist,* and that what May Be known of the doctrine will Be Either Betraïed By Deslon, or Stolen out By private Spies, are also pretty clear to Every Mind.[2]

Now, My dear Sir, instead of Helping to those transactions, don't You think the Commissaries, to whom the World Considers you as a president, Had Better Report.[3]

That What they Have Seen Gives them the idea of a Great discovery, But that Mesmer Being the Author of it, He is the fountain Head to

Franklin was welcomed home to his native Pennsylvania in 1785 after serving almost seven years as American minister plenipotentiary to France.

which You Must Apply—that Sciences and letters are frighted a way By the Hand of despotism—But that, in order to Come to the whole truth, Commissaries Must plainly, and Oppenly Go to Mr. Mesmer, and in the Same way as other people, do, Be Regularly let By Him Into His whole System.

Upon that I Have not Spoken to Mesmer. But I would Be Sorry to See a traitor triumph over an Honest man—and I am Sure You May Give a Good turn to the affair. I was very Happy in Admitting Your Grand Son into our Society.[4] Most affectionately and Respectfully Yours

LAFAYETTE

ALS (PPAmP: Franklin Papers, vol. 42, no. 138).
1. In his letter to Lafayette of May 17, 1784 [DNA: RG 360, vol. 3, pp. 449–51], Calonne informed him that announcements of the free ports were being printed.
2. Mesmer kept the ultimate "secret" of animal magnetism to himself and refused to teach it even to his best students. Deslon left Mesmer's group in 1782 and set up a rival establishment, claiming to know the true doctrine of animal magnetism. The Baron de Breteuil was minister of state with responsibilities for Paris and the king's household.
3. Franklin was a member of a commission appointed by the king, consisting of members of the Academy of Sciences and the Faculty of Medicine, to examine the evidence for animal magnetism. When Mesmer refused to appear before the commission, Deslon undertook to demonstrate its principles. The commission reported to the king in August 1784 that they were not convinced of the existence of any force called "animal magnetism" (see R. Darton, *Mesmerism and the End of the Enlightenment in France* [New York, 1968]).
4. William Temple Franklin was a member of the Society of Harmony, a group dedicated to mesmerism.

To John Adams

Paris june the 2d 1784

Dear Sir

Altho' I Have not Been Honoured With an Answer to My last letter,[1] I will not loose time in Acquainting you that My departure from l'Orient is fixed on the 22d intant. Any letter from You that Reaches Paris Before the 17th will Be Carefully forwarded By me, and in Case You Had Any to Send clear of post offices, their Being put into My Hands Will insure their Being Safely delivered to the persons to whom they are directed.

We Have letters from America as late as the 20th April. Nothing Had Been as Yet Settled By Congress Respecting their political Arrangements.[2] Unless Some passenger is on the Road with More particular dispatches than those which Have Been Received By post. But I Rather think Nothing Had Been done in that Respect. With an affectionate Regard I Have the Honour to Be Dear Sir Your obedient Humble Servant

LAFAYETTE

As I intend landing in Newyork, Your letters to your family will not Have a long way to go.

ALS (MHi: Adams Papers).
1. See Lafayette to Adams, April 9, 1784.
2. The letters Lafayette is referring to have not been found. Congress was debating whether to adjourn for the summer, and if so, whether a "Committee of the States" would be left in charge of federal affairs.

From John Adams

The Hague June 11. 1784

My dear Marquis

I received in Season, the Letter mentioned in yours of the Second of this Month, but as there was nothing in it which required an immediate Answer, I have not acknowledged the Recipt of it, untill now.

If an Express should be upon his Passage with any Arrangement of Congress, respecting their foreign Affairs I presume the Departure of Mr. Jay and Mr. Laurens for America, will disarrange it: So that I conclude to remain here, enjoying the Pleasures of the Prince of Orange's Court and the Conversation of the Dutch Patriots, who are excellent Sons of Liberty, without budging, untill I know the final Settlement of Congress, upon the Arrival of those Ministers. Whether Congress will recall Mr. Franklin and me, and pursue a frugal system of foreign affairs, whether they will join several in a Commission to treat with the maritime Powers, or whether they will Send a Minister to any other Courts, I am wholly at a Loss to conjecture, from all the Intelligence I have.[1] After a good deal of Impatience under these Uncertitudes, I have at length become quite reconciled, to them and resigned, to such a degree that I am quite indifferent whether I stay here, go to France or England, or home to America. The last is a Part which I regret not to have taken a Year Ago.

I will answer the Letters of my Friends by Mr. Reed and Coll. Herman,[2] as soon as I know what the Plan of Congress is and what is to be my Destination. At present all is Such Uncertainty that I know not what to write to Congress or to Individuals.

AL (MHi: Adams Papers).

1. Adams had not yet received notification that Congress had resolved on October 29, 1783, to make Adams, Franklin, and Jefferson commissioners to negotiate treaties of amity and commerce with the maritime powers of Europe (*JCC*, 25:754–57).

2. Colonel Josiah Harmar. Joseph Reed, a former president of the Supreme Executive Council of Pennsylvania, was then in Europe soliciting funds for the College of New Jersey (now Princeton University).

From Charles-Alexandre de Calonne[T]

Versailles, June 11, 1784

I have had assembled, Monsieur, as I promised you, the review of all the various fees imposed by the admiral, the officers of the admiralty courts, the towns, or particular noblemen, which a ship from the United States of America is obliged to pay in the ports of Marseilles, Dunkirk, Bayonne, and Lorient on its arrival or departure. These fees have been combined in a table that shows simultaneously the rights to each levy and the laws authorizing it. I have the honor to send it to you so that you may communicate it to the United States and they may mark in the column for observations the requests they want to make regarding each kind of fee. Until that is done, it would not be possible for me to propose to His Majesty any abolition, modification, or combination of these fees, since the Americans do not understand the fees themselves, and it is indispensable that the nature and the distribution of each fee be perfectly known to them.[1] When the replies from the United States reach me, I shall hasten, Monsieur, to put them before His Majesty, and I hope you will believe that the desire to do something that may please you will add still more to my desire to be useful to the United States. I have the honor to be with a sincere attachment, Monsieur, your very humble and very obedient servant,

DE CALONNE

LS (DNA: RG 360, PCC 137, vol. 3, pp. 453), translation; enclosed with Lafayette to Morris, August 14, 1784 (DNA: RG 360, PCC 121, p. 107).

1. The original, a translation, and a printed copy of the tables appear in DNA: RG360, PCC 59, vol. 4, fols. 39, 59, 99. The tables were presented to Congress on February 8, 1785, with other letters to and from Lafayette on French–American commercial relations. Jay had the tables printed for distribution to American merchants and ship owners, but he submitted no observations on the duties to Vergennes (see Robert Morris to Congress, September 30, 1784, below).

From Charles-Alexandre de Calonne[T]

Paris, June 16, 1784

M. Chardon, Monsieur, has just communicated to me the letter you wrote him this morning, in which you ask that the fees American ships are required to pay in the ports of Marseilles, Dunkirk, Bayonne, and Lorient be combined into a single fee of so much per ship of one or two masts.[1] You note at the same time that you would like to carry to the United States a decision abolishing or modifying these fees. Despite the pleasure I would have, Monsieur, in doing something agreeable for the United States and in showing you personally the value I place on the interest you take in these requests, it is not possible for me to propose them to His Majesty before your departure. The fees that the United States pay belong to the admiral, to the officers of the admiralty courts, and finally to particular towns and noblemen. All of them will be entitled to draw up claims for indemnities for the loss or reduction of their fees, and you will agree, Monsieur, that it would not be just to reduce them, or even to suspend them temporarily, without having heard from the interested parties. The same reason also weighs against making the assessment you propose of all these different fees in a single fee, determined by the number of masts on each ship. It is therefore indispensable, Monsieur, that the United States, after receiving the report on the fees that I had the honor to address to you, establish their requests precisely on each one.[2] It is only after these requests have reached me that I can put the result before the king, and the United States ought to be persuaded that they will find His Majesty disposed to give them proofs on every occasion of the friendship that is to reign between him and the United States, which will always be based on equity and his natural sense of justice. I have the honor to be with a sincere attachment, Monsieur, your very humble and very obedient servant,

DE CALONNE

The transaction that you desire, whatever diligence is brought to bear on it, will necessarily entail a period of three to four months. We shall work on it in your absence and you will be informed of the result.

I am sending back to you the report on the fees as they now are. It is always good for you to have it.

LS (DNA: RG 360, PCC 137, vol. 3, p. 457), translation: enclosed with Lafayette to Morris, August 14, 1784 (DNA: RG 360, PCC 121, p. 107).

1. The letter has not been found. Lafayette had proposed that tonnage duties be replaced by a fee based on the number of masts on each ship (see Lafayette to Calonne, February 26, 1784).

2. Calonne prepared a table of port fees and sent it to Lafayette on June 11, 1784.

From the Maréchal de Castries[T]

Versailles, June 17, 1784

The regulations for trade between the United States and our colonies, Monsieur, cannot be finished in time for your departure. I have in mind all you told me in favor of your system, but it will not be possible for us to give the degree of freedom you desire. All I foresee at this time is that there will be a free port for the Americans in each colony, that there will be no difficulties with all the goods that were formerly received there, and that the fees to be levied will be as reasonable as can be.

As for the regulations concerning flour and sugar, I cannot yet determine anything for you in that regard, but the interests of our own trade require special consideration, and as you requested, I shall discuss these subjects thoroughly with Mr. Franklin and the consul general of the United States. I have the honor to be with a sincere attachment, Monsieur, your very humble and very obedient servant,

LE MAL. DE CASTRIES

LS (DNA: RG 360, PCC 137, vol. 3, p. 461), translation; enclosed with Lafayette to Morris, August 14, 1784 (DNA: RG 360, PCC 121, p. 107).

To Adrienne de Noailles de Lafayette[T]

La Flèche, [June 20, 1784] Sunday, 1:00

Bad post coaches and bad roads, my dear heart, allowed me to get only this far. I am about to leave again so as to be in Lorient tomorrow night, and Tuesday, with an inexpressible heartache, I shall see that cursed packetboat. While our horses are being hitched up, I wanted to send you a note by the courier who is going to pass by. I wanted to repeat to you with what regret I leave you. Never was this separation so painful for me, my dear heart, and although the absence will not be so long, now that no notions of a great public good or glory any longer sustain me, the sadness I feel no longer has the slightest consolation. So far from America, I cannot yet really feel the pleasure of seeing my friends there again while I leave here those I love best. The more I see you, my dear heart, and the dearer you are to me, the more I enjoy the happiness of being united with you, of being loved by you. But the pain of leaving you also becomes more appreciable. I slept in the carriage on the road yesterday. I am feeling fine and am very satisfied with my young traveling companion.[1] Farewell, my dear heart, it is so sweet to tell you I love you that I have trouble saying farewell when I think that the farewell from Lorient will be the last you will have from Europe. I embrace you, my dear heart, and hope you know how much I love you.

AL (ALG, Courtesy of the Comte de Chambrun), translation.
1. Maurice Riquet de Caraman accompanied Lafayette on this trip to America.

To John Adams

L'Orient june the 25th 1784

My dear Sir

At the Very instant of Sailing for America, I Stop to Send You the New Modelled Regulations of the Cincinnati.[1] My principles Ever Have Been Against Heredity, and While I Was in Europe disputing about it with a few friends, My letters to the Assembly, and Still more Particularly to the president, Made them Sensible of My Opinion Upon that Matter. Untill Heredity Was Given Up, I forbeared Mentionning in Europe what Sense I Had Expressed. But Mr. Jay Being in Paris, I once Explained my Conduct to Him, and He Appeared Very well Satisfied. The Valüe I Have for Your Esteem is the Reason why I mention those particulars—and So far as Respects me, it is *for You* that I write this Minuted Account.

Mr. Jay is Named a Minister for foreign Affairs. Mon. John Adams, Franklin, and Jefferson are Appointed a Committee to Make treaties with European Powers. With Every Sentiment of an Affectionate Regard I Have the Honour to Be Dear Sir Your obedient Humble Servant

LAFAYETTE

Whatever Has Been thought Offensive, You See the Cincinnati Have Given it Up. Now the New frame Must Be Examined. In Every Circumstance, my dear Sir, depend upon it You will find me, what Ever I Have Been, and perhaps with Some Eclat—i.e.—a Warm friend to the

John Adams's disapproval of the Society of the Cincinnati prompted a cool interchange with Lafayette on the subject.

Army—a Still Warmer Advocate for the Cause of liberty—But those two things, when the army is put to the proof—you will ever aknowledge to Agree with each other.

ALS (MHi: Adams Papers).
1. Washington, as president of the Society of the Cincinnati, had sent a circular letter to the state societies with the amendments and alterations, including the abolition of hereditary succession, agreed to in the general meeting in May 1784. The state societies, however, refused to ratify the changes, and the general rules of the Society remained the same.

To Adrienne de Noailles de Lafayette[T]

Lorient, June 25, 1784

Still no wind, my dear heart, no letters from Paris. I am all alone here, repulsed by the sea, which is normally very repulsive to me, and as I have not received the letters from America or the letters from Paris I was expecting by the post from Versailles, it was as though I were already under sail, and once separated from my friends, I might as well have been at sea. I feel, however, that the moment the wind changes will bring me sadness, and although I should wish for it, my heart loathes everything that signals our departure. Having nothing to do here, I think about how to get news over there. First, in addition to the packetboat there is a Commodore Nicholson whom I like very much, and who, if he comes to see you, is entitled to a very friendly reception. He leaves again in three weeks or a month, and once letters are delivered into his hands, it is a very certain opportunity, especially if he is going to northern Virginia. You can also ask M. de Charlus to write to the ports for them to give notice when boats are leaving for America, and by this means every ship will bring me your letters and those of my friends. The letter I am enclosing has to do with the family portrait and will serve as instructions for Carter and Wadsworth.[1] I hope you have taken the latter to Barthe and very particularly recommended him. Carmichael asks that you send him an engraving of me. You know by reputation my friend Harrison, the consul in Cadiz. I have given security for some money he loaned to Littlepage, and since I received the whole sum through a letter of exchange from M. de Beaumarchais, the portion due Harrsion must be returned to him. Two more requests, my dear heart: one is that you find out if M. Wurtz got the position he wanted, and the other is that you see M. Robert de St. Vincent, attesting to him all my zeal in the interests of his son's affairs and pursuing them yourself, with Mme de Tessé, with the greatest zeal. Mme de Ségur is pursuing a matter with the king's sisters of which I would like to see the end.

Forgive me, my dear heart, for all my commissions, but it is nice to think that we are so closely united that our two interests are but one, that my affairs and yours are the same thing, and that everything, from our children to the last little tree at Chavaniac, is shared between us and everything affects us equally. Your Chavaniac trip, if it is possible, pleases me very much. I am very keen on George's going, not only because of my aunt, but especially for his health, so that he will breathe the country air and run without hindrance, and especially without fear that he will do himself harm; and finally, I would like him to be raised without any fastidiousness, and I would rather know he is with the wolves of [*illegible*] than with the nice children at the Tuileries. Don't you think as I do, my dear heart? I still have my other fantasy about the abbé's costume, and I would rather he exchanged his little collar for a sword, because throughout my childhood I never stopped envying the luck of those who had a governor.

After repeating myself over and over again, my dear heart, please say a thousand affectionate things for me to Mme d'Ayen and my sisters. Give my regards to Gouvion and Poirey. Under certain circumstances I would be very glad if the latter joined me, because besides having the pleasure of very detailed news through him, I would find him very useful. I leave you to go and dine in town, and you, who know me, understand how much that amuses me. If my room had not had a slight smell of paint, which I destroyed by a varnish that must be left to dry, I would already be aboard the packetboat. But I hope to go there tomorrow in any case. While there is some consolation in thinking that this letter is not the last, it is very cruel for me to realize that when you receive it I shall, by all appearances, no longer be in Lorient. Despite the short length of this voyage, it leaves me with a gloomy feeling of sadness. It is no longer willingly, except for my first departure, that I separate from you, that I cause you pain by leaving you. My heart suffers because of it, for you and for me, and I shall not be at peace until the moment when I can embrace you and repeat to you in person, my dear heart, how happy you make me and how much I love you.

I was elected a member of the academy in Charleston.[2]

AL (ALG, courtesy of the Comte de Chambrun), translation.
1. The letter has not been found. Lafayette considered engaging John B. Church ("Carter") and Wadsworth to ship the Lafayette family portrait to Washington.
2. The Charleston Library Society had elected Lafayette to its membership on January 13, 1784 (ScC: Minutes of the Charleston Library Society Journal, 1783–1790, p. 201).

To Adrienne de Noailles de Lafayette[T]

Aboard the *Courrier de New York,* June 28, 1784

From the look of things this morning, my dear heart, I should have thought this letter would be the last, but the wind changed during our preparations, and though it is promised we will sail tomorrow, that is still a very uncertain prediction. Expecting the wind to change, I moved on board. We are trying out our hammocks and our little bedrooms, which no longer smell, and which I have had arranged rather comfortably. As long as I stay quiet, I shall suffer only what my whole mental and physical being will always suffer at being confined. But when the *Courier* starts to move, I shall fortify myself with magnetism, camphor, and treacle tablets on an empty stomach, and drops of ether on a piece of sugar, all new remedies that I shall try and that will do nothing at all for me. In recommending that I embrace the mainmast, Mesmer did not know, and I forgot, that it is coated with tar up to a certain height, and hugging it is absolutely impossible without getting tarred from head to foot.[1] I greatly regret the time I spent here, my dear heart, and if I had foreseen this long delay, I would have brought you to Lorient. But on the other hand, you would have been wrong not to wait for your sister to give birth, which I myself am very sorry to miss. If the winds delay further, perhaps I shall have some news of the birth tomorrow at eight o'clock, and although packets arrive only on Wednesday, I have engaged our friend M. Monistrol to have a courier come tomorrow night. From the first, my dear heart, I have received no letter except yours, and I am much obliged to you for it.[2] You write me that M. de Calonne is going to be keeper of the seals, but this news deserves, I think, confirmation. I shall not bother you today with commissions, my dear heart. I shall only say goodnight to you, without being able to prevent myself from being glad that this is not yet a farewell, and wishing you, my dear heart, as much happiness as you bring me, I repeat to you with a pleasure always new that I love you with the greatest tenderness, the most total confidence, and the most perfect happiness in thinking that we belong to each other.

Embrace our children with great tenderness.

AL (ALG, courtesy of the Comte de Chambrun), translation.
1. Mesmer had suggested that by embracing the mainmast, which would act as a polar force, Lafayette could escape seasickness.
2. Adrienne de Lafayette's letter not found.

To the Comte de Vergennes[T]

Aboard the *Courrier* [*de New York*], June 28, 1784

After waiting for the winds for several days, Monsieur le Comte, we are finally about to set sail, and my next letter will probably be written from New York. The packetboat carrying us is very nice, but I shall be very shaken up and very ill. During my stay in America I shall do all I can to serve my country, and that idea consoles me a little at the moment when I am about to separate once more from my friends. On arriving here, Monsieur le Comte, I found there was some question about what the *arrêt du conseil* no longer allowed me to question. The fears of the intendant and M. d'Arlincourt about the arrangement regarding the duty and rights of the Farm; the new opinion of five or six persons, opposed to that of the whole city; the possibility of building on lands that are for sale while Lorient, which is already all built, is right there: such, Monsieur le Comte, are the ideas by which they mean to justify the problem of their going back on their word at the very moment that the *arrêt du conseil* assures the openness of the port and the city. I have taken the liberty of writing about it to Monsieur le Controleur Général,[1] and I hope you will find a better means of conciliation than that of restricting the free area to the confines of the port. You will soon have news from America, Monsieur le Comte, through the Chevalier de La Luzerne; I hope to bring you back some in December, and I shall be very eager to see my country and my friends again. That is a feeling that grows stronger the more one travels, but it cannot increase any more in my heart, and although the desire to be useful, or to get ready to become so, often makes me roam, I shall always be unhappy to leave, always be transported with joy to see my country again. Farewell, Monsieur le Comte. Present my respects to Mme la Comtesse de Vergennes and your daughters-in-law. A thousand compliments to your sons, and please accept with my farewells the homage of my very tender and respectful attachment.

AL (AAE: Correspondance politique, Etats-Unis, vol. 27, fol. 475), translation. Lafayette mistakenly addressed the letter from the *Courrier de l'Europe*. He was actually on another packet, the *Courrier de New York*.

1. On June 25 Lafayette had written the controller general, Calonne:

I saw M. d'Arlincourt the Farmer General, who told me that the addition of the town to the duty-free status of the port causes little increase in the cost of the guard. Everything I see and hear confirms me in my opinion, even if it is not wholly shared by Monsieur l'Intendant (and the town mayor, whose intentions are good even though there are few people of his opinion). These gentlemen all agree that complete exemption from duties for the town and the port is the best plan that can be adopted.[T] [ICU: Louis Gottshalk Collection; misdated by Lafayette as February 25, 1784]

To Samuel Adams

Jones's tavern in the Jersays August the 7th[1]

Dear Sir

Having it at last in My power to Visit My American friends, I Hastened to the Well known, and Heartly Beloved Shores of this Continent, and Now feel Happy to think, I once More am within the limits of the United States. From a Recollection of Past times, I the Better Enjoy the Present Quiet Situation of the people. Those Houses I Saw Burning I Now See to Have Been Rebuilt—and the poole [pole] of liberty Now Stands in Every spot Upon a firm, and I Hope Ever lasting foundation. Having Nothing to do But to Visit My friends, to Rejoice With those to Whom I Had the Honour to Be a Companion in the Noble Struggle, I am Beggining My tour By a Visit to General Washington in Virginia—after which I will Hasten to Boston and I wish the packet I Came in Had Been Bound to Your Capital, which You know is Generally the first and last place I See on the Continent. With Every Sentiment of Respect, love, and Gratitude, I Anticipate the Pleasure to Be Again Within the Walls of Boston and Among its Inhabitants. It will Be a Great Satisfaction for me, My dear Sir, to take You By the Hand, and to tell you How Respectfully and Sincerely I Have the Honour to Be Yours

LAFAYETTE

My Best Respects Waït Upon Mrs. Adams.

ALS (NN: Samuel Adams Papers).
1. Probably Jones's Tavern in Clinton, New Jersey.

Address of the Committee of Officers of the Late Pennsylvania Line, with Lafayette's Reply

[August 9, 1784]

WE, the officers of the late Pennsylvania line, deeply impressed with a gratful remembrance of your zeal and activity in the cause of our country, beg leave to welcome your return to this city.

We very sensibly feel all the warmth of affection arising from the intercourse of the field, and while we look back on the scenes of distress freedom had to encounter, we can never forget, that when destitute of foreign friends, you generously stepped forth the advocate of our rights—the noble example you gave by early bleeding in our infant cause, impresses us with an exalted idea of your patriotism. A recollection of the fortitude and patience with which you have since encountered every difficulty consequent to the situation in which you had to act, and particularly during that important crisis wherein you were called to the chief command in Virginia, endears you to us as a soldier; and while we mingle with the class of citizens, we can never forget the influence your conduct had in leading us to the liberty and independence we now enjoy.

We have the honor to be, With the most perfect esteem, Your very obedient servants, In behalf of the line,

> ARTHUR ST. CLAIR
> ANTHONY WAYNE
> WILLIAM IRVINE

[August 10, 1784]

Gentlemen,

IN the wished for meeting with my dear brother officers, in your so kind reception and most obliging address, I am more happily, more deeply affected than words can express, by my heart has long been open to you, gentlemen, and from the value it has, by your esteem and friendship, you may conceive what on this occasion, must be the feelings of my affection and gratitude. That I early enlisted with you in the cause of liberty, shall be the pride and satisfaction of my life; but while on the glorious conclusion, I rejoice with those to whom I had the honor of being a companion in gloomy times, let me once more thank you, for the peculiar obligations, which, either as a late Commanding Officer in Virginia, or as a brother soldier and affectionate friend, ever bind me to the officers of the Pennsylvania line.

I have the honor to be, Gentlemen, With the warmest sentiments of Esteem and respect, Your most obedient servant,

> LAFAYETTE

From *Pennsylvania Journal,* August 14, 1784.

To Adrienne de Noailles de Lafayette[T]

Philadelphia, August 13, 1784

At last, my dear heart, after such a long time I am able to write you. I can both give you news of me and tell you again of my tenderness for you. But this letter will be a very long time on its way to you; I know your heart and suffer to think that you will not hear anything of me until the middle of September. Our crossing was short and without incident. I was tossed about and was sick, but after thirty-five days I saw the American coast, and the smell of the pines of New Jersey is a wonderful specific for seasickness. Entering the port of New York, I experienced many feelings of pleasure, but it was eleven o'clock at night when we arrived in the city, and all my friends were fast asleep, so that when they awoke, they were quite surprised to find that I was with them. The majority of those I knew were in the country, however, and after spending two days in the city, after reveling there in the excitement of my friends and former comrades in arms (living now, like me, as common citizens), I started off across New Jersey. I stopped only at the home of Mrs. Jay, who arrived a few days before me, and at the state assembly in Brunswick.[1] All of that detained me only a few hours, and at last I saw again the beautiful city of Philadelphia. I was expected there and was met by a large cortege, which preceded me. Former officers, militiamen, and citizens accompanied me into the city, and to avoid lengthy descriptions, I shall tell you that my receptions here and in Boston were very much alike. In the crowd that surrounded me I delighted to see my former soldiers, mingled now with the other citizens. It is true, my dear heart, that each step I take here brings me a new satisfaction. The country is prosperous, tranquil, flourishing. The houses I saw burned, I see rebuilt; abandoned lands are being occupied again, and everything I come across has an air of complete recovery. In my present situation I like to think that my influence may not be useless to the domestic interests of the United States, to the union that should exist between them, in short, to the federal union. Congress will not meet until the first of November, but do not be afraid that this circumstance will delay my return. I shall arrange it so as to take care of all my other affairs by that time. What concerns me now is seeing General Washington again. In three days I shall be at Mount Vernon, and I leave you to imagine with what impatience I await that moment. Since my arrival in New York I have not even had the time to write. Every moment of my time was taken up with my friends, and among the speeches I made I shall not forget to mention the one on magnetism I delivered yesterday at the academy in Philadelphia.[2]

Speaking of science, my dear heart, I am alerting you that you will receive by stagecoach the head of a porpoise, a large ocean fish that is difficult to catch and with which I pay homage to Mme d'Aguesseau through you. You see, my dear, that I am not forgetting the commission, and particularly your recommendation. In a short time I shall send some more interesting things. It was impossible for me to refuse to give a bill of exchange for 2,000 crowns to a former servant of M. de La Luzerne, but the payment date is far off, and I warned him that for three or four months he would probably have only the interest on that sum.

Since I cannot write during the day, my dear heart, I have chosen to do so while everyone is asleep. In a few days I shall take advantage of the tranquillity of Mount Vernon, and you will have more detailed news. At this very moment I am awaiting a group of officers who will accompany me out of the city. Remember me, my dear heart, to Mme d'Ayen, to the vicomtesse, to all our sisters, to the Comtesse Auguste, and give my regards to friends who ask you for news of me. Say a thousand things for me to M. de Gouvion; I am sending him, as he asked, several American newspapers. Embrace our children a thousand and a thousand times. Pay my respects to your father and to M. de Maréchal de Noailles. Take care of your stomach, my dear heart, and give me the pleasure of returning to find you in perfect health. Farewell, farewell, my dear heart. Despite the happiness I feel here, I think very tenderly of the pleasure I shall soon have in embracing you. I foresee no business here that will delay me, and I shall be detained only by the indescribable kindness that is showered upon me. Farewell once again, my dear heart. I know that I have no need to ask you to think of me, but when you do, be aware of how happy you make me and how much I love you.

My health is excellent and I shall take good care of it. My regards to the abbé and M. de Margelay.

L (ALG, courtesy of the Comte de Chambrun), translation.

1. Lafayette stopped in New York City with the Jay family, who had just arrived on July 24 from France. On his way to Philadelphia, Lafayette was given a reception by the state assembly in Trenton, New Jersey.

2. On August 12 Lafayette addressed the American Philosophical Society for two hours on Mesmer and the doctrine of animal magnetism. The proceedings of the American Philosophical Society recorded that Lafayette

> entertained them with a particular relation of the wonderful effects of a certain invisible power, in nature, called *animal magnetism* lately discovered by Mr. Mesmer, a German Philosopher, and explained by him to a number of Gentlemen in Paris of

which number the Marquis was himself one. By this Relation it appears that persons may be so impregnated with this power (by a process which the Marquis does not think himself at liberty yet to explain) as to exhibit many phenomena similar to those of metallic magnetism. (*Early Proceedings of the American Philosophical Society* [Philadelphia, 1884], pp. 126–27).

To Adrienne de Noailles de Lafayette[T]

Mount Vernon, August 20, 1784

Though I do not know if my letter will reach you, my dear heart, I had to write you that I am at Mount Vernon and that I am reveling in the happiness of finding my dear general again; and you know me too well for me to need to describe to you what I felt. Crossing the countryside very quickly, I arrived here on the seventeenth, and as the general, though he had been anticipating my arrival, did not expect me for several more days, I found him in the routine of his estate, where our meeting was very tender and our satisfaction completely mutual. I am not just turning a phrase when I assure you that in retirement General Washington is even greater than he was during the Revolution. His simplicity is truly sublime, and he is as completely involved with all the details of his lands and house as if he had always lived here. To describe to you the life that we lead here, I shall tell you that after breakfast the general and I chat together for some time. After having thoroughly discussed the past, the present, and the future, he withdraws to take care of his affairs and gives me things to read that have been written during my absence. Then we come down for dinner and find Mrs. Washington with visitors from the neighborhood. The conversation at table turns to the events of the war or to anecdotes that we are fond of recalling. After tea we resume our private conversations and pass the rest of the evening with the family. That, my dear heart, is how we spend our time, and we often talk of you, of our children, and of anything that has to do with the family. There are in the house two small children of Mrs. Washington, who you know was married once before.[1] The general has adopted them and loves them with great tenderness. It was rather amusing, when I arrived, to see the curiosity of these two little ones, who had heard me spoken of all day and were very anxious to see if I looked like my portrait. The general read with great pleasure your letter and Anastasie's.[2] I have been asked to send the fondest regards from the whole household, and Mrs. Washington was saying the other day that since they were both old, we must not defer the pleasure they would have in entertaining you and our whole little family here. On my earlier trip, my dear heart, I made the most solemn promise to bring you with me.

Nothing is as beautiful as the location of Mount Vernon, for which the Potomac seems expressly created. The house itself is very fine, and the countryside is delightful. It is not without anguish that I resist the general's entreaties to go on a trip that he is obliged to make toward the Appalachians. He has delayed it so long for me that some of his property has become the prey of squatters. But this six-week trip would delay me too much, and in order to get the general to go there without me I had to promise to meet him again here. So I shall leave on the first of September for Philadelphia, New York, and then all of New England. I shall return at the beginning of October and travel across Virginia with the general so as to be in Trenton in the first days of November. There I shall see Congress reassembled and take leave of everyone. Thus, my dear heart, you may be sure to see me back at the end of December. The past two months seem to me to have been very long. The four months that separate me from you will also be very long, and nothing in the world will make me delay a return to which I look forward with the greatest enthusiasm.

In a few days I expect news from France, and Rousselet is to bring it to me from New York. Poor Hubert was sick in the carriage, got the itch aboard ship, and injured his knee in Philadelphia. All that aside, he is enjoying his trip and is awaiting me on one foot in the capital of Pennsylvania. Ezra went home, and Demanche, who accompanies me with Le Brun, still can't get over the fact that Americans don't understand his French.[3] But I must finish this letter, my dear heart, just as if it were leaving immediately for France. They are expecting me downstairs for tea, and the bearer of my dispatches will leave right after the last cup is finished. Give my tender respects to your father, Mme d'Ayen, and M. le Maréchal de Noailles. Say a thousand tender things to all my sisters, and tell the vicomtesse that I think of her often. My regards to the vicomte, to Ségur, Mme de Ségur, and M. and Mme de Fresnes. Remember me to your grandfather and your grandmother, to whom my porpoise head will soon, I hope, pay my respects. Embrace our dear children. Farewell, farewell, my dear heart. You know how much I love you.

AL (ALG, courtesy of the Comte de Chambrun), translation.

1. Eleanor ("Nellie") Parke Custis and George Washington ("Squire Tub") Parke Custis, children of Martha Washington's son, John Parke Custis.

2. Adrienne's letter to Washington, June 18, 1784, is in DLC: George Washington Papers, Series 2.

3. Rousselet, Hubert, Demanche, and Le Brun were Lafayette's servants. Ezra, whom Lafayette saw in Lorient before his departure, had already returned to America (see Lafayette to Adrienne, June 23, 1784).

Seven-year-old Anastasie de Lafayette's letter to the "beloved General" she had been taught to revere, which Lafayette hand-delivered during his 1784 visit to America.

Address of the Citizens of Baltimore to Lafayette and His Reply

September 1, 1784

Sir:

While the citizens of Baltimore embrace the present occasion of expressing their pleasure in again seeing you among them, they feel the liveliest emotions of gratitude for the many services you have rendered their country. They can never forget the early period in which you engaged in our cause, when our distressed and precarious situation would have deterred a less noble and resolute mind from so hazardous an enterprise: nor the perseverance and fortitude with which you shared the fatigues and sufferings of a patriotic army. They especially shall never cease to remember that the safety of their town is owing to those superior military virtues which you so conspicuously displayed against a formidable enemy during your important command in Virginia. But your love for this country has not terminated with the war. You have laid us under fresh obligations by your successful representations, to free trade from those shackles that abridge mutual intercourse. To that profound veneration and gratitude which we entertain for the singular interposition of your nation and its illustrious monarch, we have only to add our sincere wishes that you may long enjoy that glory which you, in particular, have so justly merited.

In the name and behalf of the citizens of Baltimore, we have the honor to be, with sentiments of the greatest respect, Sir, your most obedient servants,

JOHN SMITH,
SAMUEL PURVIANCE,
JAMES CALHOUN,
TENCH TILGHMAN,
NICHOLAS ROGERS.[1]

Gentlemen:—Your affectionate welcome makes me feel doubly happy in this visit, and I heartily enjoy the flourishing situation in which I find the town of Baltimore. Amidst the trying times which you so kindly mention, permit me with a grateful heart to remember, not only your personal exertions as a volunteer troop, your spirited preparations against a threatening attack, but also a former period when, by your generous support, an important part of the army under my command was forwarded—that army to whose perseverance and bravery, not to any merit of mine, you are merely indebted.[2] Attending to

American concerns, gentlemen, it is to me a piece of duty as well as a gratification to my feelings. In the enfranchisement of four ports and their peculiar situation, it was pleasing to France to think a new convenience is thereby offered to a commercial intercourse, which every recollection must render pleasing, and which from its own nature and a mutual goodwill, cannot fail to prove highly advantageous and extensive. Your friendly wishes to me, gentlemen, are sincerely returned, and I shall ever rejoice in every public and private advantage that may attend the citizens of Baltimore.

With every sentiment of an affectionate regard, I have the honor to be, gentlemen, you obedient and humble servant,

LA FAYETTE

From John Thomas Scharf, *Chronicles of Baltimore* (Baltimore 1874), p. 237.
1. John Smith, Samuel Purviance, James Calhoun, and Nicholas Rogers were among those who had advanced money for Lafayette's troops in April 1781 on Lafayette's credit (*LAAR*, 4:54n). Tilghman had been an aide-de-camp to Washington.
2. The Baltimore Troop of Light Dragoons had joined Lafayette in Virginia late in June 1781.

James Madison to Thomas Jefferson

Philada. Sepr. 7th. 1784.

Dear Sir

Some business, the need of exercise after a very sedentary period, and the view of extending my ramble into the Eastern States which I have long had a curiosity to see have brought me to this place. The letter herewith enclosed was written before I left Virginia, & brought with me for the sake of a conveyance hence.[1] Since the date of it I have learned that Mr. Short who was to be the bearer of the letter to which it refers[2] has not yet left Richmond. The causes of his delay are unknown to me. At Baltimore I fell in with the Marquis de la Fayette returning from a visit to Mount Vernon. Wherever he passes he receives the most flattering tokens of sincere affection from all ranks. He did not propose to have left Virginia so soon but Genl. Washington was about setting out on a trip to the Ohio, and cod. not then accompany him on some visits. The present plan of the Marquis is to proceed immediately to New York, thence by Rhode Island to Boston, thence through Albany to Fort Stanwix where a treaty with the Indians is to be held the latter end of this month, thence to Virginia so as to meet the Legislature at Richmond. I have some thoughts of making this tour with him, but suspend my final resolution till I get to N.Y. whither I shall follow him in a day or two.

The RELATION IN which THE MARQUIS STANDS TO FRANCE and AMERICA HAS INDUCED ME TO ENTER INTO A FREE CONVERSATION with HIM ON THE subject OF THE MISSISSIPPI. I have ENDEAVORED EMPHAT-ICALLY TO IMPRESS on HIM that the IDEAS of AMERICA AND OF SPAIN IRRECONCILABLY CLASH—THAT UNLESS THE MEDIATION OF FRANCE BE EFFECTUALLY EXERTED an ACTUAL RUPTURE IS NEAR AT HAND—THAT IN SUCH AN EVENT THE CONNECTION BETWEEN FRANCE AND SPAIN will GIVE THE ENEMIES OF THE FORMER IN AMERICA THE FAIR-EST OPPORTUNITY OF INVOLVING HER IN OUR RESENTMENTS AGAINST THE LATTER and OF INTRODUCING GREAT BRITAIN AS A PARTY WITH US AGAINST BOTH—THAT AMERICA CAN NOT POSSIBLY BE DIVERTED from HER OBJECT AND THEREFORE FRANCE IS BOUND TO EVERY EN-GINE AT WORK TO DIVERT SPAIN FROM HERS and THAT FRANCE HAS BESIDES A great INTEREST IN A TRADE VITH THE WESTERN COUNTRY THROUGH THE MISSISSIPPI. I thought IT NOT AMISS ALSO TO SUGGEST TO HIM some of the CONSIDERATIONS WHICH SEEM TO APPEAL TO THE PRUDENCE OF SPAIN—HE ADMITTED THE FORCE OF EVERY THING I SAID TOLD ME HE WOULD WRITE IN THE MOST [   ] TERMS TO THE COUNT DE VERGENNES by THE PACKET which will probably CARRY THIS AND LET ME SEE HIS LETTER AT NEW YORK BEFORE HE SENDS IT.[3] HE THINKS THAT SPAIN IS BENT on EXCLUDING US FROM THE MISSISSIPPI AND MENTIONED several ANECDOTES which HAPPENED WHILE HE WAS AT MADRID IN PROOF OF IT.

The Committee of the States have dispersed. Several of the Eastern members havg. by quitting it reduced the number below a quorum, the impotent remnant thought it needless to keep together.[4] It is not prob-able they will be reassembled before Novr. so that there will be an entire interregnum of the foederal government for some time, against the intention of Congs. I apprehend, as well as against every rule of decorum.

The MARQUIS THIS MOMENT STEPPED INTO MY ROOM & SEEING MY CYPHERS BEFORE ME DROPPED some QUESTIONS which OBLIGED ME in order TO AVOID RESERVE TO LET HIM KNOW that I WAS WRITING TO YOU. I SAID NOTHING OF THE subject, but HE WILL PROBABLY INFER FROM OUR CONVERSATION THAT THE MISSISSIPPI IS MOST IN MY THOUGHTS.

Mrs. House charges me with a thousand compliments & kind wishes for you & Miss Patsy. We hear nothing of Mrs. Trist since her arrival at the Falls of this on her way to N. Orleans. There is no doubt that she proceeded down the river thence, unapprized of her loss.[5] When & how she will be able to get back since the Spaniards have shut all their

ports agst. the U.S. is uncertain & gives much anxiety to her friends.[6]
Browze has a windfall from his grandmother of £1000 Sterling. Present my regards to Miss Patsy and to Mr. Short if he should be with you, and accept yourself Dear Sir, the sincerest affection of your friend & servant

J. MADISON JR.

ALS (DLC: James Madison Papers). Passages written in code appear in small capitals.
1. Madison to Jefferson, August 20, 1784 (Rutland, *Papers of James Madison*, 8:102–11).
2. Madison to Jefferson, July 3, 1784 (ibid., pp. 92–95).
3. See Lafayette to Vergennes, September 15, 1784. Madison wrote to Jefferson on September 15: "The M. Has shewn me a passage in his letter to the Ct. de V. in which he Sketches the idea relative to the Miss: he says he has not had time to dilate upon it, but that his next letter will do it fully" (ibid., p. 115).
4. One representative of each state was to have remained as a Committee of the States to perform necessary governmental functions until the full Congress reconvened in November 1784. For their adjournment on August 19, see *JCC*, 27:636–38. Jacob Read wrote to the governor of South Carolina on September 9 that Lafayette "laments the dispersion of the Committee of the States in Terms expressive of the deepest Concern. He thinks no step since the Peace will more deeply wound our Interests in the Courts of Europe" (Burnett, *Letters of Congress*, 7:589).
5. News of the death of Nicholas Trist arrived after his wife had set out to meet him.
6. Spain had closed the Mississippi River at New Orleans to American traffic on July 22.

To the Comte de Vergennes[T]

New York, September 15, 1784

Although the packetboat arrived, Monsieur le Comte, it did not bring me any letter from you. But I know your health was good and I hope it is the same with your whole family. Since I landed I have not stopped traveling. I am overwhelmed with kindness everywhere, and I spent two weeks at General Washington's place of retirement. Now I am on my way to treaty negotiations with the savages, and from there I shall go to New England. I'll rejoin the general and we shall continue my visits together. Toward the middle of November we shall see Congress in its revival, and at the end of the year I shall have the very warmly wished-for good fortune to see my country again.

The news from America reaches you through M. de Marbois, and in my state of pilgrimage I must put off my observations until my return. You have surely heard what has become of the Longchamps affair. It appears that indignation and good will are not lacking, but at the present time people are at a loss as to how to handle it. Until now M. de

La Luzerne and M. de Marbois have had no reason to complain, according to what the latter told me, about the dispositions of the president and the Council.[1]

The trade with England is owing to the surprising amount of credit that every American finds there. This abandon will bring about bankruptcies, and next winter will be favorable to us, provided our merchants consult the needs and tastes of the country. Some hemp arrived in Virginia and French sabots in Baltimore.

An immense population is settling near the Ohio. New arrivals go directly there and the older inhabitants are themselves moving there. America's manufacturing and even its shipping will be slowed by that, and since they intend to connect the Potomac, the Susquehanna, and the Ohio more closely by means of canals, we shall have the preference of the Illinois country and the savages for our manufactured goods. But the outlet for this whole area is the Mississippi, and prohibition of trade on the Mississippi will lead to disputes, later than is thought here but much sooner than is thought in Europe.[2] The Americans like us, but they very genuinely hate Spain.

As much as a private person can claim to do so, I try to know and serve the interests of my country here. The City of New York presented me with the *"freedom of the city,"* an English-style compliment that I assured myself beforehand was of no consequence.[3] It was published in the papers that the free status of Lorient is limited to the port. I am going to have a suitable explanation inserted.[4]

Farewell, Monsieur le Comte. Recall me to the kind thoughts of Mme la Comtesse de Vergennes and your whole family, and think sometimes of a friend who has pledged you for life the most tender and respectful attachment.

LAFAYETTE

ALS (AAE: Correspondence politique, Etats-Unis, vol. 28, fol. 201), translation.

1. In order to obtain the hand of a young woman, the Chevalier Charles Julien de Longchamps had asked Barbé de Marbois to authenticate his titles. When Marbois refused, Longchamps insulted him and later attacked him with a cane in the street. The attack went to the Pennsylvania courts, but Longchamps claimed the right as a French citizen to have the case transferred to Paris. Lafayette wrote Poix, "There is a Chev. de Longcamps here who claims he knows you and who brought me a letter from your father, but this affair being a national one as it were, you realize what course I had to take"ᵀ (September 15, 1784, courtesy of Mme André Balleyguier). Though the legal controversy centered on the law of nations, sentiment ran strongly against turning Longchamps over to French officials, and it was decided to uphold Pennsylvania's jurisdiction in the case.

2. See Madison to Jefferson, September 7, note 6.

3. On September 14 the city presented Lafayette with the freedom of the city in the form of an address enclosed in an elegant gold box.

4. The French packet *Fortune* had arrived in New York City with a report that the free-port status of Lorient was limited to the port and did not extend to the city. For the Philadelphia account, see *The Freeman's Journal*, September 22.

Barbé de Marbois's Journal of His Visit to the Territory of the Six Nations[ET]

September 23, 1784

. . . On landing at Albany, I found M. le Marquis de Lafayette, M. le Chevalier de Caraman, and Mr. Madison, a member of Congress, ready to leave to visit the Indian nations, and we soon combined our parties to go there together.

We had heard a great deal about the American Shakers. For the three years that that sect had been growing in America, we had all wanted to see their principal settlement, which was not far from our route; and in addition to ordinary motives of curiosity, M. le Marquis de Lafayette wished to examine at firsthand phenomena that seemed very similar to those associated with Mesmer, with whom he studied.

It was a Sunday. We left for Niskayuna, the place of their assembly. It is difficult to reach this village, which is in the middle of the woods, and we were obliged to go to see them on foot. At great distance we heard a slow, melancholy, but rather melodious music. All the voices were singing in unison or in octaves, and the effect was rather pleasing at a distance. We found the Shakers in the midst of their religious devotions. . . . M. le Marquis de Lafayette, one of Dr. Mesmer's adepts, wanted to try out animal magnetism on one of them. While he was magnetizing him with all his power, the poor man told us his story: "One day I fell from my wagon," he told us. "I injured my leg very badly. A kind man came to my aid while I was unconscious. When I awoke, I found myself healed. I experienced a complete change in my sentiments and beliefs. I renounced the world and its ways. I followed those of these perfect men, and from that moment, I have been infinitely happy."

This chosen one was a person of extreme simplicity, and while M. le Marquis de Lafayette was trying without success the effects of magnetism on all his poles, one of the old men—uneasy about what might result from it—came to us. He asked whether we were acting in the name of a good spirit or of an evil spirit. "Assuredly," said M. le Marquis de Lafayette, "it is in the name of a good spirit." Once he had made this avowal, you can well imagine that the Shaker pressed us hard. He even tried to persuade us to become his proselytes, and we were unable to shake him off until we left Niskayuna to continue our voyage. . . .

We continued our journey through a country that was superb but where we could still trace the image of the war—and of a cruel war, as

Robert Lefèvre pinx.

Fremy del et sculp.

The French chargé d'affaires in America, François Barbé de Marbois, accompanied
Lafayette to the negotiations with the Indian tribes at Fort Schuyler.

the savages wage it. We had with us a sack of cornmeal, which was a great resource for us. People gave us butter in abundance. If we asked for milk, they brought it to us in great wooden pails. We made a porridge out of it that was a great success throughout that country, and often our hosts, instead of feeding us, were fed by us. We were completely protected from the famine we had been led to fear. We were still better sheltered from the ill effects of the weather. Our cloaks and blankets were a great resource. I except M. le Marquis de Lafayette, however, who seemed to be impervious to heat, cold, drought, humidity, and the inclemency of the seasons. To protect himself against the rain, he had brought along an overcoat of gummed taffeta which had been wrapped in newspapers that had stuck to the gum. There had been no time to pull them off, and the curious could read on his arm or his back the *Courrier de l'Europe* or the news from various places.

Despite the devastation to which the two banks of the Mohawk have been prey, the population there has been growing rapidly. We found families with ten to twelve children, large and small all sleeping in the same bed. They surrounded us continually, as we were strange objects in a country where it is very rare to see foreigners traveling for curiosity. We lacked nothing that was of the first necessity, but things that would have been included in that category elsewhere were lacking here. It is true that the children served all purposes: if we asked for a candlestick, an urchin four or five years old was placed near us, a candle in his hand; if the heat seemed to make us uncomfortable, another stood in front of us to serve as a screen. They were most anxious to render us these little services, and often the honor of turning a wooden spit that we had devised to cook our meat disturbed the peace of the family and sowed division among brothers.

We are already meeting savages frequently, and everything announces to us that we are about to leave the settlements of white men to enter Indian territory. All of the scattered houses are still surrounded by the stockades with which people tried to protect them against those barbarians during the last war, and which did not always stop their ravages. They are made of beams sunk into the ground like piles, lined up close to each other, and surround the house, which became the refuge of all the inhabitants of the farm at the approach of the enemy. The buildings that were outside the enclosures were the prey of the flames.

We had been warned in advance about the bad condition of the roads, but we found them worse than we had expected, and after traveling eighty miles by carriage, we were obliged to give up that mode of travel on account of the continual danger of overturning and because of the horses' extreme fatigue. I left my phaeton at German Flats and turned two large carriage horses into riding horses. The blankets that fortunately I had brought along served as a saddle, and in those semi-savage trappings we made the rest of the journey to Fort Schuyler. That was the place agreed upon for negotiations between the three commissioners of Congress and the chiefs and warriors of ten Indian nations who live along the Great Lakes, which separate the United States from Canada. We found a great number of them assembled, but the commissioners had not yet arrived. The Indians, whom we justly call "savages," had hastily built some huts, and were lodging there with their families. Some of them, in spite of the cold and frost, had only shelters of branches, whose dried leaves protected them from neither wind nor rain.

As for Fort Schuyler, which for five years I had heard described as the former bulwark of the colony of New York against the savages, I was surprised to find that it was no more than a little earthen fort with four half-ruined bastions. There were two huts without flooring, their roofs covered with bark. One of these huts was filled with the presents intended for the savages. The other served as a lodging for Mr. Kirkland, a missionary who had been living among the savages for about twenty years. He has the sort of affection for them that a person ends up feeling toward those with whom he has spent a large part of his life, and he likes to present them in the most favorable light. We shared his room, which was meant to house the commissioners, and as they were expected at any moment, cabins of bark were hastily built for us.

. . . We had biscuit and some other provisions. These we distributed as if we were preparing for a famine or a journey through a desert.

We left on horseback for the Oneida Castle. . . . What is really barbarous and savage is the roads running from Fort Schuyler to the Oneida country. One of our servants seriously urged us to complain to the intendant of the province about the bad state of the bridges and roads in his department. The soil here is as rich as that on the Mohawk River, but whatever advantage posterity may derive from it, nothing is more troublesome for present-day travelers. They have to force their way through the woods on horseback, following as best they can a footpath made for the savages, who always go on foot. The streams form a continuous miry bog into which we sank at every step. Trees of immense height and girth fall from old age throughout the forest. They make the paths difficult for people on horseback, though nothing prevents the savages from climbing over them. We were traveling in overcast and rainy weather. We were lost for a time, but our guides soon found their way again. The trees serve them for compasses. They know which is the north side by the bark, which is brown and more moss-covered on that side than on the south. After traversing this long forest, sometimes on foot, sometimes on horseback, sometimes crossing fords, and sometimes making our horses swim, we arrived very wet and tired at the Oneida Castle. Moreover, we did not meet anyone on the way except an old savage sleeping in a bog and covered with half-frozen mud. Our guides woke him up and learned that the night before, he had been at the fort where he had traded his gun for a cask of brandy. He had intended to take it back to the village, but having succumbed to the temptation to taste it, he had emptied the cask and spent a very cold night in a drunken stupor.

Before entering the village, I should tell you that M. de Lafayette was taking three casks of brandy there—or to use the expression of the connoisseurs of the country, three casks of milk. Each of three savages was carrying one, and despite their weight and the difficulty of the road, they followed us quite steadily and even went ahead sometimes. One of them seemed to me so tired, however, that I had my domestic, who was on horseback, take his cask. This savage expressed his gratitude to me, and I was surprised to hear him speak in very good French. . . .[1]

A white flag flying at the principal hut indicated to us the council house, or as our people say, the town hall. There we found the chiefs and warriors of the nation assembled. They received us with the hospitality that the savages show toward all those who are not their enemies. I found an old acquaintance. It was a chief venerable for his age and his abilities. His name is the Great Grasshopper. I had seen him in Philadelphia in 1781. He received us dressed in an embroidered uniform that M. le Chevalier de La Luzerne had given him at that time and which he wears on all important occasions.[2] After the usual compliments, they brought us a large salmon that had just been caught. We had milk, butter, fruit, and honey in abundance. We prepared our supper ourselves, and some silverware that happened to be in our baggage was very useful. We drank from wooden goblets, and M. de Lafayette was honored with one of glass mended with resin.

We expressed the desire to see their dances, and immediately one of their leaders went out and, blowing on a horn, called the young people of the village and told them to dress for the dance and come to the council house right away to entertain the foreigners. . . .

. . . When the dance had gone on for two hours, we were so weary of it that we told the interpreters to ask the dancers to retire. But it was not so simple as that. They wanted to continue until daybreak, and as drunkenness had also become a part of it, the first two pleas that were made to them had no effect. The chiefs did not want to dismiss them, probably because they would not have been able to. Finally one of the dancers, who had once served under M. de Lafayette, took pity on us and spoke so eloquently that the dancers dispersed, and we were free to go to bed. . . .

. . . When we were ready to return to Fort Schuyler, the Great Grasshopper, the Smith, and the Rock Falling from the Top of the Mountains—the three chiefs of the nation—came to find us. Just as they were arriving, I was informed that my horses had strayed and that people had been searching for them since morning. The chiefs were neither surprised nor uneasy. They gave some orders, and at the end of half an hour the Rock Falling from the Top of the Mountains led them back to me himself. . . .

We were on the point of leaving when two young people 24 or 25 years old, one of whom seemed drunk, began to quarrel. The conversation grew more and more animated, and one of them struck the other violently with his club. The one who had been struck began to cry and seemed to want to return the blows he had received, but an old man took him in his arms and held him down on the ground until some women who had come led the other out of the hut. The old man was the father of these two young people, and his son, though strong, made no attempt to escape from his arms. He even consented to smoke the peace pipe with his brother. We saw him smoke half a pipe and give it to the aggressor, who finished it, and peace was made. These quarrels are all the more frequent as they stem from the war that is just over. The nations, and even families, are divided. One of the two brothers had served in the British army, and the other had joined the Americans. On several occasions we had heard the latter call his brother a Tory; for in taking part in the quarrel, the Indians adopted the names "Whigs" and "Tories," which—among them as among the Americans—serve to perpetuate the division and the violence even after the war is over.

I have reason to believe that some of our domestics were married during their short residence at the village, because at the moment of our departure we saw some very unhappy squaws, still decked out in their wedding ribbons, and the separation was quite touching. Since a missionary has been living among the Oneidas, however, these weddings of courtesy are quite rare there, and no one even proposed them to us.

On our way back to the fort we were surprised to find the drunken savage that we had met earlier on the way to the village. This poor man, back home and recovered from his drunkenness, had realized that he must redeem his rifle at any cost. He had bought another cask of brandy, and he was carrying it to the fort when, sucumbing a second time to an irresistible temptation, he fell again into the same state of inebriation in which we had found him once before.

. . . The savages had arrived from many districts during our absence, and we found representatives of eight different nations when we returned to the fort. They were the Mohawks, the Oneidas, the Onondagas, the Tuscaroras, the Cayugas, the Wolves or Stockbridge Indians, the Senecas, and some other nations from Canada, among whom those from Fort St. Louis were the most remarkable, and nearly all spoke French. The Senecas, the Cayugas, the Onondagas, and the Ganiengahagas or Mohawks were enemies of the United States during the last war and still are not very peacefully disposed. They had come to the Mohawk River at the invitation of Congress to treat with Mr. Wolcott, Mr. Lee, and Mr. Butler, commissioners of that assembly. This great council—that is the name the savages give to these assemblies of several nations—this great council gave us an opportunity to see these peoples all together in the same place and a little more conveniently than if we had had to travel through the various countries they inhabit.

. . . You will be able to estimate the value they place on keeping a man with them and how important it is to prevent the weakening of their society by the difficulty M. le Marquis de Lafayette had in obtaining a savage for a companion. Even though the Oneidas have the greatest affection for him, they were extremely reluctant to give him permission to take one of their young people to France. They had to consult the chiefs and confer with all the relatives. There were some relatives who were far from this place and whose consent was needed. They were sent messages to this effect, but although most of them are disposed to gratify him, I don't think that this important negotation has been concluded yet. . . .[3]

. . . We witnessed the reconciliation of the Oneidas with their Indian enemies. Although they had both been living near the fort for several days, they had not seen each other, and although hostilities had ceased, communication had not been re-established. The Great Grasshopper, wearing the cloak M. le Chevalier de La Luzerne had given him and followed by five other savages dressed with the same care, went to the huts of the Senecas. They walked with dignity and stopped from time to time. The chief of the Senecas came out and received them at some distance. They sat down on the grass, the two chiefs exchanged greetings, they smoked the peace pipe, and they parted. The next day the visit was returned, the Senecas going to the Oneidas with the same ceremony and the same formalities. . . .

. . . These savages still have great respect for the king of France. They speak of the French nation with reverence, even though their relations with us ended over twenty years ago. They are passionately fond of liquor, but they say that the French were their true fathers because the French refused them this poison that the British brought them in abundance. M. de Lafayette has their confidence and attachment to an extraordinary extent. Those who had already seen him were very eager to see him again. They had transmitted their enthusiasm to their friends, and they seemed proud to wear around their necks the presents he had given them before. . . .[4]

. . . We were present at the opening of the peace conference between the congressional commissioners and the savages. There were several speeches, and Monsieur de Lafayette gave one that was well composed, with the grace and nobility that you know in him.[5] The meeting took place outdoors despite the rather bitter cold. The savages, seated in a circle around a fire that was to be used only to light their pipes, listened with careful attention. There were about forty chiefs and warriors present. The warriors, armed as if for combat, were rather handsome, but others were dressed in the most bizarre and ridiculous way. One had decked himself out in a bearskin and looked rather like that animal. Another had attached ears to his head like those used to represent Midas. We also saw once more the wig whose ownership had caused a quarrel a few days earlier. These grotesque figures were in complete contrast to the gravity of the speakers. One of these spoke with a great deal of grace. He was standing, as is their custom. A piece of cloth floated from his shoulders. His left arm was bare and outstretched. His bearing was proud, his voice strong, and we listened very attentively to the interpreter who translated his speech for us. But we found nothing in it to equal what his appearance led us to expect.

October 6

We fulfilled the principal aim of our journey, which was to see the savages. Nothing kept us at Fort Stanwix any longer. We rented a small boat that had just enough space for eleven people including five oarsmen, and we traveled down the Mohawk River very comfortably in the most beautiful weather in the world. There is a waterfall called *The Little Falls* where the boat has to be taken overland.[6] It is pulled by horses, and the baggage or merchandise is put on a wagon. This portage is about half a mile long. It is pleasing to watch the increasing improvement of agriculture as one descends this river. But at the same time we were tormented by the spectacle of the barbarities committed by the savages. All the farms have been burned, and the inhabitants still lack a great number of necessities. But foodstuffs of all sorts are found there in abundance.

October 8

Here we are back in Albany, Mademoiselle. There we found in good

health all the people who mattered to us. We have been to see a waterfall that we won't tell you about, since you have seen a description of it
as beautiful as nature in Mr. de Chastellux's journal. We could not tell
you about it as well as he did.

We rejoin here a very polite and refined society, and as this journal
was only meant to acquaint you with the savages, we shall end it here
and hope that you will read it with as much pleasure as we derived
from writing it for you.

M (AAE: Correspondance politique, Etats-Unis, vol. 28, fols. 204–38), originally composed for friends, these extracts of Marbois's journal were sent by Marbois [to Vergennes?], in 1785. The sections deleted here contain his descriptions of the Indians and
their customs. For a different version of the journal, see Barbé-Marbois, *Our Revolutionary Forefathers* (New York, 1929), pp. 177–215.
    1. The "savage" was a Frenchman, Nicholas Jordan, who had been captured by the
Indians during the Seven Years' War.
    2. On July 15, 1782, La Luzerne held a celebration at Philadelphia in honor of the
birth of the Dauphin, to which he invited more than twelve hundred guests. Included
was a group of Indians from the Five Nations, among them the Great Grasshopper, to
whom La Luzerne presented a number of gifts.
    3. The Indian boy, Peter Otchikeita, was in Quebec when Lafayette left for France,
but he followed him there in 1785.
    4. See *LAAR*, 1:247, for an account of Lafayette's earlier encounters with the Indians
when he was preparing for the Canadian expedition in 1778.
    5. The speeches appear on pp. 255–59.
    6. The Little Falls portage was just below German Flats and the present site of
Herkimer, New York.

To the Commissioners of Congress

Fort Schuyller September the 30th 1784

Gentlemen

I Have the Honour to inform You that I Have Got Yesterday to this
Place, and altho' we Had Breakfasted at Mr. ShoeMaker's[1] we Arrived
By land at the fort pretty long time Before Sun Set. Doctor Courtland's
Anxiety to See You Well Accomodated Has Made Him Advise You not
to Come Before the troops Have Made Some Arrangements.[2] But I
Assure You, and in this the doctor Now Agrees with me, that You will
Be as well Here at least as Any where Upon the Road, and as Your
Baggage is partly Arrived and Getting in Every Hour, it Seems Noth-
ing Can Now detain you.

It Seems to Be Doctor Courtland's opinion that My little influence
With the indians Can in a pretty Great degree Promote your Purposes.
The Same observation Having Been Made to me By Gal. Woolcot, I

don't think Myself at liberty to leave this Before I Have told the Indians what You May wish me to Mention. But as the doctor clearly think it Sufficient for me to Speak to Such Indians as Now are within Call, I Beg leave to Represent that the twentieth Having Been Appointed for me to Be Here, I Have Consequently Made Sundry Arrangements. General Washington whose journey Has Been Cramped on My Account and Several other friends are waiting for me on Certain Periods whom My delay will disappoint.

Give me leave therefore, Gentlemen, to ask you if By Adopting Doctor Courtland's opinion, You Could Now Send for those indians, Oneïdas and others that are waïting for You at Oneïda Castle. As it is probable You will Be to Morrow on this Spot, You Might then tell me, or Send me, (if you don't Come) what You wish me to tell them on Saturday—and Sunday Next, if there is No public motive for my attendance, I will Beg Your permission to Set out for New England.[3]

I Strongly Advise You not to Ride in the Night along the Road from the German flatts to this place, as there are Some Bad places, which in the dark Might Be dangerous. With Every Sentiment of Respect I am waïting for Your orders and Have the Honour to Be Gentlemen Your Most obedient Humble Servant

LAFAYETTE

ALS (MH: bMs, Am 811.6 [124a], autograph file). The Commissioners, Arthur Lee, Oliver Wolcott, and Richard Butler, were instructed by Congress to impose final peace terms on the Indians and establish American land claims in Indian territory.

1. The Shoemaker Tavern was in the village of Mohawk, near Herkimer, New York.
2. Lafayette was referring to Dr. Samuel Kirkland, the Indian missionary.
3. As Lafayette was a foreigner and his status unofficial, his position at the Indian conference was a matter of some delicacy. Probably Lee, and perhaps Butler also, opposed his taking any action, while Washington, Wolcott, and Kirkland felt he could be of use to the Americans. During his visit to Mount Vernon, Lafayette discussed the Indian situation with Washington, and Washington may have been the one to suggest that Lafayette attend the conference. See Lafayette to Washington, October 8, 1784.

Robert Morris to the President of Congress

Office of Finance, 30th. September, 1784.
Sir.

I do myself the honor to enclose for the Inspection of Congress, a Copy of a Letter of the fourteenth of last Month, from the Marquis De la Fayette; and with it I send the Originals which were delivered by him to me.[1] The unexampled Attention to every American Interest, which this Gentleman has exhibited cannot fail to excite the strongest Emotions in his favor; and we must at the same time, admire the Judgment which he has shewn in the Manner of his Applications, as well as the Industry in selecting proper Materials. There can be little Doubt that his Interest at his own Court must always prove beneficial to this Country while the same Cordiality shall continue which now subsists between him and the venerable Plenipotentiary now resident at Passy.

I shall not hazard Opinions upon the Matters, which have employed the Attention of Monsr. de la Fayette as a Negociator from this Country to that which gave him birth. It would be intending Sentiments which will suggest themselves. But while I feel the Delicacy and perhaps Danger of asking from France the Moderation or Abolition of particular Duties, thereby establishing a Precedent for similar requests on her part—I hope Congress will pardon a Wish prompted by the general Interests of Commerce that the Statement of all those Duties might be translated and published for the Government of those who may form Expeditions to those different Ports now opened to us.[2] With perfect Respect I have the Honor to be Sir, Your Excellency's Most obedient & Humble Servant

ROBT. MORRIS

LS (DNA: RG 360, PCC 137, vol. 3, fols. 793–94).
Morris sent a copy of this letter to Lafayette on the same date with thanks for his services to America (DLC: Robert Morris Papers).
1. See Lafayette to Morris, August 14, 1784 (DNA: RG 360, PCC 121, p. 107). Enclosed with that letter and here forwarded to Congress by Morris were the following letters: Lafayette to Calonne, January 31, February 10, February 26, and March 5, 1784; Calonne to Lafayette, March 8, May 17, June 11, and June 16, 1784; and Castries to Lafayette, June 17, 1784.
2. Jay had the schedule of duties translated and printed for distribution to all American shippers (DNA: RG 360, PCC 59, vol. 4, p. 99).

Account of Lafayette's Meeting with the Six Nations[T]

October 3–4, 1784

The representatives of Congress, those of Pennsylvania, and the Marquis de Lafayette went to the Council where all the savage chiefs were, and M. de Lafayette gave the following speech in French, which was translated by the United States' interpreter:[1]

Upon rejoining my children, I give thanks to the heavens that led me into this place of peace where you are smoking the pipe of friendship together.

If you recognize the voice of Kayeheanla, remember, too, his advice and the wampum belts he often sent you.[2] I come to thank the faithful children, the chiefs of the nations, the warriors, the bearers of my words, and if a father's memory did not forget the evil sooner than the good, I could punish those who while opening their ears have closed their hearts, who, blindly raising their hatchets, risked striking their own father.

The American cause is just, I told you then; it is the cause of humanity, it is particularly your cause. At least remain neutral, and the brave Americans will defend their liberty and yours. Your fathers will take them by the hand; the white birds will cover the shore; the great Onontio, known as "the Sun," will dissipate the clouds around you, and contrary schemes will vanish like a mist that fades away.[3]

"Do not listen to Kayeheanla," they cried to you before. But they also told you that an army in the north would enter Boston in triumph, that the one in the South would take Virginia, and that the great war chief, Washington, at the head of your fathers and your brothers, would be forced to leave the country. Those who had their hands over your eyes did not fail, however, to keep their own open. Peace is accomplished! You know the terms of it, and I shall oblige some among you by abstaining, out of pity, from repeating them.

My predictions having been fulfilled, listen to the new advice of your father, and may my voice resound among all the nations.

What have you ever gained, my children, or rather what have you not lost in European quarrels? Be wiser than the white men, keep peace among you, and since the great council of the states is willing to negotiate, take advantage of its good inclinations. Do not forget that the Americans are close friends of your fathers the French; this alliance is as enduring as it has been fortunate. The great Onontio gives his hand forever to your brothers who offer you theirs, and by this means we shall form a salutary chain. To assure yourselves of this, trade with the Americans and with those of your fathers who cross the great lake. The products of France are known to you, and you are clever enough to prefer them.[4] They will be for you the symbol of the alliance. In selling lands, do not consult a barrel of rum to give them up to the first who come, but let the American chiefs and yours, joined together around the fire, conclude reasonable bargains. At the present time, my children, you know that while several are entitled to Congress's gratitude, there are many whose only resource is to be found in its clemency and whose past mistakes require amends.

If you are listening well, my children, I have said enough to you about it. Repeat my words to each other, while on the other shore of the lake, I shall receive news of you with pleasure, and until the day when we shall join pipes, when we shall lie down again under the same bark, I wish you good health, happy hunting, unity and abundance, and the success of all the dreams that promise you happiness.

The chief of the Mohawks[5] arose holding a wampum belt and said:

May the ears of Kayeheanla, a chief of the great Onontio, our father, be open to receive our words.

My father, we have heard your voice, and we rejoice that you have visited your children to give them just and necessary advice. You told us we were wrong to lend an ear to the wicked and to close our hearts to your counsel. That is true, my father. We, the Mohawk Nation, have left the true path. We acknowledge having been led astray and enveloped in a black cloud, but now we return so that you will find in us again good and faithful children.

Truly, my father, we love to hear your voice among us, which, without wounding our hearts, has done us much good. It seems that the all-powerful spirit has directed you, has led you into this place of peace where you may smoke the pipe of friendship with your children whom you have found again.

Kayeheanla, my father, as for our situation, you also spoke the truth to us, but we hope that the Great Spirit who has protected us up to now will bring us out of the wrong path to direct our steps into the right path so that our past mistakes will be forgotten, so that we may join together in the same cause and be of one mind in all our enterprises.

My father, we feel that all the words you uttered are words of truth, and experience has shown us that all your predictions have been fulfilled. Your words and your speech inspire a spirit of peace. That is our great and sole objective; it is the objective that brings us.

Kayeheanla, my father, it is an old and established rule that children must obey their father and that scolding them and punishing them when they make mistakes is the paternal prerogative. We know this, and have certainly deserved punishment. But as we said, we count on the Great Spirit on high to incline and purify our hearts so that you can be pleased to give back to your children in your Goodness the life they deserved to lose.

My father, we recall the words you said to us seven years ago,[6] and we find there is not one that is not verified. Yes, my father, we see that all you said is true, which makes us rejoice now when we look upon you and when we shall also smoke again the pipe of peace and friendship. You observed to us, my father, that the alliance between France and America was an indissoluble bond that would never be broken, and those who doubt it have only to board your ships, cross the great lake, and see for themselves.

My father, you warned us not to take counsel from strong liquor in the sale of our lands. We have much need of this salutary advice, because it is from that that all our miseries and misfortunes come, and we hope that no problem of that kind will arise in this great peace council.

Kayeheanla, my father, the words that you have uttered today will be spread throughout all of the Six Nations, and they are bound to renew and strengthen the bond of friendship that we wish to see endure forever.

My father, we shall say no more to you today, because it is not fitting to our situation to multiply words. But we rejoice in the happiness of the present moment, and we shall attend the great council of the United States, whose members we congratulate on their arrival here. You told us you were leaving tomorrow, and if we have something to add we shall communicate it to you at your quarters.

The next day there was another gathering of savages at which the speaker of the friendly nations gave the following speech:

> Kayeheanla, my father, I beg all the nations present here to open their ears to the few words I am about to say. And you, great war chief of our father, Onontio, I beg you to listen to me.
>
> Your speech yesterday contained congratulations, reproaches, and advice. We accept them all the better because we recall the words you spoke to us seven years ago. They are what kept us from being led astray by those who were fighting against America's cause. This necklace (like the wampum belt received from M. de Moncalm) was given us twenty years ago by our fathers.[7] They told us that we must hold one end of it and France the other, and that one day their voices would be heard among us again.
>
> Kayeheanla, my father, all your words have been verified by the events of this great isle. We therefore receive with pleasure the new words you say to us on this occasion.

In giving back the wampum belt the Marquis replied that he rejoiced to see that this belt had been kept so well and to think that his influence on some nations had kept them from declaring themselves against the United States; that France will always hold one end of the belt and that it will also be held by America, whose alliance with France will maintain communications between the French and their children. He thanked them for their fidelity in following his counsel by closing their ears to the enemies of the American cause.

A Huron chief arose and said:

> Kayeheanla, my father, open your ears to the few words I am about to speak at your departure. The nations of the north have been the children of the great Onontio for a long time. The words you spoke to us were pleasing to us because they were true. You began by thanking the Supreme Being for having led you to this place of peace and friendship. We recognize the same providence, and we hope it will make this council the source of the greatest blessings. We thank you for all your words, and thanking you, we take leave of you.
>
> Kayeheanla, my father, we shall add one more word to what we have said to you. In leaving the nations of the north, we received exhortations from the governor of Canada which were not foreign to the subject of your speech. He counseled us to behave with decency, to speak only soft words at the treaty negotiations that are going to be held with the thirteen United States, telling us at the same time that all hostilities were ended between Great Britain and the United States. This, my father, corresponds with the spirit of your speech. He counseled us further to observe

the same gentle conduct with all the savage nations and especially with those that might come from around Niagara.

Corn Planter, Seneca chief, arose and said:

Kayeheanla, my father, war chief of the great Onontio, open your ears to the words I am about to speak.

At the beginning of your speech you acknowledge the guidance of the Great Spirit on high, who leads you to this place where you find your children in peace. You then give us some lessons and advice in which you declare that fatherly affection forgets mistakes sooner than good actions and otherwise you would not have been willing to come and see us in this land. You also reminded us, my father, of the words you spoke to us at our first meeting seven years ago at Fort Johnson. You told us then that you knew the basis of the quarrel between America and Great Britain and that its cause was just and that the great Onontio would form a link with America that would shine forever. You called upon our memory of it for the fulfillment of your predictions. You also informed us on other subjects of great importance, while observing to us that if we followed your counsel in the present negotiations, you would hear about us with pleasure on the other side of the great lake.

My father, open once more your ears. We did not have time yesterday to reflect on your words. It is very true that no nation is free from error, and we have been led into very great mistakes, at Great Britain's instigation, in uniting against the American states. We were vanquished, but it is fitting for all nations to be concerned about each other in misfortune, and it especially becomes the victors to show this compassion to those who are vanquished. You have heard our voice, my father. Our ideas are all brought together around this council fire lit by Congress, whose representatives are here at this moment. Our hopes, our trust, are concentrated in this treaty negotiation. If the Americans speak to us kindly, all will go well and peace will spread over all the nations. My father, take this belt with you, and do not forget our words.

The Marquis' reply was that we thank the governor of Canada for his sincere wishes for the success of these negotiations and that they should also thank him for the counsel he gave them to make for themselves the best peace they can; that knowing the good inclinations of Congress, he is very pleased to see his children enlightened about their former errors; that he entreats all the savages to forget all animosity against each other; that in the situation in which he is leaving everything, he does not doubt that the treaty will be satisfactory to the United States; and that with his confidence in that, he enjoys already the return of his fatherly affection.

M (AAE: Correspondance politique, Etats-Unis, vol. 28, fols. 290–93), copy, translation.

1. Just a few weeks before this meeting, commissioners from New York met with the Indians at Fort Schuyler to settle land claims within the state. The congressional commissioners were instructed by Congress to impose final peace terms on the Indians and establish substantial land claims for the Americans. Pennsylvania sent commissioners to the Fort Schuyler meeting to buy land from the Indians within the borders of Pennsylvania. The actual treaty negotiations between the congressional commissioners and the Indians did not begin until October 5.

2. Lafayette's Indian name was Kayeheanla, not Kayenlaa, as in this manuscript, or Kayewla, as given by Lafayette in his memoir of 1779 and followed in *LAAR*, 1:247.

3. Onontio was the Iroquois name for the king of France.

4. The French were interested in the possibility of reopening the Indian trade through the Americans. Barbé de Marbois reported to Vergennes on the Indian fur trade after the Fort Schuyler meeting.

5. Probably David Hill.

6. For Lafayette's appearance at the Johnstown Conference in March 1778, see *LAAR*, 1:247–49.

7. In 1757, when Montcalm held a general conference with his Indian allies, he presented the senior Indian chief with a wampum belt of 6,000 beads, symbolizing their alliance.

To Adrienne de Noailles de Lafayette[T]

Fort Schuyler, October 4, 1784

Here I am in the country of the savages, my dear heart, surrounded by Hurons and Iroquois and very weary of the role of father of the family which has been forced on me here. I wrote you that my influence might be useful for the treaty that is being negotiated with all the Nations.[1] This consideration led me to postpone my trip to Boston. I went up the North River;[2] near Albany I visited a new sect of enthusiasts who go through incredible contortions and who claim to perform miracles, in which I have found some of the methods of magnetism.[3] From there I proceeded to the treaty negotiations over appalling roads, and on my arrival my companions were quite surprised to find that the country was as familiar to me as if I were entering the suburb of St. Germain. We spent a day in a settlement of savages where M. de Gouvion lived for a long time.[4] My personal credit with the savages—who are as much friends as enemies—has proved to be much greater than I had supposed. Although the congressional ambassadors were led by Mr. Arthur Lee, who certainly did not care to be under obligation to me, they were obliged to have recourse to me, and yesterday I mounted the speaker's rostrum. The responses having fortunately come to an end today, I am joyfully taking the road to Albany, and Mr. Lee's final observation to me was that the savages had been too occupied with me to pay attention to the commissioners. They made me great promises, and I love to think that I have contributed to a treaty that will give us a small commercial outlet and will ensure the tranquility of the Americans. At present I am going to New England; I shall embark at Newport for Virginia, which is a journey of three days, and there I shall again see General Washington. The mishaps of the voyage have fallen entirely on Demanche. He tumbled into a mire; he crossed a river, one foot in the stirrup and unable to get his right leg over; he fell through a rickety floor, and half of his body hung in the second story while the other half stayed on the third. But he has been very useful to us, doing the cooking with such zeal that, on seeing a little boy turning to the left the spit he had been turning to the right, he rushed to stop him, apparently out of fear that the boy would unroast the meat. He manages my money with great care and is a completely honest man. I am with M. de Marbois here and was not displeased to have with me the nation's chargé d'affaires to tell me how far I should go. It is with pleasure that I shall depart tomorrow, because all this savagery, despite my popularity, bores me to death, and my little bark hut is about as comfortable as a taffeta suit in the month of January. But I'll stop this babbling, my dear heart, and continue my little journal in some inn that is a bit less well ventilated. Farewell, my dear heart, I embrace you very tenderly.

Church's Tavern near Hartford, October 10, 1784

Here I am, back in the world, my dear heart, and I have left the savage forests with great satisfaction. The hope of finding some letters at Albany contributed a great deal to that feeling, but I did not have that pleasure, and although, according to the arrangements I have made, Le Brun may join me tonight, it is equally possible that I shall go to bed as unhappy as I was on my arrival at Albany.[5] Because I have been traveling across the countryside, I have nothing very interesting to tell you. People treat me with kindness everywhere, and when I arrive at a house where I am not known, my first response is always taken up with given my own news. While I remember it, my dear heart, I have to tell you about a celebrated plant called *ginseng*, of which I can only send one pot, which is addressed to you, and which I beg you to share with the Maréchal de Noailles and Mme de Tessé. Since this may be the only time in my life that we shall talk about botany, I shall add that I have found here a climbing plant, an evergreen, that will create a marvelous effect on the two walls of our terrace. When you get it, I pray you will have it sown and planted in great quantities at the foot of the two walls; and I am also sending a plant that will cover them with the most beautiful red flowers during the summer. If my study is finished, the charms of the house will lack nothing. I am quite distressed that poor Poirey has a nervous disorder, but if he is better, persuade him to learn to write in abbreviations, as quickly as a person speaks, and to have my library arranged. I have bothered you so much about our arrangements that I don't want to dwell on them again. I shall merely say that I would be glad to find my debts to the workmen paid when I return; that since General Greene is in Charleston, I don't know whether the money will be paid to me before I leave or if it will be sent to France; that the bill of exchange on Baltimore, though good, has run into some difficulties; that consequently it will be prudent to take measures with the Duc de Castries to see that I shall have a hundred louis waiting for me at Brest so that I won't lose a minute, which at that time will be more precious to me than a week in America. As for the minor domestic arrangements, I hope you will have brought my aunt back with you, and you will do well then to get our friend Desplaces established. If you find a position for Comtois, I'll confide to you that I may well bring back a young Iroquois savage, but that negotiation is not yet completed. This letter is very long, my dear heart, and to tell the truth I think that my stay at Mount Vernon has spoiled me altogether. I enclose a large packet of letters, and you will also find one for my aunt, for Gouvion, and for our dear Anastasie.[6] The first letters I receive will tell me of your trip to Chavaniac. I rejoice at all the good you will have done my aunt, and my heart loves to be obliged to you for it. Your conjugal virtues will have impressed M. de Lastic even more, and his poor wife will have glimpsed some disadvantageous reflections. I am impatient to know how our children took to the country and their father's natal air. It will be a great source of satisfaction for me if my aunt has followed you to Paris. If she hasn't consented to do so, try again in your letters to convince her. The end of my sojourn here, my dear heart, is not fixed as to the specific week of our departure, but I think that the first packet will tell you the exact time, and in the course of December, toward the end, I shall surely have the happiness of embracing you.

L (ALS, courtesy of the Comte de Cambrun), translation.
1. Letter not found.
2. The Hudson River.
3. The Shakers; see Barbé-de Marbois's Journal, September 23–October 8, 1784.
4. Gouvion was stationed at Oneida Castle in 1778 (see *LAAR*, 1:358, note 7).
5. Le Brun was coming from France to join Lafayette.
6. Letters not found.

To John Jay

Albany, October 7, 1784

My dear sir,

I am very unfortunate in my attempts to meet you, but hope at last to have better success, and sincerely wish it to happen about the middle of next month, when I hope to wait upon Congress at their next meeting.

Until a few days ago, I had no doubt but to hear you had accepted the appointment conferred upon you. My fears, however, have been raised, and with my usual frankness I assure you that your refusal could not but be attended with very bad circumstances. Setting compliments apart, I am sensible of the great injury such a denial would cause to the public, not only on account of the loss made by the United States in your person, but also for other motives.[1] I hope you will accept; I know you must: but in case you are not determined, I had rather change my plans than not to see you before you write to Congress. I wish much to hear from you at New-York, where I expect to be about the 22d.

My most affectionate respects wait upon Mrs. Jay. With every sentiment of regard and attachment, I have the honour to be Your sincere friend,

LA FAYETTE

From William Jay, *The Life of John Jay* [New York, 1883], pp. 158–59
1. Jay had been nominated for the position of secretary of foreign affairs, and Lafayette was afraid that if Jay declined, Arthur Lee would be chosen in his stead (Lafayette to Hamilton, October 8, 1784).

To Alexander Hamilton

Albany October the 8th 1784

Dear Hamilton

With all the warmth of My long and tender friendship I Congratulate You Upon the Birth of Your daughter, and Beg leave to present Mrs. Hamilton with My Most Affectionate Respects.[1]

Several delays Have Retarded the Oppening of the treaty—and when I was Upon the Ground, it Has Been found that My Influence with the Indians, Both friendly and Hostile tribes, was much greater than the Commissioners and Even Myself Had Conceived. So that I was Requested, Even By Every one of the *three,* to Speack to *those* Nations.[2] There were Some, More or less, from Each tribe. I stayed as long as the Commissionners thought I could do them Some Good, and that Has Rather Cramped My private plans of Visits.

Now, My dear friend, I am Going to Harford, Boston, Newport, from thence By Water to Virginia, in order to Save time, and about the twentieth of Next Month I Hope to Be Again with You in Newyork. But Before that time will write You from Newport. Adieu, My dear Hamilton, Most affectionately I am Yours

LAFAYETTE

I am told Mr. Jay is not determined Upon Accepting. I much wish He may Consent to it. The More So as His probable Successor A. L. does not Hit My fancy. Indeed, I very much wish Mr. Jay May Accept the Office.[3]

ALS (DLC: Alexander Hamilton Papers).
1. Angelica Hamilton was born in September.
2. Lafayette's underscoring was probably meant to emphasize Arthur Lee's acquiescence in his colleagues' wish that Lafayette be allowed to speak. Lee, one of the commissioners of Congress at the conference, had been the object of Lafayette's hostility for years (see *LAAR,* 3:190).
3. See preceding letter.

To George Washington

Albany October the 8th 1784

My dear General

Every where I Have Met with delays. But So Agreable were they in their Nature that I Cannot Complain of them. It is not Quite the Case with the Indian treaty—Altho' the Hope to Be Useful Has kept me there longer than I Had Expected. My presence at the oppening of it Had Been desired. Many Circumstances kept it off. At last it Began, and My influence with the Indians was found Greater than I myself Could Expect. I Was therefore desired to Speak—to Hearken to Answers. I took the liberty to Caution the Commissioners Upon Such Points as You Had Mentionned me—and did not leave the Ground Untill they thought they Had No farther Occasion for me.[1] But as the Business is just Beginning, I Cannot Give You any farther Intelligence, But that Great deal of intrigue is Carried on By Some tory indians of

Brant party, and that the Whigg and tory distinctions Are kept up Among those tribes to an Amasing degree of private Animosities.[2]

This day, My dear General, I am Going towards Hartfort, Boston, and Newport where the french ships Now are—and (as, if I went By land, I would Be So much kept of By my friends as to Be very late on our Appointed Meeting,) I intend Submitting Myself to the little Inconvenience of Going by Water from Rhode island to Williamsburg where I Hope to Be About the 26th and where I Will Be Happy to Receive the orders of My dear General.

Waiting Upon the Assembly in Richmond, and Visiting Frederisburg on My way to Mount Vernon would Be My plan—But Expect Your orders to know where I am to Meet You. It is possible You Had Rather Not Go to Richmond. In a Word, My dear General, as Your Paternal Goodness to me Cannot Stand Upon any Kind of Ceremony, Give me Your orders. Tell me what I Had Best to do—and I Shall Be As You well know Happy to obey them.

One thing, My dear General, I Very much wish You Might grant Me—as the time of my stay in Virginia will depend Upon Your Advice Respecting french letters which I am to Receive there, as it will Be then a last Visit for this American trip of Mine—I Will Be Happy My dear General, if without Inconvenience to Yourself You may Come with me So far, at least, as Philadelphia where Your friends depend Upon me to Have an Opportunity to See You.

Could You Pay the Virginia Visits With me, Could I meet You Some where, or Frederisburg I Suppose, where in that Case I would Go Before I visit Richmond, it Would Be to me a Most Heartfelt Happiness.

I Beg Your Pardon, My Beloved General, But I want to See You, and No Heart Can Better feel the pleasure to Be with You than the filial Heart of Your Respectfull and affectionate friend

LAFAYETTE

The chevalier Begs leave to Be Most Respectfully presented to You.[3] We United in Respects to Mrs. Washington and Compliments to Mr. Washington and Children. If you Hear from George I Beg You will Let me know it.[4]

ALS (PEL: Hubbard Collection).

1. In July–August 1783 Washington took a nineteen-day, 750-mile tour of the north country from Albany to Crown Point, stopping at Fort Schuyler on the return trip. After his return, he urged Congress to take a firm stand with the Indians, treat them as conquered enemies, and require substantial land cessions (Fitzpatrick, *Writings of Washington*, 27:133–40). Apparently Washington took advantage of Lafayette's intended visit to the conference to make known his opinions once more, though the instructions to the commissioners were already in substantial agreement with his views.

2. Joseph Brant, Mohawk war chief, was still in contact with the British in Canada and to the west.

3. Maurice Riquet de Caraman, Lafayette's traveling companion.

4. George Augustine Washington had been in the West Indies.

To Thomas Jefferson

Hartford October the 11th 1784

My dear Sir

When I Heard of Your Going to France, I Heartly lamented I Could not Have the Honour to Recieve You there, But in the Same time Anticipated the pleasure to Wait Upon You this Winter in our french Capital. Your Voyage to Europe I Ever Considered as a favourite Wish of Mine, and on Every public and private Account am Happy to think You at last Have Consented to Go.[1] Permit me, My dear Sir, farther to Carry My Wiews, and in Case our Respected Doctor Franklin is Indulged in His Wishes for Retirement, let me Hope my Country May So far Agree with You, as to obtain Your Consent for a longer Residence—an Event which, Both as a french man, and an American, I Most Warmly desire.

Upon wiewing Again these Blessed shores of liberty My Heart throbbed for joy, and Nothing Could add to my Satisfaction But the flattering Reception with which I Have Been Every where Honoured. I wish it were in My power to Make a much longer Stay, But will at least Employ the time I Have in Visiting as Many of My friends as I Can. From Mount Vernon to this place I Have Been Enjoying their Compagny in their Respective States, and am just from Fort Schuyller where it was thought my presence, and Even my personal influence with the Indians Could Be of Some public Utility. The Business is just Began, But in Case You Wish to know the temper of those people, So far as You may discover it in their Answers to me, I think You will find the whole with Count de Vergennes to whom it will Be Probably Sent By Mr. de Marbois.[2]

I am now Going to Boston, Rhode island, and By water to Virginia where Gal. Washington is again waïting for me. We will together proceed to Philadelphia, and I intend attending in Trenton By the time Congress are Met, in order to pay My Respects to them. God grant Such a foederative System May Be fairly followed By all the states, as will Insure their eternal Union, and of Course their Interior Happiness, Comercial wea[l]th, and National Consequence! Nothing New from Rhode island Respecting the import.[3] A few Indians Have broke out towards the New Settlements, But Nothing of Any Consequence.

Should a little dispute Be Mentioned, that Happened Upon the Back lands of Connecticut and Pennsylvania, it May Be Affirmed that this trifling affair is Vanishing into Nothing.[4]

My House, Dear Sir, My family, and Any thing that is Mine are entirely at Your disposal, and I Beg You will Come and See Mde. de Lafayette as you would act By Your Brother's wife. Her knowledge of the Country May Be of Some Use to Miss Jefferson whom she Will Be Happy to attend in Every thing that May Be Agreeable to Her. Indeed, my dear Sir, I would Be very Angry with You, if either You or she, did not Consider My House as a Second Home, and Mde. de Lafayette as Very Happy in Every opportunity to wait Upon Miss Jefferson.

My Best and Most Affectionate Respects Waït Upon Doctor Franklin. Be pleased also to Remember me to Mr. Barklay, Young Franklin, and other American friends. Should you Now Be with Mr. Adams, I Beg You Will present My Respects to Him. Adieu, My dear Sir, With Every Sentiment of Attachement and Regard I Have the Honour to Be Your obedient Humble Servant

LAFAYETTE

ALS (DLC: Thomas Jefferson Papers).

1. Congress had appointed Jefferson, Adams, and Franklin in December 1783 to negotiate treaties of amity and commerce with foreign powers (*JCC*, 25:824–25). Jefferson had sailed from Boston for France in July.

2. See the Account of Lafayette's Meeting with the Six Nations, October 3–4, 1784.

3. Lafayette deleted the next sentence: "But those Restrictions put on [their] exported goods into Connecticut By land By the Neighboring States May produce a good [effect]." On July 1, 1784, the General Assembly of Rhode Island refused to ratify an amendment granting Congress a 5 percent import duty, the second such amendment proposed by Congress in four years. Lafayette clearly hoped that taxes neighboring states imposed on Rhode Island products would reduce its trade enough to force it to accede to the import duty.

4. In September, Pennsylvania sent several commissioners into Northumberland County to reinstate claimants dispossessed of their lands. The *Pennsylvania Packet*, October 6, 1784, reported that the commissioners were physically attacked and a number of people killed by rival Connecticut claimants to the same lands.

To the Prince de Poix[T]

Hartford, October 12, 1784

After leaving all that I love, my dear prince, I have always gone straight ahead, and as if I hadn't had enough of being in another world, I even gave up that one to go into the wilderness. Thank God, I am back now and am finally beginning to gaze upon the east coast. I couldn't lose my scalp among the Iroquois, because one doesn't lose, says the proverb, what he doesn't have, but I lost time, and it drove me

completely wild. They thought I would be useful for this treaty negotiation, and I admit they were right. But this treaty delays my calls, and
I have a grudge against anything that prolongs this cruel exile. After
listening to the gibberish of those savages (and they said the same of
me), we finally separated, and here I am in the city of Hartford, where
I am receiving the same marks of kindness showered on me in all the
states.[1] I am detained here because of a public dinner, after which I
shall be on the road to Boston and then to Rhode Island. But since I am
always stopped in my trips on land, in order to make haste, I would
rather embark in Newport and join General Washington by sea. He
must have been expecting me for several days, and I, who never come
late, shall this time have unnecessarily upset his plans. The plan I made
to be in Paris toward the end of December is irrevocably settled. Without knowing just how, I am certain of carrying it out. Seven months'
absence, and voluntary absence, is a long enough penance, and if heav-
en takes it into account, it should serve for the sins of my whole life. If
you had the slightest bit of faith, my dear prince, I would tell you about
a new sect of Shakers who do contortions and miracles, all due to the
application of the major tenets of magnetism. I shall tell you that I can
do a book in quarto titled "Essay on Savage Dances and Especially on
the New Dance Brought from the Western Woods" (which is like the
Fitzjames or the Iroquois dance), "Applied to the Principle of Dr. Mesmer." But I am saving all these nice things to use to do myself credit
this winter, not among the profane, but at the gatherings on the Rue
Coqueron.[2] Although I am expecting papers, my dear friend, it is not
because of them that I am groaning over delays of the packetboats. But
this is my fourth letter, and as yet I have only one from you, though I
have no criticisms to make, which is always a consolation.[3] This latest
ship doesn't come. I expect my packets everywhere and everywhere my
hopes are deceived. I cannot talk about Paris except to those who are
not there, because I would not be any better informed than a lady from
whom I received a nice little note asking me for a meeting and whose
affair will have succeeded or failed three months before she receives
the short note in which I answer her. But with Maurice, who knows no
more about it than I do, I talk about France all day. Paris, Epinal, the
Noailles Regiment, and the prince come to mind every day, and morning and night we repeat the same thing with always new pleasure. The
first letters we get will set us up for a month, but meanwhile we are
beginning to repeat ourselves a bit. I am perfectly satisfied with my
traveling companion. Everyone likes him; our tour is interesting, and
he is taking good advantage of it, which gives me real pleasure. In
formulating my wishes for my return, I think very tenderly of the
happiness of embracing my dear prince. My heart can always rejoice in
it but has more need of it than ever; every day it is more convinced of

how dear your friendship is to it, and the value it puts on that friendship is easier to feel than to express. Think often of me, my dear
prince, think of me in all the tenderness of your heart. I need this
sentiment and I deserve it, my friend, for my lively, my eternal friendship. Since I am writing to several of our friends, I shall limit your
commissions today; but please speak of me to your father, your whole
family, Mme de Vauban, Mme de Durfort, Comte Etienne, and
Chevalier de Puységur. Give a thousand friendly greetings to Coigny
and my tender respects to your wife and father-in-law. Mme de Poix's
health keenly concerns me, and I hope the first letters I receive will tell
me much about it. Present my respects to her, and embrace big Charles
and little Juste for me. There you are in the good time of year, my
friend, between the regiment and a tour of duty, and consequently a
faithful inhabitant of Paris. I could be there too, if the devil hadn't
transported me to the other side of the ocean; if he offered me the
whole New World, he would not make me renounce that part of the old
one in which I had the good fortune to be born and to live. To my taste
there is nothing so charming as to be a native of the Auvergne, and
even of the Upper Auvergne, be it said without vanity, and to live in the
Rue de Bourbon in a house that, if it isn't the most beautiful, is at least
infinitely pleasing. If I could see it again for a week, that poor little
house, I would be mad enough to purchase that week of happiness with
all my friends by prolonging my exile for two months. But farewell, my
dear prince, I shall not tell you to love me dearly; my heart replies that
I should count on yours; but I repeat a thousand times that I need to be
loved by my dear prince, as he knows how to love me, and that my
affection for him will endure till my last breath.

L (courtesy of Mme André Balleyguier, Paris), translation.
1. They included an escort into town and two public banquets, one given by the
municipal authorities which included an address by the mayor. Later that month,
Lafayette and his son, George-Washington Lafayette, were granted Connecticut citizenship by the state assembly (Ct: Connecticut Archives, 1st Series).
2. The Rue de Coq Héron in Paris, where Mesmer and his disciples gathered.
3. Letter from Poix not found.

To the Comte de Vergennes[T]

Hartford, October 12, 1784

Since my last letter, Monsieur le Comte, I have had no news from
France, and since I left M. de Marbois only a short time ago, I rely on
him to send you the news from America. He will tell you about the
treaty negotiations with the savages which we attended together and in

which it was thought I could be of some use.[1] It is impossible not to take pleasure in the attachment these nations still have for us. They like our manufactured goods, and with a little care can offer us a small branch of trade. Before addressing them, I consulted M. de Marbois, and I avoided anything that might annoy England.

Some time ago, Monsieur le Comte, a rather embarrassing speech was addressed to me. I could not avoid replying to it, and I hope you will approve my moderation. I was informed that the compliment came from the Irish Volunteers, but I pretended to see only the American Revolution and formerly Irish citizens of Baltimore. At least no one can censure me with any *justified* criticism, and M. de Marbois agrees with me. But in printing the reply these gentlemen called themselves volunteers, and I took care, without affectation, to have this error corrected in the other papers.[2] I am sending you the whole thing, indicating what I had suppressed. If I go into this much detail, Monsieur le Comte, it is because I place the highest value on your approval and would be very sorry to appear imprudent to you. Some rather strange advice has come to me lately—for example, to land elsewhere than in France—but I would not think I was doing myself justice if it seemed necessary to me to reassure you of my discretion.[3]

M. de Marbois is writing you about the credits to be extended in America. His opinion is worth more than mine, but I would not be so totally exclusive, though I am far from advising the follies England is committing, of which we must take advantage to increase our American trade.[4] As for American commerce with the British West Indies, I know that a great number of Americans trade there under the British flag, and the low price of sugar confirms that assertion.[5]

Now I am on the way to Boston, Monsieur le Comte, and although the kindness showered on me everywhere greatly delays my progress, I hope soon to meet General Washington, who will be at the meeting place long before me. We shall complete my visits together, and after attending the reconvening of Congress, I hope to return to Boston early enough to pay you my respects at the end of December. Please be good enough, Monsieur le Comte, to offer my respects to Mme la Comtesse de Vergennes and to your daughters-in-law, and give my regards to your sons. Farewell, Monsieur le Comte. Maintain for me a friendship that I deserve because of my gratitude and my tender and respectful attachment.

AL (AAE: Correspondance politique, Etats-Unis, vol. 28, fols. 317–18), translation.

    1. Marbois wrote Vergennes on October 9, 1784, enclosing a copy of the addresses by Lafayette and the Indians (AAE: Correspondance politique, Etats-Unis, vol. 28, fols. 311–14).

    2. The enclosure, a copy of a newspaper article from an American newspaper, contained the following account:

At a large meeting of those Irish men, who, having arrived in America since the termination of the war, are now become citizens of Baltimore; the following address was ordered to be presented to the Marquis de la Fayette.

To the Right Honourable the MARQUIS DE LA FAYETTE, Marechal de camp of His Most Christian Majesty's Armies, and Major General in those of the United States of America.

SIR,

At a time when all our fellow-citizens seem desirous to evince that gratitude, with which the illustrious conduct of the Marquis de la Fayette, has inspired their bosoms, it would ill become the sons of Ireland, who have not been uninterested spectators of the progress of public virtue, to withhold their tribute of applause.

But, while we manifest our approbation of those great qualities, which have placed you amidst the first supporters of the rights of men, we are peculiarly induced to approve that generous philanthropy, which overpassing the bounds of modern patriotism, impelled you, even to distant regions, to assert in the face of danger and of death, the privileges of an injured people.

Signed by order of the meeting.

C. CARROL; M-J M'CRAOH, H. ROSE,

J. DEANE; J. GALLWAY

To which the marquis de la Fayette returned the following answer:

To those Irishmen, Volunteers, and others who have arrived in America since the termination of the war, are now become citizens of Baltimore,

GENTLEMEN,

WITH respectful acknowledgments of your kind and particular address, permit me to assure you, that no man could more highly prize the honour you have been pleased to confer.

In the cause of oppressed humanity, all good men sympathize, and happy are they when they can unite their efforts—During our noble contest, under unexampled difficulties, it was animating to us soldiers of liberty, that we had the eyes and good will of all friends to mankind; but in the approbation of the sons of Ireland, every admirer of true honour, liberal patriotism, and national virtue, must find a peculiar delight.

Whilst I rejoice for America in the acquisition of those, who so well know, and so much deserve the blessings of liberty, I heartily wish you gentlemen, every success you may desire, and with unfeigned gratitude, shall ever remember your so flattering attention.

LA FAYETTE

3. Apparently some Irish patriots hoped that Lafayette would go to Ireland and openly support the movement for parliamentary reform.

4. British orders in council had placed heavy restrictions on American vessels carrying goods to the British Isles—higher duties on tobacco, tar, turpentine, and rice, complete exclusion of fish, whale oil, and salt meats. They closed the markets of Newfoundland, Nova Scotia, and the West Indies.

5. Though the Privy Council had closed the West Indies to American ships and sailors on July 2, 1783, smuggling was encouraged by local officials.

James Madison to Thomas Jefferson

Philda. Octr. 17, 1784

Dear Sir

On my arrival here I found that Mr. Short had passed through on his way to N. York & was there at the date of my last. I regret much that I missed the pleasure of seeing him. The inclosed was put into my hands by Mrs. House, who recd. it after he left Philada.[1] My two last, neither of which were in cypher, were written as will be all future ones in the same situation, IN EXPECTATION OF THEIR BEING READ BY the POSTMASTERS.[2] I am well assured that this is the FATE OF ALL LETTERS at least to AND FROM PUBLIC PERSONS not only in FRANCE BUT ALL THE OTHER COUNTRIES OF EUROPE. Having now the USE OF MY CYPHER I CAN WRITE WITHOUT RESTRAINT. In my last I gave you a sketch of what past at Fort Schuyler during my stay there, mentioning in particular that the MARQUIS HAD MADE A SPEECH TO the INDIANS WITH THE SANCTION OF THE COMMISSIONERS, WOLCOTT, LEE, BUTLER. The question will probably occur how A FOREIGNER AND A PRIVATE ONE, could APPEAR ON THE THEATRE OF A PUBLIC TREATY between UNITED STATES AND THE INDIAN NATIONS and how THE COMMISSIONERS COULD LEND A SANCTION TO IT. Instead of offering AN OPINION OF THE MEASURE I will state the MANNER IN WHICH IT was BROUGHT ABOUT. It seems that most of the INDIAN TRIBES particularly THOSE OF THE IROQUOIS RETAIN A STRONG PREDILECTION FOR THE FRENCH and most of THE LATTER AN ENTHUSIASTIC IDEA OF THE MARQUIS. This idea has resulted from HIS BEING A FRENCHMAN THE figure HE HAS MADE DURING THE WAR and the arrival of several important EVENTS WHICH HE FORETOLD TO them soon after HE CAME TO THIS COUNTRY. Before HE WENT TO FORT SCHUYLER it had been suggested either in COMPLIMENT OR SINCERITY that his PRESENCE AND INFLUENCE might be of MATERIAL SERVICE TO THE TREATY. At ALBANY the SAME THING HAD BEEN SAID TO HIM BY GENERAL Wolcott. On HIS ARRIVAL AT FORT S. MR. KIRKLAND recommended an exertion of HIS INFLUENCE AS OF ESSENTIAL CONSEQUENCE TO THE TREATY painting in the strongest colours the ATTACHMENT OF THE Indians TO HIS PERSON which seemed indeed to be VERIFIED BY THEIR CARESSES and the artifices employed by the BRITISH PARTISANS TO FRUSTRATE THE OBJECTS OF THE TREATY among which was a pretext that the ALLIANCE BETWEEN THE UNITED STATES AND FRANCE was INSINCERE AND TRANSITORY and consequently the respect of the INDIANS FOR THE LATTER OUGHT TO BE NO MOTIVE FOR THEIR RESPECTING THE FORMER. Upon these CIRCUMSTANCES THE M. GROUNDED A WRITTEN MESSAGE TO THE COMMISSIONERS before THEY GOT UP intimating HIS DISPOSITION TO RENDER THE UNITED STATES any SERVICE HIS SMALL influence OVER THE INDIANS might PUT IN HIS POWER and DESIRING TO KNOW what THE COMMISSIONERS WOULD CHOOSE HIM TO SAY. The ANSWER IN MR. LEE'S HAND consisted of POLITE ACKNOWLEDGMENTS and information that the COMMISSIONERS WOULD BE HAPPY IN AFFORDING HIM AN OPPORTUNITY OF SAYING WHATEVER HE MIGHT WISH forbearing to ADVISE OR SUGGEST WHAT IT

WOULD BE BEST FOR HIM TO SAY. THE M. PERCEIVED THE CAUTION
BUT IMPUTED IT TO LEE ALONE. AS HIS STAY HOWEVER WAS TO BE very
SHORT it was NECESSARY FOR HIM TO TAKE PROVISIONAL MEASURES
before THE ARRIVAL OF THE COMMISSIONERS and particularly for
CALLING IN THE ONEIDA CHEIFS who were AT THEIR TOWN. It fell TO
MY LOT TO BE CONSULTED IN HIS DILEMMA. My ADVICE WAS that HE
SHOULD INVITE THE chief IN SUCH A WAY AS would GIVE HIM AN
OPPORTUNITY OF ADDRESSING them PUBLICLY if on a PERSONAL INTER-
VIEW WITH THE COMMISSIONERS it should be judged expedient; or OF
SATISFYING THEIR EXPECTATIONS with a friendly ENTERTAINMENT IN
RETURN FOR THE CIVILITIES HIS VISIT TO THEIR TOWN had met with.
This ADVICE WAS APPROVED but the INDIANS brought with THEM SUCH
IDEAS OF HIS IMPORTANCE AS no PRIVATE RECEPTION would PROBABLY
HAVE BEEN EQUAL TO. When THE COMMISSIONERS ARRIVED THE M.
CONSULTED THEM IN PERSON. They were RESERVED HE WAS EMBAR-
RASSED. Finally THEY CHANGED THEIR PLAN and CONCURRED explicitly
IN HIS MAKING A SPEECH IN FORM. He accordingly PREPARED ONE
COMMUNICATED IT TO THE COMMISSIONERS and PUBLICLY PRO-
NOUNCED IT, THE COMMISSIONERS PREMISING such an one as was
thought proper to INTRODUCE HIS. The ANSWER OF THE SACHEMS as
well as the CIRCUMSTANCES OF THE AUDIENCE denoted the HIGHEST
REVERENCE FOR THE ORATOR. The chief of THE ONEIDAS SAID that
THE WORDS WHICH HE HAD SPOKEN TO THEM EARLY IN THE WAR[3] had
PREVENTED THEM FROM BEING MISLED TO THE WRONG SIDE OF IT.
During this SCENE and even during the WHOLE STAY OF THE M. HE was
THE ONLY CONSPICUOUS FIGURE. The COMMISSIONERS WERE ECLIPSED.
All of THEM PROBABLY FELT IT. LEE COMPLAINED TO ME OF THE IM-
moderate STRESS LAID ON THE influence OF THE M. and evidently
PROMOTED HIS DEPARTURE. The M. WAS NOT INSENSIBLE OF IT BUT
CONSOLED HIMSELF with the SERVICE which HE THOUGHT THE INDIAN
SPEECH would witness that HE HAD RENDERED TO THE UNITED STATES.
I am persuaded that the TRANSACTION is also PLEASING TO HIM IN
ANOTHER VIEW as it will FORM A BRIGHT COLUMN IN THE GAZETTES OF
EUROPE [and that HE WILL BE IMPATIENT FOR ITS APPEARANCE THERE
without seeing ANY MODE IN which IT CAN HAPPEN OF COURSE.] As it is
BLENDED WITH THE PROCEEDINGS OF THE COMMISSIONERS it will prob-
ably not be PUBLISHED IN AMERICA VERY SOON [IF AT ALL.] THE time I
have lately PASSED WITH THE M. HAS GIVEN ME A pretty thorough
INSIGHT INTO HIS CHARACTER. With great NATURAL FRANKNESS OF
TEMPER HE UNITES MUCH ADDRESS; with very CONSIDERABLE TALENTS
[A strong THIRST OF PRAISE AND POPULARITY.] IN HIS POLITICS HE says
HIS THREE HOBBY-HORSES are the ALLIANCE BETWEEN FRANCE AND
THE UNITED STATES, the UNION OF THE LATTER and the MANUMIS-

SION of the SLAVES. The two former are the DEARER TO HIM as THEY ARE CONNECTED with HIS PERSONAL GLORY. The last DOES HIM REAL HONOR as it is a PROOF OF HIS HUMANITY. In a word, I take HIM TO BE AS AMIABLE A MAN AS [HIS VANITY WILL ADMIT] and as SINCERE AN AMERICAN AS ANY FRENCHMAN CAN BE; one WHOSE PAST SERVICES GRATITUDE obliges US TO ACKNOWLEDGE and WHOSE FUTURE FRIEND-SHIP prudence REQUIRES US TO CULTIVATE.

The Committee of the States have never reassembled. The case of Longchamps has been left both by the Legislature & Executive of this State to its Judiciary course. He is sentenced to a fine of 100 Crowns, to 2 years imprisonment, and Security for good behaviour for 7 years. On teusday morning I set off for Richmond, where I ought to be tomorrow, but some delays have put it out of my power. The ramble I have taken has rather inflamed than extinguished my curiosity to see the Northern & N.W. Country. If circumstances be favorable I may probably resume it next Summer. Present my compliments to Miss Patsy, for whom as well as yourself Mrs. House charges me with hers. She has lately recd, a letter from poor Mrs. Trist, every syllable of which is the language of affliction itself. She had arrived safe at the habitation of her deceased husband, but will not be able to leave that Country till the Spring at the nearest. The only happiness she says she is capable of there, is to receive proofs that her friends have not forgotten her. I do not learn what is likely to be the amount of the effects left by Mr. T. former accounts varied from 6 to 10,000 dollars. I am Dear Sir Yrs. very affectly.,[4]

J. MADISON JR.

ALS (DLC: James Madison Papers). Passages written in code and deciphered between the lines appear in small capital letters. Phrases in brackets were stricken by a later hand.

1. This may have been a letter to Short from Fulwar Skipwith of September 22, wishing him farewell and requesting him to look for a scoundrel thought to have left for Europe (DLC: William Short Papers).

2. Madison to Jefferson, September 15, 1784, and October 11, 1784, in Boyd, *Jefferson Papers*, 7:421–22, 439–41.

3. See *LAAR*, 1:247–49.

4. Jefferson replied on March 18, 1785, "Your CHARACTER of the M. FAYETTE is precisely agreeable to the idea I had formed of HIM. I take HIM to be of UNMEASURED AMBITION but that the MEANS HE USES are virtuous. HE is RETURNED FRAUGHT with AFFECTION to AMERICA and DISPOSED to render every POSSIBLE SERVICE" (Boyd, *Jefferson Papers* 8:39).

To Alexander Hamilton

Boston october the 22d 1784

My dear Hamilton

Every Step I move, there Comes upon me a Happy Necessity to Change My plans. The Reception I Met with in Boston no Words Can describe. At least it is Impossible to Express what I Have felt. Gratitude as well as propriety Conspired with all other Inducements to keep me Here Some time longer. Rhode island and New Hampshire I must Visit—and intend Embarking By the first or Second day of Next Month for Virginia in the Nimph frigat which Has Been Sent on My Account.[1] In less than four weeks time from this day I Hope to Be with Congress, and when My Business there is Concluded, will Come to Newyork where I Hope we will Spend Some days together. My Stay in Your City Has Been too Short—far inadequate to the feelings of my Gratitude, and to the Marks of goodness Bestowed upon me—But this time I will Be Some days longer with My Newyork friends.

Upon Reflecting to My Situation, My Circumstances, My love for America, and yet the Motives that Might Render it Improper for Her, to Employ me in a public Capacity, I Have Confined Myself to a plan which, at the Same time it gratifies my Attachement, And Serves the United States, Cannot Have Any Shadow of Inconvenience. After Having told Me they know My zeal, I wish Congress to Add me they want me to Continue those friendly, and I might Say Patriotic Exertions—that in Consequence of it, their Ministers at Home, and their Ministers Abroad will Have a Standing order to look to me as one whose information, and exertions will ever Be employed to the Service of the United States, and when they think it is wanted to Communicate with me Upon the affairs of America—that Congress will, whenever I think it proper, Be glad of my Correspondance.

Upon that General Scale, Every Minister May Conceal from me what He pleases, may write to me, Only when He pleases, and should He ever think my assistance is wanting, He Has a title to ask, I Have one to give it—and My Connection with America is for ever kept, without Giving jealousy, upon Such a footing as Will Remain at the disposition of Each public Servant of Congress.

It Seems to me, my dear friend, this idea already met with Your approbation. In Case it does, do promote it with Your delegates and others. If it does not. Write it to me By the Bearer whom I Sent By land to Apologize to the General for my delays.[2] My affectionate Respects

wait upon Mrs. Hamilton. I give my Blessing to the little family. Adieu
Yours for Ever

LAFAYETTE

Our friend Knox Has Been most affectionate and kind to me.

I Have writen to Wadsworth, and Spoken to Bostonians Respecting the
Baron's [affairs].[3] I will do the Same in Virginia [&] Maryland and
elsewhere.

ALS (DLC: Alexander Hamilton Papers).
1. The frigate *Nymphe* was sent by the French government to carry Lafayette southward and then back to France.
2. Lafayette sent one of his servants by land to have Washington's instruction for him
waiting at Yorktown (Lafayette to Washington, October 22, 1784, in Gottschalk, *Letters of
Lafayette*, p. 287).
3. Letter to Wadsworth not found. On April 15, 1784, Congress accepted Steuben's
resignation from the American service and resolved to pay him all the money due him
(*JCC*, 26:277–28). Payment had still not been made by February 1785, and Steuben was
forced to remind Congress of it. For congressional response to that request, see ibid.,
28:171, 194, and 29:771–74.

To David Humphreys

Portsmouth October 31st 1784

Dear Sir
    I Have Been lately writing to My friend Mr. Jefferson, But did not at
that time know You Had Already Sailed for Europe. I Need not tell
You, My dear Humphreys, How Happy I would Have Been to wellcome You to Paris. Altho' we Both Have long Been at Home in the
Same family,[1] Yet will it Be the first time where we Can Meet and Quietly Set down in One Another's House. With the Most Affectionate Regard, I Anticipate the Pleasure of taking You By the Hand in France,
But the Precise Instant of My departure I am not yet able to determine. In the Mean while, My dear Sir, I Beg You will Consider My
House as that of a Brother officer and Intimate friend, whose family,
in His absence, will Be Highly Happy to wellcome You, and to Be
Honoured With Your particular Acquaintance.[2] In Every Part of My
tour through these States, I am So pleasingly Retarded By My friends,
that I Can only guess I may Be with You Some time in the End of
january. The Reception I Have Met with is So flattering, So Affectionate, that No Words Can Express the feelings of My Unbounded Affec-

tionate Gratitude. My Stay in New England Has Been to me an abundant Source of the Most flattering Enjoyements. Newspapers May Convey You a part of what I Have met—and what I feel, Your own Good Heart Can Better determine, than it Could Be possible for me to describe it. Congress are Going to meet, and in a few weeks I Hope to Be with them in Trenton. An Attempt Must Have Been Made this week to Carry the five per Cent Impost in Rhode island—and should it fail, I Hope, at least, the Majority will not this time Be Very Considerable.[3] It Seems to me this winter is an Important Crisis for the Interior Arrangements of America, So far at least as Respects foederal Union, Commercial Systèm, and Militia Establishement. God Grant Every Measure May promote the Prosperity and Happiness of these Rising States!

My Best Respects Waït Upon Doctor Franklin, John Adams, Mr. Jefferson; I Beg You will present My Compliments to all American friends in France—and Believe me with Every Sentiment of Attachement and Regard Dear Sir Your obedient Humble Servant

LAFAYETTE

P.S. On my Return to Boston, I will immediately Sail for Virginia, where the General and myself are to meet again, and then Continue My tour together, to the Northard, where I Will present My Respects to Congress.

ALS (Anderson House Museum, The Society of the Cincinnati, Washington, D.C.).
1. Humphreys had been Washington's aide-de-camp.
2. In fact Lafayette advised his wife: "The embassy secretary who is now with Mr. Jefferson is Col. Humphreys the general's former aide-de-camp with whom please flirt as much as possible"[T] (Lafayette to Adrienne de Lafayette, [October 1784] [ALG: courtesy of the Comte de Chambrun]).
3. On July 1, 1784, the General Assembly had refused to ratify the amendment granting Congress a 5 percent duty on all imported articles. The Assembly did not reconsider the measure when it reconvened.

Recommendation for James

Richmond November 21st 1784

This is to Certify that the Bearer By the Name of James Has done Essential Service to Me While I Had the Honour to Command in this State.[1] His Intelligence from the Ennemy's Camp Were Industriously Collected and Most faithfully delivered. He Perfectly Acquitted Him-

Lafayette's achievements in America were a popular subject in France. This engraving pictures Lafayette with his black aide James Armistead Lafayette, whose services to the Revolutionary cause gained him his freedom.

self With Some Important Commissions I Gave Him and Appears to me Entitled to Every Reward His Situation Can Admit of. Done Under My Hand, Richmond November 21st 1784

LAFAYETTE

ADS [facsimile] (ICHi). Present location of manuscript unknown.

1. James Armistead Lafayette, a slave of William Armistead of New Kent County, Virginia, served under Lafayette from March through October 1781, frequently operating as a spy and courier. In November 1784 he asked for his freedom:

> Also, a petition of James, a negro slave; setting forth, that being impelled by a most earnest desire of gaining that liberty which is so dear to all mankind, and convinced that if he rendered any essential services to the public, that that would be his reward, he often during the invasion of the enemy in the year 1781, at the risk of his life entered into the enemy's camp, and collected such intelligence as he supposed of importance, and which he conveyed in the most expeditious manner to the Marquis de la Fayette, who then commanded the American army in Virginia; and praying that an act may pass for his emancipation; and that a reasonable compensation may be made for him, to his present proprietor. [*JHD*, October 1784 session, p. 57 (December 4, 1784)]

James was emancipated on January 9, 1787, by the Virginia legislature and was later granted a pension.

From George Washington

Mount Vernon 8th. Decr. 1784.

My Dr. Marqs.,

The peregrination of the day in which I parted with you, ended at Marlbro':[1] The next day, bad as it was, I got home before dinner.

In the moment of our separation upon the road as I travelled, & every hour since—I felt all that love, respect & attachment for you, with which length of years, close connexion & your merits, have inspired me. I often asked myself, as our Carriages distended, whether that was the last sight, I ever should have of you? And tho' I wished to say no—my fears answered yes. I called to mind the days of my youth, & found they had long since fled to return no more; that I was now descending the hill, I had been 52 years climbing—& that tho' I was blessed with a good constitution, I was of a short lived family—and might soon expect to be entombed in the dreary mansions of my father's. These things darkened the shades & gave a gloom to the picture, consequently to my prospects of seeing you again: but I will not repine. I have had my day.

Nothing of importance has occurred since I parted with you; I found my family well—& am now immersed in company; nothwithstanding which, I have in haste, produced a few more letters to give you the trouble of—rather inclining to commit them to your care, than to pass them thro' many & unknown hands.[2]

It is unnecessary, I persuade myself to repeat to you my Dr. Marqs. the sincerity of my regards & friendship—nor have I words which could express my affection for you, were I to attempt it. My fervent prayers are offered for your safe & pleasant passage—happy meeting with Madame la Fayette & family, & the completion of every wish of your heart—in all which Mrs. Washington joins me; as she does in complimts. to Capt. Grandchean[3] & the Chevr.—of whom little Washn: often speaks. With every sentimt. wch. is propitious & endearing—I am &c. &c. &c.

G: WASHINGTON

LbC (DLC: George Washington Papers, Series 2).

1. Marlboro, Maryland, is on the road from Alexandria to Annapolis. Lafayette and Washington spent several days together at Annapolis, where they were given a reception by the Maryland Assembly, a banquet, and a ball. Lafayette must have traveled back to Marlboro with Washington and from there to Baltimore.

2. Washington wrote a series of letters to Frenchmen on November 25 while he and Lafayette were at Mount Vernon and gave them to Lafayette to carry to France. He later added his letter of December 5 to La Luzerne to the packet.

3. Grandchain was captain of the *Nymphe,* which was carrying Lafayette back to France.

Address to the Continental Congress

[Trenton, December 11, 1784]

Sir

While it pleases the United States in Congress So kindly to Receive me, I want words to Express the feelings of a Heart which delights in their present Situation and the Bestowed Marks of their Esteem.

Since I joined the Standart of liberty, to this wished for Hour of My personal Congratulations, I Have Seen Such Glorious deeds performed, and Virtues displayed By the Sons of America, that in the instinct of My first Concern for them, I Had Anticipated But a Part of the Love and Regard which devote me to this Rising Empire.

During our Revolution, Sir, I obtained an Unlimited, Indulgent Confidence which I am Equally proud and Happy to Acknowledge. It dates with the time, when, an Unexperienced Youth, I Could only Claim My Respected friend's paternal Adoption. It Has Been Most Benevolently Continued throughout Every Circumstances of the Cabinet and the field, and in personal friendships I often found a Support Against public difficulties. While, on this Solemn Occasion, I Mention

My obligations to Congress, the States, the people at large, permit me also to Remember the dear Military Companions to whose Services their Country is So Much Indebted.

Having felt Both for the timely aid of My Country, And for the part She, with a Beloved King, Acted in the Cause of Mankind, I enjoy an Alliance So well Rivetted By Mutual Affection, By interest, and Even local Situation. Recollection Insures it. Futurity does But Enlarge the Prospect, and the Private Intercourse will Every day Increase which Independant and Advantageous trade Cherishes in proportion as it is well Understood.

In Unbounded wishes to America, Sir, I am Happy to observe the Prevailing disposition of the people to Strengthen the Confederation, preserve Public faith, Regulate trade, and in a proper guard over Continental Magazines and fronteir posts, in a General System of Militia, in foreseeing Attention to the Navy, to Insure Every Kind of Safety—May this Immense temple of freedom Ever Stand a Lesson to oppressors, an Exemple to the oppressed, a Sanctuary for the Rights of Mankind! and May these Happy United States Attain that Complete Splendor and Prosperity which will Illustrate the Blessings of their Government, and for Ages to Come Rejoice the departed Souls of its founders!

However Unwilling to trespass Upon Your time, I must Yet Present You with Gratefull thanks for the Late favours of Congress,[1] and Never Can they oblige me So much, as when they put it in My Power, in Every part of the World, to the latest day of My life, to Gratify the Attachment which will Ever Rank me Among the Most Zealous and Respectfull Servants of the United States.

LAFAYETTE

AMS (DNA: RG 360, PCC 19, vol. 2, p. 263).

1. On December 9, Congress resolved:

> That a committee, to consist of one member from each State, be appointed to receive the Marquis, and in the name of Congress to take leave of him. That they be instructed to assure him, that Congress continue to entertain the same high sense of his abilities and zeal to promote the welfare of America both here and in Europe, which they have frequently expressed and manifested on former occasions, and which the recent marks of his attention to their commercial and other interests have perfectly confirmed. That as his uniform and unceasing attachment to this country has resembled that of a patriotic citizen, the United States regard him with particular affection, and will not cease to feel an interest in whatever may concern his honor and prosperity, and that their best and kindest wishes will always attend him. [*JCC*, 27:673]

John Jay served as chairman of the committee. On December 10, Congress resolved that the secretary of war present Lafayette with one of the British standards captured at Yorktown "as a testimonial of the high sense Congress entertain of the great bravery and prowess evinced on many occasions by the Marquis and particularly during the seige of Yorktown . . ." (*JCC*, 27:679–80).

Congress to Louis XVI

At Trenton the 11 Decr. 1784.
Great, Faithful and beloved Friend and Ally

The various and important acts of friendship done by your Majesty to these States, have inspired them with strong attachment to your Person, and with firm confidence in your friendly disposition towards them. Both these Considerations unite in urging us to recommend to your Majesty's particular attention and favor the Marquis de la Fayette a Nobleman, who has ably promoted the Interests of both Countries, and acquired Glory by strenuous and successful endeavours to advance our mutual Honor, Prosperity and confidence.

Permit us to assure your Majesty, that we not only approve, but admire his Conduct—we entertain esteem and affection for him as a Man, we think highly of his Talents, and are convinced of his disposition to perpetuate the amity and good Understanding, which we pray God may ever subsist between France and America.

May the Author of all Good continue to bless your Majesty, your Family & People; and keep you and them under his holy Protection.

By the Unanimous Order of Congress. At Trenton the 11 Decr. 1784.

RICHARD HENRY LEE. President
attest CHA. THOMSON secy.

LS (AAE: Correspondance politique, Etats-Unis, vol. 18, fols 429–30).
President of Congress Richard Henry Lee enclosed this letter and one for Franklin with a letter to Lafayette of the same date, in which he wrote: "I assure you my dear friend that I feel myself singularly happy in observing the unanimous disposition that prevails in Congress to promote your glory for I do most sincerely wish you every felicity that this world can afford" (DNA: RG 360, PCC 16, pp. 316–17). Lafayette was to deliver both letters to Franklin when he reached France, and Franklin was to present this letter to Louis XVI.

To [John Jay]

Sunday Night [December 12, 1784]
Inclosed, My dear Sir, I Send You My Speech which Altho' it is to Be Considered as a Speech in the publication I though I Had Better Sign for Authenticity's Sake.[1] In Presenting the Chair Man With a Copy I

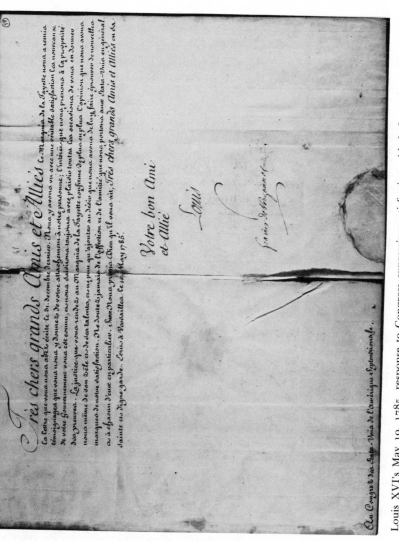

Très chers grands Amis et Alliés. Ce que quis de la fayette nous a remis la lettre que vous nous avez écrite le 31 décembre dernier. Nous y avons vu avec une véritable satisfaction les nouveaux témoignages que vous nous y donnés de votre attachement à notre gouvernement; l'intérêt que nous prenons à la prospérité de votre gouvernement vous rend connu, aurions doité avec plaisir toutes les occasions de vous en donner des preuves. La justice que vous rendez au Marquis de la fayette confirme de plus en plus l'opinion que nous avions nous même de son zèle et de ses talents, en ne peut qu'ajouter au désir que nous avons de luy faire éprouver de nouvelles marques de notre satisfaction. Ne doutez jamais de l'affection et de l'amitié que nous portons aux Etats-Unis en général ou à chacun d'eux en particulier. Sur ce nous prions Dieu qu'il vous ait, Très chers grands Amis et Alliés en sa Sainte et digne garde. Ecrit à Versailles ce 10 May 1785.

Votre bon Ami
et Allié

Louis

Gravier de Vergennes

À nos Congrès des Etats-Unis de l'Amérique Septentrionale.

Louis XVI's May 10, 1785, response to Congress expressing satisfaction with Lafayette's conduct and pledging French friendship and affection for all the United States. Signed by Louis and his foreign minister, Vergennes.

Have Clapped in a little Bit of french Sugur plumb Because I thought it fair to Bend a little on that Gentleman's Side. Inclosed are two petitions intrusted to me.[2] What the Sea officer wishes is a Brevet in the Continental Navy, But those two things don't Require Any immediate Answer. My Servant Will Call Upon You to Morrow—But [as] He Spends the tuesday at Princetown With an Aigue and fever Every dispatches Sent By Express to Him Will on Wenesday Set off with Him By the Princetown Stage—and Every thing that leaves Philadelphia tuesday Morning, is in Newyork Wenesday Evening. God Bless You, My dear Sir, Most Respectfully I am Your affectionate friend

LAFAYETTE

ALS (CtY: Benjamin Franklin Collection). Jay was chairman of the congressional committee appointed to receive Lafayette.

1. See Address to the Continental Congress, December 11, 1784.

2. On December 16 Congress considered a petition from Colonel Fleury, a former aide-de-camp to Lafayette, requesting payment of his accounts, and another petition from a Mons. Barré requesting promotion in the navy (*JCC*, 27:692). These probably were petitions brought from France by Lafayette and presented to Congress when he took leave of it.

To the President of Congress

Trenton december the 12th 1784

Sir

At the Request of Many Canadian families, I Beg leave to lay Before Congress a Subject, which, from a National Connection, and a personal Confidence in me, it Became My lot to Investigate.[1]

Such Canadians as May petition Congress are divided into three Classes—1st officers and Soldiers who Had no Particular State to Support them—2dly people who freely lent their Monney and Services, and Were Expelled from their Country 3dly others Now in Canada whose Certificates Entitle them to a payment.

To Satisfy those Claims, and to Avoid the Numberless Applications Congress will Receive I would take the liberty to Suggest the idea of an Inquiry to Be Made Into this Matter, and as Some Cases Call for Immediate Relief, as Some people draw provisions, and others are Neither fed nor Employed, I think that, Besides the public debt to Be paid a Method Could Be taken to Render these men more Useful Citizens than they Now are.

My Circumstances with Respect to them Being peculiar,[2] I Have flattered Myself that the Opinion I presume to offer would Appear

Consistent with propriety, and that the Indulgence of Congress to me would Apologize for the liberty I Have taken. With the Highest Respect I Have the Honour to Be Sir Your Excellency's Most obedient Humble Servant

LAFAYETTE

ALS (DNA: RG 360, PCC 35, p. 93).

1. The French Canadians from Quebec and Nova Scotia who joined the American army were left destitute after the war. Without state citizenship or property in America, they and their families still depended on Continental rations for their survival. Most of these refugees settled in two camps near Fishkill and Albany, New York, while they petitioned Congress for reimbursement for their losses in Canada, army pay, and land grants. Congress considered relief measures for the refugees repeatedly over 1784 and 1785 and eventually made piecemeal settlements.

2. The Canadian brigades served under Lafayette's command on several occasions during the war.

To James Madison

Newyork december the 15th 1784

My dear Sir

Before I leave this Continent, give me leave once more to Bid You adieu, and to Assure you with the Sincerity of my Heart, that One of the most pleasing Circumstances, not only of my Voyage, But also of my Life, Has Been to obtain as an intimate friend the Man who Before this last time, was only to me a valuable and Agreable Acquaintance. Hitherto You Had Been my friend as the world calls it—But now I Hope you are my friend as my Heart Reckons But few men—and once for all, I wanted to tell you that I know you, esteem you, and love you with all the warmth of my regard and affection.

I Have pretty rapidly past through Mount Vernon—Annapolis—Baltimore—Philadelphia—and Trenton. There I was Happy to find delegates from every state But Maryland—and what is Better still than a Numerous Congress, I also found a very Respectable one who, I Hope, will do great deal of good. Their most Kind Reception of me, You will find in the papers. This only I will add that some Gentlemen Having proposed I Should Be Requested to continüe my Services—all The House Said No American Could Harbour any Idea that Should make it a question—and so Confi[d]entially, and affectionately it was taken up, That it Renders almost Useless Any Recommendation which However Would Be Made on occasion.[1] But as M. Jay will I Hope Accept, and as M. Jefferson will certainly Be The Minister to France, I shall Be Very Happy in my American public Business.[2]

Give me leave, my dear Sir, to Recommend You the three little Memorials that I laid Before the Assembly.[3] Be so kind as to pay my Compliments to Mr. Harrison, M. Jones and M. Henry to whom I will write from France. I Have seen Mercer who seems to Act as well in Congress as He did once in our Virginian Army. Besides His Congressional Conduct I am pleased with His future prospect of Happiness in an Union with the fair Miss Sprig. Our friend Munro is very much Beloved and Respected in Congress—and Mr. Hardy seems to me a very distinguished Young Man.

I Have much Conferred with the General Upon The Pottowmack System. Many people Think The Navigation of the Mississipy is not an advantage. But it May Be the Excess of a very good Thing Wiz The oppening of your Rivers. I fancy it Has not changed your opinion—But Beg you will write me on The subject—in The Mean while I Hope Congress will act cooly and prudently By Spain who is such a fool That allowances must Be Made.[4]

Be so kind, my dear Sir, as to let me often, and By every packet Hear from You. I want to Hear of Your private Concern along with your public affairs, and I Beg You will let me know every thing that is interesting to you. I shall on my side do The same. The chevalier's Best Compliments wait upon you. Adieu, Your affectionate friend

LAFAYETTE

Newyork december The 17th 1784

My dear Sir

Previous to the Receipt of your letter the 4th inst I Had prepared to send you the foregoing scrawl, and am now to acknowledge your friendly communication of the Resolve which your State Have been pleased to pass.[5] I Beg you will Become an interpreter of the gratefull sense I Have of such a favour, conferred in so particular and flattering a manner. An official communication Had Been made of the first Resolve, to which my Answer did not Arrive, as it was in time of War—But Having Apologized through Gal. Washington a long time since, I think I Have Nothing official to do Now with propriety as the matter Stands. In Case I receive a letter I shall of course Answer it The Best I Can.

The printer of The irish Volunteer journal Has Been obliged to fly for His life, and Now is in Philadelphia where He sets up a paper.[6] He lives at Mr. Sutter's [House on] Front street. I think we ought to encourage this Martyr to the cause of liberty. My speech to the Indians Had Been printed By the French Consul at Newyork against my intention—But I Had This Matter put to Rights.[7]

To morrow morning I will sail.[8] Adieu, my dear friend, God bless you, write me often and believe me for ever Yours

LAFAYETTE

L (ICU: Louis Gottschalk Collection), transcript. The present location of the manuscript is unknown.

1. See Lafayette to Hamilton, October 22, 1784.

2. Lafayette had written to Jay on October 7, urging him to accept the post of secretary of foreign affairs.

3. In a letter to Benjamin Harrison on November 21, 1784 (ALS [NN: Emmet Collection]), Lafayette had forwarded the petitions to the state of Virginia for payment on behalf of Coulongnac & Cie., A. M. Chevalier, and Penet, d'Acosta & Cie.

4. Though Spain acted contrary to the terms of the peace treaty in closing the navigation of the Mississippi River to the Americans, those who wanted to control western exports by extending inland navigation of eastern rivers, such as the Potomac and Susquehanna, were not eager to see the Mississippi outlet reopened. Washington certainly held this view (Washington to David Humphreys, July 25, 1785, in Fitzpatrick, *Writings of Washington*, 28:202–5). Madison, however, was more concerned to see American navigation rights on the Mississippi upheld (Rutland, *Papers of James Madison*, 8:100–102).

5. Madison sent Lafayette a copy of the resolutions passed in the Virginia House of Delegates on December 1, 1784, providing that two busts of Lafayette be made, one to be presented to the city of Paris from the Commonwealth of Virginia and the other to be placed at the capitol in Richmond. These resolutions were a revision of earlier ones passed on December 17, 1781, ordering a bust to be made and presented to Lafayette himself. Madison's letter with the resolution enclosed has not been found.

6. Matthew Carey, publisher of the Irish *Volunteer Journal*, had recently fled from Ireland to Philadelphia under threat of prosecution for his political views. In early December, while in Philadelphia, Lafayette subscribed $400 for Carey to start a newspaper.

7. French consul St. Jean de Crèvecoeur had copies of Lafayette's speeches and the Indians' replies printed in the *Pennsylvania Packet* of November 17 and 19, 1784. From a letter to John Jay on November 25 on the same subject, it appears that Lafayette thought it improper to print the speeches before the commissioners had formally reported to Congress (ALS [DNA: RG 360, PCC 156, pp. 396–97]). Since Lafayette had tried to be sensitive to American prerogatives and protocol with the Indians, this premature publication, without American authorization, was, at the least, undiplomatic.

8. Lafayette finally sailed on the morning of December 23.

To George Washington

New York 17th. Decr. 1784

I Shou'd think myself much Obliged To Your Excellency if through Your Means Some of the Following Seeds might be Procured From Kentucke' for the use of the King's Garden viz.

The Seeds of the *Coffe Tree* which Resembles the Black oak

D.° of the *Pappa Tree.*

D.° of the *Cucumber Tree*

D? *Black berry Tree*
D? *Wild Cherry Tree*
D? *Buck-Eye Tree*
D? of *Wild Rye, Buffalo Grass—Shawane [?] Salad—Wild Lettuce—Crown Imperial Cardinal Flower—the Tulip-bearing Laurel Tree—*& the Seeds of Every thing else Curious which that Famed Country Produces.

It wou'd be Necessary Your Excellency wou'd order the whole To be Carefully Sent To the Care of the director of the French Pacquets at New York, that it might be Transmitted To Paris.[1]

God Bless You, my dear general, I am Requested By Mr. St. John to Sign this, and do it with the greater pleasure as these seeds and trees will Be very wellcome in France

LAFAYETTE

LS (PEL: Hubbard Collection). In the hand of St. Jean de Crèvecoeur; postscript in Lafayette's hand.
1. The French packets carried free of charge any plants for the three experimental gardens—the gardens of Louix XV in Versailles and the two gardens in America, the "King's Garden" at Bergen Neck, New Jersey, and a garden in New Haven. Crèvecoeur frequently sent specimens to France and asked for French and other European plants to be sent to America.

To Samuel Adams

Newyork December the 19th 1784

My dear Sir

With all the tenderness of a Gratefull Heart, I Had Been Enjoying the Hope of Paying a Second Visit to Boston. But for Several Reasons, Among which the Accident Happened to the frigat, and orders for Her Return, Have no inconsiderable weight, I now Have the Mortification to Sail Before my favourite plan is Executed.[1] Highly Sensible of the kindness of Your State and Capital in My Behalf, I feel all the Attachment which love, devoted zeal, Gratitude and Respect Can Inspire. Be pleased, my dear friend, to Express to Your Acquaintances Both My Regrests, and My Sentiments. Should it Ever Be in My power to promote the Interest of Your Country, a line from You on the Subject will Be Considered as a Great favour. I Beg You Will Request Gal. Warren to Send me Some Notes He Has promised Respecting the price of Your oils, and the Manner in which I ought to try this Business.[2] Your Correspondance, My dear Sir, will Make me Very Happy, and I Beg

You Will take Care that Your letters Reach Newyork Before the 14th of the Month. My Respect and attachment to You are Equally Sincere and Everlasting, and with the Best wishes for Yourself and family Have the Honour to Be Dear Sir Your obedient Humble Servant

LAFAYETTE

My Best Respects Waït Upon Mrs. Adams and Compliments to Your Son.

ALS (NN: Samuel Adams Papers).

1. The *Nymphe* had run aground on its passage from Virginia to New York City, and it was considered safer for it to leave with the regular packet in case it should spring a leak. This circumstance prevented Lafayette from stopping again at Boston before leaving America.

2. In a letter to John Adams of April 30, 1786, James Warren wrote: "If our [whale] Oil can find a Market in France it will, I think, disconcert the views of the British Ministry and be very advantageous to us as well as to the Commerce of France. I took great pains to impress the Marquiss de Fayate with proper Sentiments on the subject when here last, and have reason from his Letters to suppose it has had a good Effect" (*Warren-Adams Letters*, 2:272).

From George Washington

Annapolis 23d. Decr. 1784

My Dr. Marqs.

You would scarcely expect to receive a letter from me at this place. A few hours before I set out for it, I as little expected to cross the Potomac again this winter, or even to be fifteen miles from home before the first of April, as I did to make you a visit in an air Balloon in France.

I am here however, with Genl. Gates, at the request of the Assembly of Virginia, to fix matters with the Assembly of this State respecting the extension of the inland navigation of Potomac, & the communication between it and the Western waters; & hope a plan will be agreed upon to the mutual satisfaction of both States, & to the advantage of the Union at large.[1]

It gave me pain to hear that the Frigate la Numph, grounded in her passage to New York—we have various accots. of this unlucky accident but I hope she has received no damage, & that your embarkation is not delay'd by it.

The enclosed came to my hand under cover of the letter which accompanies it, & which is explanatory of the delay it has met with.[2] I can only repeat to you assurance of my best wishes for an agreeable passage & happy meeting with Madame la Fayette & your family, & of the sincere attachment & affection with which I am My Dr. Marqs. &c. &c.

G. Washington

P.S. You & your heirs, Male, are made Citizens of this State by an act of Assembly.[3] You will have an official Accot. of it. This is by the by.

LbC (DLC: George Washington Papers, Series 2).

1. On December 13 the Virginia House of Delegates resolved to appoint Washington, Horatio Gates, and Thomas Blackburne to consult with Maryland officials on a petition for citizens of both states urging the creation of a company "under the authority of the two States, for the purpose of opening and improving the navigation of the river Potomac" (*JHD,* 2:68). His report on the meeting to the Virginia General Assembly is in Fitzpatrick, *Writings of Washington,* 28:20–22.

2. The enclosed items probably included a letter of introduction for a "Mr. Ridout," a merchant traveling to France (see Washington to Baron de Montesquieu, December 23, DLC: George Washington Papers, Series 2).

3. On December 13 a bill was introduced in the Maryland Senate granting citizenship to Lafayette and his male heirs in perpetuity. On December 18 the House of Delegates approved the proposal.

PART III

STRENGTHENING
THE BONDS

January 23–December 29, 1785

... altho' American Patriotism, virtue, and wisdom Cannot But
Being Roused to Every thing that is good and great, provided you
give the people time to Consider, and judge their own faults, yet I
Cannot Hear those ideas Spocken, without Heartly wishing no time
may Be lost in Ensuring the Consequence and prosperity of the
American Confederation.

To Nathanael Greene, March 16, 1785

Immediately upon his return to France from the triumphal American tour of 1784, Lafayette turned his attention to consolidating the
fruits of victory. More than ever he felt that his role as advocate for the
American cause was critical to the development of effective postwar
relationships between the United States and Europe. Lafayette hoped
to persuade the Spanish to reach an amicable settlement with the United States over navigation of the Mississippi. In this effort he continued
to correspond with Carmichael; he also met with the French ambassador to the Spanish court. At the same time Lafayette promoted
American trade and defended the viability of the American confederation in conversations with Frederick the Great and Emperor Joseph II.
To bolster American prestige in Europe, he urged Jefferson and
Adams to encourage Congress to sponsor a multinational expeditionary force to halt the Barbary pirates' practice of demanding tribute.

Lafayette's distrust of England continued throughout this period.
He assumed that British agents were speaking ill of America at European courts. Even worse, he feared that England was attempting to
regain commercial control over the United States by dominating the
young nation's credit and carrying trade, and by dumping its manufactures on the American market.

In France, Lafayette undertook a number of projects to promote
closer relations between France and the United States. His major effort
was to encourage greater commercial ties. He sought reform of the

complicated system of regulating imports, he opposed renewal of the Farmers General's tobacco monopoly, and he toured the French provinces urging manufacturers to participate in more extensive trade with America. At the same time, he continued to urge his American correspondents to centralize foreign trade policy under Congress' authority rather than leave it to the individual states. He advised them also to resolve the country's credit problems. Lafayette spent increasing amounts of time encouraging specific commercial ventures. For his New England friends, he promoted whale oil and fur sales. For southern interests, he suggested timber and tobacco projects.

To lay a foundation for continued friendship between the two countries, Lafayette promoted the concept of educational exchanges. He offered to superintend personally the education of the sons of Greene, Knox, and Hamilton in France, and proposed that in return his own son should go to America for his studies.

For Lafayette, the primary legacy of the American Revolution was the struggle for "the rights of mankind." His return to peaceful pursuits gave him the opportunity to begin working for the cause of civil rights in France and abroad. He was becoming keenly aware of the persecution of French Protestants, and he began to communicate with supporters of a reform movement. Consistent with his heightened interest in the evils of Negro slavery, revealed in his correspondence with Condorcet, Washington, Hamilton, and Jay, Lafayette began to seek ways to contribute personally to its demise. His return to France seemed ripe with new opportunities to change the world for the better.

To Adrienne de Noailles de Lafayette[T]

Rennes, Sunday evening
[January 23, 1785]

Here I am, very near you, my dear heart, very impatient to arrive, and very happy to feel behind me the distance that has separated us. What crowns all my joy is to learn that my aunt is settled in Paris. I arrived in good health,[1] and this evening I stopped by Montmorin's intending to leave immediately, but the Estates of Brittany have assembled, and it has been decided that I should make an appearance tomorrow at eleven o'clock, with arrangements too special for me possibly to avoid it.[2] I shall arrive Wednesday evening at Versailles, surely so late that I shall not pay a visit, but since I must meet with the ministers the next day, I would rather sleep there and could pay my court Thursday, so that Friday we could go to dine with my aunt, sup at Mme de Tessé's, and take up our former way of life again. Or rather, if you prefer, we shall go on Thursday after dinner to Paris. Although I shall let you know later, to be sure of finding you alone, I am very much hoping to take you in my arms between eleven and midnight, unless we are detained en route. Give my news to Mme de Tessé, your sisters, and father and mother. I have instructed Le Brun to go to Charlus's, M. de Poix's, and the vicomte's, and I am writing a word to Mme d'Hénin and Mme de Simiane, so you see all my friends are forewarned. I am also sending a note to my aunt.[3]

Farewell my dear heart, I am very happy. I love you very much, and I am very impatient to tell you so myself.

I would very much like our children to come to Versailles. Please give my news also to Mme de Boufflers. It is late, and I want a little sleep.

AL (ALG: courtesy of the Comte de Chambrun), translation.
1. Lafayette arrived at Brest on January 20.
2. On January 24, when Lafayette entered the assembly hall of the provincial estates of Britanny, he was met with a round of applause and seated at the barons' bench, close to the *président* of the nobility. Before leaving, he delivered a speech informing the members that he hoped to join them soon (*Mercure de France*, February 19, 1785). Lafayette's maternal grandfather, Joseph, marquis de La Rivière, had been a Breton noble.
3. Letters not found.

To John Jay

Versaïlles february the 8th 1785
Dear Sir

After thirty days Passage, I Have Safely landed at Brest, and am So lately Arrived in Paris, that I Had Better Refer You to Your Ministerial Intelligences. In Consequence of Austrian demands upon the dutch, and the Gun these Have fired at fort Lillo, 40,000 Men were Sent to the low Countries By the Emperor, and a Second division was in Motion the Same Way[1]—When France Gave orders for two Armies to Get in Readiness, the one probably in Flanders and the other in Alsace. Holland is Gathering Some troops, the Greater Number purchased in Germany and Will Have at the Utmost 30,000 men in the field. Count de Maïllebois an old and able french General Has Been demanded By them.[2] Russia Seems friendly to the Emperor—and altho' the State Holder is a friend to the king of Prussia, while the Patriots are Wholly attached to France,[3] Yet Prussia will no doubt Side in politicks with France—and the State Holder will Command His own Country's troops. A Grand plan is Spoken off, where By the Emperor would Endeavour to obtain Baviera, and in Return give the low Countries to the Palatine House—a Bargain which Centers and encreases the Imperial forces.[4] Under those Circumstances, Negotiations Cannot But Be Very interesting. Altho' the freedom of Holland, and the protection of German princes are very proper objects for France to Support, Yet a War with the Emperor must Be peculiarly disagreable to Court. It will Certainly Be avoided, if Consistent with the liberties of Holland, with faith and dignity—and Upon the whole, I strongly am of opinion No War will take place, at least for this Year. The Appearance of things, However, is Still Warlike Enough to Have made it proper for me to Be Arrived at the time I am—an idea, I Confess, the More Necessary for the Situation of my mind, as I most Heartly lamented the Shortness of this Visit to America, and the obligation I Had Been under to give up favourite plans, and Break off Most Agreable Arrangements. The officers of the Regiments Under Marching orders, Colonels Excepted, Have joined their Corps. But I Hope Matters will Be Compromised. Such is at least my private opinion, and even to those who know more than I do, it would perhaps Be difficult to form a precise one.

The Ministers of Congress will no doubt Inform them of the Situation of their Negotiations in Europe. You will Have Seen Mal. de Castries's Complyance with Engagements He Had taken in a letter to me which Mr. Moriss laid Before Congress.[5] Nothing New was Granted, and atho' the Suspended decision about flour and Sugars were favourable to them, the french merchants Have Complained of what Has Been obtained.[6] In Every Country mercantile prejudices wear of By little and little. You Have desired I should make it a point to inform Court, and inform you upon the Unhappy affair of Longchamp. By all accounts the Man is a despicable wretch. It was expected By Many, He should Be Returned. The Matter, However, is taken in a Very friendly point of wiew. Allowances are made for the Situation in which the affair Happened—and the Injustice of Retroactive laws is properly felt—So that I am not Uneasy upon this point—and don't doubt But what either the Recommandation of Congress, and the laws of the States to that purpose will Be worded in such a way as will Settle the Whole affair in a Satisfactory Manner.[7]

I Beg, my dear Sir, You Will forgive the Hurry in which I write, and Will exactly inform you of Every political Event in Europe. I wish my gazettes may Some times Be agreable to Congress. Some of my opinions, and peculiarly that Respecting Longchamp's affair, I lay Before Congress Rather in a Confidential way, Because my informations are friendly if I am allowed to Speack so, and not official.

Be pleased, my dear Sir, to Remember me to all our friends, and to

present my affectionate Respects to Mrs. Jay. Mde. de Lafayette joins in
Compliments to Both and I Have the Honour to Be very Respectfully
Dear Sir Your obedient Humble Servant

LAFAYETTE

ALS (DNA: RG 360, PCC 156, pp. 400–402).

1. Austria and the United Provinces were involved in a deepening controversy over
the boundary between the United Provinces and the Austrian Netherlands. The major
issue was free navigation on the Scheldt River. In October 1784, when the imperial
brigantine *Louis* attempted to sail upstream without securing clearance, the Dutch fired
on it near Fort Lillo. In response, Austrian emperor Joseph II prepared to march 40,000
troops into the Netherlands.

2. On December 21, 1784, the French Council of State gave the Comte de Maillebois
permission to accept command of the army of the United Provinces. John Adams maintained that Lafayette had hoped for the appointment himself. Recording his January 30
meeting with Lafayette, Adams wrote: "As he went out he took me aside and whispered,
that altho he would not serve a foreign Prince, he would serve a Republick, . . . if the
States General would invite him, without his soliciting or appearing to desire it, he would
accept the Command" (*Diary and Autobiography of John Adams*, 3:172–73).

3. The *stadthouder*, Prince William V of Orange, who had married a Prussian princess,
was pro-British during the American war. The war had encouraged the development of
the Patriot party in the Netherlands, which was anti-Orange and anti-British and included both popular and aristocratic elements.

4. On December 3, 1784, the Austrian ambassador to the French court, Mercy-Argenteau, proposed to Vergennes the creation of a "kingdom of Burgundy," composed of a
large part of Belgium, Deux-Ponts, Jülich, and Berg, to be placed under the control of
the Palatinate in exchange for Austrian control over the kingdom of Bavaria (Arneth and
Flammermont, eds., *Correspondance secrète du Comte de Mercy-Argenteau*, 1:356).

5. See Castries to Lafayette, June 17, 1784. Congress referred the letter to Jay on
February 7, 1785 (*JCC*, 28:60).

6. The *arrêt* of August 30, 1784, provided some relaxation of the restrictions on
foreign trade with the French West Indies (*Recueil des anciennes lois françaises*, 27:459–64).
Even though these were not large concessions, French merchant groups vociferously
complained. A number of the merchant petitions of protest appear in AN: Colonies,
F^{4}24. See Frederick L. Nussbaum, "The French Colonial Arrêt of 1784," *South Atlantic
Quarterly* 27 (1928): 62–78.

7. For Longchamps's assault on Marbois, see Lafayette to Vergennes, September 15,
1784, note 1. On April 27, 1785, Congress instructed Jay to explain to Barbé de Marbois
that though Congress regretted the incident, the state concerned (Pennsylvania) had sole
jurisdiction over the matter. Congress resolved to urge the states to pass laws "for the
exemplary punishment of such persons as may in future by violence or insult attack the
dignity of sovereign powers in the person of their ministers or servants" (*JCC*,
28:314–15).

From George Washington

Mt. Vernon 15th. Feby. 1785.

My Dr. Marqs.

I have had the pleasure to receive your affectionate letter of the 21st.
of December—dated on board the Nymph Frigate in the harbour of

New York, & felt all that man could feel from the flattering expression of it.

My last to you, if I recollect right, was dispatched from Annapolis;[1] whither I went at the request of this State to settle a plan (to be mutually adopted by the Legislatures of both States) for improving and extending the navigation of the river Potomac as far as it should be found practicable, & for opening a Road of communication therefrom, to the nearest navigable water to the westward. In both, I happily succeeded. The Bill, of which I send you a copy, was prepared at that time, & has since passed both Assemblies in the usual forms, & must speak for itself: The road of communication is to be undertaken on public account, at the joint & equal expence of the two States. Virginia has passed a similar Act to the one enclos'd, respecting James river, & its communication with the waters of the Great Kanhawa,[2] & have authorized the Executive to appoint Commissioners to examine, & fix on the most convenient course for a canal from the waters of Elizabeth river, in this State, to those passing thro' the State of No. Carolina, & report their proceedings therein, with an estimate of the expence necessary for opening such Canal, to the next General Assembly.[3]

Hence my dear Marquis you will perceive that the exertions which you found, & left me engag'd in, to impress my Country men with the advantages of extending the inland navigation of our Rivers, & opening free & easy communications with the Western Territory (thereby binding them to us by interest, the only knot which will hold) has not been employ'd in vain. The Assembly of this State have accompanied these Acts with an other—very flattering one for me—but which has been productive of infinitely more embarrassment than pleasure. This Act directs the Treasurer of the State to subscribe fifty shares in each of the navigations, Potomac & James, for my use & benefit, which it declares is to be vested in me & my heirs forever: generous as this Act is, the reasons assigned for it, with the flattering, yet delicate expression thereof, renders it more valuable than the grant itself—& this it is which perplexes me. It is not my wish, nor is it my intention, to accept this gratuitous gift, but how to decline it with out appearing to slight the favors of my Country—committing an act of disrespect to the Legislature or having motives of pride, or an ostentatious display of disinterestedness ascribed to me, I am at a loss: but will endeavour to hit upon some expedient before the next Session, to avoid these imputations. This was the closing act of the last, without my having the most distant suspicion that such a matter was in contemplation; nor did I ever hear of it until it had passed, & the Assembly had adjourned.[4]

With what readiness the subscription Books will fill, is not in my power at this early stage of the business, to inform you; in general, the

friends to the measure are sanguine, but among those good wishes are
more at command, than money—consequently it is not only uncertain
of whom the company may consist, but (as its existence depends upon
contingencies) whether there will be one or not. Therefore at this moment we are all in the dark respecting this & other matters. One thing
however is certain, namely, if a company should be established & the
work is undertaken a skilful Engineer, or rather a person of practical
knowledge, will be wanted to direct & superintend it. I should be glad
therefore my Dr. Sir if you would bear this matter in your mind—that
if the company when formed should be disposed to obtain one from
Europe [and] should prefer France, proper characters may be applied
to without loss of time. You will readily perceive My Dr. Marqs. that
this is more a private intimation of mine, than an authorised request,
consequently how improper it would be to raise the expectation of any
Gentleman to the employment, without being able to give him the
appointment. If a company should be formed, it will be composed, no
dout of many men, & these of many minds; & whilst myself & others
may be disposed to go to France for an Engineer, the majority may
incline to send to England for one, on account of the languge, & from
an opinion that there is greater similarity between the inland navigation of the Kingdom & the improvments which are intended here, than
prevails between any in France & them; whilst others again may turn
their Eyes towards Holland. The nature of our work, as far as I have
been able to Form an opinion of it, will be first, at the principal falls of
the River to let Vessels down by means of Locks—or, if Rumsey's plan[5]
should succeed, by regular or gradual slopes—in either case, the bad
effect of Ice & drift wood in floods, are to be guarded against. 2d. As
the Canals at these places will pass thro' rocky ground, to be able to
remove these with skill & facility, & to secure the canals when made.
3dly. in other parts of the River, the water will require to be deepened,
& in these places the bottom generally is either rock under water, or
loose stone of different sizes; for it rarely happens that Sand or Mud is
to be found in any of the shallow parts of the River. I mention these
things because it is not the man who may be best skilled in Dikes; who
knows best how to conduct water upon a level—or who can carry it
thro' hills or over mountains, that would be most useful to us.

We have had a mild winter hitherto, & nothing new that I recollect,
in the course of it; for I believe Congress had determined before you
left the country, to fix their permanent seat in the vicinity of Trenton;
& their temporary one at New York.[6] The little Sprig at Annapolis, to
whose nod so many lofty trees of the forest had bowed, has yielded the
Sceptre: thursday last placed it at the feet of Mr. M: who perhaps may
wield it with as much despotism as she did.[7]

If I recollect right, I told you when here, that I had made one or two attempts to procure a good Jack Ass from Spain, to breed from. Colo. Hooe, or rather Mr. Harrison, was one of the Channels thro' which I expected to be supplied; but a day or two ago the former furnished me with the enclosed extract from the latter.[8] As it is not convenient for me to pay such a price, I have desired Colo. Hooe to countermand the order—& the same causes induce me to pray, that if these are the prices of a good Jack (& no other I would have)—that you would decline executing the commission I gave you of a similar kind.

I will use my best endeavours to procure the seeds (from Kentuckey) which are contained in your list; but as the distance at which I live from that country is great, & frequent miscarriages of them may happen, you must prepare yourself for delay.[9]

I will write as you desire, to Cary the late Printer of the Volunteer Journal in Ireland.[10] Bushrod Washington, sensible of your polite invitation, but unable to avail himself of it, wrote you a letter of grateful acknowledgments & thanks; which letter I sent under cover to the President of Congress with a request to deliver it to you, but you had sailed: I presume he has since forwarded it to you.[11]

I am possessed of the Cypher which was used by Mr. Livingston whilst he was Secretary of foreign affairs; if therefore he had not different ones, I can when necessary, correspond with you in his.[12]

Every body of this family, & those who are connected with it, join in the most sincere & affectionate wishes for you & yours, with the most affectionate of your friends

G. Washington

P.S. If it should so happen that the subscriptions for opening the navigations of the rivers Potomac & James should not (from the want of money here) fill in the time required by the acts, do you think that there are persons of your acquaintance in France who might incline to become adventurers in it? I give it as my *decided* opinion to you that *both* are practicable beyond all manner of doubt; & that men who can afford to lay a little while out of their money, are laying the foundation of the greatest returns of any speculation I know of in the world.

LbC (DLC: George Washington Papers, Series 2).

1. Washington to Lafayette, December 23, 1784.

2. For the Maryland act establishing the Potomac River Company, see *Laws of Maryland, made since M,DCC,LXIII, consisting of Acts of Assembly under the Proprietary Government* . . . (Annapolis, 1787), 1784 sess., chap. 33. The acts of the Virginia legislature establishing the James River Company and the Potomac River Company appear in Hening, *Statutes*, 11:450–62, 510–25.

3. The Virginia State Council appointed the commissioners on January 14 (*Virginia Council Journals*, 3:409).

4. The act investing Washington with an interest in the companies provided him with fifty shares of Potomac River Company stock and a hundred shares of James River Company stock (Hening, *Statutes* 11:525–26). Washington eventually accepted the stock with the understanding that the proceeds would go to philanthropic endeavors (see Washington to Patrick Henry, October 29, 1785, in Fitzpatrick, *Writings of Washington,* 28:303–4).

5. In September 1784 Washington had witnessed a demonstration by James Rumsey of his design for a boat that could propel itself up a swift-moving stream (Fitzpatrick, *Writings of Washington,* 27:468).

6. Congress decided on December 23, 1784, that it would reconvene in New York (*JCC,* 27:704).

7. Sophia Sprigg married John Francis Mercer in Annapolis on February 3, 1785.

8. No extract of the letter from Richard Harrison has been found.

9. For Lafayette's request for the seeds, see his letter to Washington of December 17, 1784.

10. Washington's letter to Matthew Carey, March 15, 1785, is in Fitzpatrick, *Writings of Washington,* 28:103–4. Lafayette recommended Carey to Washington in his letter of December 21, 1784, and asked Washington to subscribe to Carey's newspaper.

11. See Lafayette to Washington, December 21, 1784, for Bushrod's invitation. Bushrod Washington's reply not found. Richard Henry Lee informed Washington on December 26 that Lafayette had left (DLC: George Washington Papers, Series 4).

12. Livingston enclosed a copy of his cipher in his letter to Washington of June 27, 1782 (DLC: George Washington Papers, Series 4).

From [the Marquis de Condorcet][T]

Basel, February 24, 1785

Monsieur le Marquis,

I have just learned that you have honored my reflections on Negro slavery with your attention. I had made a trip to Paris in 1780; one of those writers whose pen is at the hire of anyone who is willing to pay for it took it into his head to write a defense of this slavery. I wished to reply to him in a newspaper and was unable to get permission to do so. Upon returning to my own good country, where there are no slaves, I wrote a book instead of a letter, and this is the book that you have deigned to read.[1]

No one on our continent has helped more than you, Monsieur le Marquis, to break those chains with which Europe endowed America. Perhaps the glory of overthrowing the slavery that we have imposed on the unfortunate Africans is also demanded of you. You would be, then, the liberator of two of the four parts of the world, and far superior to that Pompey we saw in another age "triumph in three days over three-fourths of the world."[2]

Perhaps without the American war Negro slavery would have been abolished within a few generations. A well-known London doctor, Dr.

Fothergill, had formed a plan for a company that was to start the African Negroes cultivating sugar. He had assigned considerable sums for this worthy undertaking, which was to lead eventually to the abolition of slavery.[3] The American war prevented the execution of this plan, and that is still another reason why you should apply yourself to reviving it or to devising a better one. A revolution to which you contributed should have accomplished only good.

Allow me, Monsieur le Marquis, to offer you my limited understanding. In my *Réflexions* I told governments that did not listen to me what justice demanded of them, and I have thought it necessary to limit myself to that. But I have looked into the same subject in other respects, and if you deign to occupy yourself with this noble undertaking, you will find me always at your command. I have the honor to be, with respect.

P.S. If you do me the honor to reply, I beg you to address your letter to M. Schwartz, poste restante, Basel.

AL (NNPM), draft, translation.

1. Condorcet's *Réflexions sur l'esclavage des negres* (Neufchâtel, 1781) had appeared under the pseudonym "M. Schwartz, pasteur du Saint-Evangile à Bienne, membre de la Société économique de B____." Written in response to a justification of slavery by Pierre-Ulrich Dubuisson (*Nouvelles considérations sur Saint-Domingue* [Paris, 1780]), the *Réflexions* attempted to refute systematically all justifications for slavery, including the argument that it was necessary if the colonial economies were to flourish.

2. Plutarch's *Life of Pompey* notes that the Roman general was honored three times with triumphal marches in Rome—for his victories on the three continents of Africa, Europe, and Asia.

3. Fothergill had proposed that Africans cultivate sugar cane in Africa "as servants for hire, and not as slaves compelled to labour by the dread of torture" (John Coakley Lettsom, ed., *The Works of John Fothergill*, 3 vols. [London, 1783–84], 3:lxvii).

To William Carmichael

Paris March the 10th 1785

My Dear Sir

A few days Ago I Had the pleasure to write You a line, inclosing Mde. de Lafayette's letter,[1] But Before I Entered into Particulars Have Been Waïting for American dispatches which did not Arrive Untill yesterday. My tour throughout the Continent Has Been a Most Agreable one. Happy to Meet My friends, I Have felt myself doubly Happy By their Affectionate Reception—and Need not tell what pleasure it is to Enjoy peace, plenty and Happiness where the Horrors of a Most

Cruel War Had Been So long Raging. Every part of America is thriving Very fast. In Your State, Baltimore Has So Amazingly improved that You Could Hardly know it Again. I am also much pleased with the General disposition of the people—the Good intention of the States— the Excellent Collection in the present Congress—and Hope the United States will attain that degree of Splendor and Energy which a free and Generous Nation Has a Right to Expect.

It is Useless for me to tell you, My dear Sir, that I Have not Neglected My absent friends. I Had Both the dictates of justice and friendship to obey—and Both induced me to Recommend the Same Measures.

By my last letters, I Hear Congress Have Removed to Newyork—But are Ready to Build one foederal town Near the falls of Delawar.[2] Delegates from Vermont Had made their Appearance. How they should Be Received it was not yet known.[3] The Appointement of Ministers Was in Contemplation. M. Jay Has Accepted His Appointement. Mr. Adams Will probably go to England—and when the doctor's Resignation is Accepted, Mr. Jefferson will Remain in France.[4] As to other points, it Was more Uncertain.

I am sorry to tell you, My dear Sir, that the people of America are not pleased with Spain. Indians are Every day attacking Virginia, who, to a man, pretend to Be Excited By the Spaniards. The Navigation of Mississipy will Be a Source of troubles—and the Beauty of it is that the interest of either party is By the wisest thought to Be directly Against their Wishes. When America Gets the Navigation, all the Back Country people, as they are Severed from the States By chains of Mountains Seventy Miles wide, will Break off their Connection with You, put themselves Under Spanish influence, and as they are Composed of Emigrants from every Nation, and of Course attached to None, they will Become a check Upon You. This is the Reason why General Washington is So Busy about oppening the Navigation of James River and the Pottowmack. Should it on the Contrary Be possible for the Spaniards to shut [up] the Mississipy, the Back Country Settlements Will Be forced into an Union With this Side of the Mountains—and as those Settlements are growing much faster than You Have Any idea off, they will influence the United States into Unfriendly Measures, or at least will it Be impossible for Congress and all the states put together to Stop those Back Country Inhabitants. Upon my Honour, I See But one plan which it is Rational and Advantageous for Spain to follow. Let them oppen the Navigation and Make New Orleans a free port. How far it is the true policy of America is a great question. General Washington thinks it Would Weaken America, and transform the Back Country people into Spaniards. But in the present disposition of minds, I know Such a plan would Be very pleasing—and So far as Respects Spain, it

Would Certainly Be Big with Advantages. By Some Confidential Secret letters, I know, (and I Beg You not to Commit my friends nor me) that England Have Been Exciting leading men Against the Spanish Settlements in a Very particular Manner.[5]

Inclosed is a letter to Mr. Harrison which I Request you Will forward.[6] Be pleased to present My Respects to Count de Florida Blanca, and my other Acquaintances in Madrid. I Have Been the more Confidential with You as I know You are a Staunch friend to the alliance. Adieu, my dear Sir Your affectionate friend

LAFAYETTE

ALS (DNA: RG 233, HR 27A-G7.4, Papers of William Carmichael, tray 742, item 104). This is another of Lafayette's letters to Carmichael intended also for the eyes of Spanish officials.

1. Neither Lafayette's letter to Carmichael nor the enclosure from Adrienne has been found.

2. On December 23, 1784, after considerable debate, Congress ordered the appointment of three commissioners "to lay out a district . . . on the banks of either side of the Delaware [River], not more than eight miles above or below the lower falls thereof, for a foedaral town" (*JCC*, 27:704).

3. The "Vermonters" favored the separation of that area from New York state, making it a free, sovereign, and independent state. The rumor that they had sent delegates to Congress was incorrect.

4. Despite Lafayette's urgings (Lafayette to Jay, October 7, 1784), Jay did not take the oath of office as secretary for foreign affairs until December 21. Congress elected Adams minister plenipotentiary to Great Britain on February 24, 1785. They accepted Franklin's resignation on March 7, and on March 10 they elected Jefferson minister plenipotentiary to France (*JCC*, 28:98, 122, 134).

5. Letters not found.

6. Enclosure to Richard Harrison not found. It probably dealt with Harrison's efforts to obtain jackasses in Spain for Washington (see Washington to Lafayette, February 15, 1785).

To Nathanael Greene

Paris March the 16th 1785

My dear Sir

It Has not Yet Been in My power to Execute Your Commands, and I Had Rather waït a few weeks, than to do the Business of the tutor in a Slight manner.[1] But you want me also to write politicks, and that it is the Easier for me to do, as I am not Equally Scrupulous on this matter. War is not Begun, or is peace made. By the inclosed declaration printed in the Leyden Gazette, you See what part France Has taken.[2] I am just Now told the Account of an intended Surprise against Mastreik is mentionned in the Hague Gazette. But altho' warlike preparations

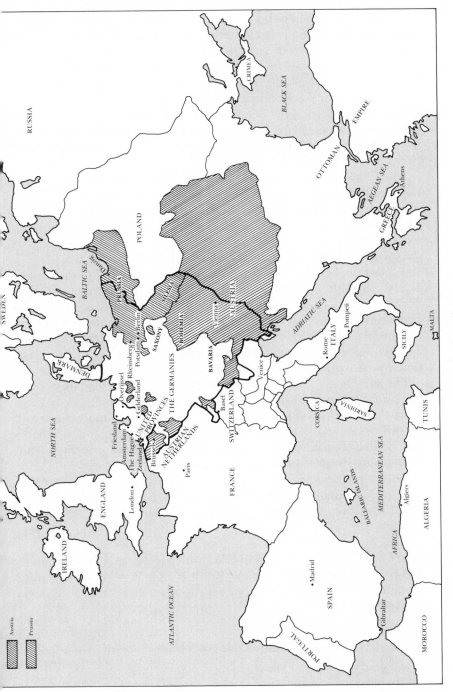

Europe in the 1780s

are Going on, Negotiations Have not Been one instant interrupted, and According to all probability they will end in [some] Arrangement where By the Dutch will give up much less than [they] were likely to loose. They are divided into two parties, and very warm on Both Sides. The patriots are decidedly attached to France. The Emperor's plan to give the Austrian low Countries to the elector of Baviera, and get that electorate in Return, Has Been opposed By the elector's Nephew and Heir, the duke of Deux Ponts who is in the french Service. I think therefore this will End quietly terminated, to the very great Credit of Count de Vergennes.[3]

You Have asked my opinion upon the Effect that would Result in Europe, in Case Congress Have powers to Regulate trade, and measures are taken to Restore public Credit. The effect, my dear Sir, would Be greater than Can Be imagined. I wish those who oppose these measures Could Come to this side of the Atlantic—Hear what is Said of the probable divisions among the States, of the Neglect that is likely to take place in Every Concerns of public faith, public Energy, public Safety. And altho' those Bad omens, are, thank God, ill founded, altho' American Patriotism, virtue, and wisdom Cannot But Being Roused to Every thing that is good and great, provided you give the people time to Consider, and judge their own faults, yet I Cannot Hear those ideas Spocken, without Heartly wishing no time may Be lost in Ensuring the Consequence and prosperity of the American Confederation.

The admission of foreigners in the West Indias Has Been the Subject of a [warm paper war between] the merchants and planters.[4] You know the articles, and I will only add that in lieu of getting more, there will Be difficulty enough to Stop the Efforts of the opponents to what is now Settled. Great Britain perseveres in Her Narrow principles—But all the trade from America goes to them.

I Beg, my good friend, you will present my Best Respects to Mrs. Greene. Remember me most affectionately to our friends in Rhode island, Carolina, and where ever you go. Adieu. Yours

LAFAYETTE

There is a Book writen By M. Necker which makes great deal of noise, and produces much exageration. But it is a great work indeed, and I thought the inclosed extract, Stating the Ressources of France might Be Agreable.[5]

ALS (MiU-C: Greene Papers).

1. Lafayette planned to send his son, George-Washington Lafayette, to America for an education and to oversee the education of Greene's son, George Washington Greene, in France. Young Greene reached France in the summer of 1788.

2. Enclosure not identified. On November 17, 1784, Louis had issued a declaration

offering to mediate the differences between Austria and the United Provinces, an offer the States General accepted on January 24, 1785.

3. On January 6, 1785, Louis had written to Joseph II that he would be willing to present the Austian exchange proposal on Bavaria, Deux-Ponts, and the low countries to the Prussians for their approval. This was in fact a polite rejection of it (Alfred Ritter von Arneth, *Marie Antoinette, Joseph II, und Leopold II* [Leipzig, 1866], pp. 65–68). On Vergennes's role in the rejection of the proposal, see Paul Bernard, *Joseph II and Bavaria* [The Hague, 1965], p. 203.

4. On the *arrêt du conseil* of August 30, 1784, see Lafayette to Jay, February 8, note 6. The conflicting arguments of merchant *chambres de commerce* and West Indian planters appeared in *Recueil de differentes pièces pour et contre l'admission des Etrangers dans les Isles Françaises de l'Amérique* [n.p., 1785].

5. The enclosure has not been found, but was probably similar to a brief transcribed extract from Necker's *De l'administration des finances de la France* (1784) enclosed with Lafayette's March 19 letter to Jay (DNA: RG 360, PCC 59, vol. 4, pp. 323–24).

To Patrick Henry

Dear Sir

Paris March the 16th 1785

Heartly Wishing for the Honour of Your Correspondance, I am not less desirous to Hope My letters may Be Entertaining. That Advantage I was Near purchasing at the expense of much European Blood. But owing to the part France Has taken in favour of the dutch, those differences Have taken a more pacific turn. The emperor's plans of an Exchange of His low Country dominions for Baviera Have, it is Said, Been also disappointed. So that the threatening war Has Been, it is Hoped, Removed—and altho' the Conditions are not known, and preparations Are Still going on, I do not doubt But what this Summer Will Be much more Quiete than Had Been expected. At the time of My Arrival, very thick Clouds were spread—which would Have Rendered it very improper for me to Have stayed in America longer than I did. My departure However was to my Reluctant Heart a painfull moment—and I would Have still more lamented it, Had I not Been Impressed with the Sanguine Expectation to pay You Before long an other Visit. Your Excellency Has no doubt Seen the french edict, permitting the intercourse with the West indias, in Every particulars except flour and Sugars, which However were Capital points.[1] But the regulation, Such as it is, [Has] Raised a Great Clamour Among the Merchants—the More So as they Compare it With the Narrow principles of England, Notwistanding which, Say they, all the trade of America is Going to them. I Hope this Matter may at last Be better Understood By the Chambers of Commerce. The Navigation of Mississipy now, in my opinion, is the great object. I Have Been, in My Representations to the french ministry, Candid, pressing, and decided. Could it depend upon their good will or their good sense, I would Be very Sanguine in my Hopes. But neither of these two Requisites, in Matters of Commerce or Boundaries, are to Be found at a Court, who Consider it as the first of Blessings to Monopolize trade, and to Hold much Ground. I think it will Be to the Honour of America to act with prudence, and a Moderation not Exclusive of firmness. There is no doubt But what England Will endeavour to Cherish dissentions they Have Been Sowing By their last treaty—and I Heartly Wish Spain may Yeld to Her own interest, to the Reasons of Congress, the advices of France, and it pleases me to think, to the first of laws, the laws of Nature, and Necessity. By Gal. Washington's last letters I Hear with great Satisfaction that the Navigation of Your Rivers will Be attended to, and that You are going to improve those Commercial channels, which, thank God, Nature Has provided for the Avantage of America, and Your State in particular.[2] I Beg, my dear Sir, You will present My Best Respects to Your family, and all our friends in Virginia and Believe me With Every Sentiment of Sincere Affection, and High Respect, dear Sir Your obedient Humble Servant

LAFAYETTE

ALS (Vi: Executive Department, Governor's Office, Letters Received).
1. See Lafayette to Jay, February 8, note 6.
2. See Washington to Lafayette, December 23, 1784.

To Richard Henry Lee

Paris March the 16th 1785

My dear Sir

What Intelligences I may think worth the while for the president of Congress to Read, I Have Communicated to their Secretary for foreign Affairs to whom I Beg leave to Refer Your Excellency.[1] But the personal tribute of My Regard and affection I Can only trust Myself to present. Those Sentiments, My Good friend, Have Been long Engraved in my Heart. To You I owe my first obligations—and to Be obliged to You, Has Ever Been to me a Most pleasing idea. Highly Sensible of Your friendship and its Valüe, I am Happy in Every opportunity to Remind you of me, and I know You will Be pleased to Hear that I am well, and Happy with My family and friends. The Situation of affairs in Europe Made it Highly proper for me to Arrive at the time I

Richard Henry Lee in 1784, the year he received, as president of Congress, an appeal from Lafayette to consider the plight of French-Canadians who had supported the American cause.

did. But matters are now taking a pacific turn, and Since my Return Has Ceased to present itself Under the idea of Necessity, I more than ever lament the shortness of a visit which I fondly Hope to Renew in a little time. What Has Been given to foreign trade in the West Indias, altho' it is Short of what Had Been demanded, Becomes a Source of Complaint among the Merchants of this Country, who Might Be More tractable, Had they a larger share in the American trade with Europe.[2] The Spirit of Great Britain Seems to me, not Hostile as Some pretend, But Averse to the United States, which, By the way is a Very foolish policy. I am glad to Hear You are Seriously taking up a plan for the Navigation of Your Rivers in Virginia.[3] You will, I fear, find the Spaniards Very obstinate. But every means must Be taken to Reason them into proper Measures.[4] Above all, my dear Sir, do attend to the Confederation, to Union, and Harmony, to Every Regulations that Can give Security to the Commerce, Energy to the Governement, faith to the public Creditors. This Congress is an Excellent one, and the fate of future Ages does probably depend Upon what will Be done this year. Impossible would it Be for me to Express the pleasure I feel when I Hear Some thing that Resounds to the Glory of America! Adieu, my dear Sir, Remember me Most affectionately to all your family, and Ludwell in particular.[5] My Best Compliments also waït Upon Mr. Arthur Lee. Should you write to the partizan, Send my love to Him. God Bless You, my good friend, with every Sentiment of affection and Respect I Have the Honour to Be Your obedient Humble Servant

LAFAYETTE

My Compliments wait Upon Your Colleagues in the delegation. I Hope Mercer is married By this time.[6]

ALS (PPAmP: Lee Papers).

1. See Lafayette to John Jay, February 8, 1785.
2. Lee replied to this complaint in his June 11 letter to Lafayette:
It is obvious, why the merchants of France, have not so great a share of our commerce as they wish; the staple states, or those which have much valuable produce to export, have at present but few ships and seamen of their own, and consequently, do not now export themselves much of their own produce; those nations, therefore, that push trade with them, by sending ships and merchandise to them, will for the reason above, certainly possess at this time, the greatest share of their trade. . . . [*Richard Henry Lee Correspondence*, 2:66]
3. See Washington to Lafayette, December 23, 1784.
4. A reference to the need for a peaceful resolution of differences with the Spanish on open navigation of the Mississippi River. Toward this end Diego Gardoqui had been appointed Spanish chargé d'affaires to the United States in autumn 1784, but he did not arrive in Philadelphia until June 1785.
5. Lee's son Ludwell had served under Lafayette in 1781.
6. Mercer, who had served under Lafayette in 1781, married Sophia Sprigg on February 3, 1785.

To James Madison

Paris March the 16th 1785

My dear Sir

Was I to found my Hopes Upon the Letters I Have from Congress, I would please My fancy with the Expectation of wellcoming You to the European Shore—and Yet, when I Remember Your obstinate plans of life, I am affraïd Least My Warm Wishes should Be disappointed.[1] In the Mean while, I will Continüe writing, and By the way will advise You to Send Your Answers By the packets Rather than By a private vessel. Those letters I Sent from Richmond are not Yet Arrived,[2] and I do not think Any letters of the Executive, nor any private dispatches from Virginia Have as Yet Got to Europe. The politics of this Country are not Yet perfectly Cleared Up. But I am firm in the opinion we Shall Have no war at this time. The Emperor's plans Have Been opposed By France. It Has on one Side Saved the Dutch, whose Sacrifices, in Comparison of what threatened them Will probably Be Small. It Has on the other kept up the Scale in the Empire of Germany, As By its dependance Upon the protection of France and Prussia, the Duke of Deux Ponts Has Been Emboldened to oppose Arrangements Betwen the Emperor and the Elector of Baviera where By this Would Have it is Said, given up His Electorate for the low Countries of the Austrian House.[3] The Conditions Betwen the Dutch and the Emperor are not Yet published—But I Send You a declaration of the king of France to the Emperor, which took place when He Entered the political field a few months ago.[4] Count de Vergennes Has acted, in My opinion, with a Moderation and firmness which does Him great Honour.

I am Every day pestering Governement With My prophesies Respecting the Mississipy. My favourite plan, they think, Cannot Be accepted By Spain, who know not How to give up what they once Have. On My Arrival, I strongly Advised, at least, to tell the Spaniards to make for themselves New Orleans a free port. I am to Have a Conference on that Interesting Subect with Duke de la Vauguion who is going Next week to Spain as an Ambassador. I Have writen letters By post to Madrid and Cadix, to Be intercepted and Read.[5] I wish theyr Ministry Were as Sensible and as well disposed as ours is. I am told Congress want to Send You there. Could'nt you Accept of it, only for a time, and in the Mean while make Your journey through France and Italy? Kantucky, its growth, Its principles, and its inhabitants are, I find, very little Understood in Europe, and not much so perhaps By many Europeans in America.

There is a Book of M. Necker Upon finances which Has made great deal of Noise. It Has Raised a party spirit where By Both Have to an Excess Hated or Adored Him. But I only Speack of the Book, which is a very sensible one, and worth Your Reading. Untill you get it, I inclose a Miniature portrait of France Made By that man who of Course knows its Ressources. Its publication may afford Entertainement.[6]

Cher. de Caraman's Best Compliments waït upon You, my dear Sir, and I Beg You Will Remember me to all friends in Virginia. M. Jefferson's Health is Recovering, But He keeps Himself too Closely Confined.[7] By my last letter from the General, He was in full enjoyment of a plan for the Navigation of the Pottowmack.[8] God Bless you, My dear friend, Remember me often, and for Ever depend Upon the Warm affection, and most High Regard of Your Devoted friend

LAFAYETTE

The Mercantile Interest is Warmer than Ever Against the New Regulations in favour of the West India trade.[9] They are Encouraged By the Narrow Conduct of England, and the total interruption of Commerce Betwen french and Americans, who are all flocking to Great Britain.

ALS (PHi: Dreer Collection).

1. On January 31 Madison had been nominated for minister at Madrid, but his name was withdrawn on February 2 (*JCC*, 28:25n). On December 8, 1784, Jefferson had also invited Madison to visit Paris, an offer that Madison declined (Boyd, *Jefferson Papers*, 7:557–60, 8:110–16).

2. Letters not found.

3. In early January 1785 the Duc de Deux-Ponts, heir presumptive to the Bavarian throne, had refused to exchange his inheritance for the Austrian Netherlands despite the efforts of the elector palatine, Charles Theodore, and the emperor.

4. Enclosure not found. See Lafayette to Greene, March 16, note 2.

5. For example, see Lafayette to Carmichael, March 10, 1785.

6. See Lafayette to Greene, March 16, 1785, note 5.

7. Jefferson had been ill from November 1784 to January 1785.

8. See Washington to Lafayette, December 23, 1784.

9. See Lafayette to Jay, February 8, 1785, note 6.

From James Madison

Orange March 20th. 1785.

My dear Sir

Your favour of the 15th. continued on the 17th of December came very slowly but finally safe to hand. The warm expressions of regard which it contains are extremely flattering to me; and the more so as they so entirely correspond with my own wishes for every thing which may enter into your happiness.

You have not erred in supposing me out of the number of those who have relaxed their anxiety concerning the navigation of the Mississippi. If there be any who really look on the use of that river, as an object not to be sought or desired by the United States I can not but think they frame their policy on both very narrow and very delusive foundations. It is true, if the States which are to be established on the waters of the Mississippi, were to be viewed in the same relation to the Atlantic States, as exists between the heterogenious and hostile societies of Europe, it might not appear strange that a distinction or even an opposition of interests should be set up. But is it true that they can be viewed in such a relation? Will the settlements which are beginning to take place on the branches of the Mississippi, be so many distinct societies, or only an expansion of the same society? so many new bodies or merely the growth of the old one? Will they consist of a hostile or a foreign people, or will they not be a bone of our bones, and flesh of our flesh? Besides the confederal band, within which they will be comprehended, how much will the connection be strengthened by the ties of friendship, of marriage and consanguinity? ties which it may be remarked, will be even more numerous, between the ultramontane and the atlantic States than between any two of the latter. But viewing this subject through the medium least favorable to my ideas, it still presents to the U. States sufficient inducements to insist on the navigation of the Mississippi. Upon this navigation depends essentially the value of that vast field of territory which is to be sold for the benefit of the common Treasury; and upon the value of this territory when settled will depend the portion of the public burdens of which the old States will be relieved by the new. Add to this the stake which a considerable proportion of those who remain in the old states will acquire in the new, by adventures in land either on their own immediate account or that of their descendents.

Nature has given the use of the Mississippi to those who may settle on its waters, as she gave to the United States their independence. The impolicy of Spain may retard the former as that of G. Britain did the latter. But as G. B. could not defeat the latter, neither will Spain the former. Nature seems on all sides to be reasserting those rights which have so long been trampled on by tyranny & bigotry. Philosophy & commerce are the auxiliaries to whom she is indebted for her triumphs. Will it be presumptuous to say that those nations will shew most wisdom as well as acquire most glory, who instead of forcing her current into artificial channels, endeavour to ascertain its tendency & to anticipate its effects. If the United States were to become parties to the occlusion of the Mississippi they would be guilty of treason against the very laws under which they obtained & hold their national existence.

The repugnance of Spain to an amicable regulation of the Use of the Mississippi, is the natural offspring of a system, which every body but herself has long seen to be as destructive to her interest, as it is dishonorable to her character. An extensive desart seems to have greater charms in her eye than a flourishing but limited empire, nay than an extensive flourishing empire. Humanity cannot suppress the wish that some of those gifts which she abuses were placed by just means, in hands that could turn them to a wiser account. What a metamorphosis wd. the liberal policy of France work in a little time, on the Island of N. Orleans? It would to her be a fund of as much real wealth as Potosi has been of imaginary wealth to Spain. It would become the Grand Cairo of the New World.[1]

The folly of Spain is not less displayed in the means she employs than in the ends she prefers. She is afraid of the growth and neighbourhood of the U. States because it may endanger the tranquility of her American possessions: and to obviate this danger she proposes to shut up the Mississippi. If her prudence bore any proportion to her jealousy she would see, that if the experiment were to succeed, it would only double the power of the U. States to disturb her, at the same time that it provoked a disposition to exert it, she would see that the only offensive weapon which can render the U. States truly formidable to her, is a navy, and that if she could keep their inhabitants from crossing the Appalachian[s], she would only drive to the sea most of those swarms, which would otherwise direct their course to the Western wilderness. She would reflect too that as it [is] impossible for her to destroy the power which she dreads, she ought only to consult the means of preventing a future exertion of it. What are those means? Two & two only. The first is a speedy concurrence in such a treaty with the U.S. as will produce a harmony, & remove all pretexts for interrupting it. The second, which would in fact result from the first, consists in favouring the extension of their settlements. As these become extended, the members of the Confederacy must be multiplied, and along with them the Wills which are to direct the machine. And as the wills multiply, so will the chances against a dangerous union of them. We experience every day the difficulty of drawing thirteen States into the same plans. Let the number be doubled & so will the difficulty. In the multitude of our Counsellors, Spain may be told, lies her safety.

If the temper of Spain be unfriendly to the views of the U. States, they may certainly calculate on the favorable sentiments of the other powers of Europe, at least of all such of them as favored our Independence. The chief advantages expected in Europe from that event, center in the revolution it was to produce in the commerce between the new & the old world. The commerce of the U.S. is advantageous to Europe in two respects, first by the unmanufactured produce which they export: secondly by the manufactured imports which they consume. Shut up the Mississippi and discourage the settlements on its waters, and what will be the consequence? First, a greater quantity of subsistance must be raised within the antient settlements, the culture of tobacco indigo & other articles for exportation be proportionably diminished, and their price proportionably raised on the European consumer. Secondly the hands without land at home being discouraged from seeking it where alone it could be found must be turned in a great degree to manufacturing, our imports proportionably diminished, and a proportional loss fall on the European manufacturer. Establish the freedom of the Mississippi, and let our emigrations have free course, and how favorably for Europe will the consequence be reversed. First the culture of every article for exportation will be extended, and the price reduced in favour of her consumers. Secondly, our people will increase without an increase of our manufacturers, and in the same proportion will be increased the employment & profit of hers.

These consequences would affect France in common with the other commercial nations of Europe; but there are additional motives which promise the U. States her friendly wishes and offices. Not to dwell on the philanthropy which reigns in the heart of her Monarch and which has already adorned his head with a crown of laurels, he cannot be inattentive to the situation into which a controversy between his antient and new allies would throw him, nor to the use which would be made of it by his watchful adversary. Will not all his councils then be employed to prevent this controversy? will it not be seen that as the pretensions of the parties directly interfere, it can be prevented only by a dissuasive interposition on one side or the other, that on the side of the U.S. such an interposition must from the nature of things be unavailing, or if their pretensions for a moment be lulled, they wd. but awake with fresh energy, and consequently that the mediating influence of France ought to be turned wholly on the side of Spain. The influence of the French Court over that of Spain is known to be great. In America it is supposed to be greater than perhaps it really is. The same may be said of the intimacy of the Union between the two nations. If this influence should not be exerted, this intimacy may appear to be the cause. The United States consider Spain as the only favorite of their ally of whom they have ground to be jealous, and whilst France hold the first place in their affections they must at least be mortified at any appearance that the predilection may not be reciprocal.

The Mississippi has drawn me into such length that I fear you will have little patience left for any thing else. I will [spare] it as much as possible. I hear nothing from Congress except that Mr. Jay has accepted his appt. and that no successr. has yet been chosen to Dr. Franklyn.[2] Our Legislature made a decent provision for [deleted? the] remittances due for 1785 from Va. to the Treasy. of the U.S. and very extensive provision for opening our inland navigation;[3] they have passed an Act vesting in Genl. Washington a considerable interest in each of the works on Js. River & Potowmac but with an honorary rather than lucrative aspect. Whether he will accept it or not I cannot say.[4] I meant to have sent you a copy of the Act, but have been disappointed in getting one from Richmd.; They also passd an act for reforming our juridical system which promises Salut[ary] effects;[5] and did not pass the Act for the [corrupting our] Religious system.[6] Whether they passed an act for paying British [debts or not,] they do not know themselves. Before the bill for that purpose had got through the last usual forms, the want of members broke up the House. It remains therefore in a situation which has no precedent, & without a precedent lawyers & legislators are as much at a loss, as a mariner without his compass.[7] The subjects in which you interested yourself were all referred to the Executive with power to do what I hope they will do better than the Assembly. I understood before I left Richmd. that you wd. receive officially from the Govor. a copy of the Resolutions which I sent you.[8] I recd. a letter a few days ago from Mr. Mercer written in the bosom of wedlock at Mr. Spriggs;[9] another at the same time from Monroe, who was well at New York. I have nothing to say of myself but that I have exchanged Richmond for Orange as you will have seen by the above date; that I enjoy a satisfactory share of health; that I spend the cheif of my time in reading, & the chief of my reading on Law; that I shall hear with the greatest pleasure of your being far better employed, & that I am with most affect. esteem Yr. Obedt. [friend] & Servt.

J.M.

AL (DLC: James Madison Papers), draft.

1. "Potosi": Potosí, in what is now Bolivia, site of the most famous silver mines of Spanish America. The position of New Orleans on the Mississippi River was analogous to Cairo's location on the Nile, which made it a favored marketplace for the treasures of the African interior.

2. John Jay had accepted his appointment as secretary of foreign affairs on December 21, 1784. Congress appointed Adams minister plenipotentiary to Great Britain on February 24 and Jefferson minister plenipotentiary to France on March 10 (*JCC*, 28:98, 134). For some of the complications in choosing Franklin's successor, see James Monroe to Madison, February 1, 1785, in *Madison Papers*, 8:237–38.

3. Virginia budgeted £120,000 annually as its portion of the interest due on the national debt. The General Assembly confirmed the allocation of funds for this purpose from the tax on land and slaves in its October 1784 session ("An Act to amend and

reduce the several acts for appropriating the public revenue, into one act," in Hening, *Statutes*, 11:433–34). The statement of public accounts presented to the Virginia House of Delegates in late December 1784 (*JHD*, October 1784, pp. 85–94) also reported on Virginia's delinquency in paying its quota for 1784 and earlier (ibid., p. 86).

4. Madison is referring to the bills establishing the James River Company and the Potomac River Company (see Washington to Lafayette, February 15, 1785, note 2). For Washington's reactions to the act giving him shares in the two companies, see his letter to Lafayette of February 15, note 4.

5. For the act establishing a system of courts of assize in place of county justices of the peace, see Hening, *Statutes*, 11:421–29. It was never implemented.

6. A final vote on a bill that would establish tax support for "Teachers of the Christian Religion" was postponed until the October 1785 session. Madison's efforts to organize opposition to the bill were influential in its final defeat. In October 1785, Madison introduced an "Act for Establishing Religious Freedom," which the assembly passed on January 19, 1786 (see *Madison Papers*, 8:295–306, 399–402).

7. The peace treaty with Britain recognized the claims of British creditors. On December 3, 1784, the House of Delegates passed a resolution fixing the period of payment and the period for which interest was due. The bills were amended but a quorum could not be obtained for final passage. As Madison explained to Jefferson: "The question to be decided is whether a bill which had passed the House of Delegates, and been assented to by the senate; but not sent down to the H. of D. nor enrolled, nor examined, nor signed by the two Speakers and consequently not of record, is or is not a law?" (*JHD*, October 1784, p. 48; *Madison Papers*, 8:229–31 [January 9, 1785]). It was decided that the bill had not been enacted into law, and a similar bill was introduced during the October 1785 session (ibid., pp. 447–50).

8. For the resolutions to present a bust of Lafayette to the city of Paris and also to cast one for Virginia, see Lafayette to Madison, December 15, 1784, note 5.

9. For Mercer's marriage, see Lafayette to Richard Henry Lee, March 16, 1785, note 6.

To the American Commissioners

Paris April the 8th 1785

Gentlemen

In Consequence of Your Desire, I Have Endeavoured to Collect informations, Relative to the presents which the African powers Usually Receive from European Nations.

By the inclosed Summary, You will get Every Intelligences I Could obtain of what Has Been done By Holland, Sweden, Danemark, Venise, Spain, Portugal, and England. The Returns Nos. 2, 5, 9, 10, 11, 12, 13, are minuted Accounts of the Presents which at Several periods Have Been delivered By those powers.[1]

As to France, it Has Been More Difficult for me to know their Exact Situation. Their Way of transacting Business with the Affricans is peculiar to them, and it is a principle with Governement Not to Divulge it. I know we are not like the other powers obliged to pay Certain tributes. Our presents are Volontary, with Respect to the time, as well as to the

Valüe, and France is Upon a much more decent footing with those pirats than Any other Nation. It Has Been Avoided to Give presents Upon fixed Occasions, like a change of princes. The king of Morocco's Envoys Have not Been Considered as Ambassadors, one Excepted who Came to present a Number of french men taken in foreign Vessels whom that king Had purchased from the Captors. Upon the king's Coronation, He Was Complimented By Tunis and Tripoly. But the permission, I am told, was not Granted Upon the delphin's Birth.

In the last treaty of peace with Tunis the present No. 3 was Sent By the late king of France. It did Cost about 50,000 livres, Besides which the french Merchants made a present of about 12,000 livres. The tunisian Ambassador who Came for the king's Coronation Received the present No. 4 which Costs 68,840 livres.

Upon the occasion of the last peace With Morocco, the present to the Emperor was worth 163,708 livres, and to His officers 74,250 livres as appears By the Return No. 6. The Ambassador from that Country, in the Circumstance I Have Mentionned, in the year 1778, was Complimented with the Articles of the Return No. 8, to the Amount of 129,063 livres.

The Return No. 14th Contains the present to the Pacha of Tripoly, By the Envoy He was permitted to Send for the king's Coronation. It is worth 34,341 livres.

It is also Costumary to pay the Expenses of those Envoys on the Road, and to Send them Back to their Country in a ship of War.

Such are, Gentlemen, the Intelligences I Could Collect. I am to Apologize for the delay. But Considering the Variety of Articles, and the Reserve of Governement Upon this point, my exertions Required Some time Before I Could gather all the Interesting particulars. With the Highest Respect I Have the Honour to Be Your Excellencies's Most obedient Humble Servant

LAFAYETTE

ALS (DNA: RG 360, PCC 98, pp. 77–78).

The American Commissioners, Adams, Franklin, and Jefferson, were appointed by Congress in May 1784 as ministers plenipotentiary to negotiate treaties of amity and commerce (see commission and instructions in Boyd, *Jefferson Papers,* 8:262–71).

In their first report, November 11, 1784, the commissioners informed Congress that they would need money before they could open negotiations with the Barbary states, since "treaties with these powers are formed under very peculiar circumstances. . . . Presents or war is their usual alternative" (in ibid., p. 496). John Jay replied to the commissioners' letter on March [11], 1785, and informed them that by resolutions of February 14 Congress had authorized them to spend $80,000 in treaties with the Barbary states. The commissioners were also authorized to appoint agents to negotiate these treaties with the Barbary princes (ibid., pp. 19–22). The seizure of American vessels by Morocco gave urgency to the commissioners' desire to negotiate a treaty, and they wrote to Vergennes on March 28 seeking information and advice on dealings with the Barbary states (ibid., pp. 61–63). In 1778 the American commissioners in Paris (Adams, Franklin, and Lee) had corresponded with Vergennes and Sartine concerning the possibility that France might intercede with the Barbary powers on behalf of the United States, but the commissioners had at that time no authority or instructions to treat with the Barbary states. Though by the trade treaty of 1778 France had agreed to intercede as far as possible to protect American shipping from Barbary pirates, Sartine replied that there was little France could do unless the Americans were prepared to pay for protection.

On April 24, 1785, Castries, to whom Vergennes had referred the commissioners' March 28 letter, made a similar reply. He also informed Vergennes that about three weeks earlier the commissioners had been provided with "extensive information concerning the payments and presents of the Christian powers and concerning the value and nature of those France made on a few notable occasions"[T] (DNA: RG 360, PCC 98, pp. 275–78). Castries was probably referring to this letter from Lafayette and its enclosures (see note 1, below).

The commissioners enclosed Lafayette's letter and its enclosures in their letter to Jay, April 13, 1785 (Boyd, *Jefferson Papers*, 8:80–83), with the comment that Lafayette's report concerning the Barbary states "will shew that the price of their peace is higher than the information heretofore communicated, had given us reason to expect." They suggested that since France and England, which could "combine the terror of a great naval force with the persuasive of pecuniary tribute," still paid enormous sums to the several powers, Congress would have some idea "of what will be required of a people possessing so weak a navy and so rich a commerce as we do." The commissioners also acknowledged their indebtedness to Lafayette, "whose means of access to the depositories of this species of information" and "zeal for the service of the United States" procured them this intelligence.

1. Lafayette enclosed a summary report, dated March 1785, of the tribute paid to the Barbary states by European nations and detailed lists of the kind and value of presents given at various times by those nations to the several Barbary powers. The enclosures and translations of them are in DNA: RG 360, PCC 98, pp. 81–94, 128–221. An endorsement in Lafayette's hand on the summary report reads: "This is the footing upon which several european powers now stand with the affrican princes" (ibid., p. 81).

To Alexander Hamilton

Paris April the 13th. 1785

My Dear Hamilton

Altho' I Have just Now writen to McHenry,[1] Requesting Him to Impart My Gazette to You, a Very Barren one Indeed, I feel within Myself a Want to tell you I love You tenderly. Your Brother Church Has Sailed for America, Since which I Had a letter from His lady who is in Very Good Health.[2] By an old letter from our friend Greene, I Have Been delighted to find He Consents to Send His Son to Be Educated with Mine.[3] The idea Makes me Very Happy. I wish, Dear Hamilton, You Would Honour me with the Same Mark of Your friendship and Confidence. As there is No fear of a War, I intend Visiting the Prussian and Austrian troops. In one of Your New York Gazettes, I find an Assossiation Against the Slavery of Negroes which Seems to me Worded in Such a Way as to Give no offense to the Moderate Men in the

Southern States. As I ever Have Been Partial to My Brethren of that Colour, I wish, if You are one in the Society, you would move, in Your own Name, for my Being Admitted on the List.[4] My Best Respects Waït on Mrs. Hamilton. I kiss Phil, and the Young lady.[5] Adieu Your affectionate friend

LAFAYETTE

Mention me Most affectionately to the doctor, His lady—Gal. Schuyller and family—Your Sister Peggy—Fish, Webb, and all our friends.[6]

ALS (DLC: Alexander Hamilton Papers).

1. Letter not found.

2. Hamilton's brother- and sister-in-law, John Barker and Angelica Schuyler Church. Letter not found.

3. Greene's letter, dated January 7, has not been found. See Lafayette to Greene, March 16, 1785.

4. The first meeting of the New York Society for Promoting the Manumission of Slaves and Protecting Such of Them as Have Been or May Be Liberated was held on January 25, 1785. Hamilton attended the organizational meeting on February 4. Hamilton did not respond to Lafayette's request to be enlisted in the association, and Lafayette again wrote to him on May 24, 1788, requesting membership (Syrett, *Hamilton Papers*, 4:652–53).

5. Hamilton's son Philip and daughter Angelica.

6. Dr. and Mrs. John Cochran, Elizabeth Hamilton's aunt and uncle; Philip and Catherine Schuyler, Mrs. Hamilton's parents; Peggy: Margaret Schuyler Van Rensselaer; Fish: Nicholas Fish; and Samuel Webb.

To Jeremiah Wadsworth

St. Germain April the 16th 1785

Dear Wadsworth

The february packet Has Been Long on the Road, and Brought Very few letters—So that we are much Retarded as to American Intelligences. I did not Hear Either from or of You By this Opportunity, which Disappoints me the more as I am Very Anxious to know the State of Your Health. British Politics will Be Explained to You By Church who Has Sailed for America.[1] The disputes of Ireland are taking a Negotiating turn—Notwistanding which I think they Will Be much puzzled to Make an Arrangement Agreable to Both.[2] Great Britain Seems in no Hurry to Have an American treaty of Commerce—and Still less So to Give up the forts.[3] In the Mean While no American trade Comes to France—Which Now and then Gives the Minister a Notion to lessen the Number of the Packets. Warlike preparations are Still going on, But there will Be, I think, no war this Year. The Dutch Quarrel, owing to the part France Has taken, Will Be Settled. The Duke of Deux Ponts, Heir to the Elector of Baviera Has opposed the Exchange of that Electorate for the Austrian Low Countries.[4] The Election of a king of the Romans, which You know is the title of the future Emperor, will Be an object for Negotiations, and Some Aprehend, for a Serious Controversy. Your friend Bxx is in England, and writes to me Now and then. I think many of Your letters to Him Have Been Intercepted.[5] There are Great Clamours in this Country Raised By the Merchants Against the Arrêt du Conseïl Respecting the West Indias.[6] But the Ministry will Stick to it—and More Cannot Be obtained for the Present. I Have the Hope Marechal de Castries will Make a demand of American Hemp, the Cultivation of which I would like to Encourage in preference to that of Russia. It Has Been the More impossible to obtain an Exemption of Duties Upon Whale oils, as it is Now the favourite Scheme of M. de Calonne to Revive that fishery. French vessels are gone upon that Expedition But I am Negotiating a proposition to Be Made to the New England Merchants By the people whose Contract it is to light Paris and Many other Cities—By Which Means I Could Raise the Demand to a Million of livres worth—But am very much Affraïd to Meet with an opposition from Government Who must absolutely Interfere.[7] I Beg You will Communicate the Information to Breeck altho' I Have nothing Certain to depend upon. I Have not Yet Received the Marks of kindness which Your city, the University of Cambridge, and the State of Mashashushet Have Been pleased [lately] to Resolve in my Behalf. I will in a few days write You again By Young Mr. Adams.[8] There is a young Indian, Son to a french Man By the Name of Stephanus, whom I intend to take with me to France as a favourite Servant.[9] The Young Man Has a Regard for me, as I was Spoken off to Him By His deseased father. He went with Brant to Quebec in the fall. The whole family who are Oneïdas, Consented to His Coming with me—and I would Be much obliged to You to Send the Inclosed to Kirland By Express,[10] and to forward the Young Indian's departure By the October packet— Because I Will then Be Back from Prussia, and Bohemia, where I am going to visit those troops. My Best Respects waït On Mrs. Wadsworth. Mention me affectionately to Daniël,[11] and the Young ladies—to all our friends. Mde de Lafayette Sends Her Most affectionate Compliments. Adieu Yours

LAFAYETTE

ALS (Ct: Joseph Trumbull Collection).

1. John B. Church, Wadsworth's business partner.

2. The Irish Parliament had requested less restrained trade between England and Ireland. British prime minister Pitt responded by offering a series of commercial propositions for completely free trade. The Irish Parliament approved the proposals on Febru-

ary 7, 1785, but, under pressure from the opposition and from manufacturing interests, the British Parliament greatly modified the propositions and the ministry was eventually forced to abandon them.

3. The peace treaty with Britain provided for British evacuation of frontier forts on Americal soil. Pitt tied that evacuation to the settlement of the claims of British creditors against American prewar debtors, because a number of states were passing legislation repudiating those obligations.

4. See Lafayette to Madison, March 16, note 3.

5. Bxx: probably Dr. Edward Bancroft.

6. The *arrêt du conseil* of August 30, 1784. See Lafayette to Jay, February 8, 1785, note 6.

7. For the offer by Tourtille Sangrain to purchase whale oil for lighting Paris, see Lafayette to John Adams, May 8, 1785, note 1.

8. John Quincy Adams.

9. The "young Indian": Peter Otchikeita.

10. Enclosure to Dr. Samuel Kirkland not identified.

11. Daniel: Jeremiah's son.

To [John Adams]

Paris May the 8th 1785

My dear friend

Inclosed you will find what I intended to carry this morning—But the Duke de Choiseuïl's death which Happened about twelve o' clock prevented my going out of town.[1] The Bargain Has Been altered over and over, and I Have at last Secured the following advantages—1stly the vessels may Be Americans 2dly the More precious part of the oil, called Spermecity may Be left out. dely By the Contract it Rests with the American Society to obtain a diminution of duties which all say at their charge. By the Passports not only foreign But also National duties are taken off, and all the Anchorage, pilotage and other plagues of the kind which give the Untertakers an extraordinary profit over and above the Common profits of other people who are admitted to sell their oils.[2]

If you think the Bargain is good, your son might Carry the proposition to our New England friends, and take charge of the Samples of oils that will Be Ready to morrow—in which case, I would propose His Meeting Mr. Jefferson where a man of the police will attend at Whatever Hour in the morning you please to appoint. When you send Back the papers, I will show them to Mr. Jefferson and know from Him if it is Convenient we should waït upon Him, your son, the police man and myself about ten in the morning. God Bless you.

L.F.

ALS (MHi: Adams Papers).

1. The Duc de Choiseul had served under Louis XV in major ministerial posts.

2. On May 7 M. Tourtille Sangrain submitted a proposal to Lafayette for the establishment of an American company to provide him with 16,000 hundredweights of whale oil for the lighting of Paris (CSt). The contents of the proposal show that it was made at Lafayette's request, and, as his comments on its provisions to Adams make clear, he was also concerned to see that all of the complicated duties and taxes in French ports would be borne by the purchasers, not by the American suppliers. Nothing came of the original proposed trading monopoly because Boston merchants preferred to have the offer made to individual American dealers in whale oil. They sent Nathaniel Barret to France in the autumn of 1785 to negotiate such contracts (J. Bowdoin to Jefferson, October 23, 1785, in Boyd, *Jefferson Papers*, 8:662–63).

To Henry Knox

Paris May the 11th 1785

My Dear friend

In Consequence of Your New Appointement I Hope this letter Will find you in Newyork, arranging the War departement, Saving our Stores from destruction, Brushing up our fine pieces, thinking of a School for Engineers and Artillers, and Reflecting upon the General's light Compagnies, the Baron's legions, and all the ways and Means to Have troops without Having an Army.[1] With all my Heart and Soul I wish you every kind of Success, my good friend. The patriot and the Soldier are nobly United in Your person. God grant Your advices may Be adopted—your pains may fructify—and Be pleased to let me know Every thing that Concerns you either as My friend Knox or the Secretary at War. À propos of war—Should you quarell either way don't forget I am Your zealous Servant. Besides which I am a french man [   ] my father and mother were Very good Roman Catholics—Circumstances which may Render me Not an Useless tool in Some Expeditions. The devil would Be getting a way from Hence. But when I did it once, it Was Still much more difficult and Unsafe. All that I tell you in Confidence, and Because the letter will Be Safely delivered. So I Beg You will keep it for *American* friends, and *Not* answer me unless it is in General terms. In a letter Some thing official I write to Mr. Jay You will find a few words upon the affair of Longchamps, a journey I intend taking to Be Back in October, and a whale oil proposal, in consequence of what You told me at Boston, which is all what I could obtain this Year.[2] I Hope it will Be agreable to our New England friends. For particulars I Refer You to my Young friend M. Adams. I

Have introduced a Gentleman to Mr. Jay, Hoping the letter would do for Both.

General Greene is So kind as to let me Have His Son to Be educated along with mine. I Cannot Express to You How Happy I am By this mark of His friendship. I wish You would do the Same. My Most affectionate Respects Waït upon Mrs. Knox, Miss Lucy, all the family. I kiss my God Son.[3] Remember me to all our friends—our military friends, our friends in Boston, in Newyork, where ever You are and Have a chance to Meet them. I am assured Billy is gone to America But in the Mean while am Hunting for Him in England and Ireland—altho' I don't doubt He Has fled from danger.[4] God Bless you. Your affectionate friend for Ever

LAFAYETTE

ALS (MHi: Henry Knox Papers).

1. Congress had appointed Knox secretary of war on March 8 (*JCC*, 28:129).
2. On the whale-oil contract, Lafayette wrote to Jay on May 11:
   As it Seems to me that favours Granted to American Importations is One of the Best Services that Can Be Rendered to American trade, I wish it Had Been possible to obtain a total abolition of duties upon whale oils. But in this Moment Governement are taken up with a Scheme to Revive that fishery in France. It Was therefore Necessary to follow a Round about Course. . . . [DNA: RG 360, PCC 156, pp. 418–19].
3. Lafayette's godson, Henry Jackson Knox, was not sent to France for his education.
4. Lafayette located brother Billy in England; see Lafayette to Knox, June 12, 1785.

To George Washington

Paris May the 11th 1785

My dear General

This is not the only letter You Will Get from me By this packet.[1] But as the opportunity is Safe, I will trust Young M. Adams With Some Matters Which I would not like to Be Ventured in the post offices of France.

PROTESTANTS in FRANCE are under intolerable DESPOTISM. Altho' oppen persecution does not now Exist, yet it depends upon the whim of KING, QUEEN, PARLIAMENT, or any of THE MINISTERS. Marriages are not legal among them. Their wills Have no force By law. Their children are to Be Bastards. Their parsons to Be Hanged. I Have put it into My Head to Be a LEADER in that affair, and to Have their Situation changed. With that wiew I am Going, under other pretences to Visit their chief places of abode, With a Consent of CASTRIES, and an other.[2] I will afterwards Endeavour to Gain VERGENNES and PARLIAMENT, with the keeper of the Seals who acts as Chancellor.[3] It is a Work of time, and of Some danger to me, Because none of them Would give me a Scrap of paper, or Countenance whatsoever. But I Run My chance. CASTRIES Could only Receive the Secret from me. Because it is not in His departement. Don't Answer me about it, only that You Had my Ciphered letter By M. Adams. But when in the Course of the fall or winter You will Hear of Some thing that way, I wanted You to know I Had an Hand in it.

IRELAND are Spent out, and Nothing for LIBERTY's Sake to do that Way.[4] I was in Hopes Holland would offer Some thing that Way. But I am affraïd not.[5] I don't think CALONNE's political life May last long, unless He leaves FINANCES for Some other Branch.[6]

Before I arrived, a letter Had gone demanding Longchamps. Since which the Ministry were Satisfied with that Business and a letter went ordering to let it drop.[7] I Hope there Will Be no war in America. But if it Was Ever the Case, either to SOUTH SPAIN,[8] to MISSISSIPY, or to the fronteer posts and Canada, I depend Upon You, my dear General, to Be offered a Command, which in one Case my Situation as a french Man May Render personally a little ticklish for me, But for which, in all Cases my Situation as Such, as well as my Roman Catholick Creed, or Supposed to Be So at least if any thing, and the Confidence You, and the public are pleased to Honour me with, may Render me a proper choice to propose. But I Earnestly Hope it Will not Be the Case that You make war—particularly with Spain—altho' a Visit to Mexico and New Orleans I would prefer to Any thing I know of. Don't answer to me about it otherwise than in general terms. Adieu, My dear General, My Best Respects waït on Mrs. Washington. Remember me to the family. Your filial and devoted friend

LAFAYETTE

When You Arrange Your papers, my dear General, I Beg You Will Send me my letters to You, which I will Send Back fortnight after I Have Received them. I Had no Copies kept of them—and wish to preserve some.[9]

ALS (PEL: Hubbard Collection). Words printed in small capitals were in code and deciphered on the manuscript. The letter is endorsed: "favoured by M. Adams, and particularly Recommended. LAFAYETTE."

1. Probably Lafayette to Washington, May 13.

2. The "other" was probably Malesherbes, a former minister of the king's household, who was interested in the issue of Protestant rights.

3. Miromesnil.

4. On Lafayette's earlier interest in Irish turmoils, see Lafayette to Wadsworth, April 16, note 2.

5. See Lafayette to Jay, February 8, 1785, note 2.

6. There were rumors at the time that Louis XVI was particularly upset by Calonne's

mishandling of major expenditures. His imminent departure from the ministry was expected. See Metra, *Correspondance secrète*, 18:119–20.

7. For the background of the Longchamps affair, see Lafayette to Vergennes, September 15, 1784, note 1. On February 10 Barbé de Marbois informed Jay that the French government was requesting the extradition of Longchamps, but Jay recommended that approval of the request be delayed since Longchamps had been sentenced by a Pennsylvania court to nearly two years' imprisonment and a fine of $200. Eventually the French decided not to press for Longchamps's extradition (Jay to Jefferson, September 14, 1785, in Boyd, *Jefferson Papers*, 8:519).

8. "South Spain": probably South America. During his stay in New York in 1784, Francisco de Miranda had broached the subject of a campaign for the liberation of Spanish America with Alexander Hamilton and Henry Knox. Hamilton had suggested Washington and Lafayette as likely candidates to participate (William Spence Robertson, *The Life of Miranda*, 2 vols. [Chapel Hill, N.C., 1929], 1:43). Yet Miranda did not share Hamilton's assessment of Lafayette. "He seems to me of mediocre character, endowed with that activity and perpetual motion of a Gallic being"[T] (William Spence Robertson, ed., *The Diary of Francisco de Miranda: Tour of the United States, 1783–1784, The Spanish Text* (New York, 1928), p. 121).

9. For Washington's first plan to have them copied by his nephew George Augustine Washington, see Washington to Lafayette, September 1, 1785. Bushrod Washington eventually wrote Lafayette on January 9, 1817, that he was forwarding the originals to him (PEL: American Friends of Lafayette Collection).

To George Washington

Paris May the 13th 1785

My dear General

My Correspondance With You Will this time Be in two Volumes and Young Mr. Adams, John Adams's Son, Has taken Care of a letter Which I Hope He will Safely forward. Your kind favour february the 15th only Came in the last Packet. I Need not telling You, My dear General, How Happy I was to Hear from You, and How Happy You will Make me By an Exact Correspondance and an Attention to Send the Letters in time for the Sailing of the Packets which now will Arrive in France at the Havre a place Very Near Paris at the Mouth of the Seine River. I am Very Glad to Hear Your Pottowmack Business Has Succeeded.[1] It is Highly important, and I feel doubly Happy By Reflecting this Good is owing to the part You Have taken in the affair. The Compliment the State of Virginia Have paid You is No doubt perplexing. I feel for You, and With you, My dear General, on the Occasion. Your Reluctance to Receive Such a present is the More pleasing to me, as I want it to Be Said in Your History—General Washington Got Every thing for His Country—and Would not Receive Any other Reward. But on the other Hand, You Certainly Wish to Avoid Every

Step which Could appear a Slight, a want of proper Respect, or of Gratitude for the Compliment which a Nation pays to an Individual. You Better know what to do than I Can tell. But if it Can Be gently turned towards Some public popular Establishement, You May perhaps Avoid a deviation from Your plan, and the Appearance of Slight or ostentation. I will look out for Subscribers when the Matter Comes to Be a little Better known—and will Have an Eye upon Your Recommendation Respecting the Engeneer.

There is not much News for the Present in this Country. Dutch affairs Seem to Be in a Good train of Pacification. But if we Believe the Rumours that were Spread Yesterday, Baviera Would Be Invaded, or Rather, with the Consent of the Elector, taken Possession of By the Imperial troops. It is trüe that Elector is a Complete fool, and His Ministry are Bought By the Emperor. But I Cannot think the Report is trüe—altho' that Baviera, or the ottoman Empire are Now more probable Grounds of a future war than the provinces of Holland. Duke de Choiseuïl died a few days Ago. Some think He was not Without Hopes, and Worked pretty Hard to Reenter the Ministry.

French Hounds are not Now Very Easely got Because the king Makes use of English dogs as Being more Swift than those of Normandy. I However Have got Seven from a Normand Gentleman Called *Monsieur le Comte Doilliamson* the Handsomest Bitch Among them Was a favourite with His lady who Makes a present of Her to You.[2] As He was very active in procuring the Best Blooded dogs, I Beg leave to propose Your writing a line to Him, containing a thankfull notice of the Comtesse, who Seems to take much pride in Being mentionned to You.

Mquis. de St. Simon Has once writen a letter to You the Answer to which did not arrive.[3] I think a Copy, or an Antidated letter would do the Business, and the Whole Will Be attributed to Naval Accidents.

M. Adams Has taken with Him Some proposals for a Contract about Whale oils which I think to Be Very advantageous to the Commerce of America, and will produce an Envoice of about 800,000 french livres. I Have Been very Busy in Bringing it on, and it is the Consolation I Had for failing in My Endeavours to obtain a General exemption of duties upon those oils. You Have Been Very Right Not to purchase the Spanish jack ass. The Best ones Come from the Isle of Maltha. Admiral Suffrein who goes there Has promised He would within these Six months Send me the Handsomest in the island with a female and the Whole Will not amount to more than fifty guineas.

My wife, children, and myself are in perfect Health, and all join With me in Most affectionate Respects to You, to Mrs. Washington, and we Send our love to the Young ones. I was very Happy to Hear George

WASHINGTON

Lafayette carried on a warm correspondence with his "adopted father," Washington, extolling the general's virtues and informing him of European political gossip.

Arrived at Charlestown in a Better State of Health. Remember me to Him, to all your family, to my friends about you, or any of them you Happen to Meet. Adieu, My dear General, I grieve to think we are Now Separated By this Immense Ocean. But my Heart is With You in Every Moment, My dear General, and I am Happy when I Can once more Mention to You the Sentiments of Respect, Gratitude, Unbounded affection which for Ever Render me, My Beloved general, Your Most devoted friend

LAFAYETTE

ALS (PEL: Hubbard Collection).
1. On the establishment of the Potomac Company, see Washington to Lafayette, February 15, 1785.
2. Lafayette wrote John Quincy Adams on May 18, 1785, that he would find the seven dogs for General Washington ready to be embarked; he wished Adams to deliver them to one of Washington's friends in New York, who would then arrange for them to be taken to Mount Vernon (MHi: Adams Papers).
3. The Marquis de Saint-Simon Montbléru had written to Washington seeking admission to the Society of the Cincinnati. Washington replied to Saint-Simon, on May 10, 1786, that it had been decided the French branch should determine the issue of his membership. It was eventually approved (Fitzpatrick, *Writings of Washington*, 28:416).

To Pierre-Samuel Du Pont de Nemours[1]

Paris 30, May 1785

Monsieur the Controller General has kindly promised me to write in favor of M. de Gouvion, lieutenant colonel on the general staff of the army, whom I have requested to talk with the merchants of La Rochelle about trade with the United States and especially with the Indians. We could then send him on to Dunkirk for the same purpose. What I have in mind, for my own part, would be to acquire some knowledge about our trade centers and our factories, with regard to the United States, and to mention to them the best American concerns, and the articles most in demand in this country, so as to contribute my poor efforts to the extension of our trade with this continent. It is with this intention that I am going myself to Auvergne by way of Lyons, and that I venture to beg Monsieur the Controller General to be so kind as to give M. de Gouvion a general letter of recommendation to present in the places he will pass through on his way to join me.

LAFAYETTE

ALS (DeGE), translation.

To Patrick Henry

Paris june the 7th 1785

Sir

I Have Been Honoured With Your Excellency's Commands dated in Council March the 30th, and find myself Happy to Be Employed in the Service of the Virginia Militia, to whom I am So particularly Bound By Ever lasting Sentiments of Regard and Gratitude.

As Soon as Your favour Came to Hand, which was only a few days Ago, I Have waïted on Mr. Barklay, and at His Request, with Mr. Jefferson's Advice, I Applied to Mons. de Gribeauval lieutenant General and Commander in chief of the french Artillery. From this Very learned Gentleman I Have Got a Return, Containing the Manner in Which the ten thousand pounds, May, Agreable to Your directions, Be laid out. As to the Expense, it May Be Reduced to the price Contracted for By the king, and the Arms and powder will Be prouved By the officers of the Royal Corps, after which I shall myself inspect them with the Most Scrupulous Attention. Those papers I Have put this day in Mr. Barklay's Hands—and By the End of the Month Hope to get farther informations from the Manufactures, Enabling us to adopt the Best and Cheapest Method to Execute Your Commands, in Which Mr. Jefferson and Myself will Be Happy to Give Mr. Barklay Every Assistance in our Power.[1]

Indeed, Sir, the Virginia Militia deserves to Be well armed and properly attended. I pray to God these warlike Stores May Never Be of Use. But Should America, Unfortunately Have Any future Occasion for Soldiers, I Hope She Will Not leave out of Her list, One, who Was Early adopted in Her Service, and who, at all times, Will most Readily and Most devotedly offer His Exertions. With Unbounded Wishes for the Complete prosperity of the State of Virginia, and with Affectionate Sentiments of the Most perfect Respect for Your Excellency I Have the Honour to Be, Sir, Your Excellency's Most obedient Humble Servant

LAFAYETTE

ALS (The Rosenbach Museum & Library, Philadelphia).

1. Henry had written letters on March 30 to Lafayette, Jefferson, and Barclay, requesting that they secure arms and ammunition for the state of Virginia (Vi: Executive Department, Governor's Office, Letter Books). For letters from Barclay to Henry on the progress of the contract, see *Virginia State Papers*, 4:49–50, 59, 81.

To Henry Knox

Chavaniac, Auvergne, june the 12th 1785

My dear friend

It Grieves me to think I am Going to wound Your Good Heart, and Yet find it My duty as a friend Rather to Give You a pain, perhaps Unnecessary, than to leave You in the Cruellest Anxiety. When I Returned to France, I Endeavoured to find out Your Brother Billy, and Intended Calling Him to me, and Persuading of Him to Return to Boston. After much Inquiries I was Assured He Had left England and Ireland, and Had Gone to America. However as I know His Heart, I Could not Be made Easy, and Continued My efforts to trace Him out. Five days ago, as I was getting into a Post Chaise, with an Aged Aunt of mine which I was Conducting into this Country Seat, I Received a letter from Doctor Bancroft,[1] a Sensible and Good Natured American, Acquainting me that poor Billy Has Been Since january last Confined in an House, and, as you probably know, and it Grieves me to Repeat, disordered in His Head—that He is However Better, and in a few weeks will Be able to Go out, which He Very Much desires. Shocked at the Intelligence as You May Conceive, my first Motion was to post off to London, and See Him properly Attended, or take Him a Way to Paris. But Upon Recollection, I thought My journey there Could not Be So Concealed as to Avoid Notice, and that if the trüe Cause was Unfortunately discovered it Would Be an object for the News papers. At last I determined to Send a Most Intelligent and trusty Person in My family to Waït on Your Brother, See Him well attended in Every Respect, and when He is permitted to Go abroad Accompagny Him to My House. I Have writen to Doctor Bancroft,[2] Recommending Secrecy to Him, [Encouraging?] Him to See that Billy is Well attended with phisicians, and Begging He will differ His Intended departure Untill they Can travel together. In a few days I will Be Back in Paris, and if My presence in London May do Him Good, I will go there Under a fictitious Name. What I Have Most Recommended is not to Hurry the treatement, and to Waït Untill the phicisians think proper. Now, my dear friend, that I Have found Him out, you may Be as easy as if You were Yourself in Europe. The doctor writes me, He was glad to Hear I Had Inquired after Him, and Spocken of Him with tenderness and Regard. But they did not deliver my former letter.[3] The last one I Have dispatched is an invitation to Come to Paris, and live in the family.[4] Towards the Middle of Next Month, Mde de Lafayette is Coming to this Country Seat, in a Remote province, where She will Spend two Months, and I think the Best way for Your Brother is to Accompagny Her and if necessary I will prevail upon Doctor Bancroft to Be one in the Partïe. On my Arrival in the City where I am just Returning, I will get more Particular Accounts and forward them Immediately. In the Mean While Rest Assured Billy is much Better, and in a fair way of Recovery.

Every plan of Mine will Be Subordonate to this Unhappy Circumstance. But in Case, By the Arrangements I will Have made, my presence is Unnecessary I will in the Course of Next Month Set off for Berlin, and Visit the prussian and Austrian troops which are to Be assembled in Several Camps for the grand Maneuvres, and I will Examine the fields of Battle in Hessia, Prussia, Bohemia, Silesia, Saxony, and perhaps Flanders, so as to Be in Paris By the End of october.

I Confidentially intrust to You, my dear Sir, that I am about purchasing a fine plantation in a french Colony, to make the experiment for Enfranchising Our Negro Brethren, god grant it may Be propagated![5]

Adieu, my good friend, my most affectionate Respects to Mrs. Knox, and a kiss to Lucy, my Son, and the little one. Your affectionate friend

LAFAYETTE

ALS (MHi: Henry Knox Papers).
1. Letter not found.
2. Letter not found.
3. Letter not found.
4. Letter not found.
5. On June 7, 1785, Lafayette authorized his attorney to purchase estates in French Guinea on condition that the owner "neither sell nor exchange any black"[T] (NIC: Dean Collection). For Lafayette's earlier proposal to Washington of an experiment to purchase an estate, free the blacks on it, and employ them as tenants, see Lafayette to Washington, February 5, 1783.

Verses Sung to Lafayette at Lyons[T]

[Lyons, June 23, 1785]

Why, friends, this obliging guest
Is this fearsome general!
This Lafayette so exalted
Is verily seated at this table.
Ah, how sweet is our fortune,
And what glory this warrior boasts!
He can battle, vanquish, and imbibe,
He deigns to sing among us.

Let us forget that ancient Hercules,
Avenger of kings and subjects;
Hercules was not a Frenchman.
He did not save America.
Ah, how sweet . . .

When he sets off at the mercy of Aeolus,[1]
Forthwith love breaks into tears;
But after a thousand triumphant deeds,
By his return he consoles it.
Ah, how sweet . . .

Dear to his king, beloved of the ladies,
Loved by Mars and by Cyprian;[2]
He turns back our enemies
And cannot imagine cruel deeds.
Ah, how . . .

Let La Pérouse, on the waves,
Go seek out new shores;[3]
Friends, here without such exertions
You see the Hero of two worlds,
Ah, how sweet is our fortune,
And what glory this warrior boasts!
He can battle, vanquish, and imbibe,
He deigns to sing among us.

[M. DELANAINE?]

From *Mercure de France*, December 10, 1785, translation.
This drinking song (to the tune *Elle aime à rire*) was sung in Lafayette's honor at a banquet at Lyons. Lafayette had gone there to promote American trade with the local manufacturers.
1. Aeolus: Greek god of the winds.
2. Mars: Roman god of war; Cyprian: a worshipper of Aphrodite, the goddess of love and beauty.
3. The celebrated French navigator the Comte de La Pérouse was planning a voyage of discovery and exploration around the world.

To Jeremiah Wadsworth

Paris july the 9th 1785
Dear Wadsworth
   Give me leave to Introduce to You M. Houdon, whom I take to Be the first Artist in Europe, and who, actuated By the love of glory more

than By Selfish Motives, is Going over to Model Gal. Washington. It is a Good opportunity for Congress or the States to order what Ever works they please to Have Executed. He is the Very Man for the Continental Brass Statüe.[1] As to the Marble one of Gal. Washington He is going to Execute for the State of Virginia, it Costs only about a thousand guineas.[2]

I Have Been lately Rambling through Some Commercial and Manufacturing towns in France where I Have Endeavoured to forward the American interest. Complaints Have Been made to me of the Slowness of Remittances, and Bad Regulations for the trade in the Continent. God grant they may Soon Be into the Hands of Congress. I am now Setting out on a tour to Prussia, Vienna, and other parts of Germany and will Be Back in Paris By the tenth of October.

Doctor Franklin is going Home. I Hope He will Be well Received, and Something May Be done for His grand Son,[3] who you know is a deserving young man and much Beloved By the doctor.

By this opportunity I Send the Passports for three whale oil vessels, and New Copies of the Contract where By the time granted to the American Merchants is Prorogued Untill Next june.[4] I Hope it will Be Satisfactory. It is directed to the Mashashushet delegates in Congress. Upon you, my good friend, I depend to Send all this a going. I Have directed a chest of paper of the Manufacturers of Auvergne to Be Sent to you in order to Make an Experiment.

By the Newspapers I Hear You are at the Head of the Newyork Bank.[5] I am very glad of it on theirs and on Your Account. My Respects waït on Your lady. Remember me to the young Gentleman and ladies. My Compliments waït on all our friends. God Bless You. Yours

LAFAYETTE

ALS (CtHi: Jeremiah Wadsworth Papers).

1. On August 7, 1783, Congress resolved to erect a bronze equestrian statue of Washington wherever Congress set up residence and to have the work done "by the best artist in Europe, under the superintendence of the Minister of the United States at the Court of Versailles" (JCC, 24:494–95). See Gilbert Chinard, ed., Houdon in America (Baltimore, 1930), pp. 15–20.

2. Benjamin Harrison had written to Jefferson on July 20, 1784, requesting him to find "the most masterly hand" in Europe to execute a statue of Washington (Boyd, Jefferson Papers, 7:378–79). Jefferson wrote to Washington on December 10, 1784, that he had discussed the idea with Houdon and that the artist volunteered to go to America to model a bust from life (ibid., 7:567).

3. William Temple Franklin.

4. Enclosures not found.

5. Wadsworth had been appointed a director of the Bank of New York.

To John Adams

Sarguesmines july the 13th 1785

My Dear Sir

Had I Been But a slow traveller, I should much Sooner Have Received, and of Course Acknowledged Your favours. But the Rapidity of my March Has Been Such, that While letters went after me One Way, I was Scampering on the other, and So on, Untill, By the Blessed fourth day of july, I found myself Magnetised to Mr. Jefferson's table, where we chearfully Began our tenth Year of Independance. I Had afterwards the pleasure to Hear from You which Had Been Intended Much Sooner,[1] and Doctor Bancroft's departure to London Gives me an opportunity to Answer. Here therefore I Stop, on the German fronteer, and looking Back to the West ward, I feel my Heart is Going Quite the Contrary Way to that My Carriage is to follow. What different Sensations Would I Experience, if on leaving this Country, I Had Before My Eyes the Happy prospect of a landing Upon the shore of Liberty! It is Said a Soldier Must Have Seen those German Armies, fields of Battles, and So on. I Hope My Military feelings may Enjoy much Satisfaction. As for My Republican Heart there will not Be Great pleasure to taste. Little Masters and Big Boned Slaves I am Going to Visit, whose Coloured Ribbonds Hang like so many Halters about their Necks. Some great Sovereigns and distinguished Characters, I Have Howevever a Great Curiosity to See. The Emperor, the king of Prussia, Prince Henry, and Duke of Brunwick are Such men in the Sight of whom one Must Be Much Interested. My Ramble about Germany will last Untill the Middle of october. I Hope, my Good friend, You will Continüe to Honour me With Your Much Esteemed Correspondance— and as my want of Exactness proceeded from Circumstances Not in my power, I Can assure You, You will Have no Reason to Complain.

I Had Been told His Britannick Majesty Was a Great dissembler. But Could not think He would Carry it So far as He Has done in Your Interview.[2] Indeed, those people are Very Right to take it kindly, now they Cannot Help it. But while they are Rational in their good Reception of You, I Hope they may Cease to Be Quite Mad in their Commercial, I don't know what, for as to plans I don't think they Have Any. Our Fanneüil Hall friends Seem to Be out of Humour With them.[3] It is trüe the British trade Has Been Carried on in a Ruinous Way, particularly for the Southern planters, whose luxuries Have Been Encouraged By the Credits of Britain, and who Now will Be plagued By their

Joseph II, King of Austria, the aspiring model of enlightened despot some European political theorists sought.

Creditors. It were to Be wished a good treaty was made Betwen England and America, and to You, my Good friend, that Glory is Reserved. In the mean while, let us advise our friends in America to make Proper Regulations for their Commerce. The want of them, I find are objected to me Every day. Altho' Matters on that Head are Much Better than people Generally think, Yet You know Great deal might Be done to attain perfection.

As on my Setting out, I told Mde. de Lafayette I would soon answer the letter that Had then Come to Hand,[4] She desired Her most affectionate Compliments to You, Mrs. and Miss Adams. Anastasie and George present their Best Respects. Mention me Most Respectfully to the ladies, and tell my friend Smith[5] I Have Not as Yet Heard from Him. I Am not Surprised, But Am However Happy to Hear He Has Answered the description I gave You of Him, which altho' dictated By warm friendship Was not in the least Exagerated. Adieu, My dear Sir, with Every Sentiment of affection and Respect I Have the Honour to Be Yours

LAFAYETTE

ALS (MHi: Adams Papers). Sarreguemines is on the Saar River in Lorraine.

1. On June 3, 1785, Adams had written to Lafayette from Westminster that he dreaded the Fourth of July "because as I shall be the focus of so many Eye-Balls I am afraid of being Scorched" (MHi: Adams Papers).

2. George III had received Adams on June 1 upon the "same footing with other foreign Powers" (ibid.) and engaged him in a cordial conversation (*Diplomatic Correspondence, 1783–1789*, 4:200–203).

3. Faneuil Hall had been the site of a reception given by the Boston merchant community for Lafayette in 1784. Growing resentment at the flood of English goods had resulted in the posting of the following handbill throughout Boston on April 6:

> Does not every Part of this Metropolis severely feel the amazing Importation of *British Manufactures*, to the Prejudice of home-made Commodities? . . . Study to discourage British Traders, as their Parliament have discouraged your Commerce,—Bid them DEPART in Peace, their Persons sacred, their Property inviolate, but let them not remain, to undermine the Basis of our Empire, by silently sucking the Blood of each Individual. [Boston *Independent Chronicle*, April 8, 1785]

4. The June 3 letter.

5. Colonel William Stephens Smith had arrived at Westminster the day before Adams to assist him as secretary of the United States legation.

To John Jay

Sarguemines on the french fronteer

july the 14th 1785

My dear Sir

Before I Begin my journey through Germany, Give me leave to Remind You of an absent friend who is Most tenderly attached to You, and wish, instead of Going Eastward, it Was in His power to take You By the Hand in Newyork. Intelligences are not for the present Very interesting, and for them I Refer You to our old friend who is going Back to His own Country where, I Hope, He will Be well Received.[1] You know the Sentiments of the people on this Side of the water. A proper attention will Be expected for a Man of His merit and His advanced age. You Have Interested Yourself in Behalf of His Grand Son and I Have only to add that Whatever is done for Him must Come from the doctor's friends. I Have Been much pleased to find You Have Stood an advocate for the Negroes[2]—and (as you know their Cause, is mine) You will not Be Surprised to Hear I am about an Experiment of which I will write You More By and Bye.[3] Be pleased, my dear Sir, to present my most Affectionate Respects to Mrs. Jay—to Remember me to Hers and Your family—to the Chancellor, the Governor, and all our friends.[4] Adieu, my dear Sir, most Respectfully and affectionately Yours

LAFAYETTE

Houdon the Celebrated artist is Going to America to model Gal. Washington. I Beg leave to introduce this gentleman to You, and I think Him the first man in Europe to Be intrusted with the Brass Statüe and Any other Commands Congress May Have for Him.[5]

ALS (NN: Berg Collection).

1. Benjamin Franklin left Passy on July 12 to return to America.

2. Along with Hamilton, Jay had been an organizer of the New York Society for Promoting the Manumission of Slaves and Protecting Such of Them as Have Been or May Be Liberated. See Lafayette to Hamilton, April 13, 1785, note 4.

3. On Lafayette's project, see Lafayette to Knox, June 12, 1785, note 5.

4. The chancellor was Robert R. Livingston; governor of New York at the time was George Clinton.

5. On the statue of Washington, see Lafayette to Wadsworth, July 9, note 1. Jay's letter of October 29 informing Congress of Lafayette's recommendation was read on October 31 (*JCC*, 29:861–62).

From George Washington

Mount Vernon 25th. July 1785.

My Dear Marquis,

I have to acknowledge & thank you for your several favors of the 9th. of February—19th. of March & 16th. of April, with their enclosures; all of which (the last only yesterday) have been received since I had the honor to address you in February.

I stand before you as a Culprit; but to *repent & be forgiven* are the precepts of Heaven: I do the former—do you practise the latter, & it will be participating of a divine attribute. Yet I am not barren of excuses for this seeming inattention; frequent absences from home—a round of company when at it, & the pressure of many matters, might be urged as apologies for my long silence; but I disclaim all of them, & trust to the forbearance of friendship & your wonted indulgence: indeed so few things occur, in the line on which I now move, worthy of attention—that this also might be added to the catalogue of my excuses; especially when I further add, that one of my letters, if it is to be estimated according to its length, would make three of yours.

I now congratulate you, & my heart does it more effectually than my pen, on your safe arrival at Paris, from your voyage to this Country, & on the happy meeting with Madame la Fayette & your family in good health. May the blessing of this long continue to them—& may every day add increase of happiness to yourself. As the clouds which overspread your hemisphere are dispersing, & peace with all its concomitants is dawning upon your Land, I will banish the sound of War from my letter: I wish to see the sons & daughters of the world in Peace & busily employed in the more agreeable amusement, of fulfilling the first and great commandment. *Increase & Multiply:* as an encouragement to which we have opened the fertile plains of the Ohio to the poor, the needy & the oppressed of the Earth; any one therefore who is heavy laden, or who wants land to cultivate, may repair thither & abound, as in the Land of promise, with milk & honey. The ways are preparing, & the roads will be made easy, thro' the channels of Potomac & James river.

Speaking of these navigations, I have the pleasure to inform you that the subscriptions, (especially for the first) at the surrender of the books, agreeably to the Act which I enclosed you in my last, exceeded my most sanguine expectation: for the latter, that is James river, no comparison of them has yet been made.

Of the £50,000 Sterl:g required for the Potomac navigation, upwards of £40,000, was subscribed before the middle of May, & encreasing fast. A President & four Directors, consisting of your hble Servant, Govrs. Johnson & Lee of Maryland, & Cols. Fitzgerald & Gilpin of this State, were chosen to conduct the undertaking.[1] The first dividend of the money was paid in on the 15th. of this month; & the work is to be begun the First of next, in those parts which require least skill; leaving the more difficult till an Engineer of abilities & practical knowledge can be obtained; which reminds me of the question which I propounded to you in my last, on this subject, & on which I should be glad to learn your sentiments. This project, if it succeeds & of which I have no doubt, will bring the Atlantic States & the Western Territory into close connexion, & be productive of very extensive commercial & political consequences; the last of which gave the spur to my exertions, as I could foresee many, & great mischiefs which would naturally result from a separation—& that a separation would inevitably take place, if the obstructions between the two Countries remained, & the navigation of the Mississippi should be made free.

Great Britain, in her commercial policy is acting the same unwise part, with respect to herself, which seems to have influenced all her Councils; & thereby is defeatg. her own ends: the restriction of our trade, & her heavy imposts on the staple commodities of this Country, will I conceive, immediately produce powers in Congress to regulate the Trade of the Union; which, more than probably would not have been obtained without in half a century. The mercantile interests of the *whole* union are endeavouring to effect this, & will no doubt succeed; they see the necessity of a controuling power, & the futility, indeed the absurdity, of each State's enacting Laws for this purpose independant of one another. This will be the case also, after a while, in all matters of common concern. It is to be regretted, I confess, that Democratical States must always *feel* before they can *see:* it is this that makes their Governments slow—but the people will be right at last.

Congress after long deliberation, have at length agreed upon a mode for disposing of the Lands of the United States in the Western territory: it may be a good one, but it does not comport with my ideas. The ordinance is long, & I have none of them by me, or I would send one for your perusal. They seem in this instance, as in almost every other, to be surrendering the little power they have, to the States individually which gave it to them. Many think the price which they have fixed upon the Lands too high; and all to the Southward I believe, that disposing of them in Townships, & by square miles alternately, will be a great let to the sale: but experience, to which there is an appeal, must decide.[2]

Soon after I had written to you in Feby., Mr. Jefferson, & after him Mr. Carmichael informed me that in consequence of an application from Mr. Harrison for permission to export a Jack for me from Spain, his Catholic Majesty had ordered two of the first race in his Kingdom (lest an accident might happen to *one*) to be purchased and presented to me as a mark of his esteem.[3] Such an instance of condescension & attention from a crowned head is very flattering, and lays me under great obligation to the King; but neither of them is yet arrived: these I presume are the two mentioned in your favor of the 16th. of April; one as having been shipped from Cadiz—the other as expected from the Isle of Malta, which you would forward.[4] As they have been purchased since December last, I began to be apprehensive of accidents; which I wish may not be the case with respect to the one from Cadiz, if he was actually shipped at the time of your account: should the other pass thro' your hands you cannot oblige me more, than by requiring the greatest care, & most particular attention to be paid to him. I have long eddeavoured to procure one of a good size & breed, but had little expectation of receiving two as a Royal gift.

I am much obliged to you my dear Marquis, for your attention to the Hounds, & not less sorry that you should have met the smallest difficulty, or experienced the least trouble in obtaining them. I was no way anxious about these, consequently should have felt no regret, or sustained no loss if you had not succeeded in your application.[5] I have commissioned three or four persons (among whom Colo. Marshall is one) to procure for me in Kentucke, for the use of the Kings Garden's at Versailles or elsewhere, the seeds mentioned in the list you sent me from New York, & such others as are curious, & will forward them as soon as they come to my hands; whch. cannot be 'till after the growing Crop has given its seeds.[6]

My best wishes will accompany you to Potsdam, & into the Austrian Dominions whenever you set out upon that tour. As an unobserved spectator, I should like to take a peep at the troops of those monarch's at their manoeuverings upon a grand field day; but as it is among the unattainable things, my philosophy shall supply the place of curiosity, & set my mind at ease.

In your favor of the 19th. of March you speak of letters which were sent by a Mr. Williams; but none such have come to hand.[7] The present for the little folks did not arrive by Mr. Ridouts Ship as you expected; to what cause owing I know not.[8] Mrs. Washington has but indifferent health; & the late loss of her mother, & only brother Mr. Barthw. Dandridge (one of the Judges of our Supreme Court) has rather added to her indisposition.[9] My mother & friends enjoy good health. George has returned after his peregrination thro' the West Indies, to Burmuda, the Bahama Islands, & Charlestown; at the last place he spent the winter. He is in better health than when he set out, but not quite recovered: He is now on a journey to the Sweet Springs, to procure a stock sufficient to fit him for a matrimonial voyage in the Frigate F. Bassett, on board which he means to embark at his return in October: how far his case is desperate, I leave you to judge—if it is so, the remedy however pleasing at first, will certainly be violent.[10]

The latter end of April I had the pleasure to receive in good order, by a Ship from London, the picture of your self, Madame la Fayette & the children, which I consider as an invaluable present, & shall give it the best place in my House.[11] Mrs. Washington joins me in respectful compliments, & in every good wish for Madame de la Fayette, yourself & family; all the others who have come under your kind notice present their compliments to you. For myself, I can only repeat the sincere attachment, & unbounded affection of My Dr. Marqs. &c. &c. &c.

G: WASHINGTON

LbC (DLC: George Washington Papers, Series 2).

1. Thomas Johnson, Thomas Sim Lee, John Fitzgerald, and George Gilpin.

2. On April 23, 1784, Congress adopted a committee report that divided the western lands into ten territories with temporary governments and indicated means by which they could become permanent states (*JCC*, 25:275–79). The Northwest Ordinance of 1787 superseded the project.

3. Jefferson to Washington, December 10, 1784 (Boyd, *Jefferson Papers*, 7:566–67); William Carmichael to Washington, December 3, 1784–March 25, 1785 (DLC: George Washington Papers, Series 4).

4. Lafayette to Washington, April 16, 1785, in Gottschalk, *Letters of Lafayette*, pp. 294–96.

5. The seven hounds, a gift from the Comte and Comtesse d'Oilliamson, crossed the Atlantic with John Quincy Adams; they arrived at Mount Vernon in late August (see Fitzpatrick, *Writings of Washington*, 28:233, 240).

6. Washington had written Thomas Marshall on May 3 enclosing a list of seeds that he wanted (Marshall to Washington, May 12, 1785, DLC: George Washington Papers, Series 4).

7. Lafayette had written to Washington March 19, "My little family have been writing to yours by Mr. Williams" (Gottschalk, *Letters of Lafayette*, pp. 292–94). These letters have not been found.

8. Thomas Ridout wrote to Washington on May 1 that Lafayette had sent him a letter dated April 8 and a few packages to forward to Washington, but the packages had not yet arrived in Bordeaux (DLC: George Washington Papers, Series 4). In fact they did not reach Mount Vernon until the following year (Fitzpatrick, *Writings of Washington*, 28:418).

9. On April 24 news reached Mount Vernon of the deaths of Martha's stepmother, Frances Dandridge, and only surviving brother, Bartholomew Dandridge (*Washington Diaries*, 4:127).

10. George Augustine Washington married Frances (Fanny) Bassett on October 15, 1785. He had set out on July 9 for Sweet Springs, whose waters were famous for relieving "all kinds of *languishing* situations" (John Rouelle, *A Complete Treatise on the Mineral Waters of Virginia* [Philadelphia, 1792], p. 17).

11. The London merchant John Hunter, while visiting Mount Vernon the following autumn, noted: "There is a fine family picture in the Drawing room of the Marquis de La Fayette, his lady, and three children—" ("An Account of a Visit Made to Washington at Mount Vernon, By an English Gentleman, in 1785: From the Diary of John Hunter," *Pennsylvania Magazine of History and Biography*, 17 [1893]:81).

To [Mme de Tessé][T]

Rheinberg 7 August 1785

If you are wishing for news of me, my cousin, I shall tell you that for the past three days I have been at Prince Henry's country house.[1] You

During his 1785 tour of Germany, Lafayette found Prussia's Prince Henry a most congenial host.

will be not very surprised that I arrived in the middle of dinner, and that every evening I give the master of the house the trouble of adding up my score at lotto; but save for my awkwardness they seem pleased with me here, and I am infinitely pleased by the kindnesses and amiability of Prince Henry. He loves our country with a really touching predilection, and I always agree with what he says about our national glory, because if I know how to defend myself a bit from personal compliments, I never have the strength to refuse praise given to my country. I am enjoying Prince Henry much more than I would have done in Paris.[2] I have scarcely finished breakfast when he comes to see me; we go for a walk by ourselves until dinner; we are close in the same way at supper as well, and in the salon except at lotto—we are always together. He replies with great civility to my questions, and the company here is very pleasant and very likable.

There was an awfully good play. They put on *The Huron,* which interested me as a Frenchman and as an Indian.[3] In a word, I am extremely pleased with my stay here, and am trying to profit from it as much as I can. Tomorrow evening I shall return to Berlin, and Friday, after having seen some troops, I leave for Silesia, where I hope to admire the king at close range, and where, since I have no doubt his health will permit him to talk, his kindness makes me hope to enjoy his conversation for a few hours. Because they tell me here that M. Custine has indeed told him a few stories about the American war and especially about the campaign in Virginia,[4] but I am not intending to discuss that subject, and not having, like him, brought along maps, I am satisfied with a bit of reputation on the whole, without disputing every inch of ground as thoroughly as I did with Lord Cornwallis.

L (*Mémoires,* 2:128–29), fragmentary copy, translation.

1. Prince Henry, a younger brother of Frederick the Great, resided at his country palace in Rheinsberg, fifty miles northwest of Berlin.

2. Prince Henry had been in Paris in 1784.

3. Marmontel's play *Le Huron.* On Lafayette's becoming an Indian in 1778, see *LAAR,* 1:247.

4. Comte Custine-Sarreck had been promoted to the rank of *maréchal de camp* for his services in the Yorktown campaign.

From George Washington

Mount Vernon 1st. Septr. 1785.

My Dr. Marqs.

Since my last to you, I have been favored with your letters of the 11th. & 13th. of May by young Mr. Adams, who brought them to New

York, from whence they came safely to this place by the Post: the first is in *cypher,* & for the communications therein contained I thank you: my best wishes will always accompany your undertakings; but remember my dear friend it is a part of the military art to reconnoitre & *feel* your way, before you engage too deeply. More is oftentimes effected by regular approaches, than by an open assault; from the first too, you may make a good retreat—from the latter (in case of repulse) it rarely happens.

It is to be hoped that Mr. Adams will bring the British Ministry to some explanation respecting the Western Posts. Nothing else can, I conceive, disturb the tranquillity of these States; but if I am mistaken in this conjecture, you know my sentiments of, & friendship for you too well to doubt my inclination to serve *you* to the utmost of your wishes, & my powers.

It gives me very singular pleasure to find the Court of France relaxing in their demand of Longchamps; to have persisted in it would have been a very embarrassing measure to this country under the Laws & Constitution of the Foederal Government, & those of the several parts which compose it.[1]

The Hounds which you were so obliging as to send me arrived safe, & are of promising appearance: to Monsieur le Compte Doilliamson; (if I miscall him, your hand writing is to blame, & in honor you are bound to rectify the error); & in an *especial* manner to his fair Competesse, my thanks are due for this favor: the enclosed letter which I give you the trouble of forwarding contains my acknowledgement of their obliging attention to me on this occasion.[2]

If I recollect right, the letter which was written by the Marquis de St. Simon was on the business of the Cincinnati, and was laid before the general meeting at Philad. in May 1784; consequently, the answer must have proceeded from the Society either specially to him, or generally, thro' the Counts de Estaing & Rochambeau, who were written to as the heads of the Naval & military members of that Society in France; but as all the papers relative to the business of the Society were deposited in the care of the Secretary General, Knox—or the assistant Secretary, Williams—I have them not to refer to; but will make enquiry & inform you or the Marqs. de St. Simon more particularly of the result.[3]

Your constant attention, and unwearied endeavors to serve the interests of these United States, cannot fail to keep alive in them a grateful sensibility of it; & the affectionate regard of all their Citizens for you. The footing on which you have established a market for whale oil must be equally pleasing & advantageous to the States which are more immediately engaged in that commerce.[4]

Having heard nothing further of the Jacks which were to be sent to me from Spain, & which by Mr. Carmichael's letter (enclosing one from the Count de Florida Blanca) of the 3d Decr. were actually purchased for me at that date, I am at a loss to account for the delay, & am apprehensive of some accident.[5] Be this as it may, if you could my Dr. Marquis, thro' the medium of Admiral Suffrein, or by any other means that would not be troublesome, procure me a male & female, or *one* of the former & *two* of the latter, upon the terms mentioned in your letter of the 3d. of May, I should think it a very fortunate event & shou'd feel myself greatly indebted to your friendship. The mules which proceed from the mixture of these Animals with the horse, are so much more valuable under the care which is usually bestowed on draught cattle by our Negroes, that I am daily more anxious to obtain the means for propagating them.

When George returns from the Springs & gets a little fixed, I will set him about copying your letters to me, which will be better than to hazard the originals at Sea, where an accident might occasion the loss of them to both of us. In my last I informed you of his intended marriage, which I suppose will take place in the early part of next month.[6]

I should have given an earlier acknowledgment of your letters of the 11th. & 13th. of May aforementioned, had I been at home when they came to this place; but at that time I was on a tour up this river with the Directors, (Johnson, Lee, Fitzgerald & Gilpin) to examine the obstructions, & to fix upon a plan of operations; which having done, we commenced our labours on the 5th of last month, under a full persuasion that the work will not prove more arduous than we had conceived before the difficulties were explored. The James River Company, by my last accounts from Richmond, is formed; a meeting of the members was summoned to be held on the 20th. of last month, but what the determinations of it were, I have not yet heard;[7] Nor (so barren are the times) have I a tittle of news to communicate to you; the several assemblies are in their recesses but will be addressed I presume at their autumnal meetings by the commercial interests of the United States to vest Powers in Congress to regulate the Trad of the union which they see clearly must be directed by one head in order to obtain consistency & respectability at home & abroad. I am My Dr. Marqs. &c. &c.

G. WASHINGTON

LbC (DLC: George Washington Papers, Series 2).

1. See Lafayette to Washington, May 11, 1785, note 7.

2. Washington's September 1 letter to the Comte de'Oilliamson is in Fitzpatrick, *Writings of Washington*, 28:245–46.

3. See Lafayette to Washington, May 13, note 3. At the time Otho Holland Williams was the assistant secretary general of the American Society.

4. On the Tourtille de Sangrain proposal, see Lafayette to [John Adams], May 8, 1785. For Calonne's decision to support the reduction of duties on American fish oil, see Lafayette to [Thomas Boylston], November 20, 1785, note 1.

5. Carmichael's letter of December 3, 1784–March 25, 1785, enclosed a letter from Floridablanca dated November 24 (DLC: George Washington Papers, Series 4). One of the Spanish jackasses arrived in Massachusetts that autumn (Washington to John Fairfax, October 26, 1785, in Fitzpatrick, *Writings of Washington*, 28:297–300).

6. For Lafayette's request for the correspondence, see Lafayette to Washington, May 11; on George Augustine Washington's marriage, see Washington to Lafayette, July 25, note 10.

7. Washington had received a letter from Edmund Randolph, dated August 8, informing him of the meeting on August 20 and of the desire of a number of members that he accept the presidency of the company (DLC: George Washington Papers, Series 4). Despite his objections (Washington to Randolph, August 13, in Fitzpatrick, *Writings of Washington*, 28:219), he was elected to that post (Randolph to Washington, September 2, in DLC: George Washington Papers, Series 4).

To Thomas Jefferson

Vienna September the 4th 1785

My Dear Sir

This letter will Be delivered By a Private Courier of Mis. de Noaïlles who Has Been in My family, and who, I am Sure will take Proper Care of my dispatch. Since I Had the pleasure to See You, I Have Been At the prussian Court, and the prussian Camps with which I was much pleased and Now am at Vienna with an intention Soon to Return to Postdam where there will Be great deal of Maneuvring. The kind Reception I met with in Every part of My journey Has Given me the Means to Hear, and to Speack much, on the affairs of America. I find the Misrepresentations of Great Britain Have not Been fruitless. The strength of the Union, the powers of Congress, the dispositions of the people and the principles of trade are points Upon which I Have Had Many opportunities to Give the Lye to false assertions of News papers, and to Set to Rights the false ideas of Misinformed people. It is Useless to observe I wish the Good Measures Now in Contemplation May Be Soon Executed. But in the Mean while, I more than Ever wish we May, in the News papers Counter act the Uncandid Accounts that are Sometimes Given.

On the first day I Saw the king of Prussia, He Spoke with me on the present Situation of American affairs.[1] The Mquis. de Luchesiny His friend paid me a visit in the after Noon, where in I Introduced the Subject of the treaty of Commerce Betwen His prussian Majesty and the United States.[2] Since which, the king Has Some times at dinner put His questions to me, on the Ressources, the Union, and the future Existence of America—and I do not think they would Have Been So properly Answered By the Duke of York, and Lord Cornwallis who

A 1788 painting of Lafayette, quite likely depicting him in 1785 on his tour of Germany and Austria.

were two of the Guests.[3] I fancy I may Have Still More particular opportunities to know His opinions, and to introduce my ideas.

On the day Before Yesterday I arrived at Vienna, and last morning waïted on the Emperor.[4] The Misrepresentations about America, the good Measures that Had Been, and Were to Be taken, the Necessity to improve this moment, and Come in Early into liberal treaties, that would oppen the door to American Importations in order to pay for Austrian goods, Such were the Points to which I directed, and Some times forced the Conversation. It Was a great object with Him to know if Americans would Be their own Carriers. The Same day, in the Evening, Prince Kaunitz their prime Minister Very willingly Came in the Subject of American trade which I Brought about in a private Conference. That Carrying trade was again the topic. I advised Him to Send Consuls, to Settle partnerships in America, as no trade Could last But Was mixed and Reciprocal. I detaïlled out the objets of American Exportations, as I Had done to the Emperor. Why then Said Prince Kaunitz don't they Make advances to us. I answered advances Had Been made, And more in my opinion than were Necessary. But they Had not Been listened to in that time, and for the present that I Had Heard Some thing, as if an Answer was Expected from the Emperor. He Said the demand Had Been an Indirect one. At last I Concluded the Conversation with telling of Him that I know Nothing of particulars, But Had Heard Congress, the People, and their Ministers in Europe Express a desire to Be upon a very friendly footing with the Emperor. That as a friend, I advised Him to loose no time, and He knew Very well no treaty Could go on without Reciprocity. I therefore thought the first Measure was to oppen the italian ports to the Salt fish of America. From our Conversation I am apt to think He may order His ambassadors to talk with you or Mr. Adams, and I wished to write You what Had past Betwen us, Wherein I Spoke as a man, who Being ignorant of particulars, Could only offer an Humble advice to His Imperial Majesty. But upon the Whole I don't think You will Have a very great trade this Way.[5]

As I think these Hints may Be agreable to our friend M. Adams, I Beg You will Send the letter By a Safe Hand as opportunities often offer. There is Such a distance Betwen Congress and myself that I will leave to You to trouble them with the News of My German tour.[6] Adieu, My dear Sir, my Compliments to Humphreys, M. Short and our other friends in Paris.[7] Most Respectfully and affectionately Yours

LAFAYETTE

ALS (DNA: RG 360, PCC 156, pp. 432–36).
1. At the time, the Prussian ambassador to The Hague was awaiting the text of the

Th:Jefferson begs the Marquis de la Fayette's acceptance
of a copy of these Notes. the circumstances under which they
were written, & the talents of the writer, will account for their
errors and defects. the original was sent to Monsr. de Mar-
-bois in December 1781. the desire of a friend to possess some
of the details they contain occasioned him to revise them
in the subsequent winter. the vices however of their original
composition were such as to forbid material amendment.
he now has a few copies printed with a design of offering
them to some of his friends, and to some estimable cha-
-racters beyond that line. a copy is presented to the
Marquis de la Fayette whose services to the American
Union in general, & to that member of it particularly
which is the subject of these Notes, & in that precise
point of time too to which they relate, entitle him to
this offering. to these considerations the writer
hopes he may be permitted to add his own perso-
-nal friendship & esteem for the Marquis.   Un -
-willing to expose these sheets to the public eye
the writer begs the favor of the Marquis to put
them into the hands of no person. on whose care
and fidelity he cannot rely to guard them against
publication.

Jefferson's note to Lafayette in a copy of his *Notes on the State of Virginia.*

proposed Prussian-American treaty of amity and commerce. He signed it on September 10. For the text of the treaty, see *JCC*, 30:269–84.

2. The Marquis Girolamo de Lucchesini was chamberlain of Frederick the Great.

3. The Duke of York and Lord Cornwallis were guests of Frederick at the August army manuevers in Silesia (Cornwallis to Ross, September 9, 1785, in Charles Ross, ed., *Correspondence of Charles, First Marquis Cornwallis*, 3 vols. [London, 1859], 1:194–95). Cornwallis' special mission for the British government was to sound out Prussian intentions toward Britain and France.

4. On September 3 the French ambassador to the Austrian court and Adrienne's uncle, the Marquis de Noailles, presented Lafayette and Gouvion to Emperor Joseph II. In the hour-long conversation that ensued, Joseph asked about the strength of the American confederation, Congress, American trade, and Washington.

5. Jefferson sent a copy of this letter to Adams on September 24, adding: "In the present unsettled state of American commerce, I had as lieve avoid all further treaties except with American powers. If Count Merci therefore does not propose the subject to me, I shall not to him, nor do more than decency requires if he does propose it" (Boyd, *Jefferson Papers*, 8:544).

6. Jefferson sent a copy of the letter to Jay on October 11 (DNA: RG 360, PCC 87, vol. 1, pp. 129–32).

7. David Humphrey was secretary of the legation; William Short was shortly thereafter named Jefferson's secretary.

To [Thomas Boylston]

Paris october the 4th 1785 [November 4?]

Dear Sir

Agreable to Appointement I Have Seen M. Tourtille Sangrain this Morning, and at the Same time I acquainted Him a friend of Mine was every Hour expecting a Ship load of Sperma Coeti oil Bound to the Havre de grace. I told Him He would Most Particularly oblige me to Give my friend the preference in His purchases. I added that the oil was of the Best kind, and fitted for the french taste, and told Him He must Immediately offer the Highest price, Because I knew my friend Had other Means advantageously to dispose of His Cargoe. Inclosed you will find the proposals He thought proper to Make, which I Requested Him to write down and Sign.[1] You will find that He Engages for about 300,000p. french Weight, at the price of fifty five french livres for Each Hundred of Weight, provided the oil, Upon His examination, Appears to Him Well Qualified. M. Sangrain tells me You will not find So good a Price elsewhere, But I would advise You to Make further Enquiries. In the Mean while Your Captain or Yourself Might Come to town With a Sample of the oil, and I will introduce You to M. Tourtille Sangrain whom we may then perhaps prevail upon to Contract for a greater Quantity, and to Any person that May promote Your Purposes.

The Entrance of foreign oil is permitted. But there are duties which M. Sangrain Says to Amount to a Sixth or fifth part of the Valüe, He Believes: as to Myself I Cannot tell, But those duties I wanted the American Vessels to Be exempt of, and that Was the Reason which Made me think of the Bargain of which You Have Heard. Hoping that a political Care of their own Manufactures would Engage this Ministry to take of all duties for one Envoice, and So By little and little that I Could obtain the end for which My efforts Had Hitherto Been fruitless. The oil Business is a Most favorite object to My Heart, Because I throughly know How far it is essential to the Very Subsistence of Many families in New England.

Any thing that depends Upon me, My dear Sir, You May entirely Command. You are an American, a Bostonian, and the National object you pursüe is Next to My Heart. So that I will Be Most Happy in Every opportunity to Convince You of the Regard I Have the Honour to Be with Your obedient Humble Servant

LAFAYETTE

How far the inclosed propositions are advantageous I am not in Any manner able to determine.

ALS (MWA).

1. Enclosure not found. Boylston was seeking a monopoly on American whale oil sales in France (Boyd, *Jefferson Papers*, 9:29–31). His proposal called for the removal of all duties on it, which proved unacceptable to the French government. Jefferson wrote to John Adams on December 10 that he had told Lafayette that he opposed "wasting our efforts on individual applications, we had better take it up on general ground, and whatever could be obtained, let it be common to all. He concurred with me" (ibid., pp. 88–89).

To the Comte de Vergennes[T]

[Fontainebleau] 16 November 1785

You were good enough, Monsieur le Comte, to tell me that Messrs. the Farmers General had replied to Mr. Jefferson's letter.[1] If it were possible for us to have that reply, perhaps Mr. Jefferson, who has a thorough knowledge of everything about tobacco, could help demonstrate that certain calculations are inaccurate. These gentlemen are so redoubtable, despite their disinterestedness, that we cannot have too many defenses against them.

We have been told, Monsieur le Comte, that the lease with the Farms is going to be renewed.[2] If this rumor is well founded, I would dare propose that the renewal of the one for tobacco, since there is still time, were just delayed longer than the others, so the proposed methods can be examined.

Pardon my importuning you, Monsier de Comte, but I wanted to communicate my two ideas to you, because you receive them kindly, and besides I am happy with every opportunity to present you the homage of my very tender and respectful attachment.

LAFAYETTE

ALS (AAE: Correspondance politique, Etats-Unis, vol. 30, fol. 412), endorsed: "negatively answered by word of mouth";[T] translation.

1. Vergennes was chairman of the council that handled the Farmers General's leases. Jefferson had written to him on August 15, proposing the suppression of the tobacco monopoly (Boyd, *Jefferson Papers,* 8:385–89). Calonne—not the Farmers General—replied on October 19 that Jefferson's criticisms were "absolutely inexact"[T] (AAE: Correspondance politique, Etats-Unis, vol. 30, fols. 359–60).

2. By royal decree of 1721, the king held the exclusive right to import and sell tobacco; it was this right that the Farmers General leased. Its 1780 lease in the name of Nicolas Salzard was not scheduled to expire until late 1786.

To Rabaut de Saint-Etienne[T]

[Paris] 20 November 1785

It is with much gratitude, Monsieur, that I received the letter with which you honored me,[1] and I value your friendship too sincerely not to be very touched by all the proofs you are kind enough to give me of it. Since I had the honor of seeing you, I have made a grand tour of Germany. A large part of these regions, including the Prussian states, flourish because of our stupidities a century ago, stupidities even more barbarous than they are impolitic, which cannot be deplored enough.[2] During my trip I found vast scope for admiration and instruction, and I divided my time between the two, to try to make this excursion militarily useful to me. Although less a soldier, thank God, than a citizen, I have a keen taste for that profession, and for all the means of improving myself in it. Your interest in me, Monsieur, occasioned this very abridged account of my trip. We could just as well talk about trade, because the United States, in rejecting British ships and cargoes, seems constantly to invite ours, and you will be surprised to learn that the Farmers General in their patriotic wisdom are sending their money to England to buy products within their purview, which because of the extraordinary duties levied in America on every British ship, they could sell cheaper in our ports, and pay in manufactured goods.[3] To continue talking about trade, I shall tell you that I have not stopped speaking of it with all the king's ministers who are favorably inclined. But in this country one fears the things that have a decided effect, one seeks to put them off, and affairs are delayed when they branch off into different departments. I do not doubt, however, that if we follow through, we shall have much better terms of trade than exist now.

The lawsuit of which you told me attracts far less attention, I believe, than Cardinal de Rohan's. But with patience and care, just causes win; I have recommended it to other judges also, and shall always be very happy to contribute to what may be agreeable to you.[4]

Since I hunt every summer, I would be sorry if your trip to Paris were deferred beyond April; but since between now and then we can, I hope, find some means of trade with the United States that is useful to the town of Nimes, I shall take the liberty of writing you in the course of the next month, or the beginning of next year. Meanwhile, please accept the assurance that an acquaintance as precious as yours brings me great pleasure, and it is with all my heart that I add the expression of attachment with which I have the honor to be, Monsieur, your very humble and obedient servant.

LAFAYETTE

ALS (BMN), translated.

1. Letter not found.

2. "Our stupidities a century ago": Lafayette is referring to the Revocation of the Edict of Nantes in 1685, which caused many French Huguenots to emigrate. The Prussian kings welcomed them for the habits and skills they brought with them. Rabaut was a prominent Huguenot; the reference would not be lost on him.

3. This is a reference to the Farmers General's acceptance of Sir Robert Herries's June 16, 1785, offer to sell them 40,000 hogsheads of tobacco.

4. A reference to Lafayette's efforts to liberalize the treatment of Protestants at a time when Cardinal de Rohan's involvement in the Affair of the Queen's Necklace was occupying public attention. Rohan, *grand aumonier* of France, stood accused of lèse majesté before the Parlement of Paris. Though Rohan was eventually found innocent, Louis XVI felt obliged to banish him from the realm.

To [Thomas Boylston]

Paris November the 20th 1785

Dear Sir

Inclosed you will find the Extract of a letter from the Contrôleur General, whereby You Will find we Have obtained a diminution of duties Upon American whale oil.[1] Altho' it is Not yet Come down to My Wishes, for what I fervently wish is a total abolition of those duties, yet is it An Advantage Already Gained, and May Be a ground work to get more.

While I Rejoice at a General diminution of duties, I Can't Help lamenting You are only partially Exempted.[2] I Hope this difference May Some what Ballance Your accounts, But, Notwistanding the opposition of farmers generals, with whom, of Course, I am Upon Bad terms, I am Going once More to try Entirely to Clear You, if possible, of all duties for that Ship which is Arrived.[3]

M. Jefferson and Myself Having joined in this affair, it is the Same whether You write to Him or to me, But we wish to know How far the oil trade May Be Benefited By this Partial exemption which is Mentionned in the Extract. I Have the Honour to Be Very Sincerely Sir Your obedient Humble Servant

LAFAYETTE

ALS (ViHi).

1. On November 17 Calonne had written to Lafayette that he had requested the king's permission to order the Farmers General to charge the same low duty on American fish oils as was being charged the Hanseatic towns (DLC: Papers of Thomas Jefferson).

2. The duties decreased from twelve livres per barrel (520 French pounds) to seven livres, ten sous (ibid.).

3. Lafayette's effort to abolish the duty altogether failed. On November 30 Vergennes wrote to Jefferson that Boylston's cargo would be subject to the same duties as the Hanseatic towns (Boyd, *Jefferson Papers*, 9:72–73).

To Jeremiah Wadsworth

Paris december the 3d 1785

My dear Sir

As this letter Goes a Round about Way and By duplicates I shall only tell You that I am well, and Not long Ago Returned from a journey throughout Prussia the Austrian dominions and Several parts of the German Empire. There is Nothing New in this Part of the World Except our treaty of Alliance With Holland,[1] And the Begining of the trial of Cardinal de Rohan in this Strange Affair of Which No doubt You Have Heard.[2]

Inclosed You Will find an Extract of My letter to M. Breeck which I Have Requested Him to Have printed in the Boston Gazette for the information of the People.[3] In Case it does not Appear shortly after You Have Received this, I Beg You will Send it to Boston and in the Mean while Have it printed in the Hartfort and Providence Gazettes.[4] Inclosed I also Send a Small extract from the Amsterdam Gazette which I want to Have published as it Answers a Very foolish piece of Intelligence Maliciously Imputed to me in order it Might Have more Weight in the public opinion.[5]

I Have so much quarrelled With the farmers generals that We Now are Upon Very Hostile terms. But I think Some New Mode May Be adopted more Satisfactory Respecting what You Have once writen to me about—of this More, in My Next letter.

My fur Merchant, a Very Rich Man, Came to me the other day and I Advised Him to Apply to You and our friends for a large Envoice. He Sent me this Note[6] Requesting the prices may Be Set down By Each Article, and if He is pleased with them, He will the first Year Send orders for thousand guineas Worth, and the Year after that for four Hundred thousand livres. Be pleased to Communicate My whole letter to Mr. McHenry and Mr. Constable for whom this May Be an opportunity to Unite with You in a french Undertaking and Such furs as are on the Back parts of Virginia and Pennsylvania Might Come By Way of Baltimore.

Altho' our friend Knox Has Nothing to do with trade I Beg You will Read My letter to Him and Give Him My Compliments.[7] Adieu, my Respects to Your lady and family and Have the Honour to Be Yours

LAFAYETTE

ALS (Ct: Joseph Trumbull Collection). An LS copy in the same collection includes the postscript: "I think upon the whole I Had Better send you Breck's letter[s]."

1. France signed a treaty of alliance with the United Provinces at Fontainebleau on November 10, 1785.

2. See Lafayette to Rabaut de Saint-Etienne, November 20, note 4.

3. Enclosure not found.

4. Lafayette's letter to Breck on the reduction of fish-oil duties did not appear in either newspaper.

5. Extract not found.

6. Enclosed note not found.

7. Henry Knox had returned to private life in Boston after completing his service as commander in chief of the Continental army in June 1784.

To James McHenry

Paris december the 3d [1785]

Dear McHenry

This is Not Intended to Answer Your Several favours for which I am much obliged to You. I am only writing By duplicates on Mercantile Concerns.

Your letter Inclosing proposals for an Envoice I found on my Return from Germany.[1] I Sent it to M. [Mäsois][2] who Said He Was going to fix a french House of His own in Philadelphia. I am Going to try [Bergasse] and Some others.[3]

Not knowing Where You are, I Have Requested Clel. Wadsworth to Communicate to You Several papers I Send Him which I also Recommend to You.[4] But the Intelligence Respecting the fish oil I want only to Have in the New England Papers, as it Must Be Given to Congress By Mr. Jefferson.[5] No Better Minister Could Be Sent to France. He is Every thing that is Good, Up Right, Enlightened, and Clever, and is Respected and Beloved By Every one that knows Him.

General Greene Will By this opportunity Have letters from me Whereby a great chance is Given Him to Contract with France for timber on a large Scale. I advise Him to form a Compagny in the Several States for the Sale of His Exportations and Particularly point out Your House to Him. I think you Had Better write to Him on the Subject.[6]

In my letter to Wadworth there is an Article about furs. How far it may Concern You, I do not know. But told Him at all events to Communicate it.

I am glad to Hear Mr. Gardochy Behaves well. Could He not Mention this letter of Florida Blanca to me in the Winter 82 to 83 which you and I wanted to Have published?[7] Your affectionate friend

LAFAYETTE

My Respects to Mrs. McHenry.

ALS (DLC: James McHenry Papers).
1. Letter and enclosed proposals not found.
2. "Mäsois": unidentified.
3. Nicolas Bergasse, a friend of Lafayette, was already involved in commercial ventures with the Americans.
4. See Lafayette to Wadsworth, December 3.
5. Jefferson informed Jay of the reduction of fish-oil duties in an enclosure sent with his letter of January 2, 1786 (Boyd, *Jefferson Papers*, 9:140).
6. Lafayette wrote Greene on December 3 that he had met with the Marquis de Castries and "found Him better disposed to purchase His naval Stores in America than ever He Had Been." Lafayette suggested that Greene prepare a sample shipment (DLC: Nathanael Greene Papers).
7. Floridablanca to Lafayette, February 22, 1783.

From John Adams

Grosvenor Square Decr. 13. 1785.

Dear Sir.

I have received your favour of the 30th. Ulto. and thank you for the extract enclosed.[1] The Commerce of New England will follow their oil, whereever it may go and therefore I think it good Policy, in the Controller General to take of[f] the duty. But there is another object of Importance I mean the sperma Coeti Chandles. Will you be so good as to inform me whether these are prohibited in France? or what duties they are subject to on Importation? whither these duties can be taken off,? whether they are at all used or known in France? Whether they cannot be brought into fashion in private families, or even in Churches? They are certainly cheaper & more beautiful than wax, & emit a purer, brighter flame. Pot ash, too: I want to know, what quaintity of Pot ash & Pearl ash, is annually consumed in France? from what Country imported? in what it is paid for? whether in Cash, Bills or Goods? & at what Prices ordinarily? This is another article, by which France may draw to herself a great share of the Trade of New England. Our Merchants will be obliged to alienate their Commerce from this Country, and transfer it in a great measure to France. They are awkward and unskilful, at present, how to effect it, and every aid you can afford them will be gratefully acknowledged.

I hope that Mr. Boylston and Mr. Barrett, will be able to compleat a Contract, with Monsieur Tourtille De Sangrain for the Illumination of your Cities. Boylston's Capital will enable him to do what he pleases, but you may depend upon it, he will do nothing but what is profitable. No Man understands more intuitively, every thing relating to these subjects, and no man is more attached to his Interest. You sent your Letter by the post I suppose, in hopes it would be opened in the Post office and sent to Court to assist me a Little in my negotiation.[2] I have the Pleasure to inform you, that your intentions were probably fulfilled, for although they conceal their art with more care in the post offices here, than they think it necessary to make use of in Paris, yet I assure you there is not less Curiosity: And your Letter upon an attentive inspection may be plainly perceived to have been opened. I am glad of it, because altho' it will not assist me much, nor make any great impression I shall at least have the Pleasure to think we tease them a little. My best respects to Madam La fayette & Love to Anastasie & George. Yours

                                                                                    J.A.

LbC (MHi: Adams Papers).
1. Letter not found. The "extract" appears to have been from Calonne's November 17 letter; see Lafayette to [Thomas Boylston], November 20, 1785, note 1.
2. Adams was attempting at this time to negotiate a trade treaty with Great Britain.

From John Adams

Grosvenor Square Decr. 20th. 1785.

Dear Sir.

I am very happy to learn by your favour of the 12th. that Mr. Barrett, is in a fair way to make a Contract between the Merchants in Boston and Messrs. Le[Couteux] '& the first Houses in yᵉ french sea ports. Where by a Channell may be opened for an Exchange of oil & Chandles for french Merchandizes.[1] This Plan, I am very sure may be matured into something very agreable & equally profitable for both Countries, & I wish it all possible success.

It is unlucky that Mr. Boylstone, did not sell his Cargo to Mr. De Sangrain: because as this Gentleman has the Contract for enlightening the Cities, he would have had an opportunity of Making experiments with this kind of oil and of satisfying himself and others that it may be used in his Lamps as cheap as the olive oil, neetsfoot oil, and whatever other Ingredients are used in the Composition of that which he now uses. I suppose Boylstone will carry his Cargo to Ireland where the Duties are lower than in England. He is a Person of a peculiar Temper & Character and alltho' intelligent and rich enough to conduct the Business as well as any Man, yet from his age, his ignorance of the Language and his impatience he is less likely to succeed.

Mr. Barrett, will be more agreable to the Merchants in Boston & his Experience in Trade, will enable him to judge of the Kinds & qualities of Goods which are suitable to the American Markett. But he should settle at Paris, and Correspond with the sea Ports, at least this appears to me the best Plan.

The Commerce between New & old England must cease, if a new Plan is not adopted, But whether any change of system takes Place or not, it is very Certain, that a great share of that Trade may be had by France if she will receive oil in Payment to facilitate the Business. I wish the Duty could be all taken off, for a hundred or an hundred and fifty Guineas upon one hundred ton of oil, is a considerable abatement of Profit to the Poor whaleman who find it hard enough to live by the Business in its best Condition.

The great point to be carried, is to penetrate Mr. De Sangrain to use, the white sperma Coeti Oil, in his Lamps, and to get the private families to burn sperma Coeti Chandles in their Houses. This once accomplished, the Commerce will be established of Course. Mr. Houdon is here, & I have introduced him to a sight of all that is Curious in the arts here, He has made his models in Plaister of the General & is impatient to be at Work.[2] I am

J.A.

LbC (MHi: Adams Papers).
1. Letter not found. Nathaniel Barrett, representing a number of Boston merchants, had arrived in Paris in December 1785 for further negotiations with Tourtille de Sangrain on his offer to purchase whale oil. On December 10, Barrett wrote to Adams:
I am happy in acquainting you that I have before me, a prospect of effecting something which may materially promote the Trade of our Country thro' the Exertions of the Marquis de lafayette in Conjunction with Mr. Jefferson to the kind Attention & politeness of both whom, I am under the highest Obligations. [MHi: Adams Papers]
2. Houdon carried the mold of Washington's face back with him, leaving the rest to be returned with his assistants (Jefferson to Washington, January 4, 1786, in Boyd, *Jefferson Papers*, 9:150).

To [the Marquis de Castries][T]

Paris 29 December 1785
Your Grace,
   I received the letter of the 23rd of this month with which you honored me, and find myself especially happy with the orders it contains, as I have long been convinced of the excellence of American naval stores and that we can pay our allies in merchandise for reliable supplies, instead of the precarious supplies for which we pay in cash to our rivals.[1]
   You will find here, your Grace, the request I made to General Greene for a thousand cubic feet of live oak in assorted curves, and a few pieces of cedarwood, which possession of Cumberland Island in Georgia enables him to furnish. I am sending this letter in quadruplicate, and the original enclosed here can remain filed in the Bureaus.[2]
   As for the tar and hemp, these two articles could be obtained from the Chesapeake Bay area. North Carolina is the state richest in tar; it is easily transported to Norfolk and Portsmouth, at the entrance to the Bay. Hemp is a bit rare, but we should, I think, encourage its cultivation at the expense of that of the Russians, and the hinterlands of Virginia would supply a lot that will be sent down the Potomac. I know of a good firm in Baltimore, one of whose heads was my aide de camp, and I would like to have a letter authorizing the *McHenry firm in Baltimore* to trade at Toulon or Rochefort for a fixed amount in tar and hemp. The arrangement would be all the better since I asked for the one in Marseilles; we could also have from La Rochelle a cargo of

The Marquis de Castries, French marine minister, to whom Lafayette directed many proposals on French policy toward the United States.

French merchandise whose shipment would ensure partial payment. If the experiment succeeds, a trade shuttle would thus be established.

I imagine the American merchants who supply the king can draw letters of exchange on him when they send the invoice, and the letter of insurance, and announce the ship's departure as they do with Messieurs Le Coulteux and probably with other trading houses.

I have the honor to be with respect, Your Grace, your very humble and obedient servant.

LAFAYETTE

ALS (CtY: Benjamin Franklin Collection), translated.

1. The Marquis de Castries wrote to Lafayette on December 23, 1785, to commend his useful observations on the value of American goods to the French naval service and to urge him to have his American mercantile friends send the following to Brest: a thousand cubic feet of live oak in assorted curves, several barrels of tar, a few bales of hemp, and a few pieces of cedarwood (ANL: Marine B^2, 429, pièce 106).

2. On December 29 Lafayette wrote to Nathanael Greene that he had been requested by the French government to obtain supplies for an "Experiment, and I very much wish the quality and cheapness of the Envoice may be Such as to encourage a Bargain with you upon a very Large scale" (CtY: Benjamin Franklin Collection).

APPENDIX I

FRENCH TEXTS

For the provenance and annotation of these texts, the reader should refer to the translated documents.

From the Comte de Vergennes

Versailles le 23 janvier 1782

Si j'avois Eu, Monsieur Le Marquis, un moment a moi j'aurois ete vous embrassér et vous faire toutes mes felicitations. Je devois vous Les adressér en Amerique, vous Les trouveres consignées dans La Lettre cijointe qui porte La date du 1er. Xbre. et qui n'est pas partie faute d'occasions. Elle peut donnér matiere a quelques reflexions et j'ai grand besoin d'en faire avec vous, Monsieur le marquis. Je ne suis pas merveilleusement Content du pays que vous quittés; je le trouve peu actif et tres Exigeant. Je vous prie de me procurér le plustot possible L'occasion de vous entretenir, j'ai besoin de vos Lumieres pour fixér mes idées. Je me flatte que l'intervalle des mers n'a point alteré Les sentiments dont vous m'avés promis La Continuation. Les miens pour vous ne peuvent avoir de terme que Celui de mon Existence. C'est sur Cette baze que pose Le tendre et sincere attachement avec Lequel j'ai l'honneur d'etre, Monsier Le Marquis, Votre tres humble et tres obeissant serviteur.

DE VERGENNES

Tous Les paquets d'Amerique m'ont ete rendus.

To the Comte de Vergennes

Paris Ce 20 Mars 1782

Vous m'avés prié l'autre jour, Monsieur le Comte, de vous envoïer par ecrit un article de mes lettres d'Espagne; d'après la Bonté du Congrès, en mandant à

tous ses Ministres de Correspondre avec moi, je me trouve instruit des offres
Americaines, et de la Repugnance des espagnols pour traiter Avec eux;
peutêtre, il sera politique de Cacher ce Sentiment, mais il Seroit trop Injuste
d'attribuër les obstacles à Ceux qui S'efforçent de Les lever.

Le 2 juïllet 1781 Les Ministres Apprirent de Mr. Jay que le Congrès Instruit
de L'objection au traité avoit Resolu de Ceder sur le point en litige; Ce point
Regardoit la Navigation du Mississipi, et Mr. Jay pria qu'on Nommat une
personne pour Regler avec lui les articles.

Le 21 juïllet le Ministre manda qu'il presenteroit la lettre à Sa Majesté.

Le 19 Septembre Le Ministre Annonça qu'il *proposeroit* au Roy la Nomination
d'une personne chargée de Conferer; au'il presenteroit au Roy Une lettre de
M. Morris au Sujet des Secours Sur lesquels il lui donna des esperances, enfin le
Ministre demanda les propositions qui devoïent devenir la Baze du traité.

Le 22 Septembre Les propositions furent Envoyées.

Le 27 Septembre une lettre du Ministre annonçant qu'on alloit Nommer une
personne pour Conférer, et ajoutant que les instructions Seroïent donnees
avant que le Cour partit pour l'Escurial.

Le 5 octobre Comme la Cour alloit partir, Mr. Jay Ecrivit Au Ministre, et lui
Manda qu'il attendroit ses ordres à l'Escurial. Celui-ci Repondit qu'il ecriroit à
l'instant ou il pourroit dire sur l'affaire quelque chose de positif.

Le 10 decembre Le Ministre Annonça La Nomination de Don Bernardo del
Campo dont les Instructions Seroïent prêtes dans Huit ou dix jours.

Le 27 decembre Mr. del Campo s'excusa de ne pas entrer en Matiere sur ce
que ses Instructions n'etoïent pas faites, elles n'etoient pas Commencées, et il ne
savoit quand elles le seroïent; Ce Mr. del Campo est le premier Secretaire du
ministre. Le premier fevrier 1782 Mr. del Campo a Repeté l'excuse du 27
decembre. Le 16 fevrier même excuse.

Quand Mr. Jay S'adresse au Ministre il est tantôt affairé et tantôt Malade, et
Renvoïe Mr. Jay à Don Bernardo del Campo. Et Don Bernardo del Campo
n'ayant pas Receu d'instructions ne peut que promettre d'en parler au
Ministre.

Ce defaut de Santé, defaut de tems, ou defaut d'instructions ont fait jusqu'ici
Negliger tous les Memoires qu'a presenté le Ministre Americain.

Je ne me permets pas, Monsieur le Comte, de juger ici la politique d'une cour
que tant de Motifs me Rendent Respectable; mais Les Americains desirent avec
Raison que les detaïls de leur Conduite ne Soïent pas inconnus au Roy, et que
celui dont les traités ont été fondés Sur la generosité et la franchise, ne puisse
douter que dans leur Negotiation avec l'Espagne ses alliés Americains ne manquent ni de Bonne foi ni de Bonne Volonté.

D'après les esperances du 19 Septembre on avoit Imaginé que les Secours de
l'Espagne passeroïent la Modique somme que l'Amerique en a Receüe; mais un
Reste de lettres de change, montant à 25,000 pounds Sterl. auroit été protesté,
si M. Franklin n'eut pas fait usage de l'argeant dont il dispose, et je vois,
Monsieur le Comte, que les droits de la France à la gloire de cette Revolution, et
à la Reconnoissance des americains ne pourront etre justement partagés par
aucune puissance de l'Europe.

Les depèches de Mr. de la Vauguion vous apprenent Surement ou en sont les affaires d'Amerique en Hollande; par ce que me mande Mr. Adams, il paroït qu'elles y prennent une tournure Avantageuse. Agreés, je Vous prie, Monsieur le Comte, l'Homage de l'attachement Respectueux avec lequel j'ai l'Honneur d'etre Votre très Humble et obeïssant Serviteur

LAFAYETTE

To the Comte de Vergennes

[20 mars 1782]

Vous etiés occupé, Monsieur le Comte, et je n'ai pas Voulu vous parlé d'affaires; Mr. Franklin m'a cependant fait part d'une idée qu'il m'a prié de Vous Communiquer.

Les Ministres Anglais, dit-il, S'exagerent les obstacles que la France Apporteroït à la paix; Mr. Forsh, creature de Lord North, ne leur Rendra pas Comte de Sa Mission; une lettre particuliere de Mr. Franklin à un ami, qui l'est aussi des *Nouveaux* ministres, pourrait Sans Inconvenient leur faire Connoitre Votre Reponse.

L.F.

To Robert R. Livingston

[March 30, 1782]

Quant à l'Espagne, j'ai une lettre de M. Jay dont les négociations n'avancent pas, et c'est la faute des Espagnols. Après en avoir conféré avec le Dr. Franklin, j'ai remis aux ministres de France un mémoire où je représentais la conduite de la Cour de Madrid sous le point de vue qui m'a paru le mieux démontrer leur tort. Je finissais par leur dire combien il serait injuste d'accuser les Américains de délais qu'on ne doit attribuer qu'à la lenteur espagnole. Ce gouvernement-ci me paraît convaincu de nos difficultés de traiter avec la Cour de Madrid. Le Dr. Franklin s'est chargé de quelques lettres de change tirées sur l'Espagne. Vous apprendrez par M. le Chevalier de la Luzerne, qu'un M. Forth est venu d'Angleterre à Paris. Il a parlé à M. le Comte de Vergennes, lui a fait sentir qu'on pourrait faire des avantages à la France. La réponse de M. le Comte de Vergennes a été comme il a déclaré, que la France ne traiterait jamais sans ses alliés. M. Forth est retourné à Londres. Cela prouve que l'indépendance est pour eux le seul obstacle à la paix; ils tâcheront probablement de faire à l'Amérique des propositions trompeuses, et je le désire pour que le Congrès ait une nouvelle occasion de leur parler avec fermeté et générosité. J'ai été bien satisfait de la réponse de M. le Comte de Vergennes. Que tout ceci soit secret jusqu'à ce que M. le Chevalier de la Luzerne vous en parle. Dites, je vous prie, à M. Morris qu'il ne m'a pas été possible jusqu'ici de faire ajouter aux millions de livres de

cette année, mais je veille à l'occasion d'avoir une augmentation, et je ne la
laisserai pas échapper. J'ai écrit à M. Morris que je ne crois pas entièrement
remplir la somme désirée. Tous les moyens d'amener les opérations vers le
continent, et d'avoir un peu plus d'argent, les occasions de servir notre cause
dans le cas où l'Anglois voudrait tout de bon traiter, seront saisi par moi avec le
zèle patriotique qui m'attache aux États-Unis. Dans la situation des choses, je
crois devoir rester encore quelque temps ici, et je crois que le Congrès ap-
rouvera ma conduite.

Les dispositions du Roi de France, du ministère de France et de la nation
française, sont telles que nous pouvons le désirer. J'en parle sans prévention; la
France est la seule vraie amie sur qui l'Amérique doive compter en Europe. La
situation des affaires est si incertaine, qu'il nous faut plus que jamais faire des
efforts. Une bonne armée en Amérique amenera la paix plus qu'on ne peut
l'imaginer. La minorité n'est pas plus notre amie que la majorité. Le Roi d'Angleterre est plus irrité qu'humilié; il faut donc bien le convaincre de l'impossibilité de nous conquérir. Si cette compagne est vigoreuse, elle sera certainement la dernière.

LAFAYETTE

Proposals for the French Campaign in North America

Paris ce 18 Avril 1782

Le plan des Ennemis est Si peu Connu, Le Notre Depend tellement de Nos
Alliés, qu'il est pour L'instant Impossible d'arrêter un projet de Campagne.
Nos operations presentes, Surtout dans les Antilles, Sont Soumises à des Cir-
comstances encore Incertaines; Mais il est des points politiques Sur lesquels on
peut Se fixer, il est des dispositions Militaires qu'on fera Surement et qui
Suivant Celles des Ennemis Se prèteront Aisement Aux Circomstances.

Envoïé par L'Amerique pour Representer Sa Situation, par Le Gal. Washington pour determiner un plan de Cooperation, je joins à ces titres celui de
francais qui Rapporte tout à l'interest de Sa patrie, et celui d'Homme Honoré
de Votre Confiance qui presente librement Ses opinions particulieres.

Les Americains Sont las de la guerre, et le peuple Soupire après la fin de Ses
Souffrances; Mais les plus tentantes propositions, faites par des Ministres Autrefois Cheris et toujours Reverés, N'obtiendront Rien de Contraire aux termes
du traité ni Même Aux devoirs de la Reconnoissance. Dans Cette Circomstance
Cependant, je Conseïlle de ne Rien Retrancher Sur les Secours demandés; ils
doivent etre les derniers et Couronneront tous les Autres. Il faudroit Au Moins
fournir les Effets dont Mr. Moriss Envoïe L'etat et qui Se Montent à une
Somme peu Considerable.

L'evacuation de Newyork, Celle de Charlestown Sont Encore problemati-
ques; dans les deux Cas il faut, ou prendre des ports qui donnent pied Aux
Anglais, ou prendre des troupes qu'ils croïent devoir poster aïlleurs; Mais il est
Surtout Necessaire que pendant l'Hivernage La flotte Alliée Soit dans La
Chesapeake. Toute Operation des Antilles aura Reussi ou Manqué; Le Repos

et La Santé des Equipages, les Approvisionements des flottes ne se trouveront que sur les Côtes des Etats Unis; Si les Ennemis ne Retirent pas Leurs troupes, il est Militairement et politiquement utile d'operer offensivement; S'ils les Retirent on doit ou tâcher de les Intercepter, ou Escorter Celles de Mr. de Rochambeau. Ce Mouvement etant donc Necessaire, Même à La Continuation de la Guerre des Isles, je puis Sans Inconvenient Assurer Le Gal. Washington, que La Flotte Alliée, pendant L'Hivernage, doit positivement Se Rendre a l'Amerique Septentrionale.

Cette Baze une fois donnée, le choix d'operations doit etre laissé au General; Newyork et Charlestown peuvent Seuls Occuper un tel Armenent; Les Autres points Sont peu importants, ou Bien par leur distance ils detournent la flotte des grands objets de son Attention.

En Examinant les Moyens d'operer, on a Reconnu la Necessité d'Augmenter La division française; c'est un point Convenu dans le Commité, Sur lequèl il est inutile de Repeter; le changement de Ministere et de Mesures a produit des Speculations Nouvelles; en Voici une qui pour la Suite me paroit devoir etre Interessants.

Plus la paix Approche, plus Nous en devons Maitriser Les points principaux; l'isle et le Banc de Terreneuve en est un important; ôter sa clef aux ennemis, ou la posseder avant Les Negotiations, Nous Assure un Grand Avantage.

Occupée d'autres objets, Veillée, et suivie par les Ennemis La flotte alliée ne peut faire cette Expedition ni en detaïl ni en totalité; elle prendroit Sa Superiorité ou son tems, et c'est partant de Brest, point assés Rapproché, qu'on peut Esperer de Surprendre Terre Neuve.

Si dans le Courant de May l'on ne tente Rien dans la Manche, les obstacles Vont en Augmentant, et l'on Renonce à ce genre d'operations; la plus Prochaine Sera donc d'envoyer pour l'Automne et des Vaisseux et des troupes aux Mers d'Amerique.

Trois Mille Hommes et quelques Vaisseaux de guerre qui en Recevroïent une partie, quitteroient Brest vers la fin de May, et seroïent à Terreneuve dans Le Courant de juïllet; Cette Expedition et celle de Penobscot ne passeroient pas la fin d'Aoust; en partant plutôt, en etant favorisés, en m'allant pas à Penobscot, on Seroit Retenu Bien Moins longtems; on se joindroit ensuite à Mr. de Grasse, comme Mr. de Barras le fit, avec cette difference, cependant, que les Ennemis ne l'y attendroïent pas; alors, si l'on n'opere pas dans le Continent, toutes les forces francaises Se porteront Aux Antilles.

L'evacuation des postes Anglais peut etre prematurée; la flotte alliée dans Ce Cas, ne S'occupera que de la flotte et de l'armée ennemies; ce n'est plus Au Continent, c'est Aux isles Même que les forces de Terreneuve Opereront leur jonction.

Vaut-il Mieux detruire ou Conserver les forts de Terreneuve? Est il à propos d'avoir une Cooperation Americaine? Penobscot ne peut il pas se prendre par un Corps Americain sous la protection et direction des Generaux de Terreneuve? L'expediton une fois Resolüe, il Seroit facile d'Arranger Ces Detaïls.

Au defaut de Ces operations, Le Gal. Washington se portera Sur le Canada; la foiblesse des Ennemis, la disposition du peuple, et les efforts de la Nouvelle Anglettere et de L'etat de Newyork Nous donnent Grande Esperance de Succès.

En S'occupant cependant de Terreneuve et Penobscot, et de preparatifs Contre Newyork ou Charlestown. l'on pourroit alors en Cas d'evacuation detourner les projets du Canada sur le Detroit, Niagara et Autres postes des derrieres qui pousseroïent Loin la fin de la Campagne. Le Second point de Discussion, Celui des limites, Se trouveroit detruit pas le fait, et ces Nouvelles Arrivant à peu pres avec Celles de L'Inde, avec celles des Antilles, tout Se trouveroit prêt a la fin de l'Hiver pour une Pacification Generale.

LAFAYETTE

P.S. Une partie de Nos dispositions etant Generale et preliminaire, il est de toute Importance qu'elles Soïent Sur le champ Communiquées au Gal. Washington, et c'est le Seul Moyen de trouver dans tous les Cas les preparatifs Necessaires.

Minutes of the Assembly of June 24, 1872, of the Worthy Lodge of Saint John of Scotland of the Social Contract[E]

24 Juin [1782]
A l'Orient de Paris

L'an de la V[rai] L[umière] 5782 le 24e jour du 4e mois la R[espactable] L[oge] de Saint-Jean d'Ecosse du Contrat Social, Mère Loge du Rite écossais en France, duement convoquée et régulièrement assemblée sous les points géométriques connus des seuls enfants de la Lumière Le F[rère] de Rouillé, v[énem]ble, éclairant, et les ff. de Chevey et Guibert, en absence des deux surveillants, inspectant les colonnes du midy et du nord, les travaux ont été ouverts en la manière accoutumée, lecture faite de la dernière planche tracée la R.L. y a applaudi Maçonniquement. . . .

Un f. M[ai]tre des Cérémonies ayant annoncé que le f. de La Fayette était dans le porche et demandait l'entrée du temple, le Vble ayant envoyé pour recevoir ce cf. plusieurs chevaliers écossais précédé de deux Maîtres de cérémonies. La R[especta]ble Loge, en recevant le fr. de La Fayette avec des honneurs qui ne sont ordinairement rendus qu'à des Maçons possédant les plus hauts grades, a voulu lui donner une Marque sensible du cas qu'elle fait de ses talents Militaires et dont l'exemple est fait pour former des héros.

Le fr. de Lafayette ayant été placé à l'Orient sans tirer de consequence La Rble applaudit par les signes et acclamations ordinaires et après qu'il a eu répondu en la manière accoutumée aux honneurs qu'il venait de recevoir, il s'est rendu au pied du trosne où il a prêté serment en qualité d'affilié de suivre à l'avenir les regts que suit et suivra la R.L.

Le Fr. Gauthier, chargé par la R[espectable] M[ère] L[oge] de tracer une planche qui portât tous les travaux qu'Elle a fait depuis l'envoi de son dernier tableau à toutes les Loges regulières, a fait part à la R.M.L. du travail qu'il avait fait et qui a été approuvé et applaudi en la manière ordinaire. La R.M.L. a arrêté qu'il serait imprimé ainsi que le tableau de ses officiers et des membres qu'Elle a reçus et affilier depuis led. Envoi; et que le tout serait envoyé due-

ment signé, timbré et scellé à toutes les Loges régulières, chargeant son secré-
taire général de La Signer par mandement de la R.M.L. et de tenir la main à
l'exécution de la présente Délibération.

Le cf. de La Fayette, obligé de Couvrir les travaux par Ses occupations civiles,
ayant demandé au Vble la permission de Se retirer, le Vble l'a fait reconduire
avec les mêmes honneurs qu'à Son introduction dans le temple. . . .

From the Comte de Ségur

A Rochefort ce 7 juillet 1782

J'ai reçu mon cher La Fayette ton aimable lettre, elle m'a infiniment touché,
je t'aime à la folie et je ne me console pas de ne point voyager avec toi. Tu vas
avoir un rôle bien honorable, et bien délicat à jouer, il faudra concilier ensemble les deux caractères de français, et d'Américain. Ménager des intérêts opposés, combler la mesure de ta gloire en ajoutant l'olive, au laurier. Et agir
même contre ton penchant en aidant à terminer d'une manière durable l'horrible fléau auquel tu dois ta célébrité. Je suis bien fâché de ne pouvoir causer avec
toi librement dans l'instant où j'en aurais le plus d'envie. Mais les lettres ne sont
pas assex sûres, et je n'ai à te dire que des choses que je ne voudrais pas qu'on
lut. Je prévois que tu vas être plus que jamais révolté de l'orgueil Anglois, de la
sotte vanité Espagnole, de l'inconséquence française, et de l'ignorance despoti-
que, tu verras que le Cabinet donne autant d'impatiences qu'un Champ de
Bataille, et qu'on fait autant de sottises dans une négotiation que dans une
campagne. Tu verras surtout combien on sacrifie le fond aux formes, et tu
diras plus d'une fois, si le hazard ne m'avait pas fait un des premiers acteurs, je
ne resterais certainement pas au théatre. Mais plus tu trouveras d'obstacles,
plus tu auras de mérite. Comment ne viendrais tu pas à bout de tout ce que tu
veux, tu as du génie, et du bonheur. C'est avoir la moitié de plus que ce qu'il
faut pour être un grand homme. Adieu mon ami je compte partir après demain me consolant assez philosophiquement de faire duex mille lieues pour
rien, mais ne me consolant pas de repoint te trouver dans un pays que je
trouverai rempli de ton nom, et de tes faits. Je m'acquitterai de toutes tes
commissions, je ferai valoir le sacrifice patriotique que tu fais de troquer pour
un moment ton Epée contre une plume. Je te recommande d'aimer ma femme,
de Caresser mes enfans, de tenir ma place auprès de mon père, et de nous
rejoindre le plus tost que tu pourras soit pour sonner la charge, soit pour battre
la retraite adieu.

To the Comte de Vergennes

Paris ce 10 Septembre 1782

J'esperois avoir l'Honneur de Vous Voir Aujourd'huy, Monsieur le Comte,
et je devois de Concert avec M. Jay Vous parler sur les Scrupules qui Embaras-

sent Notre Negotiation; Nous Vous porterons les Instructions et les Resolutions du Congrès, et Votre Opinion Reglera La Reponse des plenipotentiaires; Mais Nos Extraits ne Sont pas prêts, et d'après ce que vous m'avés dit, je ne Vois pas d'inconvenient à Retarder d'un jour cette Consulation; C'est, je crois, demain, Monsieur le Comte, que M. Jay pourra se Rendre à Versaïlles, et dans tous les Cas j'aurai l'Honneur d'y diner avec Vous, et de Vous porter l'Homage du tendre et Respectueux Attachement avec lequel j'ai l'Honneur d'etre Votre très Humble et obeïssant Serviteur

LAFAYETTE

Ne prenés pas, je Vous prie, la peine de me Repondre.

To the Comte de Vergennes

Paris Ce 22 Novembre 1782

Lorsque je quittai L'Amerique, Monsieur Le Comte, je fus chargé de Representer ici sa Situation, et dans La Circomstance Critique ou elle se trouve, Le Congress me Recommande Particulierement de Vous Exposer ses Besoins Pecuniaires; C'est d'après Leur Congé, et Leurs Instructions que je Suis Venu ici, et lorsque Sans Leur Approbation, Sans un Rang declaré dans L'armée française, je Vais M'occuper d'operations dont Le Commencement Leur est etranger, je dois au moins M'acquitter de Leurs Commissions, et Surtout Reposer ma Conscience Sur L'opinion que dans Ce Moment delicat je prends la Liberté de Vous Soumettre.

Les depêches du Congrès Sont Arrivées, celles du Cher. de La Luzerne ne Le Sont pas Encore; on peut S'etre trompé dans ses Bureaux, Comme à Bord du Bâtiment Americain, et si ces Lettres Sont Retardées, il Seroit facheux de Se jetter dans des Lenteurs, et des Incertitudes; Vous Connoissés trop Bien L'Amerique, Monsieur le Comte, pour avoir Besoin d'etre eclairé par Cette derniere depêche; d'aïlleurs, j'ai trop Causé avec le Ministre du Roy Sur l'objet en question, pour ne pas prevoir qu'il Conseïllera Le Secours que l'on Croit Instant de demander.

Les papiers que M. Franklin A Confiés Contiennent au Moins des informations; c'est à Lui, qu'ils ont eté Adressés, et si Vous en Craignés L'exageration, je dois Ajouter que les Nouvelles particulieres, ma Connoissance intime du païs, et le jugement qu'il m'est aisé de former Sur Sa Situation Actuelle, tout enfin, Monsieur le Comte, se Reunit à me persuader la Necessité de Cette Assistance Pecuniaire.

En Considerant l'Amerique, Monsieur le Comte, il est Naturel de M'attacher au point de Vüe qui interesse un francais; c'est en cette qualité seule que j'Examine les dangers de L'influence Anglaise. Le peuple est Las de la guerre, mais à present il aime la France, et deteste L'Anglettere; un Secours Accordé dans Ce Moment est une operation d'autant plus utile qu'elle Met le Sceau à toutes les autres, qu'elle Releve le Courage, et ferme la Bouche aux Emissaires

Anglais qui Sans cesse Accusent la France de Vouloir Attiser Le feu Sans L'eteindre. Je ne M'arrête pas à ces Calomnies, Monsieur le Comte, et leur absurdité doit, j'espere, en garentir L'effet; mais il n'est pas moins inutile de S'arrêter au peu d'efforts pecuniaires du peuple Americain; Sous ce point de Vüe, je L'avoüe, ils Sont Extremement Blamables; on peut dire qu'il y a peu d'Argeant dans Le païs, et je puis affirmer que les Anglais en ont moins laissé qu'on ne Croït, encore Cet Argeant est il ou dans leur Lignes, ou dans les Cassetes Enterrées des Royalistes. On peut Ajouter que les etats n'ont pu dans ces tems de trouble prendre des Mesures Convenables à L'imposition, à La Levée des taxes, que d'aïlleurs L'etendue du païs, la dispersion des Habitants en Rend la Collection difficile; il Seroit possible aussi de Remarquer La difference entre Les taxes Actuelles et celles même qui ont été une des Raisons de Mecontentement; enfin, Monsieur le Comte, les Americains diroïent que leur Commerce a Cruellement Souffert Cette Année; Mais en pensant que ces Excuses quoiqu'assés Bonnes ne Sont pas Suffisantes, je Vois aisement que le Congress M. Moriss, et tous Les chefs de la Revolution Sont interessés à ce qu'un defaut d'argeant ne les fasse pas Manquer; il est clair qu'ils doivent tâcher d'en avoir, et prendre pour Reussir tous les Moyens qui ne mettent pas en danger la Revolution elle Même.

Puisqu'ils n'ont pu en avoir, Monsieur le Comte, il devient je Croïs Necessaire que pour le Succès et la gloire de La Cause Commune, un genereux et dernier effort Soit fait en faveur des Americains; en Comparant l'argeant qu'ils demandent, avec les avances faites à Nos alliés de la derniere guerre, et Surtout en Distinguant le degré d'interest que Nous Avions à Les Soutenir, le Secours jugé Indispensable ne paroîtra pas non plus exhorbitant.

L'Armée de M. de Rochanbeau quitte L'Amerique, et si Newyork N'est pas evacué, Cette demarche trop prematurée Semble inviter à un dedomagement. Ces troupes Coutoïent treize millions, elles tiennent place d'autres troupes aux isles et d'aïlleurs ne Couteront pas autant; pour Remplacer L'envoy de deux Regiments on donna la Somme de Six millions; dans le Cas Actuel, ne pourroit-on pas donner au moins ce que le Ministre des finances avoit Surement preparé pour le Maintien annuel de Cette Armée? Je Croirois Aussi, que si la guerre dure, si surtout elle est prolongée par des interets qui ne Regardent ni les Americains, ni leurs alliés, on a pensé qu'il falloit au moins les aider un peu durant la Campagne et ce Secours prêvu joint à l'epargne imprévu Sur l'armée de M. de Rochambeau ne doit-il pas Approcher des Esperances que l'Amerique Semble avoir Conçüe.

Peut-être on Se Souviendra que Ce Continent est le Seul point ou nous avons Eu de grands Succès, et la Raison en est assés Simple puisque tout y est pour Nous, tout y est Contre les Ennemis; dans le Cas Heureux ou L'on y portera Nos forces, il faut que Nous trouvions une Armée Capable de Cooperer; jamais il n'y en eut de Maïlleure que celle des Americains, Mais Si leur patience est à la fin lassée, Si le Congrès Balance entre l'inconvenient de les garder, et l'inconvenient de les debander, S'il faut enfin prevenir une Convulsion au lieu de Conduire une operation offensive, Non Seulement il Sera impossible d'attaquer les postes Ennemis, Mais encore il leur Sera aisé de les degarnir ainsi que le Canada, et cet excedent n'etant plus Retenu Se portera Sur Nos isles.

Sous un point de Vüe politique, il paroit encore plus instant d'aider les Americains; je ne crains pas leur paix avec l'Anglettere, et Si Nous y portons la guerre, je Suis persuadé qu'on obtiendra un grand Succès; Mais pour Resserer Encore les liens de l'amitié, pour assurer les Moyens d'operer Contre l'ennemi, je ne Voudrois pas qu'on Refusat Cette instante et derniere demande; Les dispositions de l'Amerique sont Excellentes, Nous N'avons Rien à Craindre que l'impossibilité de Continuer, et encore ne Consentiroitelle jamais à s'ecarter des devoirs de L'alliance, de Ceux de la Reconnoissance; Mais en partant, Monsieur le Comte, il M'est impossible de ne pas Vous laisser mon opinion, je la donne du fond de mon Coeur, et Sans me flatter qu'elle Remplace celle du Cher. de La Luzerne, je me Reprocherois de ne pas Vous avoir dit Combien je Crois un Secours instant et Necessaire. Agreés, je Vous prie, Monsieur le Comte, l'Homage du tendre et Respectueux Attachement avec lequel j'ai l'Honneur d'etre, Votre très Humble et obeïssant Serviteur

LAFAYETTE

To [the Comtesse de Tessé]

Cadix 1er. janvier 1783

Le convoi que j'avais laissé à 20 lieues a depuis éprouvé mille contrariétés. Il est enfin entré avec celui de Toulon. Toutes ces troupes se réunissent aux francais de Gibraltar et à plus de cinq mille Espagnols. Quoiqu'en dise Vaudreuil, Mr. Destaing commande la terre et la mer. Je suis maréchal Général des logis des troupes francaises et espagnols et quoique Mr. de Falkenheim ait voulu rester je n'ai rien à démêler qu'avec Mr. Destaing qui a signifié aux troupes de suivre les ordres que je donnerais et qui a pour moi son amitié et sa confiance ordinaire . . . Je ne vous dirai rien de Cadix. Son plus grand mérite est d'être moins espagnole que les autres villes, je ne veux pas d'ailleurs empieter sur le droit de description qu'ont eu les revenans de Gibraltar et mes journaux seront tous de l'autre monde. Je n'y mettrai pas que je vois tous les jours Mr. le Cte. Orelly, mes principes s'accordent peu avec le gouverneur de la Louisiane, j'avais le projet de ne pas le voir mais sans lui l'on ne peut rien se procurer ici, et le bien public exige que je sacrifie ma répugnance. Si j'en juge par la manière dont je suis avec les troupes les craintes de Mr. de Segur étaient mal fondées, mais je me trouve fort bien comme on m'a placé; j'espère que notre campagne ira mieux que la dernière et surtout je desire qu'une bonne paix vienne rendre tous mes préparatifs inutiles.

Pendant que nous déferons ce qui a été fait et que nous tachons de mieux l'arranger, pendant que nous sommes ennuyés de beaucoup de détails nécessaires, la marine fait aussi tous ses préparatifs. Nous avons M. de Lamothe-Piquet. Il y avoit un autre officier Général M. de Bausset, mais il tient de mauvais propos et j'espère obtenir de M. Destaing qu'il le renverra tout simplement. Je monterai le *Terrible* et Mr. Destaing le *Majestueux* ces deux vaisseaux seront les plus voisins.

Aurons nous la paix, ma chère cousine, et faut-il encore se battre pour qu'on puisse s'entendre. Ma grande affaire à moi paroit être arrangée et l'Amerique est sure de son indépendance, l'humanité a gagné son procès et la liberté ne sera jamais plus sans asile. Puissent à présent nos succès déterminer la paix générale, puisse la France reprendre son rang et ses avantages et je serai parfaitement heureux, car je ne suis pas assez philosophe pour ne pas mettre un intérêt particulier aux affaires publiques.

To the Comte de Vergennes

Cadix ce 5 fevrier 1783

Je Vous fais mon Compliment, Monsieur le Comte, et je jouïs pour Vous de L'Heureuse Conclusion de Vos travaux. Ma premiere idée etoit d'aller En Amerique, mais une phrase de Vos lettre me fait penser que Vous Conseïllés mon Retour en France. M. d'Estaing m'est temoin que cela m'a determiné, et puisque Vous n'avés pas Songé à ce Voyage, c'est que Vous Croïés mon Retour plus Convenable. Dans le Courant de l'été je demanderai au Roy la permission d'aller à Philadelphie.

D'après les sollicitations de Mr. Carmichael, et l'avis de Mr. d'Estaing, et ce que me mande Mr. de Montmorin, je me tiendrai à portée de donner au Ministere Espagnol l'opinion d'un Homme qui Connoit l'Amerique, et qui etant français excitera moins leur Mauvaise Humeur. Je vous ecrirai de Madrid, Monsieur le Comte, Mais je n'ai pas voulu tarder à vous Rendre un Compte Succint de ma Conduite, et à joindre mon Compliment à l'assurance de mon Respect et de mon Attachement.

LAFAYETTE

To the Comte d'Estaing

Madrid Ce 18 fevrier 1783

J'ai Receu Votre Lettre, Monsieur le Comte, et Vous Remercie Bien des Soins que Vous prenés pour le Triomphe. Graces à Vos Precautions, j'espere qu'il ne lui Arrivera Rien, et je suis Sür qu'il Sera Bien Receu à Philadelphie. Les Anglais Vont y Envoïer le fils du Duc de Norfolk, et cela prouve qu'ils ne font pas les choses à Moitié. C'est Mr. d'Adhemar qu'on fait Ambassadeur à Londres et Le Marquis de Camarthen doit Venir à Paris. Je loge ici chès Mr. de Montmorin, Monsieur le Comte, il me temoigne une Amitié à laquelle je Suis Bien Sensible. Je lui Sais d'aïlleurs Bon gré de la Maniere dont il Vous Connoit et Vous Aime. Nous avons Hier été à la Cour, et ni mon Habit ni mes principes n'ont empêché le Roy de me Recevoir avec Bonté. J'eus Ensuite une Conversation avec Mr. de F.B., et ce Ministre doit Venir ici demain pour la Continuer.

J'ai trouvé Beaucoup de prejugés, point de Connoissances Sur le tout, et un air de Visage trop Contraint pour étre Affectueux. Sans le Consoler du Malheur de l'independance, je Consacre Cette Semaine à le prêcher pour en tirer parti, et je partirai vite pour France ou je Suis Ramené par une affreuse inquietude Sur le Sort d'une de mes tantes.

Je Suis affligé, Monsieur le Comte, de Voir Retarder Votre Arrivée à Paris. J'esperois Vous Embrasser ici, et je Serai toujours Heureux quand je pourrai Vous offrir moi Même l'Homage de mon Respect et de Ma tendresse.

To the Comte de Vergennes

Madrid Ce 18 fevrier 1783

A mon depart de Cadix, Monsieur Le Comte, j'eus L'Honneur de vous Ecrire deux Lignes, et je vous mandois Les Raisons qui Reculoïent mon Voyage d'Amerique. Mr. Le Cte. de Montmorin a aussi pensé que je pouvoit etre utile à Madrid, et je L'ai prié de me diriger dans La Conduite que j'y dois tenir. Graces à Mr. d'Estaing j'ai pu ecrire au Congrès, et en Leur parlant de la paix, je n'ai pas laissé ignorer Combien le plan de Campagne etoit Avantageux. Après m'avoir presenté au Roy, Mr. Le Cte. de Montmorin m'a Mené chès Mr. de Florida Blanca. Ce qu'on fera ici pour les Etats Unis ne partira jamais du Coeur mais en mettant à part L'interest Americain, il est, je crois, encore plus important à la France d'adoucir ces prejugés et ces Repugnances de L'Espagne. En Causant avec M. de Florida Blanca, il m'a paru qu'il aimoit peu, et qu'il Ne Connoissoit point l'Amerique, qu'il S'ettonnoit à chaque Condescendance de l'Anglettere, et que le Malheur de l'independance frappe plus ici que La Necessité d'en tirer parti. Si l'on s'en tient aux limites Anglaises, c'est par Crainte d'une dispute qui Remplîroit l'objet de Lord Shelburne. Si l'on Reçoit Mr. Carmichael c'est par crainte de voir arriver Mr. Jay qu'on N'aime pas autant. À la Lenteur Naturelle, se joint une Repugnance peu Commune, et quoique Mr. de Florida Blanca paroisse assés Bien disposé, je prevois que Le traité Espagnol Nous donnera Bien de L'embarras. Ce Ministre doit etre ici demain, et le jour suivant Nous Lui faisons une autre Visite. Je me croirois Heureux, Monsieur le Comte, Si par ma Connoissance du païs je pouvois Rendre le Ministere un peu Confiant et si en Pressant la Reception de Mr. Carmichael, ou la fixation de quelques Bazes, on pouvoit Rapprocher un peu L'Espagne des Etats Unis. Comme Mr. Le Cte. de Montmorin Vous Ecrit, et Comme Mr. Carmichael, ainsi que moi, Lui fait part de toutes ces demarches, je me Contenterai d'ajouter que je passerai ici toute cette Semaine, et que je m'efforcerai d'eclairer les prejugés du Ministere Espagnol; l'Amerique libre leur est inconnüe, et l'avantage d'y avoir été me tient lieu des Autres Connoissances qui me Manquent. Si je puis Servir les Vües de Mr. de Montmorin et celles du Congrès, je serois d'autant plus Heureux d'y Contribuer que Les sentiments actuels de l'Espagne me font prevoir des Embarras très desagreables.

Du Coté de L'Anglettere, Monsieur le Comte, Vous Voilà Bien tranquille et je Vous en felicite de tout mon Coeur. Par les lettres que je Reçois, j'apprends L'arrangement des Commissions et des Ambassades. C'est encore un travaïl pour Vous après celui de la paix. Adieu, Monsieur le Comte, Agrées, je Vous prie, l'Homage du tendre et Respectueux Attachement avec lequel j'ai l'Honneur d'etre, Votre très Humble et obeïssant Serviteur

LAFAYETTE

To the Condé de Floridablanca.

Madrid Ce 19 fevrier 1783

Monsieur Le Comte

Ayant eu l'honneur de Conferer avec votre Excellence sur les objets relatifs aux Etats-unis, et devant bientot me rendre auprès du Congrès Americain, je desire me penetrer moi même du Resultat de nos conversations. Au lieu de l'Indifference et meme des divisions qu'une autre nation aimeroit à prevoir, il m'est agreable de porter aux Etats-unis le tableau de vos bonnes dispositions. Je vous dois cet avantage, Monsieur le Comte, et pour le rendre complet, pour m'assurer que je n'oublie rien, permettez que mon rapport au Congrès soit dabord Soumis à Votre Excellence.

Sa Majesté Catholique desire qu'entre elle et les Etats-unis il S'etablisse une Confiance, une harmonie Durables. Elle est de Son Côté decidée à faire tout ce qui pourra l'Entretenir. Le Chargé d'affaires américain est reçu dès ce moment et Votre Excellence Va S'occuper à traiter les interêts des deux nations; pour presenter au Roy Mr. Carmichael, Votre Excellence qui veut marquer toutes Sortes d'Egards à Mr. Jay, attend seulement que M. Le Conte d'Aranda lui ait notifié Vos dispositions.

Pour la fixation des Limites, Sa Majesté Catholique adopte celles des préliminaires du 30 novembre entre les Etats-unis et la Cour de Londres. La Crainte d'Elever un Sujet de dispute est la seule objection qu'elle auroit à la Libre navigation du Mississipy. Le tabac de Virginie, les objets relatifs à la marine fourniroient dans le traité des Conventions reciproques, et d'après les productions de L'Amérique il S'y feroit des arrangements utiles à ses finances. Ayant eut l'honneur de vous parler pour une diminution des droits sur la Moruë, Vous m'avez répondu qu'il faudroit faire à la France le même avantage, et qu'en Vertu d'anciens traités, les Anglais auroient la prétention de la reclamer; mais Vous ferez à tous égards ce qui dependra de vous pour Satisfaire l'Amérique.

C'est avec un plaisir bien vif Monsieur le Comte que j'entrerois dans tous les détails où je prevois des Liaisons entre l'Espagne et les Etats-unis: mais ce n'est pas moi que Cet heureux travail regarde. Les Ministres du Congrès, celui que vous aller y envoyer, doivent S'en occuper et je me borne à rappeller les idées générales que Vous m'avez données. Un mot de vous m'assurera que je n'ai rien oublié. Les dispositions de Sa Majesté Catholique et la franchise de Votre Excellence ne laisseront aucun pretexte a de fausses representations. L'alliance de la maison de Bourbon avec les Etats unis est fondée sur l'interêt commun. Elle aura plus de force encore par l'affection et la Confiance que votre Excellence desire etablir.

D'Après nos conferences, Monsieur Le Comte, Voila le Resultat que je me suis formé et le Comte que je me propose de rendre Sans avoir aucune mission à Cet egard. Je Connois les Sentiments du Congrès et je Sais tout le prix qu'ils mettront à vos dispositions. En me permettant de leur soumettre ce que j'ai vû vous excités ma Reconnoissance personnelle et j'en joins l'hommage a Celui du Respect avec lequel J'ai l'honneur &a.

LAFAYETTE

From the Condé de Floridablanca

Au Pardo Ce 22 fevrier 1783

Monsieur le Marquis

Je ne puis mieux Satisfaire a vos desirs qu'en vous priant de me permettre de vous donner ici ma réponse. Vous avez compris exactement tout ce que j'ai eu l'honneur de vous communiquer sur nos dispositions à l'Egard des Etats-unis. J'ajouterai seulement que quoique l'Intention de Sa Majesté soit de Suivre à present les Limites établies dans le traité du 30 novembre 1782 entre les anglais et les Americains, elle compte prendre des Lumieres pour savoir si il y a des inconveniens, ou des prejudices, et Regler amicalement cette affaire avec les Etats-unies. J'ai l'honneur d'etre, Monsieur Le Marquis Votre tres humble et tres obeissant Serviteur

FLORIDA BLANCA

Note on Correspondence with the Condé de Floridablanca

Madrid Ce 22 fevrier 1783

En recevant la Réponse de Mr. Le Comte De Florida Blanca je lui ai demandé une explication sur l'addition relative aux Limites. Il m'a repondu que le principe etoit etabli de prendre les Limites arretées entre les anglais et les Americains, que sa remarque portoit uniquement sur des details nullement importants, qu'il desiroit avoir des Commandants Espagnols qui se regleroient amicalement et ne nuiroient point au principe général. Je lui ai demandé devant M. l'Ambassadeur de France, S'il m'en donnoit Sa parole d'honneur. Il m'a repondu qu'oui, et je pourois l'engager vis-a vis du Congrès.

LAFAYETTE

To Jean-François Joly de Fleury

Paris Ce 19 Mars 1783

En me presentant chez vous, Monsieur, pour avoir l'honneur de vous voir, j'ai été d'autant plus faché de ne pas vous y rendre mes devoirs, qu'un voyage en Auvergne me privera pour quelque tems de Cet Avantage. Mais il est un objet sur lequel je ne puis tarder à vous parler, et cette liberté m'est dictée par l'amour du bien, la confiance dont on m'honore, et ma Connoissance des affaires américaines.

C'est en commerçant avec les Etats-Unis que nous tirerons un grand avantage de la guerre, de nos dépenses et de la Revolution. Mais apres le tems perdu sur cet objet, et dans le moment où les Anglais reparent leurs Erreurs: il est je crois, important de diminuer pour les americains les entraves de notre commerce. Il est inutile de dire, Monsieur, que je ne pretend pas entrer ici dans des détails d'administration, mais après des longues reflexions sur l'intérêt commun et Sur la disposition particuliere de nos alliés, je Suis convaincu de deux Verités que mon devoir Comme Citoyen m'oblige à Vous Soumettre. La premiere est qu'il tenoit à nous d'avoir presque tout le Commerce Américain. La Seconde est que par nos entraves sur le Commerce nous Sommes en danger eminent d'en perdre la plus grande partie.

Il ne m'appartient pas d'indiquer les remedes, il Seroit trop long de Citer tous les Exemples. Mais je ne puis m'empêcher de parler de deux batiments de Tabac, que les difficultés de la ferme ont dernierement chassés de L'Orient et qui ont pris sur le Champ la route d'Angleterre. Ayant acquis le droit de Reflechir sur les interêts de la France et de l'Amerique, je Suis malheureux de penser qu'en repoussant leur commerce au lieu de l'attirer, nous Servirions bien mieux les Anglais qu'ils ne peuvent se Servir eux mêmes.

On a donné des Ports aux Americains et l'on trouvera surement nécessaire d'en ajouter d'autres. J'ai eu l'honneur d'en parler avec M. Le Cte. De Vergennes, et je me Bornerai à ce que je lui ecris aujourd'huy à ce Sujet. Mais on traite à present une affaire où les americains sont tres interéssés et Lorsque la Barre de Bayonne offre trop de difficultés il faut esperer qu'on evitera de les augmenter en gênant la communication avec l'Espagne. D'après la position de ce port, l'espoir de Cette Communication facile peut seule y attirer les Americains. Sans entrer dans les details que vous ont Soumis les deputés de Bayonne, et quoiqu'un Militaire ait droit de Juger que la Rive offre une excellente position dans Ce genre de Guerre, je me borne au devoir de vous avertir qu'une plus grande gêne Sur les debouchés produiroit un mauvais effet sur les Négociants Américains.

Les Réfléxions que je vous Soumette, Monsieur, sont plus qu'excusées par le Patriotisme qui les dicte. Accoutumé à Ce genre de Confiance, je Suis heureux de la Meriter par ma franchise et mon Zèle, et j'avoue que dans ce moment je Suis tres effraié sur nos interêts de Commerce avec les Americains.

C'est avec un grand plaisir Monsieur, que je vous porterai à mon retour l'homage du Respectueux attachement avec lequel J'ai l'honneur d'etre Monsieur Votre tres humble &a.

LAFAYETTE

To the Comte de Vergennes

Paris Ce 19 Mars 1783

Je pars pour L'Auvergne, Monsieur le Comte, et à moins que je Recoive vos ordres, je serai une Vingtaine de jours dans ce Voyage. Mais pour peu que je Vous soïe utile, ayés la Bonté de m'ecrire au Château de Chavaniac par Brioude, et je serai Heureux de Venir Vous porter mon zele public et mon Attachement particulier.

Les deputés de Bayonne sont Venus me Voir, ils sont Bien Reconnoissants de Votre interest et Bien inquiets sur le plan de Campagne des fermes et Regies. Vous etes trop de notre avis, pour que je me permette de donner ici le mien. Mais sans avoir de titre Bien precis, j'ai cru que mon devoir de citoïen suffisoit pour ecrire à Mr. de Fleury. Vous trouverés ici copie de ma lettre, et je desire Bien que vous l'approuviés. On ne sauroit trop Repeter qu'après une grande guerre et une Belle paix, il seroit Ridicule de perdre le fruit de tant de sang et de tresors, et cela pour plaire à une Classe de gens qui ne plaisent à personne. Après avoir donné des Leçons à l'Anglettere, Recevons celle qu'elle nous donne à present, et tâchons qu'en Se trouvant aussi Bien chés leurs amis que chés leurs ennemis, les Americains ne soïent pas forcés à donner aux derniers la preference.

En diminuant les inconveniens Naturels de Bayonne, en donnant aussi le Port de Marseïlles, et Rendant Dunkerque le plus Avantageux possible, j'espere, Monsieur le Comte, qu'au lieu de Port Louïs Vous Vous deciderés pour L'Orient. L'etablissement de Port Louïs est très petit, il n'offre aucune de Commodités de L'Orient, et ce dernier port est très Agreable Aux Americains. Quant aux avantages Generaux de Commerce, il seroit Bien important qu'une prompte decision Empêchat de Renoüer les liaisons de Commerce entre les Etats Unis et l'Anglettere.

Soyés assés Bon, Monsieur le Comte, pour Presenter mes Homages à Mde. la Ctesse. de Vergennes. Je me suis presenté plusieurs fois pour la Voir, mais n'ai pas été assés Heureux pour lui faire ma Cour. Agreés, je Vous prie, l'assurance de mon tendre et Respectueux Attachement

LAFAYETTE

To Adrienne de Noailles de Lafayette

Chavaniac Ce 27 Mars 1783

J'ai Receu Hier Votre aimable lettre, mon cher Coeur, et Voici la premiere occasion ou je puisse Vous ecrire. Vous avés Receu de Brioude un Mot qui Vous apprenoit le jour de mon arrivée. C'est un peu avant la nuit que je me suis Retrouvé dans ce château ou j'avois laissé deux personnes si chères et qui n'y sont plus. Le premier Moment a été terrible pour ma tante, ses cris et sa douleur etoïent faits pour effraïer. Mais elle s'est Remise peu à peu, et Malgré l'abondance de ses larmes, il s'est fait depuis mon Arrivée un changement immense. Je l'ai trouvée Horriblement changée et vieïllie; mais à present elle a plus de forces, passe la journée Hors de sa chambre, vient à table et y mange quelque chose. Depuis mon arrivée la Maison est pleine de monde, et elle s'occupe d'en faire les Honneurs. Pour moi j'ai laissé là tout Compliment, et je ne pense qu'à ma tante. Elle me parle de mes affaires, des siennes, et je lui parle de Vous, de nos enfants, et de l'Amerique. Nous avons entâmé L'affaire du Chevalier de Chavaniac; elle veut la poursuivre, et alors il faudroit Bien tâcher de la gagner. Mais j'aimerois mieux un abandon de tous ses Biens, qui nous mettroit à portée d'arranger les choses à notre fantaisie. Elle veut toujours aller à Langeac, au moins pour le moment. Mais j'espere que Cet été nous la determinerons à Venir à Paris. Je jouïs du changement que lui fait epprouver ma presence, et en verité il est miraculeux.

Quant à moi, mon cher Coeur, j'epprouverois ici un Sentiment fort doux Si je pouvois y Retrouver Ce que j'y ai laissé. Mais Chaque impression agreable est attristée par cette idée, le souvenir des choses me Rappelle Celui des personnes. Il n'y a pas un Coin dans cette Maison, pas un arbre dans les environs, ou je ne me Sente prêt à Revoir ma tante et Mde. d'Abos, et il me faut une triste attention pour penser que de nous trois il n'y a plus que moi qui existe.

Parlons un peu de nos affaires, mon cher Coeur, et je vous dirai d'abords que je consulte à chaque pas Votre petit Memoire. Le Subdelegué etoit ici Hier, et Reviendra Samedi. Il attend l'ordre pour un don de 80 septiers, et pour un prêt de 150. Je ferai Nommer par chaque Village ses Representants, et je Voudrois que le gouvernement me permit de former des greniers publics auxquels j'ajouterois du mien, et qui feroient une Banque de grains pour les Semences. On espere trente mille francs pour Votre Manufacture et cela fera un grand Bien. Vous avés Rendu au païs un Service immense. J'aurai lundi un Commité de Curés ou nous verrons ce qu'il y a de mieux à faire. Jeudi je Compte Repartir, Car il est indispensable à ma tante que je Reste jusques la. Elle ne Sait pas l'etendue du Sacrifice que je lui fais. Mais je Connois votre Coeur, et je sais que Vous insisteriés sur mon sejour ici. Il sera de dix à onze jours. Je dinerai à Brioude, Coucherai à Issoire, Vendredi je dinerai à Clermont, et lundi j'espere diner à St. Germain.

C'est un grand Bonheur pour moi, mon cher Coeur, de penser que vous partagés tous mes sentiments, et cette idée me fait trouver un double plaisir à vous les Communiquer. Je ne Vous parle pas de Votre santé, mais je vous Remercie Bien de m'en avoir parlé. Ce que vous m'en dites m'est Bien necessaire; ce que je vous en dirais vous est Bien Connu. Faites je vous prie mes Compliments au docteur. N'oubliés pas de faire presser notre Maison. Ma tante Vous aime tendrement, est Bien touchée de vos Soins, et vous ecrit, je crois, aujourdhuy. J'ai fait vos Commissions auxquelles on est Bien sensible. J'ai donné le portrait de la pauvre Anastasie. Faites en faire un de George et de Virginie, et faites aussi Copier le petit tableau que Vous avés de moi. Tout cela etant prêt, je pourrai l'envoyer à mon Arrivée. Mille tendresses à Maman, à mes Soeurs. J'embrasse Nos enfants. Adieu, mon cher Coeur, menagés vous, Soignés Bien Votre santé, aimés moi toujours, et avec cela soïes sure de mon Bonheur.

Recommendation of Lafayette for the Cross of Saint Louis

5 May 1783

M. Le Mis. de La Fayette
  né le 26 Septembre 1757
  Sert du 9 avril 1771
  Capitaine le 19 may 1774
  Mestre de camp le 3 mars 1779
est passé dans l'Amérique Septentrionale au commencement de la Guerre des Americains contre l'Angleterre. La conduite qu'il y a tenue a été Si distinguée qu'il s'est acquis une confiance entiere tant de la part du Congrès que de celle du Roi et sa Majesté, pour le récompenser a bien voulu lui accorder le grade du Maréchal de camp a la datte du 19 Octobre 1781.

Comme il n'y a point d'article dans les Réglements qui fixe le tems du Service auquel un officier Général est susceptible de la Croix de Saint Louis On Propose à Sa Majesté de l'accorder au Mis. de La Fayette.

Il est agé de 26 ans. Il en a douze de Service dont près de 6 en Amérique, ou il S'est trouvé a toutes les affaires et ou il a été très utilement emploïé d'ailleurs pour des objets de négociations, et qui a enfin obtenu le grade du Maréchal de camp par une distinction toute particuliere et rélative au zêle et aux talens dont il a donné des preuves.

To the Comte de Vergennes

Paris ce 12 juin 1783

J'ai Vu Sir James Jay, Monsieur le Comte, et j'ai appris Avec plaisir que Vous deviés Causer demain avec lui Sur le Commerce Americain. L'objet est Si important, et les instants Sont Si precieux, que je Suis Heureux toutes les fois que le gouvernement y porte Son attention. Sir James Jay m'a Communiqué ses idées, et j'en ai été Content; le principe d'aider quelques maisons ici et en Amerique me paroit avantageux, et parmi les dernieres il Seroit, je crois, juste de Comprendre celle de Sir James. Le double interest qui m'anime Servira d'excuse à la liberté que je prends, et j'y joins l'Homage de mon tendre et Respectueux Attachement

LAFAYETTE

To the Comte de Vergennes

Paris Ce 17 juin 1783

Les Ministres Americains ont été chès Vous, Monsieur le Comte, et par consequent je n'ai Rien à dire sur leurs affaires. La poste m'a porté des lettres d'Amerique, et j'imagine aussi que vous en aurés Receues. Dans celle du 1er May Mr Lewingston me fait part de la joïe publique, à la Nouvelle d'une paix generale; le Congres a été Bien aise de ce qui S'est passé entre les Ministres Espagnols et moi. On Avoit echangé les prisonniers, mais la lenteur à Evacüer Newyork Commençoit à deplaire, et le Gal. Washington alloit avoir üne entrevüe avec le le Gal. Carleton. Les preliminaires out été Ratifiés par le Congrès, et l'on m'annonce des lettres plus longues à la premiere occasion.

Celles du Gal. Washington Renferment Cinquante quatre pages, il m'y fait des detaïls Relatifs à l'armée. Nous avons la même opinion Sur la Necessité, et les moyens d'union entre les etats. Les affaires de L'armée prennent une tournure qui fait un Nouvel Honneur à leur Vertu et à leur patriotisme. Dès qu'elles Seront Reglées, le general Reprendra Sa vie privée. Voilà, Monsieur le Comte, l'extrait de mes depêches, et j'y dois Ajouter Les temoignages d'attachement, de Respect, et de Reconnoissance pour le Roy que m'exprime le General Washington et dont vous me feriés grand plaisir de Vouloir Bien lui parler.

Il me paroit qu'on etoit fort las de la guerre, et la Nouvelle de la paix en a été plus agreable. Mais si par Malheur elle eut été differée, le general Se preparoit á une Cooperation. La dissolution de l'armée va etablir des maisons de Commerce, et plusieurs officiers S'adressent à moi pour leur donner des Conseïls. J'en attends même ici, et je desire Bien leur faire etablir des liaisons avec la France.

Il y a un point, Monsieur le Comte, sur lequel je suis Souvent Consulté, et je vous prie de vouloir Bien me donner une Reponse Ministerielle. Sous la denomination de port franc, entendés vous Seulement un depôt pour les productions de l'Amerique avec permission de Les Rembarquer Sans droits? Ce qui Seroit fort au dessous de l'idée que s'en font les Americains. Ou Bien est ce Comme ils le pensent un port ou toutes les productions quelquonques du Royaume, Manufacturées ou Brutes, Arriveroïent Sans droits avec *un Acquit à Caution*, comme ce qui S'exporte aux Isles, et une fois arrivées dans la franchise, Seroïent Regardées Comme arrivées en païs etranger? Les productions ou Manufactures etrangeres Seront elles admises librement et Sans distinction dans le port affranchi, avec permission d'y Rester à volonté, de les vendre et Revendre, et de les faire changer aussi Souvent qu'on veut de proprietaires, Pour les envoyer ensuite dans tout autre port sans formalités de douanes? Bien entendu cependant qu'aucun article ne Sortiroit des limites qu'en etant Soumis aux Restrictions ordinaires dans les autres parties du Royaume. En Vous demandant cette explication, Monsieur le Comte, je me propose de la Communiquer à mes amis dont elle Reglera la Conduite.

Je vous demande pardon de ma longue lettre, Monsieur le Comte, et je vous prie de me faire donner des Nouvelles de Votre Santé. Agreés l'Homage de mon tendre et Respectueux Attachement

LAFAYETTE

From the Comte de Vergennes

A Vlles. le 29 Juin 1783.

J'ai reçu, M., la lettre que vous m'avez fait l'honneur de m'ecrire le 17. de ce mois; vous desirez Savoir ce que l'on entend par port franc.

Nous entendons par cette denomination, M., un lieu où toutes les marchandises tant nationales qu'etrangères peuvent être importées, et d'où elles peuvent être exportées librément. Vous jugerez par cette définition, M., que toutes les marchandises du Nord Sans exception pourront être importées à Lorient et exportées Sans difficulté par les américains. En un mot, Lorient sera réputé étranger à l'egard de la France relativement au commerce. Les prohibitions et les droits établis Sur les marchandises etrangères n'auront lieu que dans le cas où l'on voudroit faire entrer dans l'intérieur du Royaume les marchandises etrangères assujetties à l'un ou à l'autre.

To the Comte de Vergennes

Chavaniac Ce 21 juïllet 1783

En me Rendant ici, Monsieur le Comte, j'ai receu des lettres du Congrès dattées le 12 avril, et le President me fait passer une Resolution qui approuve mon sejour en Europe. Mais il est un point important dont le Congrès me charge expressement, et sur lequel on m'ordonne de m'adresser à Vous. Je le fais avec d'autant plus de Confiance que, par les Consequences Necessaires, notre Commerce s'y trouve Particulierement interessé.

En Reglant les preliminaires, les Ministres Americains n'ont Point fixé de terme pour le païement des dettes à l'Anglettere. Après une Pareïlle guerre, ou les uns ont été Ruinés, les Autres ont tout mis dans les fonds publics, et ou tous ont Souffert de la depreciation du papier, il est impossible que les Negotiants

Americains païent Sur Le champ Leurs dettes Anglaises. Trois ou quatre ans leur Seroïent Necessaires, et Leurs Ministres Recevront Surement des ordres à cet Egard. Mais je Voudrois Bien, Monsieur le Comte, qu'ils Vous eussent Encore cette obligation dont l'effet Seroit Excellent en Amerique. S'ils Vous doivent La Reparation de cet oubli, Vous Rendrés aussi un grand Service au Commerce français. L'impossibilité de païer leurs dettes, mettroïent les Negotiants Americains dans La main des Anglais; on ne quitte pas un ouvrier dont on ne peut Solder le Memoire, et Si l'on ne fait pas une Clause à ce Sujet, la liaison de Commerce que nous desirons doit Considerablement en souffrir.

Agreés, je vous prie, Monsieur le Comte, l'Homage de mon Bien tendre et de mon Respectueux Attachement.

LAFAYETTE

Address of Nobles of Langeac to Lafayette

[August 4, 1783]

Monsieur,

Le nom de Lafayette, grand d'origine, cher à l'Etat et répandu dans les fastes de l'histoire, vient de retentir glorieusement sur l'un et l'autre hémisphere. C'est vous, Monsieur le Marquis, qui, secondant les vues généreuses et bienfaisantes du prince, avez combattu contre ces orgueilleux et redoutables insulaires, les Anglais, nos ennemis, qui avez rendu la liberté à une nation opprimée et fixé l'attention de toute l'Europe.

Gilbert de Motier de Lafayette, l'un de vos ancêtres, se distingua à la bataille de Baugé, en Anjou. Il contribua beaucoup à chasser les Anglais du royaume et fut fait maréchal de France.

Jeune et dans l'âge où les talents s'annoncent à peine, héritier de la haine du héros contre les ennemis de l'Etat, vous vous êtes attaché à suivre ses traces; vos premières armes ont été signalées par les plus vaillants exploits, témoin Cornwallis! et déjà votre gloire a surpassé la sienne. Quelle dignité ne vous promet pas une valeur si précoce et si éclatante?

Vous avez excité l'admiration et la reconnaissance des Français. Les Auvergnats vous sont redevables pour l'honneur que vous leur faites et particulièrement nous qui avons celui d'être vos voisins.

Aussi, tous se sont-ils empressés de vous marquer le plaisir qu'ils ont de vous voir et à vous rendre les hommages les plus respectueux et les mieux mérités.

Nous n'avons pas eu l'honneur de nous montrer les premiers, mais nos sentiments et notre attachement pour vous n'en sont ni moins vifs ni moins respectueux.

Daignez, monsieur le marquis, accepter le vin que cette ville a l'honneur de vous offrir, en considération de votre naissance et de votre mérite; daignez encore être persuadé que, si les circonstances le veulent, elle sera infiniment flattée de vous appartenir pas ses possessions, comme elle est à vous de coeur.

To [Mme de Simiane?]

Paris mardi matin [21 octobre 1783]
. . . Mon diner d'hier a fort bien réussi, Mr. Pitt étoit soutenu de cinq anglais et il y avait une douzaine de rebelles en comptant les dames. Après avoir un peu politiqué, Mr. Pitt est parti pour Londres et m'a laissé fort content de son esprit de sa modestie, de sa noblesse et d'un caractère aussi intéressant que le rôle auquel sa position le destine. L'attaque parlementaire l'empêche de venir à Paris et il prètend que tant que l'Angleterre restera monarchie on ne peut gueres se flatter de me voir à Londres. Malgré cette plaisanterie j'ai bien envie d'y aller un jour. Je ferai peu ma cour au roi. Je me sauverai par l'opposition, depuis que nous avons gagné la partie, j'avoue que j'ai un plaisir extrême à voir les anglais, l'humiliation de l'avant dernière guerre et leur insolence pendant la paix m'avaient donné contre eux un sentiment d'aversion, elle n'a fait que croître avec les horreurs dont ils ont souillé l'Amérique, et l'adjonction de leur nom à celui de la tyrannie en a fait prendre à mes oreilles une habitude défavorable, mais à présent je les vois avec plaisir, et soit comme francais, soit comme soldat américain, ou bien même comme simple individu je me trouve sans embarras au milieu de cette fière nation. Ma conversion n'est cependant pas assez complete pour que dans tous les tems je ne leur fasse pas le mal qui dépendra de moi, sans avoir la fatuité de les traiter en ennemis personnels, il me suffit qu'ils soient ennemis de la gloire et de la prospérité francaises, car en fait de patriotisme je puis *étonner* le public comme on dit que je l'ai fait en sensibilité.

Observations on Commerce between France and the United States

[13 décembre 1783]
En sacrifiant à la derniere Guerre et ses trésors et le Sang de ses citoyens, la France a dû y prévoir de grands avantages. Il en est qu'aucune faute ne peut lui ôter, et tandis qu'elle a recouvré sa consideration, sa rivale perd une partie de son Commerce, un territoire immense, un grand nombre de sujets que l'Europe s'empressait à multiplier. La France a plus fait encore, elle s'est garantie d'une ruine sûre et prochaine. Aux yeux de tout ce qui connait le Nouveau-Monde, il est démontré que la veille de la Déclaration d'Indépendance, l'Angleterre pouvait s'assurer toutes nos possessions Américaines. Mais quoique pour les biens acquis et les maux évités, nous devions bénir cette révolution; quoique les lieux communs de la Critique se reduisent eux-Mêmes à savoir si cette force inévitable des Etats-Unis, à présent isolée et tranquille, serait mieux

placée dans sa réunion avec nos rivaux, il est d'autres profits encore qui nous semblaient assurés et que je vois à regret nous échaper.

Pendant l'animosité de cette querelle, nos liaisons de Commerce eussent été plus faciles; mais si nous avons attendu des concurrens il nous reste sur eux des avantages. Non que le Négoce me paraisse une affaire de sentiment; les Américains aiment la France; ils sont reconnaissans et généreux, et quand on reproche de l'excès à leur haine (au sujet des représailles ou des Refugiés, par exemple) il serait trop absurde de leur reprocher de l'amour pour l'Angleterre; Mais tout Commerçant cherche un gain, et quoique la politique des Etats-Unis nous soit très favorable, l'interêt mercantile garde l'impartialité. Son influence, il faut l'avouer, ira plus loin encore; elle conduira peu à peu des Conseils où les Negocians jouent un grand rôle. Rivaux des Anglais, et dans nos manufactures et dans notre Commerce Naval, c'est par les mêmes moyens qu'un jour s'y décidera notre rivalité politique.

Quand je parle de nos avantages, je me borne donc à dire que pour les premiers essais nous en trouverons dans la disposition Américaine; que la nature nous en a donné d'exclusif, qu'un peu de soin nous en donnerait beaucrop encore; qu'au lieu de repousser ce Commerce, il nous faudrait moins de peine pour en attirer la plus grande partie; que chaque délai, chaque faute devient un gain sûr pour l'Angleterre. Car enfin si l'Amerique n'existe pas pour nous, elle existera pour d'autres, et si cette vérité ne vaut pas des sacrifices, du moins vaut-elle une promte et bien sérieuse attention.

Interessé de bonne heure à cette révolution, je dois regretter les moindres profits que ma Patrie négligerait d'y trouver. Je dois chérir tout ce qui resserre une alliance naturelle que l'interêt commun me parait exiger. Si j'avais l'expérience d'un Négociant, j'écrirais sur le commerce avec les Etats-Unis. Il m'est impossible d'y prétendre, et si mes reflexions, ou mes rapports, m'ont donné quelques idées, elles sont trop imparfaites pour hazarder un Mémoire. Ce que j'ai appris ou pensé, je l'ai dit aux Ministres du Roi, et c'est pour leur obéir que je présente ici quelques Notes sur cette grande affaire.

Le Commerce du Royaume et celui des Colonies, quoique divisé par les Départemens, est, dans son rapport avec les Etats-Unis, impossible à séparer. En examinant la premiere partie, l'on voit d'un côté des productions crues, et de l'autre des ouvrages manufacturés; ce qui annonce un grand profit à cet échange. Si cette vérité demandait un exemple, je citerais le grand Commerce des graines de Lin, que les anciennes Colonies vendaient à l'Irlande. Depuis l'instant où elles etaient plantées jusqu'à celui où l'Amerique recevait des toiles blanchies, l'Irlande gagnait tout à y favoriser cette culture. En evitant de nuire au Commerce, nos draps fins, nos Soyeries de toute espèce, nos toiles et nos ouvrages de Mode &a. trouveront un débit considérable; mais il peut s'augmenter encore par les soins; et tandis que les Manufactures moins recherchées s'approcheront du gout américain, (car j'ai vu qu'à Boston les têtes rondes de nos cloues en empêchaient seules la vente, et que la maniere Irlandaise de plier les toiles, influait sur le débit) les autres pourraient diminuer la cherté en simplifiant leurs moyens, et quelques unes ne perdraient pas à l'adoption du principe Anglais, qui n'employe chaque personne qu'à une chose, et à chaque chose que le dégré de force absolument nécessaire. Il est singulier, par exemple, que lorsque la matiere premiere est meilleure, moins chère dans nos Colonies les ouvrages en coton de Rouen depuis la Paix soient plus chers que ceux de Manchester. Le prix de notre main d'oeuvre, le bon gout, l'intelligence qui nous distinguent, tout nous promet et d'imiter, et de surpasser les ouvrages quelconques des Etrangers.

En formant des liaisons de Commerce; en faisant gouter nos Manufactures, on doit aussi faciliter l'exportation. J'etens les Américains souhaiter qu'elle soit sur le même pied pour leur Continent que pour nos Isles; ils sont effrayés par cet établissement contre nature des Douanes intérieures. Depuis le moment où l'ouvrage sort de la Manufacture, jusqu'à celui où sans ouvrir les Caisses, à moins de formalités pires que l'incertitude, on les voit entrer dans le Vaisseau, ils se plaignent de ces difficultés sans nombre qui affligent également les nationaux. Les véxations conduisent à la Contrebande, aux friponneries: pour un Etranger ignorant la Langue et les usages, elles sont encore plus insupportables. Les fabriques Anglaises donnent un plus long crédit, reflexion moins triste que les autres, mais qui vaut la peine d'être remarquée. Quant à nos vins, nos eaux-de-vie, ils nous donnent sur l'Angleterre un avantage exclusif. Le gout des vins de France augmente tous les jours; ils sont recherchés dans le Nord, nécessaires aux païs chauds. Il faudrait étouffer ce Commerce pour que le Portugal, les Açores, et même Madère, soutinssent la comparaison.

Voilà donc une nouvelle source de richesse qui vivifie nos productions et nos Manufactures. Il serait maladroit de la tarir, il est bien plus aisé de l'augmenter. Mais cette partie du Nouveau-Monde produisant de bonnes denrées et non de riches Metaux pour faire payer nos Ouvriers, nous devons, à l'exemple de l'Irlande, encourager leurs cultivateurs. Tandis que leurs Pelleteries sont renvoyées sous la forme de chapeaux, manchons &a. que nous employons leur excellent fer, que leurs bois reçoivent ici, comme autrefois en Angleterre, outre la construction, une addition de voiles, de gréements &a. il faut aussi que leur Indigo, leur Riz, leurs Tabacs trouvent en France un marché avantageux. Leur Indigo, moins fin que le nôtre, a son emploi particulier. Le riz Américain doit être préféré à celui du Levant, quand même ce Commerce serait bien assuré. L'article essentiel, c'est le Tabac; mais il est anéanti par M[ss]rs. les Fermiers Généraux. S'il est une Nation favorisée pour la Moruë, il ne faut pas oublier que c'est la monnaie de la Nouvelle Angleterre: en un mot, si l'on veut que les Américains achetent, leurs moyens de vente ne sauraient assez être multipliés.

Loin de remplir ce but désirable, notre Sistême actuel a repoussé leur commerce. La difficulté des règles est encore plus facheuse que leur cherté. Les Préposés de la Ferme ne peuvent qu'arrêter et ne décident jamais. Le tems si précieux au Négociant est consumé par le plus leger obstacle, comme il le serait par la plus importante affaire. Ces jugemens de la Compagnie, si longtems attendus, varient arbitrairement à chaque occasion.

En arrivant dans un Port Français, on flotte entre la crainte d'une déclaration moindre qui fait confisquer, et celle d'une déclaration exagérée, qui fait payer pour ce qu'on n'a pas. Dans les cargaisons de Tabac, l'erreur est encore plus facheuse; car en se trompant à son desavantage, on est accusé de contrebande, et cette absurdité n'est suspendue que par un ordre particulier, *Sans tirer à conséquence*. En remportant les marchandises, les Américains souhaitent recouvrer les droits d'Entrée, et cette facilité leur parait essentielle au commerce. Celui du Tabac est dans ce moment perdu pour la France, et depuis la Paix, il n'en est, je crois, arrivé que deux Batimens; encore était-ce un ancien engagement, et tous les autres vont en Angleterre, en Hollande, où ils sont payés par les Manufactures. Il y a telle Cargaison gui, après avoir passé neuf mois en France, sans que M[ss]rs. les Fermiers Généraux voulussent ni l'acheter ni lui permettre d'aller à Marseille où les Italiens la demandaient, est à la fin partie pour Amsterdam. Le bon Tabac se vend à présent à Philadelphie de 50 à 60 Schellings le Quintal; arrivé en France les differentes charges le portent à 54 Livres de notre Monnaye; et tandis que dans nos Ports on n'en tire que neuf sols la Livre, il se vend, dit-on, seize Sols à Londres et à Amsterdam. Mais sans entrer dans des détails où je puis me tromper, il est clair que pour l'achat de cette denrée et pour le débit des nôtres, un Commerce direct est le meilleur; que pour s'en emparer les Etrangers sont capables de tout, même d'une perte momentannée, et qu'à moins d'éclairer le patriotisme de la Ferme, l'appât d'un gain passager, ou l'attachement aux vieux usages, pourra nuire à nos interêts mercantiles et politiques.

Depuis longtems ces abus enchainnet le Commerce, affligent les citoyens, et, de l'aveu général, ils compensent nos avantages naturels sur les autres Nations. Je ne prétends pas donner des idées neuves, mais j'indique celles dont les Américains sont frappés. Il m'appartient encore moins de décider les remèdes, mais l'exemple des Etrangers prouve qu'il en existe, et je parlerai seulement des Ports francs qu'on a longtems négligés. Le Traité en promet deux: Marseille et Dunkerque le sont de tout tems. Au moment de la Paix je représentai que l'Orient convenait fort aux Américains. On voulut bien le choisir, je fus chargé de l'assurer, et d'annoncer une Lettre en forme, qui n'a point encore paru. La conclusion de cette affaire et l'addition de Bayonne formeraient une chaine de quatre Ports suffisante au Commerce des Etats Unis. Peut-être vaudrait-il mieux pour nous que tous les Ports de France fussent libres; mais sans me permettre une idée étrangere, sans même faire valoir ici et L'Orient et Bayonne, j'ajouterai seulement que ces dispositions devraient être combinées avec les Ministres du Congrès et leur Consul en France.

Quelques soient cependant les importations d'Amérique, la France est assez heureuse pour que la balance d'exportations soit de beaucoup en sa faveur. Il s'agit donc de trouver un payement pour cet excédent, et le commerce des Etats Unis aux Isles peut Seul le procurer. Lors même que j'aurais de profondes connaissances, je craindrais de risquer un avis sur cette importante question. Les Négocians Français y semblent opposés aux Français habitans des Colonies. Le pour et le contre pouvent, dit-on, se Soutenir; mais en causant avec des gens moins ignorans que moi, voici à peu près ce qui m'a frappé sur le Commerce Américain.

Dès que son interêt nuit à notre commerce il doit être nul aux yeux du Gouvernement; Mais je n'en dis pas autant et de nos cultivateurs, de nos ouvriers en France et de nos concitoyens dans les Colonies. Le debit de leurs productions, la prospérité qui en résulte, doivent être balancés avec l'avantage des Négocians et se combiner pour le plus grand bien de la chose publique. Il y a moins de dixhuit ans que les chambres de Commerce s'opposaient unanimement à toute communication entre les Colonies et les Etrangers. Depuis ce tems elles sont devenues tolérantes sur quelques articles; elles conviennent même à présent qu'il vaut mieux tirer les Salaisons d'Amérique que d'Irlande. Ce n'est pas sans débats que la nécessité fit établir des Entrepôts à Ste. Lucie et au Môle St. Nicolas. Il y a parmi les Negocians une diversité d'avis, et toutes ces reflexions me font espérer un sistême conciliant où l'interêt national s'accorderait avec celui des particuliers.

En prenant les chairs Salées d'Irlande, nous avions le rebut des Anglais, et la difference de prix et de qualité ne sera pas comparable. Si le Poisson d'Amérique se verse dans les Colonies, les Marchés d'Europe en recevront mieux le nôtre. La concurrence peut se rétablir par des droits modérés mais tant que la Subsistance des Negres dependra des loix prohibitives ils seront moins nombreux, mal nourris; ils travailleront peu, mourront plutôt; et puisqu'enfin on a des Esclaves, ne doit-on pas écouter la double voix de l'interêt et de l'humanité? Les droits du Roi, la consommation des Manufactures, la culture des Colonies augmenteraient en proportion de la liberté. Les Colons ne sont-ils pas les meilleurs juges sur la nourriture de leurs Nègres? Et craint-on qu'ils ne leur donnent du Superflu? En recevant la Morue et les salaisons, on recevra sûrement aussi les animaux vivans, Merrains, &a. qu'a toujours fourni le Continent Américain. Je dois observer ici que les Entrepôts actuels éxigent un cabotage incommode et dispendieux; et si l'on attend quelque ressource des Espagnols, j'ajouterai que leur Commerce se réduit à des Chèvres, des peaux de leurs bestiaux lâchés dans les bois, que le manque de fourage ne permet pas d'élever autrement. L'Isle Marguerite seule a quelques pâturages, mais ce petit objet doit d'autant moins être calculé, qu'elle adoptera de plus en plus la culture de nos Isles. Repoussés par nous, les Américains encourageraient les Espagnols, et c'est en Manufactures Anglaises que ceux-ci se font toujours payer. La négligence des Gardes Côtes rend la Contrebande facile. Parmi ce peuple paresseux, quoiqu'il puisse promettre, on ne doit compter sur rien qui demande des soins personnels; mais le bois propre aux maisons, aux Bateaux, à la réparation des Navires; mais les Merrains, les Bois pour mâts et vergues; mais enfin les provisions salées que rien n'empêchera de tirer des Etats-Unis: Voila des objets sur lesquels les Espagnols ne peuvent prétendre à la concurrence.

Il est impossible de douter que les Poissons, Salaisons &a. tous les articles enfin ci-dessus nommés, ne soient admis dans nos Colonies. Les farines offrent une plus grande difficulté, que je suis bien loin de savoir resoudre. Les Colons disent que la question sur l'exportation des grains etant encore douteuse, on ne doit pas être si affirmatif sur leurs exportations aux Isles; que les Nègres ne font guères usage de farines; que si le vendeur de bled perd, le consommateur, et par conséquent l'ouvrier français y gagneront; que les champs se transformeront en vignes; que l'importation intérieure du Royaume offre un débouché; que puisqu'on porte tous les jours des farines Américaines dans les Ports d'Europe, (et la France même en a quelques fois reçu) il est cruel d'étouffer l'accroissement des Colonies par des privilèges exclusifs, dont l'effet ne sert ordinairement que les individus. Les Taffiats, les Melasses et les Manufactures de France, passeront des Isles aux Etats Unis; mais ils tiennent fort

au Commerce des sucres, du moins pour leur consommation. S'ils n'en trouvent ni chez nous, ni chez les Anglais, ils encourageront à notre détriment, ou
le Brésil, ou les Colonies Espagnoles. S'ils ont cette liberté dans les Isles Anglaises ils y reprendront des liaisons que nous devons craindre. L'amélioration
de nos Colonies doit nous interesser. Ste. Lucie, par exemple, est regardée
comme un tombeau, et peut devenir une Isle florissante. Si l'on arrêtait la
croissance d'une possession ennemie, ne croirait-on pas lui avoir fait un grand
mal? Et puisque le Commerce français ne suffit point au progrès de nos Colonies, pourquoi ne pas laisser leur Superflu à des consommateurs alliés?

En indiquant certaines Isles, ou certains Ports, et bornant la proportion de
sucres sur chaque Navire, ou bien en exigeant des gages d'une représentation
de cette denrée aux Consuls Français dans les Etats Unis, n'y aurait-il pas des
moyens pour s'assurer que ce commerce n'excède pas les besoins du Continent,
et pour que les Américains ne trouvent aucun profit à porter nos Sucres en
Europe? On craint des difficultés dans l'execution de ces Réglemens; mais ne
doit-on pas en dire autant de toutes les restrictions? Si celles ci n'embarrassent
pas assez pour faire accorder entiere liberté, pourquoi les autres effrayeraient-
elles au point d'adopter une prohibition générale? Il est d'ailleurs raisonnable
de tenter des essais et l'on ne doit pas commencer par ceux qui, faisant perdre
un commerce peu connu, nous prépareraient d'inutiles regrets. Lorsqu'on
aurait examiné ce commerce sous toutes les points de vue, il en resterait
encore un qui mérite d'être considéré. Les Etats Unis regorgeant de productions, les Isles ayant avec eux des besoins mutuels qui les rapprochent, il est à
craindre que le refus d'honnêtes liberté n'entraine une licence générale. Si tout
est également défendu, les Américains et les colons violeront tout indistincte-
ment; mais l'assurance d'un profit licite, éloignerait la Contrebande, et c'est elle
qui entraine les véxations, les animosités, qui perd tous les droits du Roi, qui
détruit toute combinaison en faveur de notre Commerce, et qui défait les liens
de la Politique.

S'il est juste de ne donner, même à nos plus chers alliés, que le superflu de
notre Commerce; s'ils ne doivent être employés qu'à sa prospérite, ou bien à
celle de nos cultivateurs, de nos ouvriers, et celle de nos Colonies pour l'avantage de la Métropole, on serait bien coupable, Sans doute, de leur sacrifier le
grand interêt de notre Navigation. Celle des Colonies détruit, dit-on, plus de
Matelots qu'elle n'en forme, et généralement les Américains n'esperent pas
pour la leur un accroissement très rapide. Il est vrai que dans le moment actuel
on se porte avec empressement sur les dernieres du païs, et qu'on est attiré vers
les précieuses terres qui attendent des cultivateurs. Cette Navigation dailleurs,
sera peut-être, plus chère qu'on ne pense. Si le bois est à meilleur marché, il
n'en pas de même de la main d'oeuvre, et le cordage est en grande partie
importé d'Europe. Leurs Matelots sont mieux payés et mieux nourris; leurs
batimens durent beaucoup moins long tems que les Nôtres. S'ils se construisent
à meilleur compte, disent les Américains, les Français en acheteront une partie
qui deviendra propriété Française. Ils prétendent enfin que plusieurs Nations
naviguent moins chèrement; ce n'est pas eux que l'on doit craindre sous ce
rapport.

Si j'ai hazardé quelques idées sur le commerce américain, j'y ai été encouragé par les Ministres du Roi, et plus encore par l'amour de ma Patrie et mon attachement aux Etats-Unis. Ces motifs, que j'ai le droit de faire valoir, excuseraient quelques prétentions sur des matieres que j'entends mal; mais je n'ai pas même ce tort à me reprocher. J'avoue que le moindre Nègociant en Sait plus que moi, et si quelques unes de mes idées paraissaient justes, on doit y croire d'autant plus, qu'exposées par un ignorant, elles ne sont pas montrées à leur avantage. Je ne donne point un Mémoire: je rassemble des Notes qu'on m'a demandées sur des vérités rebattues, ou sur des opinions américaines que mes rapports particuliers m'ont mis à portée d'entendre. Tandis que pour la prospérité de notre Commerce, de notre culture, de nos Fabriques, on facilite notre exportation, et que pour assurer un payement, on favorise l'importation américaine, il faudra qu'en Soignant notre Navigation, qu'en prévoyant, et ce qu'on doit desirer et ce qu'on ne peut empêcher, l'interêt de nos Négocians se combine avec celui de nos Manufactures et de nos Colonies, pour le plus grand bien possible du Royaume. Les Ministres du Roi Sauront mieux que moi comment remplir ces objets; mais il est deux refléxions qui ne demandent point de Science La premiere est qu'en perdant du tems, on se fait un tort irréparable: La Seconde est, que Le Ministre des Etats Unis et son Consul en France, que d'autres Envoyés Américains étant ici, il est d'autant plus important de les consulter, que leurs talens et leurs connaissances rendent les avis précieux, et que leur opinion influera beaucoup sur la disposition des Etats-Unis.

LAFAYETTE

To the Comte de Vergennes

Paris ce 16 decembre 1783

Monsieur le Comte

Après avoir Vu triompher la noble Cause qui les assembloit, les officiers Americains ont deposé leurs armes pour Reprendre leurs paisibles occupations. Mais à l'instant de cette separation, ils ont voulu se donner un gage de leur tendre fraternité, et n'ont pas moins souhaitté de perpetuer leur Reconnoissance pour la France, avec la memoire de leurs obligations.

C'est dans cette disposition, Monsieur le Comte, qu'a été institué la Societé *des Cincinnati.* Vous en Connoissés les Reglements, et je me Borne à Remplir les ordres du General Washington president de cette assossiation.

En m'adressant le Major L'Enfant, qui a été chargé de Composer les desseins et de les faire executer, le general me mande de Recevoir les souscriptions et signatures, et de distribuer les marques distinctives, pour tous les officiers En Europe qui auront Rempli dans l'armée des Etats Unis les Conditions Necessaires. Je vous supplie donc, monsieur le Comte, de vouloir Bien obtenir l'agrement du Roy pour ce que nous sommes de français qui me paroitront etre admis par les Reglements.

La societé se flatte, monsieur le Comte, que les marques de l'ordre Seront acceptées par les generaux, Amiraux, et Colonels des troupes francaises qui ont servi de Concert avec les Americains, et toute l'armée Americaine se Reunit pour demander au Roy cette permission. S'il a la bonté de l'accorder, le Depart prochain du Washington en fera Bientôt parvenir la Nouvelle.

La Societé met un grand interest, monsieur le comte, à ce que ses intentions soient clairement Connües en Europe et en Amerique. Ses Reglements seront publiés dans les gazettes etrangeres, mais vous obligerés vraiment l'assossiation en faisant inserer l'article ci joint dans la Gazette de France à l'article de Paris.

J'ai l'Honneur d'etre avec un tendre et Respectueux attachement, Monsieur le Comte Votre très Humble et obseïssant Serviteur

LAFAYETTE

From Charles-Alexandre de Calonne

Paris le 18 xbre. [décembre] 1783.

J'ai, Monsieur, un véritable regret de n'avoir pas eu l'honneur de vous voir, lorsque vous avez bien voulu prendre la peine de passer chez moi. J'ai lû avec le plus grand intérêt les observations que vous m'avez adressées sur le commerce entre la Françe et les Etats-unis. Je serai charmé de conférer avec vous de ces objets, mais comme je vais demain à Versailles et que d'ici au moment de mon départ j'ai des affaires et des rendezvous qui ne me permettroient pas de vous donner autant de tems que je le desire, je vous propose un des jours de la semaine prochaine, celui qui vous conviendra et je vous prie de m'informer du moment que vous aurez choisi. Vous avez, Monsieur, trop de titres à l'Estime universelle pour qu'il vous Soit permis de douter de mes Sentiments et de l'Empressement avec lequel je concourrai aux Vuës qui vous animent.

J'ai l'honneur d'Etre &a.

DE CALONNE

From Charles-Alexandre de Calonne

à Versailles le 25 dcbre 1783

J'ai lu, Monsieur, avec la plus grande attention, le mémoire tres intéressant que vous m'avez fait l'honneur de m'adresser concernant les facilités que l'on pourra procurer aux Etats unis de l'Amérique pour leur commerce avec la France. Les vuës que ce mémoire renferme spécialement pour la franchise des portes qui paroissent convenir le plus à leur navigation sont tres bien conçuës, et me semblent susceptibles de se concilier tout avec l'interet politique de l'Etat qu'avec celui des finances du Roy au moyen, de quelques précautions dont je vais m'occuper sans délay, et après que J'aurais concerté avec M. Le Cte. de Vergennes les mésures à prendre pour prévenir toute difficulté je m'empresserai d'en rendre compte à sa Majesté. Ses dispositions en faveur des Etats-

unis de l'Amérique sont assez connuës pour qu'il-y-ait lieu de prevoir dès
aprésent qu'elle donnera volontaire son agrément aux moyens d'assurer de
faciliter et d'etendre les relations de commerce qui sont à désirer pour l'avantage réciproque des deux nations. Je serai charmé d'en conferir incessament
avec vous, et vous pouvez compter que je ferai tout ce qui dependra de moi
pour terminer cette affaire le plus tot qu'il serait possible. J'ai l'honneur d'etre,
etc.

CALONNE

From Charles-Alexandre de Calonne

à Versailles le 9 Janvier 1784.

Monsieur,
   J'ai rendu compte au Roy des observations contenuës dans le mémoire que
vous m'avés remis concernant le commerce de l'Amérique et de celles que vous
m'avez faites dans notre derniere conférence. Je Suis autorisé à vous annoncer
que l'intention de Sa Majesté est d'accorder aux Etats-unis, les Ports de L'Orient et de Bayonne comme libres et francs, outre ceux de Dunkerque et de
Marseilles dont le premier jouit d'une franchise absolue, et le Second n'est
restraint dans l'exercice de cette franchise qu'à l'egard du Tabac qui y est
assujeti à un droit. Les Américains peuvent dès ce moment expédier Leurs
Batiments pour ces quatre ports où ils n'éprouveront aucune difficulté. Vous
pourrez S'il en est besoin, expliquer ce qu'on entend par *Ports francs* Suivant la
Signification qu'en a donné M. De Vergennes dans sa lettre du 29 Juin dernier.
Les Américains trouveront surtout à Dunkerque toutes les facilités qu'ils peuvent desirer pour la Vente de leurs Tabacs en feuille, de leurs Ris, de leurs
Mérins, et autres marchandises, ainsi que pour l'achat de celles qui peuvent
leur convenir, comme Toiles, Eaux de Vie, Etoffes de Laine, &a. &a. On se
propose même d'y former des Dépots et Magazins qui leur seront fournis à des
conditions tres avantageuses pour leur commerce. J'ai donné des Ordres aux
fermiers généraux de traiter par préference et à des prix raisonnables pour
l'achat des tabacs de l'Amérique Séptentrionale, et au surplus les Etats-unis
seront aussi favorisés en France pour leur commerce qu'aucune autre nation.
Les plaintes qu'ils vous adresseroient, ou que M. Franklin et autres ministres
américains, que je Verrai avec grand plaisir, auroient à me transmettre de leur
part, Seroient examinees avec beaucoup d'attention et le Gouvernement ne
Souffrira pas qu'ils éprouvent aucune Espece de Véxations. On prendra aussi
toutes les mesures possibles pour empêcher les envoys de mauvaises Marchandises qui, S'ils ont eu lieu jusqu'à present, ne peuvent etre attribués qu'à l'avi-
dité de quelques Négociants du dernier ordre. Je vais m'occuper de ce qui
concerne les Douanes et les droits de traite, qui gênent le commerce; c'est un
objet important et qui demande un travail considérable. Enfin, Monsieur, vous
pouvez compter que je Serai toujours tres disposé, ainsi que Mr. Le Marechal

De Castries et Mr. le Comte De Vergennes à recevoir et écouter avec attention les demandes et Representations ultérieures que vous croirez devoir faire en faveur du Commerce de L'Amerique. J'ai l'honneur d'Etre &.

De Calonne

P.S. Les ports de Bayonne et de l'Orient Seront assimilés à celui de Dunkerque pour l'Entiere franchise.

To Charles-Alexandre de Calonne

Paris Ce 31 J[anvi]er 1784.

Dans notre derniere conversation, Monsieur, je vous soumis quelques questions de Negociants américains. Vous m'en avéz demandé la Note, et vos bonnes intentions sur ce commerce, les décisions promptes qui en Sont l'effet ont ranimé mes esperances. Pendant que les partis anglais se Disputent, nous pouvons reparer des Lenteurs dont vous avez Si bien senti l'inconvenient.

Les quatre ports francs sont accordés; vous y destinés des Batiments publics à former des Magazins americains. Il est bien à Souhaiter qu'aucun des quatre ports ne Soit privé de cet avantage: l'usage de ces Magazins devroit être au plus bas prix possible. Ce qu'il faudroit determiner d'une maniere fixe, c'est la Liste des droits d'ancrage, de Bureaux, d'amirauté, tous ces droits enfin qu'on percoit d'une maniere Vague et toujours d'une maniere gênante. Ils sont moins utiles au Roy qu'incommodes aux particuliers et S'il est instant de les fixer au plus bas prix possible, il Seroit je crois tres important d'en faire entierement le Sacrifice.

En voyant les difficultés du Commerce avec la France M[ess]rs. Wadsworth et Carter, americains tres Riches, avoient abandonné toute idée de ce genre. Je leur montrai votre lettre, et ils se determinerent à faire des Essais. Ils acheterent des Soïeries, et autres articles et les destinoient pour un batiment qui part de l'Orient. Mais le Domaine de Monsieur se trouvant Sur le chemin, il a fallu ou payer des droits qui absorboient le profit ou comme ils ont fait perdre l'occasion et augmenter la depense en prenant un detour.

Ces Messieurs desirent envoyer en Amérique quarante Mille bouteilles de Vin de Champagne, il leur seroit Commode de l'embarquer à Brest, et un de leurs batiments y passe en Revenant d'Angleterre, ils demandent S'ils n'Eprouveront pas de difficultés, et quels droits il faudra payer pour l'entrée et Sortie du Batiment.

M. Nesbit Negociant à L'Orient me mande que M. Pignon lui a dit que le tabac de Virginie Se prendroit pour 45 lt. et celui du Maryland pour 40 lt. Il est forcé de perdre Sur celui qu'il a deja reçu, mais ses amis et lui ont donné des ordres pour que leur tabacs aillent directement d'Amérique dans les ports Etrangers. Ce monopole du tabac est un grand malheur pour le Commerce avec l'Amérique, mais puisqu'il faut que m[ess]rs. Les fermiers generaux en

achetent je cherche quelles vuës ils peuvent avoir en degoutant les americains
de le porter ici, quand la même qualité se vend beaucoup plus cher dans les
autres ports d'Europe.

M[ess]rs. Wadsworth et Carter dont toute l'armée de M. De Rochambeau
peut vous parler, m'ont fait une observation tres juste. C'est que l'Angleterre
diminue les droits Sur les articles Exportés en Amérique: et Si la France en
faisoit autant, sur les glaces, par Exemple, et toute cette branche de verrerie,
elle auroit l'avantage sur les manufactures anglaises.

En Recevant Votre Réponse sur Ces notes, Monsieur Je Rendrai compte aux
negocians americains de ce qui peut les intéresser. Ils Sont Ranimés par votre
activité et votre décision et c'est fort àpropos que vous êtes venu detourner le
Courant qui portait en Angleterre tout le Commerce des Etats Unis. J'ai &.

To Charles-Alexandre de Calonne

Paris Ce 10 f[évri]er 1784

Etant sur le point d'écrire en Amérique, Monsieur, je voudrois y Continuer
l'envoy de Nouvelles favorables. Après l'affranchissement des Ports, il faudroit
achever votre ouvrage, en y déterminant et peut être même en abolissant les
droits d'amirauté, ancrage, Pilotage et autres gênes du commerce dont j'ai eu
l'honneur de vous ecrire. Il seroit intéréssant de rassurer les americains sur la
Vente de leurs Tabacs; je vous ai fait parvenir quelques plaintes Recentes, et
j'augure mal de la commission donnée par la ferme pour des Tabacs de Virginie. On en tire à present de Luckraine, et generalement au lieu d'acheter
ceux d'Amerique, la ferme en prend à Vil prix dont la qualité se trouve tres
mauvaise. Vous avez été si genereux sur les Ports francs, qu'il seroit indiscret de
presenter une Nouvelle idée de ce genre. Mais plusieurs americains m'ont dit
que Si Le Havre avoit des privileges, ils assureroient la Supériorité aux manufactures de Normandie, et faciliteroient le debit des articles fabriqués à Paris.
Un batiment chargé en Angletere viendroit encore prendre quelques productions francaises dont il Seroit tenté par le Voisinage et la Commodité. Ce que
j'ai l'honneur de vous en dire, Monsieur, doit être attribué à l'envie de n'oublier
aucune des Representations americaines. Agreez l'homage de ma Reconnoissance et du Respect &a.

To Charles-Alexandre de Calonne

Paris Ce 26 f[évrier] 1784

Monsieur Le Controleur General trouvera ici les Etats qu'il a bien Voulu me
Confier; et pour remplir ses intentions je lui soumets l'avis de Negociants

Américains que j'ai consultés. Les droits à Payer dans les ports francs sont moins facheux par leur Prix que par leur multiplicité. Les abolir entierement seroit peut être difficile mais on pourroit les diminuer d'abord, et ensuite les Reunir sous une Seule denomination, qui se paieroit, tant pour un batiment à trois mats, tant pour un à deux mats, et ainsi de Suite, Sans se jetter dans l'embarras du Jaugeage. Cette methode ne priveroit personne parceque la Subdivision des profits Se Seroit par ceux qui y pretendent; elle preveindroit les Exactions, et les infidelités auxquelles les etrangers peuvent etre Soumis; elle degageroit tous les embarras de ce genre dont les Americains se plaignent et Surpasseroit de Beaucoup la methode anglaise. Apres Cet Arrangement, il faudroit envoyer deux etats, l'un des anciens droits, et l'autre de la nouvelle forme adoptée et ce nouveau Reglement seroit imprimé dans tous les papiers Américains.

Il va partir une occasion pour l'Amerique et Si Mr. Le controleur general veut bien donner une decision sur cet objet, et quelques autres points de mes Lettres, je m'empresserai à Remplir ses Vuës en Communiquant ses dispositions; S'il lui convient de me recevoir ou samedy à Paris ou dimanche à Versailles avant ou apres le Conseil, Je me Rendrai aux Ordres qu'il voudra bien me donner. Je le prie d'agreer

To Charles-Alexandre de Calonne

Paris Ce 5 Mars 1784

Pour me conformer aux intentions de Mr. Le Controleur General je me suis rendu chez M. Chardon, et quoiqu'il eut été saigné deux fois il a bien voulu s'occuper de notre affaire. Il n'a pas crus que ce travail put se faire avant d'avoir de nouveaux Etats plus précis, mais d'après le compte qu'il a dû rendre aujourd'huy j'espere recevoir deux lettres qui rassureront les americains Sur la disposition des deux departements.

Outre cette Lettre que Mr. Controleur general m'a promis je prends la liberté de lui representer qu'on a reçu depuis un mois à Newyork l'annonce des quatre ports francs. On doit en consequence attendre des Batiments tous les Jours, et comme il ne reste plus à faire qu'une simple formalité, il Seroit à desirer qu'on la terminat le plutot possible. J'ai même arrêté l'officier americain dans l'espoir que le voyage de Dimanche à Versailles me mettroit a portée d'envoyer l'Imprimé.

En causant avec Les americains sur l'Importation de leur farine aux Isles l'un d'eux m'a dit que nous pourrions prendre des mesures pour les faire payer en partie par des Vins ou des ouvrages manufacturés. Cette obligation à faire contracter aux Americains pourroit S'allier avec l'Excellente idée d'un droit modique reversible en prime dont Mr. Le Controleur General a bien voulu me faire part et que M. Le Comte d'Estaing m'avoit aussi donné. J'ai l'honneur &.

L.

From Charles-Alexandre de Calonne

Versailles le 8 mars 1784

J'ai examiné, Monsieur, avec beaucoup d'attention les Representations que vous m'avez fait l'honneur de m'adresser sur les droits que les Navires americains sont obligés de payer dans les quatre Ports francs que Sa Majesté leur a assignés. Vous vous plaignez, Monsieur, de la chérté de ces droits, de leur multiplicité et de la facilité qu'y trouvent les gens de mauvaise foy, pour tromper des Etrangers qui ignorent la Langue française ainsi que les usages Locaux. Vous demandez la Suppréssion de la plus grande partie de ces droits, et que tous ceux qu'on laissera Subsister soient reduits sous la dénomination d'un Seul exigible en raison de la grandeur de chaque Batiment à trois ou à deux mâts ainsi de Suite; afin d'Eviter le détail de l'imposition de droit en raison de la continance du Navire par tonneau et de Son Jaujage. Je dois d'abord vous observer, Monsieur, d'un coté, que les droits qui Se perçoivent sur les navires americains dans les ports de France, Sont les mêmes pour les Navires étrangers; et d'un autre coté qu'ils n'excedent pas les droits exigés par les anglais. Mais vous representés que les americains ne Sont pas instruits de la Nature et de la qualité des droits éxigibles en France sur leurs navires, comme sur tout autre. Je ne puis à cet égard proposer aucune décision à Sa Majesté, avant d'avoir constaté par des Renseignements certains en quoi consistent ces droits, au profit de qui ils Se levent, et Sur quel titre ils Sont établis. C'est pour parvenir à cette connoissance que j'ai engagé Sa Majesté à faire adresser des ordres aux amirautés des quatres Ports francs pour que ces Tribunaux ayent à envoyer Sans delay un Etat precis et certifié d'eux, de tous les Droits quelconques qu'un Navire americain est dans le Cas de payer au moment de Son arrivée dans le Port, ou à celui de Son depart. Lorsque ces Etats me Seront parvenus, je m'empresserai d'en mettre le Resultat Sous les yeux de Sa Majesté et C'est alors que je pourrai lui proposer de prendre des mesures pour diminuer ces droits autant qu'il Sera possible que pour reunir en un Seul ceux qui Seront conservés, et les faire payer en raison de la grandeur des Batiments. Ce Sera pour moy une nouvelle occasion de prouver aux Etats Unis les dispositions favorables de notre Cour pour tout ce qui les intéresse. Vous devez être convaincu que je n'en laisse échaper aucune, et la détermination que Sa Majesté Vient de prendre Sur mon Raport de Suprimer tous les droits de traite à l'Exportation de nos Eaux de vie est encore une preuve de l'attention qu'elle donne à toutes les parties de notre Commerce avec les Etats-Unis. Je me flatte que vous Rendez Justice au desir que j'ai de vous temoigner tous les Sentiments que je vous ai voués. J'ai l'honneur d'Etre Votre tres humble &a.

DE CALONNE

To [Simon-Nicolas-Henri Linguet]

Paris ce 20 avril 1784

Il est Bien vrai, Monsieur, que je n'oublie pas Mr. Baumier; mais jusqu'ici ma Recommandation est Bien infructueuse; je ne Conçois pas Comment toutes ses esperances s'evanouïssent successivement; mais Ce Malheureux est Vraiment persecute par son etoile; si d'ici à mon depart, il n'est pas en meïlleure situation, je Consentirai à le mener avec moi en Amerique. Le Voyage que j'y ferai, Monsieur, sera fort Court; j'y suis depuis longtems attendu par mes amis, et quoique la Revolution soit achevée les treize etats ont encore à travailler Sur leur Constitution foederative. Quelques personnes m'engagent à etre temoin de leurs travaux a cet egard; et quand je me Rends à leur amitié en les allant trouver je voudrois avoir une partie des talents qui pourroient servir l'Amerique, et y Consolider encore, s'il est possible, le temple de la liberté, mais au moins serai-je Spectateur très Benevole, et dans le Courant de l'Hiver prochain je Viendrai vous Renouveller l'assurance de mon tendre attachement; il n'est egalé que par ma Reconnoissance pour Votre interest et le prix que je mets à votre opinion. C'est Dans Ces sentiments, que j'ai l'Honneur d'etre pour toute ma Vie, Monsieur, Votre très Humble et très obeissant Serviteur.

LAFAYETTE

To the Comte de Vergennes

Paris ce lundi [10 mai 1784]

Vous aurés demain, Monsieur le Comte, la Visite de Mr. Jay qui Retourne en Amerique; après avoir pris Congé de Vous, il souhaitte, si c'est l'usage, prendre aussi Congé du Roy; Sans etre Bien Habile sur l'etiquette diplomatique, je lui ai dit que cette idée me paroissoit Convenable.

Mr. Barklay a Receu de Mr. Moriss des ordres sur lesquels il desire Conferer avec Vous; il est aussi chargé d'une lettre du Docteur Franklin, et tout cela est Relatif à l'affaire des saisies faites en Bretagne dont j'ai souvent eu l'Honneur de Vous parler. Je lui ai dit que demain matin Vous seriés occupé, mais si vers six Heures vous avés la Bonté de le Recevoir, je vous prie de me donner vos ordres, ou pour ce moment, ou pour tout autre qui vous Conviendroit. Agreés, je Vous prie, Monsieur le Comte, mon tendre et Respectueux Homage.

LAFAYETTE

From *Charles-Alexandre de Calonne*

Vlles. Le 11 Juin 1784

J'ai fait rassembler, Monsieur, ainsi que je vous l'avois annoncé, la Notice de tous les differents Droits appartenants a M. l'Amiral, aux officiers des Amirautés, aux Villes, ou a des Seigneurs particuliers, qu'un navire des Etats Unis de l'Amerique est dans le Cas de payer dans les Ports de Marseille, Dunkerque, Bayonne et L'Orient, a son arrivée, ou lors de son départ; ces droits ont été reunis dans un Tableau qui presente en même tems les titres de chaque perception et Loix qui L'autorisent; J'ai l'honneur de vous l'envoyer afin que vous puissiez le Communiquer aux Etats Unis, et qu'ils marquent dans la Colonne des observations les demandes qu'ils ont a former sur chaque nature de droit; Il ne me Seroit pas possible jusques là de proposer à Sa Majesté aucun parti sur la supression, la modification, ou la reunion de ces droits, puisque les Etats Unis ne les connoissoient pas eux même; et qu'il est indispensable que la Nature et la quotité de chaque droit leurs Soient parfeitement Connus. Lorsque les reponses des Etats Unis me Seront parvenues, Je m'empresserai, Monsieur, de les mettre sous les yeux de Sa Majesté, et J'espere que vous me rendez la Justice de croire que le desir de faire une chose qui pourra vous être agreable ajoutera encore a celui que J'ai d'être utile aux Etats Unis. J'ai l'honneur d'être avec un Sincère attachement Monsieur, Vôtre très humble et très obeissant Serviteur.

De Calonne

From *Charles-Alexandre de Calonne*

Paris le 16 Juin 1784

Mr. Chardon, Monsieur, vient de me communiquer la lettre que vous lui avez ecrite ce matin, par la quelle vous demandez que les droits que les Navires americains sont dans le cas de payer dans les ports de Marseille, Dunkerque, Bayonne et L'Orient, soyent reünis sous une Seule denomination de tant par navire d'un, ou deux mâts. Vous marquez en même temps que vous desireriez porter aux Etats-unis, une decision sur la Supression, ou la modification de ces droits; malgré le plaisir que j'aurois, Monsieur, a faire une chose agréable pour les Etats-unis, et a vous marquer personellement, Le cas que je fais de l'interêt que vous prenez a ces demandes, il ne m'est pas possible de les proposer avant votre depart a sa majesté; Les droits que payent Les Etats-unis appartiennent à Mr. L'amiral, à des officiers des amirautés, et enfin à des villes et des Seigneurs particuliers: Les uns et les autres seront dans le cas de former des réclamations en indemnité de la privation ou de la reduction de leurs droits, et vous conviendrez, Monsieur, qu'il ne seroit pas juste de les reduire, ni même de les suspendre provisoirement, Sans avoir entendu les parties interessées: La même raison s'oppose egalement a faire l'evaluation que vous proposez, de tous ces differens droits en un Seul, determiné en raison du nombre de mâts de chaque Navire. Il est donc indispensable, Monsieur, que les Etats Unis, après avoir pris communication de l'Etat des droits que j'ai eu l'honneur de vous adresser, etablissent avec précision leurs demandes Sur chacun; ce n'est qu'après qu'elles me seront parvenües, que je pourrai en mettre le resultat sous les yeux du Roy, Et Les Etats Unis doivent être persuadés qu'ils trouveront Sa majesté disposée a leur donner dans toutes les occasions des preuves de l'amitié qui doit regner entre elle et les Etats Unis et dont l'Equité et Sa justice naturelle seront toujours la baze. J'ai l'honneur d'être avec un Sincere attachement, Monsieur, Votre très humble et très obeissant serviteur

De Calonne

L'operation que vous desirez quelque diligence qu'on y apporte entraine necessairement un espace de 3 a 4 mois. On s'en occupera en votre absence et vous seres instruit du resultat.

Je vous renvoye L'etat des droits tels qu'ils existent. Il est toujours bon que vous L'ayés.

From the Maréchal de Castries

Versailles le 17 Juin 1784.

Le Reglement de Commerce entre les Etats Unis et nos Colonies, Monsieur, ne peut pas être terminé pour votre départ; tout ce que vous m'avez dit en faveur de votre sistème est présent à mon esprit, mais il ne nous sera pas possible de donner le dégré de liberté que vous desirez. Tout ce que je prévois dans ce moment ci, c'est que dans chaque Colonie il y aura un Port franc pour les Américains; que tous les objets qu'on recevoit autrefois n'y Souffriront pas de difficultés et que les droits à percevoir seront les plus moderés qu'il se pourra.

Quant aux reglements concernants les farines et les Sucres, je ne puis encore vous rien fixer à cet égard; mais les interêts de notre propre commerce demandent une considération particuliere et comme vous m'en avez prie, je traiterai à fonds sur ces objets avec Mr. Franklin et le Consul général des Etats Unis. J'ai l'honneur d'etre avec un Sincère attachement, Monsieur, votre très humble et très obéissant Serviteur

Le Mal. De Castries

To Adrienne de Noailles de Lafayette

La Flêche [20 juin 1784]
ce dimanche 1 He.

Les mauvaises postes et les mauvais chemins, mon cher Coeur, ne m'ont permis que d'arriver ici; je vais en Repartir pour etre demain au soir à l'Orient, et mardi je verrai ce maudit paquebot avec un Serrement de Coeur inexprimable; pendant qu'on met nos chevaux, j'ai voulu vous dire un mot par le Courier qui va passer; j'ai voulu vous Repeter avec quel Regret je m'eloigne de vous; jamais cette separation ne me fut si penible, mon cher Coeur, et quoique l'absence soit moins longue, à present qu'aucune idée d'un grand Bien public ou de gloire ne me soutient plus, le chagrin que j'epprouve n'a plus l'ombre de Consolation. Si loin d'Amerique, je ne puis encore Bien sentir le plaisir d'y Revoir mes amis, tandis que je laisse ici Ceux que j'aime le mieux. Plus je vous vois, mon cher coeur, et plus je vous trouve aimable pour moi, plus je jouïs du Bonheur de vous etre uni, d'etre aimé de vous; mais aussi la peine de vous quitter en devient plus sensible. J'ai Couché Hier en chemin, j'ai dormi en voiture; je me porte fort Bien, et je suis fort Content de mon jeune Compagnon de Voyage. Adieu, mon cher Coeur, il m'est aussi doux de vous dire que je vous aime que j'epprouve de peine à vous dire adieu, quand je songe que celui de l'Orient sera le dernier que vous Recevrés d'Europe. Je vous embrasse, mon cher coeur, et j'espere que vous savés combien je vous aime.

To Adrienne de Noailles de Lafayette

L'Orient Ce 25 juin 1784

Point de Vent encore, mon cher Coeur, point de lettres de Paris, je suis tout Seul ici, Repoussé par la mer qui [naturellement] est pour moi très Repoussante, et sans Recevoir les lettres d'Amerique ni les lettres de Paris que j'attendois à une poste de Versailles, j'etois deja Comme sous voile et une fois separé de mes amis, autant vaudroit-il etre à la mer. Je sens cependant que l'instant où le vent tournera me fera epprouver une impression triste, et quoique je doive le desirer, mon Coeur Repugne à tout ce qui devient signal de depart. Ne faisant Rien ici, je Songe aux moyens d'avoir des nouvelles là Bas. Il y a dabords outre le paquebot un Commodore Nicholson que j'aime Beaucoup, et qui s'il vient vous voir a droit à une Reception très Amicale; il Repart dans trois semaïnes ou un mois, et une fois que les lettres seront Remises en ses mains, c'est une occasion Bien sure, pourvû surtout qu'il aïlle au Nord de la Virginie. Vous pouvés aussi prier Mr. de Charlus d'ecrire dans les ports qu'on l'avertisse des occasions pour l'Amerique, et par ce moïen tout les Bâtiments m'apporteroïent

Vos lettres et celles de mes amis. La lettre que je joins ici a Rapport au portrait de famille, et servira de Renseignement à Carter et Wadsworth. J'espere que Vous aurés mené celui-ci chès [Barthe?] en le lui Recommandant Bien particulierement. Carmichael vous prie de lui envoyer ma figure gravée; Vous Connoissés de Reputation mon ami Harrison Consul à Cadix; j'avois Repondu pour quelque argeant prêté par lui à Littlepage, et comme j'ai Receu le tout par une lettre de change de Mr. de Beaumarchais, il faudra Rendre à Harrison la partie qui le Regarde. Encore deux Recommandations, mon cher Coeur, l'une est de savoir si Mr. Wurtz a eu la place qu'il desire, et l'autre de voir Mr. Robert de St. Vincent, en lui temoignant tout mon zele pour les affaires de son fils, et les suivant par vous même et Mde. de Tessé avec le plus grand zele. Mde. de Segur suit auprès de Mesdames une affaire dont je voudrois voir la fin.

Pardon, mon cher Coeur, de toutes mes Commissions; mais il m'est doux de penser que nous sommes tellement unis que nos deux interets ne font qu'un, que mes affaires et les votres sont la même chose, et que depuis nos enfants jusqu'au dernier petit arbre ce Chavaniac, tout est Commun entre nous, et tout nous touche Egalement. Votre Voyage de Chavaniac, s'il est possible, me fait grand plaisir; je tiens Beaucoup au Voyage de George, non seulement à Cause de ma tante, mais surtout pour sa santé, pour qu'il Respire l'air de la Campagne, qu'il Courre sans aucune gêne, et Surtout sans les craintes qu'il ne se fasse mal et enfin, je voudrois qu'il fut elevé sans aucune delicatesse, et j'aime mieux le savoir avec les loups du [*illegible*], qu'avec les jolis enfans des Thuileries. Ne pensés vous pas Comme moi, mon cher coeur? J'ai encore mon autre fantaisie sur le Costume de l'abbé, et je voudrois qu'il troquant son petit Collet Contre une epée parceque dans toute mon enfance, je n'ai Cessé d'envier le sort de ceux qui avoïent un gouverneur.

Après avoir Bien Rabaché, mon cher coeur, je Vous prie de dire pour moi mille tendresses à Mde. d'Ayen et mes soeurs. Faites mes Compliments à Gouvion et à Poirey. Dans Certain Cas, je serois fort aise que celui-ci vint me joindre, Car au plaisir d'avoir par lui des nouvelles Bien detaïllées, j'unirai l'utilité que je puis en Retirer. Je vous quitte pour aller diner en ville, et vous qui me Connoissés, vous sentés Combien cela me divertit; si ma chambre n'avoit pas un peu senti la peinture, ce que j'ai detruit par un vernis qu'il faut laisser Secher, je Serois dejá á Bord du paquebot. Mais j'espere m'y Rendre demain dans tous les Cas. S'il y a quelque Consolation à penser que cette lettre-ci n'est pas la derniere, il est Bien cruel pour moi de sentir que lorsque Vous la Recevrés je ne serai plus suivant toute apparence à l'Orient. Malgré la Courte durée de ce voyage, il me laisse une sombre impression de tristesse. C'est plus volontairement, excepté le premier depart, que je me Separe de Vous, que je Vous fais de la peine en vous quittant. Mon coeur en Souffre, et pour vous et pour moi, et je ne serai tranquille qu'au moment ou je pourrai Vous embrasser et vous Repeter moi même, mon cher coeur, combien vous me Rendés Heureux et combien je Vous aime.

Je suis elu membre de l'Academie de Charlestown.

To Adrienne de Noailles de Lafayette

A Bord du Courier de Newyork
ce 28 juin 1784

D'après les apparences de ce matin, mon cher Coeur, je devois croire que cette lettre-ci seroit la derniere; mais le vent a tourné pendant nos preparatifs, et quoiqu'on en promette pour demain, c'est encore une prediction Bien incertaine; en attendant ce changement, je me suis etabli à Bord; nous y essaïons nos Hamacks et nos petites chambres qui n'ont plus d'odeur, et que j'ai fait arranger d'une maniere assés Commode. Tant que j'y serai tranquille, je ne souffrirai que ce toute ma personne morale et phisique souffrira toujours a etre Renfermée. Mais quand la sourriciere Commencera à Remuër, je me fortifierai de Magnetisme, de sachets de Camphre et de theriaque sur le creux de l'estomac, et de gouttes d'oether sur un morceaux de sucre, tous Remedes Nouveaux que je tenterai, et qui ne me feront Rien du tout. En me Recommandant d'embrasser le grand mât, Mesmer ne savoit pas et moi j'ai oublié qu'il est jusqu'à une Certaine Hauteur enduit de goudron, et que l'accolade devient absolument impossible, à moins de Se goudronner des pieds jusqu'à la tête. Je Regrette Bien le tems que j'ai passé ici, mon cher Coeur, et si j'avois prevu ce Retard si long, je vous aurois emmenée jusqu'à l'Orient; mais d'un autre Coté, Vous auriés eu tort de ne pas attendre les couches de votre soeur que je suis moimême Bien affligé de manquer; si les vents Retardent encore, j'en aurai peutêtre des nouvelles demain à 8 Heures, et quoiqu'on n'ait les paquets que mercredi, j'ai engagé notre ami Mr. Monistrol à faire arriver le Courier demain au soir. Depuis le premier, mon cher coeur, je n'ai Receu de lettre que la votre, et je vous en suis Bien obligé. Vous me mandés que Mr. de Calonne va etre garde des sceaux; mais cette nouvelle merite, je crois, Confirmation. Je ne vous ennuïerai pas aujourd'huy de Commissions, mon cher coeur, je vous dirai seulement Bonsoir, sans pouvoir m'empêcher d'etre Bien aise que ce ne soit pas encore un adieu, et vous souhaittant, mon cher coeur, autant de Bonheur que vous m'en procurés, je vous Repete avec un plaisir toujours nouveau, que je vous aime avec la plus vive tendresse, la plus entiere Confiance, et le plus parfait Bonheur de penser que nous sommes l'un à l'autre.

Embrassés Bien tendrement nos enfans.

To the Comte de Vergennes

à Bord du Courier de l'Europe
ce 28 juin 1784

Après avoir attendu les Vents quelques jours, Monsieur le Comte, nous allons enfin mettre à la voile, et ma premiere lettre Sera vraisemblablement dattée de Newyork. Le paquebot qui nous porte est fort joli, mais j'y serai Bien Secoué, et Bien malade; pendant mon Sejour en Amerique, je ferai tout ce qui dependra de moi pour servir mon païs, et cette idée me Console un peu dans le moment ou je vais me separer encore plus de mes amis. En arrivant ici, Monsieur le Comte, j'ai trouvè en question ce que l'arrêt du Conseïl ne me permettoit plus de Revoquer en doute. Les craintes de Mr. l'intendant et de Mr. d'Arlincourt sur l'arrangement Relatif au devoir et aux droits de ferme; le nouvel avis de cinq ou six personnes opposé à celui de toute la ville; la possibilité de Bâtir sur des terrains à Vendre, tandis que l'Orient tout Bâti est à coté. Telles Sont, Monsieur le Comte, les idées par lesquelles on veut justifier l'inconvenient de se dedire au moment même ou l'arrêt du Conseïl assure la franchise du port et de la ville. J'ai pris la liberté d'en ecrire à Monsieur le Contrôleur general; et j'espere Bien que Vous trouverés un meïlleur moyen de tout Concilier, que celui de Reduire la franchise à l'enceinte du port. Vous aurés Bientöt des Nouvelles d'Amerique, Monsieur le Comte, par le Cher. de La Luzerne; j'espere Vous en Rapporter au mois de decembre, et je serai Bien pressé de Retrouver mon païs et [mes] amis. C'est un Sentiment qui Se fortifie à mesure qu'on voyage, mais il ne [peut] plus augmenter dans mon Coeur, et quoique le desir d'etre utile, ou de me preparer à le devenir me fasse souvent Courir les champs, je serai toujours malheureux de partir, toujours transporté de joie en Revoiant ma patrie. [Adieu,] Monsieur le Comte, presentés mes Homages à Madame la Comtesse de Vergennes, à Mesdames Vos Belles filles, mille Compliments à Messieurs vos fils, et agreés avec mes adieux l'Homage de mon Bien tendre et Respectueux attachement.

LAFAYETTE

To Adrienne de Noailles de Lafayette

Philadelphie, ce 13 aoust 1784

Enfin, mon cher coeur, après un si long intervalle, il m'est permis de vous écrire; je puis et vous donner de mes nouvelles, et vous reparler de ma tendresse; mais cette lettre sera bien longtemp en chemin; je connois votre coeur, et je souffre de penser qu'avant le milieu de septembre vous n'aurés pas entendu parler du moi; notre traversée a été courte, et heureuse; j'ai été balloté, et malade; mais après trente cinq jours, j'ai vu la terre américaine, et l'odeur des pins de Jersay est un grand spécifique contre le mal de mer; en entrant dans le port de New-York, j'ai eu des jouissances de plus d'un genre; mais il étoit onze heures du soir quand nous sommes arrivés dans la ville, et tous mes amis étoient profondément endormis, ce qui fait qu'en se réveillant, ils ont été bien ettonnés de me trouver auprès d'eux. La plus grande partie de mes connoissances étoit cependant à la campagne, et après avoir passé deux jours dans cette ville, après y avoir jouï de l'empressement de mes amis, de mes anciens compagnons d'armes, vivant à présent comme moi, en simples citoïens, je me suis mis en marche à travers le Jersay, je ne me suis arrêté que chès Mme Jay arrivée peu de jours avant moi, et auprès de l'assemblés de l'etat de Brunswick. Tout cela ne m'a retenu que quelques heures, et j'ai enfin revu la belle ville de Philadelphie; comme mon arrivée y étoit attendüe, j'ai trouvé un nombreux cortège qui venoit au devant de moi; les anciens officiers, les milices, les citoïens m'ont accompagné dans la ville, et pour ne pas m'arrêter en descriptions, je vous dirai que ma réception ici, et celle de Boston se ressemblent infiniment. Parmi la foule qui m'entouroit, je jouïssois de reconnoitre mes anciens soldats, confondus à présent avec les autres citoïens. Il est vrai, mon cher coeur, que chaque pas ici me procure une satisfaction nouvelle. Le païs est heureux, tranquille, florissant; les maisons que j'ai vû brulées, je les vois rebâtir; on occupe les terrains abandonnés, et tout ce que je rencontre a l'air d'une parfaite convalescence; dans ma situation présente j'aime à espérer que mon influence peut n'être pas inutile aux intérests domestiques des Etats-Unis, à l'union qui doit régner entre eux, enfin à l'union foedérative. Le Congrès ne se rassemble qu'au premier novembre, mais ne craignés pas que cette circomstance retarde mon retour. Je m'arrangerai pour avoir fini dans ce tems-là toutes mes autres affaires; celle qui m'occupe dans ce moment est de retrouver le Général Washington; dans trois jours je serai à Mount Vernon, et je vous laisse à penser avec quelle impatience j'attends ce moment. Depuis mon arrivée à New-York, je n'ai même pas eu le tems d'écrire; tous mes instants sont pris par mes amis, par des visites, par des discours ou des lettres à recevoir et à répondre, et parmi mes oraisons je n'oublierai pas celle que j'ai faite hier sur le magnétisme à l'Académie de Philadelphie.

A propos de science, mon cher coeur, je vous donne avis que vous recevrés par la diligence une tête de marsoûin, gros poisson de mer qu'on prend difficilement, et dont je fais hommage par vos mains à Mme d'Aguesseau. Vous voïés, mon coeur, que je n'oublie pas la commission et surtout votre recommandation. Dans quelque tems, je vous enverrai des choses plus intéressantes; il m'a été impossible de refuser à un ancien domestique de Mr. de La Luzerne une lettre de change pour deux mille écus qu'il me donne; mais le païement est éloigné, et je l'ai prevenu qu'il n'auroit peut-être pendant trois ou quatre mois que les intérêts de cette somme.

Ne pouvant pas écrire dans la journée, mon cher coeur, j'ai choisi le tems où tout le monde dort; dans quelques jours vous aurés des nouvelles plus détaïllées, et je profiterai de la tranquillité de Mount Vernon. Dans ce moment même, j'attends un corps d'officiers qui m'accompagne hors de la ville; parlés de moi, mon cher coeur, à Mme d'Ayen, à la Vicomtesse, à toutes nos soeurs, à la Comtesse Auguste, et faites mes compliments aux amis qui vous demanderont de mes nouvelles. Dites mille choses pour moi à Mr. de Gouvion; je lui envoie comme il m'en a prié quelques gazettes américaines. Embrassés mille et mille fois nos chers enfants; présentés mes homage à Mr. votre père et à Mr. le Maréchal de Noaïlles; Ménagés votre estomac, mon cher coeur, donnés-moi le plaisir de vous retrouver en parfaite santé; adieu, adieu, adieu, mon cher coeur, malgré le bonheur dont je jouïs ici, je m'occupe bien tendrement de celui que j'aurai bientôt de vous embrasser. Je ne vois point ici d'affaire qui me retarde, et je ne serai retenu que par les bontés inexprimables dont on me comble; adieu, encore une fois mon cher coeur. Je sais que je n'ai pas besoin de vous prier de penser à moi, mais en y sachés combien vous me rendés heureux et combien je vous aime.

Ma santé est excellente et j'en aurai bien soin. Mes compliments à l'abbé et à Mr. Margelay.

To Adrienne de Noailles de Lafayette

Mount Vernon, ce 20 aoust 1784.

Sans trop savoir si ma lettre vous parviendra, mon cher coeur, j'ai besoin de vous mander que je suis à Mount Vernon, que j'y jouïs du bonheur d'avoir retrouvé mon cher général, et vous me connaissés trop bien pour que je sois obligé de vous décrire ce que j'ai senti. Après avoir traversé très rapidement le païs, je suis arrivé ici le dix-sept. et comme après avoir été au-devant de moi, le général ne m'a tendoit plus de quelques jours, je l'ai trouvé établi dans sa campagne où notre entrevûe a été bien tendre, et notre satisfaction bien mutuelle. Ce n'est pas pour faire une phrase que je vous assure que dans la retraite le général Washington est plus grand encore qu'il ne le fut jamais pendant la Révolution. Sa simplicité est vraiment sublime, et les détaïls de sa terre et de sa maison l'occupent d'aussi bonne foi que s'il y avoit toujours demeuré. Pour vous rendre compte de la vie que nous y menons, je vous dirai qu'après déjeuner le général et moi causons ensemble quelque tems; après avoir bien parlé du passé, du présent, et du futur, il se retire pour ses affaires, et me donne à lire de qui s'est écrit pendant mon absence; ensuite nous descendons pour diner, et nous trouvons Mme Washington avec des visites du voisinage; la conversation à table roule sur les évènements de la guerre, ou sur les anecdotes que nous aimons à rappeler. Après le thé, nous recommençons nos conversations particulières et le reste de la soirée se passe en famille. Voilà, mon cher coeur, comment nous emploïons notre tems, et nous parlons bien souvent de vous, de nos enfans et de tout ce qui peut intéresser la famille. Il y a dans la maison deux petits enfants de Mme Washington que vous savés avoir été mariée deux fois. Le général les a adoptés et les aime avec une grande tendresse; il étoit assés drôle à mon arrivée de voir la curiosité de ces deux petites figures qui entendoient parler de moi toute la journée, et qui avoient bien envie de savoir si je ressemblois à mon portrait. Le général a lu avec grand plaisir votre lettre, et celle d'Anasthasie; je suis chargé des plus tendres compliments de toute la maison, et Mme Washington me disoit aujourd'huy qu'étant vieux l'un et l'autre, il ne falloit pas différer le plaisir qu'ils auront à vous recevoir ainsi que toute notre petite famille; au premier voyage, mon cher coeur, j'ai pris le plus solemnel engagement de vous mener avec moi; il n'y a rien de beau comme la position de Mount Vernon pour lequel le Pottowmack semble fait exprès. La maison elle-même a fort bon air, et c'est une campagne charmante. Ce n'est pas sans peine que je résiste aux instances du général pour un voyage qu'il est obligé de faire vers les Appalaches. Il l'a retardé si longtems pour moi, qu'une partie de ses biens a été la proïe du premier occupant: mais cette course de six semaines me retarderoit trop, et pour engager le général à y aller sans moi, il a fallu promettre de le retrouver ici. Je partirai donc le premier septembre pour Philadelphie, New-York et ensuite toute la Nouvelle-Anglettere; je serai de retour au commencement d'octobre, et parcourrai avec le général la Virginie, pour être à Trenton dans les premiers jours de novembre. C'est là que je verrai la réunion du Congrès et que je prendrai congé de tout le monde. Ainsi, mon cher coeur, soïés sure de me voir arriver à la fin de décembre; les deux mois passés me semblent avoir été bien longs; les quatre mois qui me séparent de vous seront bien longs aussi; et rien au monde ne me fera retarder un retour que je souhaitte avec la plus vive ardeur.

Dans peu de jours, j'attends des nouvelles de France, et Rousselet doit me les apporter de New-York. Le pauvre Hubert a été malade en voiture, a pris la galle à bord, s'est estropié le genouï à Philadelphie. A cela près, il se trouve très bien de son voyage, et m'attend sur un pied, dans la capitale de Pennsylvanie. Esra est dans son païs, et Demanche qui me suit avec Le Brun ne revient pas encore de ce que les Américains n'entendent pas son français. Mais il faut finir cette lettre, mon cher coeur, tout comme si elle allait partir sur le champ pour la France; on m'attend là bas pour le thé, et le porteur de mes dépêches s'en ira tout de suite après la dernière tasse. Présentés mes tendres homages à Mr. votre père, Mme d'Ayen, Mr. le Maréchal de Noaïlles; mille tendresses à toutes mes soeurs, et dites à la vicomtesse que je suis bien occupé d'elle. Mes compliments au vicomte, à Ségur, à Mme de Ségur, Mr. et Mme de Fresnes. Parlés de moi à Mr. votre grand-père, et Mme votre grand-mère, à qui ma tête de marsouin fera, j'espère bientôt mes honneurs. Embrassés nos chers enfans. Adieu, adieu, mon cher coeur, vous savés combien je vous aime.

To the Comte de Vergennes

Neywork Ce 15 Septembre 1784

Quoique le Paquebot Soit arrivé, Monsieur le Comte, il ne m'a point porté de lettre de Vous; mais je sais que Votre Santé etoit Bonne et j'espere qu'il en est de même pour toute la famille. Depuis que j'ai debarqué, je ne cesse de Courir; partout on m'a Comblé de Bontés et j'ai passé quinze jours dans la Retraite du Gal. Washington. Me Voici en chemin pour un traité de sauvages; de là j'irai dans la Nouvelle Anglettere; je Rejoindrai le general et nous Continuerons ensemble mes visites. Vers le milieu de Novembre nous verrons le Congrès dans Sa Resurrection, et à la fin de l'année j'aurai le Bonheur Bien Vivement desiré de Revoir ma patrie.

Les Nouvelles Americaines vous parviennent par Mr. de Marbois, et dans mon etat de pelerinage, je dois Remettre au Retour mes observations. On Vous mande surement ou en est l'affaire de Longchamp. Il paroit que l'indignation et la Bonne volonté ne manquent pas; mais dans le moment actuel, ils sont embarassés sur la maniere; jusqu'ici Mr. de La Luzerne, et Mr. de Marbois, n'ont pas eu à se plaindre, à Ce que m'a dit Ce dernier, des dispositions du president et du Conseïl.

Le Commerce avec l'Anglettere vient du credit ettonnant qu'y trouve tout americain. Cet abandon produira des Banqueroutes, et l'Hiver prochain nous sera favorable, pourvû que nos negotiants consultent les Besoins et les gousts du païs. Il est arrivé du Chanvre en Virginie, et des Sabots de France à Baltimore.

Il s'etablit vers L'Oyho une population immense; les arrivants y vont tout droit, les anciens Habitants S'y transportent eux mêmes. Les Manufactures et même la Navigation d'Amerique en Seront Retardées, et Comme on Veut Rapprocher par des Canaux la Communication du Pottowmak, de la Susquehana, et de l'Ohyo, nous aurons la preference des Illinois et des Sauvages pour nos Manufactures; mais le debouché de tout ce païs est le Mississipy, et la prohibition entrainera des disputes, plus tard qu'on ne le croit ici, mais Beaucoup plutôt qu'on ne pense en Europe. Les americains nous aiment, mais ils Haïssent l'Espagne très Cordialement.

Autant qu'un particulier peut y pretendre, je tâche de Connoitre et de Servir ici les interests de mon païs. La ville de Newyork m'a presenté *la liberté de la ville*, Compliment à l'anglaise que je me suis assuré d'avance etre sans aucune Consequence. On a mis dans les papiers que la franchise de l'Orient est Reduite au port. Je vais y [faire] inserer une explication Convenable.

Adieu, monsieur le Comte, Rappellés moi aux Bontés de Madame la Comtesse de Vergennes, et de toute la famille, et pensés quelquefois à un ami qui vous a voué pour la vie le plus tendre et respectueux attachement.

LAFAYETTE

Barbé-Marbois's Journal of His Visit to the Territory of the Six Nations[E]

23. 7bre. [septembre] 1784

. . . En débarquant Je trouvai M. le Mis. de La Fayette, Mr. le Chever. de Caraman, et M. Madisson delegué du Congrès, prêts à partir pour aller voir les nations Sauvages; et nous eumes bientot lié partie pour nous y rendre ensemble.

Nous avions beaucoup entendu parler des Convulsionaires américains. Depuis trois ans que cette Secte a fait des progrès en Amérique, nous desirions tous de Voir leur principal établissement qui étoit peu éloigné de notre route; et aux motifs ordinaires de curiosité Mr. le Mis. de La Fayette Joignoit ceux d'examiner de près des phénomènes qui paroissent avoir beaucoup d'analogie avec ceux de Mesmer, a l'école de qui il a étudié.

C'étoit un dimanche: nous partimes pour Neschiune, lieu de leur assemblée. Ce Village Situé dans le milieu de Bois, est de difficile accès, et nous fumes obligés de mettre pied à terre pour aller les chercher. Nous entendimes de fort loin une musique lente, mélancolique, mais assès mélodieuse: toutes les Voix chantoient à l'unisson, ou par octaves, et l'effet en étois assés agréable à quelque distance. Nous trouvames les Secouans dans l'Exercice de leurs pratiques réligieuses. . . . M. le Mis. de La Fayette, un des adeptes du Dr. Mesmer, voulut tenter Sur l'un d'eux les epreuves du magnétisme animal: pendant qu'il le magnétisoit de toute Sa force le pauvre homme nous faisoit Son histoire: "Je tombai un Jour de mon chariot, nous dit-il; "Je me fis une profonde blessure à la Jambe, un "homme charitable vint me Secourir pendant que j'étois privé de "connoissance, à mon reveil Je me trouvai guéri. J'eprouvai un "changement total dans mes Sentimens et mes inclinations; Je renonçai "au monde et à Ses Voyes. J'ai Suivi celles de ces hommes parfaits et "depuis ce moment Je Suis infiniment heureux."

Cet élu etois d'une extrême Simplicité, et pendant que Mr. le Mis. de La Fayette tentoit Sans Succes Sur tous Ses poles les effets du magnétisme, un des anciens inquiet de ce qui pouvoit en resulter, vint à nous. Il demanda Si c'étoit au nom d'un bon esprit ou d'un mauvais esprit que nous agissions. Assurément, dit M. le Mis. de La Fayette, C'est au nom d'un bon esprit. Ce principe une fois accordé, Vous imaginés bien que le Secouant nous mena loin; il voulut même nous persuader de nous rendre Ses proselytes et nous ne pumes nous débarasser de lui qu'en partant de Neshiune pour continuer notre Voyage.

. . . Nous poursuivimes notre voyage à travers un pays Superbe, mais où tous nous rétraçoit encore l'image de la guerre, et d'une guerre cruelle, telle que les Sauvages la font. Nous avions avec nous un Sac de farine de maïs, qui nous fut d'une grande ressource. On nous fournissoit du beurre en abondance; Si nous demandions du lait, on nous en apportoit dans de grands Sceaux de Bois; Nous en faisions une bouillie qui eut un grand Succès dans tous ce pays, et Souvent nos hôtes, au lieu de nous nourir, le furent par nous. Nous étions parfaitement à l'abry de la famine qu'on nous avoit fait craindre. Nous étions encore mieux garantis des Injures du tems; les manteaux, les couvertures nous furent d'une grande ressource: J'Excepte cependant Mr. le Mis. de La Fayette qui paroit être à l'epreuve du chaud, du froid, du Sec. de l'humide, et de l'intempérie des Saisons. Il avoit pris pour Se garantir de la pluye un Surtout de taffetas gommé qui avoit été envéloppé dans des gazettes qui S'étoient attachées à la gomme. On n'avoit pas eu le tems de les arracher, et les curieux pouvoient lire Sur Son bras ou Son dos le courier de l'Europe ou les nouvelles de divers endroits.

Malgré les dévastations auxquelles ont été enproye les deux rives de la Mohawk, la population y fait des progrès rapides. Nous trouvions des familles de 10 à 12 enfans, couchant tous dans le méme lit, grands et petits. Ils nous environnoient continuellement comme des objets nouveaux pour eux dans un pays où il est fort rare de Voir des étrangers voyageant par curiosité. Tout ce qui est de 1ere. [première] nécessité ne nous manquoit pas; mais ce qui Seroit mis ailleurs dans cette classe nous manquoit ici. Il est vrai qu'on faisoit Servir les enfans à tous: Si nous demandions un chandelier un marmot de quatre ou cinq ans étoit placé près de nous, une chandelle à la main. Si nous paroissions incommodés de la chaleur, un autre Se mettoit devant nous pour nous tenir lieu d'Ecran. Ils avoient le plus grand empressement à nous rendre ces petits offices, et Souvent l'honneur de tourner une broche de Bois que nous avions inventée pour cuire nos viandes troubla la paix de la famille et mit la division parmi les freres.

Nous rencontrons déjà fréquemment des Sauvages et tout nous annonce que nous allons quitter les Etablissemens des hommes blancs pour entrer chès les Indiens. Toutes les maisons éparses Sont encore environnées des Stocades par lesquelles on a Voulu pendant la derniere guerre les protéger contre ces barbares, et qui n'ont pas toujours Suffi pour arrêter leurs ravages. Ce Sont des poutres enfoncées comme des pilotis, rangées les unes près des autres, et qui environnent la maison qui devenoit la refuge de tous les habitans de la ferme aux aproches de l'ennemi. Les Batimens qui étoient hors de l'enceinte, etoient la proye des flammes.

On nous avoit prevenus d'avance Sur le mauvais Etat des chemins; mais nous les trouvames pires que nous n'avions imaginé; et après avoir fait 80 milles en Voiture, nous fumes obligés d'y rénoncer à cause du danger continuel de Verser et de l'Extrême fatigue des chevaux. Je laissai mon Phaëton aux German Flats, et transformai deux grands chevaux de Carosse en chevaux de monture. Les couvertures dont Je m'étois heureusement pourvu, me Servirent de Selle; et dans cet équipage à motié Sauvage nous fimes le reste du chemin Jusqu'au Fort Schuyler: c'étoit le lieu convenu pour une négociation entre trois commissaires du Congrès et les chefs et guerriers de dix nations Sauvages qui habitent le long des grands lacs qui Séparent les Etats Unis du Canada. Nous en trouvames un grand nombre de rassemblés; mais les commissaires n'étoient point encore arrivés. Les Indiens que nous appellons à Juste titre Sauvages, avoient construit à la hâte des cabanes où ils logeoient avec leurs familles; quelques-uns mêmes, malgré le froid et la gélée, n'avoient que des abris de branches d'arbres dont les feuilles déssechées ne les garantissoit ni du vent ni de la pluye.

Quant au Fort Schuyler, dont J'avois entendu parler depuis cinq ans comme de l'ancien Boulevard de la colonie de Newyork contre les Sauvages, Je fus Surpris de voir qu'il Se reduisoit à un petit fortin en terre, avec quatre Bastions à moitié ruinés. Il y avoit deux Baraques Sans plancher, et dont le toit étoit couvert d'Ecorce. Une de ces cabanes étoit remplie des présens destinés aux Sauvages, l'autre Servoit de logement à Mr. Kirkland missionnaire établi parmi les Sauvages depuis environ Vingt ans. Il a pour eux l'affection qu'on finit par prendre pour ceux avec qui on a passé une grande partie de la Vie, et il aime à les présenter Sous le point de Vue le plus favorable. Nous partageames Sa chambre qui étoit destinée à loger les Commissaires, et comme ils étoient attendus de moment en moment, on Se hata de nous construire des cabanes d[e] l'ecorce.

. . . Nous avions du Biscuit et quelques autres provisions. Nous en fimes la distribution comme Si nous nous fussions disposés à une famine ou bien à Voyager dans un desert.

Nous partimes à cheval pour la Bourgade des Onéidas. . . . Ce qui est réellement barbare et Sauvage, ce Sont les chemins qui conduisent du Fort Schuyler chès les Onéidas. Un de nos gens nous exhorta de bonne foi à porter nos plaintes à l'Intendant de la province touchant le mauvais Etat des ponts et chaussées de Son département. Le Sol est aussi riche ici que Sur la Riviere des Mohawks, mais quelqu'avantage que la postérité puisse en tirer rien n'est plus facheux pour les Voyageurs d'a présent. Il faut Se faire Jour à cheval à travers les Bois, en Suivant du mieux qu'on peut un Sentier pratiqué pour les Sauvages qui vont toujours à pied. Les Ruisseaux forment une continuité de marais bourbeux où nous enfoncions à chaque pas. Des arbres d'une grandeur et d'une grosseur démesurée tombent de Vieillesse dans toutes les parties de la forêt; Ils embarassent les Sentiers pour les hommes à cheval, quoique rien n'empêche les Sauvages de les Escalader. Nous Voyagions par un tems obscur et pluvieux. Nous nous égarames un moment; mais nos guides retrouvoient bientot leur chemin: les arbres leur Servent de Boussole, et ils reconnoissent le nord à l'ecorce qui est brune et plus couverte de mousse de ce côté que de celui de Sud. Après avoir traversé cette longue forêt, tantôt à pied, tantôt à cheval, quelquefois au gué, quelquefois en faisant nager nos chevaux, nous arrivames bien mouillés et bien las à la Bourgade des Onéidas. Nous ne fimes au reste aucune rencontre chemin faisant, Si ce n'est celle d'un vieux Sauvage dormant dans un marais et couvert de boue à demie gelée. Nos guides le reveillerent et Sûrent que la Veille il avoit été au fort où il avoit engagé Son fusil pour un baril d'eau de vie; Son intention étoit de la rapporter à la bourgade, mais ayant Succombé à la tentation de la gouter, il avoit vuidé le barril, et passé une nuit bien froid dans une profonde yvresse.

Avant d'entrer dans la Bourgade, Je dois vous dire que M. de La Fayette y portoit trois barrils d'eau de vie, ou pour me Servir de l'Expression des amateurs du pays, trois barrils de lait. Trois Sauvages en portoient chacun un, et malgré le poids et la difficulté du chemin, ils nous Suivirent assés constamment, et même nous évancerent quelquefois. L'un d'eux me parut Si fatigué cependant que Je fis porter Son barril par mon domestique qui étoit à cheval. Ce Sauvage m'en témoigna Sa réconnoissance, et Je fus Surpris de l'entendre me parler en très bon françois. . . .

Un drapeau blanc arboré à la principale cabane nous indiqua la maison du conseil, ou, comme disent nos gens, l'hôtel de Ville. Nous y trouvames les chefs et guerriers de la nation rassemblés. Ils nous y reçurent avec l'hospitalité que les Sauvages exercent envers tous ceux qui ne Sont pas leurs ennemis. Je retrouvai une ancienne connoissance: C'étoit un chef respectable par Son age et Son habileté. Son nom est la Grande Sauterelle: Je l'avois vù à Philadelphie en 1781. Il nous reçut revêtu d'un uniforme brodé que M. le Chevr. de La Luzerne lui avoit donné à cette époque; et qu'il porte dans toutes les occasions importantes. Après les complimens d'usage, on nous apporta un grand Saumon qu'on venoit de prendre. Nous eumes du lait, du beurre, des fruits et du miel en quantité. Nous aprêtames notre Souper nous mêmes, et un couvert qui Se trouve par hazard dans notre bagage nous fut d'une grande ressource; nous bûmes dans des gobelets de bois, et M. de la Fayette en eut par distinction un de verre racommodé avec de la gomme.

Nous témoignames le desir de voir leurs danses et aussitôt un des principaux Sortit, et Soufflant dans un cornet, il appela les Jeunes gens de la Bourgade, et leur det de S'habiller pour le bal, et de Se rendre Sans délai à la maison du Conseil pour amuser les étrangers. . . .

. . . Le Bal ayant duré deux heures, nous en fumes Si ennuyés que nous dimes aux interprêtes d'engager les danseurs à se retirer: la chose n'étoit pas facile; ils Se proposoient de continuer Jusqu'au Jour, et l'yvresse S'en étant mêlée, les deux premieres harangues qu'on leur fit n'eurent aucun effet. Les chefs ne vouloient pas les congédier, probablement parcequ'ils n'en avoient pas le pouvoir. Enfin un des danseurs qui avoit autrefois Servi Sous Mr. de la

Fayette nous prit en pitié, et parla Si éloquemment que les masques Se disperserent; et nous eumes la liberté de nous coucher.

. . . Quand nous fumes prêts à retourner au Fort Schuyler, la Grande Sauterelle, le Forgeron, et le Rocher Roulant du Haut des Montagnes, les trois chefs de la nation vinrent nous trouver. Comme ils arrivoient, on m'apprit que mes chevaus étoient égarés, et qu'on les avoit cherchés depuis le matin. Ils n'en furent ni Surpris ni inquiets: ils donnerent quelques ordres, et au bout d'une demie heure le Rocher Roulant du Haut des Montagnes me les ramena lui même. . . .

Nous étions Sur le point de partir lorsque deux Jeunes gens de 24 à 25 ans, dont l'un paroissoit yvre, commencèrent à se quéreller, et la conversation devenant de plus en plus animée, l'un d'eux frappa l'autre de Son Cassetête avec violence. Le battu Se mit à pleurer, et paroissoit vouloir rendre les coups qu'il avoit reçus quand un Vieillard le prit dans ses bras, et le tint couché à terre Jusqu'à ce que des femmes étant venues, elles emmenerent l'autre hors de la cabane. Le Vieillard étoit pere des deux Jeunes gens, et Son fils, quoique vigoureux, ne fit aucun effort pour Se dégager de ses bras. Il consentit même à fumer la pipe de paix avec Son frere. Nous le vimes fumer à demi une pipe, et la présenter à l'agresseur qui l'acheva, et la paix fut faite. Ces querelles Sont d'autant plus fréquentes qu'elles ont pour cause la guerre qui vient de finir. Les nations, et mêmes les familles, ont été divisées: l'un des deux freres avoit Servi dans l'armée angloise, et l'autre avoit Joint les américains. Nous avions entendu plusieurs fois celui ci appeller Son frere tory: car les Sauvages en prenant part à la querelle ont adopté les dénominations de Wighs et de torrys qui Servent chès eux comme chès les américains à perpétuer la division et les violences même après la guerre est finie.

J'ai lieu de croire que quelques-uns de nos gens Se marierent pendant leur courte résidence à la bourgade car au moment de notre départ nous vimes quelques Squaws fort affligées, encore parées des rubans de nôces; et la Séparation fut fort touchante. Au reste depuis qu'un missionaire habite chès les Oneïdas ces nôces hospitalieres y Sont fort rares, et l'on ne nous en fit pas même la proposition.

En revenant au fort nous fumes Surpris de retrouver le Sauvage yvre que nous avions déjà rencontré en allant à la Bourgade. Ce malheureux de retour chès lui, et Sorti de Son yvresse, avoit compris qu'il lui falloit dégager Son fusil à quelque prix que ce fut. Il avoit acheté un autre barril d'eau de vie, et il le portoit au fort Lorsque Succombant une Seconde fois à une tentation insurmontable il étoit retombé dans le même état d'yvresse où nous l'avions déjà trouvé une fois.

. . . Les Sauvages étoient arrivés de plusieurs cantons pendant notre absence, et nous en trouvames de huit nations différentes à notre retour au fort. C'étoient les Mohawks, les Onéidas, les Onondagas, les Tuscaroras, les Cayagas, les Loups ou Stockbrige, les Senecas et d'autres nations du Canada, parmi lesquelles les gens du Fort St. Louis étoient les plus remarquables, et parloient presque tous françois. Les Senecas, les Cayoucas, les Onondagas et les Agniés ou Mohawks ont été les ennemis des Etats Unis pendant la derniere guerre, et n'ont pas encore des dispositions bien pacifiques. Ils S'étoient rendus à la Rivierre des Mohawks Sur l'invitation du congrès pour traiter Avec M[ess]rs. Woolcot, Lee et Buttler commissaires de cette assemblée. Ce grand conseil (c'est le nom que les Sauvages donnent à ces assemblées de plusieurs nations) ce grand conseil nous fournissoit l'occasion de voir ces peoples réunis au même lieu, et un peu plus commodement que Si nous avions été obligés de parcourir les différens pays qu'ils habitent.

    ... Vous Jugerés du prix qu'on met à conserver un homme, et de l'importance dont il est de ne pas Souffrir l'affoiblissement de la Société, par la difficulté que M. le Mis. de La Fayette a trouvée à Se procurer un compagnon Sauvage. Quoique les Onéidas ayent la plus grande affection pour lui, ils ont eu une peine infinie à lui accorder la permission d'emmener un de leurs Jeunes gens en France; il a fallu consulter les chefs, conférer avec tous les parens; il y en a d'éloignés de ce lieu et dont il faudra avoir le Consentement; ou leur enverra des messages à cet effet; et quoique la pluspart Soient disposés à le Satisfaire, Je ne regarde pas encore cette importante négociation comme conclue.

    ... Nous fumes témoins de la réconciliation des Onéidas avec les Sauvages ennemis. Quoiqu'ils habitassent depuis quelques Jours les uns et les autres près du fort, ils ne Se voyoient pas, et malgré la cessation des hostilités la communication n'étoit pas rétablie. La Grande Sauterelle couvert du manteau de Mr. le Chever. de La Luzerne et Suivi de cinq autres Sauvages vêtus avec la même recherche Se rendirent aux cabanes des Senecas: leur marche étoit composée, et ils S'arrêtoient de tems en tems. Le Chef des Senecas Sortit et Vint les recevoir à quelque distance. Ils S'assirent Sur le gazon, des compliments furent faits par les deux chefs; on fuma le calumet de paix, et ils Se Separérent; le lendemain la Visite fut rendue par les Senekas aux Onéidas avec le même appareil et les mêmes formalités.

    ... Il reste à ces Sauvages un grand respect pour le Roi de France; ils parlent avec vénération de la nation françoise quoique leurs relations ayent cessé depuis plus de Vingt ans. Ils aiment les liqueurs avec passion; mais ils disent que les françois étoient leurs véritables peres puisqu'ils leur refusoient ce poison que les anglois leur fournissoient avec abondance. Mr. de La Fayette possede leur confiance et leur attachement à un point extraordinaire: ceux qui l'avoient déjà vu, avoient un grand empressement à le revoir encore. Ils avoient communiqué leur enthousiame à leurs amis, et ils paroissoient fiers de porter à leur col quelques présens qu'il leur avoit fait autrefois.

    ... Nous fumes présens à l'ouverture des conférences pour la paix entre les commissaires du congrès et les Sauvages. Il y eut plusieurs discours, et M. de La Fayette en prononça un très bien composé avec la grace et la noblesse que Vous lui connoissés. La Séance Se ténoit en plein air malgré un froid assès vif; les Sauvages assis en rond autour d'un feu qui n'étoit destiné qu'à allumer leurs pipes, écoutoient avec une attention particuliere. Il y avoit une quarantine de chefs ou guerriers présens; les guerriers armés comme pour le combat avoient assès bonne mine; mais d'autres étoient vêtus de la maniere la plus bizare et la plus ridicule. L'un S'étoit affublé d'une peau d'ours, et ressembloit assès à cet animal. Un autre avoit attaché Sur Sa tête des oreilles Semblables à celles avec lesquelles on représente Midas. Nous revimes aussi la péruque dont la possession avoit causé une querelle peu de Jours auparavant. Ces figures grotesques contrastoient parfaitement avec la gravité des orateurs. L'un de ceux ci parla avec beaucoup de grace; il étoit debout Suivant leur usage. Une piéce de drap flottoit Sur Ses épaules. Il avoit le bras gauche nud et étendu; l'air fier. la Voix haute; et nous écoutames fort attentivement l'interprête qui nous traduisit Son discours; mais nous n'y trouvames rien d'égal à ce que l'apparence nous avoit annoncé.

6. 8bre. [octobre]

Nous avions rempli le principal but de notre Voyage, qui étoit de Voir les Sauvages. Rien ne nous retenois plus au Fort Stanwix. Nous frettames un petit Bateau où il y avoit Justement place pour onze personnes, y compris cinq rameurs, et nous descendimes la Riviere des Mohawks très commodément et par le plus beau de tems du monde. Il y a une cataracte appellée *The Little Fall*, où il faut mettre le batteau à terre. On le fait trainer par des chevaux et les effets ou marchandises Sont mises Sur un chariot. Ce portage est d'environ un demi mille. il est agréable de Voir les progrès de la culture à mesure qu'on descend cette riviere: mais nous étions en même tems affligés par le Spectacle des barbaries commises par les Sauvages. Toutes les fermes ont été brulées, et les habitans Sont encore dénués d'une foule de choses necessaires; mais les Subsistances de toute espéce S'y trouvent en abondance.

8. 8bre. [octobre]

Nous voila de retour à Albany, Mademoiselle; nous y avons trouvé toutes les personnes qui nous intéressoient en bonne Santé. Nous avons été Voir une cascade dont nous ne dirons rien parceque Vous en avès vu dans le Journal de Mr. de Cahttellux une description aussi belle que nature, et que nous ne pourions dire aussi bien que lui.

Nous retrouvons ici une Société très civile et très polie et comme ce Journal n'a eu pour objet que de vous faire faire connoissance avec les Sauvages, nous le finissons ici, et nous desirons que Vous le lisiés avec autant de plaisir que nous en avons pris à l'écrire pour vous.

Account of Lafayette's Meeting with the Six Nations

Relation de ce qui s'est passé à l'ouverture du
Traité entre les Etats-Unis et les nations Sauvages
au Fort Stanwix le 3 et 4 october 1784

Les deputés du Congrès, ceux de Pensilvannie, le Mis. de la Fayette s'etant rendus au conseil, où étoient tous les chefs Sauvages, Mr. de la Fayette prononça en français le discours suivant, qui fut traduit par l'interprete des Etats-unis:

En me rapprochant de mes enfants, je rends graces au ciel qui me conduit dans ce lieu de paix où vous fumé ensemble le Calumet d'amitié.

Si vous reconnoissés la voix de Kayenlaa rappelés vous aussi ses conseils et les colliers qu'il vous a souvent envoiés. Je viens remercier les enfans fideles, les chefs des nations, les guerriers, les porteurs de mes paroles, et si la memoire paternelle n'oublioit pas plutot le mal que le bien, je pourrois punir ceux qui en ouvrant les oreilles ont fermé leur coeur, qui levant aveuglement la hâche, ont risqué de frapper leur propre pere.

La cause Americaine est juste, vous disois-je alors, c'est la cause de l'humanité, c'est particulierement votre cause. Restés neutres au moins, et les braves Americains defendront leur liberté et la votre. Vos peres les prendront par la main; les oiseaux blancs couvriront le rivage; le grand Onondio, connu le soleil, dissipera les nuages autour de vous, et les projets contraires s'evanouiront comme un brouillard qui tombe.

N'ecoutés pas Kayenlaa, vous crioit-on ailleurs; mais on vous disoit aussi qu'une armée du nord, entreroit triomphante à Boston; que celle du sud prendroit la Virginie; que le grand chef de guerre Washington, à la tete de vos peres et de vos freres, seroit forcé de quitter le païs. Ceux qui avoient la main sur vos yeux ne laissoient cependant pas que d'ouvrir les leurs. La Pais est faite! Vous en savés les conditions, et j'obligerai quelques uns d'entre vous, en m'abstenant par pitié de les repeter.

Mes predictions étant accomplies, écoutés les nouveaux avis de votre pere, et que ma voix retentisse parmi toutes les nations.

Qu'avés vous jamais gagné, mes enfants, ou plutot que n'avés vous pas perdu aux querelles Européenes? Soiés plus sages que les blancs, conservés la paix entre vous, et puisque le grand conseil des Etats veut bien traiter, profités de ses bonnes dispositions. N'oubliés pas que les Américains sont amis intimes des françois vos peres: cette alliance est aussi durable qu'elle a été heureuse. Le grand Onondio donne pour toujours la main à vos freres qui vous tendent la leur et par ce moien nous formerons une chaine salutaire. Pour vous en assurer, commercés avec les Americains, avec ceux de vos peres qui traversent le grand lac. Les manufactures de France vous sont connues et vous etes assés habiles pour les preferer. Elles seront pour vous le signe de l'alliance: en vendant des terres ne consultés pas un barril de Rum, pour les livrer au premier venu. Mais que les chefs Americains et les votres reunis autour du feu concluent des marchés raisonables. Dans le moment actuel, mes enfans, vous sáves que si plusieurs ont droit à la reconnaissance du Congrès, il y en a beaucoup dont la seule ressource est dans sa clemence et dont les fautes passées exigent des reparations.

Si vous écoutés bien, mes enfans, je vous en ai dit assés, repetés vous mes paroles les uns aux autres, tandis que sur l'autre bord du lac, je recevrai avec plaisir vos nouvelles et jusqu'au jour où nous joindrons nos pipes, ou nous coucherons encore sous la même écorce, je fous souhaite bonne santé, chasses heureuses, union et abondance, et le succès de tous les rêves qui vous promettront du bonheur.

Le chef des Mohawks se leva tenant un collier et dit:

Que les oreilles de Kayenlaa, un chef du grand Onondio, notre pere, soient ouvertes, pour recevoir notre parole.

Mon pere.

Nous avons entendus ta voix, et nous nous réjouissons que tu ai visité tes enfans, pour leur donner des avis justes, et necessaires. Tu nous a dit que nous avions eu tort de preter l'oreille aux mechants, et de fermer nos coeurs à tes conseils. Cela est vrai, mon pere, nous la Nation des Mohawks avons quitté le bon chemin, nous reconnaissons avoir été egarés et enveloppés dans un nuage noir, mais nous revenons à present afin que tu retrouve en nous de bons et fideles enfans.

Vraiment, mon pere, nous aimons à entendre ta voix parmi nous, qui sans blesser nos coeurs, nous a fait beaucoup de bien. Il semble que l'esprit tout puissant t'ait dirige, t'ait conduit en ce lieu de paix, où tu peux fumer le calumet d'amitié, avec tes enfans retrouvés.

Kayenlaa, mon pere.

Quant à notre situation, tu nous as aussi parlè vrai; mais nous esperons que le Grand Esprit, qui nous a jusqu'ici protegé, nous sortira aussi du mauvais chemin pour diriger nos pas dans le bon sentier que nos fautes passées seront oubliées, afin que nous puissions nous joindre dans la meme cause et etre unanime dans toute nos entreprises.

Mon pere.

Nous sentons que toutes les paroles que tu as proferées sont les paroles de la verité, et l'experience nous a montré que toutes les predictions se sont accomplies. Tes paroles et ton discours inspire un esprit de paix, c'est notre grand et seul objet, c'est l'objet qui nous conduit.

Kayenlaa, mon pere.

C'est une regle ancienne et établie que des enfans doivent obeïr à leur pere et que de les gronder et de les punir quand ils font des fautes, est la prerogative paternelle; nous le savons, et l'avons certainement meritée. Mais comme nous l'avons dit, nous comptons que le grand esprit d'en haut disposera et purifiera tellement nos coeurs, que tu pourras te feliciter de rendre à tes enfans dans ta Bonté, la vie qu'ils ont merités de perdre.

Mon pere.

Nous nous rappellons les paroles que tu nous as dites il y a sept ans et nous trouvons qu'il n'y en a pas une qui ne se soit verifiée. Oui mon pere nous voïons que tout ce que tu dis est vrai, ce qui nous fait jouir à present lorsque nous te regardons et que nous fumons encore aussi la pipe de paix et d'amitié. Tu nous as observé, mon pere, que l'alliance entre la France et l'Amerique étoit une chaine indissoluble, qui ne se romperoit jamais et ceux qui douteront n'ont qu'à entrer dans vos vaisseaux, passer le grand lac et voïr par eux mêmes.

Mon pere.

Tu nous as averti de ne point prendre conseil des fortes liqueurs dans la vente de nos terres; nous avions bien besoin de cet avis salutaire, car c'est de là que viennent toutes nos miseres et tous nos malheurs, et nous souhaitons qu'il ne survienne pas d'inconvenient de ce genre dans ce grand conseil de Paix.

Mon pere.

Les paroles que tu nous as prononcés aujourdhui, seront publiées parmi toutes les Six Nations, elles doivent renouveller et renforcer la chaine d'amitié que nous désirons voir durer toujours.

Kayenlaa mon pere.

Nous ne t'en dirons pas d'avantage aujourd'hui, parceque il ne convient pas à notre situation de multiplier les paroles. Mais nous jouissons du bonheur du moment present et nous asisterons au grand conseil des Etats-unis, dont nous felicitons Les membres, sur leur arrivé ici. Tu nous as dit que tu partois demain et si nous avons quelque chose à ajouter nous te le communiquerons chés toi.

Le lendemain il y eut une autre assemblé Sauvage ou l'orateur des Nations [amies?] prononça le discours suivant:

Kayenlaa mon pere.

Je prie toutes les nations ici presentes d'ouvrir les oreilles au peu de mots que je vais dire; et toi, grand chef de guerre de notre pere Onondio, je te prie de m'écouter:

Ton discours d'hier contient des felicitations, des reproches, et des conseils; nous les recevons d'autant mieux que nous nous rappellons les paroles que tu nous as dites il y a sept ans. Ce sont elles qui nous ont empeché d'etre égarés par ceux qui combattoient la cause de l'Amerique. Ce collier (comme le collier receu de Mr. de Moncalm) nous fut donné il y a vingt ans par nos peres. Ils nous dirent que chacun devoit en tenir un bout et qu'un jour leurs voix seroient encore entendues parmi nous.

Kayenlaa mon pere.

Toutes tes paroles ont été verifiées par les événements de cette grande Isle, nous recevons donc avec plaisir les nouvelles paroles que tu nous dis en cette occasion.

En rendant le collier le Marquis repondit qu'il jouissait de voir qu'on eut si bien gardé ce collier et de penser que son influence sur quelques nations les eut empechées de se declarer contre Les Etats-unis, que la France tiendra toujours un bout du collier et qu'il sera aussi tenu par l'Amerique, dont l'alliance entretiendra la communication entre les francois et leurs enfans. Il les remercia de leur fidelité à suivre ses conseils en fermant l'oreille aux ennemis de la cause Americaine.

Un chef huron se leva et dit:

Kayenlaa mon pere.

Ouvre tes oreilles au peu de mots que je vais prononcer à ton depart. Les Nations du Nord ont longtems été les enfans du grand Onondio. Les paroles que tu nous as dites, nous ont été agréables, parcequ'elles étoient vraies. Tu as commencé par remercier l'Etre Suprême de t'avoir. Conduit dans ce lieu de paix et d'amitié. Nous reconnoissons la même providence et nous esperons qu'elle rendra ce conseil la source des plus grandes bénédictions. Nous te remercions de toutes tes paroles en te remerciant, nous prenons congé de toi.

Kayenlaa mon pere.

Nous ajouterons encore un mot à ce que nous t'avons dit. En quittant les nations du nord, nous reçumes des exortations du Gouverneur de Canada, qui ne sont pas étrangeres au sujet de ton discours. Il nous [conseilla] de nous conduire avec decence, de ne prononcer que des paroles douces, au traite de Paix qui va se [tenir] avec les treize Etats-unis; nous disant en meme tems que toutes les hostilités étoient finies entre la Grande Bretagne et les Etats-Unis. Ceci mon pere se rapporte à l'esprit de ton discours; il nous conseilla de plus d'observer la même conduite douce avec toutes les nations Sauvages, et particulierement celles qui pourroient venir des environs de Niagara.

Towanoganda chef Seneca se leva et dit:
Kayenlaa mon pere chef de guerre du Grand Onondio, ouvre [tes] oreilles aux paroles que je vais prononcer.

Au commencement de ton discours tu reconnois la Surintendance du grand Esprit d'en haut, qui te conduit dans ce lieu, où tu trouves tes enfans en paix. Tu nous donne ensuite quelques Leçons et quelques avis dans Lesquels tu declare que l'affection paternelle, oublie plutot Les fautes que les bonnes actions, et sans cela tu n'aurois pas voulu nous venir voir sur ce terrein. Tu nous as aussi rappellé, mon pere, les paroles que tu nous dis à notre premiere entrevue il y a sept ans au Fort Johnson. Tu nous dis alors, que tu connoissoit le fondement de la querelle entre l'Amerique et la Grande Bretagne et que la cause en étoit juste et que le Grand Onondio formerait une chaine avec l'Amerique qui seroit brillante à jamais. Tu en as appellé à notre memoire pour l'accomplissement de tes predictions. Tu nous as aussi averti sur d'autres objets de grande importance; en nous observant que si nous suivions tes conseils au traité actuel, tu entendrois parler de nous avec plaisir de l'autre coté du grand lac.
Mon pere.

Ouvre encore une fois tes oreilles, nous n'avons pas eu le tems hier de deliberer sur tes paroles. Il est très vrai qu'aucune nation n'est exempt d'erreurs et nous avons été conduit à de très grandes fautes, par les instigations de la Grande Bretagne, pour nous unir contre les Etats Americains. Nous avons été vaincus, mais il convient à toutes les nations de s'interesser l'une à l'autre dans le malheur et il sied bien surtout aux vainqueurs de montrer cette compassion à ceus qui sont vaincus. Tu as entendus notre voix, mon pere, nos idées sont toutes reunis sur ce feu de conseil qui est allumé par le Congrès, dont les representants sont dans ce moment-ci present. Nos esperances, notre Confiance sont concentrées dans ce traité. Si les Americains nous parlent avec bonté tout ira bien et la paix s'etendra sur toutes les nations; Mon pere, emporte ce collier avec toi, et n'oublie pas nos paroles.

La Reponse du Marquis fut: que nous remercions le Gouverneur du Canada de ses voeux sinceres, pour le succès de ce traité et qu'ils doivent aussi le remercier du conseil qu'il leur donna, de faire pour eux la meilleure paix qu'ils pourront. Que connoissant les bonnes dispositions du Congrès, il est bien aise de voir ses enfans éclairés sur leurs anciennes erreurs. qu'il engage tous les Sauvages à oublier toute animosité les uns contre les autres, que dans la situation où il laisse toutes choses, il ne doute pas que le traité ne soit satisfaisant pour les Etats-Unis et que dans cette confiance il jouit deja du retour de son affection paternelle.

To Adrienne de Noailles de Lafayette

Fort Schuyller, ce 4 octobre 1784.

Me voici dans le païs sauvage, mon cher coeur, entouré de Hurons et d'Iroquois, et fort ennuïé du métier de père de famille qu'on m'a forcé de faire ici; je vous ai mandé que mon influence pouvoit être utile au traité qui se négocie avec toutes les nations; cette considération m'a fait différer mon voyage de Boston, j'ai remonté la rivère du Nord, j'ai visité auprès d'Albany une nouvelle secte d'entousiastes qui font des contorsions incroïables, et qui prétendent faire des miracles où j'ai trouvé des procédés magnétiques. De là je me suis rendu au traité par des chemins affreux, et à mon arrivée, mes compagnons ont été bien surpris de me trouver en païs de connoissance comme si j'entrois dans le faubourg St. Germain. Nous avons été passer une journée dans un établissement sauvage que Mr. de Gouvion a longtems habité; mon crédit personnel sur les sauvages, tant amis qu'ennemis s'est trouvé bien plus grand que je ne l'avois imaginé; quoique les ambassadeurs du congrès soïent conduits par Mr. Arthur Lee qui ne se soucioit point de m'avoir obligation, il leur a fallu recourir à moi, et j'ai monté hier dans la tribune aux harangues; les réponses étant heureusement finies aujourd'hui, je reprends avec joïe le chemin d'Albany, et Mr. Lee m'observoit dernièrement que les sauvages étoient trop occupés de moi pour faire attention aux commissionaires. Ils m'ont fait de grandes promesses, et j'aime à penser que j'ai servi à un traité qui nous donnera une petite branche de commerce, et assurera la tranquillité des Américains. Je vais à présent dans la nouvelle Anglettere, je m'embarquerai à New-Port pour la Virginie, ce qui est une traversée de trois jours, et j'y retrouverai le Général Washington. Les accidents de voyage n'ont tombé que sur Demanche; il a culbuté dans un bourbier; il a traversé une rivière avec un pied à l'étrier sans pouvoir passer la jambe droite; il a enfoncé un plancher peu solide, et la moitié de son corps pendoit au premier étage, tandis que l'autre moitié restoit au second; mais il nous a été très utile, a fait la cuisine avec tant de zèle que voyant un petit garçon tourner en sens contraire la broche que jusqu'alors il avoit tourné à droite, il s'est empressé de l'arrêter, de peur apparament qu'il ne dérôtit la viande; il ménage mon argeant avec grand soin, et c'est un homme parfaitement honnête. Je suis ici avec Mr. de Marbois, et je n'ai pas été fâché d'y avoir le chargé d'affaires de la nation, pour savoir jusqu'à quel degré je devois aller. C'est avec délices que je m'embarquerai demain, car toute cette sauvagerie, malgré ma popularité, m'ennuie à périr, et ma petite cabane d'écorce est à peu près aussi commode qu'un habit de taffetas dans le mois de janvier. Mais je vais finir ce bavardage, mon cher coeur, et dans quelque auberge un peu moins aërée, je continuerai mon petit journal. Adieu, mon cher coeur, je vous embrasse bien tendrement.

Church's Tavern près d'Hartfort, ce 10 octobre 1784

Me voici rentré dans le monde, mon cher coeur, et j'ai quitté les bois sauvages avec une grande satisfaction. L'espoir de trouver des lettres à Albany ne laissoit pas que d'y contribuer beucoup; mais je n'ai pas eu ce bonheur, et quoique, d'après les arrangements que j'ai pris, il soit possible que Le Brun me joigne ce soir, je pourrois bien aussi me coucher aussi triste que je l'ai fait à mon arrivée à Albany. Comme je cours à travers champs, je n'ai rien de bien intéressant à vous mander; partout je vois qu'on s'occupe de moi avec bonté, et quand je débarque dans une maison où je ne suis pas connu, ma première réponse est toujours emploïée à donner de mes propres nouvelles. Tandis que je m'en souviens, mon cher coeur, il faut que je vous parle d'une fameuse plante, appelée *genzing*, dont je ne peux envoyer qu'un pot qui vous est adressé, et que je vous prie de partager avec Mr. le Maréchal de Noaïlles et Mme de Tessé. Comme c'est peut-être la seule fois de ma vie que nous parlerons botanique, j'ajouterai que j'ai découvert ici une plante grimpante, toujours verte, qui fera un merveilleux effet sur les deux murs de notre terasse. Quand elle vous parviendra, je vous prie de la faire semer, et planter en grande quantité au pied des deux murs, et j'en envoïe aussi qui pendant l'été les couvrira des plus belles fleurs rouges. De manière que si mon cabinet est fini, rien ne manquera aux charmes de la maison. Je suis bien faché que ce pauvre Poirey ait mal aux nerfs, mais s'il se porte mieux, persuadés lui d'apprendre à écrire en abbréviation aussi vite que la parole, et de faire arranger ma bibliothèque. Je vous ai tant ennuïée de nos arrangements, que je ne veux pas en radoter encore; je dirai seulement que je voudrois bien voir mes dettes d'ouvriers païées à mon retour; que le Général Greene étant à Charlestown, je ne sais pas si l'argeant me sera remis avant mont départ, ou envoïé en France; que la lettre de change sur Baltimore, quoique bonne, a souffert quelques difficultés; que par conséquent il sera prudent de prendre des mesures avec le Duc de Castries pour que je trouve cent louïs à Brest sans perdre une minute qui dans ce moment là me sera plus précieuse qu'une semaine d'Amérique. Quant aux petits arrangements intérieurs, j'espère que vous aurés ramené ma tante, et vous ferés bien alors d'établir notre ami Déplaces. Si vous disposés de Comtois, je vous prêterai Le Brun, ou Lêon pour faire le service chés vous quand vous en aurés besoin; et je vous confierai que je pourrois bien ramener un jeune sauvage iroquois: mais cette négociation n'est pas encore terminée. En voilà bien long, mon cher coeur, et en vérité je crois que le séjour de Mount Vernon m'a tout à fait gâté. Je joins ici un gros paquet de lettres, et vous en trouverés aussi une pour ma tante, pour Gouvion, et pour notre chère Anastasie. Les premières lettres me parleront de votre voyage à Chavaniac; je jouïs de tout le bien que vous aurés fait à ma tante, et mon coeur aime à vous en avoir l'obligation. Vos vertus conjugales auront encore bien mieux frappé Mr. de Lastic, et sa pauvre femme en aura attrappé quelques réflexions désavantageuses. Je suis impatient de savoir comment nos enfans se sont trouvés de la compagne, et de l'air natal de leur père. Si ma tante vous a suivie à Paris, ce sera pour moi une bien grande satisfaction. Dans le cas où elle n'y auroit pas consenti, tachés encore de la déterminer par vos lettres. Mon séjour ici, mon cher coeur, n'est pas fixé à une semaine près; mais je pense que le premier paquebot vous apprendra le moment précis de notre départ, et dans le courant de décembre, vers les derniers jours, j'aurai surement le bonheur de vous embrasser.

To the Comte de Vergennes

Hartford Ce 12 octobre 1784

Depuis ma derniere lettre, Monsieur le Comte, je n'ai pas Receu de Nouvelles de France, et Comme j'ai peu quitté M. de Marbois, je m'en Rapporte à lui pour Vous mander celles d'Amerique. Il vous parlera du traité Sauvage ou nous avons été ensemble, et ou l'on a cru que je pouvois être de quelque utilité. Il est impossible de ne pas jouïr de l'attachement que ces nations ont Conservé pour Nous; ils aiment nos Manufactures, et peuvent, avec un peu de soin, nous offrir une petite Branche de Commerce. Avant de leur parler, j'ai Consulté M. de Marbois, et j'ai evité ce qui pouroit choquer l'Anglettere.

Il y a quelque tems, Monsieur le Comte, que j'ai Receu une adresse un peu embarassante; je ne pouvois eviter d'y Repondre, et j'espere que Vous approuverés ma moderation. Il m'etoit annoncé que le Compliment venoit de Volontaires d'Irlande, mais j'ai affecté de ne voir que la Revolution Americaine et d'anciens irlandois citoïens de Baltimore; on ne peut de moins me faire aucun Reproche *fondé*, et Mr. de Marbois est de mon opinion. Mais ces messieurs en imprimant la Reponse se la sont adressée Comme Volontaires, et j'ai eu soin dans les autres papiers, Sans affectation, de faire Redresser cette erreur. Je vous envoïe le tout, avec la marque de ce que j'ai fait Retrancher. Si j'entre dans ce detaïl, Monsieur le Comte, c'est que je mets le plus grand prix à votre approbation, et que je Serois Bien fâché de Vous paroitre imprudent. Il m'est venu dernierement des Conseïls assés etranges, comme par exemple de debarquer aïlleurs qu'en France, mais je croirois ne pas me Rendre justice, s'il me paroissoit necessaire de Vous Rassurer Sur ma Sagesse.

M. de Marbois vous ecrit Sur les credits à faire en Amerique; Son opinion Vaut mieux que la mienne, mais je ne serois pas si entierement exclusif, quoique je Soïe Bien loin de Conseïller les folies que fait l'Anglettere, et dont nous devons profiter pour augmenter notre Commerce Americain. Quant à celui des isles Anglaises, je sais qu'un grand nombre d'americains y Commerce sous pavillon Britannique, et le Bon marché du sucre Confirme cette assertion.

Me voici Sur le chemin de Boston, Monsieur le Comte, et quoique les Bontés dont on me Comble partout Retardent Beaucoup ma marche, j'espere Retrouver Bientôt le Gal. Washington qui sera au Rendés vous longtems avant moi; Nous acheverons mes visites ensemble, et après avoir assisté au Rassemblement du Congrès, j'espere Regagner Boston assés tôt pour Vous faire ma Cour à la fin de decembre. Soïes assés Bon, Monsieur le Comte, pour offrir mes Homages à Madame la Comtesse de Vergennes, à Mesdames vos Belles filles, et faire mes Compliments à Messieurs vos fils. Adieu, monsieur le comte, Conservés moi une amitié que je merite par ma Reconnoissance et par mon tendre et Respectueux attachement.

To the Prince de Poix

Hartford Ce 12 octobre 1784

Après avoir quitté tout ce que j'aime, mon cher prince, j'ai toujours été droit devant moi, et comme si je n'en avois pas assés d'etre dans un autre monde, j'ai encore passé Celui-là pour entrer dans le monde sauvage. Graces à dieu m'en voilà Revenu, et je commence enfin à Regarder du coté de l'orient: Chès les Iroquois, je ne pouvois pas perdre ma chevelure, Car on ne perd, dit le proverbe, que ce qu'on a; mais j'ai perdu du tems, et j'en ai enragé de tout mon Coeur. Ils ont cru que je serois utile à Ce traité, et j'avoüe qu'ils avoïent Raison; mais ce traité Retarde mes visites, et j'en veux à tout ce qui prolonge ce cruel exil; après avoir ecouté le Baragouïn de ces sauvages, et ils en ont dit autant du mien, nous nous sommes à la fin separés, et me voici dans la ville d'Hartfort ou je Recois ces marques de Bonté dont on me Comble dans tous les etats. Je Suis Retenu ici par un dîner public après lequel je m'acheminerai vers Boston, et ensuite vers Rhode Island. Mais Comme je suis toujours arrêté dans mes Voyages terrestres, j'aime mieux, pour faire diligence, m'embarquer à Newport, et joindre par eau le Gal. Washington. Il doit m'attendre depuis plusieurs jours, et moi qui n'arrive jamais tard, j'aurai cette fois-ci fort inutilement derangé ses projets. Celui que j'ai formé d'etre à Paris vers la fin de decembre est fixé irrevocablement. Sans trop Concevoir Comment, je suis sûr de l'executer. Sept mois d'absence, et d'absence volontaire, sont une penitence assés longue, et si le ciel m'en tient Compte, elle doit servir pour les pechés de toute ma vie. Si tu avois le plus petit grain de foi, mon cher prince, je te parlerois d'une nouvelle secte de trembleurs qui fait des Contorsions et des miracles; le tout appliquable au profit des grands principes magnetiques. Je te dirois que je puis faire un livre in 40. intitulé, essai sur les danses sauvages, et particulierement sur la nouvelle danse apportée des Bois de l'occident, (ce qui est Comme la Fitzjames ou la tracite des Iroquois) appliquées au principe du Docteur Mesmer. Mais je garde toutes ces Belles choses pour me faire Honneur Cet Hiver, non parmi les Prophanes, mais aux assemblées de la Rüe Coqueron. Quoique j'attende les cahiers, mon cher ami, ce n'est pas pour eux que je gemis du Retard des paquebots. Mais voici ma quatrieme lettre, et je n'en ai encore qu'une de toi, sans cependant avoir d'injures à dire, ce qui est toujours une Consolation. Ce dernier Bâtiment n'arrive point, j'attends mes paquets partout, et partout je suis trompé dans mon espoir. Je ne puis parler de Paris qu'à Ceux qui n'y sont pas; Car je ne serois pas plus au Courant qu'une dame dont j'ai Receu un joli petit Beillet pour me demander un Rendés vous, et dont l'affaire aura Reussi ou manqué trois mois avant le petit Billet que je lui Reponds. Mais avec Maurice qui n'en sait pas plus long que moi, je parle de France toute la journée; Paris, Epinal, le Rgt. de Noaïlles, et le prince Reviennent tous les jours, et matin et soir nous Repetons la même chose avec un plaisir toujours nouveau. Les premieres lettres nous monteront pour un mois, mais en attendant nous commençons un peu à Rabacher. Je suis parfaitement Content de mon compagnon de Voyage; il est aimé de tout le monde; notre tournée est interessante, et il en profite Bien, ce qui me fait un veritable plaisir. En formant des voeux pour mon Retour, je songe Bien tendrement au Bonheur d'embrasser mon cher prince. Mon Coeur sait en jouïr toujours, mais il en a plus Besoin que jamais; il est tous les jours plus Convaincu à quel point ton amitié lui est chere, et le prix qu'il y met est plus aisé à Sentir qu'à exprimer. Penses Souvent à moi, mon cher prince, penses y dans toute la tendresse de ton Coeur; ce sentiment m'est necessaire, et je le merite, mon ami, par ma vive mon eternelle amitié. Comme j'ecris à plusieurs de nos amis, je Bornerai aujourdhuy tes Commissions; mais je te prie de parler de moi à ton pere, toute ta famille, Mde. de Vauban, Mde. de Durfort, le Cte. Etienne, le Cher. de Puysegur; mille amitiés à Coïgni; mes tendres Homages à sa femme et à son Beaupere. La santé de Mde. de Poix m'occupe Bien vivement, et j'espere qu'on m'en parlera Beaucoup dans les premieres lettres; presente lui mes Homages, et embrasse pour moi le grand Charles et le petit Juste. Te voilà dans le Bon tems, mon cher ami, entre le Regiment et le quartier, et par consequent fidele Habitant de Paris. Je pourrois y etre aussi, si le diable ne m'avoit pas transporté sur l'autre Bord de l'ocean; quand il M'offriroit tout le nouveau monde, il ne me feroit pas Renoncer à la partie de l'ancien ou j'ai eu le Bonheur de naitre, et ou j'ai celui de vivre. Il n'y Rien à mon gré de si charmant que d'etre auvergnac, et même de la Haute Auvergne soit dit sans vanité, et d'Habiter la Rüe de Bourbon, dans une maison, qui si elle n'est pas la plus Belle, est au moins infiniment gentille. Si je pouvois la Retrouver pour Huit jours, cette pauvre petite maison, je serois assés fou pour acheter ces Huit jours de Bonheur avec tous mes amis, pour une prolongation de deux mois d'exil. Mais adieu, mon cher prince, je ne te dis pas de Bien m'aimer; mon coeur me Repond que je dois Compter sur le tien; mais je te Repete mille fois qu'il m'est necessaire d'etre aimé de mon cher prince, comme il sait m'aimer, et que ma tendresse pour lui, durera jusqu'à mon dernier soupir.

To Adrienne de Lafayette

Rennes Ce dimanche au Soir
[23 Janvier 1785]

Me voici Bien près de vous, mon cher Coeur, Bien impatient d'arriver, et Bien Heureux de Sentir derriere moi tout Cet espace qui nous Separoit; ce qui met le Comble à ma joïe est d'apprendre l'etablissement de ma tante à Paris. Je Suis arrivé en Bonne Santé, et Ce Soir j'ai debarqué chés Montmorin avec l'intention de partir sur le champ. Mais les etats de Bretagne sont assemblés, et il y a été decidé que je ferois une visite demain à onze Heures, avec des attentions trop particulieres pour qu'il m'ait été possible de m'en dispenser. J'arriverai Mercredi au soir à Versaïlles, si tard Surement que je ne ferai pas de visite, mais Comme le lendemain il me faudra voir des ministres, je voudrois y

Coucher, et pourrois faire ma cour jeudi par la même occasion de Maniere que Vendredi nous irions diner avec ma tante, souper chés Mde de Tessé et Reprendre l'ancien train de vie; ou Bien si vous aimés mieux nous irons jeudi après diner à paris. Quoique je m'annonce plus tard pour etre Sûr de vous trouver seule, j'espere Bien Vous embrasser vers onze Heures ou Minuit à moins que nous ne soïons arrêtés en chemin. Donnés de mes nouvelles à Mde de Tessé, vos soeurs et peres et meres; j'ai chargé le Brun d'aller chés Charlus, M de Poix et le Vicomte, et j'ecris un mot à Mde d'Henin, et Mde de Simiane, ainsi voilà les amis et amies Averties. [J'envoie] un Billet aussi à ma tante. Adieu, mon cher Coeur, je suis Bien Heureux, je vous aime Bien, et je suis Bien impatient de vous le dire moi même:

Je Voudrois Bien que nos enfans puissent venir à Versailles. Donnés aussi de mes nouvelles à mde de Bouflers. Il est tard, et je veux dormir un peu.

From [the Marquis de Condorcet]

Basle ce 24 fevrier 1785

Monsieur le Marquis,

Je viens d'apprendre que vous avez honore de quelque attention mes reflexions sur L'esclavage des negres. J'avais fait un voiage à Paris en 1780, un de ces auteurs dont La plume est vendue a quiconque veut la paier, s'avisa de faire L'apologie de cet esclavage, je voulus lui répondre dans un journal, et je ne pus en obtenir la permission. Retourné dans mon bon pays ou il n'y a pas d'esclaves, j'ai fait un livre au Lieu d'une lettre et c'est ce livre que vous avez daigné Lire.

Aucun homme de notre continent n'a plus Contribué que vous M. le Marquis a rompre ces fers que L'Europe donnait à L'Amerique, peut être la gloire de detruire la Servitude que nous avons imposée au malheureux affricains vous est aussi reclamée. Vous Seriez alors le libérateur de deux des quatre parties du monde, et bien Superieur à Ce Pompée que L'on a vu autrefois triompher en trois jours des trois parts de La terre.

Peut être Sans la guerre d'Amérique L'esclavage des negres aurait-il eté detruit d'ici a quelques generations. Un celebre medecin de Londres le docteur Fothergill avait formé le plan d'une compagnie qui devait etablir parmi les negres d'Afrique La culture du Sucre. Il avait destiné des Sommes très Considerables à cette brave oeuvre qui devait amener à La Longue La destruction de l'esclavage. La guerre-d'Amerique a empeché l'exécution de ce projet: et c'est une raison de plus pour que vous vous occupiez de la renouveller ou d'en former un meilleur. Il faut qu'une revolution a laquelle vous avez Contribué n'ait fait que du bien.

Permettez-moi, Monsieur Le Marquis, de vous offrir mes faibles lumieres, *dans Mes reflexions* j'ai dit aux gouvernemens qui ne m'ont pas ecouté ce que La justice exigeait d'eux: et j'ai cru devoir m'y borner. Mais j'ai etudié le mème objet Sous d'autres rapports, et Si vous daignez vous occuper de ce grand ouvrage vous me trouverez toujours a vos ordres. J'ai L'honneur d'ètre avec respect.

P.S. Si vous me faites L'honneur de me répondre, je vous prie d'addresser votre lettre à M. Schwartz à Basle poste restante.

To Pierre Samuel Du Pont de Nemours

Paris ce 30 may 1785

Monsieur le Contrôleur general a Bien Voulu me promettre d'ecrire en faveur de M. de gouvion lieutenant Colonel dans l'etat Major de l'armée, que j'ai prié de Causer avec les Negotiants de la Rochelle sur le Commerce des etats unis, et particulierement sur celui des Sauvages. Nous pourrions ensuite l'envoïer à dunkerque pour le même objet. Celui que j'ai en vüe pour moi même, seroit d'acquerir quelques Connoissances sur nos villes de Commerce et Nos Manufactures dans le Rapport des etats unis, et de leur nommer les meïlleures maisons Americaines, et les articles les plus Recherchés dans Ce païs, afin de Contribuer de mes foibles efforts à l'extension de notre Commerce avec Ce Continent. C'est dans cette intention que je vais moi même en Auvergne par Lyon, et que j'ose supplier Monsieur le Contrôleur general de Vouloir Bien donner à M. de gouvion une lettre generale de Recommandation à montrer dans les endroits ou il passeroit en venant me Rejoindre.

LAFAYETTE

Verses Sung to Lafayette at Lyons

[Lyon, le 23 juin 1785]

AMIS, quoi, ce convive aimable
Est ce Général redouté!
Ce la Fayette si vanté
Est donc assis à cette table.
Ah! combien notre sort est doux,
Et que ce Guerrier a de gloire!
Il sait combattre, vaincre & boire,
Il daigne chanter avec nous.

OUBLIONS cet Hercule antique,
Vengeur des Rois & des Sujets;
Hercule n'étoit pas François,

Il n'a pas sauvé l'Amérique.
Ah! combien, &c.

QUAND il s'embarque au gré d'Eole,
Aussitôt l'Amour est en pleurs;
Mais après mille exploits vainqueurs,
Par son retour il le console.
Ah! combien, &c.

CHER à son Roi, chéri des Belles,
Aimé de Mars & de Cypris;
Il renverse nos ennemis,
Et ne peut trouver de cruelles.
Ah! combien, &c.

QUE la Peyrouze, sur les ondes,
Aille chercher de nouveaux bords;
Amis, ici sans tant d'efforts,
On voit le Héros des deux Mondes,
Ah! combien notre sort est doux,
Et que ce Guerrier a de gloire!
Il fait combattre, vaincre & boire,
Il daigne chanter avec nous.

[M. Delanaine]

To [Mme de Tessé]

Rheinsberg 7 aout 1785

Si vous souhaitez de mes nouvelles, ma cousine, je vous diroi que depuis trois jours je suis à la campagne du Prince henry. Vous serez peu surprise que j'y sois arrivé au milieu du diner et que j'y donne tous les soirs au maître de la maison la peine de faire mes comptes au loto, mais aux gaucheries près, on paroit content de moi ici et je le suis infiniment des bontés et de l'amabilité du prince henry, il aime notre nation avec une préférence vraiment touchante, je conviens toujours de ce qu'il dit à notre gloire, parce que si je sais défendre un peu ma personne des compliments, je n'ai jamais eu la force de refuser un éloge qu'on donne à mon pays. Je jouis beaucoup plus du Prince henry que je ne l'eusse fait à Paris. À peine ai-je déjeuné qu'il arrive chez moi, nous nous promenons tête à tête jusqu'au diner nous y sommes voisins ainsi qu'au souper, et dans le salon excepté au loto, nous sommes toujours ensemble. Il répond avec une grande complaisance à mes questions, et la société qui est ici est fort douce et fort aimable. Il y a un fort bon spectacle. On a donné *le huron* qui m'intéressait comme francais et comme sauvage. En un mot je suis extrêmement satisfait de ma course ici et je tache d'en profiter autant que je puis. Demain au soir je retournerai à Berlin, et vendredi après avoir vu quelques troupes, je pars pour la Silésie où j'espère admirer de près le roi, et où, comme je ne doute pas que sa santé ne lui permette de causer, ses bontés me font espérer de jouir de sa conversation pendant quelques jours. Parce que j'entends ici, Mr. Castine a bien fait quelques contes sur la guerre d'Ámerique et particulierement sur la campagne de Virginie, mais je ne cherche pas à traiter ce sujet, et n'ayant pas porté comme lui des plans, je me contente d'un peu de réputation en gros sans disputer autant le terrain que je l'ai fait à lord Cornwallis.

To the Comte de Vergennes

fontainebleau ce 16 novembre 1785

Vous avés eu la Bonté, Monsieur le Comte, de me dire que Mers les fermiers Generaux avoïent Repondu à la lettre de M. Jefferson; S'il nous etoit possible d'avoir cette Reponse, peut-être M. Jefferson qui Connoit à fonds tout ce qui Regarde les tabacs, pourroit-il servir à demontrer la fausseté de quelques Calculs. Ces messieurs Sont Si Redoutables, Malgré leur desinteressement, qu'on ne Sauroit assés Multiplier les Moïens de defense.

On Nous a dit, Monsieur le Comte, que le Bail des fermes va Se Renouveller. Si Ce Bruit est fondé, j'oserois proposer que le Renouvellement de celle du tabac, puisqu'il Reste encore du tems, fut Seulement plus Retardé que les autres, afin de pouvoir Examiner les Methodes proposées.

Je vous demande pardon de Vous importuner, Monsieur le Comte, mais j'ai voulu Vous Communiquer mes deux idées, parceque Vous les acceuillés avec Bonté, et d'ailleurs je suis Heureux de toutes les occasions ou je puis Vous presenter l'Homage de Mon Bien tendre et Respectueux Attachement.

LAFAYETTE

To Rabaut de Saint-Etienne

Paris, ce 20 novembre 1785

C'est avec Bien de la Reconnoissance, Monsieur, que j'ai receu la lettre dont Vous m'Honorés, et je mets un prix trop sincere à Votre Amitié, pour n'être pas Bien touché de tous les temoignages que Vous Voudrés Bien m'en donner; depuis que j'ai eu l'honneur de Vous voir, j'ai fait une grande tournée en allemagne; une grande partie de ces Contrées, en y comprenant les états prussiens, fleurit par nos sottises du siecle passé, par ces Sottises Barbares encore plus qu'impolitiques, et que nous ne pouvons assés déplorer. Dans le Voyage que j'ai fait, j'ai trouvé un Vaste champ pour l'admiration et pour l'instruction, et j'ai partagé mon tems entre les deux, pour tâcher que cette Course me fut militairement utile. Quoique moins soldat, graces à Dieu, que citoïen, j'ai un gout très vif pour Ce métier, et pour tous les moïens de m'y perfectionner. Votre interest pour moi, Monsieur, souhaittoit ce compte bien abregé de mon Voyage; nous pourrions Bien aussi parler Commerce, Car les états unis, en Repoussant les Navires et les chargements Anglais, semblent inviter Sans Cesse les notres, et Vous Serés ettoné d'apprendre que les fermiers generaux, graces à leurs lumières patriotiques, envoïent leur argeant en Angletterre pour y acheter les objets de leur ressort, que d'après les droits extraordinaires levés en Amerique sur tout Bâtiment anglais, ils pourroïent avoir dans nos ports à meilleur marché, et païer en Manufactures. Pour Continuer à Causer Commerce, je Vous dirai que je n'ai pas cessé d'en parler à tous les minstres du Roy qui Sont Bien disposés. Mais dans ce païs-ci l'on craint les choses qui font un certain effet, on cherche à les Reculer, et les affaires sont arrêtées lorsqu'elles embranchent sur differents departements. Je ne doute pas cependant qu'avec de la suite, nous n'aïons Beaucoup plus de facilités de Commerce qu'il n'en existe à present.

Le procès dont Vous me parlés occupe, je crois, Beaucoup moins que Celui du Cardinal de Rohan. Mais avec de la patience et de la douceur, les Causes justes se gagnent; je l'ai Recommandée à d'autres juges aussi, et Serai toujours Bien Heureux de Contribuer à Ce qui peut Vous être agréable.

Comme je Cours tous les étés, monsieur, je serois faché que Votre Voyage à Paris fut differé plus tard que le mois d'avril; mais comme d'ici là, nous pourrons, j'espere, trouver quelque moïen de Commerce avec les états unis utile à la ville de Nismes, je prendrai la liberté de Vous ecrire dans le Courant du mois prochain, ou les premiers jours de l'autre année. Agréés, en attendant, l'assurance de tout le plaisir que me procure une Connoissance aussi precieuse que la votre, et c'est de tout mon coeur que j'y ajoute l'expression de l'attachement avec lequel j'ai l'Honneur d'être, Monsieur, Votre très Humble et obéissant Serviteur.

LAFAYETTE

To [the Marquis de Castries]

Paris ce 29 decembre 1785

Monseigneur,

J'ai receu la lettre du 23 de Ce mois dont Vous m'Honorés, et me trouve [d'autant] plus Heureux des ordres qu'elle Contient, que je suis depuis longtems Convaincu [de la] Bonté des munitions Navales Americaines, et que nous pouvons païer en Marcha[ndise] à Nos alliés des fournitures sûres, au lieu des fournitures precaires que nous païons [en] argeant à nos rivaux.

Vous trouverés ici, Monseigneur, la demande que je fais au General [Greene] de mille pieds cûbes de chêne verd assortis en Courbes, et de quelques pieces de [Bois de] Cedre, que la possession de l'isle de Cumberland en Georgie le met à portée de [fournir]. J'envoïe Cette lettre par Quadruplicata, et l'original que je joins ici peut Rester [deposé aux] Bureaux.

Quant au goudron et au chanvre c'est de la Baïe de chesapeack qu'on [pourroit] tirer Ces deux articles. La Caroline du Nord est l'etat le plus Riche en goudron, [on en] transporte aisement à Norfolk et Portsmouth à l'entrée de la Baïe. Le chanvre [est] un peu Rare, mais nous devrions, je crois, encourager cette Culture aux depends de [celle de] Russes, et les derrieres de la Virginie en fourniroïent Beaucoup qu'on fera descendre le pottowmack. Je connois une Bonne maison à Baltimore dont un des chefs etoit [mon aide-de-camp], et je voudrois avoir une lettre qui authorisat *la maison de McHenry à Baltimore* [de commercer] à toulon ou à Rochefort pour une Valeur determinée de goudron et de chanvre. L'arrangement Vaudroit d'autant mieux que j'ai demandé pour celle à Marseïlles, [on peut] aussi avoir de la Rochelle une Cargaison de Marchandises françaises dont [l'envoy] assureroit en partie la païement; et si l'experience Reussit on etabliroit par là une Navette d'echanges.

J'imagine que les Negociants Americains qui fournissent le Roy peuvent [tirer] sur lui des lettres de change en envoïant la facture, lettre d'assurance, et annonçant le depart du Bâtiment Comme ils font avec Mmr le Coulteux et vraisemblablement avec les autres maisons de Commerce.

J'ai l'Honneur d'etre avec Respect Monseigneur Votre très Humble et obeïssant Serviteur.

LAFAYETTE

APPENDIX II

CALENDAR OF
OMITTED LETTERS

Fr at the end of an entry indicates that the document is in French.

1782

[1782?] AM [memorandum on preliminary articles for treaty with Great Britain] (DLC: Benjamin Franklin Papers).

[1782] LS from Ségur [congratulating Lafayette on his glorious campaigns] (NIC: Dean Collection), *Fr.*

[1782] from Charles Grant [asking Lafayette to petition Congress for land for him] (PPU), *Fr.*

[1782] AL [draft] from John Jay [presenting his compliments] (NNC: John Jay Papers).

[1782] AL [draft] from Jay [expressing gratitude for Lafayette's efforts on behalf of the United States] (NNC: John Jay Papers).

[1782] AMS [summary of conversation with Vergennes on America, written at the minister's request] (AAE: Mémoires et documents, Etats-Unis, vol. 2, fols. 97–99), *Fr.*

[1782] L from Castries [concerning Lafayette's appointment as quartermaster general] (AN: Marine, C⁷ 157, dossier de Lafayette), *Fr.*

January 3. ALS [draft] from Robert Livingston [presenting greetings and congratulations] (NHi: Robert R. Livingston Papers).

January 18. ALS to John Hanson, president of Congress [announcing his arrival] (DNA: RG 360, PCC 156, p. 260).

January 18. ALS to Robert Livingston [telling of his arrival in Lorient and subsequent departure for Versailles] (NHi: Robert R. Livingston Papers).

January 22. L to Franklin [apologizing for delay in visiting him] (PPAmP: Franklin Papers, vol. 24, no. 39), *Fr.*

January 29. ALS to Livingston [discussing England's determination to continue the fighting and his appeals to the French ministers on America's behalf] (NHi: Robert R. Livingston Papers).

[February] ALS [endorsement on memorial] to Ségur [for promotion of Gimat] (SHA: Ya 514), *Fr.*

February 1. ALS to John Adams [enclosing other letters] (MHi: Adams Papers).

February 3. LS from Maillebois [introducing himself] (NIC: Dean Collection), *Fr.*

February 12. LbC from Franklin [thanking Lafayette for all his efforts] (DLC: Benjamin Franklin Papers, Series 1, vol. 7).

February 21. D [copy] [endorsement of Louis-Pierre Laneuville's memorial to Congress] (DNA: RG 360, PCC 41, vol. 5, p. 332), *Fr.*

February 25. M [copy] [list of officers for whom Lafayette requests his king's consideration] (SHA: Ya 514), *Fr.*

February 26. ALS [draft] from Benjamin Rush [discussing British movements in America and the coming evacuation of Charleston] (DLC: Lafayette Papers).

February 28. L to Franklin [requesting to see Franklin] (PPAmP: Franklin Papers, vol. 43, no. 170), *Fr.*

[February–March] AL to John Adams [requesting information on money affairs for presentation to Vergennes] (MHi: Adams Papers).

March 5 [1782–1783] AL to Franklin [announcing arrival of frigate *Hermione*] (PPAmP: Franklin Papers, vol. 42, no. 139).

March 6. AL [draft] to Gaston Louis, comte de Jarnac [concerning prisoner exchange with England] (DLC: Benjamin Franklin Papers).

March 10. LbC from John Adams [discussing British movement in America; recognition of United States by United Provinces] (MHi: Adams Papers).

March 13. L [copy] to de Grasse [congratulating him on military victories in America] (MH: Sparks Mss. 85, vol. 2), *Fr.*

March 20. ALS [copy] to Robert Morris [discussing French-American trade and Franklin's efforts to get military stores to America] (*Henkels Catalogue,* January 16, 1917).

March 23. ALS to James Searle [informing of arms to be shipped to Pennsylvania] (PHi: Conarroe Papers).

March 28. LbC from Franklin [plan for securing release of American prisoners and bringing them to France] (DLC: Benjamin Franklin Papers).

March 30. ALS to John Hanson, president of Congress [apologizing for delay in returning to America] (DNA: RG 360, PCC 156).

March 30. ALS to Robert Livingston [discussing siege of Gibraltar; taking of St. Kitts; state of British internal affairs] (NHi: Robert R. Livingston Papers).

March 30. LS to Robert Morris [concerning Franklin getting vessels to carry supplies to America; purchase of arms for Pennsylvania] (*Parke-Bernet catalogue,* January 22–24, 1941; October 18, 1955).

[April–June] AL to Franklin [requesting return of a paper to be sent to George Washington] (PPAmP: Franklin Papers, vol. 42, no. 137).

April 12. L [transcription of deciphered letter] to [Robert Livingston] [state of British internal affairs; American campaign] (DNA: RG 360, Misc. PCC, Letters Relating to Spain and Barbary States), *Fr.*

April 12. ALS to Livingston [introducing Chevalier de Lameth] (NHi: Robert R. Livingston Papers).

April 12. ALS to Livingston [introducing Comte de Ségur; justifying his remaining in Europe] (NHi: Robert R. Livingston Papers).

April 12. ALS to Livingston [introducing Prince de Broglie] (NHi: Robert R. Livingston Papers).

April 12. ALS to Benjamin Lincoln [introducing Prince de Broglie] (MHi: Benjamin Lincoln Papers).

April 12. ALS to Benjamin Lincoln [introducing Comte de Ségur] (MHi: Benjamin Lincoln Papers).

April 12. ALS to Benjamin Lincoln [introducing Chevalier de Lameth] (CSmH: Rare Book 48644).

April 12. ALS to Henry Knox [introducing Chevalier de Lameth] (MHi: Henry Knox Papers).

April 12. AL to La Luzerne [explaining reasons for not returning immediately to America] (AAE: Correspondance politique, Etats-Unis, supplément, vol. 14, pp. 272–72½), *Fr.*

April 12. AL to Robert Morris [introducing Chevalier de Lameth] (DLC: Lafayette Papers).

April 12. ALS to Robert Morris [sending of supplies to America; introducing Comte de Ségur] (PHi: Simon Gratz Collection).

April 12. ALS to Alexander Hamilton [discussing British affairs and explaining his delay in returning to America] (DLC: Alexander Hamilton Papers).

April 12. L [printed copy] to George Augustine Washington [introducing Comte de Ségur] (*Proceedings of the Massachusetts Historical Society,* 2d series, 6 [1890–91]:170).

April 12. L [copy] to George Washington [introducing Prince de Broglie] (MH: Sparks Mss. 88).

April 13. L to Franklin [suggesting a commission he was performing for Franklin be delayed until the folowing day] (PPU), *Fr.*

April 24. ALS to Vergennes [sending proposals for French campaigns in America, April 18] (AAE: Mémoires et documents, Etats-Unis, vol. 2, fol. 94), *Fr.*

April 28. L to Franklin [dinner invitation] (PPAmP: Franklin Papers, vol. 43, no. 167), *Fr.*

May 12. LS from the Marquis de Ségur [responding to Lafayette's recommendations for compensation and positions for various French officers who served in America] (AN: Section moderne, C 358, 1901, pièce 6), *Fr.*

May 16. ALS to Jacques le Brigant [discussing American independence from Britain] (InU: Lafayette Mss. I), *Fr.*

May 21. M [copy] from La Luzerne [making a table of American commerce] (AAE: Correspondance politique, Etats-Unis, vol. 21, fols. 212–20), *Fr.*

[June 10.] AD [draft] [granting conditional parole by Lafayette to Cornwallis and his aides] (DLC: Benjamin Franklin Papers).

June 21. ALS to Franklin [British emissary met with Vergennes; Lafayette will wait on Franklin next day] (DLC: Benjamin Franklin Papers).

June 25. ALS [draft] from Franklin [mentioning Jay's arrival] (DLC: Benjamin Franklin Papers).

[June 25] ALS to John Jay [welcoming Jay to Paris; explaining reasons for not having returned to United States] (NNC: John Jay Papers).

June 25. AL [draft] from John Jay [expressing satisfaction at prospect of seeing Lafayette] (NNC: John Jay Papers).

June 29. ALS to Alexander Hamilton [apologizing for not having returned to America; speaking of de Grasse's defeat] (DLC: Alexander Hamilton Papers).

June 29. ALS to John Hanson, president of Congress [explaining motives for staying in Europe] (DNA: RG 360, PCC 156 p. 294).

June 29. ALS to Livingston [explaining reasons for remaining in Europe] (NHi: Robert R. Livingston Papers).

June 29. ALS to George Augustine Washington [apologizing for remaining in France; announcing Jay's arrival in Paris] (PHi: Society Collection).

July 9. L [printed copy] from Franklin [discussing changes in British ministry] (*The Works of Benjamin Franklin . . . with Notes and a Life of the Author,* ed. Jared Sparks [Chicago, 1882], p. 360).

July 9. ALS to Jay [announcing Grenville's arrival in Paris] (NNC: John Jay Papers).

July 9. L [printed copy] to Franklin [announcing Grenville's arrival in Paris] (*The Works of Benjamin Franklin . . . with Notes and a Life of the Author,* ed Jared Sparks [Chicago: 1882], p. 359).

July 11. ALS to [Linguet] [sending sum of money to help an acquaintance] (PHi), *Fr.*

July 16. ALS to Vergennes [discussing Grenville's messengers] (MH: Autograph File), *Fr.*

August 6. L [fragmentary copy] from Henry Laurens [thanking Lafayette for credit of 500 livres; discussing upsets in British ministry] (NN: Bancroft Transcripts).

[September] AM [memorandum to Franklin proposing, on behalf of Vergennes, that a sentence be added to Oswald's commission] (DLC: Benjamin Franklin Papers), *Fr.*

September 1. [printed copy] to Benjamin Lincoln [introducing the Chevalier de Lameth] (*Pennsylvania Archives,* ser. 1, 9:627).

September 1. L [copy] to Washington [introducing the Chevalier de Lameth; apologizing for delay in returning] (MH: Sparks Mss. 88).

[September 3] AL to Sarah Livingston Jay [offering to accompany her to the theater] (NNC: John Jay Papers).

September 9. DS [power of attorney for Morizot] (NNPM), *Fr.*

September 13. LbC from Franklin [Jay's reaction to Rayneval's departure; asking Lafayette to continue efforts for America] (PHi: Franklin Papers).

September 17. L to Franklin [announcing birth of daughter Virginie] (PPAmP: Franklin Papers), *Fr.*

September 18. LbC from Livingston [expressing disappointment at Lafayette's delay in returning; instability of British ministry] (DNA: RG 360, PCC 118, p. 307).

September 19. ALS to Henry Laurens [British unwillingness to treat with America on equal footing] (ScHi: Henry Laurens Papers).

September 27. ALS from Robert Morris [thanking Lafayette for his kind attention to his boys in France] (*Henkels Catalogue*, January 16, 1917).

October 7. LbC from Morris [introducing Joshua Barney; also addressed to Franklin, Jay, Adams, and Carmichael] (U.S. Naval Academy Museum: Robert Morris Letter Book).

October 14. ALS to Livingston [state of peace negotiations; failure of Gibraltar siege; Dutch recognition of American independence] (NHi: Robert R. Livingston Papers).

October 14. ALS to Washington [apologizing for delay; discussing de Grasse's defeat; birth of daughter] (PEL: Hubbard Collection).

October 28. L [copy] from John Barry [announcing arrival in France and the seizure of nine prizes] (DLC: Papers of Commodore John Barry).

October 31. L [copy] from John Barry [asking after peace prospects] (DLC: Papers of Commodore John Barry).

November 2. ALS [typescript] to John Barry [expressing pleasure over his arrival] (Louis Gottschalk Collection, private collector).

November 2. L to Gouvion [errands for Gouvion to perform in America] (NIC: Dean Collection).

November 3. L [copy] from Hamilton [had been expecting Lafayette's arrival; becoming member of Congress; death of John Laurens] (DLC: Alexander Hamilton Papers).

November 7. L [draft] from Vergennes [concerning Ridley's request for arms] (AAE: Correspondance politique, Etats-Unis, vol. 22, fol. 427), *Fr.*

November 17. LbC from John Barry [thanking Lafayette for letter; announcing imminent departure] (DLC: Papers of Commodore John Barry).

November 20. ALS to Ségur [discussing Lafayette's joining with Franco-Spanish expeditionary force and other military matters] (SHA: A^1 3732, pièce 114), *Fr.*

[November 26] ALS to [Franklin] [announcing granting of 6-million-livre loan to the United States] (DLC: Benjamin Franklin Papers).

November [28] LbC from Adams, Franklin and Jay [expressing approval of Lafayette's actions] (MHi: Adams Papers).

December 3. AL to Prince de Poix [announcing imminent departure on expedition] (Mme André Balleyguier), *Fr.*

December 3. L to Gouvion [discussing expedition against England] (NIC: Dean Collection).

December 3. ALS to Elias Boudinot, president of Congress [Franco-Spanish expedition against British; explaining reasons for remaining in France] (DNA: RG 360, PCC 156 p. 304).

December 4. AL to Prince de Poix [imminent departure of expedition] (Mme André Balleyguier), *Fr.*

December 4. AL to Prince de Poix [Lafayette's unhappiness at leaving friends and family] (Mme André Balleyguier), *Fr.*

December 4. ALS to Franklin [imminent departure of expedition] (DLC: Benjamin Franklin Papers).

December 6. L [copy, fragment] to Mme de Simiane [farewell] (NIC: Dean Collection), *Fr.*

December 6. AL to Poix [returning because of bad winds; discussing gossip over Mme de Simiane] (Mme André Balleyguier), *Fr.*

December 7. ALS to Livingston [expedition against British West Indies; recommending William Temple Franklin] (NHi: Robert R. Livingston Papers).

December 8. ALS to Franklin [expressing desire to serve the United States any way he can] (DLC: Benjamin Franklin Papers).

December 8. AL to Poix [winds changed, fleet departing again] (Mme André Balleyguier), *Fr.*

December 13. AL to Poix [repeating affection for Poix and all his family] (MMe André Balleyguier), *Fr.*

December 15. L [draft] from Montaran [discussing expedition] (AN: F^{12} 1376), *Fr.*

December 15. ALS from Washington [awaiting outcome of negotiations; evacuation of Charleston and New York] (DLC: George Washington Papers).

December 24. AL to Poix [announcing arrival at Cadiz] (Mme André Balleyguier), *Fr.*

December 31. AL to Poix [prospects of peace; Spanish women] (Mme André Balleyguier), *Fr.*

1783

[1783] ALS to [unknown] [discussing affair with Abbé Murat] (CtY: Benjamin Franklin Collection), *Fr.*

[1783] ALS to Sarah L. Jay [announcing desire to escort her and Mr. Jay to theater] (NNC: John Jay Papers).

[1783] AL [draft] from Jay [welcoming Lafayette back] (NNC: John Jay Papers).

[1783] from Jay [declining dinner invitation] (NNC: John Jay Papers).

January 1. ALS to Vergennes [prospects of peace] (AAE: Correspondance politique, Etats-Unis, vol. 23, fol. 3), *Fr.*

January 2. AL to Poix [thanking for letters; expressing affection] (Mme André Balleyguier), *Fr.*

January 2. ALS to Vergennes [discussing peace negotiations] (AAE: Correspondance politique. Etats-Unis, vol. 23, fol. 28), *Fr.*

January 13. AL to Poix [peace will disappoint his plans; satisfaction with composition of expedition] (Mme André Balleyguier), *Fr.*

January 16. AL to Poix [uncertainty over his plans if peace comes] (Mme André Balleyguier), *Fr.*

January 21. AL to Poix [imminent departure from Cadiz] (Mme André Balleyguier), *Fr.*

January 28. AL to Poix [asking whether there will be peace or war] (Mme André Balleyguier), *Fr.*

February 5. ALS to Nathanael Greene [discussing peace; need for unity in America] (DLC: Nathanael Greene Papers).

February 5. L [copy] to [Matthias Ogden] [concerning signing of peace preliminaries] (MH: Sparks Mss. 49.3).

February 7. ALS to d'Estaing [sending *Triomphe* to Philadelphia with news of peace] (AN: Fonds de la Marine, C^7 157, dossier de Lafayette), *Fr.*

February 11. L [copy] from d'Estaing [reporting on sending *Triomphe* to Philadelphia; hoping to see Lafayette in Madrid] (AN: Fonds de la Marine B³ 801, dossier 3), *Fr.*

February 15. L [copy, fragment] to [Mme de Simiane] [concerning departure from Madrid and return to Paris] (NIC: Dean Collection), *Fr.*

February 15. AL to Poix [at Madrid, will be delayed] (Mme André Balleyguier), *Fr.*

March 2. ALS to Washington [discussing difficulties with Spanish court] (PEL: Hubbard Collection).

March 3. ALS to Samuel Adams [congratulating on general peace; expressing disappointment over not being able to annex Canada] (NN: Samuel Adams Papers).

March 11. ALS from d'Estaing [discussing Lafayette's efforts in Spain] (NNPM), *Fr.*

March 17. ALS from d'Estaing [fleet departing for Brest] (NIC: Dean Collection), *Fr.*

March 27. AL to Aglaé d'Hunolstein [bidding farewell] (RPJCB), *Fr.*

[March 30] AL to Adrienne de Noailles de Lafayette [business concerns with his aunt] (ALG), *Fr.*

March 30. ALS to Montaran [received his memoir on commerce] (AN: F¹² 1375), *Fr.*

April 7. ALS to Franklin [discussing Franklin's proposed visit to Vergennes] (PPU).

April 12. L [printed copy] from Elias Boudinot [thanking Lafayette for sending news of peace] (Burnett, *Letters of Congress,* 7:135–36).

April 26. ALS to La Colombe [prospects for La Colombe's military career] (AN: Section moderne, C 358, 1901, pièce 7), *Fr.*

[ca. May 10] ALS to Ségur [writing on behalf of Gimat to obtain pension for him] (CtY: Benjamin Franklin Collection), *Fr.*

May 10. ALS from Washington [British evacuation of New York; Lafayette's efforts in Spain; hostilities with Indians] (DLC: George Washington Papers).

May 12. ALS from Clinton [responding to Lafayette's request to set the record straight on remarks concerning American troops] (MiU-C), *Fr.*

May 12. ALS to John Dickinson [letter of introduction] (PPAmP: Logan Papers).

May 12. AL to d'Ormesson [means of attracting American commerce] (AN: 144 AP [Archives d'Ormesson] 133, dossier 5, pièce 30), *Fr.*

May 13. LbC from Henry Laurens [expressing appreciation of Lafayette's role in peace negotiations] (ScHi: Henry Laurens Papers).

May 18. LS from Castries [discussion of Captain Fanning] (PPAmP: Society Collection), *Fr.*

May 18, ALS to Livingston [letter of introduction] (NHi: Robert R. Livingston Papers).

May 18. ALS to Washington [letter of introduction] (PEL: Hubbard Collection).

[May] 21. L to William Temple Franklin [letter of introduction] (PPAmP: Franklin Papers), *Fr.*

[June] M from Lafayette [memorandum on American commerce, recommending interests of Carter and Wadsworth] (AAE: Correspondance politique, Etats-Unis, vol. 24, fols. 418–21), *Fr.*

June 6. L to Franklin [dinner invitation] (PPAmP: Franklin Papers, vol. 28, no. 143).

June 10. ALS to Livingston [letter of introduction for Dr. Bancroft] (NHi: Misc. Mss. Livingston).

June 10. ALS to Nathanael Greene [explaining his delay in returning to America] (MiU-C).

June 12. ALS to Washington [letter of introduction] (PEL: Hubbard Collection).

June 16. AL to Franklin and Jay [will stop by for information from America] (NNC: John Jay Papers).

June 16. AL [draft] from Jay [indicating that neither he nor Franklin has new information] (NNC: John Jay Papers).

June 20. LbC from Henry Laurens [concerning British maneuverings in negotiations] (ScHi: Henry Laurens Papers).

June 21. L to Franklin and Jay [sending them American newspapers] (PPAmP: Franklin Papers, vol. 43, no. 168), *Fr.*

June 26. L to Franklin [dinner invitation] (PPAmP: Franklin Papers, vol. 28, no. 190).

June 30. ALS to d'Estaing [will forward note from Captain Roux] (AN: Fonds de la Marine, B⁴ 210, fol. 160), *Fr.*

[July] AL [autograph envelope] to James McHenry (DLC: James McHenry Papers).

[July 1] ALS to d'Estaing [recommending requests of various officers] (AN: Fonds de la Marine, G 171, pièces 174–75), *Fr.*

July 17. ALS to d'Ormesson [recommending Colonel Ogden] (AAE: Correspondance politique, Etats-Unis, vol. 25, fol. 47), *Fr.*

July 17. ALS to Vergennes [recommending Colonel Ogden] (AAE: Correspondance politique, Etats-Unis, vol. 25, fol. 46), *Fr.*

July 20. L [copy] from Castries [enclosing a copy of his response to Vergennes and a memoir of the Farmers General] (AAE: Correspondance politique, Etats-Unis, suppl., vol. 11, fol. 277½), *Fr.*

July 22. ALS to the American Peace Commissioners [Franklin, Jay, Adams, Laurens] [addressing issue of American debt to England and its effect on commerce] (MHi: Adams Papers).

July 22. D Lafayette [memoir on spinning establishment in Auvergne] (AN: F¹², 1376), *Fr.*

August 7. L to Franklin [enclosing a memoir] (PPAmP: Franklin Papers, vol. 42, no. 148), *Fr.*

August 24. ALS to [Ségur?] [requesting passport to visit Austrian troops] (InU: Lafayette Mss. III), *Fr.*

August 26. ALS to Vergennes [endorsing petition of Grubb & Co.] (AAE: Correspondance politique. Etats-Unis, vol. 25, fol. 227), *Fr.*

August 29. DS [power of attorney for sale of lands at Lislaval] (NjMoHP: The Park Collection), *Fr.*

September 8. AL to Adrienne de Noailles de Lafayette [telling of difficult voyage] (ALG), *Fr.*

September 10. AL to Adrienne [discussing illness of friend Roger] (ALG), *Fr.*

September 17. AL to Adrienne [discussing Roger's illness] (ALG), *Fr.*

September 28. ALS to Jay [Jay's imminent departure from Europe] (NNC: John Jay Papers).

October 17. L to Franklin [dinner invitation] (PPAmP: Franklin Papers, vol. 30, no. 28).

October 22. LS to William Temple Franklin [discussing American commercial interests in France] (PPAmP: Franklin Papers, vol. 105, no. 133).

October 30. LbC from Washington [enclosing list of requested silver items] (DLC: George Washington Papers).

November 1. L [draft] from Washington [letter of introduction] (DLC: George Washington Papers).

November 9. ALS from Nathanael Greene [recommending Governor Reed] (NHi: Reed Papers, vol. VII, no. 77).

November 29. ALS to Washington [recommending Sailly for improvement of mines in Virginia] (PEL: Hubbard Collection).

[December] ALS to Vergennes [mentioning Laurens's ill health and decision to return to the United States] (AAE: Correspondance politique, Etats-Unis, vol. 26, fol. 269), *Fr.*

[December?] D [draft] from Lafayette and Chastellux to Franklin [recommending Dr. Coste] (PPAmP: Franklin Papers, vol. 57, no. 123), *Fr.*

December 1. LbC from Washington to Franklin and Lafayette [letter of recommendation] (DLC: George Washington Papers).

December 4. LbC from Washington [canceling earlier order for plated ware] (DLC: George Washington Papers).

December 9. LbC from Washington [recommending Dr. Witherspoon] (DLC: George Washington Papers).

December 10. ALS to Secretary of American Philosophical Society [concerning French balloon experiments] (PPAmP).

December 14. ALS [draft] from Henry Knox [discussing American independence and friendship for Lafayette] (MHi: Henry Knox Papers).

December 18. L to Franklin [dinner invitation] (PPAmP: Franklin Papers, vol. 30, no. 133).

December 20. ALS to [Ségur] [letter of introduction] (PPAmP: Feinstone Collection), *Fr.*

December 25. ALS to Vergennes [discussing American commerce and its need to break ties with England] (AAE: Correspondance politique, Etats-Unis, vol. 26, fol. 251), *Fr.*

December 26. ALS to Thomas Mifflin, President of Congress [relating news of British internal affairs] (DNA: RG 360, PCC 156, p. 365).

1784

January 3. L to Franklin [dinner invitation] (PPAmP: Franklin Papers, vol. 31, no. 7).

January 8. L to Franklin [dinner invitation] (PPAmP: Franklin Papers, vol. 31, no. 12).

January 10. L [draft] from Castries [discussing situation with Griffin Greene] (AN: Fonds de la Marine B^2 427, fols. 7, 13), *Fr.*

[January] 18. L to Franklin [dinner invitation] (PPAmP: Franklin Papers, vol. 31, no. 37½).

January 19. LS to La Colombe [discussing the Society of the Cincinnati] (AN: Section moderne, C 358, 1901, pièce 8), *Fr.*

January 20. ALS [draft] from George Clinton [discussing Washington's plans] (NN: George Clinton Papers).

January 23. ALS to Rayneval [announcing his brother's acceptance into the Society of the Cincinnati] (PHi: Dreer Collection), *Fr.*

February 5. ALS from Thomas Mullens [testifying to his service in the army] (Papers of the Society of the Cincinnati, Washington, D.C.).

February 10. L to Franklin [dinner invitation] (PPAmP: Franklin Papers, vol. 31, no. 66).

February 26. ALS to [Jay] [announcing four free ports for American merchants] (CtY: Benjamin Franklin Collection).

February 26. L to Franklin [dinner invitation] (PPAmP: Franklin Papers, vol. 31, no. 90).

March 5. ADS [endorsement of Jay's statement on complaints about Chevalier de Quésney's conduct] (AN: Fonds de la Marine, B^2 426, pièce 84).

March 6. L [printed copy] from John Dickinson [naming of Pennsylvania county for Lafayette] (*Maryland Gazette*, August 26, 1784).

March 8. ALS to Robert Morris [discussing payment for subscription in the Society of the Cincinnati] (DLC: Digges-L'Enfant-Morgan Papers).

March 9. L to Franklin [dinner invitation] (NNC: DeWitt Clinton Collection).

March 9. ALS to Washington [supporting claims of French naval captains to be included in the Society of the Cincinnati] (PEL: Hubbard Collection).

March 9. ALS to Washington [forwarding du Bouchet's claims for Society membership] (PEL: Hubbard Collection).

March 17. ALS to Jeremiah Wadsworth [detailing changes in British ministry; plans to go to America] (CtHi: Jeremiah Wadsworth Papers).

March 22. L [copy] from Sir Edward Newenham [recounting British politics and state of American maufactures] (PPAmP: Franklin Papers, vol. 31, pt. 2, no. 118).

March 23. ALS to Antoine-Lewis Chaumont de la Millière [dealing with overtaxation and lack of good transportation networks] (CtY: Benjamin Franklin Collection), *Fr.*

March 24. L [copy] from Nathanael Greene [thanking Lafayette for his offer to advance money to Griffin Greene] (CSmH).

March 27. L to Franklin [accepting dinner invitation] (PPAmP: Franklin Papers, vol. 43, no. 169). *Fr.*

March 30. L to Franklin [dinner invitation] (PPAmP: Franklin Papers, vol. 31, no. 130).

March 31. L [copy] from Henry Laurens [discussing problems of trade restrictions] (NN: Bancroft Transcripts).

April 4. L [copy] from Washington [inviting Adrienne to stay with his family;

hoping to see Lafayette soon; thanking him for the plated ware] (DLC: George Washington Papers).

April 5. AL [draft] from Jay [declining dinner invitation] (NNC: John Jay Papers).

April 9. ALS to Washington [concerning applications for the Society of the Cincinnati] (PEL: Hubbard Collection).

April 10. ALS to Vergennes [bringing Colonel Harmar to Versailles] (AAE: Correspondance politique, Etats-Unis, vol. 27, fol. 275), *Fr.*

April 16. ALS to Jeremiah Wadsworth [complaining of lack of American trade] (Ct: Governor Joseph Trumbull Collection).

April 19. ALS to Wadsworth [will be leaving for America in June] (CtHi: Jeremiah Wadsworth Papers).

April 20. ALS to [Linguet?] [planning trip to America] (InU: Lafayette Mss. I), *Fr.*

April 22. ALS to Wadsworth [discussing upcoming trip to America] (CtHi: Jeremiah Wadsworth Papers).

April 28. L to Franklin [dinner invitation] (PPAmP: Franklin Papers, vol. 43, no. 167), *Fr.*

May 5. LbC from Washington [letter of introduction] (DLC: George Washington Papers).

May 8. ALS [draft] from Jay [discussing travel plans] (NNC: John Jay Papers).

[May 9] ALS to Jay [expressing disappointment at not being able to travel with him] (CtY: Benjamin Franklin Collection).

May 15. ALS to [Ségur] [recommending Gouvion and Laumoy for their military service] (NIC: Dean Collection), *Fr.*

May 17. LS from Calonne [granting four free ports] (DNA: RG 360, PCC 137, vol. 3, appendix, p. 449), *Fr.*

[May 17] ALS to [Franklin] [announcing *arrêt du conseil* for free ports] (PPU).

May 17. L [draft] from Washington [informing Lafayette that French naval captains are now eligible for membership] (Papers of the Society of the Cincinnati, Washington, D.C.).

May 25. L to William Temple Franklin [suggesting someone wishes to use title of Benjamin Franklin's secretary in order to obtain free passage to America] (PPAmP: Franklin Papers, vol. 42, no. 146), *Fr.*

[June] AL to Adrienne [giving last instructions and notifying of planned return in January] (ALG), *Fr.*

[June 3] ALS to Franklin [relating American news and planned departure for America] (PPAmP: Franklin Papers, vol. 32, no. 3).

June 12. L [draft] from [Castries] [discussing French purchase of American naval supplies] (An: Fonds de la Marine, B² 427, fol. 349), *Fr.*

June 13. L from [Castries] [discussing purchase of ship *La Flore*] (AN: Fonds de la Marine, B² 426, fols. 148–49), *Fr.*

[June] 25 ALS [photostat] to [Calonne] [discussing addition of another free port] (Louis Gottschalk Collection, private collector), *Fr.*

[June] 30. AL to Adrienne [expressing love and sorrow over leaving her] (ALG), *Fr.*

August [10] ALS to Washington [announcing expected arrival at Mount Vernon] (private collector).

August 13. AL to Prince de Poix [announcing his arrival in America and his reception] (Mme André Balleyguier), *Fr.*

August 13. ALS to Vergennes [announcing his arrival in America] (AAE: Correspondance politique, Etats-Unis, vol. 28, fol. 135), *Fr.*

August 13. M [printed copy] from the Pennsylvania State Assembly [expressing gratitude for all Lafayette's efforts for America] (*Maryland Gazette,* August 26, 1784).

August 13. M [printed copy] [reply to address by the Pennsylvania State Assembly (*Maryland Gazette,* August 26, 1784).

August 14. LbC to Robert Morris [announcing free ports in France and enclosing a memo from Castries] (DNA: RG 360, PCC 121, p. 107).

August 19. ALS to Chevalier d'Antérroches [will see him soon] (MH: Autograph File), *Fr.*

August 20. AL to Poix [announcing arrival at Mount Vernon; joy at being with Washington] (Mme André Balleyguier), *Fr.*

August 29. L to Adrienne [announcing departure from Mount Vernon and giving household instructions] (ALG), *Fr.*

[September–December] AL to Matthew Carey [inviting him to dine at French consul's] (Davis Memorial Library, Methodist College).

September 14. ALS to Washington [letter of introduction] (PEL: Hubbard Collection).

September 15. AL to Poix [reception in America; plans to go to Indian negotiations] (Mme André Balleyguier), *Fr.*

September 24. ALS to [unknown] [delayed at Fort Schuyler; will arrive Hartford later] (PHi: Gratz Collection).

September 30. L [copy] from Morris [thanking Lafayette for services rendered to America] (DLC: Offical Letter Book, Robert Morris Papers).

[October] D [resolution granting citizenship to Lafayette and his son from the state of Connecticut] (Ct: Connecticut Archives, 1st series).

October 1. AL [draft] from the Commissioners of Congress [announcing imminent arrival at Fort Schuyler] (MH: Autograph File).

October 1. ALS from Livingston [expressing regret at having missed Lafayette] (NHi: Robert R. Livingston Papers).

October 12. L to Adrienne [announcing his arrival at Hartford, disappointment at finding no letters for him there] (ALG), *Fr.*

October 12. M [printed copy] from Thomas Seymour [welcoming Lafayette to the city of Hartford] (*Connecticut Courant and Weekly Intelligencer,* no. 1030, October 19, 1784).

October 12. M [printed copy] [Lafayette's reply to address by the mayor of Hartford] (*Connecticut Courant and Weekly Intelligencer,* October 19, 1784).

October 16. AMS [Lafayette's speech to his former officers in Boston] (MeHi: S. H. Fogg Autograph Collection).

[October 22] AL to Poix [describing his reception in Boston and his plans for returning to Virginia] (Mme André Balleyguier), *Fr.*

October 22. ALS to [Madison] [explaining that he was delayed by his reception in Boston] (Phi: Dreer Collection).

October 22. ALS to Washington [explaining his delay in Boston] (PEL: Hubbard Collection).

October 25. M [printed copy] [address to Lafayette by former Rhode Island officers] (*Newport Mercury,* no. 1205).

October 25. M [printed copy] [reply to address from Rhode Island officers] (*Newport Mercury,* no. 1205).

October 25. M [speech in honor of Lafayette by the mayor of Newport, Rhode Island] (RNHi).

October 26 M [LbC] [address of welcome to Lafayette from the Rhode Island General Assembly] (Rhode Island Colony Records, vol. 12, State of Rhode Island and Providence Plantations).

October 26. M [LbC] (Lafayette's reply to the Rhode Island General Assembly (ibid.).

October 29. M [printed copy] [address to Lafayette by the gentlemen of Salem] (*Massachusetts Centinel,* 2, no. 13 (November 3, 1784).

[October 29] AMS [Lafayette's response to welcome at Salem] (MSaE).

November 4. ALS to Livingston [expressing regret at missing him thus far in his trip] (NHi: Misc. Mss. Livingston).

November 21. ALS to Benjamin Harrison, Jr. [presenting petition of some French merchants in the United States) (NN: Emmet Collection).

November 25. ALS to [Jay] [apologizing for the publication of preliminary accounts of negotiations at Fort Schuyler by St. Jean de Crèvecoeur] (DNA: RG 360, PCC 156, p. 396).

November 30. L [copy] to [William Paca] [addressed to the Governor and the Council of Maryland] (MH: Sparks Mss. 29).

December 6. ALS to Richard Henry Lee, president of Congress [announcing impending departure from America] (DNA: RG 360, PCC 19, vol. 2, p. 253).

[December 9] AL [draft] from John Jay [announcing the appointment of a committee of thirteen to take formal leave of Lafayette] (NNC: John Jay Papers).

December 14. LbC from Richard Henry Lee [bidding farewell; requesting transport of letter to Franklin in Paris] (DNA: RG 360, PCC 16, p. 316).

December 16. ALS to Henry Knox [farewell; asking Knox to send his son to France for education with his own] (MHi: Henry Knox Papers).

December 17. ALS to [unknown] [introducing John McHenry] (DLC: James McHenry Papers).

December 19. L [printed copy] to Elbridge Gerry [regretting inability to return to Boston as planned] (James Austin, *Life of Elbridge Gerry* [Boston, 1828–29], vol. 1, p. 468).

December 19. L [printed copy] to the President of the Charleston Library Society [thanking the Society for electing him to its membership] (*Newport Mercury,* no. 1234).

December 19. ALS to [James Monroe] [announcing departure for Europe] (NN: Monroe Papers).

December 19. ALS to [unknown] [taking leave] (PPT: Manuscript no. 1320).

December 19. ALS to Jonathan Trumbull [announcing departure and apologizing for being unable to return to Connecticut] (Ct: Jonathan Trumbull, Sr., Papers).

December 21. ALS to Washington [bidding farewell; will see Washington again; continued trouble with Britain] (PEL: Hubbard Collection).

1785

[1785] ALS to Louis-Hardouin Tarbé [introducing an American merchant] (InU: Lafayette Mss. II), *Fr.*

[1785–1786] ALS to Thomas Jefferson [sending him a consultant for tobacco affairs] (MHi: Jefferson Papers).

January 19. AL [draft] from Jay [requesting Lafayette's help in getting trade restriction lifted from the Indies] (NNC: John Jay Papers).

February 9. ALS to Nathanael Greene [announcing arrival in Paris; giving news of Griffin Greene] (OCl WHi).

February 9. ALS to Henry Knox [reporting safe arrival in Paris] (MHi: Henry Knox Papers).

February 6. LS [copy] from Jacques Le Maire to [Lafayette?] [hoping he will return to his military career] (Vi), *Fr.*

February 9. ALS to Washington [safely arrived; giving Europe's political news; thanking him for his letters to Anastasie de Lafayette] (PEL: Hubbard Collection).

February 14. L to Jefferson [sending a copy of Floridablanca's letter] (DLC: Thomas Jefferson Papers), *Fr.*

February 15. L to Franklin [dinner invitation] (PPAmP: Franklin Papers, vol. 33, no. 32), *Fr.*

[March] M [memorandum on tributes paid to the Barbary States by European nations; enclosed in L to American Commissioners, April 8, 1785] (DNA, RG 360, PCC 98, pp. 89–94), *Fr.*

March 6. L to William Temple Franklin [reporting American news; Congress convening] (PPAmP: Franklin Papers, vol. 106, no. 147), *Fr.*

March 10. L [copy] to [William Carmichael] [discussing troubles with Spain; Indian attacks on United States settlements] (DLC: Thomas Jefferson Papers).

March 14. L to Abigail Smith Adams and Miss Adams [dinner invitation] (DSI: Hull Collection, 53206).

March 14. L to Franklin [dinner invitation] (PPAmP: Franklin Papers, vol. 33, no. 52).

March 15. ALS to [Franklin] [introducing a Canadian] (PPAmP: Franklin Papers, vol. 33, no. 52).

March 16. ALS to Henry Knox [informing him of European political affairs] (Knox Memorial Association).

March 16. ALS to Elbridge Gerry [reporting trouble with the commercial concessions] (DLC: Elbridge Gerry Papers).

March 16. ALS to Elias Boudinot [relaying European political news] (NjHi).

March 16. ALS to Samuel Breck [mentioning political affairs] (CtY: Benjamin Franklin Collection).

March 19. ALS to Washington [discussing Potomac Company; European politics; possibilities of European war] (PEL: Hubbard Collection).

March 19. ALS to [Jay] [necessity of federal union in America; difficulties with the Spanish; American commercial concerns] (DNA: RG 360, PCC 156 p. 408).

March 22. L to William Temple Franklin [letter of introduction] (PPAmP: Franklin Papers, vol. 108, no. 86), *Fr.*

March 24. ALS to Grattepain Morizot [expressing satisfaction with his services] (J. Fromageot Tonnere), *Fr.*

March 30. L [printed copy] from Patrick Henry [requesting arms for Virginia] William Henry, *The Life, Correspondence and Speeches of Patrick Henry* [New York, 1891], 3:289–90).

April 5. L to Franklin [dinner invitation] (PPAmP: Franklin Papers, vol. 33, no. 73).

April 9. L to Thomas Ruston [dinner invitation] (PHi: Tench Coxe Papers).

April 12. ALS from Washington [letter of introduction] (PPAmP: Feinstone Collection).

April 16. ALS to Nathanael Greene [regarding tutors for Greene's son] (MiU-C).

April 16. ALS to Washington [complaints of French merchants against *arrêt;* jackasses and hounds are being shipped] (PEL: Hubbard Collection).

April 18. ALS to [Jay] [petitioning for aid to an orphan child] (DNA, RG 360, PCC 156, p. 412).

April 18. ALS to [Jay] [letter of introduction] (DNA: RG 360, PCC 156, p. 422).

April 18. L to Jonathan Williams [arranging a time to see him] (PPAmP: Feinstone Collection), *Fr.*

April 19. L to Franklin [dinner invitation] (PPAmP: Franklin Papers, vol. 33, no. 84).

April 26. L [printed copy] to La Colombe [discussing Colombe's military prospects] (Ulysse Rouchon, *Un ami de La Fayette, le Chevalier de La Colombe* [Champion, 1924], p. 22), *Fr.*

April 26. L to Franklin [dinner invitation] (NHi: Misc. Mss. Lafayette).

[ca. April 29] ALS to William Temple Franklin [discussing Congress's acceptance of Benjamin Franklin's resignation; asking for American news] (PPAmP: Franklin Papers, vol. 108, no. 43).

[May] ALS to Nathanael Greene [promoting French interest in buying American naval supplies] (CtHi).

May 3. L to Franklin [dinner invitation] (PPAmP: Franklin Papers, vol. 33, no. 95).

May 7. D [agreement between Pierre Tourtille-Sangrain and Lafayette for the procurement of American whale oil for lighting of Paris] (CSt: Manuscripts Division, Department of Special Collections), *Fr.*

[May 8] ALS to William Temple Franklin [announcing Choiseul's death; will delay his visit to Benjamin Franklin] (PPAmP: Franklin Papers, vol. 197, no. 96).

[ca. May 9–10] AL to John Adams [letter of introduction for Cadran] (MHi: Adams Papers).

[May 10] ALS to Cadran [enclosed with AL to Adams, ca. May 9–10, asking Cadran to assist Adams] (MHi: Adams Papers), *Fr.*

May 10. L to John Quincy Adams and Miss Abigail Adams [dinner invitation] (DSI: Hull Collection, 53123).

May 11. ALS to Jay [European political affairs and prospects of war] (DNA: RG 360, PCC 156, p. 418).

May 11. ALS to Jeremiah Wadsworth [planning trip to south of France for American commercial interests] (Ct: Governor Joseph Trumbull Collection).

May 11. ALS to Washington [letter of introduction] (PEL: Hubbard Collection).

May 12. LbC from Washington [letter of introduction] (PEL: Hubbard Collection).

May 13. ALS to William Constable [urging more powers for Congress; French response to *arrêt du conseil* removing trade restrictions from Americans] (NNC: John Jay Papers).

May 14. LS to John Quincy Adams [concerning American commercial concerns] MHi: Adams Papers), *Fr.*

May 18. ALS to John Quincy Adams [asking him to convey commercial news; informing him of seven dogs he is to deliver to Washington] (MHi: Adams Papers).

June 1. ALS from Nathanael Greene [recommending John McQueen] (S. Harold Goldman).

June 1. ALS to Patrick Henry [accounts to be settled] (CU-BANC).

June 1. L [copy, fragment] from Livingston [relaying his unwillingness to serve abroad as a foreign minister] (NN: Bancroft Transcripts).

June 3. LbC from John Adams [announcing his arrival in London; pleased with Colonel Smith] (MHi: Adams Papers).

June 4. ALS to [unknown] [letter of recommendation] (CtNhHi).

[June 6] D [recommendation for Dr. Coste for membership in the Society of the Cincinnati, with endorsement in Lafayette's hand] (PPAmP: Franklin Papers, vol. 33, no. 129), *Fr.*

June 6. L to Franklin [encloses Coste recommendation] (PPAmP: Franklin Papers, vol. 33, no. 129).

June 7. DS [statement of conditions for land purchase in French Guiana] (NIC: Dean Collection), *Fr.*

June 11. L [printed copy] from Richard Henry Lee [explaining commercial problems; announcing arrival of Spanish envoy] (*Richard H. Lee Correspondence*, vol. II, p. 66).

June 12. ALS to John Quincy Adams [sending passports and Tourtille-Sangrain proposal] (MHi: Adams Papers).

June 12. ALS to Patrick Henry [letter of recommendation] (NHi: Gallatin Papers).

June 12. ALS to Nathanael Greene [concerning education of his and Lafayette's son] (MiU-C).

June 22. L [printed copy] from Rabaut de St. Etienne [thanking Lafayette for his help in lawsuit against Protestants] ("Les Promoteurs de l'édit de 1787", *Bulletin de la Société de l'Histoire du Protestantisme français*, 1855), *Fr.*

June 30. LS to Vergennes [concerning United States arms seized at Nantes] (AAE: Correspondance politique, Etats-Unis, vol. 30, fol. 85), *Fr.*

July 9. ALS to John Dickinson [letter of introduction for Jean-Antoine Houdon] (PHi: Gratz Collection).

[ca. July 9] ALS to [William Temple Franklin] [concerning renting of Franklin's house after his departure] (PPAmP: Franklin Papers, vol. 108, no. 39).

July 9. ALS to Samuel Geary [concerning whale-oil commerce] (Papers of the Society of the Cincinnati, Washington, D.C.).

July 9. ALS to Washington [letter of introduction for Houdon] (PEL: Hubbard Collection).

July 13. LS to John Quincy Adams [passports and contracts for vessels carrying whale oil] (MHi: Adams Papers).

July 14. AL to Franklin [saying farewell] (PPAmP: Franklin Papers, vol. 33, no. 161).

July 14. ALS to Washington [beginning German travels; will purchase estate for experiment with slaves] (PEL: Hubbard Collection).

July 15. AL [draft] from Jay [arrival of Gardoqui; difficulties getting Britain to evacuate frontier posts] (NNC: John Jay Papers).

July 16. L to Adrienne [describing travels through Germany] (ALG), *Fr.*

July 26. AL [draft] from Elias Boudinot [French reaction to lifting of trade restrictions for Americans; sending herbs for pregnant women] (Rosenbach Museum and Library, Philadelphia).

July 30. L to Poix [describing his travels] (ALG), *Fr.*

August 5. DS [receipt for 2,400 livres] (PEL: American Friends of Lafayette Collection), *Fr.*

August 10. L to Poix [leaving Berlin for Silesia] (ALG), *Fr.*

August 13. L [printed copy] from Jay to Adrienne [describing life in America] (*The Correspondence and Public Papers of John Jay,* ed. Henry Johnston [New York, 1890–93], pp. 162–64).

August 17. L [copy] from Calonne [indicating no duties to be levied on the whale-oil commerce with America] (MHi: Adams Papers), *Fr.*

September 3. ALS to James McHenry [introducing André Michaux] (DLC: James McHenry Papers).

September 3. ALS to [Thomas Bee] [introducing André Michaux, sent to collect seed and plant specimens for the king] (DLC: Thomas Bee Papers).

September 3. ALS to Washington [introducing André Michaux] (PEL: Hubbard Collection).

September 6. ALS to Jay [letter of introduction] (DNA: RG 360, PCC 156, p. 436).

September 9. L to Poix [travels between Prussians and Austrians] (ALG), *Fr.*

September 16. AL [draft] from Jay [concerning case of M. Barré] (NNC: John Jay Papers).

Setpember 25. LbC from John Adams [letter of introduction for Thomas Boylston] (MHi: Adams Papers).

September 27. L to Poix [events at Potsdam] (ALG), *Fr.*

September 29. ALS to Frederick William II [describing Lafayette's German tour and encounter with a beautiful spy] (CtY: Benjamin Franklin Collection), *Fr.*

October 12. L to Poix [returning from German tour] (ALG), *Fr.*

October 15. ALS from Lachlan McIntosh [letter of introduction] MH: bMs AM 1649.6).

October 21. LbC from Jay [concerning Barré affair] (DNA: RG 360, PCC 121, p. 145).

October 30. L [printed copy] from Richard Henry Lee [praising Louis XVI as supporter of the rights of man] (*Richard Henry Lee Correspondence*, vol. II, p. 68).

November 2. ALS from l'Enfant [Houdon's success in America] (MHi: Henry Knox Papers), *Fr.*

November 8. LbC from Washington [mentioning Houdon's visit; Dr. Franklin's achievements] (DLC: George Washington Papers).

[ca. November 13] L [printed copy] from Jefferson [whale-oil agreement; Thomas Boylston's proposals] (Boyd, *The Papers of Thomas Jefferson,* 9:29–31).

November 17. L [extract] from Calonne [whale-oil commerce and duties] (DLC: Thomas Jefferson Papers), *Fr.*

November 20. ALS to [Thomas Boyston] [announcing dimunition of whale-oil duties] (ViHi: Beverly Randolph Wellford Papers).

December 2. LbC from John Adams [discussing whale-oil propositions] (MHi: Adams Papers).

December 3. ALS to Ségur [returning a pension granted to him; 3 petitions on behalf of others] (SHA: LG 1261, 1ʳᵉ série), *Fr.*

December 3. ALS to Nathanael Greene [buying of American naval supplies by France] (DLC: Nathanael Greene Papers).

December 7. ALS to Jeremiah Wadsworth [working for American commercial interests] (Ct: Governor Joseph Trumbull Collection).

December 12. ALS to [William Stephen Smith] [Mr. Barret arrived to work on mercantile plan between France and England] (MHi: DeWindt Collection).

December 17. ALS to Antoine-Cristophe Merlin [petitioning on behalf of Comte de Talobre (SHA: LG 1261, 1ᵉʳ série), *Fr.*

December 23. L from Castries [asking him to secure naval supplies from Greene] (AN: Fonds de la Marine, B² 429, pièce 106), *Fr.*

December 29. LS to Nathanael Greene [requesting supplies of wood] (MiU-C).

December 30. L [draft] from Ségur [informing Lafayette that his pension will be redistributed to others, as requested] (SHA, LG 1261, 1ʳᵉ série), *Fr.*

INDEX

This index is designed to complement the volume's annotation. The biographical information provided here covers the period of this volume. People are generally indexed under regularized spellings of the names by which they are called in the documents, and the titles and offices attributed to them are those they held during the period of this book. Cross-references are provided from other names and titles. Given-name preferences are printed in small capitals.

Places are indexed under regularized spellings of their eighteenth-century names, with cross-references from their modern names. Significant deviant spellings of the names of both places and people are given in parentheses.

Alphabetization is letter by letter. French names that incorporate "La" or "Le" are indexed with the L's, except in the case of ships' names.

Page references to illustrations appear in boldface type. The prefatory sections and French texts are not indexed.

The editors gratefully acknowledge the generous assistance of Charles T. Cullen in the preparation of this computer-assisted index. They also wish to thank Gary T. Buhrmaster of Cornell Computer Services for his patience in helping with program modifications and the staff of the Princeton University Computer Center.

Abos, Louise-Jean-MARIE-Catherine de Guérin de Chavaniac, marquise d' (1756–78), L's cousin, 117, 118n
Académie Royale des Sciences de Paris, 222n
Adams, Abigail (Nabby) (1765–1813), daughter of John, 333
—letters to, calendared, 440, 442
Adams, Abigail Smith (1744–1818), wife of John, 333
—letter to, calendared, 440
Adams, Elizabeth Wells, wife of Samuel, 233, 289
Adams, John (1735–1826), minister to United Provinces (1782–85), commissioner to negotiate peace with Great Britain (1782), minister to Great Britain from 1785, **228**; on campaign plans, 18, 19; on commerce, 357; and commercial negotiations, 60n, 61, 149, 205n, 224n, 227, 294, 316n, 347, 350n, 356, 358n; and concern about reputation, 123, 124n; and concern over future, 223; and Congress, 15, 122, 148, 164, 222, 123, 223, 267n; on dangers to America, 121–24; and Dutch, 17n, 33, 34n, 37n, 46; on foreign influence, 147n; on Franklin, 124n; and French ministry, 53; in Great Britain, 164, 166, 188, 192, 301, 302n, 314n, 335n; ill health of, 14–15; and L, 123, 151, 185, 192, 202, 213; on L, 122, 123, 295n; and peace

negotiations, 19n, 28n, 33–34, 39n, 45, 55n, 59, 150n; on Society of Cincinnati, 201, 203n, 209, 211–12; summons American commissioners, 132n; and Vergennes, 124n, 139; and views on government, 37–38; and war debt to Great Britain, 143, 144, 146; on whale oil trade, 444; and Willem V, 223; mentioned, 10n, 17, 36n, 45, 48, 69n, 71n, 74, 75n, 76, 126, 130n, 144n, 147n, 159n, 267, 277, 289n, 324, 349n, 442
—letters from, 14–15, 25–26, 37–39, 59–60, 211–12, 223–24, 355–56, 357–58; calendared, 428, 431, 442, 444; to James Warren, 121–24
—letters to, 18–19, 36–37, 60–62, 68–69, 131–32, 136, 201–3, 213–14, 222–23, 227–29, 315–17, 320–21, 333–35; calendared, 428, 431, 434, 441
Adams, John Quincy (1767–1848), son of John: and L, 320–22, 323n, 324, 325, 342; and Washington's dogs, 327n, 340n, 442; mentioned, 319, 320n
—letters to, calendared, 442, 443
Adams, Samuel (1722–1803), former member of Congress from Massachusetts, cousin of John: letters to, 233, 288–89; calendared, 433
Adams, Samuel (c. 1750–88), son of Samuel, 288

Adhémar, Jean-Balthazar, comte d', French
    ambassador to London, 97, 126
Africa, 216, 300n, 314n, 315
Aguesseau de Fresnes, Jean-Baptiste-Paulin,
    comte d' (1701–84), grandfather of L's wife,
    238
Aguesseau de Fresnes, Mme d', wife of Jean,
    stepgrandmother of L's wife, 236, 238
Aigle, L' (Eagle), French frigate, 64, 66, 67n
Albany, N.Y.: and Canadian refugees, 285n; L
    awaits letters at, 261; and L's visit to Shakers,
    260; mentioned, 121, 241, 245, 252, 263,
    264, 272
Alexander, William (1729–1819), merchant of
    Edinburgh and Richmond, 194n
Alexander, William (Lord Stirling) (1726–83),
    American major general, 121
Alexandria, Va., 160, 280n
Algiers (Alger), 162, 165n
Alliance, American frigate, 11, 21, 215n
Alsace, France, 293
America, American frigate, 66, 67n
America, United States of: John Adams on, 38,
    211–12; and affairs in Europe, 78; and al-
    liance with France, 21, 23, 33, 34n, 46, 55n,
    62n, 66, 67n, 71, 76, 80, 81, 86, 137, 168,
    179, 219, 225–26, 256, 257–59, 272, 273,
    281, 282, 313; and alliance with France and
    Spain, 82, 126; and alliance with France,
    Spain, and United Provinces, 32n; and al-
    liance with United Provinces, 14–15; and
    annexation of Canada, 84; and Barbary
    States, 316n; Barbé de Marbois on, 247; and
    boundary disputes with Spain, 72, 74n, 102;
    British evacuation of, 320n; and Canadian
    refugees, 285n; and claims against Britain,
    38; 168–75, 178, 182, 195, 219, 224; and
    commercial relations with Great Britain, 113,
    144n, 176n, 211n, 271n, 305, 310, 318,
    356n; and compliance with treaty, 130n;
    dangers to, 149, 164; and debt to Great
    Britain, 434; and demand for French goods,
    169–70; and desire for fishing rights off
    Nova Scotia, 48n; effects of war on, 245;
    European view of, 304; as example to Eu-
    rope, 79; and financial difficulties, 13n, 69,
    74, 114, 144; French dissatisfaction with, 6n,
    9; French friendship for, 9; French-Spanish
    forces in, 26; and gratitude to France, 30,
    119, 168, 176; and judicial system, 314,
    315n; L as spokesman for, 345, 347; L desir-
    es to represent at treaty ratification, 89; L
    on, 77, 159, 235; L perceives danger for, 88;
    L's absence from, 7; L's assistance to, 11, 15,
    21, 30, 39, 45, 50, 68, 74n, 75, 80, 83, 85,
    86, 89, 92, 137, 143, 149, 153, 188, 192, 240,
    254, 255n, 273, 274n, 275, 281n, 317n, 343,
    427, 430, 432, 438; L's departure from, 18,
    23, 29, 116n, 305; L's desire to serve in
    future campaigns, 328; L's influence in, 241;
    L's reception in, 243, 266, 268, 269n, 276,
    280, 300, 438; L's return to, 4, 15, 23, 27,
    29, 35, 37, 42, 43n, 47n, 48, 50, 59, 62, 67,
    68, 69n, 83, 84, 89, 90n, 91, 94, 96, 98, 116,
120, 121, 124, 132, 134n, 137, 144, 146, 150,
    153, 155, 164, 186, 188, 192, 200, 201, 207,
    212, 214, 215n, 216, 220, 222, 225–27, 229,
    232, 233, 266, 428–31, 434–37; and legal
    questions, 315n; and Longchamps affair,
    294; Madison on, 311; and military stores,
    55; and Mississippi navigation, 311; and
    naval supplies, 10; and negotiations with
    British, 61, 63; and negotiations with Indi-
    ans, 258, 272; and postwar relations with
    Britain, 47; and tax collection, 70; reception
    of news of peace, 128, 139; rejects Russian
    mediation, 132n; and religious freedom,
    314, 315n; and requests for French aid, 69;
    slavery in, 299; and Spain, 20, 87, 98, 99,
    106, 242, 301, 308n, 312; and western ex-
    pansion, 311–13; mentioned, 5n, 8, 9, 14n,
    21, 57, 65, 91, 96, 117, 118n, 127n, 134,
    136, 176, 202, 205, 210, 215, 216, 238n, 262,
    263, 288, 310, 317, 318, 322, 329, 332n
American commerce: John Adams on, 356
    Barbary threats to, 317n; with Brazil, 173;
    and British customs duties, 351, 357; con-
    gressional regulation of, 344; and fishing
    industry, 344n; with France, 111, 112, 134,
    135n, 139, 142, 147n, 148, 151, 168–75,
    178, 182, 190n, 192, 195, 219, 224, 270, 281,
    294, 308n, 310, 327, 352, 355n, 357, 428,
    429, 433, 437, 441, 442; and free ports in
    France, 111–13, 132, 139, 140, 143, 144n,
    148, 171, 182, 183, 188, 189, 193, 195, 199,
    203, 204, 208, 216, 226, 436–38; and free
    ports in Italy, 347; and French customs du-
    ties, 111, 205, 219, 224, 225–26, 232n, 255,
    350, 353n, 354n, 357; and fur trade, 354;
    with Germany, 347; with Great Britain,
    107n, 124, 125n, 194, 244, 338, 434, 435;
    and hemp trade, 358; with Ireland, 169; and
    Irish customs duties, 357; and Jefferson,
    349n; L on, 277; L's efforts on behalf of,
    153, 164, 167–75, 178, 183–85, 187, 188n,
    190, 193, 195, 198, 199, 203, 205, 207, 208,
    218, 220n, 225–26, 232, 240, 255, 266,
    281n, 289n, 306, 309, 316, 319–21, 325,
    327, 331n, 332, 343, 345, 347, 349, 351, 353,
    358, 360n, 433, 435, 437, 440, 442, 443;
    Madison on, 312; and market for French
    goods, 173; Morris on, 219; with Prussia,
    345; regulation of, 333; and Society of Cin-
    cinnati, 207; with Spain, 87, 101, 105, 111,
    128, 166, 167n, 173; with Spanish colonies,
    173; and tobacco trade, 170, 171, 189, 194,
    198, 350–51, 440; and United Provinces, 33;
    in West Indies, 150n; and whale oil trade,
    319–21, 322n, 325, 332, 343, 349, 350, 352,
    354n, 355, 357, 441, 443, 444
American Constitution, Washington on, 119
American independence: assurance of, 85;
    British efforts to undermine, 21, 44; British
    recognition of, 45, 47n, 55n, 59, 61, 67, 106;
    as central issue of peace negotiations, 36;
    dangers to, 122; Dutch recognition of, 18,
    22, 27, 33, 34n, 36, 428, 431; L on, 77;
    Spanish recognition of, 17n, 82, 97, 98, 104,

American independence (cont.)
127n; Spanish view of, 312; tenth celebration of, 333; world recognition of, 60; mentioned, 143, 311, 429, 435
American Intercourse Bill, 212
American Philosophical Society, 236n
—letter to, calendared, 435
American Revolution (American cause): and abolition of slavery, 300; Canadian assistance to, 284, 285n; and Dutch, 295n; end of, 214; and final campaigns, 8, 9, 14n, 21, 30–32, 43n, 47n, 62, 65, 66, 70, 74n, 78, 114, 115, 116n, 428; and funding difficulties, 70; Indian participation in, 257; L compares to birth of daughter, 57; and L's campaign plans, 75; L's zeal for, 7n, 23, 26, 37, 48, 56n, 65, 81, 83, 91, 94, 102n, 113, 116n, 120, 169, 201, 202, 214, 233, 240, 255, 281; principles of, 180n; success of, 29; Washington on, 154n; mentioned, 237, 270, 342
American states: and ability to raise funds, 70, 78, 114, 196n; and Articles of Confederation, 79; and conflict with Congress, 4n, 114, 130, 157, 167, 196, 267n, 301, 338; constitutions of, 211–12; and enactment of trade laws, 338; and federal constitution, 214; and lack of unity, 79n, 106, 304, 312; oppose pay of soldiers, 136; sovereignty of, 88, 295n; Washington's letter to, 162, 165n; and western expansion, 311
Amsterdam, United Provinces (now Netherlands), 14–15, 25, 112n, 171, 201, 353
Animal magnetism: claims of, 218n, 220; L explains in Philadelphia, 236; L on, 216; and L's experiments with Shakers, 245, 260, 268; mentioned, 222n
Annapolis, Md.: Congress in, 195; L's visit to, 285; mentioned, 280n, 289, 296, 297, 299n
Antérroches, Joseph-Louis, chevalier d' (1753–?): letter to, calendared, 438
Antilles, 30–32
Antony, France, 25
Appalachian Mountains, 238, 312
Aranda, Pedro Pablo Abarca de Bolea, conde de (1718–99), Spanish ambassador to France: and negotiations with America, 61, 62n; and Jay, 99, 126; and peace negotiations, 41n; mentioned, 18n
Arlincourt, Charles-Adrien-Prévost d' (1718–94), French Farmer General, 232
Armistead, William, 279n
Arnold, Benedict (1741–1801), American major general, defected to British Sept. 25, 1780; British brigadier general, 5, 9, 10n
Articles of Confederation, 79, 212n; John Adams on, 203n, 211–12; L on, 88, 92
Artois, Charles-Philippe de Bourbon, comte d' (later Charles X) (1757–1836), brother of Louis XVI, 46–47, 48n
Asia, 300n
Athens, Greece, 38
Atlantic Ocean, 27, 304, 340n
Austria: and commercial relations with America, 347; and dispute with United Provinces,

293, 295n, 305n, 309, 318; L's visit to, 330, 339, 353
Austrian Netherlands, 5
Auvergne, France: L's spinning establishment in, 434; L's visit to, 110, 112; and trade with America, 327, 332; mentioned, 118n, 269
Ayen, Henriette-Anne-Louise d'Aguesseau, duchesse d' (1737–94), L's mother-in-law, wife of Jean, 118, 230, 236, 238, 293
Ayen, JEAN-Paul-François de Noailles, duc d' (1739–1824), L's father-in-law, maréchal de camp in French army, 236, 238, 293
Azores, 170

Bahama Islands, 339
Baltimore, Md.: L on, 240; L's visit to, 240–41, 285; and recovery from war, 301; and trade with France, 244, 358; mentioned, 160, 241, 262, 269, 271n, 280n, 354
Baltimore Troop of Light Dragoons, 241n
Bancroft, Edward (1744–1821): discovered to be double agent, 133n; and William Knox, 329; and L, 132, 155, 157n, 333; mentioned, 76, 141, 142n, 319, 320n
Bank of New York, 332
Barbary States, 315–17, 440, 443
Barbé de Marbois, François (1745–1837): secretary to French legation and chargé d'affaires in America (1783–85), **246;** and L, 261, 269; and Longchamps, 244n, 324n; journal of, 245–53; and Vergennes, 243, 260n, 270; mentioned, 262, 266
Barber, Francis (1751–83), American lieutenant colonel, 121
Barclay, Thomas, American consul in Paris: and commercial negotiations, 124, 148, 149, 175, 183, 215, 226; congressional instructions to, 143; and examination of American accounts abroad, 126, 127n; and free ports, 202; in Great Britain, 188, 192; and Henry's request to secure arms for Virginia, 328n; on L, 150n; mentioned, 267, 328
Barney, Joshua (1759–1818), 431
Barras, Jacques-Melchior Saint-Laurent, comte de (?–ca. 1800), French naval commander, 31
Barre, M., 284, 444
Barrett, Nathaniel, Boston merchant, 321n, 356, 357, 358n
Barrington, Samuel (1729–1800), British rear admiral, second in command under Howe, 27–28
Barry, John (1745–1803), commodore, Continental navy, 11, 13, 431
—letters from, calendared, 431
—letter to, calendared, 431
Barthe, M., 229
Basel, Switzerland, 299, 300
Basset, Frances (Fanny) (1767–96), 339, 340n
Bath, England: as health resort, 141, 166, 210; mentioned, 142n, 192, 212
Battle of the Saints, 48n, 67n
Baumier, M., publicist, 214, 215n

Bausset, Antoine-Hilarion de (1725–90), *chef d'escadre*, 77
Bavaria (Baviera): and Joseph II, 294; and proposed exchange of, 295n, 304, 305, 319, 325
Bayonne, France: deputies from, 112; fees for American ships at, 224–26; as free port for America, 113n, 143, 148, 171, 183, 188–90, 192, 203, 204; and obstacles to American trade, 111, 112n; and tobacco trade, 176n
Beaumarchais, Pierre-Augustin Caron de (1732–99), playwright, 229
Beaune (Baune), M. de, French officer, 155, 157n
Bedford, American merchant ship, 107n
Bee, Thomas (1740–1812): letter to, calendared, 443
Berckel, Pieter Johan van, minister to America from the United Provinces, 156, 157n
Bergasse, Nicolas (1750–1832), friend of L, 355
Bergen Neck, N.J., 288
Berlin, Prussia, 330, 342, 342n, 443
Bermuda (Burmuda), 339
Bernis, François-Joaquim de Pierre de, comte de Lyon, cardinal (1715–94), 9, 10n
Biddle, Clement (1740–1814), former quartermaster general for Pennsylvania, 160
Blackburne, Thomas, 290n
Black Sea, 146, 149, 150n
Bohemia, Austria, 330
Bordeaux, France: and grain monopoly, 218n; and trade with America, 183, 216; mentioned, 102, 128, 134, 340n
Boston, Mass.: British occupation of, 256; harbor of, 67n; honors L, 319; Jefferson's departure from, 267n; L's visit to, 233, 235, 260, 264–66, 268, 270, 275, 288, 335n, 438, 439; and relations with L, 353; and trade with France, 321n, 357, 358n; and trade with Great Britain, 333, 335n; mentioned, 61, 66, 241, 277, 289n, 321, 329, 350
Boudinot, Elias (1740–1821), member of Congress from New Jersey, President of Congress (Nov. 1782–Nov. 1783), 67, 144n, 152, 196n
—letters from, calendared, 433, 443
—letters to, 84–85, 142–44, 148–50; calendared, 431, 440
Boufflers, Marie-Françoise-Catherine de Beauveau, marquise de (1711–86), 293
Bougainville, Louis-Antoine, comte de (1729–1811), *chef d'escadre, maréchal de camp*, 179
Bouillé, François-Claude-Amour, marquis de (1739–1800), L's cousin, governor of Guadeloupe and Windward Islands, 4n, 5n
Bourbon (now Réunion), 218, 220n
Bourbon, Louis-Henri-Joseph, duc de (1756–1830), 47
Boylston, Thomas (1720?–98), American merchant: John Adams on, 357; and customs duties, 353n; and whale oil trade, 350n, 356–57, 444; mentioned, 344n

—letters to, 349–50, 352–53
Brandywine, Battle of, 30n, 56n
Brant, Joseph (1742–1807), Mohawk Indian chief, 265, 319
Brazil, 173
Breck (Breek), Samuel (1747–1809), 319, 353, 354n
—letter to, calendared, 440
Brest, France: and American supplies at, 27; American trade at, 193; collection of stores at, 11; convoy from, 5, 9, 10n, 23, 28n, 31, 56n, 74, 88n, 185; convoy to, 13n; and L's return to France, 262, 293; mentioned, 72, 86
Breteuil, Louis-Auguste Le Tonnelier, baron de (1730–1807), *ministre d'état* (1783), 220, 222n
Bridgen, Edward, of North Carolina, 210
Brioude, France, 112, 117, 118
British army: and departure for West Indies, 115; evacuation of, 18, 19, 28n, 30, 78, 115, 128, 130n, 156; and final campaigns in America, 30, 63; inactivity of, 66; losses of, 8; troops remaining in America after peace, 125n
British navy, 13, 22, 26, 66
Brittany, France, 215; Estates of, 292, 293n
Broglie (Broglio), Charles-Louis-Victor, prince de (1756?–94), friend of L, 5, 28n, 64n, 67, 429
Broglie (Broglio), Victor-François, maréchal duc de (1718–1804), 5
Brunswick, Karl Wilhelm Ferdinand, duke of (1735–1806), Prussian field marshal, nephew of Frederick II, 333
Brunswick (now New Brunswick), N.J., 235
Brussels (Bruxelles), Austrian Netherlands, 53
Burgoing, Jean-François, chevalier de, French chargé d'affaires in Spain, 126, 167
Burgundy, 295n; Estates of, 48n
Burke, Edmund (1729–97), member of Parliament, privy councillor and paymaster of British forces, 44
Burnet (Burnett), William (1730–91), member of Congress, surgeon general of Eastern District of Continental army, 115, 116n
Butler, Richard (1743–91), American brigadier general, appointed Indian commissioner in 1784: and L, 264, 272, 273; and negotiations with Indians, 251, 252, 254n, 255, 257, 263, 265n; and report to Congress, 287n; mentioned, 259
—letter from, calendared, 438
—letter to, 253–54

Cabinda, Angola, 218n
Cadiz (Cadix), Spain: American consul at, 229; French convoy at, 77; French-Spanish expedition from, 119; L's arrival at, 75, 80, 432; mentioned, 81, 82n, 83–88, 90, 93, 98, 104, 119, 134n, 309, 338
Cadran, M., 441
—letter to, calendared, 442
Cairo, Egypt, 312, 314n

Calais, France, 201n
Calhoun, James, deputy quartermaster general, Maryland, 241n
Calonne, Charles-Alexandre de (1734–1802), French controller general of finances, appointed Nov. 1783, **181;** and American fishing industry, 344n; on American trade, 184, 189, 190, 191n; and commercial negotiations, 182n, 183, 205n, 232n; on customs duties, 203, 204, 224–26; downfall of, 323, 324n; and free ports for America, 182, 193, 198, 204, 222n; as keeper of seals, 231; L's discussions with, 352; replaces d'Ormesson, 162, 165n; on tobacco monopoly, 351n; and whale oil trade, 319, 352, 353n, 356; mentioned, 167, 176n, 184, 190, 192, 220, 255n, 356n
—letters from, 178, 182, 189–90, 203–4, 225–26; calendared, 437, 443
—letters to, 193–94, 198–200; calendared, 437
Camden, Charles Pratt (1714–94), Lord Chancellor, 44, 157
Campo, Bernardo, marqués del, Spanish minister, first secretary to Floridablanca, 16, 94, 96
Canada: and American campaign plans, 84; British expedition from, 8; British troops in, 71, 115; governor of, 258, 259; L hopes for campaign against, 323, 433; L's invasion of, 85n, 86, 89, 91; and refugees, 63, 284, 285n; Washington plans tour of, 156; mentioned, 248, 251
Cape St. Mary, 75
Caraman, Maurice-Gabriel-Joseph de Riquet, chevalier de (later comte de), (1765–1837), L's traveling companion to America in 1784, 227, 245, 265n, 268, 280, 286, 310
Carey, Matthew (1760–1839), publisher of *Volunteer Journal,* 286, 287n, 298, 299n
—letter to, calendared, 438
Carleton, Sir Guy (Baron Dorchester) (1724–1808), lieutenant general, commander in chief of British forces in America (1781–83): on Americans, 195; and compliance with treaty, 130n, 142n; and final campaigns in America, 63; and prisoner exchange, 128, 139; and reconciliation efforts, 46, 47n; mentioned, 128
Carmichael (Carmichaell), William (?–1795), secretary to American legation in Spain, chargé d'affaires to Spain from 1783: and L, 20n, 84n, 86, 94, 96, 106, 229, 302n; L on, 302; and negotiations, 98, 294; recognition by Spain, 82n, 96, 98, 99, 104, 105, 106n, 166, 167n; mentioned, 8, 20, 34, 76, 86, 87, 88n, 96, 104, 310n, 338, 340n, 343, 345n
—letters to, 81–84, 126–27, 166–67, 300–302; calendared, 440
—letter to, from Morris, calendared, 431
Carolinas, 19, 57, 304
Carroll, Harriet Chew, friend of G. Washington, 121
Castries, Charles-Eugène-Gabriel de La Croix,

marquis de (1727–1801), French minister of marine, **359;** and commercial negotiations, 189, 226; and Franklin, 13; and L, 9, 11, 23, 262; on loss of *Matilda,* 186n; as mediator, 317n; and Protestants, 322; and purchase of American naval supplies, 355n, 358, 360n, 437, 444; and requests for American goods, 55, 319; resignation of, 133, 146; and supply convoys, 27; mentioned, 5, 13n, 15, 42, 56n, 124, 155, 167, 176n, 192, 255n, 293, 294, 295n, 433
—letters from, 226; calendared, 427, 433, 434, 436, 437, 444
—letter to, 358–60
Catherine II (the Great) (1729–96), empress of Russia, 150n, 216
Cayuga Indians, 251
Censeur, Le, French frigate, 74
Ceylon, 39n
Chardon, Daniel-Marc-Antoine (1730–95?), French commissioner for inspection of shipping, fishing, and maritime duties, 199, 200n, 225–26
Charles III (1716–88), king of Spain, **100;** and final campaigns in America, 91; and jackasses for Washington, 338; L on, 20; L's reception with, 97, 98, 104; and relations with America, 86, 99, 101, 104, 167n; mentioned, 15–17, 41n, 83
Charles Théodore (1724–99), elector of Palatinate and Bavaria, 304, 309, 310n, 319, 325
Charleston (Charlestown), S.C.: and American campaign plans, 23, 27, 31, 32, 49, 72; British evacuation of, 9, 22–23, 28, 30, 61, 63, 78, 79n, 80, 115, 116n, 428, 432; British forces in, 4, 8, 19; honors L, 230; mentioned, 133, 262, 327, 339
Charleston Library Society, 230n, 439
Charlus, Armand-Charles-Augustin de La Croix de Castries, comte de (1756–1842), *commandant-en-second* of *gendarmerie,* friend of L, 4–5, 24, 64, 229, 293
Chase (Chace), Samuel (1741–1811), Maryland delegate to Congress and agent in England (1783), 185, 186n
Chastellux (Chartellux, Chattellux), François-Jean de Beauvoir, chevalier de (1734–88), *maréchal de camp,* friend of Washington: *Journal* cited, 253; as messenger for Washington, 125, 126n, 155, 157n; mentioned, 113, 116, 125
—letter from, to Franklin, calendared, 435
Chaumont de la Millière, Antoine-Louis (1746–1803): letter to, calendared, 436
Chavaniac, chevalier de, brother-in-law of Mme de Chavaniac, 117, 118n
Chavaniac, Louise-CHARLOTTE du Motier de Lafayette de, baronne de Montioloux (1729–1811), L's aunt, 117, 230, 292
Chavaniac, Château de, L's birthplace in Auvergne: and Adrienne, 118, 262; and L, 262, 433; and peasants, 118n; mentioned, 112, 117, 142, 144, 145, 230, 329
Chesapeake Bay, 92, 358

Choiseul, Etienne-François, duc de (1719–85), former French minister of foreign affairs, 320, 321n, 325

Church, Angelica Schuyler (1756–1814), wife of John Barker, 200, 201, 317, 318n

Church, John Barker (1748–1818), supplier of army commodities: business ventures of, 155n; and Hamilton, 317; and L.'family portrait, 218n, 229, 230n; reports on British politics, 318n; as supplier to Rochambeau, 194n; and trade in France, 193, 194, 201n, 434; as Wadsworth's business partner, 319n; mentioned, 201, 318n

Cincinnatus, Lucius Quintus, 137n

Clermont, France, 118

Clinton, George (1739–1812), governor of New York, 336
—letter from, calendared, 436

Clinton, Henry (1738?–95), British commander in chief in America, governor of Limerick, 127, 128n, 141, 142n
—letter from, calendared, 433
—letters to, 127–28

Clinton, New Jersey, 233n

Cochran, Gertrude Schuyler (1724–1813), wife of John, 317–18

Cochran, John (1730–1807), director general of Medical Department of United States, 317–18

Coigny, François-Marie-Casimir de Franquetot, marquis de, friend of L, 269

College of New Jersey (now Princeton University), 224n

Combahee Ferry, S.C., Battle of, 64n

Commerce. See American commerce.

Commissioners of Congress, letter to, 253–54

Committee of Secret Correspondence, 124n

Committee of the States, 223n, 242, 243n, 274

Comtois (Cornu, called Comtois), L's valet, 262

Condorcet, Marie-Jean-Antoine-Nicolas-Caritat, marquis de (1743–94): letter from, 299–300

Congress. See Continental Congress.

Connecticut: grants citizenship to L and son, 269n, 438; and Indians, 267; and Pennsylvania, 79, 267n; mentioned, 57, 440

Constable, William (1752–1803), New York City merchant, partner of Robert Morris, 218, 354
—letter to, calendared, 442

Constantinople, treaty of commerce at, 150n

Continental army: John Adams on, 122; Henry Clinton on, 127; condition of, 55; disbanding of, 139, 141, 176, 187, 188n, 191; and financial difficulties, 78, 79n, 89, 114, 120, 121n, 135, 136, 149, 150; and French, 9, 27, 62, 84, 124n; and Knox, 354n; L on, 21, 71, 154, 187, 209; L's attachment to, 202; and L's command in Virginia, 279n; and L's desire to rejoin, 27, 50, 50, 65; L's friendships in, 24; L's leave from, 68, 90n; L's light infantry corps, 10n; L's service in, 185, 191; L's support for, 227; Livingston on, 66; and payment of soldiers, 196; and peacetime

army, 92, 114, 281, 321; receives news of peace, 128; reduction of, 120, 135; and Society of Cincinnati, 137, 158, 158n; and takeover of New York, 195; treatment of, 164; Washington on, 116n, 120, 136n, 139, 145, 147n; Washington's support of, 162; mentioned, 74

Continental Congress: and ability to raise funds, 304; accepts Franklin's resignation, 441; and Adams, 15; adjournment of, 223n, 255n; and appointments in Spain, 88n; appoints Adams to Great Britain, 314n; appoints Barclay to examine American accounts, 127n; appoints foreign commissioners, 267n, 301, 316n; appoints Knox secretary of war, 322n; assembly of, 235, 238, 440; and Austria, 347; and Barbary States, 316n, 317n; and British proposals, 21; and Canadian refugees, 284; and capture of *Three Friends*, 215n; and Carleton, 47n; and communications with ministers abroad, 43; and commercial negotiations, 205n; and compliance with treaty, 130n; and conflict with states, 114, 165n, 267n, 295n, 338; and Continental army, 120, 135; and disputes with Du Coudray, 124n; federal powers of, 92, 242, 243n; and final campaign plans, 19, 114; and final peace treaty, 148; and foreign relations, 105, 223; and France, 67n, 78, 93n, 143, 182n, 224n; and funding difficulties, 4n, 70, 78, 116n, 130, 142n, 157, 167, 267n, 277n; and gratitude to L, 90n, 128, 156, 218, 219n; instructions on peace negotiations, 39, 54; and instructions to Barry, 13n; and instructions to ministers abroad, 14–17, 34, 81, 84, 122, 275; and Jay's appointment, 314; Joseph II questions L on, 349n; L's assistance to, 7, 9, 66, 68, 98; and L's leave from army, 18, 21, 23, 37, 39, 62, 68, 69n, 84, 91, 116n, 144n; L's visit to, 263, 266, 270, 275, 277; and Laurens' appointment, 54; location of, 195, 297, 302n; and Longchamps affair, 294; memorials to, 428; and Mullens' commission, 197n; and negotiations with Indians, 248, 251, 252, 254n, 255, 257, 259, 260, 287n; and orders for Houdon, 332, 336; and payment of Canadians, 285n; and payment of soldiers, 121n, 188n; and peace commissioners, 28n, 47n; and petitions for land, 427; and presidency of, 67; and prisoner exchange, 39, 40n, 128; ratifies provisional treaty with Great Britain, 130n; receives Dutch minister, 157n; and relations with L, 25, 29, 40, 42, 45, 69, 74n, 89, 90, 99, 102, 113, 123, 124, 132, 139, 142, 143, 149, 150, 153, 164, 183–86, 192, 254, 275, 280–82, 284n, 285, 301, 306, 307, 345, 442; and Spain, 17n, 82, 102, 286, 306; and site for American capital, 156, 162, 166, 184; and statue of Washington, 332n, 336n; and Steuben's resignation, 276n; temporary assembly in New York, 299n; and trade regulations, 304, 332, 338, 344; and treaties of

Continental Congress (*cont.*)
amity and commerce, 224n; and war debt to
Great Britain, 143, 144, 146; and Washington, 162, 165n, 195; Washington recom-
mends L to, 116; and western expansion,
301, 338, 340n; and whale oil trade, 355;
mentioned, 11, 30n, 47n, 48, 53, 72, 85n,
88n, 96, 98, 101, 106, 121, 150n, 151, 154n,
176n, 186n, 190, 196n, 197, 205, 207, 208,
222, 223, 245, 284n, 294, 295n, 309, 431
—letters from: to Louis XVI, 282; calendared,
439
—letters to, 6–7, 84–85, 142–44, 148–50,
284–85; calendared, 427, 428, 430, 431, 435,
439; from Franklin, calendared, 437; from
Robert Morris, 254–55
Continental navy, 284
Conway (Connway), Henry Seymour
(1721–95), British general, commander in
chief of British armies (March 1782–Dec.
1783), 18, 19
Conway, Thomas de (1733–1800), American
major general, *maréchal de camp*, 197, 208n
Cork, Ireland, 13
Cornwallis, Charles, marquess and earl
(1738–1805), British lieutenant general, second in command to Clinton: arrival in England, 10n; capture of, 68; and
correspondence with Clinton, 127; and defeat at Yorktown, 127–28n; downfall of, 4;
L's battle with, 342; parole of, 429; and
release from parole, 39, 40, 49; supposed
capture of, 9; surrender of, 65; and visit to
Prussia, 345, 349n
Coste, Dr. Jean-François, 442
Courrier de l'Europe, French packet boat, 232n,
247
Courrier de New York, French packet boat, 231,
232
Creutz, Gustaf Philip, greve (1731–85), Swedish ambassador to France, 34n
Crèvecoeur, Michel-Guillaume St. John de
(1735–1813), French consul at New York,
286, 287n, 288, 439
Crimea (Krimee), Russian annexation of, 125n,
133n, 146, 149, 165n
Cumberland Island, Ga., 358
Custine-Sarreck, Adam-Philippe, comte de
(1740–93), *marèchal de camp*, 342
Custis, Eleanor (Nelly) Calvert (1754–1811),
wife of John Parke, 216
Custis, Eleanor (Nellie) Parke (1779–1852),
daughter of John Parke, 154, 164, 216, 237,
238n, 325
Custis, George Washington (Squire Tub) Parke
(1781–1857), son of John Parke, 154, 216,
237, 238n, 280, 325
Custis, John Parke (Jack) (1755–81), aide-de-
camp to Washington at Yorktown, son of
Martha Washington, 238n

Damas, Roger de, brother to Mme de Simiane,
155, 435

Dana, Francis (1743–1811), American minister
to Russia (1781–83), member of Congress
from Massachusetts (1784), associate judge
of Massachusetts Supreme Court (1785), 122
Dandridge, Bartholomew (1737–85), Supreme
Court justice, brother of Martha Washington, 339, 340n
Dandridge, Frances (Fanny) (?–1785), stepmother of Martha Washington, 339, 340n
Danzig (Dantzick), Poland, 162, 165n
Deane (Dean), Silas (1737–89), former Ameri-
can commissioner to France, 5, 20n, 122,
124n
Declaration of Independence, 165, 168
De Grasse, François-Joseph-Paul, comte
(1722–88), *chef d'escadre*, commander of
French West Indies fleet: and Caribbean de-
feat, 46, 48, 49, 68, 202, 430, 431; congratu-
lates L, 428; delivers treaty preliminaries to
Vergennes, 56n; and French campaigns, 31;
and L's campaign plans, 49n
—letter to, calendared, 428
Delaware Bay, 64n
Delaware Falls, 156
Delaware River, 301, 302n
Demanche, L's servant, 238, 261
Denmark, 38, 60, 315
Deslon, Charles (1750–86), disciple of Anton
Mesmer, 220, 222n
Desplaces, Jean-Baptiste Machillot, L's valet,
262
Detroit (now in Mich.), 32, 156
Deux-Ponts, Charles-Auguste-Christian, duc de
(1746–95), heir presumptive to Bavarian
throne, nephew of Charles Théodore, 304,
309, 310n, 319
Dickinson, John (1732–1808), president of Su-
preme Executive Council of Delaware and
Pennsylvania: letter from, calendared, 436;
letters to, calendared, 433, 443
Digby, Robert (1732–1815), British rear admi-
ral, 13n, 47n, 128, 130n
Digges, Thomas (1742–1821), native of Mary-
land and British agent, 19n, 34n
Dillon, Edouard, comte de (1750–1840?), colo-
nel of Régiment de Dillon under d'Estaing,
179
Dominica, West Indies, 76n
Dorchester, S.C., 8n
Dover, England, 216
Draper, William (1721–87), lieutenant gover-
nor of Minorca, 22, 24n
Du Bouchet, Denis-Jean-Florimand Langlois de
Mautheville, marquis (1752–1826), major in
French army, 436
Dubuisson, Pierre-Ulrich (1746–94), 299, 300n
Du Coudray, Philippe-Charles-Jean-Baptiste
Tronson (1738–77), engineer, major general
in Continental army, 122, 124n
Dunkirk, France: fees for American ships at,
224, 225–26; as free port for America, 112,
143, 148, 171, 183, 188–90, 192, 203, 204;
and trade with America, 327

Dunning, John Adams on, 38
Du Plessis, Thomas-Antoine, chevalier de
  Mauduit (1753–91), lieutenant colonel in
  Continental army, 207
Dupont de Nemours, Pierre-Samuel
  (1739–1817), French controller general: let-
  ter to, 327
Duportail (Portail), Louis Le Bègue de Presle
  (1743–1802), brigadier general of engineers,
  Continental army, 5, 195
Durfort, Etienne-Narcisse, vicomte de
  (1753–1837), friend of L, 269
Durfort, Mme de, 269

East India Company, 38
East Indies (East Indias), 5, 26, 33, 47, 61
Edict of Nantes, Revocation of, 352n
Éliot, James Edward (1758–97), Lord of Treas-
  ury, friend of William Pitt, 157, 158
Elizabeth River (Va.), 296
Enabling Act, 47n, 49, 50n
English Channel, 26, 31
Estaing (Estaign), Charles-Henri-Théodat, comte d' (1729–94), French vice admiral: ap-
  pointed governor of Touraine, 127n; arrives
  in Paris, 97; dispatches news of peace to
  America, 85; and expedition against Savan-
  nah, 180n; and L, 76, 77, 86; promised
  governorship, 126; and Society of Cincinnati,
  179, 205, 208n, 343; and Spanish, 76; and
  West Indies expedition, 65, 69n, 71n, 72, 77,
  79n, 84; mentioned, 68, 93, 98, 200
—letters from, calendared, 433
—letters to, 97; calendared, 432, 434
Europe: and America, 299, 313; and Barbary
  States, 315–17; conflicts in, 306, 441; mentioned, 272, 300n, 309, 311, 312, 329
Ezra, L's servant, 238

Faculté de Médicine, Université de Paris, 222n
Falkenhayn, M., de, 77
Faneuil Hall, Boston, 333, 335n
Fanning, Captain, 433
Farmers General: and fees charged by, 193;
  and L, 353, 354; L on, 351, 434; and obstacles to American trade, 111, 112, 113n, 170,
  171, 189, 350–51; and tobacco trade, 112n,
  155n, 194, 198, 350–51, 352n; and whale oil
  trade, 353n
Federal union: John Adams on, 122, 123;
  French view of, 150n; Joseph II questions L
  on, 349n; Knox on, 137; L on, 85, 88, 92,
  139, 143, 149, 150, 154, 164, 188, 214, 235,
  243n, 266, 273, 277, 281, 304, 307, 441;
  Livingston on, 130; Madison on, 311, 312;
  necessity of, 106; Paine on, 150n; Washington on, 343
Fish, Nicholas (1758–1833), major, 2d New
  York Regiment, lieutenant colonel (1783),
  adjutant general of New York (1784),
  317–18
Fishkill (Fishkills), N.Y., 66, 136n, 137n, 285n
Fitzgerald, John, former Continental lieutenant
  colonel, 337, 340n, 344

Fitzherbert, Alleyne, British minister plenipo-
  tentiary for negotiating peace with United
  States, 53, 136n
Fitzroy, George Henry, earl of Euston (later
  4th duke of Grafton) (1760–1844), member
  of Parliament, friend of William Pitt, 157,
  158
Flanders, France, 155, 293, 330
Fleury, François-Louis Teissèdre de (1749–?),
  former aide-de-camp to L, 284n
Flint River, Ga., 62n
Flora, American merchant ship, 134
Florida, 87, 88
Floridablanca, José Monino y Redondo, conde
  de (1728–1808), Spanish minister of finance,
  chief minister to Charles III: announces ap-
  pointment of minister to negotiate with
  Americans, 16; and French, 76; and igno-
  rance of America, 104; and Jay, 15–17; L
  on, 166; and negotiations with L, 97, 98,
  102, 104, 105, 106n, 128, 139, 355; view of
  America, 98; mentioned, 17n, 83, 94, 97n,
  302, 344, 345n, 355n, 440
—letters from, 101–2
—letters to, 99–101
Fontainebleau, France, 350–51
Forster Frères, 215n
Forth (Forsh), Nathaniel Parker, agent of Lord
  North to Paris peace negotiations, 17, 18n,
  21
Fort Johnson, N.Y., 258
Fort Lillo, 293, 295n
Fort Schuyler (Fort Stanwix), N.Y.: L's visit to,
  252, 253, 438; and negotiations with Indians,
  241, 248, 260n, 266, 272, 439; physical condition of, 248; mentioned, 250, 260
Fortune, La, French packet boat, 244n
Fothergill, John (1712–80), 300
Fox, Charles James (1749–1806), leader of Opposition in Parliament, secretary of state for
  foreign affairs (1782), formed coalition with
  North (April–Dec. 1783): on American independence, 125n; and coalition with Lord
  North, 125n; downfall of, 186n, 193n; L on,
  25, 44; as member of opposition, 216; and
  peace negotiations, 26, 37n, 44, 47n; and
  return to power, 192; and Rockingham administration, 25; mentioned, 35, 36n, 209
France: John Adams on, 203n; and advantages
  of American trade, 169, 170, 171, 173, 174,
  183, 219; and alliance with America, 33,
  34n, 40, 41n, 44, 46, 47n, 55n, 61, 62n, 68,
  71, 76, 79n, 81, 137, 168, 169, 174, 179,
  190n, 202, 204, 256–59, 272, 273, 281, 282,
  284n, 302, 313, 317n, 358; and alliance with
  America and Spain, 82; and alliance with
  America, Spain, and United Provinces, 32n;
  and alliance with Spain, 86; and alliance with
  United Provinces, 14–15, 353, 354n; and
  American canal plans, 297; American dependence on, 78; American gratitude to, 70, 81;
  and Barbary States, 315, 317n; and claims
  against Britain, 38; and commerce with Indians, 256; and commercial relations with

France (*cont.*)
America, 111, 112, 135n, 139, 140n, 143,
144, 148, 167–75, 178, 182, 192, 216, 219,
220n, 224, 240, 270, 289n, 332, 350n, 351,
355–57, 360, 428, 435, 439; and commercial
relations with Great Britain, 136n; and commercial relations with Spain, 101; and concessions to American trade, 294, 295n, 304n,
305, 306, 310, 319, 320, 322n, 344n, 352,
353n, 354n, 355n, 357, 437, 440–43; and
conspiracy against America, 124n; and declaration of rights, 165n; and desire for fishing
rights off Nova Scotia, 48n; and efforts to
maintain peace, 162; and European disputes,
293, 302, 305, 309, 318; and expedition
against Cabinda, 218n; and final campaigns
in America, 78, 429; Greene's commercial
interests in, 134n; and Indians, 252, 260n,
272; and internal difficulties, 133; and Ireland, 165n; Jefferson's journey to, 266; and
joint expedition with Spain, 431; and Joseph
II, 294; L on, 159; L's arrival in, 4; L's
influence in, 123, 241, 254; L's return to, 93,
269, 329; L's service to, 232; and Longchamps affair, 244n, 343; Madison on, 312;
as mediator, 242, 317n; and negotiations
with England, 18n, 55n, 56n, 86; and obstacles to American trade, 124, 140, 148, 150n,
169–70, 171, 173, 175, 176n, 183, 189, 193,
194, 198–200, 203–5, 209, 216, 225–26,
240, 255, 308n, 321n, 332, 436, 442; prestige of, 77; and Protestants, 322, 352, 442;
and provincial governorships, 127n; and regular communications with America, 144,
148, 151, 160, 162, 166, 229, 318, 322, 324;
and relations with America, 313; resources
of, 304, 310; and rivalry with Great Britain,
219, 304; and Russian-Turkish dispute, 146,
149, 151; Ségur on, 51; and Society of Cincinnati, 343; and Spain, 106, 306; and trade
with colonies, 176n; and views on American
alliance, 21; Washington's proposed visit to,
24, 93, 120, 164; mentioned, 5n, 6, 18, 23,
28, 38, 60, 62, 92, 96, 97, 132, 136, 155,
158, 160, 187, 201, 215n, 216, 223, 262, 272,
276, 280n, 284n, 285, 288, 289, 298, 302n,
309, 314n, 322n, 324
Franklin, Benjamin (1706–90), American minister to France (1778–85), commissioner to
negotiate peace with Great Britain (1782),
12, 221; John Adams on, 124n; and American supplies, 27, 32n, 428; and animal magnetism, 220, 222n; and commercial
negotiations, 149, 175, 183, 189, 205n, 224n,
226, 227, 294, 316n; and Congress, 7n, 43,
66, 125, 148, 164, 223, 267n; and free ports,
202; and French ministry, 53; and Grenville,
45; illness of, 13n, 41n, 57, 192, 193n; in-
quires about Rayneval's trip, 56n; and L,
69n, 151, 255, 282n; on L, 40n, 43n; L's
assistance to, 6, 11, 15, 34, 122, 185, 429; L's
displeasure with, 185, 192; as minister to
France, 126n; as peace commissioner, 28n;
and peace negotiations, 17–18, 33–36, 37n,
41n, 45, 55n, 59, 150n; and prisoner exchange, 39, 40n, 49, 428; replacement for,
314n; resignation of, 301, 302n, 441; retirement of, 266; returns to America, 332, 336;
on Society of Cincinnati, 209; on Spain, 37n;
and Spanish bills of exchange, 17, 19, 20;
and Swedish ambassador, 34n; and
Veimérange, 13n; and Vergennes, 69, 71n,
139; and war debt to Great Britain, 143,
144, 146; Washington on, 444; mentioned,
9, 10n, 18n, 25, 29, 36, 47, 48, 49n, 60n, 75,
76, 80, 126, 130n, 136n, 144n, 147n, 159n,
176n, 183, 186n, 215, 221, 267, 277, 439
—letters from, 57; calendared, 428–31
—letters to, 10–15, 39–43, 55–57, 59, 68–69,
74–75, 131–32, 157–58, 167, 220–22,
315–17; calendared, 427–37, 440–43
Franklin, William Temple (1759?–1823), secretary to and grandson of Benjamin: and L,
88n, 332, 336, 432; and Society of Harmony,
222; mentioned, 10, 11, 75, 159n, 267, 332n
—letters to, 165; calendared, 433, 435, 437,
440, 441, 443
Frederick II (the Great) (1712–86), king of
Prussia: John Adams on, 38; and army maneuvers, 349n; and Danzig, 162; and European dispute, 294; and Henry, 342n; L on,
90; L's visit to, 333, 342, 345; and Russian-
Turkish dispute, 151
Fredericksburg, Va., 265
Frederick William II (1744–97), crown prince
of Prussia: letter to, calendared, 443
French aid to America: and advantages for
French, 70; American hopes for, 60; American need of, 78; and American war debt to
Great Britain, 144; for commercial ventures,
135n; difficulties in obtaining, 6, 9, 10, 15,
18; L's efforts on behalf of, 7n, 8, 14n, 27,
30, 36, 61, 69, 70, 71n, 87, 185, 202; limita-
tions of, 10n; and 6-million-livre loan, 15n,
431
French army: in America, 30–32, 50, 62, 63,
66, 68, 70, 114; departure from America,
78, 79; and foreign orders, 176n; L's rank
in, 69, 113, 123; and Society of Cincinnati,
137n, 158, 176, 179, 187, 188n, 191, 202,
205, 207n–8n; in West Indies, 84; mentioned, 201n
French Guiana, 330n, 442
French navy: and Battle of Saints, 46, 48n,
67n; vs. British fleet, 22; departure from
America, 70; and expeditions with Spanish,
26; and final campaigns in America, 31, 49,
68, 72, 91, 114; L's assessment of, 23; and
L's campaign plans, 46, 66n; Livingston's
assessment of, 67; and needed supplies, 33;
and Society of Cincinnati, 178n, 179, 191,
202, 207, 208n, 436, 437; in West Indies, 75,
77, 88n; mentioned, 27
Friesland, United Provinces, 17n

Gallitzin (Gullitzin), Dmitri Alekseyevich, prince (1734–1803), Russian minister to The
Hague, 25, 26, 60

Gallitzin, Dmitri, II, prince (?–1793), Russian minister to Vienna, 216, 218n

Gálvez, José de, marqués de Sonora (1729–86), Spanish minister of Indies from 1775, 105

Ganiengahas, 251

Gardoqui (Gardochy), Diego María de (1735–98), Spanish consul in London (1783), chargé d'affaires in United States (1784), Spanish minister to United States, 126, 308n, 335, 443

Gates, Horatio (1728–1806), former major general in Continental army, president of Virginia Society of Cincinnati (1783), 289, 290n

Gazette de France, 176, 179, 180n

Geary, Samuel: letter to, calendared, 443

Gelderland (Guelderland), United Provinces, 17n, 34n

George III (1738–1820), king of Great Britain and Ireland: and John Adams, 333, 335n; dismisses Fox-North coalition, 193n; and efforts to undermine American sovereignty, 46; and freeing of American slaves, 142n; and internal affairs, 211; irritation of, 21; L on, 44, 159; and peace negotiations, 47n, 61, 67, 124; and recognition of American independence, 45; and Shelburne, 44; and trade with America, 213n; mentioned, 19, 130n, 144

Georgia, 57, 62n, 87, 156, 358

Gérard de Rayneval, Joseph-Matthias (1746–1812), first secretary, French foreign ministry, 55, 56n, 74, 430
—letter to, calendared, 436

Germain (Germaine), George Sackville, Lord (1716–85), British secretary of state for American colonies in North administration, 9

German Flats, N.Y., 247, 253n, 254

Germany: and commercial relations with America, 347; L's visit to, 330, 332, 333, 335, 347, 351, 353, 354, 443; mentioned, 201

Gerry, Elbridge (1744–1814), member of Congress from Massachusetts: letters to, calendared, 439, 440

Gibraltar: British withdrawal from, 77; siege of, 22, 33, 34, 46, 61, 67, 72n, 75, 79n, 428, 431; Spanish cession of, 87; Spanish desire for, 39n

Gillon, Alexander (1741–94), commodore, South Carolina naval forces, delegate to Congress (1784), 56n

Gilpin, George, 337, 340n, 344

Gimat (Gemat), Jean-Joseph Sourbader, chevalier de (1743?–92?), lieutenant colonel in Continental army, formerly L's aide-de-camp, 113, 427, 433

Gouvion, Jean-Baptiste de (1747–92), colonel of Continental engineers, formerly L's aide: and French merchants, 327; and Indians, 260; and Joseph II, 349n; and L, 114, 437; L on, 200; military career of, 201n; at Oneida Castle, 262; and Washington, 116n; Washington on, 135; mentioned, 5, 65, 72,

74n, 115, 120, 136, 137, 183, 184, 190, 230, 236, 262
—letters to, calendared, 431

Grafton, Augustus Henry Fitzroy, 3d duke of (1735–1811), 44, 157, 158n

Grandchain, Guillaume-Jacques-Constant Liberge, comte de (1744–1805), commander of frigate *Nymphe*, 280

Grant, Charles (1746–1823), member of Parliament and director of East India Company: letter from, calendared, 427

Grattepain-Morizot, Jacques-Philippe, L's steward, 430, 441
—letter to, calendared, 441

Great Britain: and John Adams, 45, 301; and American canal plans, 297; American distrust of, 70; and American sovereignty, 18, 27, 32n, 33, 55n; and American war debt, 144n, 314, 315n, 320n; and Austrian Netherlands, 295n; and Barbary States, 317n; and boundary settlements with America, 102, 105; and commercial relations with America, 111–13, 124, 125n, 135n, 136n, 148, 150n, 151, 166, 168–70, 173, 176n, 193, 194, 199, 204, 210, 211n, 212, 213, 244, 270, 271n, 289n, 304, 305, 310, 333, 335n, 338, 351, 356, 357, 434, 435; and compliance with treaty, 130n, 141, 142n, 443; desperation of, 9, 26, 33, 427; and efforts to disrupt American alliances, 306, 345; and American campaigns, 119, 428; Floridablanca on, 98; and France, 18n, 26, 56n, 147, 169, 197n, 198, 219; and Indians, 252, 256, 259, 265n, 272; and internal difficulties, 24n, 25, 27, 29, 38, 43, 44, 46, 124, 141, 142n, 146, 186n, 188, 192, 193, 201, 209, 211, 318, 428, 430, 435, 436; and Ireland, 162, 165n, 166, 216, 271n, 318, 319n, 323; L on, 43–48, 61, 82; L's relations with, 270; L's visit to, 90n; and mistreatment of prisoners, 53; and Nova Scotia fisheries, 48n; and peace negotiations, 65, 79n, 132, 427, 434; and proposals for American reconciliation, 5n; and Russia, 349n; and recognition of American independence, 59, 60, 82; and relations with America, 87, 93n, 97, 141, 164, 242, 258, 259, 307, 311, 318, 440; and Spain, 26, 101, 166, 302; and Russian-Turkish dispute, 146, 149, 151; Ségur on, 51; as threat to America, 88, 89, 99; and Washington, 106; Washington on, 63; and West Indies campaigns, 28n; mentioned, 4, 10n, 22, 28, 56n, 67, 68, 89, 98, 121n, 132, 159, 165, 201, 215n, 223, 302n, 322, 329

Great Grasshopper, Indian chief, 249, 251, 253n

Great Lakes, 156, 248

Greene, Catherine (Kitty) Littlefield (1755–1814), wife of Nathanael, 304

Greene, George Washington (1775?–93), son of Nathanael, 302, 304n, 317, 322, 441, 442

Greene, Griffin (1749–1804), cousin of Nathanael, 133, 134n, 436, 440

Greene (Green), Nathanael (1742–86), Ameri-

Greene, Nathanael (*cont.*)
can major general, commander in chief of
Southern department: and agreements with
British, 78; as commander of American
forces, 29, 122; and commercial ventures in
France, 355, 358, 360n; at Dorchester, 8;
and estimate of British forces in New York,
115, 116n; and French purchase of naval
supplies, 441; and L, 134n, 186, 262; and
purchase of American naval supplies, 444;
sends son to France, 317, 322; mentioned,
24, 310n, 318n
—letters from, 133–34; calendared, 435, 436,
442
—letters to, 302–5; calendared, 432, 434,
440–42, 444
Grenville, Thomas (1755–1846), member of
Parliament, peace emissary (1782), 35, 41n,
430; and peace negotiations, 37n, 40, 45, 47,
50; mentioned, 35, 36n, 49
Gribeauval, Jean-Baptiste Vaguette de
(1715–89), lieutenant general and commander of French artillery, 328
Guadeloupe, West Indies, 76n
Guichen, Luc-Urbain de Bouëxic, comte de
(1712–90), lieutenant general in French
navy, 13, 23

Hague, The, United Provinces, 25, 26, 33, 59,
211–12, 223, 302
Haldimand, Frederick (1718–91), governor of
Canada, 258, 259
Halifax (Hallifax), Nova Scotia, 63, 115
Hamilton, Alexander (1757–1804), former
aide-de-camp to Washington, member of
Congress from New York (1782–83): and L,
90, 125, 317; as member of Congress, 431;
as member of Washington's staff, 24n; and
Miranda, 324n; and New York Society for
Promoting the Manumission of Slaves, 336n;
mentioned, 24, 28n, 130, 263, 287n
—letter from, calendared, 431
—letters to, 263–64, 275–76, 317–18; calendared, 429, 430
Hamilton, Angelica (1784–1857), daughter of
Alexander, 263, 264n, 276, 318
Hamilton, Elizabeth (Betsy) Schuyler
(1757–1854), wife of Alexander, 263, 276,
318
Hamilton, Philip (1782–1801), son of Alexander, 276, 318
Hanson, John (1721–83), member of Congress
from Maryland, president of Congress (Nov.
1781–Nov. 1782): letters to, 6–7; calendared, 427, 428, 430
Harmar (Herman), Josiah (1753–1813), brevet
colonel, 1st U.S. regiment (1783), carrier of
ratification of definitive treaty of peace to
France (1784), Indian agent for northwest
territory (1785), 223, 224n, 437
Harrison, Benjamin (1726?–91), governor of
Virginia (1782–84), 196, 286, 287n, 332n
—letter to, calendared, 439
Harrison, Richard (1750–1841), American consul at Cadiz: and jackasses for Washington,
298, 338; as Jay's replacement, 87; and L,
86, L on, 87; 88n, 89, 229; mentioned, 167,
299n, 302
Harrison, Robert Hanson (1745–90), American
lieutenant colonel, Washington's military secretary, 76, 90
Hartford, Conn.: L's visit to, 264, 265, 268,
269n; and relations with L, 353; mentioned,
66, 261, 266, 267, 269, 438
Hartley (Hartlay), David (1732–1813), member
of Parliament, British commissioner for
peace negotiations (1782): arrives in Paris,
124, 126; and commercial negotiations,
136n; L suggests contact with, 18n; and
peace negotiations, 125n, 132n, 136, 150n;
proposes withdrawal of British troops, 130n;
mentioned, 18
Havana (Havanna), Cuba, 76
Hénin, Adélaïde-Félicité-Etiennette Guignot de
Monconseil, princesse d' (1750–1824), friend
of L, 293
Henry (1726–1802), prince of Prussia, brother
of Frederick II, 333, 340, **341**, 342
Henry, Patrick (1736–99), governor of Vir-
ginia (1784–86), 286, 314, 328n, 441
—letter from, calendared, 441
—letters to, 305–6, 328; calendared, 442
Herkimer, N.Y., 253n, 254n
Hermione, French frigate, 23, 64n, 428
Herries, Sir Robert, 352n
Hill, David, 260n
Hispaniola, West Indies, 77n
Holland, Province of, 17n
Hood, Samuel, 1st viscount (1724–1816), Brit-
ish rear admiral, second in command to
Rodney in West Indies, 13n, 23
Hooe, Robert Townsend, colonel, 298
Houdon, Jean-Antoine (1741–1828), French
sculptor: and bust of Washington, 332n, 336,
357, 358n; L's introduction of, 331, 443; and
success in America, 444
House, Mary, 242, 272, 274
House of Commons, 19, 107n, 125n, 130n, 192
House of Lords, 213n
Howe, Richard, Viscount Langar (1726–99),
British admiral, commander at Gibraltar,
First Lord of Admiralty (1783), 74, 75n
Hubert, L's servant, 238
Hudson (North) River, 260, 262
Humphreys, David (1752–1818), American
captain, Washington's personal aide
(1783–84), secretary to American legation in
France (1784), 277n, 347, 349n
—letter to, 276–77
Hunter, James, Virginia munitions manufac-
turer, 133, 134n
Hunter, John, London merchant, 340n
Huron Indians, 258, 260

Illinois River, 156
India: Dutch ports in, 39n; and French, 10n,
13n, 32; and trade with America, 219; mentioned, 219

Indian Ocean, 220n
Indians: and affection for L, 252, 259, 260;
   and American Revolution, 250; appearance
   of, 252, 253; and attacks against settlements,
   252, 266, 301, 440; Barbé de Marbois on,
   248, 249; and France, 256, 260n, 270, 327;
   and hostilities with America, 433; L's influence with, 243, 253, 254n, 260, 264, 266,
   267, 270, 272, 273, 438; L's relations with,
   245–53, 255–60, 263, 286, 342n; and peace
   negotiations, 255, 258, 263; and proficiency
   in French, 251; Washington's view of, 265n
Ireland: and America, 169, 170, 357; and
   France, 165n, 172; and England, 162, 165n,
   166, 216, 271n, 318, 319n, 323; L's interest
   in, 200, 323n; mentioned, 211, 287n, 298,
   322, 329
Irish Parliament, 218n, 319n
Irish Volunteer Association, 162, 165n, 166,
   167n; and L, 270, 271n, 286
Iroquois Indians, 260, 262, 267, 268, 272
Irvine, William (1741–1804), Continental brig-
   adier general, 234
Isle de France (now Mauritius), 218, 220n
Issoire, France, 118
Italy, 309, 347

Jamaica, 26, 49, 65n, 213
James River, 296, 301, 337
James River Company: establishment of, 298n,
   315n, 344; Washington on, 295–99; Wash-
   ington's role in, 337, 345n; Washington's
   stock in, 296, 299n
Jarnac, Gaston-Louis, comte de (1758–1818),
   French soldier wounded at Yorktown: letter
   to, calendared, 428
Jay, James (1732–1814), physician, member of
   New York Senate (1778–82), elder brother
   of John, 134, 135n
Jay, John (1745–1829), American minister to
   Spain, peace commissioner in Paris (1782),
   secretary of foreign affairs (1784), **95;** arrives in France, 42, 45, 429; and Barbary
   States, 316n; and commercial negotiations,
   149, 224n, 255n; and Congress, 66, 148,
   164; and Franklin, 37n; and French ministry, 53; in Great Britain, 188, 192; and
   Harrison, 87; health of, 80, 166; and L, 43n,
   55, 56n, 69n, 105, 121, 151, 185, 192, 218n,
   227, 248n, 427; as minister of foreign affairs, 227; and New York Society for Promoting the Manumission of Slaves, 336n;
   and peace negotiations, 28n, 37, 41n, 54,
   55n, 59, 150n, 317n; returns to America,
   127n, 216, 223; as secretary for foreign affairs, 263, 264, 285, 287n, 301, 302n, 306,
   314n; on slavery, 336; on Society of Cincinnati, 209; and Spain, 16, 17n, 20, 26, 46, 61,
   62n, 80, 87, 96, 98, 99, 105, 106, 126, 143;
   and trip to England, 164; and Vergennes,
   139, 215; and war debt to Great Britain,
   143, 144, 146; mentioned, 8n, 10n, 18, 47,
   48, 56n, 74, 75n, 85, 101n, 102n, 130n,
   136n, 144n, 147n, 159n, 236n, 287n, 305n,

306n, 308n, 310n, 320n, 321, 322, 323n,
   349n, 355n, 432
—letters from, 79–80; calendared, 427,
   430–32, 434, 437, 439, 440, 443, 444; to
   Adrienne de Lafayette, calendared, 443
—letters to, 7–8, 19–20, 33–34, 68–69, 75–77,
   94–97, 131–32, 263, 282–84, 293–95,
   335–36; calendared, 430, 434–37, 439,
   441–43; from Morris, calendared, 431
Jay, Sarah (Sally) Van Brugh Livingston
   (1756–1802), wife of John: and L, 235, 430,
   432; mentioned, 8, 20, 34, 76, 80, 96, 236n,
   263, 295, 336
—letters to, calendared, 430, 432
Jefferson, Martha (Patsy) (1772–1836), daughter of Thomas, 242, 267, 274
Jefferson, Thomas (1743–1826), American
   peace commissioner in Paris (1782), minister
   to France from May 1785: appointed peace
   commissioner, 28n; and commercial negotiations, 205n, 224n, 227, 267n, 294, 316n,
   349n, 350n, 353, 358n; commissions bust of
   Washington, 332n; departs for France, 276;
   and Farmers General, 350–51; and Henry's
   request for arms, 328n; illness of, 310; and
   Madison, 310n; on L, 274n; L on, 355; as
   minister to France, 126n, 285, 301, 302n;
   Notes on the State of Virginia, **348;** and tobacco
   monopoly, 351n; and whale oil trade, 355;
   mentioned, 244n, 277, 315n, 320, 328, 333,
   338, 340n, 349n
—letter from, calendared, 444
—letters to, 226–67, 315–17, 345–49; calendared, 440; from Madison, 241–43, 271–74
Johnson, Thomas (1732–1819), member of
   Congress from Maryland, 337, 340n, 344
Joly de Fleury, Jean-François (1718–1802),
   French controller general of finances (May
   1781–March 1783), 112, 113n, 124, 125n
—letter to, 110–12
Jordan, Nicholas, 253n
Joseph II (1741–90), king of Germany and
   Holy Roman emperor, **334;** John Adams on,
   38; and America, 347; and Bavaria, 304,
   305, 309, 310n, 325; as king of Romans,
   319; and L, 333, 347, 349n; and Morocco,
   316; and peace negotiations, 132; and Russian-Turkish dispute, 133, 143, 146, 151,
   162; travels of, 192; and United Provinces,
   293, 295n; mentioned, 147n

Kanawha (Kanhawa) River, Va. (now W. Va.),
   296
Karamanli, Ali, pasha of Tripoli, 316
Kaunitz-Rietberg, Wenzel Anton, prince von
   (1711–94), Austrian chancellor, 347
Kentucky, 287, 298, 309, 339
Kirkland (Courtland), Samuel (1744–1808),
   missionary to Indians, 248, 253, 254n, 272,
   319, 320n
Knox, Henry (1749?–1806), American brigadier general, commissioner to arrange exchange of prisoners with British, founder of
   Society of Cincinnati, secretary of war from

Knox, Henry (*cont.*)
   1785, **138;** as commander in chief, 188n;
   and L, 137, 187, 276, 322, 329, 435, 439;
   and Miranda, 324n; retirement of, 354n;
   and Society of Cincinnati, 137n, 343; as secretary of war, 321, 322n; mentioned, 24,
   28n, 141, 142n, 336n, 354
—letters from, 137; calendared, 435
—letters to, 186–88, 321–22, 329–30; calendared, 429, 439, 440
Knox, Henry (Harry) Jackson (1780–1832),
   son of Henry, L's godson, 137, 188, 322n,
   330, 439
Knox, Lucy Flucker (1776–1854), daughter of
   Henry, 188, 322, 330
Knox, Lucy Flucker (1756–1824), wife of Henry, 137, 188, 322, 330
Knox, William (Billy), Jr. (1756–95), brother of
   Henry: in Europe, 137n; health of, 187, 329;
   and L, 322, 329; mentioned, 188n

Lafayette, ANASTASIE-Louise-Pauline du
   Motier de (1777–1863), L's daughter:
   growth of, 8; L's affection for, 231, 236,
   262; and letter to Washington, 237, **239;**
   portrait of, 216, 339, 340n; taught to revere
   Washington, 50; Washington's letter to, 440;
   mentioned, 28, 117, 118, 121, 125, 133, 136,
   142, 154, 164, 192, 196, 208, 230, 237, 238n,
   262, 280, 290, 293, 325, 333, 337, 356
Lafayette, GEORGE-Washington-Louis-Gilbert
   du Motier de (1779–1849), L's son: and
   Connecticut citizenship, 269n, 438; education of, 304n, 317, 322, 439, 442; growth of,
   8; inoculation of, 132, 133n, 157; L's affection for, 231, 236, 262; and Maryland citizenship, 290; portrait of, 216, 339, 340n;
   and Washington, 28n, 50, 91; mentioned,
   10n, 28, 64, 117, 118, 121, 125, 133, 136,
   142, 154, 164, 192, 196, 208, 230, 237, 280,
   290, 293, 325, 333, 337, 356
Lafayette, James Armistead (ca. 1759–1830),
   black spy, **278,** 279n
Lafayette, Marguerite–MADELEINE de (Mlle du
   Motier) (?–1783), L's aunt, 97, 117, 118n
Lafayette, Marie-ADRIENNE-Françoise de
   Noailles, marquise de (1759–1807), L's wife:
   and birth of Virginie, 57, 113; health of,
   118; and Humphreys, 277n; and Jeffersons,
   267; and W. Knox, 330; L's affection for,
   227, 230, 231, 235, 236, 238, 293; L's commissions for, 230; and Laurens, 29, 53; and
   d'Ormesson, 125n; portrait of, 216, 339,
   340n; pregnancy of, 50; and spinning mill in
   Auvergne, 118n; and Washington, 237, 436;
   Wilberforce on, 159n; mentioned, 5, 10, 23,
   28, 64, 65, 76, 79, 90n, 93, 96, 117, 121,
   125, 133, 136, 137, 142, 146, 154, 155, 157,
   161, 164, 188, 192, 196, 208, 211, 218n, 280,
   290, 295, 300, 302n, 325, 333, 337, 356
—letters from, to Franklin, calendared, 437
—letters to, 117–18, 226–27, 229–30, 231,
   235–38, 260–62, 292–93; calendared, 433,

434, 437, 438, 443; from Jay, calendared,
   443
Lafayette, Marie-Antoinette-VIRGINIE du
   Motier de (1782–1849), L's daughter: birth
   of, 57, 113, 430, 431; L's affection for, 231,
   236, 262; portrait of, 216, 339, 340n; mentioned, 117, 118, 121, 125, 133, 136, 142,
   154, 164, 192, 196, 208, 230, 237, 280, 290,
   293, 325, 337
Lafayette, Marie-Joseph-Paul-Yves-
   Roch-GILBERT du Motier, marquis de
   (1757–1834), **ii, 278,**

CHARACTER

—assessments of: by John Adams, 122–23; by
   Barrett, 358n; by Congress, 282; by Franklin, 7n, 40n, 43n; by French Masons, 41–42;
   by Jay, 43n; by Madison, 241, 273–74; by
   Morris, 254–55; by Nobles of Langeac,
   147–48; by officers of Pennsylvania Line,
   233–34; by Pennsylvania State Assembly,
   438; by Ridley, 56n
—attitudes: toward Bancroft, 132–33; toward
   British, 24–25, 29, 53, 61, 72, 159, 333, 427,
   430, 433; toward Castries, 11; toward De
   Grasse's defeat, 48–49, 68, 430, 431; toward
   diplomacy, 50; toward Farmers General,
   112, 232, 350, 351; toward George III, 21,
   44, 333; toward Irish, 166, 270–71n, 286,
   323; toward La Luzerne, 69; toward Longchamps affair, 244, 294; toward Louis XVI,
   7, 21, 36; toward Marie-Antoinette, 4; toward Mississippi navigation, 286, 301, 306,
   309; toward O'Reilly, 76, 77; toward republicanism, 201, 295n, 333; toward Rockingham, 44; toward Schuyler, 125; toward
   Shakers, 260; toward Shelburne, 44; toward
   slave emancipation, 91–92, 273–74, 317–18,
   329–30, 336, 443; toward Society of Cincinnati, 176, 179–80, 185, 191, 201–2, 207,
   209, 227; toward Spanish, 20, 61, 72, 86–87,
   106, 308; toward strong federal union, 85,
   88–89, 143, 149–50, 164, 188, 214, 266,
   277, 280–81, 304, 308, 335, 441; toward
   Vergennes, 21;
—interest in American flora, 287–88; requests
   copy of Declaration of Independence, 165;
   and use of classical allusions, 55, 106

MILITARY CAREER

—American service: desires campaign to retake
   Charleston, 27, 31–32, 46, 48–49; desires
   campaign to retake New York, 31–32, 46,
   48–49, 65; desires to command light infantry, 23; desires to serve in field, 50
—French service: and expedition to West Indies, 65, 72, 84–85, 431, 432; promoted to
   maréchal de camp, 131, rank in, 65; recommended for Cross of St. Louis, 131

PRIVATE LIFE

—family: children, 56–57, 230, 293, 430; wife,
   226–27, 229–31, 293, 437

Lafayette: private life (*cont.*)
—friendships: with Castries, 23; French, 155, 268–69; with Hamilton, 263; with Humphreys, 276–77; with Jefferson, 266–67; with Knox, 187, 321, 329–30; with Laurens, 28, 30n, 53; with R. H. Lee, 306; with Livingston, 88; with Madison, 285; with Marie-Antoinette, 4; with Wadsworth, 154–55; with Washington, 10, 90–93, 145, 151–54, 192, 208, 327;
—health, 231, 235; desires to establish public granary, 117–18; interest in mesmerism, 216, 220–22, 260; invites Washington to visit France, 153–54; servants, 238, 261

ROLE IN AMERICA

—advice on ways to preserve good relations between France and America, 9; desires to carry ratified treaty to England, 89, 92–93; efforts to obtain arms, 11; efforts to promote French-American trade, 240–41, 244;
—honored: by Connecticut, 268–69, 438; by Maryland, 290; by New York City, 244; by Rhode Island, 439
—mediates with Indians, 245–52, 255–60, 263–64, 272–73; motives for participating in American Revolution, 214; relations with Congress, 90n, 143, 280–81; supports American neutrality, 188; supports pay of Continental troops, 89, 149–50, 164; supports presidency of Washington, 89; Virginia authorizes bust of, 153, 286;
—visit to America, 124, 132, 164, 186, 187, 192, 207, 216, 233–90; Albany, 263–65; Baltimore, 240–41; Boston, 235, 275–76, 288, 438; Hartford, 266–70, 438; Mount Vernon, 235, 237–38, 438; New York, 275, 285–89; Philadelphia, 235; Portsmouth, 276–77; Trenton, 235, 280–85; Virginia, 265

ROLE IN EUROPE

—advice on cruise of *Alliance*, 11; advises Americans on Barbary States, 315–16; desires to represent France at peace negotiations, 75; discusses U.S. with Austrians, 347; discusses U.S. with Prussians, 105, 345
—efforts: to obtain arms for Virginia, 328; to obtain clothing, 11; to obtain French aid for America, 9, 22, 30–32, 45, 68–69; to obtain loans and monetary aid, 9, 21, 76; to promote French-American trade, 111–13, 124, 134–35, 139–40, 143, 148–49, 150n, 164, 167–75, 178, 182–84, 190, 192–94, 198–200, 203–5, 232, 294, 319–20, 321n, 327, 332, 349–50, 351–55, 358–60, 428, 433–37, 440–44
—informs Congress of peace, 84–85; interest in education of Americans in France, 317, 322, 439, 441; intermediary between Franklin and French government, 6, 11, 13, 15, 17–18, 34, 40–41, 54–55, 69–71, 428; negotiations with Floridablanca, 83, 86, 98–102, 104–5, 166; supports religious freedom, 322, 351, 422

Lafayette, Marie-Louise-Julie de La Rivière, marquise de (1737–70), L's mother, 321
Lafayette, Michel-Louis-Christophe-Roch-GILBERT du Motier, marquis de (1732–59), L's father, 321
La Flèche, France, 226
Lake Erie, 62n
Lake Huron, 62n
Lake Michigan, 156
La Luzerne, Anne-César, chevalier de (1741–91), French minister to America (1778–83); and assessment of American military prospects, 71n; and Congress, 244; dispatches from, 13; and Great Grasshopper, 249, 251, 253n; L makes loan to former servant of, 236; mentioned, 7, 9, 21, 69, 71, 113, 232, 280n
—letter from, calendared, 429
—letter from, calendared, 429
La Marck, Marie-Françoise-Augustine-Ursule Le Danois de Cernay, comtesse de (Comtesse Auguste) (1757–1810), friend of L, 236
Lameth, Charles-Malo-François, comte de (1757–1832), aide-de-camp to Rochambeau, friend of L, 205, 208n
Lameth, Théodore, chevalier de (1756–1854), French army officer, 28n, 428, 430
La Motte-Picquet. See Picquet de La Motte.
La Neuville, Louis-Pierre Penot Lombart, chevalier de (1744–?), former colonel in Continental army, 428
Langeac, France, 117, 147–48
La Pérouse, Jean-François de Galaup, comte de (1741–88), *capitaine de vaisseau*, French navy, 207, 331
La Rivière, JOSEPH-Yves-Thibault-Hiacinthe, marquis de (?–1770?), L's maternal grandfather, 293n
La Rochelle, France, 327, 358
Lastic, M. de, 262
Latouche, Louis-René-Madeleine, comte de (later known as Le Vassor, comte de Latouche-Tréville) (1745–1804), *capitaine de vaisseau*, commander of *L'Aigle* (1782), 64n, 207
Laumoy, Jean-Baptiste-Joseph, chevalier de (1750–1832), colonel of engineers in Continental army (1777–83), 437
Laurens, Henry (1724–92), American peace commissioner in Paris (1782), **52;** John Adams on, 37n; arrives in Paris, 124, 126; capture and imprisonment of, 28n, 428; and commercial negotiations with Great Britain, 125n; and Congress, 30n, 164; in Great Britain, 164, 166, 188, 192; ill health of, 53, 54n, 141, 210, 212, 435; and L, 122, 142n, 185, 192, 430; L's assessment of, 29; parole of, 28, 29; as peace commissioner, 28, 34n, 37n; returns to America, 45, 223; mentioned, 76, 132n
—letters from, 210–13; calendared, 430, 433, 434, 436
—letters to, 28–30, 53–54, 131–32, 141–42; calendared, 430, 434

Laurens, Henry, Jr. (1763–1821), 29, 30n, 53, 54n, 142, 212

Laurens, John (1754–82), American lieutenant colonel, son of Henry, 29, 30n, 53, 54n; death of, 64, 431

Laurens, Martha (1759–1811), daughter of Henry, 142, 211

Lauzun (Lauzen), Armand-Louis de Gontaut, duc de (1747–93), colonel in French army, 24, 64

Laval, Anne-Alexandre-Marie-Sulpice-Joseph de Montmorency, marquis de (1767–1826), 64n

La Vauguyon, Paul-François de Quelen de Stuer de Caussade, duc de (1746–1828), French ambassador to The Hague, 17, 26, 60, 309

Le Brigant, Jacques (1720–1804), philologist; letter to, calendared, 429

Le Brun, L's servant, 238, 261, 262, 293

Le Couteulx (Couteux), Mme, 360

Le Couteulx (Couteux) de Cantelu, Jean-Barthélemy (1746?–1818), 357

Lee, Arthur (1740–92), American peace commissioner to Indians: and Indians, 251, 252, 254n, 255, 257, 263, 265n; and L, 254n, 260, 263, 264, 273; and report to Congress, 287n; mentioned, 259, 307
—letter from, calendared, 438
—letter to, 253–54

Lee, Charles (1731–82), American major general, retired Jan, 1780, 64, 202, 203n

Lee, Ludwell (1760–1836), son of Richard Henry, 307, 308n

Lee, Richard Henry (1732–94), delegate to Virginia Assembly (1780–84), president of Congress (Nov. 1784–Nov. 1785), **307**; on American commerce, 308n; and L, 282, 306; mentioned, 298, 299n, 308n, 315n
—letters from, calendared, 439, 442, 444
—letters to, 284–85, 306–8; calendared, 439

Lee, Thomas Sim (1745–1819), governor of Maryland (1779–83), member of Congress (1783–84), 337, 340n, 344

Leeds, Francis Goldolphin Osborne, 5th duke of (1751–99) (marquis of Carmarthen), British secretary of state for foreign affairs, 97

Le Havre, France, 198, 324, 349

Le Huron, French play, 342

Le Maire, Jacques: letter from, calendared, 440

L'Enfant, Pierre-Charles (1754–1825), architect and engineer, appointed major in Continental army (1783): as L's messenger, 209; returns to America, 205; and Society of Cincinnati, 158, 176, 178n, 179, 191
—letter from, calendared, 444

Le Vache Le Brun, Jean, 186n

Le Vache Le Brun, Mme, 185

Liège, Austrian Netherlands (now Belgium), 196

Lincoln, Benjamin (1733–1810), American major general, secretary of war, 28n, 39, 49
—letters to, calendared, 429, 430

Linguet, Simon-Nicolas-Henri (1736–94), 215n

—letters to, 214–15; calendared, 430, 437

Lislaval, France, 434

Littlepage, Lewis (1762–1802), member of expedition against Minorca and Gibraltar, 96, 126, 159n, 166, 229

Livingston, Mary (Polly) Stevens (?–1814), wife of Robert, 90

Livingston, (Lewingston), Robert R. (1746–1813), American secretary of foreign affairs until June 1783, chancellor of state of New York, **129**; on French advantages in America, 36; and L, 93n, 130, 136, 156; and official cipher, 298, 299n; and requests for French aid, 36; resignation of, 141, 142n, 155; and unwillingness to serve abroad, 442; mentioned, 7n, 14–15, 22, 24n, 27, 28n, 43n, 48, 49n, 50n, 60n, 71n, 82n, 84, 91, 92, 96, 97n, 101n, 113, 116n, 121n, 136n, 139, 167n, 336, 336n
—letters from, 66–67, 78–79, 128–31; calendared, 427, 430, 438, 442
—letters to, 20–21, 43–48, 86–90, 102–7; calendared, 427, 428, 430–33, 439

London, England, 9, 21, 26, 34, 38, 106, 112n, 157, 158n, 159, 166, 171, 187, 192, 210, 212, 329, 333, 339

London Gazette, 213

Longchamps, Charles-Julien: and Barbé de Marbois, 244n, 274, 295n; and extradition proceedings, 323, 324n, 343; L on, 244n, 294, 321; mentioned, 243

Lorient, France: American ships at, 111, 224–26; as free port for America, 112, 132, 133, 140, 143, 148, 171, 176n, 183, 188–90, 192, 202, 204, 232, 244; L's arrival in, 4, 6, 8, 427; L's departure from, 222, 226, 238n; and obstacles to American trade, 112n; mentioned, 7n, 13, 14n, 113n, 193, 194, 204n, 227, 229, 230, 231

Louis, Austrian brigantine, 295n

Louis XV (1710–74), king of France and Navarre, 316, 321n

Louis XVI (1754–93), king of France and Navarre: and John Adams, 36, 38; and America, 16, 21, 225–26, 281, 282; and American plant specimens, 443; and American trade, 190n, 353n, 360; and animal magnetism, 222n; and Bavarian exchange, 309; and Calonne, 323n; coronation of, 316, 316n; and customs duties, 172, 174, 182, 193, 204, 224–26; and free ports, 189, 203; gardens of, 287, 288, 339; and Indians, 251, 256–59, 260n; and Jay, 215; and L, 7, 9, 14–15, 94, 284, 331, 428; R. H. Lee on, 444; Madison on, 313; as mediator, 305n; and peace negotiations, 45; and Protestants, 322; and Rohan, 354n; sisters of, 230; and Society of Cincinnati, 176, 179, 180n; and *Three Friends*, 215n; and tobacco monopoly, 351n; and use of English dogs, 325; and Vergennes, 40; and Washington, 9, 119, 139; mentioned, 9, 27, 46, 69, 114, 140n, 194n, 282n, 328
—letter from, to Congress, **283**

Louis XVI (*cont.*)
—letter to, from Congress, 282
Louis-Joseph-Xavier (1781–89), dauphin, 4, 5n, 253n, 316
Lucchesini (Luchesiny), Girolamo, marquis de (1751–1825), chamberlain of Frederick II, 345, 349n
Lyons, France, 327, 330–31

Maastricht (Mastreik), Austrian Netherlands, 302
McDougall (McDougal), Alexander (1732–86), American major general, 78, 79n
McHenry, James (1753–1816), major, Continental army, member of Maryland senate (1781–86), Maryland delegate to Congress (1783–86): and Congress, 116n, 186; as member of Washington's staff, 24n; resigns from military, 115; and trade with France, 358; and Wadsworth, 354; mentioned, 24, 65, 66n, 90, 317
—letters to, 184–86, 354–55; calendared, 434, 443
McHenry, Margaret (Peggy) Caldwell (1762–?), wife of James, 355
McIntosh, Lachlan (1725–1806), American major general from Sept. 1783, member of Congress from Georgia (1784), congressional commissioner to southern Indians: letter from, calendared, 443
McQueen, John, American merchant, 442
Madagascar, 220n
Madeira Islands, 170
Madison, James (1751–1836), member of Congress from Virginia, chairman of Ways and Means Committee (1783), delegate to Virginia legislature from 1784: and desire to travel, 274; and L, 241, 245, 273, 285, 309, 310; on Mississippi navigation, 287n, 311, 313; nominated as minister at Madrid, 310n; on religious freedom, 314, 315n; mentioned, 244n, 320n
—letters from, 310–15; to Jefferson, 241–43, 271–74
—letters to, 285–87, 309–10; calendared, 438
Madras, India, 61, 62n
Madrid, Spain: L's visit to, 85, 88n, 91, 92, 106, 120, 148; peace negotiations at, 96; mentioned, 7, 20, 37n, 45, 83, 86, 87, 89, 94, 96–99, 104, 126, 166, 167, 242, 302, 309, 310n, 433
Magnifique, Le, French frigate, 66, 67n
Mahon, Minorca, Balearic Islands, 22, 24n, 87
Maillebois, Yves-Marie Desmarets, comte de (1715–92), French lieutenant general, 122, 124n, 293, 295n
—letter from, calendared, 428
Mail service, 7, 18, 20, 37, 51, 60, 76, 82n, 83, 94, 141, 167n, 272, 309, 319, 322, 356
Majestueux, Le, French ship, 77
Malesherbes, Crétien-Guillaume de Lamoignon de (1721–94), former director of Librairie and Imprimerie, president of Cour des Aides, 323n

Malta (Maltha), 325, 338
Manchester, George Montagu, 4th duke of (1737–88), British ambassador to Paris peace negotiations (April–Dec. 1783), 124, 126, 136
Margarita (Marguerite), Cuba, 172
Margelay, M. de, L's tutor, 236
Marie-Antoinette (1755–93), queen of France: and affair of necklace, 352n, 354n; and L, 4; miscarriage of, 162; and Protestants, 322; mentioned, 220
Markov, Arkady Ivanovich, Russian intermediary to United Provinces, 25, 26
Marlboro (Marlbro'), Md., 279, 280n
Marmontel, Jean-François (1723–99), French playwright, 342n
Marseilles, France: fees for American ships at, 224–26; as free port, 112, 143, 148, 171, 183, 188, 189, 192, 203, 204; and trade with America, 358; mentioned, 171
Marshall, Thomas (1730–1802), American colonel, surveyor general of Kentucky from 1783, 339, 340n
Martinique, West Indies, 33, 34n, 76n
Maryland: and delegates to Congress, 285; grants citizenship to L and son, 290; and Potomac River navigation, 289, 290n, 296, 306; and recovery from war, 300; mentioned, 37n, 194, 276
Maryland Assembly, 280n
Maryland Senate, 90
Masois, M., 354, 355n
Massachusetts (Mashashushet), 57, 319, 332, 345n
Masserano, Carlo Ferrero Fieschi, prince of, Spanish diplomat, 33
Matilda, American merchant ship, 186n
Maurepas, Jean-Frédéric Phélypeaux, comte de (1701–81), French minister of state and chief of council of finances, 4, 10n
Meade (Mead), Richard Kidder (1746–1805), American lieutenant colonel, Washington's aide-de-camp, 192
Mediterannean Sea, Russian navy in, 146
Mercer, John Francis (1759–1821), American lieutenant colonel, 286, 297, 299n, 307, 308n, 314, 315n
Mercure de France, 150n, 154n
Mercy-Argenteau (Merci), Florimand-Claude-Charles, comte de (1727–94), Austrian ambassador to France, 295n, 349n
Merlin, Antoine-Christophe (1762–1833): letter to, calendared, 444
Mesmer, Franz Anton (1734–1815): and L, 216, 218n, 220, 231, 236n, 245, 268; and meeting of disciples, 269n; secretiveness of, 222n
Mexico, L desires to visit, 323
Michaux, André (1746–1802), botanist, 443
Mifflin, Thomas (1744–1800), president of Continental Congress (1783–84): letters to, calendared, 435; from Franklin, calendared, 437

Miranda, Francisco de, Venezuelan revolutionary (later general in French revolutionary army and dictator of Venezuela), 324n
Miromesnil, Armand-Thomas Hué de (1723–96), keeper of seals, 323
Mississippi River: and border dispute with Spain, 61, 74n, 87, 101n, 106, 242, 243n, 308n, 323; compared to Nile, 314n; free navigation of, 17n, 74n, 99, 104, 286, 287n, 301, 305, 309, 311, 312, 338; L on, 243n, 244; Madison's concern over, 242, 313; settlements on, 311, 312; Washington plans trip down, 156
Mithon de Genouilly (Mitton), Claude, comte de, French naval captain, 33, 34n
Mohawk Indians, 250, 251, 257
Mohawk River, 247, 248, 251
Môle Saint-Nicolas, Saint-Domingue, 172
Monistrol, M., 231
Monroe (Munro), James (1758–1831), lieutenant colonel for Virginia State Line, representative to Virginia Assembly (1782), member of Congress from 1783, 286, 314
—letter to, calendared, 439
Montaran, intendant of commerce for Auvergne: letter from, calendared, 432
—letter to, calendared, 433
Montcalm (Moncalm) Gozon de Saint Véran, Louis-Joseph, marquis de (1712–59), French brigadier general in Canada, 258, 260n
Montmorin, Armand-Marc, comte de (1746–92), French ambassador to Spain: desires to know state of political affairs, 76; and L, 97, 98; and role in negotiations, 102, 104, 105; and Spanish, 76; and view of America, 80; mentioned, 7, 83, 88, 94, 96, 98, 126, 166, 292
Montréal, Canada, 91
Morocco, 316
Morris, Jacob (1755–1844), representative to New York State legislature, 160
Morris, Robert (1734–1806), American superintendant of finance (1781–84): on American commerce, 184n; and American financial difficulties, 61, 70; and commercial negotiations, 215, 218, 219; European image of, 183; and French customs duties, 209; and L, 21, 18, 190n–91n, 255n, 431, 438; requests French aid, 18, 30, 87; requests supplies, 32n; threatens to resign, 141, 142n; on trade with France, 219n; mentioned, 9, 10n, 15–17, 21n, 28n, 60, 62n, 71n, 127n, 176n, 178n, 182n, 184, 188, 192, 198n, 199n, 208n, 209n, 224n, 225n, 226n, 294
—letters from, 218–20; calendared, 431–38; to Adams, calendared, 431; to Carmichael, calendared, 431; to Congress, 254–55; to Franklin, calendared, 431; to Jay, calendared, 431
—letters to, 182–84, 190–91, 204–5; calendared, 428, 429, 436, 438
Mouchy, Philippe de Noailles, maréchal-duc de (1715–94), father of Prince de Poix and

Vicomte de Noailles, L's wife's great-uncle, 244n, 268
Mount Vernon, Va.: beauty of, 238; L's arrival at, 216, 437, 438; L's visit to, 235, 237, 241, 254n, 262, 265, 266, 285; Washington retires to, 191; mentioned, 64, 121, 156, 164, 194, 208, 216, 236, 279, 280n, 295, 327n, 336, 340n, 342
Muhammad ibn 'Abd Allah (1757?–90), sultan of Morocco, 316
Mullens, Thomas (1736–?), major, Continental army, 197
—letters from, 196–97; calendared, 436
Murray, James (1725?–94), governor of Minorca, 22, 24n

Nancy, France, 148, 151, 154
Nantes (Nantz), France, 112n, 134, 443
Nassau-Siegen, Charles-Henri-Nicolas Othon, prince de (1745–1805), colonel in French army, 166
Naval superiority: John Adams' views on, 26; allied need of, 31; French views on, 22; L on, 22, 49, 65, 68, 72
Necker, Jacques (1732–1804), French director general of finances (1777–81), 113n, 176n, 304, 305n, 310
Nesbitt, John Maxwell (c. 1728–1802), director of Bank of North America, 194
Netherlands, Austrian (Austrian Flanders), 295n.
Newburgh, N.Y., 113, 119, 135
Newburgh Affair, 121n, 136n, 150n
New England: L's visit to, 243, 254, 261, 277; and trade with France, 319–21, 350, 355; and trade with Great Britain, 357; and whale oil trade, 355; mentioned, 32, 238
Newenham, Sir Edward (1732–1814), Irish member of Parliament: letter from, calendared, 436
Newfoundland, 31, 32, 72, 271n
New Hampshire, 275
New Haven, Conn., 288
New Jersey, 235
New Kent County, Va., 279n
New Orleans, La.: compared to Cairo, 314n; as free port, 301, 309; L wishes to visit, 323; Washington plans trip to, 156; mentioned, 242, 312
Newport, Rhode Island, 261, 264, 265, 268, 439
New York City: American army at, 321; and American campaign plans, 31, 32, 49, 65, 72, 78, 115, 116n; American takeover of, 195; British evacuation of, 9, 13, 22–23, 28, 30, 66, 70, 80, 128, 130n, 139, 141, 156, 161n, 187, 191, 195, 432, 433; British forces in, 61, 63, 115, 116n; British retreat to, 8; honors L, 244; L's visit to, 235, 236n, 263, 264, 275; and Loyalist refugees, 63; as temporary location of Congress, 297, 299n, 301; mentioned, 10n, 120, 130n, 160, 199, 222, 232, 238, 241, 243, 271, 284–86, 288, 289, 296, 314, 327n, 332, 336, 339

New York Society for Promoting the Manumission of Slaves, 317, 318n
New York State: and final campaigns, 32; and Indians, 248, 260n; roads in, 248, 260; Vermont secedes from, 302n
Niagara, N.Y., 32
Nicholson, James (1737–1804), commodore, Maryland navy, 229
Nîmes (Nismes), France, 352
Niskayuna, N.Y., 245
Nivernais (Nivernois), Louis-Jules Barbon Mancini-Mazarini, duc de (1716–98), minister to London, 34
Noailles, Angélique-Françoise-d'Assise-ROSALIE de (1767–1853?), L's sister-in-law, 118, 230, 236, 238, 293
Noailles, Anne-Jeanne-Baptiste-Pauline-Adrienne-LOUISE-Catherine-Dominique, vicomtesse de (1758–94), L's sister-in-law, wife of Louis-Marie, 118, 230, 236, 238, 293
Noailles, Anne-Paule-Dominique (called Pauline) de (later marquise de Montagu) (1766–1839), L's sister-in-law, 118, 230, 236, 238, 293
Noailles, Clotilde de (later marquise de Rouré and vicomtesse de Thesan) (1763–88), L's sister-in-law, 118, 230, 236, 238, 293
Noailles, EMMANUEL-Marie-Louis, marquis de (1743–1822), French ambassador to Austria, L's wife's uncle: as ambassador to England, 75, 90n; and Gallitzin, 216, 218n; and L, 89, 349n; mentioned, 236, 238, 261, 345
Noailles, LOUIS-Marie, vicomte de (1756–1804), L's wife's cousin and brother-in-law: and Gibraltar siege, 67; and King's Cavalry, 64n; mentioned, 5, 10, 24, 64, 67n, 159n, 238, 293
Norfolk, Charles Howard, 10th duke of (1720–86), 97
Norfolk, Va., 358
Normandy, France, 80, 198, 325
North, Frederick (Lord North) (1732–92), British prime minister (1770–82): downfall of, 186n, 193n; and Fox coalition, 125n; ministry of, 5n, 22; and peace negotiations, 43, 125n; and possible return to power, 44, 192; and proposals for peace, 19n; replaces Shelburne, 106; resigns, 18n, 19, 22, 24n, 25, 28; mentioned, 17
North Carolina, 4, 156, 296, 358
Northwest Ordinance, 340n
Nova Scotia, 48n, 271n
Nymphe, Le, French frigate, 275, 276n, 280n, 288–89, 295

Ogden, Matthias (1754–91), colonel in Continental army, 130, 140n, 142, 434
—letter to, calendared, 432
Ohio River, 241, 244, 337
Oilliamson, comtesse d', wife of Marie-Gabriel, 325, 340n, 343, 344n
Oilliamson, Marie-Gabriel-Eléonore, comte d' (1738–1830), 325, 340n, 343
Olainville, France (near Paris), 124

Oneida Castle, N.Y., 248, 249, 254, 262
Oneida Indians, 250, 251, 273, 319
Onondagas Indians, 251
Orange, Va., 310, 314
O'Reilly, Alejandro (1725–94), governor of Louisiana, 76, 77
Orléans, Louis-Philippe-Joseph de Bourbon, duc d' (1747–93), brother of Louis XVI, 48n
Ormesson, Henri-François de Paule Lefèvre d' (1751–1807), French controller general of finances (March–Nov. 1783): and commercial negotiations, 183; downfall of, 162, 165n; succeeds Joly de Fleury, 124, 125n; mentioned, 140n
—letters to, calendared, 433–434
Oswald, Richard (1705–84), British Peace commissioner (1782): commission of, 430; departs for London, 80; and L, 35; and peace negotiations, 34n, 35, 36, 37n, 47n, 53, 55n, 79, replaced, 125n; mentioned, 36n
Otchikeita (Otsiquette, Ouekchekaeta), Peter, Indian boy, 251, 253n, 319, 320n
Ottoman Empire, 133
Overijssel (Overysul), United Provinces, 17n

Paca, William (1740–99), governor of Maryland: letter to, calendared, 439
Paine, Thomas (1737–1809), clerk of Pennsylvania Assembly, 150n
Paris, France, 198; and bust of L, 287n, 315n; Carmichael at, 82; Forth arrives in, 21; and Gibralter siege, 48n; Jay at, 80, 85; L's home in, 118n; and L's homesickness, 268; L returns to, 4, 87, 91, 96, 102n, 143, 268, 337, 440; lighting of, 319, 320n, 321n, 357, 441; and Longchamps affair, 244n; peace negotiations at, 34, 36, 37n, 39n, 45, 59; Wadsworth arrives in, 154; mentioned, 6, 8, 10, 14–18, 26, 28, 30, 33, 35, 36, 38, 39, 43n, 45, 47, 49, 53–55, 57, 59, 60, 62, 64, 68, 69, 89, 94, 97, 110, 112, 117, 121, 127, 131, 132, 134, 136, 139, 141, 157, 158, 162, 164–67, 176, 178, 179, 182, 184, 186, 190, 191, 193, 196–201, 204, 205, 207, 208, 210, 213–16, 222, 225–27, 229, 236n, 262, 266, 269, 276, 288, 292, 293, 299, 300, 302, 305, 306, 309, 315, 317, 320–22, 324, 327–31, 342, 347, 349, 351–54, 356, 358, 430, 433, 439
Parliament, British: and commercial relations with America, 125n, 335n; confusion in, 22; dissolving of, 211, 212, 213n; and Enabling Act, 49; and Ireland, 319n; opposition in, 142n, 216; mentioned, 25, 65, 159, 209
Passy, France (near Paris): and Franklin, 43, 336n; mentioned, 15, 35, 57, 59, 255
Peace negotiations: John Adams on, 25, 38; between America and Great Britain, 19n, 67n, 71, 320n; American anxiety over, 78; and American sovereignty, 32n, 33, 34n, 44, 59; between France and Great Britain, 56n; between Great Britain and Spain, 87; British obstacles to, 21, 28, 29, 33, 36, 38, 41n, 43, 44, 55n, 61; British role in, 37n,

Peace negotiations (*cont.*)
39n, 125n, 430, 434; between United
Provinces and Great Britain, 15, 26; and
boundary disputes, 32; and final campaigns,
116n; and final treaty, 156, 162, 187; and
fisheries, 46, 48n; and general peace, 83, 84,
85, 86, 88, 90, 94, 98, 102, 116n, 119, 144n,
170, 433; L on, 49, 50, 53, 72; L's role in,
22–23, 45, 48, 74, 75n, 89, 202, 433;
Livingston on, 67; and preliminary articles
between America and Great Britain, 75, 76n,
80, 99, 128, 142n, 427, 432; and prisoner
exchange, 428; progress of, 60, 62, 64, 65,
72, 77, 79n, 80, 82, 83, 120, 431, 432; and
Russian mediation, 132; Ségur on, 51; and
Spanish compliance, 287n; and treaty
ratification, 92, 93n, 96, 102, 121n, 124, 135,
139, 141, 146, 151, 164, 166; and war debt
to Great Britain, 144, 146, 148; mentioned,
39
Peace of Paris of 1763, 36n
Pennsylvania: arms shipment to, 428; and disputes with Connecticut, 79, 267n; and fur
trade, 354; and Indians, 255, 260n, 267; and
L, 233–34, 436, 438; and Longchamps affair, 244n, 295n, 324n
Pennsylvania Line, 233
Pennsylvania Assembly, 438
Penobscot, Me., 8, 31, 32, 72, 115
Pensacola, Fla., 156
Philadelphia, Pa.: arrival of Dutch minister at,
156; L's visit to, 235, 265, 266, 285; peace
negotiations at, 96; and trade with France,
355; mentioned, 60, 64, 66, 78, 85, 88, 90,
94, 97, 113, 115, 120, 128, 132, 160, 171,
195, 235, 238, 241, 249, 271, 284, 286, 287n,
308n, 343, 432
Picquet (Piquet) de La Motte, Toussaint-
Guillaume (called La Motte-Picquet)
(1720–91), *capitaine de vaisseau* in French
navy, 77
Pignon, Michel, Farmer General of France,
194
Pigot, Robert (1720–96), British lieutenant
general, 63
Pitt, William (1759–1806), first lord of treasury
and chancellor of exchequer (1783): desires
to meet Franklin, 157; and L, 158; proposes
free trade with Ireland, 319n; and rise to
power, 192, 193n, 216; and role in opposition, 141, 142n; visits to France, 158n; mentioned, 159n, 209
Pitt, William, 1st earl of Chatham (1708–78),
38, 39n, 44
Poirey, Joseph-Léonard, L's secretary, 230, 262
Poix, Anne-Louise-Marie de Beauvau, princesse de (1750–1834?), wife of Philippe, 269
Poix, Philippe-Louis-Marc-Antoine de Noailles
de Mouchy, prince de (1752–1819), L's
wife's cousin, 244n, 268, 269, 293, 432
—letters to, 267–69; calendared, 431–33, 438,
443
Poland, 165n
Pompey, Roman general, 299, 300n

Porter, Andrew (1743–1813), major in Conti-
nental army (1782), appointed commissioner
to run boundary lines of Pennsylvania
(1784), 14–15
Port Louis, France, 112, 113n, 176n
Portsmouth, N.H., 124, 276
Portsmouth, Va., 358
Portugal, 170, 216, 218n, 315
Potomac River: and canal plans, 244; naviga-
tion of, 289, 296, 301, 310; and trade with
France, 358; and western expansion, 337;
mentioned, 124, 208, 216, 286, 287n
Potomac River Company: establishment of,
298n, 315n, 327n; Washington on, 295–99;
Washington's role in, 324, 337, 344, 441;
Washington's stock in, 296, 299n; and west-
ern expansion, 337
Potosí, Peru, 312, 314n
Potsdam, Germany, 339, 345
Pratt, John Jeffries (1759–1840), Teller of Ex-
chequer, 157, 158
Princeton, N.J., 155, 159, 284
Protestants, L on treatment of, 322
Provence, Louis-Stanislas-Xavier de Bourbon,
comte de (later Louis XVIII) (1755–1824),
brother of Louis XVI, 193, 194n
Providence, Islands of, 88
Providence, R.I., 353
Prussia: and commercial relations with Amer-
ica, 345; and France, 349n; and Great Brit-
ain, 349n; and Huguenots, 352n; L's visit to,
330, 331, 332, 345, 351, 353; and Russian-
Turkish dispute, 149
Purviance, Samuel, Jr., 160, 241n
Puységur, Jacques-Maxime-Paul, vicomte de
(1755–1820?), friend of L, 269

Québec, Canada, 253n, 319
Quésney, chevalier de, 436

Rabaut St. Etienne, Jean-Paul (1743–93), Prot-
estant pastor: letter from, calendared,
. 442
—letter to, 351–52
Randolph, Edmund (1753–1813), 345n
Rayneval. *See* Gérard de Rayneval, Joseph-
Matthias.
Reed, Joseph (1741–85), president of Supreme
Executive Council of Pennsylvania, elected to
Congress in 1784, 223, 224n, 435
Rennes, France, 292
Rheinsberg (Rheinberg), Germany, 340, 342n
Rhode Island: and Congress, 277; L's visit to,
266, 268, 275, 439; mentioned, 241, 265,
304
Rhode Island General Assembly, 267n, 277n,
439
Richelieu, Louis-François-Armand du Plessis,
maréchal duc de (1696–1788), *maréchal de
France*, 9
Richmond, Va.: and L, 265, 287n; mentioned,
241, 274, 279n, 309, 314, 344
Ridley, Matthew, Maryland agent in Europe,
37–38, 56n, 59, 203n, 431

Ridout (Ridouts), Thomas (1754–1829), American merchant, 290n, 339, 340n

Rivington's New York Gazette, 79n

Rochambeau, Jean-Baptiste-Donatien de Vimeur, comte de (1725–1805), lieutenant general in French navy: and French expeditionary force in America, 13, 24n, 31, 51n, 137; L on, 191; leaves America, 70; and Society of Cincinnati, 178n, 179, 180n, 188n, 191, 201, 203n, 205, 208, 343; and supplies, 194n; mentioned, 197

Rochefort, France, 51, 358

Rockingham, Charles Watson Wentworth, 2d marquis of (1730–82), British prime minister (1782–83), 18, 24n, 25, 29, 44, 124

Rock Rolling from the Top of the Mountains, Indian chief, 250

Rocky Hill, Conn., 158

Rodney George Brydges, baron (1719–92), admiral and commander in chief of British navy in West Indies, 9, 10n, 13, 48n

Rogers, Nicholas, 241n

Rohan-Guémené, Louis-René-Edouard, prince de (1734–1803), *grand aumonier* of France, 352, 353, 354n

Rome, Italy, 38, 56n, 137n, 300n

Ross, Alexander (1742–1827), British brevet major, aide-de-camp to Cornwallis, 39, 40n

Rouen, France, 79, 169

Rousselet, L's servant, 238

Roux, M., 434

Royal Gazette, New York loyalist newspaper, 5n

Rumsey, James (1743?–92), American inventor, 297, 299n

Rush, Benjamin (1745–1813), former physician general of Continental army: letter from, calendared, 428

Russia: and ambassador to London, 26; and Austrian-Dutch dispute, 293; and Crimea, 133n, 165n; and France, 319, 358; minister from, at Hague, 60; offers to mediate between England and United Provinces, 14–15, 25, 27; and peace negotiations, 132; and Turkey, 124, 125n, 133, 143, 146, 149, 150n, 151, 156, 162, 165n; mentioned, 38, 201

Ruston, Thomas (1739?–1804); letter to, calendared, 441

Rutland, Charles Manners, 4th duke of (1754–87), lord lieutenant of Ireland, 216, 218n

Sailly, M., 435

St. Clair, Arthur (1737–1818), American major general, 234

St. Domingue, West Indies, 74n

St. Eustatius (St. Eustatia, Statia), West Indies, 4, 5n

St-Germain (near Paris), France, 42, 43, 48, 118, 126, 260, 318

St. Kitts (St. Christophe), West Indies, 19–20, 22, 428

St. Lawrence (Laurens) River, 84, 156

St. Lucia, West Indies, 76n, 88, 173; as free port, 172, 176n

Saint-Simon-Montbléru, Claude-Anne de Rouvroy, marquis de (1743?–1819), French naval captain, 325, 327n, 343

Saint-Vincent, Robert de (?–1799), 229

Salem, Mass., 439

Salzard, Nicolas, French merchant, 351n

Sarguesmines, France, 333

Sartine, Antoine-Raymond-Jean-Gualbert-Gabriel de, comte d'Alby (1729–1801), 317n

Savannah (Savahna), Ga., 8, 115, 179, 180n

Saxony, 330

Scheldt River, 295n

Schuyler, Catherine Van Rensselaer (1734?–1803), wife of Philip, 317–18

Schuyler, Philip John (1733–1804), American major general, commissioner for Indian affairs, 125, 155, 317–18

Searle, James (c. 1730–97), Pennsylvania merchant: letter to, calendared, 428

Ségur, Antoinette-Elizabeth-Marie Daguesseau, comtesse de (1756–1828), L's wife's aunt, wife of Louis Philippe, 51, 230, 238

Ségur, Louis-Philippe, comte de (1753–1830), friend of L, 27, 28n, 64n, 67, 239

—letter from, 51

Ségur, Philippe-Henri, marquis de (1724–1801), French minister of war: and Franklin, 13; and L, 11, 427; on Society of Cincinnati, 179, 180n; mentioned, 13n, 27, 51, 77, 135, 201n, 293

—letters from, calendared, 427, 429, 444

—letters to, calendared, 427, 431, 433–35, 437, 444

Seneca Indians, 251

Seran, M. de, 126

Serpent, French frigate, 74n, 75

Seven Years' War, 36n, 51n

Shakers (American religious sect), 245, 260, 262, 268

Shakespeare, William (1564–1616), 211

Sheffield, John Baker Holroyd, 1st earl of (1735–1821),colonel of light dragoons, 210, 211n

Shelburne, William Petty Fitzmaurice, earl of (1737–1805), British secretary of state for foreign affairs under Rockingham: John Adams on, 38; and coalition with Rockingham, 24n; and French, 76n; L on, 44, 53, 87; Laurens on, 54n; Livingston on, 67; ministry of, 125n; and peace negotiations, 33, 34n, 35, 37n, 44, 47n, 75, 87, 98; and prisoner exchange, 49; resigns, 106, 107n; and Rayneval, 56n; and role in opposition, 142n; mentioned, 35, 36n, 61

Sheldon, Elisha (1740–1805), colonel in American army, 63

Shoemaker Tavern, Mohawk, N.Y., 253, 254n

Short, William (1759–1849), Jefferson's secretary, 241, 243, 271, 347, 349n

Silesia, 330, 342, 349n, 443

Simiane, Diane-Adelaïde de Damas d'Antigny, comtesse de (1761–1835), friend of L, 90n, 115n, 293, 432
—letters to, 158–59; calendared, 431, 433
Six Nations, Indian Confederation, 255–60, 267n
Slavery: Condorcet on, 299, 300n; Hamilton on, 336n; Jay on, 336n; L on, 274, 317, 443; L's experiment concerning, 91, 330, 330n, 336; Washington on, 121
Smith, John, Baltimore merchant, 241n
Smith, The, Indian chief, 250
Smith, William Stephens (1755–1816), American lieutenant colonel, secretary of U.S. legation in England (1785), 333, 335
—letter to, calendared, 444
Society of Harmony, 222
Society of the Cincinnati: John Adams on, 201, 203n, 211–12; and claims to membership, 197, 205; diploma of, **206**; finances of, 208n; formation of, 137, 158, 176, 203n; and French, 185, 187, 207, 343; and hereditary membership, 229n; insignia of, 158, **177**, 178n, 179, 187, 188n, 191, 197; L's defense of, 180, 185, 202, 205, 209, 227; L's involvement with, 179, 437; membership in, 180n, 207n–8n, 327n, 343; opposition to, 180n, 207, 209; principles of, 158n, 176, 178n, 179, 213; and Washington, 437; mentioned, 192, 442
South America (South Spain), 323, 324n
South Carolina, 4, 8, 64, 156, 243n
Spain: John Adams on, 26; and Algiers, 162, 165n; and alliance with America, France and United Provinces, 32n; and America, 15–17, 20, 61, 80, 82, 84, 86, 87, 97, 98, 101, 104, 106, 127n, 128, 142, 166, 242–44, 286, 287n, 301, 306, 307, 308n, 309, 311, 312, 314n, 323, 433, 440, 441; and Barbary States, 315; and boundary disputes with America, 62n, 74n, 76, 98, 99, 102, 104, 105; and British, 55n; colonies of, 159n, 166, 172; and commercial relations with America, 166, 167n, 173, 183, 185; and commercial relations with Great Britain, 136n; and European campaigns, 37; and free navigation of Mississippi, 301, 311, 312; French influence on, 313; and Gibraltar, 39n, 67, 72n; and jackasses for Washington, 302n, 343, 345n; L on, 15–17, 20, 22, 37, 72, 92; L's voyage to, 74n; Livingston on, 78; and loans to America, 15–17, 22, 76, 80, 86, 94, 96, 101, 105; Madison on, 312; and peace negotiations, 38, 80; Ségur on, 51; and West Indies expedition, 27; mentioned, 33, 38, 60, 112n, 143, 151, 183, 201, 202, 298
Spanish navy, 49, 67, 75, 77
Sprigg, Sophia, 286, 314, 297, 299n, 308n
Stephanus, Oneida Indian, 319
Steuben, Friedrich Wilhelm Augustus, baron von (1730–94), Continental major general, 276, 321
Suffren (Suffrein) de Saint-Tropez, Pierre-An-

dré, chevalier de (1729–88), French naval captain, 325, 344
Susquehanna land controversy, 79n
Susquehanna River, 244, 287n
Sutter, Mr., 286
Sweden, 34n, 38, 315

Talobre, comte de, 444
Tauride Peninsula, 150n
Terrible, Le, French warship, 77
Tessé, Adrienne-Catherine de Noailles, comtesse de (1741–1814), L's wife's aunt, 230, 261, 293
—letters to, 77–78, 340–42
Thomson, Charles (1729–1824), secretary of Congress (1774–89), 122, 123n, 282
Three Friends, British frigate, 215n
Tilghman, Anna Maria, cousin to and betrothed of Tench, 121
Tilghman, Tench (1744–86), aide-de-camp and secretary to Washington, Baltimore merchant, 24, 93, 121, 160, 241n
Tilly, Arnaud Le Gardeur de (1740–?), capitaine de vaisseau, 207
Tobago (Tabago), West Indies, 88
Toulon, France, 77, 358
Touraine, France, 127n
Tourtille de Sangrain, Pierre, 320n, 321n, 344n, 349, 356, 357, 358n, 441, 442
Trenton, N.J.: Congress at, 266, 277, 280, 282, 285, 297; L's reception at, 236n; mentioned, 238, 284
Triomphe, Le (Triumph), French frigate: carries news of peace, 85, 86, 92, 97, 102, 116n, 432; mentioned, 115, 128, 130, 132, 141, 142, 144
Tripoli (Tripoly), 316
Trist, Eliza House, wife of Nicholas P., 242, 243n, 274
Trist, Nicholas P. (?–1784), 242, 243n, 274
Trumbull, Jonathan (1710–85), governor of Connecticut: letter to, calendared, 439
Tunis, 316
Turkey: and commercial relations with Russia, 150n; and dispute with Russia, 124, 125n, 143, 148, 149, 151, 156, 162, 165n; and state of army, 162
Tuscarora Indians, 251

Ukraine, tobacco from, 198
United Provinces: John Adams on, 25; and aid to America, 22; and alliance with America, France, and Spain, 32n; and alliance with France, 353, 354n; and alliance with France and America, 14–15; and alliance with France and Spain, 26; and American canal plans, 297; and Barbary States, 315; and British, 55n; and Austria, 293, 295n, 302, 305n, 309, 318, 323, 325; and commercial relations with America, 18, 33, 36, 46, 59, 60n, 61, 170; and Danzig, 165n; and French, 4; and French-guaranteed loans to America, 13n, 14n; and loans to America, 18, 25, 36,

United Provinces (cont.)
  38, 59; and minister to America, 157n; and
  ports in India and Ceylon, 39n; and recognition of America, 19, 22, 27, 33, 428; mentioned, 17

Valley Forge, Pa., 29, 90
Van Rensselaer, Margaret Schuyler
  (1758–1802), 317–18
Vauban, Mme de, 269
Vaudreuil, Louis-Philippe de Rigaud, marquis
  de (1724–1802), French lieutenant general,
  chef d'escadre under de Grasse in 1782: arrives at Boston, 61, 66; and d'Estaing, 77;
  and Society of Cincinnati, 179, 180n, 205;
  squadron of, 67n
Vaux, Noël de Jourda, comte de (1705–88),
  French lieutenant general, 197
Veimérange (Veymerange, Vermerange), Pal-
  teau, chevalier de, French commissary of
  war, 10, 11, 13n
Venice, 315
Vergennes, Anne de Viviers, comtesse de, wife
  of Charles Gravier, 112, 232, 244, 270
Vergennes, Charles Gravier, comte de
  (1717–87), French minister of foreign affairs: John Adams on, 124n; and aid to
  America, 71n; on America, 427; and American ministers, 53; on American war debt to
  Great Britain, 144–6; and Bavarian exchange, 305n; and British, 18n, 21, 33, 34n;
  and Burgundy, 295n; and commercial negotiations, 167n–68n, 182, 189, 224n, 232,
  353n, 428; and free ports, 140, 184n, 189;
  and Franklin, 13; on French naval campaigns, 22; and friendship for America, 21;
  and Grenville, 40; and L, 9, 11, 15, 20, 27,
  309, 352; on loans to America, 13n; as mediator, 62n, 242, 304, 317n; and packet boats,
  318; and peace negotiations, 36, 41n, 44, 46,
  47, 50, 55n, 93, 99, 131, 136, 162; as president of conseil des finances, 351n; and Protestants, 322; and Rayneval affair, 56n;
  mentioned, 10, 13, 14n, 21n, 26, 48n, 55,
  56n, 59, 111, 112n, 133n, 144n, 147n, 150n,
  167, 176n, 179, 180n, 182n, 184, 190, 192,
  243n, 266, 293, 295n, 324n
—letters from, 6, 140; calendared, 431
—letters to, 15–18, 54–55, 69–72, 93–94,
  98–99, 112–13, 134–35, 139–40, 144–45,
  176, 215, 232–33, 243–44, 269–71, 350–51;
  calendared, 429, 430, 432, 434, 435, 437,
  438, 443
Vermont, 301, 302n
Verplanck (Verplanks point), N.Y., 62
Versailles, France: American minister at, 332n;
  diplomatic corps at, 60; L's departure for, 4;
  Louis XVI's gardens at, 288; as possible site
  of peace negotiations, 47n; mentioned, 6n, 7,
  8, 11, 15, 35, 39, 40, 41n, 54, 75, 87, 94,
  140, 167, 178, 182, 183, 185, 189, 192, 199,
  200, 202, 203, 220, 224, 226, 229, 292, 293,
  339, 427, 437

Vienna, Austria, 216, 332, 345, 347
Vioménil, Antoine-Charles du Houx, baron de
  (1728–92), maréchal de camp, French lieutenant colonel, 64n, 79n
Virginia: arms for, 441; and British campaigns,
  256; and fur trade, 354; and Houdon, 332;
  Indian raids in, 301; and James River Company, 298n; and James River navigation,
  306, 307; L names daughter after, 57, 57,
  113; L petitions for payments to French
  firms, 287n; L's command in, 234, 240,
  241n, 342; L's visit to, 233, 265, 266, 275,
  277; L to secure arms for, 328, 328n; mines
  in, 435; and national debt, 314; and Potomac
  River navigation, 289, 290n, 296, 307; tobacco from, 101, 198; and trade with France,
  244, 358; and Washington's stock in Potomac
  River Company, 324; mentioned, 133, 157,
  194, 238, 241, 261, 276, 279n, 289n, 309,
  310, 328, 438
Virginia campaign, 68
Virginia House of Delegates: and bust of L,
  153, 196, 315n; and gift to Washington, 296;
  L's memorials to, 286; and Potomac River
  navigation, 289, 290n; and public revenues,
  314n; and resolutions on L, 4n, 286, 287n
Volunteer Journal, Irish rebel paper, 286, 287n,
  298

Wadsworth, Catherine, daughter of Jeremiah,
  332, 354
Wadsworth, Daniel (?–1848), son of Jeremiah,
  320n, 332, 354
Wadsworth, Hannah, daughter of Jeremiah,
  332, 354
Wadsworth, Jeremiah (1743–1804), Connecticut merchant: and Bank of New York, 332;
  business ventures of, 155n; and commercial
  negotiations, 192; and L, 155, 354; and L
  family portrait, 229, 230n; on Society of
  Cincinnati, 209; as supplier to Rochambeau,
  194n; and trade in France, 193, 194, 201n,
  434; mentioned, 210, 276, 323n, 336n, 355
—letters to, 154–55, 200–201, 318–20,
  331–32, 353–54; calendared, 436, 437, 442,
  444
Wadsworth, Mehitable Russell, wife of
  Jeremiah, 332, 354
War of the Austrian Succession, 51n
Warren, James (1726–1808), American major
  general, president of provincial congress of
  Massachusetts, 147n, 288, 289n
—letters from John Adams, 121–24
Washington, Bushrod (1762–1829), nephew of
  George, 298, 299n, 324n
Washington, Elizabeth Foot, wife of Lund, 154,
  192
Washington, George (1732–99), commander in
  chief of Continental forces, resigned Dec. 23,
  1783, **163, 326;** and adoption of Martha's
  grandchildren, 237; and advice to L, 343;
  British image of, 211; British on, 256; bust
  of, 336, 358; and Canada, 32; cancels order

Washington, George (cont.)
for plated ware from L, 161n; and Carleton, 47n, 128, 139, 142n; as commander in chief, 68; and commission for L, 30; and concern for George Augustine, 64n; and concern over reputation, 296; and Congress, 162; on Continental army, 136; and departure of L, 279; desires world peace, 337; and end of military service, 135, 139, 154, 156, 191, 195; equestrian statue of, 332n; European image of, 145, 153, 162; family of, 5, 10, 28, 50, 65, 74, 93, 146, 154, 209, 298, 323; and final campaign plans, 114, 116n, 436; on free navigation of Mississippi, 338; French opinion of, 9; and friendship for L, 119, 121, 125, 155, 157, 159, 196, 208, 279, 296, 337, 340, 343, 437; and gift of hounds, 339, 340n, 343; on government, 39, 119; government role of, 89; and Houdon, 332; on inland navigation, 287n; and James River Company, 314, 315n, 344, 345n; and James River navigation, 301; and Joseph II, 349n; and journey with L, 266; and L family portrait, 218n, 230n; L on, 91, 237, 324; L's affection for, 125, 132, 145, 146, 151, 153, 164, 191, 207, 209, 216, 265, 323, 324, 327, 438; L's assurances to, 31; and L's leave, 116n; and L's proposal to free slaves, 330n; L's respect for, 202; L's visit to, 233, 235, 237, 243, 261; and meeting with L, 268, 270, 275, 276n, 277, 280n; on military affairs, 18; and military command, 122; military family of, 276, 277n; on needs of army, 114, 116n; and Newburgh Affair, 121n; on New Orleans, 301; as possible leader of campaign against South America, 324n; and Potomac River Company, 314, 315n, 441; and Potomac River navigation, 290n, 296, 301, 306, 310; and proposed visit to France, 120; relations with L, 10, 64, 72, 91, 93n, 115; requests plated ware from L, 159, 193n; resigns as commander in chief, 154n, 188n, 195; and Society of Cincinnati, 158, 176, 178n, 180, 201, 203n, 213, 227, 229n, 343, 437; and Spanish jackasses, 298, 302n, 325, 338, 343, 345n; statue of, 162, 165n, 186, 336n; travels of, 241, 265n; and views on Continental army, 120; and views on naval superiority, 24n; and western expansion, 296, 337, 338, 343; mentioned, 29, 42, 67n, 69n, 74n, 75, 85n, 88, 90, 130n, 137, 141, 163, 167n, 176n, 197, 208n, 214n, 241n, 254, 286, 306n, 308n, 310n, 321, 326, 428
—letters from, 62–64, 113–16, 119–21, 135–36, 155–62, 194–96, 279–80, 289–90, 295–99, 336–40, 342–45; calendared, 432, 433, 435, 436, 437, 441, 444; to Franklin, calendared, 435
—letters to, 4–5, 8–10, 21–28, 48–51, 64–66, 72–74, 90–93, 124–26, 132–33, 145–47, 151–54, 162–65, 179–80, 191–93, 205–9, 216–18, 264–66, 287–88, 324–27; calendared, 429–31, 433–35, 437–43
Washington, George Augustine (1763?–93), former aide-de-camp to L, nephew of George: arrives at Charleston, 327; illness of, 64, 64n, 115, 125, 126n, 344; improved health of, 339; marriage of, 339, 340n, 344, 345n; and L, 116n, 324n; in West Indies, 265n; mentioned, 5, 10, 24, 65, 66n, 74, 93, 146, 154, 164, 192, 209, 265
Washington, Lund (1737–96), cousin of George, estate manager at Mount Vernon, 154, 192, 265
Washington, Martha Dandridge Custis (1732–1802), wife of George: and departure for Virginia, 157; and home life, 237; and loss of mother and brother, 339; mentioned, 5, 10, 24, 28, 50, 64, 65, 74, 93, 121, 125, 133, 146, 154, 164, 192, 196, 208, 216, 237, 265, 280, 323, 325, 340
Washington, Mary Ball (1708–89), mother of George, 93, 339
Washington, America warship, 141, 176, 185, 186, 191
Wayne, Anthony (1745–96), Continental brigadier general commanding Pennsylvania Line, 234
Webb, Samuel Blatchley (1753–1807), American brigadier general, co-founder of Society of Cincinnati, 317–18
Wengiezski, Polish count, 155, 157n
West Indies (West Indias): British expeditions to, 13n, 61, 63, 63, 71, 115; and dependence on North America, 32n; French expeditions to, 5, 10n, 13n, 23, 31, 32, 49, 65, 70, 74n, 78; French-Spanish expedition to, 22, 26, 72, 75, 432; L's plantation in, 91; and provisions to French colonies, 218n; and slave markets, 141; Spanish possessions in, 88; Spanish preoccupation with, 27; and trade between America and British colonies, 210, 213, 270, 271n; and trade between America and French colonies, 150n, 172, 173, 176n, 183, 216, 295n, 304–6, 310, 319, 440; mentioned, 126n, 265n, 339
Westminster, England, 216, 335n
West Point, N.Y., 66, 135, 137
Wilberforce, William (1759–1833), friend of William Pitt, 157, 158, 159n
Willem V (1748–1806), prince of Orange, stadholder of United Provinces, 223, 293, 295n
Willet, Marinus (1740–1830), American lieutenant colonel, 8
Williams, Mr., 339, 340n
Williams, Jonathan (1750–1815), Franklin's grandnephew, 194n
—letter to, calendared, 441
Williams, Otho Holland (1749–94), assistant secretary of Society of Cincinnati, 343, 344n
Williamsburg, Va., 265
Wilmington, N.C., 4, 8
Wolcott, Oliver (1726–97), peace negotiator with Indians: and L, 253, 264, 272, 273; and negotiations with Indians, 251, 252, 254n, 255, 257, 263, 265n; and report to Congress, 287n; mentioned, 259

Wolcott, Oliver (*cont.*)
—letter from, calendared, 438
—letter to, 253–54
Wolf Indians, 251
Wurtz, M., 229

York, Frederick Augustus, duke of
   (1763–1827), second son of George III, 345,
   349n

Yorktown (York Town), Va.: American victory
   at, 6n, 127n–28n, 281n; and L's meeting
   with Washington, 276n; siege of, 5n, 281n,
   342n; mentioned, 29, 208n
Young, Moses, secretary to Henry Laurens, 29,
   30

Zeeland, United Provinces, 17n

Library of Congress Cataloging in Publication Data
(Revised for vol. 5)

Lafayette, Marie Joseph Paul Yves Roch Gilbert du Motier, marquis de, 1757–1834.
    Lafayette in the age of the American Revolution.

    (His The papers of the Marquis de Lafayette)
    Vol. 5: S. J. Idzerda and R. R. Crout, editors.
    "French texts": v. 1, p.
    Includes bibliographical references and indexes
    Contents: v. 1. December 7, 1776–March 30, 1778.—v. 2. April 10, 1778–March 20, 1780—[etc.]—v. 5. January 4, 1782–December 29, 1785.
    1.Lafayette, Marie Joseph Paul Yves Roch Gilbert du Motier, marquis de, 1757–1834. 2. United States History Revolution, 1775–1783 Sources. 3. United States History Confederation, 1783–1789 Sources. 4. Generals United States Correspondence. 5. Generals France Correspondence. I. Idzerda, Stanley J. II. Crout, Robert R. III. Series: Lafayette, Marie Joseph Paul Yves Roch Gilbert du Motier, marquis de, 1757–1834. The papers of the Marquis de Lafayette.
E207.L2A4   1977   944.04'092'4 [B]   76-50268
ISBN 0-8014-1576-4